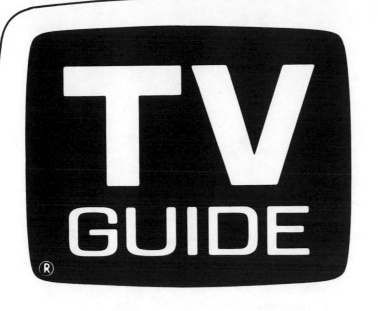

THE FIRST 25 YEARS

Compiled and Edited by JAY S. HARRIS
in association with
the Editors of TV GUIDE Magazine

SIMON AND SCHUSTER   NEW YORK

Published by Simon and Schuster, A Division of Gulf & Western Corporation
Simon & Schuster Building
Rockefeller Center, 1230 Avenue of the Americas
New York, New York 10020

Designed by Helen Barrow
Manufactured in the United States of America
1   2   3   4   5   6   7   8   9   10

Library of Congress Cataloging in Publication Data

Main entry under title:

TV guide, the first 25 years.

Includes index.
1.   Television broadcasting—United States—Addresses,
essays, lectures.   I.   Harris, Jay S.   II.   TV guide.
PN1992.3.U5T18   791.45'7   78-8936
ISBN 0-671-23065-4

ACKNOWLEDGMENTS

I would like to extend my gratitude and appreciation to the following people who have helped to make this book possible: to my good friend Fredda Stoll for her help and support in countless ways throughout; to my brother-in-law, Stephen S. Scheidt, M.D., who reviewed my initial selections and made thoughtful and useful suggestions; to Caroline Abady for a cheerful but grueling week printing thousands of pages from the microfilm machine; to Margie DeGovann and Henriette Roberts of *TV Guide* for their assistance and cooperation; to those on *TV Guide*'s staff whom I did not meet but who I know gave their time to the project; to Vincent Virga for his help in collecting the photographs; to Joel Avirom for designing such a beautiful cover; to Helen Barrow for re-creating the look and feeling of the magazine so well; to *TV Guide*'s David Appel, from whom I wish I had needed more; to Mary Jane Connell, my secretary, for so many things; to Jonathan Coleman, my editor, for his diligence, enthusiasm and competence; to Michael Korda, for knowing immediately; and to the talented men and women who wrote the words and took the pictures. A very special thanks goes to Merrill Panitt, who through the first 25 years has been *TV Guide*'s Managing Editor, Editor, and now Editorial Director, for his wise counsel, his warm support, and above all, his trust.

JAY S. HARRIS

For Jenny and Jesse, my children,
L. Arnold Weissberger, my partner,
and
Nat and Leah, my parents

PREFACE

TV Guide, in the first twenty-five years since its birth, in April 1953, has published more than 10,000 articles and features touching on virtually every aspect of television in the United States and, to some extent, in foreign countries. This book is a selection of pieces that have appeared in the magazine during that period. The articles have been reprinted intact. However, because of the unavailability of some of the original photographs, new ones, with new captions, have been substituted. Also, the nightly network fall program schedules in the Appendix for 1953–1961 were reconstructed to follow the format that began in 1962 and continues to the present. All the articles were written either by the magazine's own staff members or by prominent free-lance writers. Fortunately, I was able to pick and choose from an abundance of talent.

TV Guide is a consumer's magazine with a consumer's point of view. The consumer in this case is the television viewer. Everyone! It certainly is not a fan magazine, nor a mere listings magazine. Rather, it is a keen and articulate observer and critic. It carefully watches and reports not only what is on television, but why it's on television, what is going on behind and to the sides of it, and what effect it is having on us and our society.

This book is intended to be a mixture of entertainment, nostalgia and history. In putting the pieces together, it was my purpose to profile the outstanding personalities that have appeared on the screen, from Edward R. Murrow to Farrah Fawcett-Majors; to view the programs that occupy a unique place in television's history, from "Dragnet" to "Roots," from the Oscars and quiz shows to soaps and the Olympics; to rekindle the memory of stunning and shattering national and world events, including the incredible four-day chronicle of television's activities in November 1963, when President John F. Kennedy was assassinated; to examine the serious issues that have arisen from the business and essence of the medium itself—issues such as the portrayal of violence, the medium's effect on children, its impact on our political system; ratings, commercials; race, family life, feminism; regulation by the Federal Communications Commission, pay-TV, public television, television journalism, and television's effect on other media.

Some of the pieces are intended simply to amuse, such as the reprinting of the famous Abbott and Costello "Who's on First" routine. The familiar TV Guide Close-ups highlight the most spectacular of television's spectaculars, including the Jets-Colts 1969 Superbowl Game line-ups and the first television showing of the original "King Kong." There are photographs accompanying nearly every article, as well as a special color section of memorable TV Guide covers.

TV Guide has published hundreds of special articles of literary and scholarly merit by some of the best writers and thinkers of our time as supplemental information to upcoming programs. Although most of them have not been directly related to television, some have, such as the article by attorney Louis Nizer concerning the blacklisting of John Henry Faulk which previewed the docudrama "Fear on Trial."

With the exception of the concluding article, the material has been arranged chronologically to give the book a lively sense of feeling and flow, with the month and year of publication marked on every page, and, in certain cases, even the day. In this way, I hope the book can be an experience—an enjoyable one for all who turn its pages, as well as an educational one for those who wish to probe deeper into serious aspects of the medium. I wanted to cover everything but, naturally, that proved impossible. I have included pieces that I hope are the best—the most important, the most interesting, the most memorable and the most provocative—all together creating a twenty-five-year portrait in words and pictures of the story of television as seen through the pages of TV Guide.

Jay S. Harris
New York, New York
March 1978

CONTENTS

A COLOR SECTION OF 400 TV GUIDE COVERS

OF THE LAST 25 YEARS FOLLOWS PAGE 160.

Channel numbers used throughout the book refer to stations listed in *TV Guide*'s
New York Metropolitan edition. The national network affiliates in New York City
are Channel 2, CBS; Channel 4, NBC; Channel 7, ABC; and Channel 13, PBS.
There are also three independent VHF stations in the city, Channels 5, 9 and 11,
and two UHF stations affiliated with PBS, Channels 25 and 31.
The edition also lists some network affiliates and independent stations
in New Jersey and Connecticut.

Here's why 180,389* Philadelphia Families Read TV Digest Magazine <u>Cover</u> to <u>Cover</u>!

TV FANS look forward to the sprightly stories about their favorite stars each week. Currently, Arthur Godfrey is featured. Next week, TV Digest presents the parenthood problems facing Lucille Ball and Desi Arnaz.

BEHIND THE SCENES goes TV DIGEST with its exclusive features, Video Vignettes and TV News Flashes. All the latest inside stories, the program plans and news of television stars. It's information and reading pleasure PLUS!

READERS ARE TELLING US what they think and asking us questions. Each week hundreds of alert, enthusiastic readers take time to write us their own views—and to read the views of others.

BACKSTAGE goes TV DIGEST's cameraman to get for readers unusual, informal shots of favorite TV personalities. Every week TV DIGEST features a section of behind-the-scenes pictures plus a weekly pin-up.

SPORTS FANS get up-to-the-minute reports, gossip and features about every sports program on local channels. And to bring it to them is one of their favorite reporters—Philadelphia's own Harvey Pollack.

NO KIDDING the youngsters—they love TV DIGEST, and they influence the buying of lots of products. A recent Roy Rogers coloring contest drew over 6,000 entries.

CRITICAL OPINION and helpful information about TV programs are offered by columnist Hank O'Hare. His comments help readers get the complete television picture with TV DIGEST.

BEST LIST YET! No other publication devotes as much space and gives as detailed programming as TV DIGEST. Tune-in advertisers receive extra merchandising assistance to promote their show.

More Than a Reference Book ... It's A Preference Book!

Some advertisers mistakenly regard TV DIGEST solely as a reference book for television viewers—but take a good look at these sample pages and you see our position.

True... TV DIGEST offers the best television listings in print. But more than that, TV DIGEST today is loaded with editorial matter that keeps 577,244 faithful cover-to-cover readers coming back for more week after week.

The same buying urge that moves millions of movie magazines off newsstands has pushed TV DIGEST into the position of the Philadelphia area's dominant magazine. *No other magazine ever attained so large a circulation and consumer acceptance here.*

TV DIGEST outsells every national weekly in the Philadelphia area, including such favorites as Life and The Saturday Evening Post. Yes, TV DIGEST has emerged a full-fledged consumer magazine.

Now entering our fifth year, TV DIGEST is a powerful force to help you sell the bigger-than-ever Philadelphia market.

Put Yourself In Philadelphia's TV Picture With TV DIGEST

TV DIGEST's cost per thousand... only $2.56 per page, makes it Philadelphia's best magazine buy—by far. Remember, you don't have to be a TV sponsor to sell with TV DIGEST. If you want more details... if you want a specific plan for your product... if you want to place an order... dial KI 6-0807 today!

* *November 8, 1952 Issue, Net Paid.*

TV DIGEST
Member Audit Bureau of Circulations

15¢ at all newsstands

DELIVERS MORE NEWSSTAND CIRCULATION IN PHILADELPHIA THAN <u>ANY</u> OTHER MAGAZINE!

Because this November 19, 1952, advertisement appeared in the competing *Philadelphia Bulletin* instead of in his *Philadelphia Inquirer,* Walter Annenberg began asking questions that led to his creation of *TV Guide.*

INTRODUCTION

TV GUIDE is an extremely successful magazine.

That's an understatement. *TV Guide* has the largest circulation and the highest advertising income of any magazine in publishing history.

People keep asking why. Why do so many millions pay thirty cents for TV listings when their daily newspapers carry free TV listings? The people who ask that question obviously are not *TV Guide* readers. *Readers.*

Television, despite its overcommercialism and the frivolity of regular prime time programming, has an impact on all of us. The magazine covers—and criticizes—a communications medium that has become an important force in our lives. Whether we realize it or not, and whether we like it or not, television affects not only our mores, but just about every other aspect of our society—business, education, politics, government, international affairs, and human relations. Because television covers all of the world we live in, and because *TV Guide* concerns itself with whatever television touches, the magazine has not only broad and interesting subject matter but subject matter that is vital to its readers. And while our listings are as accurate and complete as some 350 dedicated staff members in 24 cities and a gigantic computer complex can make them, if all viewers want to know is when *Laverne and Shirley* is on, they don't need *TV Guide*. If, however, they also want intelligent, objective coverage of television as an entertainment medium and as what may be the most powerful force for change in our society, they do need *TV Guide*.

This book's purpose is to show the past 25 years of television as it has been reflected in the pages of the magazine. Because so much of television is filled with people entertaining us, a great many of these pages are filled with articles about television performers. That is as it should be; but it should also be noted that week in and week out *TV Guide* presents a balanced editorial content—making it possible, some years ago, for Professor Barry Cole of the University of Indiana to compile a volume of articles from the magazine dealing with serious aspects of television, how it works, and how it is changing us and our environment. That work, now being updated for a new edition, is used as a text in a number of college communications courses. The magazine itself is required reading in many such courses and, we are pleased to note, in a number of writing courses.

We have indeed come a long way since the night in late November of 1952 when I received a rather irate telephone call from Walter Annenberg, the president of Triangle Publications. I was his administrative assistant then, and as a sort of hobby wrote a television column for his morning newspaper, the *Philadelphia Inquirer*.

"Why was that full-page ad for *TV Digest* in tonight's *Bulletin* instead of in our newspaper?" he demanded.

I said I didn't think it was because the *TV Digest* people had anything against the *Inquirer*, but probably because they only had enough money for a weekday ad, and of course the *Bulletin* had a bit more circulation than we did on weekdays.

That seemed to mollify him—a little. "The ad says *TV Digest* has a circulation of 180,000. Is that possible?"

TV Digest was a little television magazine that carried listings for the Philadelphia stations and was sold in the area covered by those stations. The publishers were trying to interest advertisers in buying space in the magazine—hence the ad in the *Bulletin.*

"The 180,000 figure is okayed by ABC (Audit Bureau of Circulation)," I said, "so it must be accurate."

There was a long pause. When you talk to Walter Annenberg on the phone you get used to long pauses and you don't try to fill the dead air. You let him think. Quietly.

Next question: "Aren't there some other magazines like *TV Digest* around the country?"

There were. "There's one called *TV Guide* in New York with a circulation of about 400,000 and one in Chicago called *TV Forecast* that has about 100,000."

Pause. "Do they have anything in common?"

"I don't think so. Editorially, *TV Forecast* hates television; *TV Guide* is a fan magazine. *TV Digest* can't seem to make up its mind. They and a couple of others—in Boston and Washington and one just starting in Pittsburgh—all get their own listings and do their own stories. Every so often one of them hits on a story idea and a cover blurb that sell extra copies and the others will pick it up. But by and large, though, I think they are independent operations."

Then a long pause. I began to wonder whether we hadn't been cut off.

"How would it be," he finally said, "if we were to print a color section with national articles in our Philadelphia rotogravure plant, ship that section around the country, and in each city we'd print the local listings and bind them inside the national color section?"

This time *I* paused. It was a wild idea, but television was booming and I knew from reader response to the *Inquirer* television column how much interest there was in the medium.

"Sounds possible," I said.

He developed the idea some more during that phone call. Staffs in each city. Emphasis on network shows. Complicated publishing logistics that would have to be worked out somehow. Advertising could be either national or local. We could sell magazine space the way radio and television sell time, with the advertiser buying as much coverage as he wanted.

For the next few weeks Walter Annenberg personally spot-checked newsstands in New York, Chicago and Philadelphia to confirm his judgment that the plan he was fashioning was feasible. He'd buttonhole buyers of the TV magazines and ask them to explain why they were paying for information that was available in their newspapers. Apparently the answers he heard satisfied him, because within two months Triangle had spent several million dollars to purchase *TV Digest, TV Guide* and *TV Forecast.* New York's *TV Guide* had some ownership interest in the Washington magazine and it was included. Publishers of TV magazines in Boston, Davenport, Iowa, Minneapolis and—of all places—Wilkes Barre, Pennsylvania, were franchised to buy our national section. (Triangle eventually bought the franchised editions.) Teams were dispatched to Los Angeles and Cincinnati to set up offices and editions in those cities.

When word of the project got out, a number of prominent publishers called their friend Walter to offer condolences. Mike Cowles, whose company owned *Look* magazine, newspapers and broadcast stations, pointed out the impossibility of turning out a magazine that was both national and local. The late Norman Chandler, publisher of the *Los Angeles Times,* explained that once newspapers started carrying comprehensive television sections, no magazine featuring listings could survive. There were others equally certain that it was doomed.

Viewed from outside the company, the team selected to run *TV Guide* didn't exactly inspire confidence either. Roger Clipp, manager of Triangle's radio and television stations, was named general manager of the new magazine—in addition to his other duties. Michael J. O'Neill, who had been managing Philadelphia Inquirer Charities, became advertising director. The late James T. Quirk, the *Inquirer*'s promotion manager, took on promotion of the magazine as well as the newspaper. And I, a newspaperman, was given the title of national managing editor. Annenberg always seeks to operate within interior lines—stressing economy—but there wasn't ten minutes of solid magazine experience in the lot.

We learned fast. It was soon evident that *TV Guide* (the name barely won out over *TV Digest*) was a full-time job. Within a few months Roger Clipp went back to his primary interest, broadcasting, and Jim Quirk became publisher of the magazine. The editor of New York's *TV Guide,* Harold Clemenko, was the regional managing editor, and the *Inquirer*'s assistant managing editor, Alexander H. Joseph, had been transferred to *TV Guide* as my assistant managing editor. (Alex insisted on a letter from Mr. Annenberg guaranteeing that if *TV Guide* came a cropper he could have his job back on the *Inquirer*. He still had the letter when, as executive editor, he retired in 1976.)

The first issue of the new magazine was dated April 3, 1953. By that time, of course, we had to have four issues in various stages of preparation behind it. Not bad for a magazine that had been conceived four months earlier. That first issue had editions in 10 cities and a total circulation of 1,560,000. The next week it dropped to 1,492,000. The following week it fell to 1,485,000. Alex Joseph kept rereading the letter guaranteeing his *Inquirer* job. Our offices (the old *TV Digest* quarters over a popcorn distributor on Philadelphia's South Broad Street) were permeated with gloom as well as the smell of hot popcorn.

All that long hot summer of 1953 we watched the figures drop. We opened new editions in Rochester, Pittsburgh, Detroit, Cleveland and San Francisco, but they didn't help much. By mid-August the circulation was 200,000 under what it had been for the first issue. Weekly magazines are expensive to produce. Triangle was losing money—lots of it—on *TV Guide*. We editors consoled ourselves by saying that television viewing *always* dropped in the summer and that things would be better in the fall. To make certain, we planned a Fall Preview issue hailing the new season.

Sure enough, the September 4th issue zoomed to 1,600,809 and the next week our Fall Preview issue hit 1,746,327. And, allowing for seasonal fluctuations, the circulation has been increasing ever since. It's more than 20 million a week now, with 94 editions in the United States. (We had eight editions in Canada but when the Canadian Parliament passed a law making it all but impossible for an American publisher to do business in that country, Annenberg made a reluctant decision to sell. "You have no choice when they're holding a gun to your head," he told me. We do still work closely with the Canadian who eventually bought the editions.)

Advertising that first year totaled $760,000. The figure rose very slowly. In 1962 Mike O'Neill, now publisher of *Field and Stream,* left Triangle and was replaced by Eric Larson, the biggest advertising director in magazine publishing. (He stands 6 feet 8 inches in his size 15 shoes and weighs in—on his infrequent thin days—at 350. I'm convinced his IQ must be around 350 too.) Last year we reached $175 million in ad revenue.

Triangle is a unique company. It is, first of all, a privately owned company, with Walter Annenberg and his sisters being the only individuals who hold stock. Mr. Annenberg's closest adviser is Joseph M. First, for nearly 40 years his executive vice president, and now a consultant. There are three vice presidents—Brian Bradfield, in charge of operations (and *TV Guide*), Albert Grifone, the treasurer, and Harry Coles, general counsel. These few men make up the entire top echelon of a major publishing company.

Walter Annenberg is in charge, whether he is at his estate in California, spending five years as ambassador to the court of St. James's, or occupying his beautiful offices at the TV Guide Building in Radnor, near his Wynnewood, Pa., residence. He receives the usual profit and loss figures and statistics, and reports from the vice presidents, division and department heads. Those are routine. His real contact with us is in person or by phone, and since he holds that an executive is on duty 24 hours a day, he feels free to call us at any time during those 24 hours. Well, not quite. He has never called me before 7:30 A.M. or after 12:30 A.M.

When he was in London as ambassador he was as much in command and as close to his business as if he had been in his Radnor office. He'd phone us in the late afternoon at our offices and then at night he'd return to the residence after a diplomatic affair and start phoning us at our homes. Sometimes when he got to me it was 1 A.M. in London. He sounded tired, but he wanted to know what was going on, what was being planned for the magazine, what editorials were upcoming, were we commenting on this or that television development. He had suggestions for articles, comments on the latest issue. He'd ask that I send a note to a writer complimenting him on a good job. Or he'd complain that a cover was awful. "But don't worry about it; Babe Ruth struck out on occasion too." I wish I had a dollar for every time I've heard that.

About a thousand people are involved in taking Walter Annenberg's ideas and his direction and transforming them into the magazine you see each week. All of them—from Estelle Carroll, who enters new subscribers' names on a computer list, and Socrates Dendrinelis, a circulation field representative, to Roger Youman, the executive editor and Sho Kaneko, production manager in the Los Angeles office—take an extraordinary amount of pride in their work. For all of us who have worked at *TV Guide* during these 25 years, it has been tremendously rewarding work.

MERRILL PANITT
Editorial Director

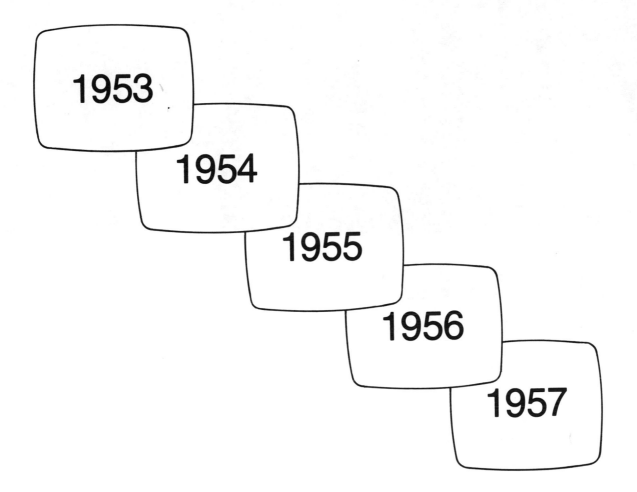

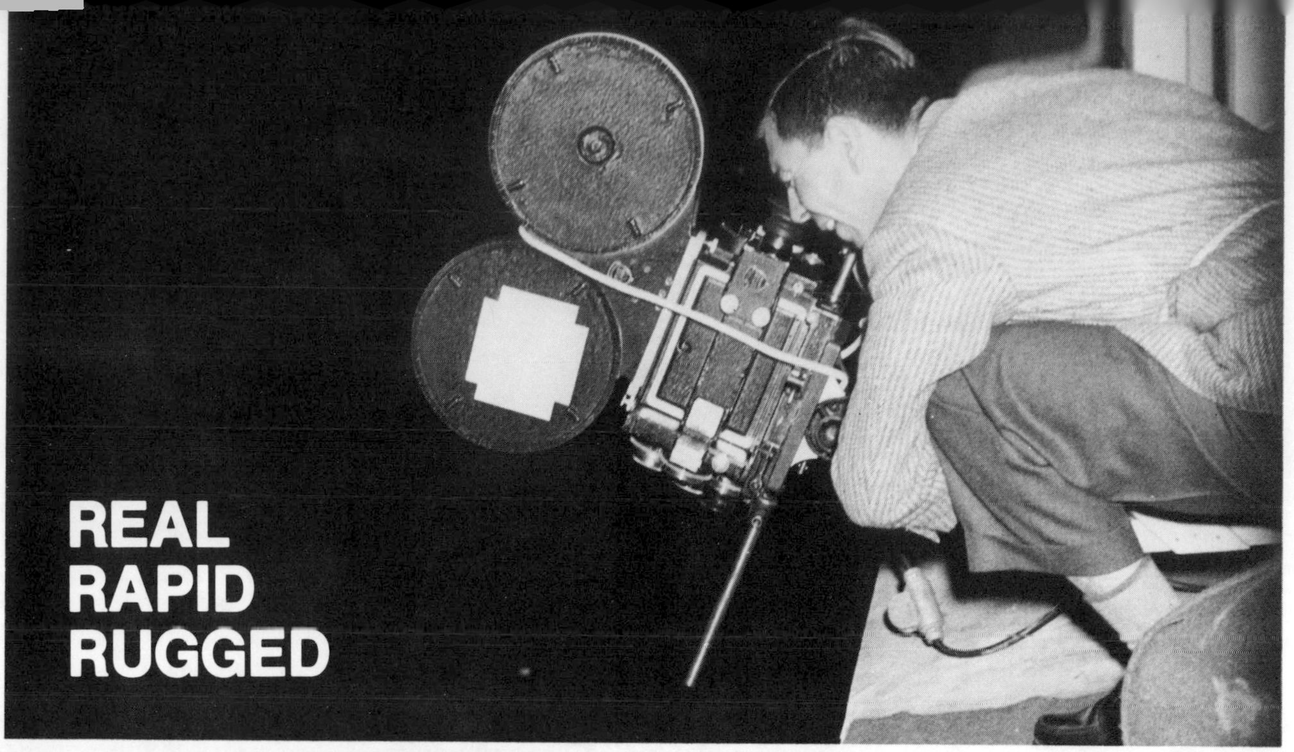

**REAL
RAPID
RUGGED**

DRAGNET

Catches 38 million viewers

Jack Webb, a professional actor who learned about realism as an Air Force B-26 pilot during the Second World War, has made it pay off as star and director of *Dragnet,* the NBC thriller which plays weekly to some 38,000,000 faithful viewers across the country.

Now in his early 30s, Webb has come to represent for the American public the ideal of the regular police detective, as contrasted with the "private eye," and with real police methods, as contrasted with fictional melodrama.

His slim frame—he's six feet tall and weighs 165 pounds—and his clipped underplaying of scenes have become as much a trademark to the American public as the stamp of Mark VII Productions, which terminates his show.

He plays every television scene as if it were a real police case.

He achieves the unbelievable

Webb has achieved the unbelievable for fictional detective work—a show which is pleasing alike to public, press, police and even penitentiary inmates. But success wasn't achieved without struggles, and it's maintained by tireless attention to detail.

For Webb, who had played radio private detectives in San Francisco, his real career began one day on the Hollywood set of the motion picture "He Walked By Night," in which he played a police lieutenant.

Idly, he asked Sergeant Marty Wynn, of the Los Angeles Police Department, technical adviser on the film, about the possibility of doing a radio program based on actual police file cases.

Wynn liked the idea, so Webb collected information from the police department, developed characters and a format and cut an audition record for NBC officials. They offered him a sustaining spot.

Then, "hat in hand," Webb went to C. B. Horrall, then Los Angeles police chief, and asked for his cooperation.

Police promise help

"You're on the right track," Horrall told him. "You don't make heroes of cops and you're reflecting the day-to-day drudgery of police work." He promised his cooperation, and the radio show was launched successfully.

The idea of the television show originated in 1951, with the president of the cigaret firm sponsoring the radio program. Webb made up a sample film, which clicked. On December 5, the order came for 13 episodes, with the first to be shown January 1.

In less than a month Webb assembled a top-notch staff, selected stories and cast, pushed production at breakneck speed and beat the deadline. He's been clicking along at that rate ever since.

The Mark VII trademark was "dreamed up over coffee" by Webb and co-producer Michael Meshekoff and has no special meaning. The use of the hammer and stamp is based "somewhat" on the use of a hammer and gong to open J. Arthur Rank's British productions.

To date, Webb's production unit has turned out 60 episodes, each using 12,000 feet of film. It's the equivalent of 20 feature-length motion pictures, all made in a shooting time of less than nine months!

Working at the Walt Disney Studios near Hollywood, Webb's production unit is now holding to a rigid episode-in-three-days schedule. Webb not only directs, but plays the lead role of Sergeant Joe Friday.

For a typical episode, he and writer John Robinson will pore over case histories furnished them by three policemen, from the Los Angeles police files. When the two have agreed on a case, they prepare a script for the radio show, which later is adapted for television use.

The script is submitted to the police for technical corrections. The City Attorney's office then checks for legal implications. A policeman from the appropriate detail—robbery, homicide, forgery, etc.—stands by during the filming to check on authenticity.

Dragnet is filmed on a budget of about $30,000 for each episode, which holds cast, sets and wasted scenes to a minimum.

Webb's present schedule enables him to make four episodes in two weeks, then lay off for two weeks. As a result, he has two weeks free out of each month for careful planning and editing.

He makes considerable use of Teleprompters to avoid "fluffed" lines and wasted film.

Moreover, Webb knows just what he wants to do with *Dragnet*. The show is intended to entertain and to sell products, but Webb says there "never will be anything in *Dragnet* that I wouldn't want my own two kids to see."

Each story accurate

Furthermore, there is no dramatic license taken with the cases. Each is related factually, but in such a manner that even the criminal would not recognize his own case. Webb is dedicated to the idea that the show should do nothing to harm a man who already has paid legally for his misdeed.

The success of *Dragnet* isn't based on violence, a milestone for such programs. In all the episodes filmed to date, Webb says, only 15 bullets have been discharged and there have been but three fights and a half-dozen punches.

Webb takes to a 9th-story window ledge in downtown Los Angeles to thwart a suicide (NBC)

Ben Alexander, capable veteran, who plays Detective Frank Smith, Webb's official partner (NBC)

Webb says flatly that the format is what the public wants and the popularity of *Dragnet* supports his view. He receives about 400 letters weekly and estimates that each letter represents similar views of 10,000 lookers.

He not only answers each letter, but he keeps a file of what viewers have to say. If 10 letters suggest a certain change, Webb will consider making it, on the grounds that this may represent the feeling of 100,000 listeners.

If 10 letters complain that the background music is too high, for example, or that Webb's voice is too soft, he will order prompt changes.

In the intensively competitive world of television, the system has paid off by keeping *Dragnet* consistently third among all TV programs. Yet *Dragnet* serves the public by realistically bringing home the fact that crime does not pay.

This, too, is one of Webb's aims, which is why he is proud of the letters which pour in from police authorities praising the work of the program. The following letter from an attorney, quoted in part, is virtually typical:

"Not only do you provide wholesome entertainment, but you are doing more for law enforcement than anyone else in the entertainment field.

"As a former FBI agent, deputy city attorney and prosecuting attorney, I'm particularly grateful for the public service you are rendering."

For Webb, such notes make the *Dragnet* show really worth all the effort he puts into it.

young producer

Barbara Walters
of "Ask the Camera"
is at 22 responsible
for an important local program

Television, like radio in its early days, is filled with bright young people in responsible jobs. A good example is 22-year-old Barbara Walters, producer of ❹'s *Ask the Camera* (Monday, Tuesday, Thursday, Friday, 6:30–6:45 P.M., Wednesday, 6:35–6:45 P.M., ❹); she may be youngest in the field.

Despite her youth, she's no newcomer to show business. She was born and brought up in it—her father is Lou Walters, who owns the Latin Quarter clubs in New York and elsewhere.

Barbara was born in Boston, where, when she was eight, her father opened his first Latin Quarter. A few years later the family moved to New York when a L.Q. was opened here. Then, when Miami was graced by a L.Q., the Walterses kept shuttling between there and Manhattan.

When Barbara was of college age, the family finally settled down in New York. Barbara went to Sarah Lawrence, with a teaching career her goal.

However, the summer after her graduation, she took a part-time secretarial job with an advertising agency—and that proved the end of her teaching ambitions. She began to do a little advertising copywriting.

After a year with the ad agency, she moved to NBC as assistant publicity director of WNBC and WNBT. When, early this year, a new special-events section was created, Barbara was chosen as one of the unit's producers. Then came *Ask the Camera*.

No matter what their names, to millions of children they are
Clarabell, Howdy Doody, Princess Summerfall Winterspring and
Buffalo Bob, citizens of a wonderland (NBC)

How those tots howl for

HOWDY DOODY!

Just 50 youngsters can be crowded into the gallery for the *Howdy Doody* show (NBC) while their parents wait in a nearby corridor. The demand for tickets is heavy.

For the lucky tots who get in, the show provides plenty of laughter as they watch such familiar performers as Buffalo Bob (Bob Smith), Clarabell (Bobby Nicholson), the Princess (Judy Tyler), Chief Thunderthud (Bill Lecornec) and Howdy. Lee Carney operates the puppet, replacing Rhoda Mann, who was with the program when it started.

Howdy keeps them engrossed, as the accompanying picture demonstrates.

A typical scene in Doodyville, an important section of New York, during a broadcast (NBC)

JUNE 15, 1953

9:00 (2) (4) (7) FORD 50TH ANNIVERSARY SHOW

Credits

Producer	Leland Hayward	Set designer	Paul Barnes
Director	Clark Jones	Choreographer	Jerome Robbins
Musical director	Bernard Green	Writers	Frederick Lewis Allen,
Costume designer	Irene Sharaff		Agnes Rogers, and Howard Teichman

A two-hour, half-million-dollar panoramic capsule history of the past 50 years, recreating in song, dance, comedy, and drama famous events between 1903 and 1953. The show will utilize three studios, eight cameras, 25 stagehands, 45 engineers, a cast of more than 50, and a 24-piece orchestra.

Program

(Not necessarily in order listed.)

Ethel Merman (left) and Mary Martin (Slim Aarons)

MUSIC AND DANCE NUMBERS

(1) Mary Martin and Ethel Merman in a number of duets and medleys.
(2) Marian Anderson sings folk songs.
(3) Oliver J. Dragon (Ollie) sings "There's Nothing like a Model T" from the 1947 production "High Button Shoes."
(4) Ethel Merman sings "Alexander's Ragtime Band," written by Irving Berlin in 1911, accompanied by a Dixieland band.
(5) Mary Martin does a skit on the fashion changes in the feminine silhouette from 1903 to 1953, to the tune of "There Is Nothing Like a Dame," from the 1949 production "South Pacific."
(6) A dance history of the last 50 years.
(7) Ethel Merman sings "Mademoiselle from Armentières." (tentative)

DRAMATIC SEGMENTS

(1) Dorothy Stickney and Howard Lindsay in a scene from the 1939 production "Life with Father."
(2) Oscar Hammerstein II is the Stage Manager in a scene from the 1938 play "Our Town," with Mary Martin.
(3) Ollie and William L. Laurence, science reporter of the New York Times, participate in a survey of the atomic age.
(4) Freeman Gosden and Charles Correll, creators of Amos 'n' Andy, do "Madame Queen's Trial."
(5) Edward R. Murrow, Mary Martin, and Oscar Hammerstein II comment on World War II, using film clips for illustration.
(6) Movie scenes: "The Jazz Singer" (Al Jolson), "Tillie's Punctured Romance," "Birth of a Nation," "All Quiet on the Western Front."
(7) Star scenes: Greta Garbo, John Gilbert, Rudolph Valentino, Charlie Chaplin.

SPORTS EVENTS—FILMS

(1) Jack Dempsey hurtles through the ropes after being hit by Luis Firpo. (1923)
(2) Red Grange in sensational broken-field runs. (1923-25)
(3) Babe Ruth's 60th homer. (1927)
(4) Helen Wills Moody in the championship tennis matches at Forest Hills. (1923)
(5) Lou Gehrig's farewell to baseball at the Yankee Stadium. (1939)
(6) Gertrude Ederle swimming the English Channel. (1926)
(7) Bobby Jones adds another golf title to his laurels. (1923-30)

Also: Eddie Fisher, Teddy Wilson, Rudy Vallee, Frank Sinatra. Leaders in science, industry, and government join the cast.

Marion Dougherty, who'll be busy casting both *Kraft* plays, interviewing actors (ABC)

Corinth House scene: public response convinced sponsor to double schedule (ABC)

One Sponsor, Two Networks and . . .

104 Plays a Year

With television assuming top position in the entertainment industry, a TV show has become the biggest single theatrical enterprise in history. It's *Kraft TV Theater,* now telecasting two hours of live dramatic shows over two networks on two nights every week in the year.

The *Kraft* program is now in its seventh year on NBC Wednesday nights, and has never taken a summer vacation. On October 15, a completely separate *Kraft Theater* was launched on ABC and is being telecast each Thursday night, making a total of 104 hours of plays a year. By comparison, the Theater Guild, the biggest production firm on Broadway, has never produced more than five or six legitimate shows a year.

A top musical show on Broadway seldom costs more than $300,000 to stage. Even if the Theater Guild were to produce only high cost musicals—which is not the case, of course—it would spend at the most about $1,800,000 a year. The *Kraft* producers will be spending close to $8,000,000 each year for its two TV programs. In addition, viewers will be able to see on the two *Kraft* shows alone almost two-thirds as many hours of drama each year as are staged by all producers on Broadway.

Besides this windfall of good drama for viewers, the two *Kraft* productions each week can mean new prosperity to actors. *Kraft Theater,* since it first took the air on NBC in 1947, has employed more than 1500 actors and actresses. Now that there are two programs each week, the available work for actors will be doubled.

In fact, the *Kraft* casting offices, located in the offices of the J. Walter Thompson Co., the advertising agency which produces the shows, during the last few weeks have resembled Grand Central Station during a peak holiday travel season.

Shortage of stories

Looking at the crowded reception room, one producer declared that "the supply of acting talent is certainly going to be plenty big enough." He put the finger on another question of supply, which is the chief anxiety of the *Kraft* men at this time. That is the potential shortage of stories. With the advent of *U.S. Steel Hour* and the new *ABC Album* this month, the new *Kraft Theater* will raise the total of full-hour TV dramatic shows to seven. Producers of these shows have scraped bottom in their search for plays, novels and short stories.

Because of this, the key men in the expanded *Kraft Theater* operation are the script editor, Ed Rice, and his associate, Arthur Heineman. During the 6½ years that *Kraft* was on NBC alone, Rice and his staff of readers had to study carefully about 10 scripts each week before selecting the one to put on the air. With 104 shows to produce each year, that means they will now be reading an average of 1040 scripts yearly.

Original plays needed

"We've already run through most of the available Broadway plays," Rice said. "What we plan to do is find more short stories and novels we can adapt for TV. We'll naturally be on the lookout also for original plays, and that may eventually become our chief source of story material." Rice indicated that his agency may sign some writers to work exclusively for *Kraft Theater,* a move already made by such TV producers as Fred Coe and Robert Montgomery in order to insure a steady flow of good stories. He also conceded that *Kraft* may be forced from time to time to repeat the plays found most successful.

Free Wheeling Free-for-All

The Roller Derby is back on television

Gerry Murray (left), and Midge "Toughie" Brasuhn fight for the lead position (UPI)

Referee Jerry Donovan blows the whistle on Toughie for elbowing her way past Helen Licursi (UPI)

The whistle doesn't stop Toughie from going down fighting and taking Helen with her (UPI)

If you are among those who find themselves waking up nights with the nagging question, "What ever became of the Roller Derby?" you can go back to sleep now.

Nothing happened to it. It just went away for a while, to Europe, of all places. It's home now, though, and all is forgiven. It's spending Sunday afternoons on television, in case you don't believe us.

Life is just one mad whirl for the Roller Derby crowd. A sort of wheeled version of the wrestling matches, its scoring has something to do with a skater passing one or more other skaters while the rest of the mob beats the whey out of each other. They have a couple of referees who blow whistles occasionally, and a scoreboard, and rules which defy sane analysis, but the slugging is obviously what all the fuss is about.

The Roller Derby used to be a pretty big deal on television. When it went off the air, there was loud grouching all along the coaxial cable, except in Los Angeles, which has its own road show on locally and didn't get the national version anyhow.

Originally, the Derby disappeared in some towns because it couldn't get local clearance. But when it vanished completely, it was because of the European trip—which was a huge success, incidentally, especially in Paris, a city not unlikely to go for this sort of mayhem.

The frequent brawls are not supposed to be part of the game, which has led to the thought in some quarters that maybe the Roller Derby is not as legitimate as it might be. Most of the fisticuffs and strong words take place among the "lady" participants, a sight that unquestionably has some fascination, and it could be concluded that the girls are instructed to have a go at one another. It couldn't hurt the gate.

A Gerry Tuff affair

The box-office success of the Roller Derby owes something, too, to several of its more popular skaters. A couple of hoydenish types, Midge "Toughie" Brasuhn and Gerry Murray, are currently the big draws at the gate. Toughie is just about her league's best player and a girl of violent impulses, which she obeys. Gerry is of a similar homicidal bent. Both girls are at their nasty best when confronting each other, and regularly give each other a clobber when skating by. It's all part of their day's work.

Has its own fans

Whether it's legitimate, whether it's in good taste, whether it's even worth classing as a sport, all are matters that play no part in the Roller Derby's popularity. It has been going now for 17 years and is immensely popular still.

It would not be unreasonable to predict a big revival in its TV popularity, especially on Sunday afternoons with that large kid audience. And there's nothing like it anywhere on the Sunday schedules. But, then, girls on roller skates gouging each other's eyes are not a familiar sight any other day either.

With color TV, the Derby would really come into its own. Just think of that bright red blood, and all those purple bruises.

Special Dateline

BEHIND-SCENES AT THE ARMY-McCARTHY HEARINGS

WASHINGTON. Coverage of the Senator Joe McCarthy vs. the Army Hearings marks another milestone of public service by the television networks. The job is costing them more than $1,000,000 in cancelled commercial programs and actual expenses. By far the biggest expense is borne by NBC.

Estimated audience before television screens for this show is much more than 30,000,000 daily. What gives these hearings a larger audience than saw the Kefauver crime sessions is the fact that there are now nearly 300 more television stations operating, and millions more sets in the homes . . .

The Senate Committee made a deep bow to television in its preparations. Normally, in a controversial hearing, opposing factions would be placed at opposite ends of the long committee table. If you watched this one, you noticed that Senator McCarthy and his top aides, and Secretary of the Army Robert T. Stevens and his assistants sat right next to each other . . . this was to make it easier for the television cameras to cover them both.

The first day, the McCarthy team sat at the end of the table with the Army team at right angles to them, near the end. Thereafter they exchanged positions daily. Reason was to give each group an equal chance at full-face and profile views for the cameras.

Senator Karl Mundt, acting chairman of the Investigating Committee, was responsible for a new "first." He permitted erection of a three-tiered platform along one wall for the newsreel cameras. Five of these 10 cameras have been working for television. Although CBS has one of the newsreel cameras, Edward R. Murrow had another one there exclusively to make shots for his own shows.

If you noticed people perspiring, the heat came from the big hot lights illuminating the scene for the newsreel cameras. TV is not that harsh.

Reports are strong that Ray H. Jenkins, Tennessee Republican who is chief counsel for the Investigating Committee, plans to use the hearings and the opportunity to reach millions via TV as a springboard to launch a campaign for the U.S. Senate. This would create a most unusual situation. His opponent would be Senator Estes Kefauver, running for re-election in Tennessee. Kefauver made a national reputation and nearly won the Democratic presidential nomination, thanks to his televised crime hearings.

WHO'S ON FIRST?

Lou Costello has been asking Bud Abbott for the last 17 years

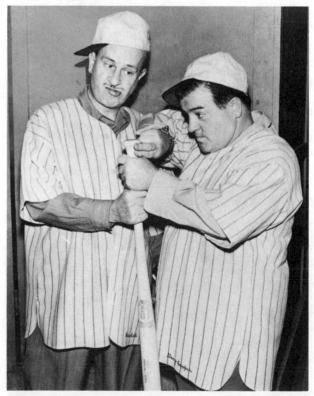

Still another baseball problem confronts comedians Bud Abbott (left), and Lou Costello

Practically everyone's chuckled at Abbott and Costello's "Who's on First?" routine, one they've performed more than 10,000 times during the past 17 years. Given the same material, can you get the same laughs? By publishing, for perhaps the first time, part of the famed skit, TV Guide *now offers you a chance to find out.*

ABBOTT—You know, strange as it may seem, they give ballplayers nowadays very peculiar names. Now, on the St. Louis team Who's on first, What's on second, I Don't Know is on third.

COSTELLO—That's what I want to find out. I want you to tell me the names of the fellows on the St. Louis team.

ABBOTT—I'm telling you. Who's on first, What's on second, I Don't Know is on third.

COSTELLO—You know the fellows' names?

ABBOTT—Yes.

COSTELLO—Well, then, who's playin' first?

A.—Yes.

C.—I mean the fellow's name on first base.

A.—Who.

C.—The fellow playin' first base.

A.—Who.

C.—The guy on first base.

A.—Who is on first.

C.—Well, what are you askin' me for?

A.—I'm not asking you. I'm telling you. Who is on first.

C.—I'm asking you, who's on first?

A.—That's the man's name!

C.—That's whose name?

A.—Yes.

C.—Well, go ahead tell me!

A.—Who.

C.—Have you got a first baseman on first?

A.—Certainly.

C.—Then who's playing first?

A.—Absolutely.

C.—Well, all I'm trying to find out is what's the guy's name on first base.

A.—Oh, no, no. What is on second base.

C.—I'm not asking you who's on second.

A.—Who's on first.

C.—That's what I'm trying to find out.

A.—Now, take it easy.

C.—What's the guy's name on first base?

A.—What's the guy's name on second base.

C.—I'm not askin' ya who's on second.

A.—Who's on first.

C.—I don't know.

A.—He's on third.

C.—If I mentioned the third baseman's name, who did I say is playing third?

A.—No, Who's playing first.

C.—Stay offa first, will ya?

A.—Well, what do you want me to do?

C.—Now, what's the guy's name on first base?

A.—What's on second.

C.—I'm not asking ya who's on second.

A.—Who's on first.

C.—I don't know.

A.—He's on third.

C.—There I go back to third again.

A.—Please. Now what is it you want to know?

C.—What is the fellow's name on third base?

A.—What is the fellow's name on second base.

C.—I'm not askin' ya who's on second.

A.—Who's on first.

C.—I don't know. (Makes noises) You got an outfield?

A.—Oh, sure.

C.—The left fielder's name?

A.—Why.

C.—I just thought I'd ask.

A.—Well, I just thought I'd tell you.

C.—Then tell me who's playing left field.

A.—Who's playing first.

C.—Stay out of the infield. I want to know what's the fellow's name in left field.

A.—What is on second.

C.—I'm not asking you who's on second.

A.—Now take it easy, take it easy.

C.—And the left fielder's name?

A.—Why.

C.—Because.

A.—Oh, he's center field.

C.—Wait a minute. You got a pitcher?

A.—Wouldn't this be a fine team without a pitcher?

C.—Tell me the pitcher's name.

A.—Tomorrow.

C.—You don't want to tell me today?

A.—I'm telling you, man.

C.—Then go ahead.

A.—Tomorrow.

C.—What time tomorrow are you gonna tell me who's pitching?

A.—Now listen. Who is not pitching. Who is on—

C.—I'll break your arm if you say who's on first.

A.—Then why come up here and ask?

C.—I want to know what's the pitcher's name.

A.—What's on second.

C.—Ya gotta catcher?

A.—Yes.

C.—The catcher's name?

A.—Today.

C.—Today. And Tomorrow's pitching.

A.—Yes.

C.—I'm a good catcher too, you know.

A.—I know that.

C.—I would like to catch. Tomorrow's pitching and I'm catching.

A.—Yes.

C.—Tomorrow throws the ball and the guy up bunts the ball.

A.—Yes.

C.—Now when he bunts the ball—me being a good catcher—I want to throw the guy out at first base, so I pick up the ball and throw it to who?

A.—Now, that's the first thing you've said right.

C.—I DON'T EVEN KNOW WHAT I'M TALKING ABOUT.

A.—Well, that's all you have to do.

C.—Is to throw it to first base.

A.—Yes.

. . . AND WHAT'S ON SECOND?

C.—Now who's got it?

A.—Naturally.

C.—Who has it?

A.—Naturally.

C.—O.K.

A.—Now you've got it.

C.—I pick up the ball and I throw it to Naturally.

A.—No you don't. You throw the ball to first base.

C.—Then who gets it?

A.—Naturally.

C.—I throw the ball to Naturally.

A.—You don't. You throw it to Who.

C.—Naturally.

A.—Well, naturally. Say it that way.

c.—I said I'd throw the ball to Naturally.

a.—You don't. You throw it to Who.

c.—Naturally.

a.—Yes.

c.—So I throw the ball to first base and Naturally gets it.

a.—No. You throw the ball to first base—

c.—Then who gets it?

a.—Naturally.

c.—That's what I'm saying.

a.—You're not saying that.

c.—I throw the ball to first base.

a.—Then Who gets it.

c.—He better get it.

a.—That's it. All right now, don't get excited. Take it easy.

c.—Now I throw the ball to first base, whoever it is grabs the ball, so the guy runs to second.

a.—Uh-huh.

c.—Who picks up the ball and throws it to what. What throws it to I don't know. I don't know throws it back to tomorrow—a triple play.

a.—Yeah. It could be.

a.—Another guy gets up and it's a long fly ball to center. Why? I don't know. And I don't care.

a.—What was that?

c.—I said, I don't care.

a.—Oh, that's our shortstop.

c.—(Makes noises—steps close to Abbott and they glare at each other.)

This is Murrow...

Ed Murrow, whose slow, pedantic voice is as familiar to Americans as that of the President of the United States, has, after 19 years of broadcasting, finally become a controversial figure. Last March, Murrow raised his voice in protest against the investigative methods used by Senator Joseph McCarthy. TV's top newsman immediately found himself labeled a communist by the McCarthyites and the greatest champion of freedom since Patrick Henry by anti-McCarthyites.

Despite the hullabaloo, Murrow is neither of these, although he certainly is on the side of freedom. He doesn't believe TV is a pulpit from which to preach his own "prejudices"—a word he uses freely. "If we snuck our own ideas in," he says, "it would be an abuse of a monopolized opportunity."

In his small smoke-filled, book-lined CBS office, the lanky newsman described his stand and his "prejudices" and explained his constant use of the term. "Everyone is a prisoner of his own experiences," he says. "No one can eliminate prejudices—just recognize them."

Ed headed CBS radio in Europe during World War

(CBS)

II. In 1938, when the Nazis marched into Austria (the whole staff then consisted of Murrow and William Shirer), Ed began his broadcasting career "sort of in desperation and without authorization." Of this experience, he says, "I saw the Anschluss at Vienna. I saw the Austrians and Czechs lose their freedom. I saw terror and fear so strong that when I saw the McCarthy tactics, I felt obliged to speak my piece. But I labeled is as clearly as I knew how."

He went on to say, "Any reputation I may have for impartiality, I stand or fall on. To use the loudspeaker as an instrument to reflect or regurgitate my own convictions or prejudices is an abuse of our privileges of the press. We will do what our judgment tells us is of interest."

No one—CBS, sponsor Aluminum Company of America or the Republican Party—told Ed what to do about McCarthy. This was a conscience piece. Ed says, "I have a wonderful arrangement with my sponsor. They make aluminum and I make film. I have no contract with CBS. I know nothing about ratings. I do the best job I know how. If I got involved in ratings I might be tempted to 'hot up' the copy. And I never want to do that."

Whether Murrow was right or not depends largely on the side of the political fence from which you view him. But Murrow believes what Will Rogers called "the big, normal majority," or what the late Chief Justice Harlan F. Stone once referred to as "the long, sober, second look of the American people" will eventually find the truth. "We're not a people to be terrorized into silence," Murrow says.

What Murrow tries hardest to get listeners to understand is that "They are not to think they're thinking when they are only rearranging their prejudices. The basic obligation of anybody of the press is not to say, 'This is what I think,' but 'These are the basic facts which led me to this conclusion.' If their conclusion is different from yours, that's okay, too," he added.

Ed grew up on farms and in logging camps in the West, where his father worked. Last year, for *See It Now*, Murrow and crew visited a logging camp. Ed watched as a lumberjack lined up his apparatus, trying to maneuver a particularly heavy log. Murrow suggested, "Why don't you tight-line it?" He was ignored. After a while, he yelled, "Whistle them down, you dope, you'll break all the rigging."

After that, he was given the respect due one of the boys, instead of a visiting college professor from the East—a status many people erroneously attribute to him. As a matter of fact, his education is quite unspectacular. He was graduated from Washington State College, class of 1930, with "an appetite to study law, but not the money."

His slow, studied manner of speaking once prompted CBS speech consultant W. Cabell Greet to comment, "He sounds like an unfrocked bishop." But it wasn't always this way. Ed says that between 1933 and 1935 he spent a lot of time with a professor who had been flung out of Germany. "As the professor's speech improved, my rate of speaking slowed down."

With a touch of pride, he points out that he spent nine years in England as European director of CBS radio and "consciously did *not* develop an English accent." Off camera, he likes to sprinkle his speech with colloquialisms. His favorite word is *ain't*.

He considers himself an outdoorsman and says, "I get more satisfaction out of understanding the nomenclature of a logging operation than writing a piece on Western European defense." He plays golf and hunts and is teaching his son, Casey, nine, to shoot on his farm in Dutchess County, New York.

Although Murrow, at 46, is on a first-name basis with many of the top-ranking brass and statesmen of the world, he doesn't like being top brass himself. He calls his brief tenure as a CBS executive a "sentence." He dislikes budgets, meetings and the occasional necessity of firing someone. "Who am I to play God?" he asks. "The person you have to fire is usually someone who just made a down payment on a new house or whose wife just had a baby. I happen to come from working-class people and that's where I like to be. When the story of labor is involved, I always have to go around to the other side of the desk. It's the same with British policy. You can't live with a people for nine years and not develop a fondness for them. That's what I mean when I say you can't eliminate prejudices. You can only recognize them."

His visits, via *Person to Person*, to the homes of the great, the near-great or the well-known have revealed that Murrow owns an enormous curiosity. He believes the real genesis of this show is that even the most sophisticated person can't resist looking into open windows. "So we decided to show unordinary people doing ordinary things. The show is dramatic only because people are dramatic."

Ed goes visiting: he has friends in both the Democratic . . . (CBS)

For a *Person to Person* visit, a crew of 15 moves in to set up TV connections. About 100 people work on this show. This includes linemen, artists, travel department employees, editors, publicity writers, engineers, secretaries, typists, photographers. Co-producer Jesse Zousmer explained it: "A man of his stature can't take chances or say, 'Well, if the line breaks down, I'll kid around.'"

Murrow feels that moving his crew into a home is akin to an invasion. "I always act like a guest in the house. I wouldn't dream of throwing anyone a curved question."

According to Zousmer, many viewers "bawl us out for not going into the deep, heavy stuff," but the staff agrees it would be unfair to ask people to perform professionally. "We got Jayne and Audrey Meadows to sing 'Jesus Loves Me' in Chinese," Zousmer says. (The girls lived in China as children.) "And Paddy De Marco to sing 'All of Me.' But if we asked Lily Pons to sing an opera, we'd be obligated to pay her for one."

Zousmer explained that Ed constantly reaches for contrast on this show. When they visited Arthur Godfrey on his Virginia farm, they achieved contrast by following with a visit to a young, unknown actor, Bill McCutcheon. Bill earns approximately $4000 a year, has a new car, wife, baby, tiny apartment and is as happy as any man ever was.

If Ed can't visit the home of the person to be interviewed prior to the telecast, a photographer is sent out to get a complete picture layout. Despite the hectic schedule of preparing for five 15-minute radio shows and two half-hour TV shows a week, Ed will go several hundred miles for an interview. If the distance is too great for him to take the time for traveling, Ed sends

. . . and the Republican Parties (CBS)

one of his co-producers—Zousmer, John Aaron or John Horn.

"Keep 'em guessing," is Ed's theory about this show. And, so far, he has unpredictably combined such pairs as Martha Raye and Muhammad Ali; Perle Mesta and Bert Lahr; Archbishop Cushing and Lilly Dache.

Ed's greatest lament is that he has to cut too much of the material on *See It Now*. His headline-making interview with atomic physicist Dr. J. Robert Oppenheimer was pared down from 2½ hours of film. Murrow and crew were three days and three nights at Remembrance Rock with Carl Sandburg, and wound up with six hours of film. "He is the most remarkable man alive. At 76, he has total recall. He's as close to Lincoln as you'll ever get—and we had to cut his film to 26 minutes."

In Ed's office is a picture of Sandburg standing near the Lincoln Memorial. It is inscribed, "To Ed—reporter, historian, inquirer, actor, ponderer, seeker." If Ed ever thinks of himself as any of these things, it is as a reporter. And at that, it's a nebulous thought. "A reporter is always concerned with tomorrow," he says. "There's nothing tangible of yesterday. All I can say I've done is agitate the air 10 or 15 minutes and then *boom!*—it's gone."

Zousmer says, "Sure, maybe that's all he does. But one thing about Ed, whatever he does, he does with integrity. He ain't going to lie to you. He doesn't need money. He's a success. He has a happy home life. He hunts, travels, shoots. If he wants to go to Korea, he goes. If he wants to talk about Eisenhower or McCarthy, he talks. And I think he's been right more often than not."

Kathy Pedell

A SUMMER SHOW
HITS THE JACKPOT

$64,000 prize, carefully picked contestants keep nation glued to its television sets

George Burns, Gracie Allen, Jack Benny and Mary Livingstone were vacationing in New York recently. They had arranged one evening to see "Bus Stop," a hit Broadway show. Suddenly Benny remembered that on that same night Mrs. Catherine E. Kreitzer was to appear for her final round on *The $64,000 Question*. They immediately cancelled their "Bus Stop" reservations and stayed at their hotel to see whether Mrs. Kreitzer would take her $32,000 or go on to the $64,000 question.

That's just one example of how this new jackpot quiz program has captured the public imagination. On a hot July evening, when the most avid viewers usually would

shun their TV sets to stay outdoors, millions of people throughout the country rushed to tune in *The $64,000 Question*. You can walk down almost any residential street when the show is on and hardly miss a word of the dialogue. The program probably has caught on faster with viewers than any show since Milton Berle first hit television.

Although *The $64,000 Question* reaped the usual advance publicity, no one could have predicted that its rise to the top of the rating lists would be so phenomenal. The program was launched June 7. Within four weeks it had zoomed to No. 1 spot in the Trendex line-up with a 23.1 rating. A week later, on the night Mrs. Kreitzer decided to go home with her $32,000 winnings, the rating almost doubled at 43. Even more striking was the fact that 79.4 percent of all TV sets in use that night were tuned to *The $64,000 Question*. No show in his company's history, says a Trendex spokesman, has done so well in the summer.

Numerous TV Guide readers have written in to ask how the sponsor can afford to give away all that money. Actually, even with the jackpot prizes, the program is not expensive in terms of current TV budgets. While producer Louis G. Cowan declines to reveal the show's cost, the best trade estimate puts it at about $15,000 a week (exclusive of network time charges). That includes the salaries paid emcee Hal March, the orchestra, camera crew and stagehands, the sets, props and incidentals. In the first six weeks, some $65,000 was awarded in prizes, or an average of $10,833 a week. Even adding that to the show's budget, the total would be only about $25,833. And in terms of the millions of viewers who see the sponsor's commercials each week, the cost of the program is almost unbelievably low.

Other Top 10 shows cost much more. Last season's *Jackie Gleason Show* cost $72,500 and the Milton Berle and *Disneyland* shows were $90,000 a week each. *The Jack Benny Show*, a half-hour program like *The $64,000 Question*, cost $42,500. Groucho Marx's is $35,000; George Gobel's is $35,000 and Arthur Godfrey's *Talent Scouts* is about $30,000. Among the panel quiz shows, *I've Got a Secret* cost $22,500 and *What's My Line*, about $27,500. All these figures exclude network charges. The sponsor of *The $64,000 Question* is the first to admit that he has a good "buy." A new product introduced on the show the second week had become the company's best-seller within five weeks.

Why has the show caught on so fast? According to producer Cowan, it's because "What is happening in front of the audience is real—it's pure TV." He compared it to watching a baseball telecast, where the audience doesn't know the winning team until the final out is made. "Even in our office there was almost a 50-50 split opinion on whether Mrs. Kreitzer would go ahead," he said.

The sponsor's advertising agency believes it is "empathy" that has made the show a success—an emotional quality that brings viewers into the show and makes them more than just onlookers. All that may be true, of course; but don't forget the prizes. Where else can a TV contestant win $64,000?

"Now for $8,000 . . ." Hal March pops the question to Bayard MacMichael (CBS)

Left, Redmond O'Hanlon and his wife, Marguerite, are jubilant with his $16,000. Right, Catherine E. Kreitzer: she quit when she was $32,000 ahead (Both photos Wide World)

Actually, what with the tax bite (see table below), a contestant must be a very confident—and a very reckless—person to try for the $64,000. There have been rumors that the show may be revised after the first 26 weeks to take care of this problem. Cowan, however, denies it. Meanwhile, March, the master of ceremonies, is quoted as saying he is convinced that no one will take a crack at the jackpot.

Cowan, a veteran independent packager of radio and TV shows (*Stop the Music* and *Juvenile Jury*), dreamed this one up while vacationing in the West Indies last February. He sold it to a sponsor a week after he returned to New York. Originally, it was to have a lot of gimmicks and gags but immediately took a turn to the serious side.

How can the average person get a crack at all that loot? Write a letter to *The $64,000 Question*, CBS, 485 Madison Avenue, New York 22, N.Y.

The letter should include as much personal information about yourself as possible—the type of work you do, the books you have read, your hobbies, education, family life. The producers also would like a snapshot of you, and photostats of any pertinent documents (such as your college diploma), but only if these can be spared, because they cannot be returned.

You may state the category of questions you'd like to try (Mrs. Kreitzer wrote in, saying, "Add the Bible as a category and I will show you how to win $64,000"), but this isn't necessary.

If, after reading your letter, the producers think you'd make a good contestant, they will get in touch with you. In other words: Don't call them—they'll call you.

Applicants are carefully screened, for a number of reasons: age, sex, occupation and locality (to provide a nicely rounded group); personality ("We want to bring into the American home the kind of people who would be welcome in anyone's living room"); and appearance—not necessarily good looks but "clean, decent-appearing persons."

Then the research starts to make certain the applicants have not misrepresented themselves. Cowan's of-

fice checks with their ministers, priests or rabbis, with their banks and their places of work. Finally, a check is made on the applicants' knowledge and abilities.

The show originates in New York. Suppose an applicant from California sounds as though he might be a good contestant. How would Cowan's office check his qualifications? "If we think such a person sounds good enough, we'll fly a man out there to interview him," he said. "Either that or bring him to New York. We've flown several people here only to find that we could not use them. We also fly our contestants to and from their homes for the show each week, once they get past that important level of $8000 and answer only one question a week."

It should be noted that Cowan's care in selecting contestants has paid off handsomely for the program. That Staten Island cop Redmond O'Hanlon was an all-American choice—a husband, a father, a New York policeman and a Shakespearean scholar. And Mrs. Kreitzer impressed so many people that Ed Sullivan immediately hired her to do a series of Bible readings on his *Toast of the Town*.

All of which has added up to a hot summer's hottest show. If any more proof be needed, there are just two more factors to be considered: First, the vast amount of page 1 newspaper space devoted, week by week, to the program has poured fuel on the fire of suspense. Second, there's that matter of ratings. Despite the weather, (which broke all sorts of records—and every one in the wrong direction), viewers have remained glued to their TV sets. At least on Tuesday evenings.

Bob Stahl

How much does a contestant have left, after taxes, at the various stages of The $64,000 Question? *Assuming a wife and two children, a gross annual income of $5,000 and the standard 10% tax deduction, here is how much he has:*

PRIZE	AFTER TAXES
$ 1,000	$ 820
$ 2,000	$ 1,640
$ 4,000	$ 3,246
$ 8,000	$ 6,324
$16,000	$11,956
$32,000	$21,220
$64,000	$34,460

The Truth Behind

GODFREY'S FEUD WITH THE PRESS

PART I

The Decline and Fall of Arthur Godfrey in the esteem of newspapermen has been one of the most startling reversals in television's brief history.

Only two years ago Godfrey was virtually enshrined by the press. At the time of his hip operation in May 1953 even the fact that he tied a shoelace was recorded in respectful tones.

Newspapers printed adulatory columns and sentimental editorial cartoons. And this was a lead editorial appearing in the New York Daily News:

BE SEEING YOU, ARTHUR

Just want to wish Arthur Godfrey the best of luck and then some, in his forthcoming hospital hitch.

So great was the veneration displayed by the press that a trade magazine, Broadcasting-Telecasting, was moved to observe: "The deification of Arthur Godfrey has been in process for some time, but his triumph over illness and the opportunities it made for the CBS publicity factory have rendered it complete. It is only a matter of time until the second syllable of 'Godfrey' will be forgotten."

And then, in the course of just a few months, the entire picture changed.

First, on October 19, 1953, came the on-the-air firing—for lack of "humility"—of one of Godfrey's "Friends," Julius La Rosa. The newspaper keynote was Disillusionment.

Wrote Ben Gross in the New York Daily News: "There's no star who can't be replaced—and forgotten ... The Great Godfrey legend has been deflated!"

And Jack Gould in the New York Times: "The carefully nurtured illusion that his supporting company was one happy family has lost some of its luster. What always has been common knowledge in the trade is now public knowledge: Mr. Godfrey likes his own way and is decidedly the stern master of his own household."

And Terrence O'Flaherty in the San Francisco Chronicle: "Unfortunately for a well-preserved myth, the La Rosa situation has shown Arthur Godfrey is a small man in a very big job."

And Washington TV columnist Bernie Harrison, a Godfrey admirer since his Washington disc jockey days:

"Anyone can pick the wrong word and Arthur certainly picked a beauty in 'humility.' But Arthur's insistence that he had a perfect right to fire La Rosa on the air because he hired him on the air seems to me to be his grandest blunder."

And syndicated columnist John Crosby: "The Godfrey show is one big happy—(happy my eye!)—family and once you become a little Godfrey, you got to stay home and bring the master his pipe and slippers ... Of all the people in the world I'd pick as being least aware of the meaning of humility, Godfrey is way up at the top of the list, jostling Jackie Gleason and Milton Berle."

Even International News Service columnist Jack O'Brian, who had long been one of Godfrey's most avid drum-beaters, sadly termed the La Rosa firing "unfortunate reasoning or whim."

Godfrey's often contradictory explanations—that La Rosa had asked for his release; that he wanted to help the young singer increase his earnings; that lack of air time had cut short a big send-off—failed to convince New York newspapermen.

Wrote Theo Wilson in the News: "Arthur Godfrey, who can sell anything from tea to soup, put on a two-hour unrehearsed program yesterday in which he sold 'The Godfrey Story' to an audience of newspapermen invited to his sixth-floor inner sanctum."

And Robert Williams in the Post: "Arthur Godfrey, who gave the sack to crooner Julius La Rosa ... appeared to be holding one today as the knocks continued to pour in."

And Fern Marja, in the same paper: "Of thousands of letters ... an absurdly small percentage backed Godfrey and his whim of iron."

However, no matter what the newspapermen wrote, a huge and loyal legion of admirers has never swerved in its devotion to Godfrey, and has met every derogatory comment in the press with letters and phone calls of protest.

Just when the public pressure was beginning to ease on Godfrey, came the Teterboro Airport "buzzing" incident, which for six months cost him his pilot's license. Godfrey attempted to make light of the whole affair. On his morning show, he held up a newspaper and said: "Boy, did you see that? Ain't that a beaut? . . . I never thought I'd get headlines like that until I was dead ... 'Godfrey Cited As Wild Flier. Port Authority Files Charge.' Roop-di-doo-dee rocky woe!"

Newspapermen didn't share his jollity. Columnist Ed Sullivan, a fellow CBS television star, wrote angrily: "The flippancies of Arthur Godfrey, in answering charges of reckless operation of his DC-3 ... are shocking. Godfrey is 50 years old—hardly the age for a hot-rodder. . . . Such fliers are as dangerous as a drunk with a loaded gun."

Martin Kivel, in the News, referred to Godfrey as a "television entertainer, second only to Captain Video as TV's most daring pilot." And the Philadelphia Inquirer observed editorially, "Godfrey's reactions have been those of an immature person ... Humility has its place, and it need not be confined to Godfrey underlings."

Godfrey again suffered a bad press last December, when Larry Puck was dropped as producer of Godfrey's Wednesday night show, reportedly because Puck was planning to marry Marion Marlowe—a report Godfrey emphatically denied. And in April the wholesale dismissal of Miss Marlowe, Haleloke, the Mariners and three writers loosed still another torrent on Godfrey's graying red head.

"Working for Arthur Godfrey these days," Ben Gross mused, "is about as risky as being a commissar in Moscow." And Jack Gould felt that "Arthur Godfrey has chosen an odd way to start his comeback. His decision to plow under a few of the little Godfreys is no surprise, but the form of his spring housecleaning would seem to suggest that he is neither the most tidy nor tactful soul in television."

(There has been an occasional breach in this solid wall of anti-Godfreyism. Washington's Bernie Harrison, for instance, commented: "What's all the fuss about? He tried to handle the dismissals properly this time, with a CBS official by his side. . . . He was eminently correct in his procedure, heartless as it might seem. The wonder, to me, is that he didn't axe some of his performers long ago.")

No man to run from a fight, Godfrey has done his share of "dishing it out." He has countered newspaper comment with a barrage of choice invectives. Among them: "Dope!" (for Ed Sullivan), "Liar!" (or words to that effect, for columnist–*What's My Line* panelist Dorothy Kilgallen and for columnist Danton Walker), "Fatuous ass!" (for John Crosby), "These jerk newspapermen!" and "Muckrakers!" (for all and sundry).

On a recent radio broadcast he labeled most news stories about himself as "pure canard, pure manufactured lies, no basis in fact at all. It really amuses me what people do to try to make headlines. . . . I don't give a—[pause]—what they print!"

Just after the "buzzing" incident, Godfrey told Frank Parker on the air: "I've learned the hard way . . . Nothing. I tell them [reporters and photographers] nothing. That's the only thing you can do. If you say anything to them whatsoever, they'll foul it up."

Yet, some time earlier, Godfrey announced gleefully: "Anything I love to do, it's cross up a newspaper."

Ironically, the same Arthur Godfrey credits a newspaperman with catapulting him to fame and fortune. Columnist Walter Winchell heard an all-night Godfrey broadcast when Godfrey's future looked bleak.

"He had some celebrities with him," Godfrey recalled years later, ". . . including Billy Rose, Ben Bernie, Ruth Etting and Jimmy Cannon. He asked me to kid Ben Bernie. Next day he had a swell plug for me in his column. Then he put more plugs in and I got 30 offers from Broadway. Put down January 26, 1934, as the luckiest day in my life and Walter Winchell as the guy who made it that way."

PART II

Shortly after the firing of Julius La Rosa and its backwash of press comment, Arthur Godfrey told an American Weekly interviewer: "I learned a long time ago to read as little as possible about myself. First they build you up; then they tear you down.

"While they were building me up, I quit reading the stuff because it embarrassed me. When the tide turned this year and the boys began tearing me down, a couple of good friends of mine told me not to read it. They said I've got enough to do without taking on any extra worries.

"I thought about it for a while and decided they were right, because, no matter what they say about me on the front page, there are a couple of lines on a back page which say that from 10 A.M. until 11:30 A.M. I'll be on radio and television five days a week, and on Monday and Wednesday nights, and, by golly, I *know* that's right."

But the fact is that American newspapers have been printing laudatory tidbits about Godfrey for years. A New York Post article termed Godfrey's newspaper coverage "probably the best press ever accorded a celebrity, in or out of show business."

"Dames and guys, city slickers and country rubes, all like him," declared columnist Earl Wilson. "If he'd been around, Hatfield and McCoy would never have feuded—they'd have been down at the barbershop, laughing about Arthur Godfrey."

Adding to the chorus of praise were:

Columnist Robert Ruark: "I love this ancient urchin . . . His energy is limitless, his wit the liveliest, his friendship boundless, and . . . he should live, already, another 100 years."

John Crosby: "His freckles and ruddy complexion contribute a good deal to a personality that is easily one of the wonders of our times."

Jack Gould: "Visually Mr. Godfrey is a wow—the freshest, most personable and most engaging comedian to be seen in years."

Kay Gardella, New York Daily News: "Arthur Godfrey will definitely return . . . This is the best news we've heard yet—even better than those color-TV stories. You can keep your tinted video. Just give us Godfrey."

But these halcyon days are past. With relatively few exceptions, the nation's newspaper writers now seem hostile to their onetime buddy. Circumstances alter cases, of course. But were circumstances—or changes in the Godfrey personality—to blame?

It's no longer the same Arthur Godfrey, suggested the New York Daily News's Ben Gross, who two years ago summed up the secret of Godfrey's appeal in these words: "It is his friendliness, his good cheer, his small-

Press was most sympathetic to Godfrey at time of his 1953 hip operation in Boston (Wide World)

boy mischievousness and his kindly philosophy . . . Or maybe it's his magnetism, his personal attractiveness."

Last May, Gross was singing a considerably less friendly tune: "Arthur complained that most radio-TV writers who slam him don't know a thing about him . . . But what he forgot to add is that to see the Great Man requires the eating of more humble pie than trying to interview the Queen of England. He is the master of the brush-off, with a generally contemptuous manner toward newspapermen."

This wasn't true in his Washington days, when Godfrey maintained a sizable bar-equipped office and used to tell newspapermen: "I built the place for you fellows."

In November 1950 Bernie Harrison, now with the Washington Evening Star, was writing: "I see very little difference between the Godfrey of the networks and the Godfrey of WJSV. His red hair may be fading, but his puckish sense of humor is still intact. Maybe you can't reach him as easily as you could, but then more people are trying to reach him now."

At almost the same time, the San Francisco Chronicle's Terrence O'Flaherty wrote: "In his relations with columnists [Godfrey] has often been split-tongued and slithery-tailed . . . ungentlemanly."

John Crosby, one of the most caustic critics of Godfrey and just about everyone else on TV, thought Godfrey's physical condition might have something to do with his peevishness.

"Godfrey seemed tired and heavy-hearted on his last show, and for good reason," Crosby wrote at the close of the 1953–54 season. "He has been in pain and he has had a pretty bad press this year. He's not entirely blameless for the bad press. Discussing the drinking habits of his associates on a national network is not calculated to endear him to just everyone. Still, the pain in his hip can be blamed at least partly for the Godfrey indiscretions."

Actually, however, the Godfrey characteristics which have been getting him into hot water with the press have *always* been part of the Godfrey makeup—as was duly noted.

Reported Time in February 1950: "Close associates say that Godfrey's contrariness is his outstanding characteristic. . . . He is confusingly shy one minute and brash the next, sentimental and savage, generous and stingy, as quick to unreasoning affection as unreasoning dislike. Every confirmed Godfrey fan knows that from one moment to the next he may erupt into ribaldry, beery pathos or waspish exasperation."

This analysis seems as accurate now as then. So why did the press stop finding these traits "lovable"?

The answer seems to lie in the fact that most Americans sympathize with the underdog. They prefer to root for David rather than Goliath. When Godfrey played fast and loose on the air with commercials, sponsors, his network employers or Congressmen, he was a brash, but admirable individualist battling against opponents stronger than himself.

The La Rosa firing, however, suddenly changed the complexion of things. Godfrey's role was suddenly switched—from hero to villain, from crusader to bully.

Godfrey is now embarked on an all-out feud with the press. In recent interviews with favored newspapermen, he has dwelled on past "errors" by their colleagues. He has promised to even the score in an upcoming autobiography.

Some people believe that in again taking on a huge institutional opponent like the press, rather than individuals, Godfrey may be making a bid to regain the backing and affection of those of his TV and radio fans who have left him.

If so, he may be making a mistake. He may be alienating them even further. But it's a calculated risk.

MARCH 5, 1956

7:30 ⑨ KING KONG — Movie

Somewhere in the South Seas lies lonely, forbidding Skull Island. It is uncharted and almost unknown to man. The island's principal architectural point is a gigantic wall which separates the two sets of inhabitants: On one side lives a tribe of superstitious natives; on the other, animals—prehistoric animals. These beasts (tyrannosaurus, pterodactyl and others) have a self-appointed master, the mighty terror of the uncivilized world—King Kong. Kong, who measures 50 feet high, has a penchant for murder. To placate him, the tribe, at intervals, offers up one of its maidens as a human sacrifice.

Carl Denham has heard strange tales of Skull Island. This fabulous and rather foolish moviemaker has in his possession a map showing the island's location, and plans to shoot a film there. He hires Ann Darrow, a down-and-out actress, to play the role every other actress in Hollywood has turned down. He charters a boat and a handful of seamen and they set sail, ignorant of the terror they are soon to let loose upon humanity.

Made in 1933, the movie, with its spectacular visual effects, paved the way for future "monster" films. To this day, producer-director Merian C. Cooper has refused to divulge how some of the effects were produced.

CAST

Ann Darrow	Fay Wray
Carl Denham	Robert Armstrong
Driscoll	Bruce Cabot
Capt. Englehorn	Frank Reicher
Weston	Sam Hardy

New York City is menaced by King Kong
(Museum of Modern Art/Film Stills Archive)

Milton Berle (NBC)

Do you remember . . .

when some stars started to bloom
(and others quickly wilted)
in a decade under the TV sun?

In 1947, according to the late Fred Allen, television looked like "a collection of passport photos." In '47 NBC had a four-station network (New York, Schenectady, Philadelphia and Washington) and CBS was preparing to shut down its studio operation almost completely after its TV color system had been turned down

"Chicago School": Dave Garroway and friends set a style in early TV days (NBC)

"New York School": Arthur Godfrey and friends (CBS)

Ed Murrow (CBS)

Bob Smith with Howdy Doody (NBC)

by the Federal Communications Commission.

Nevertheless, 1947 was the year TV first really caught the fancy of the American public. On January 2, 1947, TV reached an important milestone. It brought from Washington the opening of the 80th Congress. Later in the year President Truman was visited in the White House; and millions of fans—most of them tarrying in neighborhood spas—watched the nation's first World Series telecast. *Kraft Theater, Howdy Doody* and *Meet the Press* all began their TV careers in '47; so did a singer named Kyle MacDonnell, who later owned a basset hound named Morgan, also a TV star.

In 1948 TV continued to grow. CBS, abandoning its early indifference to network programming, announced it was building "the world's biggest TV studio" in Grand Central Station. *Broadway Open House,* starring Jerry Lester, Morey Amsterdam and Dagmar, was the first late-night variety network show at NBC; and during the season José Ferrer did "Cyrano de Bergerac" for *Philco Playhouse* (total cost of this early hour-long "spectacular": $23,000). Ed Sullivan, Milton Berle and Arthur Godfrey made their debuts in '48 and Edward R. Murrow (he was just plain "Ed" in those days) and Don Hollenbeck teamed up for one of TV's first commentary and interview programs. In '48, ABC opened its flagship TV station in New York, and that summer the networks combined their facilities to provide the first nationwide coverage of a political convention. And—oh, yes!—in the studios it was often so hot under the set lights that girls modeling fur coats for commercials wore nothing underneath.

At NBC, Roger Bower had a show called *Stop Me If You've Heard This One,* in which he bandied jokes with Morey Amsterdam, Cal Tinney and Lew Lehr. *Ted Mack's Amateur Hour* was as successful then as it is now. Lanny Ross, the first recognizable male voice on TV, was singing "Let's Have Another Cup of Coffee" on NBC's *Swift Show,* and Faye Emerson did *Paris Cavalcade of Fashions.*

By fall, the networks were full of "name" shows (*The Bob Howard Show, Mary Kay and Johnnie, The Fitzgeralds*); of panel shows (*Meet the Press, Author Meets the Critics, Court of Current Issues, Riddle Me This*), and of dramatic hours (*Kraft TV Theater, Ford Theater*). But funnyman Bobby Clark wanted no part of it. Asked where the great comics of the future would come from, if not from TV, he said: "There won't be any."

New York's TV Guide began publication June 14, 1948, with a picture of Gloria Swanson (whose chitchat show was billed as "the most glamorous hour on TV") on its cover. In the nation there were then some 30 stations, located in 15 states and Washington, D.C., dispensing entertainment to approximately 400,000 home sets, and an uncountable number of viewers in groggeries. In fact, bistro viewing soon reached the point where Henny Youngman's brother couldn't get a job as a bartender because, Henny complained, "He didn't know how to fix the TV set."

But by the spring of the following year 2,000,000 Americans were peering happily at Faye Emerson's neckline through 600,000 receivers. Berle, on *Texaco Star Theater,* had become the biggest name on the air; and wrestling matches and roller-skating derbies had fanatical followers.

Cal Tinney and Benny Rubin were the Martin and Lewis of TV in 1949, and Wendy Barrie and Faye Emerson had replaced Kyle MacDonnell and Roberta Quinlan as first in the hearts of their countrymen. Hooper ratings established Berle, Godfrey, Sullivan and *Broadway Revue,* starring a new comic named Sid Caesar, as tops.

Rapidly the infant TV was growing up. Big names were moving in from radio, the stage and screen. Bob Hope and Perry Como, Dinah Shore and Frank Sinatra, Eddie Cantor and Jack Benny—all were joining TV.

President Truman's inauguration was televised in 1949. Sid Caesar joined Max Liebman's *Show of Shows* in '50. And in Chicago, a new school of TV technique was developing. Its champion was easygoing Dave Garroway, whose *Garroway at Large* was slow, low-pitched, easy-to-look-at TV. Eventually, *Garroway* and two other Chicago-bred shows, *Down You Go* and *Kukla, Fran and Ollie,* were seen coast to coast. Groucho Marx went on the air and in his first show established the pattern that has made *You Bet Your Life* unique among quizzes.

Color came out of the laboratories and into a few of the living rooms in 1951. That year daytime TV began in earnest—and, with the Kefauver investigations of politics and crime, TV cracked the nation's newsfronts.

By this time Jackie Gleason was starring in *Cavalcade of Stars* and Jackie Kelk was starring in *Young Mr. Bobbin.* It was touch and go as to who would make good. *I Love Lucy* made its debut in 1951 and soon topped all other programs in the ratings.

In 1953 Godfrey started firing people (first casualty: Julius La Rosa); and Berle, slipping at last in the ratings, revamped the format of his program, transforming himself from a pie-throwing clown into an actor. New sensations were Wally Cox and Red Buttons; dead ducks were Jerry Lester, Parkyakarkus, Doodles Weaver. *One Man's Family* was wavering.

A year later, Godfrey was still firing and Berle was still making a comeback. Sid Caesar and Imogene Coca, the stars of *Your Show of Shows,* split. NBC launched *Home* and *Tonight,* and the world met Senator McCarthy, George Gobel and Liberace.

The season of 1955–56 was the season of *The $64,000 Question, The Phil Silvers Show* and the *Mickey Mouse Club.* It was also the season when Milton Berle was finally outrated.

TV—in 1957—is undergoing a transformation. No longer do comedians wear women's clothes and throw pies at each other. The accent now is on drama—from Shakespeare to Shaw to Serling; on musical comedy brought to TV direct from the Broadway stage; on news coverage; on programming—even giveaway shows—that has grown in taste. All in all, it was quite a decade.

"Faysie": Miss Emerson was always on TV. With her is Morey Amsterdam (William Kahn)

Set style: Roscoe Karns, as Rocky King, a famed early TV sleuth (DuMont)

How it began: the original audition of *I Love Lucy.* **The date: June 1951.** (CBS)

Ed Sullivan (CBS)

Mickey Mouse (ABC)

Jerry Lester with Dagmar (NBC)

Hal March (CBS)

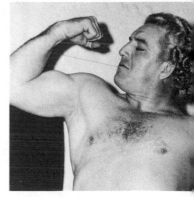

Two on a candle: Lanny Ross and Susan Shaw light up. He was one of the first singing sensations on TV (NBC)

Top cowhand: William Boyd, who owned TV rights to Hopalong Cassidy and cleaned up in early '50s (NBC)

Guess who? He's Jackie Gleason in *The Life of Riley,* **1949, his first show** (William Kahn)

Long hair: Gorgeous George (Wagner), wrestler, shows his muscle. He was tops (UPI)

Historic: the Harry S. Truman inaugural in 1949, the first to be telecast (Wide World)

Big screen: Dennis James, center, in '47, stages first TV show projected onto a movie screen in New York (DuMont)

In his library: On the wall is a portrait of his son, Richard, now seriously ill (CBS)

A Comedian Faces a Tragedy

Red Skelton reveals his thoughts on the serious illness of his son

"There's no point in kidding ourselves. Doctors today lay it on the line. They don't hold out any false hopes. At first, like any other parents, we grabbed hold of the belief that maybe tomorrow somebody, somewhere, would come up with a miraculous new drug. But it doesn't work that way. They'd have to talk about it for six months, and then it would take another six months to write and read all the papers on the subject, and six more after that to test it out. That's 18 months. Come on downstairs. I want to show you something."

Red Skelton was discussing his nine-year-old son, Richard. Last January it was revealed that Richard had leukemia, a malignancy of the white blood cells that is usually fatal. Skelton led the way down to an office at the front of his Bel Air house, a sprawling 27-room place comfortably cluttered with the memorabilia of a comedian's lifetime in show business. Maxine Davis, his secretary of long standing, was busy at a typewriter. Stacks of neatly typed letters lay on a window seat waiting for Skelton's signature.

"I sign hundreds of these every day," he said. "It's a form letter, but we've got it set up so that each one is automatically typed and looks exactly like a personal letter. We used to have two girls just to handle the normal fan mail. Now we have five. We're six or eight weeks behind. The letters have come in by the thousands—300,000, I think the last count was—but we're getting through them as fast as we can. These people took the trouble to write. Most of them don't expect an answer, but they're going to get one. I never knew people cared so much.

"I sign them all myself," he repeated. "We have four or five people around here who can sign my name so that it would fool everybody but the guys at the bank, but I sign them myself. Every one of them."

Skelton, at 44, is a gregarious man who lives in a constant state of almost compulsive laughter. If he isn't laughing, he is leading up to a laugh. The contrast when he turns momentarily serious is marked. His high-pitched voice takes on an earnestly sincere, speech-making quality. He is not a man to come to the point quickly, preferring to circle it, back off from it, even leave it entirely in favor of a readily presented laugh.

"These letters," Skelton said, his hand sweeping the office with a gesture. "I think they've given me the answer. A little girl, for instance. She wrote that her little kitty had died and she was pretty broken up about it. But then she read about Richard and saw me on the air, making people laugh, and she said it was an inspiration to her. If I could laugh, then she figured she could laugh, too.

"I've been reading a lot of religious books. There's a message in this somewhere. I'm not yet sure just what it is, but I think it means we all have a purpose in life. I don't think anyone's purpose is any greater than anyone else's, and I think mine is to make people laugh."

He plowed on, the role of serious talker weighing a little uncomfortably on his angular frame.

"We're doing something else, too. A lot of these letters, from all over the world, tell us about cures or drugs, or doctors who think they have something. We make a report of every one of them and forward them along to our doctor at the UCLA Medical Center. Every lead he hasn't already heard of gets tracked down.

"If all this can result in just one doctor or one research man's working just a little bit harder and a little bit longer for just one day, we'll feel we've accomplished something."

Skelton wandered back into the large memento-filled library that serves as the family living room. Maxine Davis looked after him and then turned back to her visitor. "It isn't easy, I know," she smiled, "but you're going to feel much better about it after you've left. That man has been an inspiration to us every single day."

Back in the library, Skelton was playing with a large and beautifully colored macaw that had appeared with him on a show and which he had impulsively bought. The bird perched on Skelton's shoulder and clucked and shrilled. "That first week in the hospital," he said, "the word apparently got around somehow and Richard asked me if he were going to die. I'm not at all sure he really knows what it means. To a child, life is unconsciously eternal.

"I said, 'Well, Richard, we all die sometime. You know when you watch television and see one of the cowboys get killed? And the very next night there's that same cowboy back again? It's something like that.' He seemed to accept that and has never mentioned it again.

"Richard now is in a period of remission. That means the disease is being controlled by drugs to the point where it's neither getting any better nor getting any worse. Nobody can tell us how long this will last. They have a boy at Harvard, at the medical school back there, they tell me has been in this remission stage for seven years now, I think the longest time on record."

"We treat him as though nothing were wrong," his wife, Georgia, broke in. "We discipline him and we try not to shower too much attention on him."

"Yes," Skelton nodded, "we have to do that. It's the only normal way of life. If we took the attitude that he should have everything his own way and then suddenly a miraculous cure were discovered, we'd have a monster on our hands. We cannot create a monster. Hitler's mother should have knocked his block off the very first time he picked up a brush and said he was going to paint the wall *his* color. She'd have saved the world a lot of grief.

"Frankly, it's harder on the others than it is on me. I'm the focal point. I get all the attention and the sympathy. But Georgia carries the load without much help.

"We had to make one more important decision right at the beginning. We had to choose a course and we chose the medical one. You'd be amazed at the number of letters we get recommending faith healers. We've got nothing against faith healers. In many instances, they do help people. But we had to make one firm choice and stick with it. We're sticking with the doctors. We're going the medical way.

"We're sticking with the doctors because we believe that through Richard they will learn a little more. And one of them, one of these days or one of these years, is going to find an answer and that answer is going to save a lot of other people. I think that's our purpose, too.

"They found the vaccine for polio. They found it because a lot of people had to sit by and watch their children suffer. And let me tell you, these American people and these people from all over the world, these 'little people,' these people *felt* this thing and they wrote these wonderful letters and everybody got behind the drive, year after year, and all of a sudden there was this vaccine. And our daughter, Valentina, will never get polio. We have a lot of people to thank for that."

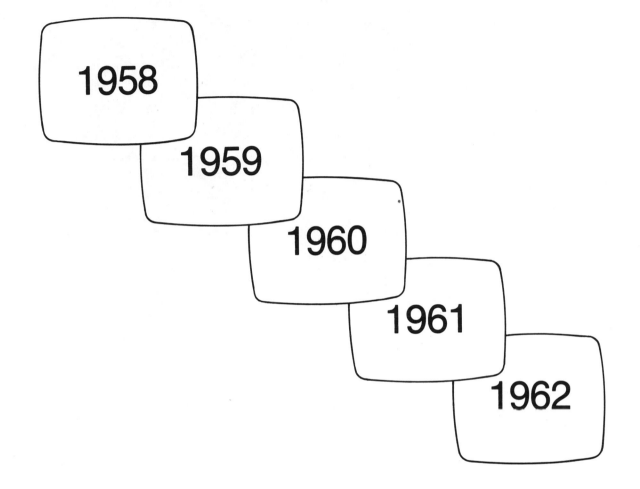

WHY "GUNSMOKE" KEEPS BLAZING AWAY

Chester (Dennis Weaver), Marshal Dillon (James Arness), and Doc Adams (Milburn Stone) are three reasons for show's success (William Read Woodfield/Globe)

The inside story of television's most popular show

Any way you look at it, *Gunsmoke* is a prodigy among TV shows. It has been in the vanguard of the "adult" Westerns and of the so-called psychological Westerns, although its makers deny any responsibility for the latter. It was—and still is—the most literate Western. It has transformed its actors from little-known bit players into celebrities mobbed everywhere they go; made tidy fortunes for its creators; and sold enough cigarets to stretch several times around the world.

Even more amazing under the circumstances, it is the most popular show of any sort on the air today—and has been right at the top ever since its beginning in radio. This despite the fact that it very often has no story in the commonly accepted sense of the word, sometimes being little more than a character sketch or vignette. Since everyone envies—and no one argues with—success, it inevitably has become the most widely imitated show. Some of the things Matt Dillon does, which used to be thought pretty daring, have become clichés because every Western does them. Thus it is fair to say

Gunsmoke is also the most influential of its kind.

How did it get that way? And what's more to the point, how does it manage to stay that way?

Like most successes, this one was achieved partly by accident and partly by dogged perseverance over the chorus of "experts" who swore it couldn't be done.

Back in 1952 there were laboring in the vineyards of CBS radio a couple of young men named Norman Macdonnell and John Meston. Meston, a Dartmouth graduate, is an angular-faced, strangely inarticulate-seeming man—a Colorado product who had spent a good deal of time working on southern Colorado ranches. Macdonnell, on the other hand, had come by his love of cowhands and their patois through a stable he had acquired in—of all places—Hollywood.

They had the notion that a Western might be done for radio which would be, as Macdonnell puts it, "non-horse-operatic," where everyone would behave more or less as human beings behave in real life, where the characters would resemble the real articles. They sat down and made out a list of all the things they planned *not* to do. No one would be allowed to say "sidewinding varmint," no one would carry two guns slung low on the hip, no one would have a favorite horse, much less one that did tricks.

Instead, the show would operate on the revolutionary but entirely valid principle that in the early West the most hated man in town was usually the marshal.

"Half the time the town tamers were worse than the gunmen they were hired to tame," explains Macdonnell. "And they were constantly suspect, no matter what good guys they were. And Matt Dillon is no exception. If you look closely you will see that there are only three in the world who care at all whether Matt lives or dies. One is Doc, who digs the bullets out of him; another is Chester, who admires him and calls him Muster Dellon; and the other is Kitty, the dance-hall girl, who loves him."

So Meston wrote a radio show called "Jeff Spain." When they showed it to a then top executive of CBS, Harry Ackerman, he told them they must be out of their minds. "Westerns are for children," he said flatly, and the idea was dropped.

However, a month or so later a show called "Operation Underground" suddenly went off the air and the network was left with an embarrassing gap in its programming. Ackerman, as it turned out, had his own title for a Western—"Gunsmoke."

"After that," says Meston, "everything was simple. We simply did 'Jeff Spain' and called it 'Gunsmoke.'"

The show was an immediate success. Even the hardest-to-please critics were impressed. Then three months later something transpired which made Macdonnell and Meston look like heroes. A movie called "High Noon" was released and suddenly the adult Western came into almost universal public acceptance. "Gunsmoke" was off and running so far ahead of the field that no one could catch it.

Three years later the transition was made to television. For this delicate operation a new producer-director was brought in, an ebullient gentleman named Charles Marquis Warren, while Macdonnell functioned as associate producer and Meston continued to write the radio scripts. It was Warren who cast the television version—and on this score he fought both Macdonnell and Meston, who were determined to simply use the radio cast, regardless of whether or not the actors suited their roles visually.

Warren won—luckily, because his casting was inspired: Big Jim Arness (whose best-known previous credit had been the title role in "The Thing"), hulking, fatherly, capable of great toughness and tenderness; Dennis Weaver, the slightly comic yet human and dignified hanger-on around the jailhouse; Milburn Stone, perfect as the elder statesman and wise man, "Doc"; and Amanda Blake, whose Kitty strikes a perfect balance between the hardness of her profession and the softness which makes her acceptable in every American home.

As it had in radio, *Gunsmoke* immediately proved a smash. What's more, the TV version had what amounted to an inexhaustible supply of scripts. The radio shows—for the most part—were adapted to the new medium. Then success began to go to everyone's head. According to Warren, "It reached the point where I'd arrive on the set in the morning only to have Arness tell me that 'Matt Dillon wouldn't say a line like that!' Everybody suddenly got to be a self-appointed authority."

After a year of this, Warren left, and the show reverted to Macdonnell and Meston.

And it should be said that it is primarily their taste and judgment that make the show what it is today. What's their secret?

"Well," says Macdonnell, "we try to capture some of the real feeling of the West. As well as something real in the people. As soon as your lead becomes a hero, you're in trouble. Sometimes we'll sit down and say to ourselves, 'You know, this fellow Dillon is just getting too noble. Let's fix him.' So we do. John writes a script where poor old Matt gets outdrawn and outgunned and pulls every dumb trick in the book. It makes him, and us, human.

"Then there is the trick of underwriting. John used to underwrite so much he'd drive everybody crazy, especially on radio. You know—with the sparse dialogue and long pauses. They kept telling us, 'You can't do it.' Every time somebody'd come up with that one, John would ask in his mumbling way, 'Where in the book does it say you can't?' So we did.

"We both like the sound of real cowboy talk. Some of it gets on the show. Like the time I heard a cowhand of mine admiring a new mare. 'Looks as if she might run a hole in the wind,' he said. John used the line in a script."

Meston's principal preoccupation is with character. Indeed, he has been accused of not being able to write stories at all. Be this as it may, he has written some 160 radio scripts and each one of them has begun, he says, with a phrase, a scrap of dialogue or some minute aspect of Western Americana that just happens to please him. "I like to write with great simplicity," he says. "And I like to have my people solve real problems realistically. I like character better than story, and to tell the truth I like radio writing better than television. In radio there is more play for the imagination."

It was Meston who conceived of the Chester character always calling Matt "Muster Dellon." This would not be unusual except that it has always seemed so inexorably right. Warren invented Chester's limp (to explain away Chester's constant presence around the marshal's office). Again, like almost everything in *Gunsmoke*, it is somehow fitting.

Says Warren, who is currently producing a fancy new Western of his own called *Rawhide:* "Gunsmoke? It proves that people will still go for folksy persiflage and that get-nowhere dialogue. But, you know, it's got something. Just don't ask me what."

Dwight Whitney

Betsy Palmer, Jackie Gleason in "The Time of Your Life" (CBS)

Review

"PLAYHOUSE 90"

Playhouse 90—now in its third season—has established itself this year as the foremost dramatic program, live *or* film, on television.

There have been ups and downs on the CBS program this year, of course, and some of the "downs" have been practically subterranean. There was a deplorable adaptation of Joseph Conrad's "Heart of Darkness," for instance, and something called "A Quiet Game of Cards"—quite possibly the most unlikely script ever turned out by Reginald Rose.

On the other hand, some of the "ups" were skyscrapers. J. P. Miller's "The Days of Wine and Roses" was easily the best original TV drama of the year, and Horton Foote's version of William Faulkner's "Old Man" was surely the best adaptation.

The dramatic semidocumentary "Seven Against the Wall" was a tremendously exciting account of gangland's St. Valentine's Day massacre in Chicago; George Balanchine's staging of "The Nutcracker" was a fine Christmas ballet; and Meade Roberts did a fine rewrite job on Henry James's "The Wings of the Dove."

A particular delight was *90*'s boozily poetic production of William Saroyan's "The Time of Your Life," while "Child of Our Time" was a heartbreakingly beautiful 90 minutes.

More recently, the show spent over $300,000 on a two-part adaptation of Ernest Hemingway's "For Whom the Bell Tolls," to make it one of the most impressive "specials" of the year.

Even some of the near misses on *90* were noteworthy. The almost slanderous "The Plot to Kill Stalin" got CBS expelled from Soviet Russia. And Rod Serling's "The Velvet Alley" rattled skeletons all over Hollywood.

Playhouse 90 producers this year included John Houseman, Fred Coe, Herbert Brodkin. Among the directors were John Frankenheimer, Ralph Nelson, Tom Donovan and Franklin Schaffner. Among the stars: Maria Schell, Jackie Gleason, Melvyn Douglas, Edward G. Robinson, Piper Laurie, Jason Robards Jr.

To these people—and particularly to Coe, Houseman and Brodkin—must go the lion's share of the credit for *90*'s esthetic success this year. Their daring, their flair and their imagination have made the program a symbol of television at its best—a program with a point of view, a program unafraid of controversy, a program alive with a sense of excitement. Long may it be with us.

Frank DeBlois

APRIL 19, 1959

A TV Guide Close-Up

CASTRO

6:00 **4** "MEET THE PRESS"— Interview

Fidel Castro, Premier of Cuba, is interviewed in Washington, D.C. Dr. Castro is in the United States on an unofficial visit at the invitation of the American Society of Newspaper Editors.

The Cuban revolutionary leader recently proposed that his country follow a neutralist course in the cold war. He will probably be questioned about this and about his criticism of U.S. restrictions on sugar imports; the trials and executions of followers of ousted dictator Batista; Communist influence in the revolution; and anti-U.S. sentiment in Latin America.

The interviewers are May Craig of the Portland (Maine) Press Herald, Richard Wilson of the Cowles Publications, Herb Kaplow of NBC and Lawrence Spivak. Ned Brooks moderates.

From Our Readers

In the past few years, Negro performers have found more and more doors opening for them in Hollywood and on Broadway. To list just a few films and plays, we have seen "The Defiant Ones," "Jamaica," "Raisin in the Sun" and the soon-to-be-released "Porgy and Bess." Yet television, the greatest influence on American life with the largest audience of any of the media, is notably lacking in the presentation of Negro performers. With the exceptions of *Green Pastures* and *Amos n' Andy,* Negro performers are limited to a few songs and dances on the variety shows. There is almost no chance for a good Negro dramatic actor. Why can't some of the detective and comedy series work Negroes into their scripts, making them an ordinary part of television life as they are an ordinary part of everyday life?

Mrs. F. Palombo, Valhalla, New York.

THE PHRASE IS FAMILIAR . . . to Late-Show Fans, at Least

Breathes there a fan, with soul so dead, who never to himself has said, "Haven't I heard that line before?" We refer, of course, to those lines in TV movies. If the dialogue that follows sounds familiar, you're a member in good standing of the Late Show Bromide Club. No dues, no officers—no surprises.

HISTORICAL

"Give me three ships, Your Highness, and I'll drive the Spanish Armada from the seas!"

"Mr. Jackson, fire a shot across her bow and run up our colors!"

"The peasants are storming the palace gates, m'lord. Unless we leave now I cannot guarantee the safety of Lady Charlotte!"

"A king's ransom to the man who brings me Captain Morgan—alive!"

SHOW BUSINESS

"Ah, gee, honey, don't let it get you down. The big lug wasn't worth it!"

"Look, kid, I've been in this business a long time. Take my advice and speed up the tempo a bit. Okay, take it again from the top!"

"Baby, you're not going out there wearing that outfit! We take off this feather . . . rearrange this sash . . . tear off the frills. . . . Baby, take a look! You're a sensation!"

WORLD WAR II

"Somebody's got to tell the captain! If we stay here we'll all die like rats! [Slap] . . . Thanks, Joe. I needed that!"

"You men have been hand-picked for this job. The training will be the toughest you've ever experienced. You'll see no one, talk to no one—not even your wives!"

"My brother went down on the *Finsterwald,* sir. That's why you've got to let me go on this mission!"

"You're not a man, you're a machine with ice water in your veins and a heart of steel!"

"Don't say it, darling. The time has come for you to go with your squadron. Leave now and let me remember the precious hours we shared in each other's arms!"

SCIENCE FICTION

"I'm afraid you won't be able to ask him any questions, Inspector. Whatever the old man saw died with him!"

"Not a word of this must leak out to the newspapers! If the public learns about the disappearance of the Rothwell formula, there'll be panic in the streets!"

"Oh, Tom, it was horrible! This creature had one yellow eye, the head of a night crawler, the body of a seal, and stood 10 stories high!"

"Commissioner, get all your available men and the militia down to the Lincoln Tunnel. We'll try to trap IT before the 5 o'clock rush!"

PRIZE FIGHTING

"Baby, this is my last fight! I promise! After tonight we'll be on easy street!"

MYSTERY

"Now that you're here, Geoffrey, I'm no longer afraid."

"What—you didn't call me, Charles? Good heavens! Muriel is alone at Bleakwell Manor! We must get there before it's too late!"

"Sir Claude out on the moor? That crazy fool, I *told* him not to go out there alone!"

"Lock the door behind me, Martha, and don't open it for anyone. Remember, if you need me, just call!"

"They all laughed at me! Even *you!* I don't like to be laughed at! . . . Don't try to run, my dear! You can't escape, no one can hear you!"

COPS AND ROBBERS

"George, I don't know what to think—this is so sudden! Certainly I'd love to fly to South America, but what about the children? . . . George, is everything all right at the bank?"

———

"This is the end of the line, Red. Get out and start walking!"

———

"Play ball with me, O'Reilly, and I'll take care of ya! If ya don't, you'll be poundin' a beat in the sticks within a week!"

———

"Look, Louie, I didn't rat on ya! Ask anyone, they'll tell ya! Go on, Nick, tell Louie I didn't talk! . . . Go ahead, Nick, tell him! . . . Nick!"

———

"Put me on the case, Lieutenant! I want to meet up with the guy that killed my brother!"

———

"Look, Falcon, it's a simple case of suicide. So stay out of this case and let the police handle it!"

———

"The boys tell me you been shootin' off your mouth all over town, Harry."

PRISON DRAMA

"The parole board turned me down again! Okay, Joe, count me in on the break!"

WESTERNS

"That's a Comanche arrow, Major. See them red stripes? We're in for a heap o' trouble!"

———

"If we ration the water we can hold out for three days, maybe. Right now I need a man to try to get through to Laramie!"

———

"I'll draw their fire—you boys go around back!"

———

"On your horse, mister, and git! Paw and me don't want no Johnson boys on our land!"

———

"I ain't never met a girl like you before, Miss Molly."

———

"We can't take another charge like that last one, Lieutenant! One man travelin' light could make it back to the fort!"

HORROR

"You think I'm mad, don't you, Valerie? Well, I'll show you! I'll show them all!"

———

"Think of it, Dr. Throckmorton, the perfect creation—with the body of an ape, the strength of 500 men, the brain of a genius!"

———

"Back—all of you! There's enough GL-35 in this bottle to destroy this entire city!"

John Oblinger

———

A TV Guide Close-Up   SEPTEMBER 27, 1959

6:00 **4** **8** **KHRUSHCHEV VISIT** — Talk

PREMIER KHRUSHCHEV

Special/Color

Soviet Premier Nikita S. Khrushchev delivers a 60-minute talk to the American people.

Mr. Khrushchev's visit to the United States, which began September 15, ends tonight. His words will be watched for evidence of the effect of 13 days in America on the Russian leader.

But while many Americans wanted the Premier to come here so he could learn about America, he himself wants us to learn about the Soviet Union, and looks on his visit as a chance to teach us his version. During his talk, which originates live from Washington, he will pause periodically while his sentences are translated.

The Quiz Scandals—An Editorial

Thanks to his own miserable sense of timing and some thoroughly inept public relations advice, Charles Van Doren seems to have won the role of official goat in the current quiz investigation. This, despite the fact he has denied receiving help.

Public indignation thus is directed away from the networks, agencies, producers and sponsors who profited considerably more than Van Doren's mere $129,000 from the phony shows. But Van Doren was in the public eye, a low-salaried college instructor who by sheer weight of intellect (we all thought) became popular, famous and rich. He even came darned close to making eggheadism acceptable.

If, as has been reported (his testimony is due November 2), Van Doren received the questions before the show, he certainly deserves the contempt of the nation. Intellectuals are supposed to be above cheating for the sake of a buck, perspiring on cue, following a director's instructions to furrow the brow and grimace as from sheer mental effort. Discovering that their idol may have had a brain of clay was a bitter disappointment to the millions of viewers who thought him as worthy of their admiration as athletes, cowboys and over-endowed actresses.

But the contestants who received questions, answers, or both, were mere prawns in the teeth of the quiz show sharks. These willing well-paid dupes—sacrificed or spared according to the whim of the sharks—may not have planned the moral crime of deceiving the American people, but they certainly are guilty of being accessories. And they are more to be condemned than pitied.

The men who should be the object of public indignation are fortunate in having a Van Doren around to bumble his way up to the Harris subcommittee's altar with his neck stuck out. The spotlight's on him, not on the conscienceless hucksters whose utter disregard for the laws of decency brought him to this sad state.

We refuse to accept the sorry excuse that the actions of the quiz show producers are merely symbolic of our nation's preoccupation with material wealth. Honesty and truth still are respected above easy money in America. And the proof is in the fact that viewers *are* angry because of the dishonesty now revealed.

While most of the onus is on the producers, it is difficult to believe that they could have continued their practices without the knowledge of the networks, agencies and sponsors concerned. Rumors were rife in the industry that contestants were being fed questions and answers so that those of them with the most audience appeal would remain on the air. Libel laws prevented publication of the rumors without proof, and proof, as is now evident, was hard to come by. But it was impossible for the networks, agencies and sponsors to be unaware of the rumors. *They* could have taken action. They chose to avoid acting decisively. The shows were profitable. Viewers still were accepting them at face value. Why upset the apple cart?

The reckoning finds the networks defenseless, shrugging off questions by denying they knew of the quiz fixing, and, in the case of CBS, dropping all big-money quiz shows.

A detailed explanation of exactly what happened is past due. And with it a promise that never will the networks fail in their responsibility to keep faith with viewers.

THOSE RATINGS— TV'S SLAVE OR MASTER?

Can they be rigged?
Science or mumbo jumbo?
Responsible for quiz scandals?
. Inspire copycat programs?
Do 1050 dictate to nation?

Were TV quiz shows rigged because sponsors and ad agencies insisted the shows get top ratings?

Have ratings themselves been rigged?

How can electronic gadgets in only 1050 homes measure accurately what 112,000,000 viewers are watching?

Are the rating systems television's master or slave? Do ratings, as has been frequently charged, wield life-or-death influence over every program? Do networks and sponsors select programs on the basis of ratings, rather than quality or balance? Are ratings responsible for program copycatting? (One Western such as *Gunsmoke* gets a good rating: everybody wants Westerns.)

What are the facts?

A Senate investigating committee is still trying to find out. One member of the investigating group, Senator A. S. (Mike) Monroney (D., Oklahoma), is already on record as saying that "the struggle for rating supremacy led to rigging of TV quiz programs."

Meanwhile, TV Guide has put its own queries to network, agency and sponsor representatives, as well as research experts and rating-company spokesmen. The consensus:

Ratings as such are not to blame for TV's ills. They serve a useful and necessary purpose in the business. The fault lies in the way ratings are *constantly* misused.

"Ninety percent of the time ratings are used, they are actually being misused," says Hugh M. Bevill Jr., NBC's vice president in charge of planning and research. "Even today only a few people in TV know how ratings are compiled, or their limitations."

How should ratings be used? "They're designed to serve only as a guide in making program judgments, said Max Banzhaf, advertising director of the Armstrong Cork Co., which sponsors *Armstrong Circle Theater*. "Instead, ratings too often are used as a substitute for judgment."

Do ratings dictate which programs you'll see? ABC president Oliver Treyz says, "The size of the audience as indicated by ratings is only one factor in any program decision." NBC's executive vice president Walter D. Scott, however, concedes that "there are advertisers who are guided almost entirely by ratings."

And what about program copycatting on the basis of rating returns? NBC's Bevill simply asks, "Is it wrong to give the people what they indicate they want?"

In such thinking, it is charged, lies one of the most blatant misuses of ratings. Historian Arthur Schlesinger Jr., writing in these pages recently, said it is the network's duty to elevate public taste. Schlesinger declared:

"The television industry must see its job, not as that of catering to the worst or even the average taste of its audiences, but in part as that of *elevating* taste. . . . It must assume responsibilities of leadership."

Marion B. Harper Jr., president of McCann-Erickson, Inc., one of the nation's largest ad agencies, recently insisted that networks must telecast more shows of quality than the ratings indicate the public wants to see. Harper said:

"It's proper that broadcasters should hold the reins but sponsors and their agencies should exert a strong influence—first, to select out of the total audience those viewers who are the best prospects for a sponsor's products; second, to keep up with, and ahead of, audience tastes in order to provide a favorable environment for his selling messages; and third, to help networks provide more choices in kinds of programming."

The public, not the ratings, dictates the quality of programs, according to Richard A. R. Pinkham, executive of Ted Bates & Co., Inc., one of the largest ad agencies dealing in TV. "The rating services only measure public taste," Pinkham said, "so it's the public that's at fault.

"I believe the dictates of public taste must upgrade programming but it will be a long, slow process. Eventually, though, TV will do what the eggheads now want it to do."

How do the entertainers feel about ratings? They reply with a question: "Is a comedian any funnier when he gets a 30 than when he gets a 20?"

"Suppose the comedian gets a 20 when he has a really good show," says Garry Moore. "His audience will talk up the show to friends; more people will tune in the following week. So he may get a 30 rating that second week and not have as good a show. Wouldn't that mean he was funnier with a 20 rating than with a 30?"

Like most performers, Garry agrees that ratings are necessary. "It's just unfortunate that ratings don't show whether viewers buy the sponsor's product."

Most TV executives agree that ratings are necessary because they constitute the best system found so far for determining the size of an audience. A movie or theatrical producer knows the size of his audience by the number of tickets sold.

"Don't forget that it was the sponsors who started ratings," said NBC's Beville. "As long as we have our commercial system of TV, we'll have ratings. It's inconceivable that any advertiser would spend $5- to $10,000,000 a year for a TV show without a measure of his audience size."

Beville did not take into account, however, that some sponsors of one-shot big-budgeted specials have been willing to gamble hundreds of thousands of dollars with no advance indication of the size of the audience.

How are TV ratings compiled?

The A. C. Nielsen Company attaches to the set an electronic gadget, called an Audimeter, which records the channel to which the set is tuned. Nielsen has Audimeters operating in 1050 scientifically selected "cross-section" homes across the country.

The American Research Bureau compiles its network ratings on the basis of viewing "diaries" kept by 1600 families. ARB also employs an instantaneous rating device, the Arbitron, which electronically "queries" 530 homes in seven cities once every 90 seconds to determine what shows those homes are watching. (Nielsen has a similar device for New York.)

Trendex ratings are based on telephone calls. Each half hour a battery of callers phones 1000 homes selected at random in 25 cities. Videodex provides a national rating on the basis of viewing diaries kept in 9200 homes. The Pulse, Inc., shows TV families a roster of programs televised within the past 24 hours, asks them to check the ones they watched.

Another charge leveled against ratings is that they cannot be accurate when they poll so small a sample of the total TV audience. An impartial observer, a life insurance actuary, observes, however: "If it can be proven that Nielsen's 1050-home sample has all the characteristics of the entire TV set-owning public, then you can say that the ratings are valid. You can get amazing results with a small representative sample."

Ratings are often accused of inaccuracy because two companies will come up with different figures for the same program. Nielsen, for example, might give Perry Como a 25 rating while Trendex gives him a 20.

The reason? Nielsen samples homes throughout the country. Trendex samples only those homes with telephones in 25 major cities in which the three networks compete.

Nielsen's 25 rating means that 25 percent of all TV homes able to receive the program are tuned to it. Nielsen also projects this percentage figure to the *number* of homes reached. In other words, with approximately 44,500,000 TV homes in the country, a 25 rating indicates 11,120,000 homes are tuned to Como. Using a general estimate of 2.7 viewers per set, that would mean 30,000,000 viewers.

Trendex's 20 rating, on the other hand, means that 20 percent of the homes phoned by Trendex are tuned to Como. Trendex makes no attempt to project its rating figure in terms of millions of homes or of viewers.

Are ratings fixed? Robert Hurleigh, president of the Mutual Broadcasting System, recently declared that the Senate investigating committee has evidence that ratings have been rigged. Not so, says Senator Monroney.

"When our committee investigated ratings in June 1958, we concluded that rating samples are inadequate, that ratings receive far too much emphasis in the industry," the Senator explained. "You can say that the quiz scandals were a direct outgrowth of this overemphasis. But we never charged that ratings were rigged."

In clarifying his remarks, Hurleigh said he hadn't meant rigging in the sense that figures were changed. He was alluding to what is known in the trade as hypoing. Trendex, for example, takes its ratings during the first week of each month. Networks and sponsors, to get higher ratings, book special guests for that rating week and intensify promotion to boost the audience.

Radio stations have used shadier hypo methods, Hurleigh said. He explained it this way. Suppose the manager of a station that concentrates on rock 'n' roll music wants a special rating taken. He persuades the rating service to restrict the survey area only to those neighborhoods in which he knows rock 'n' roll is popular. The resultant rating then favors that station over non–rock 'n' roll competitors.

Could a rating be rigged by having somebody tamper with the figures? It's possible, says an employer of ARB, but highly improbable. "I suppose it's possible to rig anything, but I've never heard of a rating being rigged," says NBC's Beville.

"I'd be amazed if I ever heard that ratings were rigged, but I'm constantly being startled at developments in this business," says ad-man Pinkham.

Good statisticians, of course, can often manipulate figures to serve their own purposes. Researchers for individual networks often publicize only favorable figures from ratings reports.

There is no clear-cut answer to all of this.

Beville of NBC offers only "If properly used, the rating service we now receive is adequate for us to decide when to renew or cancel a show. But ratings are too often misused. The only remedy for that is education of broadcasters, sponsors and agencies.

"I would also suggest that the press—newspaper critics and columnists—are not expert enough in ratings to write about them. I am convinced, consequently, that ratings should have no place in the press."

A constructive approach to the problem was outlined by Dr. Frank Stanton, president of CBS, Inc. He said:

"Ratings, properly taken, serve a useful purpose. They provide a yardstick for the measurement of audiences. But what ratings do, at best, is to reveal the choice that viewers have made among the programs available. . . . But beyond ratings, both quantitative and qualitative, we need to know something else—what people *want* to look at. It is not satisfactory to have indications of approval or disapproval of what we are doing. We need constantly to know what the audience thinks we *ought* to be doing."

Stanton revealed that CBS has commissioned outside public-opinion samplers to survey what people want from TV. That survey is now underway.

Meanwhile, there are always the ratings.

Bob Stahl

(NBC)

Comedian with Convictions

Why Steve Allen speaks up on serious topics

The late Fred Allen once observed that "for a man to remain only an actor all his life, he must have the mind of a child." Steve Allen, no kin to Fred, is one actor who has taken the remark to heart and is actively engaged in doing something about it.

"I'm not an egghead," said Allen. "I'm not sure what the term means. I'm not even sure just what I am. But when people ask me why I get into such things as, for instance, being Hollywood co-chairman with Bob Ryan [the actor] of the National Committee for a Sane Nuclear Policy, I can only say: 'Why doesn't everybody get into it?' Everybody is for peace, sure, but we still have wars.

"Somebody, I'm not sure who, once said, 'All that is required for the triumph of evil is for good men to do nothing.' I don't feel that I'm doing enough, but I'm doing what I can.

"I like to mention good new books on my TV show, books I pick at random but which, by and large, tend to stimulate thinking. The minute I started this, of course, I got swamped with new books and I haven't any room for them. They make dandy Christmas presents.

"I've been criticized occasionally for speaking out on our nuclear policy," Allen continued. "I've even had the pinko finger pointed at me, but it doesn't bother me. If

I'm a pinko for having supported the United States policy of a moratorium on nuclear tests, then so are the President, the Vice President and a lot of others."

Asked if he thinks all actors should become interested in such controversial activities, Allen said, "Well, I think all human beings should, and I presume it's safe to say that actors are human beings."

Allen the actor (and human being), a 38-year-old jack-of-all-trades who is billed principally as a comedian but who has written more than 2000 songs, strode into a bare, uninspiring rehearsal hall on a smoggy Los Angeles afternoon for a rehearsal session. Seated in a semicircle on battered folding chairs were three of his writers, a couple of secretaries and script girls and three of his second bananas—Louis Nye, Don Knotts and Pat Harrington Jr.

They ran swiftly through the comedy sketches. The writers laughed long and loud at every sally, as writers always do. Allen read his lines like a man scanning a letter, pausing only occasionally to rewrite a line or make a change ("I don't like this joke any better today than I did yesterday"). Nye, a quietly solid pro, warmed up as things went along and began to improvise bits of business. Knotts, who someday will be mistaken for a wet dishrag and hung out to dry, gave it his all the first time around. An hour later the session ended.

Back in his office, Allen relaxed as much as he is capable of relaxing, and explained his reasons for moving his show to Hollywood last fall. It was, he said, simply a matter of being near his three boys by his former wife. "I gave the staff one year to think about it back in New York," he said, "but I suppose they didn't really begin to think about it until a month before we all packed up and left. Everybody came except Tom Poston.

"Actually," Allen went on, "NBC wanted me to expand the show to 90 minutes. I didn't like the idea, but we at least gave it as fair a try as we could under the circumstances. I sat down and wrote a memo to the staff. In it, I assumed that we were now to do a 90-minute show and would they please kick it around and see what they could come up with. The result was what we'd all felt all along—that it's tough enough to create material for 60 minutes every week without having to tack on another half hour."

Unlike such performers as Milton Berle and Jackie Gleason, Allen has no long-term contract and doesn't want one. "A long-term contract is like a prison sentence as far as I'm concerned," he said. "The longest I've ever signed was for three years.

"My current deal with NBC expires with our last show, June 6, and I don't know exactly what will happen beyond that. We may do the hour show on a three-weeks-out-of-four basis next season, or we may do just eight or 10 specials. I don't know. But I wouldn't agree to the specials unless the entire staff could make a living.

"For myself, I prefer to live on a year-to-year basis. Life is exciting, and you have to keep making it exciting. I see nothing exciting in being tied to a 25-year contract."

Asked where he is living in Hollywood, Allen grinned weakly and said, "Here," waving his hand at his office. He currently is in the process of putting the finishing touches on his autobiography, doing a weekly hour-long show, lecturing, writing songs and continuing his work with "Sane."

"When you're living in a time when a couple of bombs can pretty well wipe out the world," Allen said, "I feel I should do what little I can to help keep it from happening."

The move to Hollywood has been in the nature of a homecoming for Allen. Nine years ago he was something of a local success as a late-night disc jockey. He is still doing, on a more elaborate scale, exactly what he was doing then—playing the piano, chatting with guests and making wry and often philosophic comments on the state of the nation and the world.

He doesn't, however, think of himself as a boy who has made good in the big city and come home as a celebrity.

"I've been in show business 15 years," he said soberly, "and it's been a long, slow development. I don't feel any different now than I did when I started. I don't think of myself as a celebrity. That's something that exists only in other people's minds.

"I don't think of myself as a comedian, either. I've been a writer and a songwriter ever since I was a kid. I still am. Most writers, myself included, don't make much money. And songwriting is vastly overrated as a source of income.

"I'll tell you what a writer should have," he said. "A writer should have a TV show on the side. It helps."

Ten Years For Dinah

About to begin a new season, she talks about her life, public and private

Fanny Rose Shore Montgomery, a little girl out of Nashville, Tennessee, via Hume Fogg High and Vanderbilt University, is today the reigning queen of television, ranks ninth on the most recent list of "Most Admired Women," has won a total of five Emmys and next week will start her 10th season on TV as the star of her own show.

Reminded of all these achievements one recent noon, Mrs. Montgomery, known professionally as Dinah Shore, hugged herself, looked both pleased and embarrassed, tried to laugh it off and finally said, "I don't know. Sometimes I think it's all happening to somebody else."

A TV Guide Close-Up

9:30 NIXON-KENNEDY DEBATE

Vice President Richard M. Nixon
(Wide World)

Senator John F. Kennedy
(Wide World)

Special

In an unprecedented event, the citizen in his living room witnesses a campaign debate staged specifically for him. Vice President Richard M. Nixon, Republican candidate for President of the United States, meets Senator John F. Kennedy, the Democratic candidate, in face-to-face discussion. Originating live from Chicago, this nationally televised program is seen locally over Chs. 2, 3, 4, 7 and 8.

This is the first of four joint telecasts by the two candidates. Topic of this one is domestic policy, Howard K. Smith of CBS is the moderator, and here is the order of business:

Opening Statements. These are limited to eight minutes each, with Senator Kennedy leading off.

Questions. There should be time for two from each newsman: Robert Fleming of ABC, Stuart Novins of CBS, Charles Warren of Mutual Radio and Sander Vanocur of NBC. The questions are addressed to the candidates in turn, with Senator Kennedy getting the first. Answers are limited to two and a half minutes.

Comments. Each candidate may comment on the other's answer, and has a minute and a half to do it.

Summations. For their closing statements, the two men divide the remaining time. The Vice President is first.

Quotes from the candidates

Nixon: "We believe that the Republican program is based on a sounder understanding of the action and scope of government. There are many things a free government cannot do for its people as well as they can do them for themselves. There are some things no government should promise. . . ."

Kennedy: "My chief argument with the Republican Party has been that they have not had faith in the free system. Where we would set before the American people the unfinished business of our society, this Administration has set ceilings and limitations."

There is really no "somebody else" in Dinah's makeup. What she appears to be on the TV screen to some 20,000,000 viewers is what she pretty much is—an attractive and vivacious woman with an abundance of nervous energy, a quick mind and an instinctive knack for remaining very much the female while still holding sway in what is supposed to be a man's world.

This last facet of her personality is an extremely important one to Dinah. "Right from the beginning," she says, "they wanted me to be a female emcee. And right from the beginning that's one thing I've fought against. It's a man's world, and thank heaven for it. Neither men nor women like to see a woman out there in front running things. On those occasions when I absolutely have to introduce a guest, I sort of slide into it. I just don't want to be that awful word, a 'femcee.' "

As a female, Dinah can fall in love with a song, a guest's performance, an entire show, a dress, a book or anything else that attracts and holds her attention. She is particularly in awe of talent.

"I'm still star-struck," she admits. "I love and admire talent. I try to adapt myself to my guests' talents and I

(Philippe Halsman)

learn something new every time I do. When I did a dramatic scene with Joseph Schildkraut two seasons back—well, I didn't want to do it at first. He was just too good and I felt that I was sort of intruding, holding him back. But he worked with me with the patience of Job. He almost literally pulled me up to somewhere decently near his level. He had me doing things dramatically I never thought I could possibly do."

Dinah has sometimes been criticized for her "eternal smile," but she brushes the criticism aside with a look of near-astonishment. "What am I supposed to do?" she asks. "Snarl at everybody? The minute you try to defend yourself against something like this, you're dead. Smile and you're a Pollyanna. Look glum and you're temperamental. I'm sensitive to criticism—who isn't? But if somebody wants to accuse me of smiling all the time, I just can't be bothered to explain it.

"Look here, I've been married to the same husband [TV and movie star George Montgomery] for more than 16 years, thank heaven, and it's never been a tiger pit to keep it that way. I adore my two children. I love my work. Time flies so fast, and there is so little of it. I have so much to be grateful for—why should I waste time worrying about whether or not I smile too much? If I'm going to cry about something, I'll do it in the privacy of my own home.

"I don't even cry in my dressing room. A magazine not long ago said I once threw a hairbrush across my dressing room in a fit of rage. I don't know where they get hold of such things. I never threw a hairbrush in my life. Why on earth should I?

"I love this business. Television made me. And I get mad with people who are always sounding off about the tawdry side of show business. It's like any other business, like life itself—you give to it, and it gives back to you, measure for measure.

"Television has never seemed like a rat race to me. I work because I love it. That's the only reason I've ever worked. I never worked just for the money but because it's what I've always wanted to do."

There was a widespread report that Dinah was ready to quit and would probably retire at the end of last season. Faced with this one, Dinah's eyebrows go up almost to her hairline.

"Quit!" she exclaims. "Who said?"

Dinah is particularly close to her two children, Melissa (Missy), 12, and Jody, six. She was a little annoyed last winter when a national magazine made the statement that she even knew when her daughter's hair was washed.

"That," she bridles, "sounds as though I keep track of my children through written reports. Of course I know when Missy's hair is washed. Who do you think washes it? I do."

For some years, Dinah was an ardent tennis addict. She played almost every weekend and was winning tournaments in Palm Springs. But she gave it up about two years ago.

"It was a Sunday morning," she recalls, "and we were down at the Springs. I had a game of tennis in mind, but it just didn't seem to materialize. Instead, George and I spent the day hiking, riding and painting with the children. I think we both suddenly realized, without anything actually being said, that the tennis was shutting us off from Missy and Jody. I haven't played very much since, and I really haven't missed it.

"You move on to new interests, and it's infinitely more rewarding to share those interests with your children. They grow up pretty fast, you know, and the first thing you know they're gone."

The Montgomerys have been somewhat unsettled in the past, having lived in five different homes during the past seven years. They owned three of them, rented the others. George, a talented and experienced builder, built one home in Beverly Hills several years ago in which they lived for two years, but he received an offer for it that they couldn't turn down. It is now the residence of Nanette Fabray and her husband, screenwriter-director Ranald MacDougall. (Meantime, Montgomery had built a new home not far away.)

"Tourists still think Dinah lives here," Nanette says, "and they're constantly banging on our front door. We just tell 'em blandly that Dinah is having a party in the back room with some of the boys and that stops them cold."

Dinah, a crusader at heart, is constantly crusading to keep her private life private. Sample campaign: to outlaw the "movie star maps" that are sold in profusion to visiting tourists.

"When I'm on," she says, "I'm on and I know what's expected of me. But when perfect strangers—and many of them ill-mannered—hang over your fence and demand to take pictures of your children, that's where I draw the line."

THE HEAT'S ON "THE UNTOUCHABLES"
Show's under fire from a pressure group and in a sponsor shakeup

On March 9 Anthony (Tough Tony) Anastasia marched in a picket line. He was just one of a couple of hundred demonstrators parading outside ABC's New York headquarters, protesting that the network's series *The Untouchables* unfairly stereotyped Italian-Americans as criminals. But Tough Tony got most of the attention.

He threatened to order longshoremen to stop handling the products of Liggett & Myers, *The Untouchables'* biggest sponsor. As boss of the Brooklyn waterfront he is in a position to carry out his threat. The Federation of Italian-American Democratic Organizations, organizer of the demonstration, announced that it was launching a boycott of L & M products.

Four days later L & M revealed that next fall it would not renew sponsorship of *The Untouchables* and two other ABC series—*Adventures in Paradise* and *Asphalt Jungle* (which starts April 2). L & M's advertising agency denied that the boycott had prompted the pullout. The agency explained that ABC had crossed it up by assigning later, less desirable, time periods to the three shows. It said that the decision to drop *The Untouchables* came five or six weeks ago—before the big flareup—but was announced on the day options were to be renewed, on Monday the 13th. "It hurt most to drop *The Untouchables*," a spokesman explained, "because the sponsor is Chesterfield Kings, and sales of that cigaret rose 12 percent last year. But it was a matter of principle."

Some important industry executives who have been close to the situation privately pooh-poohed this explanation, alleging that the boycott was the real reason and that L & M withdrew from the other two shows to establish the time-change excuse. And another source at L & M's agency conceded unofficially that the Italian-Americans' pressure had been "influential."

ABC president Oliver Treyz says that the network has already recouped 8½ million of the 9 or 10 million dollars lost to ABC in L & M's move. *The Untouchables,* he says, will be back next fall, fully sponsored.

Italian-American spokesman, Representative Alfred E. Santangelo (D., N.Y.), told TV Guide that he was pressuring L & M to drop out now, not when the contract expires in October. "Till I hear from them," he said, "we're not getting in touch with other sponsors or calling off the boycott.

"I don't know Mr. Anastasia. We didn't solicit his support. As an American he protested, as he has a right to do. I think L & M is afraid of Anastasia."

On St. Patrick's Day came peace. Desi Arnaz, whose studio produces the show; ABC; and the chairman of the Italian-American League to Combat Defamation agreed:

1. There will be no more fictional hoodlums with Italian names in future productions.

2. There will be more stress on the law-enforcement role of "Nick Rossi," Ness's right-hand man in the show.

3. There will be emphasis on the "formidable influence" of Italian-American officials in reducing crime and emphasis on the "great contributions" made to American culture by Americans of Italian descent.

AS WE SEE IT

An open letter to Newton N. Minow,
new chairman of the
Federal Communications Commission

Sir:

By law, broadcasters must be licensed by your Commission, and one of the requirements for renewal of licenses is that the broadcasters operate in the public interest. We believe that all of the following circumstances affect the public interest and demand immediate action by the Commission in the form of investigations, recommendations to Congress and, most urgent of all, meetings with industry leaders:

Program quality during peak viewing hours is supervised by networks, which are not directly licensed to operate in the public interest. Only stations are so licensed, and in practice they have no control over the network programs they carry.

Television violence is making our youth callous and damaging America's image abroad. Despite network pledges to curtail violence, there still is a cumulative impression of violence for the sake of violence on television.

Informational shows have increased in quantity and quality on the networks this season. But many of these programs are not carried by a number of local stations.

Tribute in the form of part-ownership of shows is being paid to networks by producers in order to get their shows on the air.

Rating services, however honest and accurate, are concerned only with numbers. By using these numbers as the criterion for retaining or dropping programs, networks and advertisers are forcing down the quality of entertainment and constricting the variety of entertainment.

A few talent agencies which control most of the important talent in television now reach into all aspects of the medium and often exercise almost dictatorial control over programming.

It has been argued that some of these matters are not the direct responsibility of the Federal Communications Commission. We submit that they all affect the public interest in broadcasting, which definitely *is* your responsibility.

Neither Government control nor Government censorship is involved here. What *is* involved is marshaling public opinion to correct practices which are harmful to television and—more important—harmful to the viewer.

The Editors

FCC CHAIRMAN REPLIES TO TV GUIDE

Newton N. Minow asks public's help in improving programs
and warns TV of its responsibilities

The Editors
TV Guide

Gentlemen:

On April 8th you wrote me an Open Letter . . . and I want to answer it openly.

Your Open Letter states: that networks control *program quality* during peak viewing hours; that networks often demand *part-ownership* of programs selected for broadcast; that *violence* is still too much the fashion in television programming; that local stations do not use enough of the many network *informational shows;* that mere *rating numbers* govern program selection; and that "almost dictatorial" programming power is held by a few *talent agencies.*

Your Open Letter calls for action on these problems by the Federal Communications Commission.

I am new to the FCC. Under the able leadership of my predecessor, Frederick Ford, and my fellow commissioners, many constructive steps have already been taken. I want you to know some of the things we are doing and will continue to do.

I start with the proposition that the public owns the air waves. Broadcasters are entrusted with use of this precious resource to operate stations in the public interest. Congress has given certain responsibilities to the Federal Communications Commission to make sure that broadcasters serve the public interest.

As part of our job, we at the FCC are actively concerned with television programming. And Senators Magnuson and Pastore, Congressmen Harris and Moulder, the members of their respective committees and President Kennedy himself are all very much aware of this important problem.

The broadcasting industry should be and now is equally concerned. Under the distinguished leadership of Governor LeRoy Collins, the National Association of Broadcasters is displaying a responsible approach to the moral and legal obligations of broadcasting to serve our nation's interest and to express its highest aspirations. The voluntary efforts of the industry, expressed by its Seal of Good Practice, are to be commended and encouraged.

Under our law, each broadcasting station is licensed by the FCC, usually for a three-year period. As each license period ends, the broadcaster must come before the FCC and demonstrate that the station has operated in a manner consistent with "the public interest, convenience and necessity." If the FCC questions whether a renewal of the license is justified, a hearing is then conducted to examine the broadcaster's record and determine whether his over-all performance has been in the public interest.

These hearings are open to the public and, where appropriate, are held in the station's local area. And what I say now is addressed to the public: If you parents feel the station is emphasizing too much violence, *you* should say so. Personally, as the father of three little girls, I think *too many* programs teach our youngsters that the solution to most problems is a punch in the jaw or a bullet in the belly. If informational shows are rarely carried by your station and you want more information and less entertainment, say so. If you think too much attention is paid to the television ratings, come forward with your opinion. Most broadcasters *want* to be responsive to the public and responsible about their use of your air waves.

But as your Open Letter points out, networks—which are *not* licensed directly by the FCC—provide most of the programs during prime time, and individual broadcasters who are licensed have little voice in the selection of programs. Recent programming patterns in television may indicate that present licensing controls are inadequate. The FCC has a special group which is studying the operation of the television networks, including the ways that network programs are selected and produced.

This study includes questions of the range of program choice, local clearing of network shows, the use of rating services, network ownership or partnership in independently produced programs, and talent agency influences. In some instances we have met evasion and resistance; in others, cooperation and assistance. *I intend to see that this study is pressed to a speedy conclusion, with useful results.*

Legislation has been proposed in Congress to license the networks in order, among other reasons, to provide a periodic review of whether the networks' program offerings as a whole are in the public interest. We at the FCC will cooperate with Congress in every way to find the right answers to these proposals.

There is another very important question you do not mention which should be discussed: the need for *more stations.* I am convinced that most television problems stem from a shortage of outlets. Eighty-five percent of available television broadcasting frequencies are hardly used.

The reason: our failure to utilize fully the UHF television band. The potential use of this sleeping giant came late to the broadcasting industry. Most television sets are not equipped to receive UHF broadcasts and so the service is a risky investment for broadcasters. The resolution of the problem will take time and thought—but when it is resolved, and it will be, we will be able to provide every community with enough stations to permit all parts of the public to receive programs directed to their particular interests. Programs with a mass-market appeal required by mass-product advertisers certainly will still be available. But other stations will recognize the need to appeal to more limited markets and to special tastes. In this way, we can all have a much wider range of programs. There will be time to prove that television stations can make money by appealing to our highest capacities instead of our lowest.

Television is the most powerful instrument ever devised for reaching the minds and hearts of men. It has produced brilliant programs, brought us education, information, adventures in the arts, exciting and fine entertainment. It has often lengthened our vision and deepened our understanding. Its future is without limit.

In my own determination, and that of the Commission, to serve the public interest, we need the continual enlightened, compelling support of the public. We can, and we will, provide leadership, but the best leadership rarely can take people where they do not want to go.

I offer TV Guide, as a distinguished and influential voice in broadcasting affairs, an Open Invitation to help us in making it clearly understood that television has a responsibility to serve the nation's needs as well as its whims; that television must assist in preparing a generation for great decisions; that television has a deep obligation to guide our country in fulfilling its future.

Sincerely,
Newton N. Minow

(NBC)

So long, Jack!

An analysis of Paar's strange hold on stay-up-late America

by Samuel Grafton

PART I

A television era will end when Jack Paar gives up his late-night show on the last Thursday of the month. (Friday will be a "Best of Paar" rerun.) But, in contradiction to what the poet said, this era will end not with a whimper but a bang. Paar is quitting at the top of his form and the top of his success. His success can't be measured in terms of money alone (though a quarter of a million dollars flows into his pockets each year), nor in size of audience (8,000,000 people); you need other

yardsticks besides riches and ratings to get the true size of the position Jack Paar has built for himself. In an industry which is often timid he is the only major broadcaster who regularly scolds the press, denouncing by name publications with which he differs, often Time and Newsweek, though he will sink his teeth into a newspaper too when he feels like it. And he frequently gives even Congress the back of his hand. (The other night he referred to a group of Congressmen as "those clowns," which would be a far-out comment in any medium.) He has won a peculiar kind of immunity for himself. "Nobody can hurt him" is what they say about him in the broadcasting parlors of midtown Manhattan, and they don't understand why he is leaving.

One of TV's mysteries

As to how a man could build this kind of conspicuous personal platform in a business which, little over two years ago when the quiz-show scandals broke, looked as if it would never be able to hold its head up again or say boo to a mouse, is one of the mysteries of the entertainment world. It is even more mysterious that Paar has been able to win his unique place by doing what seem to be quite ordinary things: by spending some 2000 hours in random talk with guests and by playing (rather ineptly) with toys and gadgets. He has varied this routine occasionally by bursting into tears and, in one instance, by quitting his job in full view of the audience. Paar quit after telling a mildly off-color story about a water closet, which NBC refused to put on the air.

Traditionally, broadcasters can be fired for an impropriety; it is revelatory of how different Paar is from most of the people in the industry which nurtures him that after *he* told a story which sailed too near the wind, he quit—and was humbly welcomed back.

"The guts of a burglar"

Obviously we are dealing with a man who, though he admits he is perpetually frightened and who is certainly thin-skinned, has resources of nerve upon which to draw. "He has the guts of a burglar," says Peggy Cass, one of his favorite guests. To find a figure in the entertainment world with a position comparable with Paar's you have to go, improbably enough, to someone like

Greta Garbo of the Hollywood '30s, who also used to upset the rules and snoot the press; and if Garbo marked a certain newly mature stage in the films, it may even be that in Paar's career television has, to some degree, and rather nervously, come of age.

It did not look as if he would head out in these directions when he started his midnight revels on July 29, 1957. He had been picked for the spot by NBC vice president Mort Werner, a programming genius, who has as sure a touch in selecting broadcasters as Casey Stengel has in picking outfielders. Werner had previously spotted Dave Garroway for the morning *Today* show and had put Steve Allen into the original *Tonight* stanzas. Paar had substituted for Allen a couple of times when Allen was preparing to leave, and had caught Werner's eye. "We expected a kind of variety show from him," says Werner.

The first reviews were not favorable. One New York paper found the show "by no means praiseworthy" and called it "strained." Most of that first show consisted of chitchat with the old-time movie actor Franklin Pangborn and was highlighted by a solo in which Johnny Johnston tried to sing a song while playing pool. Jack Gould of the New York Times found it "a very ragged affair" and predicted that if the show continued to feature gags, its viewers would give it up for an early bedtime. But, added Gould sensitively, "if *Tonight* is made over in the image of Mr. Paar's subdued and literate style, all might turn out well."

Live broadcasting itself was in trouble at the moment; the tendency was strong to put everything on tape or film, and in the can. It is hard to clear late-night hours for a network program. Local stations can run old movies at that time, sell their own spots, be boss in their own shops and make money. NBC alone has tried to keep a network image alive in the late hours, and it is another of Paar's accomplishments that, by building his list of stations to its present total of 170, he has done more than any other broadcaster to keep unrehearsed human speech going out over the coaxial cables. (Quite a number of CBS stations carry him in one-station towns.)

Programs are taped

Paar programs are actually taped, but this is done merely as a matter of convenience. The taping sessions start at 8 P.M. (ET), which makes life easier for the star and the studio audience. There is no time for reshooting the tapes before the 11:15 P.M. countdown. About the only editorial advantage NBC gets from the taping is that its press department has time to brace itself and be ready with comment should Paar have said or done anything unusually explosive. Mention is seldom made of time, and no clock is ever shown.

Paar did not build up to this high estate (and to the $15,500,000 the program grosses annually) in a hurry. He floundered for a while, gradually building a guest list which included Stanley Holloway, Hans Conried and Helen O'Connell. The first real moment of typical Paar-type tension arose when Carol Burnett sang a parody on the show entitled "I Made a Fool of Myself over John Foster Dulles." In the mushmouth world of broadcasting, this kind of irreverence toward a stately government figure was new; the nation gasped.

Dulles let it be known he was highly amused, and Paar was on his way. He had created a moment, and it is as a merchant of moments, a retailer of unexpectedness, that he has thrived ever since. "It's the only show where you watch the interviews and hope they'll postpone the entertainment," says Joey Bishop, a frequent Paar guest. "You don't know what stunning thing will build up out of the talk."

The fate of Dody Goodman

An early break was Dody Goodman, a former dancer with a naive comedy style. She went on the show on July 31, 1957, two days after Paar started, and appeared every single night until December 24. Paar was wildly enthusiastic about her and so were the fans; for a while one-third of all the mail which came into the show was addressed to Dody. This raised one of those troublesome questions which sometimes flare up in the entertainment business, like: Whose show is it? A certain snappiness of temper became obvious; there were embarrassing moments as when Dody turned up on Halloween night with masks and costumes for everybody and Paar stiffly refused to play. Fans took sides, and the dramatic question of whether Dody Goodman was going to stay on the show reached the newspapers. It was like a soap opera that was for real. Fans tried to read Dody's and Jack's expressions as they performed together. "All of a sudden it dawned on me," said Dody later, "that I was being discouraged. I was just sitting there. It doesn't dawn on you for a long time that somebody who has been so nice to you is turning against you."

How Jack profited

Ultimately Dody's appearances dwindled, and it remained, of course, Jack's show. It is highly probable that Paar learned a good deal from the incident. He learned that the public adores having a little reality leak through the 23-inch screen, that it loves watching people in their emotional undress, with all their human snappishness, pettiness, resentments and other earthy humors. In any case Paar has seemingly not bothered to conceal any emotion ever since. Whatever his show may be, he says in his new book, "My Saber Is Bent," "it is always real." And reality may be almost anything, from his public scolding of Mickey Rooney as a man who, Paar said, is talented but should never appear on an unrehearsed show, to another famous moment when he had Mimi Hines and Phil Ford on his program being funny, and he suddenly said to Mimi: "You're kidding with your singing. Sing straight for me"—and she movingly sang a straight song, "Till There Was You," so that as Paar listened tears came into his eyes, and at the end he made her sing it a second time, with probably a good many of his 8,000,000 viewers crying with him. Somewhere along the line Paar had discovered that people like to see human beings being human. It is one of the most sensational discoveries in the history of show business.

Paar doesn't put on a show. He is the show, a man with his heart on his sleeve. This brings up the key question: Is Jack Paar sincere? Are the tears and angers and rages genuine or are they designed to win him publicity? Perhaps only Paar can answer that. His friends swear he is a shy and sincere man, who has to be what he is.

Paar, a counterpuncher

Curiously enough, the little evidence available seems to bear them out. Paar does not start fights, he simply overreacts to real or imagined slights. When bruised—and a powder-puff tap turns him black and blue—he strikes back viciously, more often at the groin than the jaw. It's an effective, if less than gentlemanly, fighting style. His famous campaign against columnist Dorothy Kilgallen began only after she had criticized his defense of Castro's Cuba, early in the Castro story. During the feud with Kilgallen he made distinctly ungallant remarks about her looks, then called her a puppet who never moved her lips when she talked. "She must use Novocain lipstick," he said. When a guest on Paar's show charged that Walter Winchell did not bother to vote, and Winchell refuted the accusation, Paar cracked that Winchell had a "high, hysterical voice," which led to a joke in questionable taste.

Paar is extremely effective in this kind of infighting. When Ed Sullivan became annoyed over the fact that he had to pay from $5000 to $10,000 per appearance to stars who turned up on the Paar show quite cheerfully for $320 a night, Paar screamed as if the Constitution were being torn up, yelled that stars appeared on his show for less because his show made them look better and challenged Ed Sullivan to a public debate. When Sullivan, who had nothing to gain from such a debate, declined, he was made, of course, to look like the loser, especially to Paar's fans.

Paar's anger against Congress stems from the day a number of Congressmen attacked him on the floor of Congress, on the charge (which later proved to be wrong) that he had almost created an international incident at the closed Berlin border by getting the U.S. Army to draw up in force so that he could take pictures. (When Paar's Berlin story appeared on the air it turned out to be a mildly informative little show, revealing a good many humble details of life along the Berlin border that more pretentious television treatments of the crisis had omitted. But the lightweight chatter between Paar and Peggy Cass seemed out of place, and the show was, as critic Harriet Van Horne said, "essentially trivial." Jack Gould called it a "display of puerility" and a "coarse disaster.")

Paar does not start great events moving; he is not a man who acts in the field of public affairs; he reacts. He does not open up on his Congressional targets on behalf of some great cause, for example. His fury, as we have seen, is in self-defense. Politically he is rather naive. He had met Castro in the early days of the Cuban dictator's rise to power and had been much impressed; in the spring of 1960 he publicly deplored "the untruthful things I've read about what was happening in Cuba. This man Castro is beloved by these people." Challenged with being a Castro hero-worshiper, Paar insisted: "I do know that they have an honest government for the first time in the history of Cuba." Later Paar withdrew his support of Castro and acknowledged his error, but the affair illustrates his tendency for swimming in waters that are too deep for him.

A seeming paradox

The upshot of all Paar's wars is that, for a man with seemingly tremendous influence, Paar is not very influential. He doesn't look for key spots at which to apply his power; it all seems to be happenstance. A word from him can make almost any book a best-seller. He does not search out good neglected books to praise, useful volumes he thinks the public should know about—he will lend his influence to a funny book, written by a gag writer appearing on his show, or to the latest anecdotal volume by his favorite guest, Alexander King. For a man who has climbed high, Paar operates close to street level.

PART II

An appraisal of his influence as his late-night era ends, and a prediction about his future

It is part of the Jack Paar paradox that he has developed more power and more freedom of action than any

Jack Paar on his daytime CBS show before going to NBC and his nighttime success (CBS)

other television broadcaster has ever had, and that he uses these for basically trivial ends. He has smashed a dozen concepts of television censorship, proving, for example, that one can use words like "buttock" on the air, or tell mildly sexy jokes, without causing a cataclysm. All this has an "adult" tone, but that is where it ends; the new freedom hasn't been used for, say, a constructive, mature discussion of some problem relating to sex—Paar has merely freed himself for more mildly sexy gags. ("They are banquet-type sex jokes, not poolroom-type jokes," says a friend, which hardly seems an important distinction.)

Paar sits on top of an enormous apparatus of 170 stations. "He virtually runs a network of his own, for an hour and three-quarters every night," says NBC's Joseph Cunneff, director of night programming. An advertiser can spend as much as $1,500,000 a year with Paar, or as little as $10,000; he can buy a single spot or ride along with every show—though he has to take a minimum of 66 stations. The show is an immense business structure in itself, equaling many a good-sized corporation, but Paar seems happiest with this whole complex machine when it produces a simple yak, as, say, in the form of a comment by Alexander King about some actress's decolletage. It is a little bit as if Tom Paine had fought for freedom of speech in order to be able to tell a funny story. The Paar mountain labors, but its chief product is mice.

He does venture into controversial subjects from time to time, but he tends to handle them cutely, from an angle, and to oversimplify them. His story on the closing of the border in Berlin, filmed on the spot, gave the country some admirable shots of life and incidents along that international barrier; but Paar's whole presentation sounded rather as if he were discussing some nasty people who had built a spite fence somewhere in the suburbs—the sweep and movement of history was not in it. Paar likes to say he has had men with first-rate minds on his show, such as Peter Ustinov and Robert Morley, but these too are show people rather than philosophers and savants. That Paar's forum is big enough to hold anybody is shown by the eager appearances of 1960 Presidential aspirants John F. Kennedy and Richard M. Nixon. But most nights it's an unused forum.

For people he thinks have brains, or knowledge, Paar has a kind of undiscriminating "gee whiz!" attitude. It is a form of idolatry, like a small boy's admiration for big boys, for what he considers intellectual stuff, whether it is a case of Hugh Downs explaining that the ancient Romans had a life expectancy of only 20 years, or Dr. Albert Burke showing how to use world resources to defeat communism. Paar has a tendency to accept ideas at face value, lost as he is in admiration for anybody who has them. He has in the past spoken admiringly of the late Senator Joseph McCarthy and late attorney Joseph Welch, who fought and defeated McCarthy at the famous Senate Army investigation. So moved in Paar by human brilliance—anybody's brilliance—that he even devotes a page of his book "I Kid You Not" to the thrilling story of how he once stood next to Frank Lloyd Wright, the famous architect, in a line waiting to get into a men's room at the theater.

But Paar does seem happiest on the lower slopes of the intellectual hills, as when Hugh Downs is explaining, rather ponderously, some gimmicky principle—such as what keeps a water-skier from sinking. Paar does not use television irresponsibly, except when clawing back at his real or fancied enemies with half-truths. He is not an irresponsible man, except insofar as it may be considered irresponsible to use an elephant gun to shoot gnats. One does not expect big contributions to public discussion from, say, Garry Moore; but then Garry Moore isn't always hollering about his rights and his freedom and his integrity. Paar is, and he creates expectations that are left unfulfilled, which may account for the curious resentment he stirs up in many quarters.

Akin to Godfrey, Garroway

Basically Paar is a broadcasting pro. He has been in the business all his working life. He has a superb sense for timing, for smuggling over a tiny joke at the precise split second at which it will produce a big laugh, for turning his back on a dull guest, letting him wither beyond camera range, for hitting commercials and station breaks on the nose. When he does early-evening special shows, as he does occasionally, his professionalism shows itself; he abandons the "blue" jokes which might be in order later in the night when there are no youngsters in the audience. One is sure that if he ran a children's show in the afternoon he would do it with taste and with that superb broadcaster's sense of how to keep every moment alive. (It is interesting that nearly all of the men who have been able to keep one-man shows going on television for years have been professional lifelong broadcasters: Arthur Godfrey, Dave Garroway, Steve Allen, Garry Moore, for example. What this tells us is that there is such a thing as pro broadcasting, as sharply distinct a profession as acting or baseball playing.)

A matador of men

In this medium a pro is basically a matador of men; he "plays" his guests as a good bullfighter plays his bulls, not to show their weaknesses but their strength. Paar does this unmatchably well. Like the bullfighter, he is not detached but part of the show, deeply in it, and he prods his guests along to excel themselves, using as weapons his marvelously shifting expressions, of shock, dismay, hope, admiration. He makes his guests do things they don't even know they can do. "I even found out on his show that I didn't have to be funny to be interesting," says Joey Bishop. "He taught me that if I'm once accepted as a human being I can talk about my father and my mother, or maybe how I forgot to register to vote, and it comes out all right."

Because Paar is fairly contented with his shifting menagerie of guests and uses them over long periods, giving them enormous, skillful exposure, he has become, by all odds, the world's greatest current star maker.

The list is awe-inspiringly long. From Dody Goodman, the names run on through Joey Bishop, Shelley Berman, Phyllis Diller, Peggy Cass, Bob Newhart, Elaine May and Mike Nichols, Phil Ford and Mimi Hines; he has made established comics of men who were not even performers before he reached out for them, such as Pat Harrington Jr. and Jack Douglas—and a woman too, Selma Diamond.

The list could ramble on as long as you like—Geneviève, the Smothers Brothers; Paar has been a pioneer in introducing Negro comedians to television, providing debuts for Dick Gregory and Nipsey Russell.

Besides starting new talents cold, he has given powerful boosts to seasoned performers, such as Buddy Hackett and Jonathan Winters. He plucked Cliff Arquette (Charley Weaver) out of retirement on a California farm to give him a second career. Among Paar's discoveries Bob Newhart and Joey Bishop have shows of their own; Peggy Cass found a place in a series. Most of the others have gone on to frequent guest appearances on prime-time shows, for fees much higher than the standard $320 which the Paar budget allows performers.

Paar's greatest influence on television has been to people it with this cast of characters. He himself hasn't been imitated very much, perhaps because he can't be; it would be hard to find in anyone else this precise combination of a thin skin and a tough mind that makes Jack Paar a strange, easily wounded man who sometimes leaves his opponents stretched out dead on the field of battle.

Yet there are signs that, in the years ahead, Paar may prove to have had a bigger influence on television than merely to act as its recruiting agent. If a relaxed communion with real people takes over in American television (another step in this direction is Mike Wallace's *P.M.*) at the end of each long, long broadcast day devoted to make-believe, this will be, in a very real sense, Paar's doing. And these midnight sessions may yet improve and become America's real Main Street, where one meets everybody.

Next season Paar is scheduled for a one-hour-a-week show in earlier evening time on NBC. How will he make out? "The show will almost of necessity have to have more formality," says NBC's Joseph Cunneff. Relaxation may suffer in shortened time, in a big-budget, high-pressure operation. "It probably means higher pay for the guests," says Peggy Cass. "But if I got $2000 to talk, I couldn't open my mouth. How could I ad-lib for that kind of money? They can keep on paying me $320, or I'll get frightened." It seems clear the show will have to depend more on Paar's own talents, instead of investing long waiting minutes in the hope of prodding unexpectedness out of a guest.

The problems are many. But Paar, as the archetype of the pro broadcaster, has the needed responses in his blood; ex-actors and ex-nightclub comics fade into oblivion on television, after brief whirls, more often than do the professionals of this art. On form, it figures that you have to bet on Paar.

Reginald Rose (in shirt sleeves), creator of the series, discusses a script point with stars Reed (left) and Marshall (Curt Gunther)

THE ETERNAL CONFLICT BETWEEN
GOOD AND EVIL

. . . is waged on "The Defenders" every Saturday night—with some surprising results for the heroes and the viewers

In living rooms from coast to coast the voices are intense:

"Does the government have the *right* to take a human life?"

"Is mercy killing morally justified?"

"Killing in self-defense is legal—but is it always moral?"

"What's the difference between morality and law, anyhow?"

Since the heyday of *The Mike Wallace Interview* there has not been so much television-inspired discussion going on in the American home as there is today. The cause: a CBS dramatic series called *The Defenders*, created by a young man named Reginald Rose, produced by Herb Brodkin (of *Playhouse 90* fame) and starred in by E. G. Marshall and Robert Reed.

Filmed on location in New York, with its scripts written and directed by various people, the series—which is cast around a father-and-son lawyer team—has a unique trademark: Almost every show explores one or more ethical questions, many of them controversial, and presents arguments for and against the major positions.

For example the show called "The Attack," written by John Bloch, asks: Does a man whose five-year-old daughter is attacked have the right to kill the youth who attacked her?

In "The Quality of Mercy," written by Reginald Rose, the question is: Should a doctor who destroys a Mongolian idiot at birth be found guilty of murder?

In "The Benefactor," a forthcoming show written by Peter Stone, the question is: Should teen-agers who become pregnant be given a choice of whether they want to become mothers?

What is even more unusual about *The Defenders* is that the shows, on the whole, offer answers to the questions they raise—either explicitly or by loading the scales artistically (if not legally) in favor of a certain position.

Item: The father who is opposed to an operation is a crude bully—and the abortionist, found guilty by law, is a warmhearted "benefactor."

Item: The doctor who kills the Mongolian idiot is also portrayed as a kind and loving man who even impresses the district attorney with his nobility of soul—and gets off with a manslaughter charge.

Item: The man who thought he was right to shoot the attacker—i.e., to take justice into his own hands—turns out to be a murderer; the evidence has been misleading and he has killed an innocent man.

This is a show with a "message" and a powerful dramatic technique for communicating it to the public. One could hypothesize from its artistic and intellectual consistency that a single mind was dominating it from behind the scenes. But when one meets the producer, the writers and the actors, it ceases to be a hypothesis and becomes established fact. The man behind *The Defenders* is script editor Reginald Rose.

"*The Defenders*," says producer Brodkin, "*is* Reggie. He dreamed it up. He created it. He lives with it. He provides the consistent point of view."

Rose the guiding spirit

"It's Reggie's mind that dominates the show," says star Robert Reed. "He has a total grasp of every play that is unusual. You can *feel* in the writing his concern with ethics, with issues of right and wrong. You can feel it when you're *acting*."

Even the free-lance writers who provide *The Defenders* with its scripts concede, against all ordinary writers' tradition, that their literary brainchildren have a co-father: editor Rose.

"Two qualities determine the show," says writer Ernest Kinoy, "—whom they hire to write it, and what Reggie considers to be appropriate ideas."

"He sends you back and back and *back* for rewriting," says Peter Stone. "My first draft never has human beings in it. He is always telling me, 'Go back and put the *conflicts* in.'"

"In my case," says writer John Vlahos, "I get so involved with the people, I have practically no story. He's always sending me back to put the *story* in."

The result of being sent "back and back and *back*" is invariably a script with the Reginald Rose hallmark—no matter whose by-line is on it: a logically constructed drama built around a severe ethical conflict, intelligently complicated by a few more brain-cracking ethical conflicts, and building to a sharp climax. Characterization, too, bears the Rose brand of moral paradox: The character who commits an action deemed evil by law and/or public opinion usually turns out to be a "good guy" with noble motives; while the character who commits an action normally thought good turns out to be a

"bad guy" with wicked motives. Although Rose's heroes and villains are by no means in the classical American tradition—his "good" characters are all Albert Schweitzer in one guise or another, his "bad" suffer from such vices as "certainty" or "oafishness"—they are as stylized in their virtue or vice as any cop or robber. "I like my heroes to be heroic, and my villains villainous," he says.

One of the favorite activities of those who write for and act in *The Defenders* is to argue, like the Saturday night public itself, about the over-all "message" of the show. There are almost as many interpretations as interpreters:

"One of the main purposes of the show," says star E. G. Marshall, "is to clarify the difference between morality and justice. Morality is the way you *feel* about an act. Justice is a rational interpretation of the facts."

"The show's basic assumption," declares writer Peter Stone, "is that there is a pure absolute morality—the Judeo-Christian morality—which is true, regardless of the public's view of morality at any time. The series says that public morality may be *wrong*."

"The show fundamentally reflects Justice Holmes's concept," says Kinoy, "that the law is a historical phenomenon that lags behind social needs."

"It's a *liberal* show," says producer Brodkin. "I'm a conservative Republican in my personal life, but I'm a reeking liberal in my artistic life. Maybe I do it to shock. I'd call this the most liberal show on the air."

How the stars feel

And, like the Saturday night public, those who are closest to *The Defenders* are inclined to argue endlessly over the specific ethical issues in the shows. Co-stars Marshall and Reed are often to be seen in deep discussion, during shooting breaks, over the right and wrong of the ideas in the plays.

E. G. Marshall agrees with many of Rose's views—particularly with his concern over the rehabilitation of criminals. "Once a murder has been committed," he says vehemently, "my compassion does not go to the victim. The victim's dead. It's the criminal who's alive, and who needs our help."

Robert Reed disagrees with a number of Rose's views. "Mercy killing—that's one example of an idea I don't agree with at all," he says equally vehemently. "I don't think any man has a right to take life." And then the young actor adds soberly, "Fortunately, in the mercy-killing script, Reggie presented both sides. If it had been a pure advocacy of killing, I wouldn't have been in it. I couldn't consciously participate in any play that advocated ideas I think are wrong."

One of the most fascinating aspects of *The Defenders* to its creators and participants—whatever their attitude toward the social and ethical views of the series—is the fact that it is one of the 10 highest-rated shows on TV today—one of the few new shows this season to enter this category.

"I've heard one interpretation of our success," says producer Brodkin. "Someone pointed out to me recently that *The Defenders* has one element in common with other high-rating dramatic shows—such as the cops-and-robbers and the cowboy shows. And this is that, despite their differences, all of them are really *ethical* shows—morality plays. The central dramatic conflict is always between good and evil. It seems that the public is interested in the whole subject of morality."

To Reginald Rose, the man behind *The Defenders,* the idea that ethics are a highly salable commodity in the world of drama is not new. "Good drama," he says, "*always* projects a writer's moral values. A dramatic plot is always the story of a *moral* struggle. Plot conflict *is* moral conflict. I can't *bear* stories without plot conflict— and neither can the public."

His view is supported by the statistics. An estimated 21,000,000 viewers tune in every Saturday night to discover which bewildering ethical dilemmas the Prestons, father and son, will be involved in next. They are held by the plots, enjoy the controversy.

But perhaps most significant of all where ratings are concerned is the fact that the law, as it exists today, has the last word in *The Defenders.* The viewers remain secure in their knowledge that, before the hour is up, justice will triumph over the procession of high-minded lawbreakers and murderers. In the universe of Reginald Rose, good intentions still pave the road—if not to hell—to jail.

Edith Efron

TELEVISION '62. Sixth of a series of authoritative articles by prominent Americans exploring the status of television today and its impact on life in the United States

IT HAS BATTERED ITS RIVALS

OUT OF SHAPE

A social critic considers the impact of television on other mass-communications media

by Martin Mayer

Author of "Madison Avenue, U.S.A.,"
"The Schools," and other books

Nobody will ever be able to calculate the impact of television on the United States, because nobody can imagine what America would be like in the 1960s without television. Its influence reaches deep into the culture and spreads wide across the population. The influence has been most obvious, of course, on superficial levels, especially in the media marketplace, where television competes directly with older forms of organized entertainment and communication.

Radio broadcasting and periodical publishing have been battered completely out of shape by the power of a medium that within a few years of its introduction commanded the largest share of people's recreation time and industry's advertising dollar. Even where advertising plays no role, in movies, theater and book publishing, the rise of TV has changed the seller's attitude toward his work and the buyer's attitude toward his amusements.

Everything that happens in the world of human activity springs from many causes, and it is hard to say exactly how important television was in creating some of the recent changes in American entertainment and information habits. The light-romantic lending-library novel, for example, a staple of the 1920s and 1930s, has died the death in mid-century America, and presumably television killed it by offering great quantities of bland fantasy in the home, free of charge. But this same period saw an enormous expansion in magazine circulation, and the rise of the paperback publisher, nonexistent 30 years ago and now selling a million "pocketbooks" a day. With or without television, people have only so much time for reading. What killed the light-romantic lending-library novel?

Again, the big-city newspaper is in bad trouble while small suburban papers flourish like radishes all across the country. Clearly television did it. Television can present national and big local news before the papers hit the streets; television competes with the city papers for "national advertising" (advertising by manufacturers rather than by local stores). The suburban paper is free of these problems: it concentrates on the small local story which television has no time to cover, and it lives off the storekeeper who cannot afford the costs or profitably employ the area-wide coverage of TV's advertising. But the move to the suburbs would have happened without television. Everybody likes to read about himself, a desire the suburban paper can most easily meet. Perhaps the crisis of the big-city papers would continue if all the TV stations shut down.

Elsewhere, the influence of television seems clearly paramount. Television can be credited with the virtual destruction of the very bottom layer of American popular culture—the comic book, the pulp magazine, the radio serial, the hillbilly movie. Newton Minow's wasteland has been in fact a flood over an abyss which used to be filled by garbage a good deal worse than the featureless rubble of routine television. Particularly in the hinterlands, and in the city slums where residents had made almost no contact with the middle-class mainstream of American culture, TV has had an essentially civilizing effect.

The cold winds of competition from television were felt first, and most keenly, by what might be called "the majority media"—radio and movies, both of which aimed to sell their wares to *most* of the people. Both changed radically and rapidly.

Driven from the living room to the kitchen, the bedroom and the car, radio after some floundering came to concentrate on reality, and on special products for minority markets. News, comments and interviews now alternate with the latest pop-music horrors for adolescents and with "good music," mostly on FM, for the more serious and literate minority of adults (whose patronage is sought by television only a few hours a week). Such programs are cheap to provide, and radio broadcasting equipment is cheap to operate. When TV stole most of their audience, radio stations were able to lower ad rates and still operate profitably.

Movies went the other way. For half a dozen years the movie companies battled television, refusing to sell their old films or to make new films for broadcast use. Finally, however, the assorted King Canutes of Hollywood realized that every time the tide came up they got wet. Theaters were closing by the thousands, the routine movie was losing money and the Eastern bankers and stockholders were becoming upset. Eventually, nearly all the film studios took on low-cost producing units to service the needs of television. Meanwhile, for theater use, much of the industry turned to the wide screen, the stereophonic sound track, the superspectacular production which television could not hope to match. In movies as in radio, the adolescent market became more important, and a large number of well-developed juveniles were made into stars by the publicity departments of the studios. Probably because TV had spread the big-city culture more evenly through the country, moviemakers were able to treat "controversial" and "unwholesome" subjects more honestly than they had in the 15 years before large-scale TV; and European producers suddenly found U.S. theaters ready to buy foreign films.

From TV to Broadway

Movies, television and theaters all require similar talents, and the same people will operate in all three forms. Of the three, television needs the most, pays the lowest prices for top talent and (thanks to union rules) the highest prices for minor talent. Inevitably television has served as a training arena for gladiators who would later move to combat with the larger animals. The theater especially has been dominated of recent years by directors and producers who made their mark filling a small screen, and each Broadway season sees half a dozen plays by writers who began with television scripts. At the same time television made possible the growth of the off-Broadway theater. Occasional television appearances (at $320 and up) enable actors to work in the converted lofts and brownstones of Greenwich Village for $30 a week—and the chance of catching the eye of a television producer makes actors willing and eager to work at minimum rates under miserable conditions off-Broadway.

Network television's longest and bloodiest war, still continuing, has been with the magazines. Culturally and commercially, network television serves functions the magazine industry had abbrogated to itself over the last two generations. For the first quarter of this century, magazines were a force uniting the widely scattered people of a single nation—or, at least, uniting that social and educational level which reads magazines. Businessman, farmer, lawyer, teacher; residents in Chicago, Atlanta, Seattle—all read the same magazine every week. Manufacturers attempting to build national brands advertise nationally in magazines.

Radio broke the magazines' monopoly of national coverage, but people listen less carefully than they read (which is saying a good deal), and of course radio could have little influence on visual styles. Television struck the magazines where they lived: in what was *looked at* in middle-class households, nationwide. Consciously or unconsciously, the people who ran television centered their broadcast offerings at roughly the cultural and intellectual level of "the slicks" in the year 1950. But television also reached working-class households, as most of the "mass magazines" did not. With the rapid rise in wages in postwar America, this added market was more attractive to advertisers.

Culturally and intellectually, the magazines found an answer: They moved up the scale. Like radio, they have come to concentrate more and more on reality, on relatively serious articles and opinion rather than cheerful short stories and abridgments of popular novels. A national community made more sophisticated by television could be sold more magazines than ever. Nearly every slick magazine published today sells two to five times as many copies as it did 20 years ago. But the economics of most magazines are such that each copy sold costs the publisher more than he ultimately receives from the purchaser, after the deduction of selling costs. In their attempt to keep up with TV in sheer numbers of people reached, the magazines have placed themselves in a position where they need ever greater advertising revenue to stay afloat.

The relative effectiveness of magazine and television advertising is a matter of debate between the two industries; there is no simple answer. But in its war with the magazines, TV has had a simple weapon of enormous power, which even men in the business do not always understand.

Most people believe that "television has taken advertisers from magazines," a statement which conjures an image of advertisers like migratory birds flying from one perch to another. In fact, this mass movement has not occurred: Most companies that advertised in magazines a decade ago still advertise in magazines today. But they are less susceptible to the suggestion of the extra page, and it is the extra page that makes the difference between profit and loss.

The fight is less than fair

A magazine may budget the sale of 60 advertising pages for a November issue, while a television network budgets the sale of 60 half-hours of evening time in its fall schedule. Space salesmen for the magazine sell the first 50 pages easily, and time salesmen for the network quickly dispose of their first half-hours. Thereafter, however, the going gets rough. And the magazine salesman must, by the rules of his business, sell his last 10 pages at the same price as the first 50—while the television salesman, by the laws of *his* business, is permitted to wheel and deal in program and perhaps even time prices to sell his last 10 half-hours. The undecided advertiser, then, can get a bargain from the network, while he must pay full price to the magazine; and soon he is no longer undecided.

Generally the public benefits by fights between media, as the consumer benefits by real competition between producers of any goods or services. But the fight between television and the magazines is something less than fair. At present, it appears that television may kill the magazines, not because it is necessarily superior as an entertainment or advertising medium, but because it operates under more lenient rules. If the federal government is looking for a sensible way to regulate the television networks, it could start in this area. Under-the-table competition poisons relations among the networks themselves almost as badly as it rigs the fight against the magazines. By carrying over from Wall Street the key principle of full disclosure—by requiring that all contracts for the purchase of programs and network time be made a matter of public record—the FCC might greatly reduce the negative impact of television upon at least one of the other media.

Television is by its nature a greedy medium—it demands more time from people than they really want to give it, more talent than the world can supply, more money than advertisers can afford to spend, more praise for accomplishments and forgiveness for sins than a reasonable critic can honestly offer. Yet the greed is at least partially justified, for television is the central medium of entertainment and information in American life, and the biggest bang in the mass-producer's arsenal of selling weapons.

Ultimately, in a market economy, questions of cultural influence reduce to questions of dollars and cents. Media, like other economic goods, compete in terms of value for money. But the market for media is peculiar, because the consumers who enjoy the product pay only part of the costs—and the advertisers who foot the big bills have no very accurate way of judging the value of what they buy. Economic competition is pretty irrational at best; media competition, even further removed from reason, rapidly grows frantic: "When in trouble, / When in doubt, / Run in circles, / Scream and shout."

The question: How large is the lion's share? And can't a civilized community find an answer, without resorting to the law of the jungle?

TV GUIDE VIEWS "BEN CASEY"

CASEYITIS

How the epidemic started and why it spread

by Richard Gehman

While haranguing some of his followers in a Hollywood nightclub one night last spring, Mort Sahl, the conscience of a small nation of intellectuals and sophisticates, began speculating upon what might happen if sponsors and network executives behaved like the performers they hire.

Sponsors of Western shows would shoot it out for prime time, Sahl said. Gangster-show owners would raid the talent agencies and kidnap guest stars, whose

Vincent Edwards, flanked by Bettye Ackerman, Sam Jaffe
(Julian Wasser)

parents then would hire lawyers from lawyer shows to get them back. And, The Conscience went on, it would not be hard for one to imagine a sponsor saying, "Ben Casey, you have 39 weeks to live."

O Mort, O Mort, how wrong you were! You and I may be mortal, but *Ben Casey* bids fair to be all but immortal in its appeal to eager viewers. This masterfully contrived medicine cabinet of torn emotions and mended nerves, of hope communicated by brooding frowns, of continual crisis relieved occasionally by comedy in the most minor of all possible keys was the smash-hit dramatic series of last season.

How it came about, this phenomenon, makes for interesting speculation. I like to think that when Newton Minow, Chairman of the Federal Communications Commission, called television a "vast wasteland," thereby cribbing the phrase from the poet T. S. Eliot, the ears of Oliver Treyz pricked up. Treyz then was head of the ABC network. He is now operating elsewhere. It is just possible that Treyz called a conference of his three-buttoned executive board.

A new kind of violence

"Men," Treyz may have said, in a voice that could have rattled the windows at Brooks Brothers, "we've got to go easy next season, violence-wise. Or we've got to have a new kind of violence. We've got to have *high-minded* violence."

Trundling in from the West on a jet came an angular Quixote named James Moser, a writer-producer, bearing not a lance but a lancet—in the form of a pilot film.

"I called my show *The Medicine Man*," Moser said recently. "It was an allegorical title. I guess Treyz doesn't dig allegory. He wanted it to be called *Ben Casey*. That's his kind of allegory."

Allegorical or not, *Ben Casey* unbuttoned his wrinkled tunic and cut his way to the heart of America, if perhaps not to its brain. It went on in the autumn of 1961; by spring of this year it was in the Top 10 of a national rating service, claiming a weekly audience of 32,000,000.

The first noteworthy network hospital show, *Medic*, starring Richard Boone and also created by Moser, had been successful, but the frowning, impatient neurosurgeon Ben became a national preoccupation—not just on the minds of the lay public, but on those of the medical profession as well.

Doctors and nurses reacted

The curfew for student nurses at St. Vincent's Hospital in New York City was 10:30 P.M. On nights when *Ben Casey* was on duty until 11, everyone was permitted to stay up to watch him grimace his way through to the end. All over the country nurses off duty, who should have been sleeping, preferred to keep their eyes open and be tranquilized by the ill-tempered resident.

The name of the show became a part of hospital argot. When a doctor exhibited temperament or extraordinary diligence or notable exasperation, underlings would say, "He's pulling a Ben Casey."

Little boys and girls began wearing *Ben Casey* tunics and uniforms.

All this was extremely distressing to a hypochondriac such as the oversigned. Hospitals, uniforms and the mere mention of aspirin make this beloved American journalist as nervous as Newton Minow made Oliver Treyz. If I hear the name of a disease, such as subacute bacterial endocarditis, I at once develop subacute bacterial endocarditis. My work suffers until I hear the name of another disease I've never heard of before. Then I come down with that one.

Now there are hypochondriacs and hypochondriacs. Some actually watch *Ben Casey*, a psychiatrist told me, because they enjoy being assaulted by strange new symptoms, the more frightening the better. One thing that many hypochondriacs have in common is an unwillingness to consult a real doctor. They live in a never-never land of instantaneous health. Therefore they consult Ben in their minds.

Some go so far as to consult him in person. Because he seems to be a kind of father image, albeit a youngish one, people write him or call him up on his unlisted number or stop him on the street to tell him of their twinges and tremors. They hope he will scowl at them and make everything all better.

The ludicrousness of all this has not escaped the comedians, nearly all of whom have added *Ben Casey* jokes to their routines. So have newspaper columnists. And network executives, those unconscious comedians, are adding some *Ben* jokes by scheduling, if not an epidemic, at least a slight rash of medical shows.

Everywhere one looks around the studios in Hollywood these days, actors are sheathing themselves in surgical garb and setting their ears for stethoscopes. Actresses are talking earnestly to costumers, conceivably asking if they might lower those nurse uniform necklines a trifle.

"It will not be possible to watch television in the 1962–63 season without having one's hospitalization paid up," my wife remarked recently. My wife is a lady hypochondriac.

The bad case of—excuse me—Ben(d)s now molesting the nation is in large part due to Vincento Eduardo Zoino, an actor of 31 who operates as Vincent Edwards.

Curiously enough, Treyz did not buy the series for ABC because of Edwards. The pilot film starred him, but it was the concept that was bought more than the actor.

Vincent Edwards, nevertheless, became the focal point of the show as far as the public was concerned. His story already has been told in this magazine. He was born in Brooklyn, he wanted to be an actor, he was working his way into obscurity in Hollywood by making mediocre movies—22 of them—when Bing Crosby Productions, producers of *Ben*, discovered him.

"We'd tested dozens of actors in Hollywood and New York," Jim Moser, the creator, told me. "Then one day Vince came in. He had the build, he had the look. All I thought was, If only he can act!' "

Edwards' acting consisted chiefly of an inability to appear any way but grim. Yet he projected something that people believed in and were drawn to—some force, some magnetism, some illusion of sincerity. He at once elbowed his way into the front rank of the new breed of inarticulate actors. His fan mail began flooding in.

In the opinion of some who have worked with him, as his national popularity rose, his personal popularity dropped. Those who now regard him as a dedicated savior of mankind, as Ben, will be sorry to learn that there are those who regard him as a dedicated savior of Vince, as Vince.

Edwards has been accused of being chronically late, which is costly to the company; he has been accused of being possessed of an unmanageable temper; he has been accused of coming in without having his lines firmly fixed in his mind.

If these accusations are true, as many actors have said they are, they are defended by Jim Moser; or they were when I discussed Edwards with him last spring.

"Oh, I get a little beefed at him, because he's sometimes . . . uh . . . what shall I say?" He debated this with himself for a while. "Well, they gotta be that way or they wouldn't be actors."

Edwards made unusually high demands toward the close of last season, declaring that for his services this season he ought to get what, if reports were correct, was a salary higher than any actor in any dramatic series then was getting.

While he was holding out, I asked Matthew Rapf, the show's No. 2 executive, what would happen if Edwards did not sign. Rapf nervously said that Moser would replace him. Other stars have been replaced in series. William Bendix became *Riley* after Jackie Gleason was through enjoying *The Life of* him. John McIntire replaced the late Ward Bond on *Wagon Train.* How many mothers has that kid on *Lassie* had? How many Lassies have there been?

"Do you think it will hurt the series if Edwards goes?" I asked Matthew Rapf.

He trembled like a man facing a *Ben Casey* operation. "It would take us a while to build back up without him, but I think we could do it."

There is no disputing Vincent Edwards' popularity, but Rapf was right. The appeal of *Ben Casey* extends far beyond that of one actor's personality, especially since that actor is essentially more individualistic than talented. The appeal of this show lies in our thirst for violence—one aspect of our hypochondria.

A TV Guide Close-Up

OCTOBER 1, 1962

(NBC)

11:15 **4** "TONIGHT"—Johnny Carson

Color

It's not really a debut if you come right down to it. Steve Allen once ruled this particular roost, and Jack Paar also made the feathers fly. But tonight's the night Johnny Carson takes over, after a brief interregnum following Paar's abdication.

Johnny doesn't face the music (provided by Skitch Henderson and crew) alone. He has brought along Joan Crawford, who acts; Tony Bennett and Rudy Vallee, who sing; and Mel Brooks, who writes comedy lines and delivers them too. Keep an ear peeled for references to Joan's current film-making—she's co-starred with another great lady of the cinema, Bette Davis.

Otherwise, the *Tonight* show will follow a format not unlike Paar's. There will be plenty of Carson's satiric shafts; plenty of guests paying encore visits; plenty of off-the-cuff conversation; and, they hope, plenty of commercials. Ed McMahon handles the announcing.

Review

by Gilbert Seldes

"THE BEVERLY HILLBILLIES"

The thumping success of *The Beverly Hillbillies* has already sent some serious thinkers to the wailing wall, and when you tune the program in, you are supposed to ask yourself, "What is America coming to?" As I am still laughing, I think back to the days when custard pies and Keystone Cops were flying through the air and a lot of people were convinced America was a cultural "desert"—the 1920 word for "wasteland." (A question I asked then has never been answered: What can you do with a custard pie except throw it?)

The single simple, and to some people outrageous, fact is that *The Beverly Hillbillies* is funny. It is funny the way comic strips used to be funny before they became long continued stories in which nothing ever happens. The people in it are funny the way ordinary clowns are funny (not the Chaplin type) and the proof of it is that you never smile at what they are up to—you laugh out loud or you wait for the next absurdity. One of the formulas for comedy is "real people in unreal situations." Here you have *un*real people in *un*real situations.

The Keystone comedies had the advantage of silence. *The Beverly Hillbillies* has to use words. Many of the words are in a language new to most of us: Paw sees Elly May all dressed up and tells her she's "slicker'n a cow's belly" and when another dress is said to look "like it came from Saks," the indignant answer is that it was "made up from boughten goods." Paw says the man who bought his oil-rich land is going to pay him between 25 and 100 dollars—"a new kind of dollars: million dollars." When the banker advises Paw to put some of his millions into stocks, you get cattle, not pieces of paper.

When the characters go into action, the words mesh with the deeds. When Elly May has been outfitted by the banker's secretary, it is a pleasure to follow the camera dotingly along her figure from her head to—bare feet. And a moment later, when a very correct young man bends over her hand to kiss it, she spins him flat on his back, explaining that "he was fixin' to bite me." Even when the whole family in Ozark clothes is taken for trick-or-treaters by swanky neighbors on Halloween, the action is so fast and the situation so absurd that the scene comes off in high spirits.

In principle I object to the fundamental notion (which is not in the Declaration of Independence) that ignorant people are wiser than informed people. I'm not even sure you have to be ignorant in order to have a good time. I think you can be howlingly funny without misspelling or mispronouncing words. I have known athletic college professors and enchanting (women) librarians. The whole notion on which *The Beverly Hillbillies* is founded is an encouragement to ignorance—in a time when our only salvation lies in education.

But it *is* funny. What can I do?

One thing the sponsor can do. Stop ruining the characters by making them dramatize his commercials. *They* are not funny.

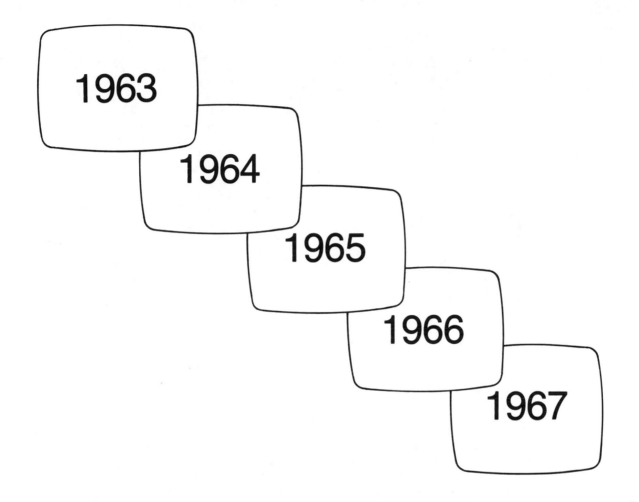

(Zinn Arthur)

IT WAS MY MEDIUM

Never a happy man, the comedian was
miserable away from television

by Richard Gehman

PART I

Since 1958, when he passed from regularly scheduled
television into an enforced exile, Sid Caesar, one of the
medium's legendary figures, had been stalking through
the split-level corridors of his own Elba, which, appropriately enough, is located at Kings Point, Long Island,
waiting like an itchy, oversized Napoleon for the telephone call that would tell him his subjects wanted him
back.

During this period he had received emissaries from
other kingdoms—films, the stage, nightclubs and even
radio—offering him kings' ransoms to rule therein, but
except for a few nightclub appearances and some TV
guest shots, nothing could tempt him.

Caesar passed his time in a variety of ways. He sat for
hours staring at pretenders who had usurped his
power. He cleaned and recleaned his large collection of
guns and, although he uses these weapons only for target practice, it may have occurred to him, occasionally,
to turn one or another toward the set and pull the trigger. He also discovered, attacked and captured the Civil
War.

"Sid read so many Civil War books that eventually he
got the idea that the whole thing had happened just to

give him a new hobby," one friend says. Caesar's new
company, not so oddly, is called Stonewall Productions.

Studying old actions may have furnished Caesar with
a psychological valve through which his anguished restlessness could hiss out. The enforced separation from
his huge television audience affected him more than it
would have a lesser monarch.

"He is not a comedian," says a close associate. "He is
more like the traditional clown. His humor comes from
inner grief and despair. He is a miserable man. He's
happy only when he is being a character—as himself,
he's tormented. People used to call him and ask him to
be an emcee—the idea frightened him to death.

"Have you watched him introduce sketches on his
own show? He almost stammers. He is not nervous
when he is performing . . . and yet he must be *fundamentally* nervous, for in his eagerness to be funny when
he *is* performing he often goes too far."

Caesar's own melancholy is so much a part of his root
personality his friends say he will never find its medicine. They accept it; just possibly they treasure it, realiz-
ing it is indeed the source of his public hilarity. Over
and over they tell stories about it. "There was this like
bacchanal we used to have at this restaurant like after
every show," says this (like) gag writer. "Sid was always
tired and mostly gloomy. One night he sat at the table
staring into space from 10:30 P.M. to about 3:30 A.M.
Everybody else was laughing and carousing.

"At about 3:34 A.M. his wife said, 'Sid, come on, let's
go home.' He looked at her angrily. 'Whadya mean,
home? I'm havin' a good time.' "

Caesar always has been an inarticulate, uncommunicative man. The person with whom he seems most at
ease is his handyman, a deaf-mute. He will sit with family and friends for long periods in mummified silence.

Perhaps in an effort to endure the captivity of his
own unarticulated problems, Caesar at one point began
drinking more than usual. "It wasn't just a lot of shots;
it was tumblers," an ex-writer says. Just as abruptly, he
gave it up. "Sid never does anything halfway. It's all or
nothing."

Although she has been living with Caesar's enormities
since 1943, Florence Levy Caesar, who met her husband at a Catskill Mountains resort operated by her uncle (Caesar was a *tumler* there), admits that the life of a
lady-in-waiting to a ruler in chains has not been precisely easy, although she did originally realize that it
might not be.

"Your husband is going to be a big, big star," Max
Liebman, Caesar's producer on *Your Show of Shows,* said
to her soon after Caesar went on TV.

She looked apprehensively wistful. "Couldn't he just
be a *little* star?"

He could not, of course. His determination to be a
dominant figure was as immense as his strength—and
the latter is awesome. "A cab driver insulted Sid once,"
a friend recalls, "and Sid tried to pull him out of the
cab through a four-inch space between the top of the
window and the roof . . . by his ear." Another time,
Caesar complained that the sink in his dressing room

wasn't working properly. When he arrived the following week and saw that it had not been fixed, he grabbed it and wrenched it away from the wall.

"Was he difficult to live with when he wasn't on the air?" I asked Florence Caesar recently.

She is a tall, warmly pretty woman, thoroughly feminine yet possessed of a guileless candor. "Well . . . I guess he was. He's not a gay, happy person, you know. He's serious and quiet. Most comedians I've met seem to be that way—very introverted."

Possibly as another way of diverting his thoughts from his idleness, she went on, Caesar developed a new interest in the crown prince (Rick, 10) and the two princesses (Shelley, 15, and Karen, 6). "He became much less aloof with the children," Mrs. Caesar said. "He began to enjoy them, especially Rick. You know—the two men against the rest of us."

Caesar's own view of the four-year period when the cameras were not his serfs once each week is an interesting definition of the seemingly warring halves of his nature. On the one hand there was his admitted need to perform; on the other, the artist's awareness that creation is dependent upon contemplation.

"There comes a time when the brain says, 'That's it, let's recharge,' " he told me. "I'd been on the air continuously since 1949. I had to sit back and take it in, drink in life a little bit, see what was going on."

It was impossible for him to do that gracefully. "He could have gone into other media, but he wouldn't," says Rosette Plesser, a longtime associate. "He had his heart set on returning triumphantly to TV, I think. I don't think he ever accepted the fact that his career might be over."

"Well, after all," said Caesar to me, "I grew up in television. It was *my* medium."

Thus did the mighty monarch pace off the days, the weeks, the months that grew into four years. And presently the telephone did ring. It was Jack Mogulescu, a cigar-roller who previously had hired the late Ernie Kovacs and was looking for someone who could do the nine shows he was to have done this season. Mogulescu and Caesar held a two-power conference, in which the former said he was prepared to render unto Caesar what the latter felt was his due.

"I finally got the kind of sponsor I wanted to work with. 'Do what you feel and don't feel obligated about ratings or about this or about that as long as it's in good taste, and, uh, go ahead.' " So Caesar says Mogulescu said. And he girded himself and went into rehearsal.

At about the same time, Caesar was signed by Stanley Kramer, the film producer, for an important part in "It's a Mad, Mad, Mad, Mad World." And producers Feuer and Martin hired him to do not one but seven different parts in their current Broadway musical "Little Me."

Thus Caesar returned not just as a king but as a conqueror at the head of an avenging army. Whether or not he will continue to prevail may depend in large part upon his ability to restrain himself; so some believe, for they claim that one reason he went off the air was his inability to control or edit his material. They believe the king's view that the king could do no wrong was responsible for the king's dethronement.

Others take the opposite view. They say that Caesar's excesses were what made him great originally, and that he cannot, and will not, ever learn restraint. And although some may view part of his behavior with alarm, most believe that his performing strengths stem from his weaknesses.

PART II

Why he often finds it easier to make millions laugh than to smile himself

Six years ago, when Sid Caesar was one of the overlords of comedy on the nation's networks, extracting a reported $25,000 a week for coruscating with such brilliance that serious critics compared him to Chaplin, he sat down with a reporter—your obdt. svt., the oversigned—to write a magazine article about his hard—one might even say agonizing—life.

Literally, I wept as Caesar recalled the extended trauma that was his childhood. To hear him tell it, this period, which began on September 8, 1922, in Yonkers, N.Y., was one long series of emotional wounds and bruises.

"I felt like a midget among giants," Caesar told me. One brother, Abe, was 15 years older; another, Dave, was 10 his senior. The parents were always bickering. This turned him inward: "I couldn't talk until I was three," he said.

At four he was packed off to school. His parents operated the St. Clair Buffet and Hotel, a run-down establishment; they worked hard all day long because they could not afford help, and they sent him away to get him out of the house.

"One summer," he told me, "my father shipped me to Asbury Park, New Jersey, where my mother was with some relatives. He put me on a train with a tag around my neck. When my train pulled in, I saw my mother on another train there, ready to pull out.

"Some relatives found me in the station, but nothing they said or did could relieve my anxiety and rejection."

The father was a bitter, sarcastic man, made that way, perhaps, by his dominating wife. One day he made as though to reach into his pocket for a quarter to give the boy to go to the movies. The delighted little Sid extended his hand, only to have Max Caesar give him a slap that bounced him off a wall.

Such experiences—there were others—caused Caesar first to withdraw and then to attempt to find an outlet in performing. He told me of his early days as an entertainer-musician (he played the saxophone) on the Borscht Circuit in the Catskill Mountains, of his service in the Coast Guard, of his appearance in the Broadway revue "Make Mine Manhattan" (in which he was hailed as a great find), and of his association with the former summer-camp-show producer Max Liebman, who helped him become famous on TV.

None of these accomplishments helped him find happiness, he said. Nor did his marriage to an agreeable, loving and patient wife who bore him three children. Much as he loved his work, he mainly was miserable. Parties depressed him.

"I was a mess," he told me. "I couldn't stand myself, and neither could anybody else."

Psychoanalysis eventually helped him to control himself, to find satisfaction in his performances, and even—a rather dubious reward—to talk on the telephone without trembling.

There was no denying that Caesar had become a happier man, or at least had in his own mind; but there also was no denying that he hardly had become a Dr. Norman Vincent Peale. Always the embodiment of excess, he remained excessive—in manner, clothing, facial expressions, appetite, everything. He still is that way.

A friend saw him in Palm Springs, having dinner. "I swear the piece of meat was six inches thick," he said. "It was a whole two-rib roast."

Another friend recalls Caesar at the height of his career riding home after a day's work. "He was sitting in the back seat of his Cadillac, which was the longest one ever made, wearing the biggest pearl-gray hat ever made, and wearing a suit with shoulders so wide there wasn't room for anybody else on the back seat.

"He was sipping a martini as his chauffeur drove him along, except that he wasn't just sipping; he would take a drink and then make about a dozen faces—real Sid Caesar comedy, coughing, smacking his lips, blinking, wrinkling his nose, everything exaggerated."

This private behavior has always carried over into public performances. Caesar never has seemed to know when to stop. On the air he almost invariably extended sketches far beyond their prescribed limits. To his staff this was especially amazing because he was aware that he was doing it. Yet he seemed constitutionally unable to follow scripts as written.

When he was preparing a nightclub act, he asked an associate, Rosette Plesser, to get him some material from old TV shows. She began running kinescopes. "Get it from the scripts," Caesar said. "I can't," she said. "They're completely different from what you did on the air."

Caesar created his material in an atmosphere of contention and commotion. Some psychoanalysts claim that people unconsciously repeat the behavior patterns of their childhood, and it may be that he could function only if all around him were arguing.

Sheldon Keller, a writer, recently told me, "The average meeting consisted of Sid, Carl Reiner, Howie Morris, Sid's stand-in, his TV wife of the moment—Imogene [Coca], Nanette [Fabray] or Janet Blair—and seven or eight writers, plus his brother Dave—everybody yelling."

Brother Dave tried to be a stabilizing influence. He answered telephones and went out for sandwiches. His humor, the writers say, was as sharp as Sid's, but quieter. One recalls, "Dave had gone for so many sandwiches that one day he handed me a piece of Swiss cheese and said, 'My card, sir.'" Sometimes Dave made suggestions for the script.

"If you interrupt us once more, Dave, I'm going to get you demoted to cousin," the writer Aaron Ruben once warned.

All Dave's efforts could not keep the meetings from becoming explosive. Caesar would walk in, saying sarcastically, "Well, everybody goofin' off again, eh? All right, let's hear the brilliance."

To show they had not been idle, everyone would speak at once. "This isn't a job, it's a great big dirty tenement family," the writer Mel Tolkin said one day.

Inevitably the writers clashed as they competed for Caesar's attention. Loud arguments, laced with profanity, were common. Savage feuds developed.

Miraculously enough, the tumult seemed to stimulate Caesar. Sometimes the writers would try to set him off. He is a fearfully tidy man about his person and surroundings. If, during a lull, he left the room, Aaron Ruben would push a venetian-blind slat crooked. Caesar would see it at once—and be so irritated that his creativity would begin to gush.

Long-lasting grudges

Anger, bitterness and tension lingered among the writers long after the show went off the air. Two once met in the street; the first knew the second hated him, and tried to make a gesture of atonement. "Why don't you and your wife come for dinner some night?" he said. "We can't—we don't eat any more," said the second coldly.

Yet, surprisingly enough, none of the men hate Caesar. They came to accept his explosiveness as Neapolitans accept Vesuvius.

Caesar does not apologize for his excesses. "Sure, I used to try to start things. I did it on purpose to get them thinking, to get myself thinking.

"Once I start to spout material, I try to go at it from every angle, get things going that way. It's better if you argue about it a little. One idea leads to another."

Few of Caesar's friends and associates feel that his tendency to carry things beyond normal limits was necessarily bad. Howard Morris, formerly one of his second bananas, told me:

"Look—I have only the greatest respect for this man's genius. People criticizing his excesses bug me. This is a big man. A Titan? Is that the word? The very things we love him for come out of that bigness, that ability to go on attacking, attacking in areas, big areas of social comment, where nobody else goes.

"Look, this is a big, big man. He thinks big, he eats big, he dresses big, he dreams big. You ever see his cuff links? It's not a guy's profile on them, it's his whole face!

"You can't have genius without some arrogance."

This season, Caesar claims, he is being more restrained. The half-hour time limit of *As Caesar Sees It* does not give him as much room in which to expand. When I saw him in California last August, he seemed fit, fairly relaxed and eager to be back on the air. He was no longer in psychoanalysis; his doctor had discharged him four years ago.

"What I hope to do this season," he said, "is make myself happy, as comfortable and happy as I can. If I can do that, that'll come across to the audience. The main thing will be to have fun."

Old friends hooted at this as loudly as they did at an article about psychoanalysis that Caesar once wrote. (It was called ironically, "What Psychoanalysis Did For Me.") They declare he never will be happy; the childhood ghosts are still haunting him. Secretly, they may be pleased by this; for if this comedian's strength comes from his weakness, as I have mentioned previously, the ironic fact is that the unhappier he is, the happier he makes the rest of us.

(Jay Thompson)

(Peter Oliver/Topix)

The Girl in the Rubber Mask

When you peel it away,
what do you find?
by Edith Efron

Now that America's most raucous female comic has signed her first million-dollar contract, one is increasingly hearing the question: "What is Carol Burnett *really* like?" The question, invariably provoked by any significant degree of fame, sounds more innocent than it is. It tacitly assumes that behind the well-known public face of a celebrity lies an unknown secret face.

In the case of Carol Burnett, whose public face is exclusively composed of rubber-faced grimaces, grotesque contortions and raucous cries, the assumption is correct. What kind of a private face does Carol Burnett have?

The first thing that must be revealed is that the Carol Burnett who lunches in New York restaurants or wanders around her spacious New York apartment bears only a faint physical resemblance to the Carol Burnett known to the public. She might be her own second cousin—from the better side of the tracks. For one thing, her features are substantially more delicate than they seem to be on screen; her teeth take up only the ordinary amount of room in her mouth and her mouth takes up only the ordinary amount of room in her face. She looks neither rubbery nor horsy, but pleasantly and normally human. Indeed, she's so normal-looking that she would seem quite at home on a college campus, behind a stocking counter at Macy's, or in a teller's cage in a small-town bank. One's first-glance impression of her can be summed up in two words: average girl.

She is an outgoing and friendly person. When she talks about show business she is enthusiastic, and she has a personal way of coming at things. For instance:

"I'll *never* do a TV series. That's it. Once you've been a series character, you're that character for *life*. They would probably name me *Gertrude* or *Agnes*, and that's all I'd be forever."

Or: "I've been offered commercials, but I'll *never* do them unless I'm starving in the streets. You get identified as a car salesman or as a soap salesman. They see you three times a night on TV pitching products. Suddenly you're in a show as somebody altogether different. It confuses fantasy with reality. I don't *like* it. You can make a *bundle*, but I'm not interested."

Or: "You don't have to be a rotten rat to get ahead in show business."

As is the case with many show-business people, Carol is almost entirely preoccupied with her work. "I haven't done much for the past few years except work and sleep," she says, "but it's not really work, it's love." Her career has been meteoric: Within 11 years she has moved from the UCLA campus, through a few minor TV roles to a New York nightclub, where her rendition of a song called "I Made a Fool of Myself over John Foster Dulles" precipitated her onto the Paar, Sullivan and Dinah Shore shows, and ultimately led to her role on *The Garry Moore Show* in the fall of 1959.

Last season she left *The Garry Moore Show*. "I knew it was time to stop shoving myself down people's throats every week," she said at the time. "How many times can you do a pratfall or cross your eyes without the audience beginning to second-guess you?" Her timing was good. She left at the height of her success and in August 1962 CBS offered Carol Burnett one million dollars to do a series of specials over the next 10 years. The first will be telecast this Sunday (February 24).

If there is any quality for which Carol Burnett has received almost universal tribute, it is her modesty in the face of success. All those who know her well report that her fame is not "real" to her. Dorothy Kilgallen, whose pen is not infrequently tipped with acid, sums up the standard opinion of those who know Carol superficially, thus: "Carol is about as unphony and normally blueberry pie as you can get and still stay in show business."

Is her normalcy an illusion?

On the other hand, those who deal closely with her often claim that her "blueberry pie" normality is illusory. Her eager dedication to her career seems to be an iron wall that cuts her off from most of reality. A systematic query of her associates reveals the peculiar fact that no one has ever heard Carol Burnett converse in a sustained fashion on any subject which does not relate in some way to the entertainment world. "I don't believe we've talked more than two pages' worth of anything but show business since I've known her," says Garry Moore. "I don't think she spends much time, so far, thinking about anything else," says Joe Hamilton, producer of *The Garry Moore Show* and Carol's official beau. A CBS official says, "She has a pleasant, nonabrasive personality. No strong opinions on anything except her work. Off stage she's a dullish girl."

Carol, too, thinks she's a "dullish" girl. "I've always been a little wishy-washy," she says. "I'm afraid to get people mad at me." As a matter of fact, she is a member in good standing of that curious group of show-business folk who are in chronic pursuit of what they variously term their "egos," "identities" or "selves." Carol confides the details of this quest to everyone who interviews her. "I have not developed my *self*," she says. "The hardest thing for me to do is to come on and talk to an audience as myself. If I'm not in character, I feel *naked*."

It is a curious form of selflessness and is sometimes interpreted as a charming modesty, but most often it is viewed as "Carol's problem." Says Garry, "Carol lacks self-confidence. She is unsure of herself as a person."

But these are minor matters as compared with Carol's negative attitudes toward her own femininity—attitudes which emerge in her comedic style and which account for most of the psychologizing done about her.

There is no doubt that Carol belongs to what might be called the "gargoyle" school of comedy (Martha Raye, Imogene Coca, Nancy Walker) as opposed to the sophisticated or romantic school (Carole Lombard, Kay Kendall, Mary Tyler Moore, Nanette Fabray). Where the romantic comediennes remain enchantingly feminine and glamorous throughout their capers, the members of the gargoyle school turn themselves into objects of ridicule and seem desperately intent on annihilating in themselves the last trace of feminine allure. As one writer puts it in describing Carol on stage, "The TV camera seems to throw her into spasms of compulsive mugging and self-uglification."

"This making herself ugly," says Garry Moore, "it all comes from Carol's not believing that she's feminine, and trying to cover it up by making fun of herself. Carol is really an attractive girl, but she thinks of herself as an ugly duckling. According to a certain theory, it's this feeling of feminine inadequacy that drives women to become comics."

Carol is highly inclined to punctuate her conversation with rueful, self-deprecatory "jokes" which bear out Garry's thesis. She has referred to herself as "slobby." Recently, in discussing her younger sister Christine, whom she has supported since the death of their parents, she said, "She's 5 feet 9 and built like Sophia Loren. I'm embarrassed to take a bath in front of her. I cry myself to sleep thinking about it."

It does not appear to be an accident that Carol's most successful comedy vehicles to date have been dedicated to a compulsive undercutting of romance. On *The Garry Moore Show*, when Carol got her hands on the Cinderella legend, the enchanting little heroine turned into a raucous 20th-century dame with a hangover. And when Carol interpreted the theme of a sensitive young girl at her first ball, what emerged was a flat-footed adenoidal wreck whose own mother could not love her.

Carol dislikes the psychological speculations which surround her. Recently she sounded off about a reporter. "He asked me, 'Why do you do comedy? Is it because you want to have people love you? Is it because you suffer a deep sense of insecurity?' He was a *beady-eyed* little man who made me feel as if I were under analysis." She also dislikes the charge that her comedy style is anti-feminine, and discusses it in a strangely equivocal fashion.

She too divides comediennes into two classes, but she calls the romantic comediennes like Carole Lombard and Kay Kendall "actresses" and the "self-uglifiers" like Imogene Coca and Martha Raye "clowns." What's the difference? "An actress," says Carol, "responds to the humor of a specific characterization. She's not always 'on.' A clown is one who is constantly funny—both on and off stage." It's a curious distinction that ignores the fact that both types of comediennes are actresses, and allows Carol to glide right over the sensitive issue of "self-uglification." "*I'm* not the kind who's always on," she says. "So I'm an actress, not a clown."

It is not surprising that, to date, Carol Burnett's romantic life has been troubled. She was married for several years to young actor Don Saroyan. Carol blames the ensuing break-up on her success in show business.

Until recently she was seriously devoid of beaus. Just last year she reported, "I've almost quit dating, I've gotten so discouraged."

Reported romance

In August 1962, a new development in Carol's life was announced to the world in an exclusive front-page story in the New York Journal-American, by-lined by Dorothy Kilgallen. The headline read: "CAROL BURNETT'S IN LOVE WITH A WONDERFUL GUY." The wonderful guy in question was Joe Hamilton. Carol informed Dorothy: "I'm madly in love with him." Joe informed Dorothy: "The feeling is mutual." Joe, a slick, sharp-featured man who looks like a denizen of Madison Avenue, admires Carol greatly. "She's a real kook," he says. He seems unconcerned by Carol's various problems. "That's how comics are," he says. "That's what makes them clowns." He is separated from his wife, and, at last report, divorce proceedings were being discussed. It is highly possible that Carol will marry him. And if she does, her wedding will have that extravagant note that seems so inescapable in Carol's universe: She will step away from the altar to find herself the stepmother of eight children.

What is Carol Burnett *really* like? There is no simple answer. She is a complex individual, bright and dull, open and closed, brave and timorous, ambitious and limited, inhibited and exhibitionistic, self-affirmative and self-attacking. She's a mass of contradictory attributes, under a surface that's as "normal as blueberry pie."

(Gene Trindl)

Jack Benny & Co.

In 30 years on radio and television, they've never missed a dividend, thanks to a stock of blue-chip jokes

Jack Benny, the 69-year-old comedian who looks about 50 but still says he's 39, has been a fixture of radio and/ or TV for 30 years. During that time he has collected more medals, both real and imagined, than a Nicaraguan general.

Early in his career, his bouts with the late Fred Allen drastically altered the course of radio comedy. ("Benny," said Allen, "couldn't ad-lib a belch after a Hungarian dinner.") And by the 1940s, he had sold so much Jell-O that they switched him to Grape Nut Flakes. In 1948 he all but started a broadcasting war by defecting (for a reported $2,500,000) from one network to another. In TV, he has managed to hold his own impressively. And yet times have been changing rapidly. How has Benny changed?

Recently Benny sat with his four writers, whose combined time of servitude totals 68 years. They were discussing the script which they would be taping later that week. The guest star was to be Rod (*Twilight Zone*) Serling, and the idea of the show was that Benny, burdened in the script with writers who could barely write their names, was to hire Serling to give his writing staff some "class."

Jack Benny, Dennis Day, Eddie (Rochester) Anderson and Don Wilson above are respectively 1, 2, 3, and 8. The writers are Hal Goldman (4), Sam Perrin (5), George Balzer (6) and Al Gordon (9). Frederick De Cordova (10) is producer-director, and No. 7 in Irving Fein, executive producer and president of J&M Productions.

The jokes that week, as every week, were vintage Benny. In the beginning Jack is discovered washing his own windows—he is too cheap to hire anybody to do it for him. The Cheap Jokes and the Ego Jokes drop like heavy dew up to and through the moment of Serling's entrance. Serling is to come into Benny's office and explain why he is late: Benny's window-washing bucket has fallen off the ledge and hit him on the head.

Benny stops the read-through. "Fellows," he says soberly, "after my line, 'Gee, that's a shame, Rod,' how about if I say, 'Uh, you didn't bring it back up with you, did you?' Then Rod says, 'What did you say?' and I say, 'Oh, nothing.'" After the laughter has subsided, Cheap Joke #9999 is duly incorporated into the script.

Benny has been telling the Cheap Joke without cessation or apology since he first started in vaudeville during the 1920s. Explain its singular attraction and you explain Jack. Thriftiness is a universally human trait with which almost everyone can identify, and writer George Balzer (20 years with Benny) has said many times, "Everybody has an uncle who's cheap—just like Jack."

George Burns, Benny's oldest show-business friend and official Boswell, says, "With Jack it's not so much the Cheap Joke as the Cheap Man. He's always been in character." Burns, like Benny a great comedy technician, tends to see Jack as a man whose technique—particularly his masterful use of the Benny look—is so polished as to constitute an end in itself. "He is secure on the stage," says Burns. "He never sweats. The tempo is easy. If he tells a pointless joke and fails to get a response, he'll stop and do the look and the hand gesture. And if he holds it long enough, he'll *get* the laugh. He's such an institution they'll laugh because they're afraid there really is a point."

Benny has a simple explanation of his own comedy. "I emphasize character," he says. "The best humor I can possibly get is out of a stingy one. You can go as wild as you want. The audience has a point of reference: Everybody knows somebody who's real tight."

Jack's concern is only what he does *with* a joke. He likes to boast about his ability as an editor and about his eagle eye for contrived straight lines or for jokes—often

very funny ones—which are inconsistent with the character he has spent 40 years creating. He is proud, too, of his sense for keeping his comedy techniques fresh.

He believes, for example, that one Cheap Joke prop that stood up for 20 years—the ancient Maxwell automobile—now is dated. But another familiar device, the bank vault where the Stingy One keeps his money, is still valid. "At some time I would have gotten rid of the Maxwell," he says, putting himself in the shoes of the fictitious tightwad he has created. "If I had a car, it would be a used car, but not a Maxwell. I wouldn't want to appear *that* cheap in public. On the other hand, a bank vault is a private affair.

"Oh, I've made other changes, too. Once I'd take out a loud-mouthed, homely-looking broad; today I take out a halfway decent one. You have to do that." He pauses. "The stingy character you can't help. If a man is stingy, he's stingy all his life."

Benny's writers point out that, except for Don Wilson, the members of the old stock company—Rochester, Dennis Day, Mary Livingstone, the French violin teacher, Mr. Kitzel, the parrot, the telephone operators, etc.—appear less frequently or not at all. This is attributable partly to the fact that television is less flexible than radio, which could build unlimited sets and situations in the imagination, and partly to the fact that the format calls for guest stars, around whom a protracted sketch must be built.

Jack the man is by and large totally different from Jack the comedian. He is truly generous and well organized, paying his real writers excellent salaries. If his comedy is "the comedy of frustration," as he says, then he is frustrated in at least one respect: He still seems to yearn to be the greatest violinist in the world. He owns a Stradivarius (an excellent one, says Isaac Stern) and practices two to three hours a day.

Next to most other comedians Benny sometimes seems all too colorless and workaday, a point about which he is sensitive. He prides himself on the fact that he is well liked, and urges would-be profilers to "go see my enemies—if you can find any."

Indeed, they are hard to come by. However, there are those who take a slightly less charitable view of the Benny comedy. "Benny can wring laughter out of a stone," says one highly placed comedy writer privately. "But he has to wring. I think all comedy is basically hostile. But Benny's is the comedy of petulance. For instance, when he begins to query his guest star Carol Burnett about her ex-boss, we know immediately what the joke is going to be. He wants Carol to knock Garry Moore and she won't do it. Benny is not only the most hostile comic going, but the one who most relentlessly satirizes the smallness of his fellow man."

That may explain something. But not everything. Philosophically, Benny is perhaps best left unexplained. Suffice it to say that at 69 he is still the most conscientious craftsman in the business. There is something rather touching about his devotion to just one joke—like a man playing a violin sonata on just one string.

But on that one string, ah! he is brilliant!

... and no regulation ... shall be promulgated ... by the
[Federal Communications] Commission
which shall interfere with the right of free speech ...

SECTION 326, COMMUNICATIONS ACT, 1934

TELEVISION

AMERICA'S TIMID GIANT

Despite official freedom from censorship, a self-imposed silence
renders network documentaries almost mute on many great issues of the day.
This special report reveals TV's shocking taboos and reasons for them.

by Edith Efron

Officially, television is free of censorship.

Such freedom is not only guaranteed by the Constitution, but the Communications Act of 1934 explicitly ensures "the right of free speech by means of radio communication" and forbids all Government censorship. And just last month Federal Communications Commission Chairman Newton Minow declared to a convention of the National Association of Broadcasters: "We have encouraged you to take positions on issues, to be unafraid of controversy, to editorialize, to help mold and lead public opinion. ... We have repeatedly protected you against those who would water down your convictions ... or suppress your freedom."

Nevertheless, there has been a growing awareness, among both television people and newspapermen, that TV is not making full use of its "freedom"—indeed, that news and public affairs departments seem to be actively avoiding certain critical areas of coverage. To quote just a few of these observers:

Says Chet Huntley, NBC: "There's an unhealthy avoidance of national politics in public affairs departments."

Says Fred Friendly, executive producer of *CBS Reports:* "There's insufficient research and first-hand reporting being done in national affairs. Too many men are trying to do 'safe' stories. They stay away from controversy."

Says John Secondari, ABC: "Public affairs programming has limited itself to certain subjects, certain themes. What's outside the limits? *We're* outside the limits! *America* is outside the limits!"

Says one of the most prominent newspaper editors in New York City: "TV coverage is unintelligible—it's *fragmented.* They're obviously keeping away from all kinds of national issues."

Says Arthur Krock of The New York Times, dean of Washington's political press corps: "I've been observing for a long time that the networks are avoiding national political issues. It's *very* noticeable on the air."

Are these just idle impressions? What accounts for their singular uniformity? What precisely is going on in network news departments to provoke such criticism?

When responsible TV newsmen are questioned intensively, many of them make very disturbing charges:

They contend that there are "taboos" in the coverage of national affairs. They insist that these taboos are "tacit" and "unstated"—and that they are not being imposed explicitly by the networks but are imposed by many men on themselves, in cautious "self-censorship."

What are these "unstated taboos"?

One of them is coverage of business and industry. "Not many men," says Fred Friendly, "are in a position to do a story that might arouse the criticism of a multimillion-dollar industry. I was able to do the cancer-cigaret story because I'm in a privileged position. I'm a senior in my company. A good many of the men in the field, however, are in insecure positions. They prefer to do safe stories."

Another taboo: coverage of government, the type that might air anti-Administration sentiment. Mr. X., a stellar CBS news figure, reports that "the networks are definitely skittish about the Kennedy Administration," and blurts out, "I resent it. I resent it bitterly."

An expanded list of taboos is offered by Gerald Green, producer of *Chet Huntley Reporting:* "I suspect that these taboo areas include any coverage that might

Fred Friendly: "Too many men are trying to do 'safe' stories. They stay away from controversy." (CBS)

air criticism of government, big business, unions or the big pressure groups. There are exceptions to this rule, of course—maybe, over all the years, 15 or 20 exceptions. But not nearly enough of this kind of original reporting is going on. People don't specifically tell you not to do shows like this. There's just a tendency not to do them."

Essentially, the same list of taboos is given by Howard K. Smith, ABC news commentator. He angrily indicts the "self-censorship" as "vicious" ("It's the worst kind of censorship!") and declares: "You get into trouble if you criticize big business. The roof falls in if you criticize Congress. And we're getting increasingly cautious in criticizing the Administration. The pressures are getting worse."

And again, the same taboos are named by Mr. Y., a producer of some of CBS's most important news shows. "You want the truth?" he demands. "I'll tell you why coverage of America is so sparse. The ad agencies panic if you take off against big business. In the area of labor, the networks themselves don't want to rock the boat. *They're* big business, and big business does *not* antagonize big labor. As for criticism of government, the nets operate by government *permission*. They're not going to antagonize the Administration. The networks don't want to antagonize *anyone*."

And then this gentleman adds: "These are the real ground rules of public affairs. They're not written. They're not spoken. But we all know them. The miracle is that we give the public as much news as we do, considering the straitjacket we're in."

These are serious charges. Indeed, it is almost impossible to bring more serious charges against a communications system which purports to be covering "public affairs." Government, business and labor are not merely three subjects like any others. They are the three elements of which the body politic consists, and their activities and relationships are the very stuff of our democracy. As historian Henry Steele Commager, another severe critic of TV's national coverage, puts it: "A public affairs department that fails to cover government, business and labor is like an educational system that fails to cover reading, writing and arithmetic!"

To what extent is this fundamental coverage missing from TV? There is only one way to find out: by checking on what has been on the air. To be sure, hard newscasts move across the broad spectrum of news and public affairs, as do panel discussions and interview shows; but they are not organized to provide in-depth coverage. The great bulk of the news and public affairs specials and series *are* so organized, and they are the programs that must be surveyed.

A reveiw of three years—1960, 1961 and 1962—of such programs * provides an illuminating insight into national coverage by network TV.

On the surface, the breakdown of the total of 1580 subjects covered on these shows seems sensible: 421 were developments abroad; 695 were U.S. domestic issues—political, economic and social; and 464 comprised a hodgepodge of subjects, from auto shows and Miss America to modern art and Shakespeare. When one examines the details of the breakdown more closely, however, one sees a remarkable distinction between the coverage of foreign and domestic affairs.

Foreign coverage is extremely varied. There are, for example, 76 shows on the UN, 75 on Europe, 65 on Latin America, 42 on Africa, 42 on the Orient, 22 on Russia and its satellites, 13 on India, and six on the Middle East. In addition, the proportional pattern of coverage is intelligible: The cameras clearly are following the critical news. There are 30 shows on Germany compared with two on Sweden; 30 shows on Cuba compared with one on Haiti; 11 shows on Algeria compared with two on Ghana, etc.

U.S. coverage, on the other hand, follows the critical news intensively in some areas, and almost ignores it in others. Almost 80 percent of the 695 shows on domestic subjects are concentrated on five areas: the President (236 shows), elections (126 shows), space (108 shows), arms and disarmament (42 shows), and racial conflict (30 shows).

The President, elections, space, arms and race are important subjects. But should they constitute 80 percent of the coverage accorded domestic issues? According to experienced newsmen, they should not. A top editor of The New York Times calls the proportion "absolutely ridiculous." A top editor of Newsweek magazine calls it "silly" and "distorted." Both instantly point out that their publications allot "at least as much, if not more," coverage to Congress, business, labor and the rest of government as they do to the President—and "infinitely" more to these subjects than to space, arms, race and elections.

It is not a coincidence that the standards of a major paper and a major newsmagazine are identical in the matter of a national political "beat"—or that they are identical to the standards of a major historian—or that they are identical to the standards of the critical TV newsmen. That government, business and labor play crucial roles—and equally crucial roles—in national life

---

* Each of the three networks has supplied a list of its news and public affairs programs for this three-year period, identifying the subject (or subjects) covered by each show. The statistics in this article were derived from these lists.

The shows included: all news specials, plus these series: *Accent, Adlai Stevenson Reports, Bell Science Series, CBS Reports, Chet Huntley Reporting, Close-Up!, David Brinkley's Journal, Editor's Choice, Expedition!, Eyewitness, Frank McGee's Here and Now, Howard K. Smith—News and Comment, JFK Reports, NBC White Paper, Project 20, Purex Special For Women, The Campaign and the Candidates, The Nation's Future, The Twentieth Century, Winston Churchill—the Valiant Years, World Wide 60.*

is not a matter of personal opinion. It is a matter of objective fact.

Nonetheless, in 1960, 1961 and 1962, the major part of this critical "beat" was taken care of in about 20 percent of the TV time devoted to national affairs. Certain details of the coverage during this period are worth noting:

Item: In three years, only 18 shows were done on Congress—an average of two per network per year.

Item: In three years, only one show was done on the Vice President.

Item: In three years, only one show was done on the Supreme Court.

Item: In three years, only one show was done on the Department of Agriculture.

Item: In three years, only one show was done on the Department of Health, Education and Welfare. (No shows at all were done on the Departments of the Interior, Commerce and Labor.)

Item: In three years, only four shows were done on the FCC. (None was done on the six other powerful, controversial regulatory agencies, which include the Securities and Exchange Commission, the Federal Trade Commission and the Interstate Commerce Commission.)

Item: In three years, only 29 shows were done on major political-economic controversies. More than one-third of these were on two subjects alone: Medicare (six shows) and Civil Defense (four).

Item: In three years, only 11 documentaries were done on state and city politics. (Most of the major political events in 50 states were acknowledged only by local TV.)

Item: In three years, only 10 shows were done on big business—five of these on steel crises.

Item: In three years, only three shows were done on little business.

Item: In three years, only four shows were done on labor.

Item: In three years, only three shows were done on farmers and agricultural problems.

Is it possible that these were uneventful years for government, business and labor? Not in the least. They were unusually stormy years, but the storms were unseen on TV, save for occasional flashes of lightning on the short newscasts. Between 1960 and 1963 there were major Congressional investigations into big business and labor unions. Executives of major industrial firms were sent to jail under the anti-trust acts. Strikes repeatedly imperiled national defense. Congress came under attack for its methods of operation and the privi-

Richard Salant, CBS News Chief: "These men agree that nobody is censoring them. In that case, it's their problem." (CBS News)

leges of its members. Supreme Court decisions provoked strong opposition from different sectors of the population. Criticism of the regulatory agencies became increasingly acute. Major political scandals broke over some of the highest-placed heads in Washington. A severe stock-market collapse created violent repercussions in the business community. Deep rifts within both major political parties were intensified.

In short, titanic conflicts—of which these are just a sampling—took place in the very areas which were so shortchanged by TV.

During this same period of inhibition on the home front, TV had no difficulty in producing strong, visually dramatic documentaries on such matters as Cambodian neutralism, Italian communism, European colonialism, African nationalism and the decline of British imperialism, as well as a host of other high-powered political and ideological issues in foreign lands.

In sum: There is substantial reason to take the charge of "tacit taboos" in domestic affairs seriously.

What do the network news bosses have to say about this performance? They deny that their coverage of vital national issues has been inadequate—and point with pride to some of the shows that have been on the air. William McAndrew of NBC points with pride to David Brinkley's exposure of highway scandals and to the *NBC White Paper* on "The Battle of Newburgh." Richard Salant of CBS points with pride to shows on birth control, on the possible link between cigarets and cancer, and on water pollution. And James Hagerty of ABC points with pride to a show on airport safety. When the pointing with pride comes to an end—as it does with remarkable speed—all three men acknowledge that there is "room for improvement" but concede no shortages in critical areas.

When asked about the repetitious concentration on just a few issues and the apparent taboos on others, CBS's Salant simply denies both phenomena. "There is no repetitiousness and there are no subjects we won't cover," he says. ABC's Hagerty says, "Sure we're repetitious. We don't have crystal balls. We don't know what others will be doing." NBC's McAndrew also denies any evasion of controversial coverage. He attempts to account for the repetitiousness thus: "Depth coverage tends to follow critical news events. If a man goes up into space, a rash of shows on space will follow."

When the executives are informed that men on their own staffs report the existence of "tacit taboos" and say they are enforced by "self-censorship," the reaction is one of anger.

"Howard *Smith* talks of self-censorship!" exclaims Hagerty. "He has more freedom than *anyone*. He's a

Howard K. Smith: "The roof falls in if you criticize Congress. And we're getting increasingly cautious in criticizing the Administration." (ABC)

Chet Huntley: "After some controversial stories, you've got six weeks of absolute agony ahead of you..." (NBC)

commentator!" Then he calms down and concedes that he is familiar with the phenomenon. "I am aware that self-censorship exists," he says. "But I try to pay no attention to it. We've *got* to get the controversial stories on the air."

Richard Salant denies violently that "self-censorship" exists in *his* organization. Then he declares: "These men agree that nobody is censoring them. In that case, it's *their* problem. Anyone who knows what a *hero* Fred Friendly is in our network and can't see where *courage* gets you, is just plain stupid!"

William McAndrew counterattacks with sarcasm: "A lot of these men are very brave when they're being interviewed, but how many of them have the *guts* to do more of the stories they're talking about?" "Yeah," interjects Julian Goodman, McAndrew's second-in-command. "I suspect a lot of them are waiting around for other guys to do the brave stuff. It's the 'I'll hold your coat' attitude."

Unfortunately, the indignant tone of Messrs. Hagerty, Salant and McAndrew is belied by their choice of words. The artless admission that to break controversial stories requires "courage," "bravery," "guts" and "heroism" is more eloquent than all the official denials.

Eventually, as the subject is further discussed, this seems to become obvious to the network news bosses themselves.

Richard Salant acknowledges that, after all, he *is* aware of the phenomenon of taboos—but he prefers to locate it in TV's dark past. "Some years back, there *was* this fear and timidity," he says. "Television *didn't* touch the raw-nerve political and social issues. But now, we do shows on *integration!*" He even goes so far as to concede that "self-censorship" at CBS is not entirely unknown to him. "A couple of fellows *have* called up," he admits. "They've said, 'I'm thinking about doing something. Maybe we'd better not.'" And he shrugs a little contemptuously. "They read so much in the papers about television getting into trouble with the pressure groups that they think *they* will. But it's a myth. They *shouldn't* give in to it. The minute *anybody* gives in to it, it snowballs."

And William McAndrew also admits that television was a fearful medium "a few years ago." "We've done more controversy than in past years," he says. "We've made a lot of progress. Of course, there are problems. If viewers complain, you get requests from the FCC to answer and sometimes even submit scripts. But we're not afraid of trouble. We take it in our stride." And then he adds, candidly, "We don't say we're over the

hump. How courageous can you *be* on how many points?"

The unpalatable fact is that some kind of courage *does* seem to be required for national reporting—courage which is not required for foreign work. And despite their fluid denials, there is every reason to suppose that the news bosses are aware of, and even share, this attitude. As Howard K. Smith, who has worked for both CBS and ABC, puts it: "The networks are delighted if you go into a controversy in a country 14,000 miles away. They don't want real controversy, real dissent at home." And as New York Times TV critic Jack Gould puts it: "The networks are courageous abroad and cowards in Washington."

Why? What is the danger that threatens television on the home front? What is the industry afraid of?

Some staff men blame the trouble on pressure groups. "They're so organized," says Chet Huntley, "that they can create real havoc within a network. After some controversial stories, you've got six weeks of absolute agony ahead of you, with yelling and meetings and endless correspondence, and lawyers and suits, and shipping scripts back and forth to the FCC. It's real agony."

Howard Smith attributes the fear to a generalized "dread of dissent." He declares: "Timid people are at the top. Journalists are not in control of TV. It's run by *lawyers.*"

Some men prefer not to answer questions pertaining to network fear at all. Fred Friendly remarks warily, "I'm not the one to talk to about that," and changes the subject.

Others simply go off the record and explain the fear in terms of different pressures emanating from Washington. The three quoted here, coincidentally, are CBS men:

Says a newscaster: "The broadcasters are afraid because they're regulated. The FCC can refuse to renew a station's license any time it pleases. People don't know what their Constitutional rights are. The whole industry is boiling with political tension."

Says Producer Y: "The networks, basically, are keeping away from the power structure. They don't want to antagonize any *part* of it. Get six Congressmen sore, and they'll change the laws on option time, on network structure."

Says another producer: "The Justice Department cut one radio network in half, years ago. Now the talk is building up that the networks have too much control of programming. They're afraid the ax may fall at any moment."

William McAndrew, NBC News Chief: "How courageous can you be on how many points?" (UPI)

Political analyst Arthur Krock gives the same type of explanation—on the record. "The fear," he says, "is an inevitable result of the licensing situation. The broadcasters *must* be licensed if they are using government property. But it creates serious problems because the regulation is political. The FCC is a political entity, every commissioner owes his job to the President. So, everybody walks on eggs! The networks are afraid of being harassed if they are critical. They don't want to do *anything* that might unnecessarily irritate the men in power. I tell you quite frankly, if I were running a network, I'd be *just* as scared."

If one were to boil down all these different types of diagnoses of the TV industry's trouble into one phrase, it would be: *floating political anxiety*. It is an anxiety caused by a continuous awareness of *potential* political danger—a danger that might spring from any one of dozens of possible sources—a danger that might strike tomorrow, next week, next year, or never. It is so omnipresent an emotion that the men in TV have apparently grown used to it, and automatically act to inhibit direct coverage of national affairs.

TV, in other words, is a medium of communication which is Constitutionally and legally guaranteed freedom of speech but which does not dare to use it. It is that most anomalous of journalistic entities: a censored medium without a censor.

This is clearly not a temporary aberration which has descended on American television within the past three years. Self-censorship—with its highly publicized exceptions—has always been characteristic of the medium. And if the network news bosses are right and progress has been made, that progress has been slow.

True, there are more network public service shows on the air now than there were a few years ago and this season has been notable for provocative documentaries on the Supreme Court, on gerrymandering, on highway scandals, on the House Rules Committee and on other controversial domestic issues. But solid, independent reporting on vital national affairs is still the glaring exception rather than the rule. And most of the staff men interviewed tend to be either resigned or actively pessimistic.

Only one man, NBC's Gerald Green, describes himself as "optimistic." "The arbitrary taboos must disappear," he says. "They've *got* to. We're all so tired of working within these limits." But he offers no reasons for his hopefulness.

Doubtless, solutions to the problems do exist. But no one interviewed by this reporter at the networks has any idea of what should be done. Arthur Krock had a suggestion—a highly controversial one. "Congress," Krock said, "should get rid of the FCC and set up a publicly owned commercial corporation like the satellite corporation. This is the only thing I can think of that would get political fear out of network coverage."

Whether this is the solution or not is open to question. What is *not* open to question is that the anxiety afflicting this medium is severe—and that the problem should be publicly aired, once and for all, and solved.

(Carl Perutz)

THE DAVID
WHO WANTS TO BE GOLIATH
Susskind has worked hard to make himself a giant in television—while dodging the slings and arrows of outraged colleagues and critics

by Richard Gehman

Until recently, David Susskind was the least controversial personality in the television industry. Nearly everybody hated his guts.

There was a time when it was hard to turn on a set of an evening without confronting a Susskind-produced show.

He has been associated with many of the most important shows in the medium: *Philco Television Playhouse, Armstrong Circle Theater, Mr. Peepers, Kaiser Aluminum Hour, Du Pont Show of the Week, The Play of the Week, Festival of Performing Arts,* and any number of other series and specials. For the past five years he also has been the immoderator on *Open End,* which some call "Open Mouth."

This activity has not prevented Susskind from also posturing as a self-appointed industry conscience. It used to be even harder to pick up a newspaper TV section without reading a Susskind attack that made Newton Minow's Wasteland speech sound like the murmurings of a gentle old lady.

The industry's uncommon scold

Suddenly, this season, there seems to be a different David Susskind. He is not as acrobatically active as formerly. He is producing the new *East Side/West Side* on CBS; he will do seven segments of *Show of the Week* on NBC; he is bringing on as many specials as he can sell, including "Hedda Gabler," telecast two months ago by CBS; and he is keeping his mouth open—but only in public, on Channel 11 in New York and in a few other cities. Suddenly, in private, the industry's uncommon scold seems to have taken the advice of Allan Sherman in "My Son, the Folk Singer":

Little David Susskind, shut up!

Yet to many who have been wounded by his barbs and offended by what they consider to be his commercial barbarism, Susskind still is eminently hateful.

Whispers begin the minute he enters Sardi's East in New York at about 12:30 P.M. each day his business, or his rampaging appetite for more of it, takes him there. The entrance is never dramatic. Susskind is a sturdy figure in an expensively unobtrusive suit—a short man who nevertheless communicates a wiry and somehow lean and skinny energy. He moves from table to table like some short Nureyev, shaking a hand here, bending for a whispered word there, his clipped hair parted straight as an Amishman's furrow above his regular features, which most often shine with the upturned lips of a clown's smile.

To some who know him, Susskind is indeed a clown, symbolically and classically, for it may be that his antic performances in the names of culture and commerce are ways he chooses to forget deep hurts and grievances, or feelings of inadequacy he is determined to conceal.

Susskind is extremely sensitive to criticism. When he gets a bad review, he cannot eat anything substantial. The witnesses in Sardi's do not know this private side. They see him only as he operates, engineering his adroit magnetism and persuasion, selling always, and always selling Susskind as well as the product.

Such is the force of Susskind's salesmanship that many people overlook the fact that he is approximately the size of a Hollywood talent agent (which he once was, in fact), and that he is possessed of that small breed's special, unrelenting fury, which is frequently rooted in terror—fury enough to direct it at people who say his passport exaggerates when it sets his height at 5 feet 9.

"David *insists* he's 5 feet 9," says a lady who knows him. "He gets almost apoplectic when people say he's smaller."

Susskind's size, and his defensive attitude about it, are emphasized here because they are, excuse me, part of the measure of the man. They, plus certain nameless and perhaps unidentifiable insecurities developed in childhood, plus the pressures of a market-minded society—all these things churn in him continually and will not let him rest. "I can't take a vacation," he says.

It must be hard to be as driven as David Susskind is, but it is even harder on those who work and deal with him. He scents a property, swoops down on it, seizes it and shakes the last possible sales potential out of it—then abruptly loses interest and leaves it to be picked at by critics and carpers. Yet he somehow manages to do this in a way that leaves the buyers ready to buy more, and his own sellers ready to work for him again.

"He is an amazingly likable man in private and an amazingly hateable man in public, " says Pierre Berton, the Canadian television interviewer who has had Susskind as a guest on his show. "I find him stimulating."

So do all who know him—although practically nobody knows him well. "I find I tend to fatigue people," Susskind said recently to me. In their state of overstimulated fatigue, people regard him with envy, incredulity, and often with rage. *Most* often. And the roots of this widespread anti-Susskindism are nourished as he treads into three media of the entertainment world, for he is not only a producer, packager, salesman and performer in TV, he is in the theater and films as well.

In a highly specialized society, no sin is less forgivable than versatility. Just beneath that transgression is a zest to produce a good deal; the prolific man is regarded as a pariah by those less gifted.

That Susskind sometimes flops does not reassure those who function less freely. He does flop; his three plays and three of his films were not box-office bonanzas, he admits. "But they all had something to say," he says.

He has been so successful so many times, and in his critics' view has spread himself so thin, that his failures bring them a special joy.

Some are particularly critical of Susskind's fondness for long words. Others also have objected to his logorrhea and his occasional malapropisms. "He is a kind of Sam Goldwyn in reverse," says one. "Sam cuts up the language, David elongates it."

Susskind reads a good deal (he says; his enemies say, "When would he get time?" and "In 10 years with David I never saw him open a book"). "I have a deep need to know, and a desire to spread knowledge," Susskind says. In Harvard he thought for a time he might become a teacher. He was graduated *cum laude* in 1942, majoring in political science.

If he reads as much as he says he does, Susskind's detractors ask, how can he do some of the dreadful things he does—and on important shows, too? At least one *Open End*—the show discussing my book on Frank Sinatra, in which I was a regretful participant—may someday take its place among the five worst panel shows ever seen. And Susskind's interview with Khrushchev was regarded as a triumph of egotism.

By far the most serious charge in the industry itself is that Susskind has taken credit for creation when actually he only has sold somebody else's. This is hard to pinpoint. In any TV endeavor, as the producer Lewis Freedman has remarked, "Nine out of 10 of the guys concerned are claiming credit for originating it."

A question of credit

"If you don't listen to David carefully, you get the idea *he* created *Philco Playhouse*," one man says. "But on the other hand, it's tough to listen to David carefully because he talks so much." Susskind does sometimes sound as though *Philco Playhouse* shot like a spark off his own internal grindstone, and he did in fact sell it. Fred Coe, who actually created the show, says, "I suggested David as producer in my place because I wanted to take some time off." He does not feel that Susskind appropriated creative credit.

When Susskind talks about past *Play of the Week* achievements, he mentions "The Iceman Cometh." He has done some shows, but not *that* one. It is hard to tell who, exactly, among the people associated in the series really *did* do it, but usually the industry gives credit to Worthington Miner. Miner says he isn't aware Susskind claims it.

Some industrialists are not as modest as Miner. Some are angry over what they regard as seized credit. One such is Ted Cott, who is generally given credit by people close to the programs for thinking up both *The Play of the Week* and *Open End.* Susskind has said they both were *his* ideas. The idea of running a two-hour play seven nights a week on one station certainly was revolutionary, and so was the idea of a discussion show with no time limit. Both originated on Cott's station WNTA. Susskind was called in to produce one and be leader of the other, Cott says.

"On the other hand, Cott always fought David's desire to do courageous things, " says yet another producer.

Cott today says flatly, but not altogether maliciously, "David has creative kleptomania." He refers to Susskind with a kind of weary tolerance.

Susskind was born December 19, 1920. Articles have said he was born in Brookline—outside Boston; to me he said it was Brooklyn—outside Manhattan. "So—you could say I'm one of those rare birds, a native New Yorker," he said.

An energetic little boy and youth, Susskind was indoctrinated with a desire for self-improvement by his father, who used to take him to public forums on Sunday afternoons. "I heard the great speakers of the day," he says. And went out and tried to imitate them: In school he was president of practically everything, played football despite his smallness, and wrote for the newspaper. And his endurance increased after he left school and the Navy and went to work first at Warner Brothers and later at Universal as a press agent.

"He was impatient in those jobs," says an acquaintance. A talent agent named Al Levy helped him move out of the press business into that of pressing to sell. They formed a firm called Talent Associates. Susskind added a "Ltd." to it because he felt it lent tone.

After a year, MCA, the biggest talent agency in the business, made him an offer he could not refuse. He handled such stars as Dinah Shore and Jerry Lewis. The latter remembers him with grimacing distaste. "He hustled too hard," he says. But Lewis' antipathy was nothing as compared with Susskind's toward MCA. He returned gratefully to partnership with Levy. By 1959, mainly due to his efforts, they had shows on the networks with a combined budget of around $15,000,000.

He hustles harder than ever

Al Levy is now dead. Susskind is hustling harder than ever. His hustling does not give him much time for personal life. Married for 24 years to the former Phyllis Briskin, he is the father of two daughters, 20 and 17, and a son, nine. The marriage is over. He and his wife are separated and probably will be divorced.

There is reason to believe the failure of this partnership troubles him. All failures do—which may be one reason he tries so hard to identify personally with projects in which his has been only one of the willing hands, usually the selling one.

Susskind watches a good deal of television and many films and plays, but watching makes him nervous. "If it's bad, I hate it; if it's good, I can't stand it because it isn't mine," he says.

This is not the remark of a man bent on making a fortune. His father was well off; Susskind never has known poverty. Today he could write a check for $250,000, for he owns 5000-odd shares of Paramount stock, which he acquired by trading a half-interest in Talent Associates. But his casual attitude toward money is evinced by his having spent around $480,000 of his own, not his company's, producing two segments of a series about former President Harry Truman. He could not sell it to a sponsor, and finally turned it over to Screen Gems. Susskind seems curiously pleased with the $180,000-odd loss he took on the sale. "That's putting your money where your mouth is," he says.

Of late, Susskind has not been putting his *mouth* where his *money* is—or at least not as much as he formerly did. Some say this is because he has sold fewer shows in recent seasons and realizes that he has alienated many people. Others believe his new attitude—he is now saying that television is growing up, and approaching new levels of taste and maturity—is directly attributable to his close friendship with James C. Aubrey, president of CBS-TV. Aubrey says, "I did what I could to keep this fellow on the track, because I feel he has one hell of a contribution to make to our industry."

The restlessness, the overpowering drive nevertheless have not waned. "If you never did another thing, you could rest on the Olivier version of 'The Power and the Glory,' " I told him.

"I can't rest on anything," Susskind said quickly.

What does he really want?

And so the question of what he really wants arises. Those who know him well offer different answers.

Ted Cott says: "A blank check to produce everything he wants to."

Robert Alan Aurthur, the writer-producer, says: "No. Power."

Alexander Cohen, the Broadway producer, says: "No. Political power."

Susskind smiles when political aspirations are mentioned, but he does not dismiss them. He will say only about himself that imps of ambition prod him into sleeplessness. He never gets more than five or six hours of rest per night, and that fitful. "I keep dreaming these short dreams, each of them little wild ones, and waking up."

It may be that these little stories are Susskind's ways

of keeping himself from facing his central in-boned problem. He is bright but not creative, says an associate; and he detests himself for selling and not originating. Another says, "He is—or can be—such a warm, human, charming, considerate, *dear* fellow . . . but he hardly ever takes time to allow himself to be."

Thomas B. Morgan once wrote that in Susskind's frenetic existence, "the self is lost." It is more possible that there never has been a chance for a real self to develop. The activity has been spread too thin; the desire to

achieve has been too gluttonous. Sometimes he may consider going into psychoanalysis. He does not admit this, but his questions about it to people who have been in do indicate a deep, perhaps a troubling interest.

"I hope he never does," says his friend Alexander Cohen. "It could break down his machine . . . and they never could put that together again. Some are thinkers, some are doers. If Susskind stopped to think about how he gets things done, he might not get anything done." There seems to be no danger of that.

NOVEMBER 22–25, 1963

AMERICA'S LONG VIGIL

by Dwight Whitney

Television's remarkable performance in communicating news of President John F. Kennedy's assassination and the events that followed was a source of sober satisfaction to all Americans.

It acted swiftly. It acted surely. It acted intelligently and in impeccable taste.

On that unforgettable weekend in November, 1963, television provided a personal experience which all could share, a vast religious service which all could attend, a unifying bond which all could feel.

I take this opportunity to add my voice to those who already have recognized television's historic contribution.

LYNDON B. JOHNSON
PRESIDENT OF THE UNITED STATES

From the moment the first TV news bulletin cut through the sticky story line of a soap opera called *As the World Turns,* at exactly 1:40 (EST) on Friday afternoon, the world of communications—if not the world—was to be a vastly different sort of place, never to be quite the same again. It was not just the sudden, senseless cutting down of a young, vigorous President that made the experience cut so deep, but the fact that no one had ever lived a national tragedy in quite these terms before. When Lincoln was assassinated by a frenzied actor at Ford's Theater in 1865, Americans had time to assimilate the tragedy. Most people in the big cities knew within 24 hours, but there were some in outlying areas for whom it took days.

In the new world of communications there was no

time for any such babying of the emotions, no time to collect oneself, no time for anything except to sit transfixed before the set and try to bring into reality this monstrous, unthinkable thing. Because the word was not only instantaneous but visual, and because at no time did the television reporters know any more than the viewers did, 180,000,000 were forced to live the experience not just hour to hour, or minute to minute, but quite literally from second to second, even as the reporters themselves did. According to Nielsen statistics, a point was reached during the funeral on Monday afternoon when 41,553,000 sets were in use, believed to be an all-time high. For four days the American people were virtual prisoners of an electronic box.

Thus what happened on the television screen became

The photographs in the original TV Guide *article were taken from the television screen. Because of their unavailability, substitute photographs have been used in all but one instance.—Ed.*

in every sense an epic drama four days long, in which the viewers were not so much spectators as participants. The insistent commercial, the thin, strident melodrama and the pleasantly foolish prattle of the quiz game had suddenly been stilled, as a blizzard stills the clamor of a big city. No pat endings here. In their place came the endless images of human frailty, dignity and grace, until it seemed the spirit could absorb no more: Mrs. Kennedy, vibrant testimony to the heights to which the human spirit can rise. The new President, constantly reminding us by his actions that there was still someone in charge—"Now then, let's get this airplane back to Washington." The endless thousands filing by the casket of the late President in the rotunda. Robert Kennedy, a man so shattered he seemed almost to be walking in his sleep. The solid phalanx of visiting heads of state advancing on the church and looking for all the world like factory workers at closing time. The tum-tum-tum-ta-tum of the muffled drums crossing Arlington Memorial Bridge. John-John's heart-stopping salute to his father on the steps of St. Matthew's. Blackjack, the riderless horse, ancient symbol of the fallen hero, all skittish and full of spirit. The white-gloved hands during the flag-folding at Arlington National Cemetery. The bugler who played the sour note during taps—"The bugler's lip quivered for the nation," Edward P. Morgan observed later.

The nasal voice of Richard Cardinal Cushing, whose burial service seemed at times more like a cry of anguish. Counterpointed against all this, the jarring impact of the alleged assassin's own murder, so quick, so unexpected, so nightmarish in its implications and so immediate because an already-staggered nation saw it as it happened on TV. "It was as if the sacrifice of a President were not enough," Charles Collingwood said.

Most unforgettable of all were the faces of the crowd, especially the teen-age Negro girl, she of the beautiful face, in Rockefeller Center, minutes after the President's death was announced. Chet Huntley said that she spoke for all the world when, asked how she felt, she replied, "I really couldn't say. . . . Really right now I don't know what to do . . . I don't even know where to go . . . or what to say. There is nothing for me to say."

The intense personal involvement of the ordinary man, so evident throughout the four days of broadcast, was heightened by still another circumstance: John Fitzgerald Kennedy was, more than any other public figure in history, a product of television. Young, personable, fast on his feet, he seemed born to the medium.

First reactions: "I don't even know where to go . . . or what to say. There is nothing for me to say." (Wide World)

His wife seemed in every way the perfect visual complement to such a man. A young woman faced with older responsibilities, she bore them with a dignity and grace surpassed only by her near-superhuman behavior after her husband's death. Together, they were the perfect embodiment of the American success story, and it was TV that had heralded the fact.

No wonder then that, exposed to the tragedy's every agonizing detail through television, 180,000,000 people reacted as they did.

A permanent record of what we watched on television from Nov. 22 to 25, 1963

Walter Cronkite, the anchor man of the CBS team, was the first on the air with the bulletin. At 1:30 (EST), when the soap opera *As the World Turns* went on live, Cronkite was preparing his regular evening news show, and in every sense the day was an ordinary one, at least judging by the trials and tribulations of the characters in the soap opera. In retrospect, the hero's sudsy dilemma as to whether or not he should remarry his divorced wife, and his mother's subsequent conversation with his grandfather about it, seems about as eerily remote as another galaxy. Actress Helen Wagner was just saying, "I gave it a great deal of thought, Grandpa," when the program was interrupted.

Cronkite's voice came through, dolorous but contained, as a bulletin slide was displayed on the screen.

"Bulletin . . . In Dallas, Texas, three shots were fired at President Kennedy's motorcade. The first reports say the President was seriously wounded, that he slumped over in Mrs. Kennedy's lap, she cried out, 'Oh, no!' and the motorcade went on . . . The wounds perhaps could be fatal . . ."

Viewers tuned to ABC and NBC at the moment heard similar bulletins. At that point CBS switched back to the soap opera. The actors, unaware, continued their performance, but the show was cut off at the second commercial. ABC and NBC blacked out a variety of local and regional shows. Bulletin:

(Wide World)

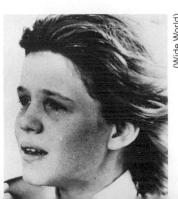

(Wide World)

A joyful moment before tragedy struck. The Kennedys are welcomed warmly at the Dallas airport (UPI)

The Kennedys riding in motorcade approximately one minute before the shots (Wide World)

"Further details . . . The President was shot as he drove from the Dallas airport to downtown, where he was scheduled to speak at a political luncheon in the Dallas Trade Mart . . . Three shots were heard . . . a Secret Service man was heard to shout, 'He's dead!' . . . The President and Mrs. Kennedy were riding with Governor [John] Connally of Texas and his wife . . ."

It was shortly after this that the video portions of the broadcasts came on (almost simultaneously on all networks), and the last entertainment or commercial that anyone would see for three and a half days had run its course. Thus there began what Cronkite was later to describe as "the running battle between my emotions and my news sense." Yet, of all the newsmen who covered the first tense hours (Ed Silverman and Ron Cochran of ABC; Bill Ryan, Chet Huntley and Frank McGee of NBC; Charles Collingwood and Walter Cronkite of CBS), it was Cronkite who agonized the most and controlled it best. For a man obviously deeply affected by the tragedy, he was able to exercise precise control without seeming to cancel out what he was feeling. Huntley, while almost as well controlled, met the situation with righteous indignation. At one point Friday he talked bitterly of "pockets of hatred in our country and places where the disease is encouraged. You have heard," he said, "those who say, 'Those Kennedys ought to be shot!' . . . It seems evident that hatred moved the person who fired these shots . . ."

That sort of talk did not come easily from Cronkite, let alone from Cochran, a more formal kind of man who prides himself on a rigid professional detachment from emotion. Yet it was Cochran who several times on Friday afternoon visibly shook. All three men seemed to be trying desperately to stave off the inevitable news that the President was dead, and all three advanced as gingerly through the reports as a buck private through a minefield.

Still the reports kept coming. Governor Connally, shot in the chest, is "serious but not critical." The President is now in the emergency room. Mrs. Kennedy is unhurt. The Vice President is unhurt. Representative Albert Thomas (D., Texas) reports, "The President is still alive but in very critical condition." Blood transfusions are being given. In Washington David Brinkley calls the White House to see if they have any late information. "No," replies a sniffling member of the White House staff. "We were watching you to see if you had any."

An abrupt switch to the Dallas Trade Mart, where the camera hammers the tragedy home by lingering on the lectern where the President was to speak, by panning over the milling guests and the uneaten luncheon—and a waiter drying an eye with a napkin. Two priests are reported entering Parkland Hospital. A small boy saw the fatal shooting by a man in the window of the Texas School Book Depository building near the underpass where the shooting took place. The stock market slumps, the stock exchanges close. Connally is quoted as saying, "Take care of Nellie."

It is now 2:32 (EST). The two priests say the President is dead. UPI reports at 2:35 (EST) that the President has died. Cochran, lowering his voice, says that government sources now confirm that the President is dead. Over at NBC, Bob MacNeil is relaying the news from Dallas: The White House says the President is dead. At CBS, at 2:38 the awful news is finally announced without qualification:

"From Dallas . . . a flash . . . The President died at two o'clock Eastern Standard Time . . . The President is dead . . ."

On a New York street NBC focuses its cameras on a chicly dressed, middle-aged woman wearing dark glasses and a tailored hat at the moment the news comes over an auto's loudspeaker. The woman starts, lets out a cry and falls back into the crowd.

At that moment there began something which could only happen in the age of TV. As a nation we were able to live out our grief in concert and at the same time begin the arduous business of picking up the pieces. Moreover, we were able to prepare ourselves for the new order of things. At the end of the four days we were to know the new President intimately—who he was, where he came from and, most important of all, how he behaved in a time of extreme stress.

As Cronkite was later to comment: "We saw before our very eyes a smooth transition of government. No confusion. Only a man in command moving ahead to the problems at hand."

And Cochran was to add: "Television had actually become the window of the world so many had hoped it might be one day."

Through that window now came many things: ABC's brilliant tapes (obtained through its Dallas affiliate) of the President's arrival at the airport that morning, for example. This footage, among the most heart-stopping to be seen during the whole coverage, showed the smiling President, alive and vibrant, moving through a sea of outstretched hands which wanted only to touch him. ABC was to follow this later with an interview with James C. Hagerty, in which the onetime Eisenhower

Presidential press secretary, now a broadcasting executive, illuminated the nature of the security problem.

"This is the President's way of saying thank you to the people," Hagerty declared, referring to the scenes at the airport. "How can you stop it? I don't think you want to stop it. . . . It's rather difficult, while guarding the President, to argue that you can't shake hands with the American people or ride in an open car where the people can see you."

By late afternoon the great and small were trying to find the right words. And TV was recording every halting one. Harry S Truman was reported so distraught that he was unable immediately to make a statement. The following day the cameras caught up with a saddened ex-President at the Truman Library at Independence, Missouri. Mr. Truman, his voice low, paid a forthright tribute. Kennedy was "an able President, one the people loved and trusted," he said. At the end a reporter asked him how he felt the new President would do. The former Chief Executive perked up. "Perfectly capable of carrying out the job," he snapped. "Don't you worry about him." If the nation had been in a cheering mood, it would have cheered.

President Kennedy's predecessor, Dwight D. Eisenhower, came on at about 5 o'clock Friday. He felt, he said, not only shock and dismay, but indignation. His voice verged on anger when he spoke of "the occasional psychopathic thing," then he assured us that we are a nation "of great common sense." We are not going to be "stampeded or bewildered."

Lyndon B. Johnson is sworn in as President in the cabin of Air Force One, the presidential plane (Wide World)

Shortly after 3 P.M. (EST) the President's casket was moved aboard the Presidential airplane. Mrs. Kennedy, still wearing the bloodstained pink suit in which she had started out the day, never left her husband's side except to attend the swearing-in of the new President.

The swearing-in, conducted by U.S. District Judge Sarah T. Hughes, took place in the airplane itself with no television coverage. The still pictures were broadcast, and showed a stunned Mrs. Kennedy, hard by the side of the new President.

All afternoon the air was alive with film from Dallas, terrifying in the confusion it showed—milling crowds in the police station, parade-route spectators flattened on the grass at the moment of the shooting, motorcycle policemen with slightly dazed looks on their faces, footage of the Texas School Book Depository from which the shots were alleged to have come, and visual reconstruction of the killer's supposed route. Then there was the young construction worker, who stood 20 feet away from the President when the shot was fired, who described the scene in almost too-vivid detail: "We heard a shot and the President jumped up in his seat. I thought it scared him because I thought it was a firecracker."

"Stunned disbelief" became the byword, and if Huntley used it once he must have used it a score of times. In late afternoon the networks announced the cancellation of all regular programming until after the funeral. General Douglas MacArthur told the nation that "The President's death kills something in me." And Adlai Stevenson, speaking from the UN, said, "And all men everywhere who love peace and justice and freedom will bow their heads." Later he observed, "It's too bad that, in my old age, they couldn't have spent their violence on me and spared this young man for our nation's work."

On the streets total strangers consoled each other. At the White House aides wept openly in the corridors. In Dallas, Governor Connally was pronounced out of immediate danger. And in New York Charles Collingwood came in to relieve harassed Walter Cronkite in the CBS anchor position. "Where's your coat, Walter?" asked Collingwood. For the first time Cronkite realized he had been too busy to put it on.

As the nation groped for meanings, the Presidential airplane put down in Washington's Andrews Air Force

The President is hit by the assassin's bullets (Wide World)

Shots ring out, people crouch in fear (UPI)

Mrs. Kennedy, still wearing blood-stained pink suit, arrives in Washington with the body (Wide World)

Robert Kennedy escorts his brother's widow. (UPI)

Base shortly after 6 (EST). The television eye hungrily devoured every detail as the hydraulic lift lowered the casket and the honor guard placed it in the waiting ambulance. It was followed closely by Mrs. Kennedy, never far from her husband and still wearing the pink suit. The step from lift to runway was long and somehow symbolic. An aide made the actual assist down to the level of the ambulance, but it was clearly made in the name of every American. In a way hard to define, it was one of the most moving moments of the four days—the small determined figure, devastated but not undone. And America marveled.

As the ambulance with Mrs. Kennedy and the casket sped away, the new President, Mrs. Johnson at his side, walked purposefully out of the airplane to face a barrage of cameras. "This is a sad time for all people," said Lyndon Baines Johnson in the first public pronouncement of his Administration. "We have suffered a loss that cannot be weighed. . . . I will do my best. That is all I can do. I ask for your help—and God's."

In Dallas there was emerging in grisly counterpoint the portrait of the man who was ultimately to be charged with the President's murder. In midafternoon the networks reported that "a Dallas policeman had been shot while apprehending the suspected assassin." The arrest of one Lee Harvey Oswald, 24, had taken place in the Texas Theater, some six blocks from the spot where he had allegedly gunned down Officer J. D. Tippit. Television cameras had a field day photographing the marquee. "Battle Cry" and "War Is Hell," it said. But it took until much later to confirm that the police had found the murder weapon, an Italian-make rifle with a telescopic sight, beside the sixth-floor corner window of the Texas School Book Depository—along with a sackful of chicken bones. And that the onetime defector to Russia and militant espouser of pro-Castro causes had already undergone hours of intensive questioning.

At 7:30 (EST) viewers got their first good look at the man. He was preceded into the bedlam of the Dallas police station by an officer holding the rifle aloft over

Lee Harvey Oswald, the accused assassin, was puffy-eyed, morose, uncommunicative (Wide World)

the heads of the milling throng of reporters. Oswald entered, an animal-like figure looking puffy-eyed and morose, flanked by beefy, stone-jawed police, and wearing the T-shirt about which he was later to complain because no one had offered him a clean one.

Viewers got only a fleeting glimpse as, handcuffed, he was whisked away to a fifth-floor cell. Later the cameras offered vignettes of Oswald's Russian wife, a pathetic figure with her two young children, and his mother, who could only murmur, "But he's really a good boy."

Later that night the Dallas police formally charged Lee Harvey Oswald with the murder of John F. Kennedy.

As the image faded, most Americans felt a sinking feeling in the pits of their stomachs. The inescapable truth, as it came through so clearly on television, was that Oswald was beneath contempt, unworthy of the emotions we all felt toward him—anger and outrage.

Saturday, November 23

Saturday was a day to shore up the human spirit, a time to prepare for the massive emotion of the lying-in-state at the Capitol on Sunday and the funeral on Monday. In Hyannis Port, Massachusetts, Mrs. Rose Kennedy was with son Ted, the Massachusetts Senator, and daughter Eunice, wife of Sargent Shriver. She went to the 7 A.M. Mass, stayed through another at 7:30, then returned home, where Ted broke the news of the President's death to the ailing Joseph Kennedy, the late President's father.

Very early in the morning (4:30 A.M.) the President's body had been moved into the White House and placed in the East Room on a catafalque similar to the one on which Lincoln had rested. At 10:30 the Washington Kennedy family members attended a private Mass in the East Room. Later, dignitaries arrived to view the casket. Former President Eisenhower came first, followed later in the day by Chief Justice and Mrs. Warren, former President Truman, Governor and Mrs. Rockefeller and the new President. In between times a steady stream of government officials, Senators, Congressmen, the military and friends of the family filed past the bier.

The camera caught them all, heads bowed as they mounted the steps of the White House.

At one point during the morning the new President crossed the street to the White House to confer with Secretary of State Rusk, whose plane had turned around in mid-Pacific (he had been on his way to Tokyo for an economic conference) to return to Washington. As Rusk came out, Secretary of Defense McNamara

Former President Eisenhower arrives at the White House to pay his respects (Wide World)

went in. The nation took silent comfort in this reassuring visual evidence that the government was still functioning.

Saturday was the day, too, when the reaction began to pour in. By relay satellite we saw and heard Pope Paul from Rome, who was "profoundly saddened," he said in hard-to-follow English, "by so disturbing a crime" and prayed that "the death of this great statesman may not damage the cause of the American people, but rather reinforce it." England's Prime Minister, Sir Alec Douglas-Home declared that the President had left "an indelible mark on the entire world."

The camera offered us a glimpse of just how indelible by taking us to see the crowds outside the American Embassy in London, where the faces again told the story. Premier Khrushchev was later to appear personally at the embassy in Moscow to pay his respects. General de Gaulle let it be known that he intended to attend the funeral, as did 19 other chiefs of state and heads of government and three reigning monarchs before the weekend was done. We saw faces of Frenchmen, Italians, Germans, crying. In London, the regular cast of *That Was the Week That Was*, the outrageously irreverent British TV satire on the week's events, tossed out their regular script and in just 16 hours prepared as moving a tribute as was seen during the entire four days, rendered even more moving in that it came spontaneously from the hearts of Englishmen whose stake in an American President was presumably not as great as ours. The tape, flown over by jet, ran on NBC Sunday night and was repeated on Monday. One of the young men said, "There wasn't anything anyone could do about it." Another talked of "the All-American human-

ity of the man." And still another said that "Behind the rocking chair . . . and Caroline's pony . . . behind the trappings of the image, [the President] was the first Western politician to make politics a respectable profession for 30 years." And another: "Death has become immediate to people all over the world." Housewives wept.

Former Vice President Richard Nixon, speaking from his New York City home, said, "President Kennedy yesterday wrote the finest and greatest chapter in his 'Profiles in Courage.' The greatest tribute we can pay is to reduce the hatred which drives men to do such deeds."

Senator Barry Goldwater in a news conference at Muncie, Indiana, paid an extravagant and typically American compliment to his late political opponent. From the South came the voices of those staunch segregationists, Governors George Wallace of Alabama and Ross Barnett of Mississippi, who found in the man in death qualities which they apparently could not find in life.

There were other forms of reaction, too. The networks were deluged with mail. Particularly poetry.

Later Cronkite was to comment: "This was real mail. Not fan mail. People were desperate to express themselves about this thing. And poetry seemed a natural form. They seemed intent either on finding a way to accept the guilt we were all feeling or laying it on someone or something else, or simply eulogizing the man."

Edward P. Morgan and Chet Huntley reported similar reactions. Morgan says in retrospect: "It is probable that when all this is over we will find it created a more personal response than any other event in history."

There were negative responses, too. There was the word from Peking that there would be no expressions of regret forthcoming from Red China. There was the man on the street who could only advocate an eye for an eye. "I hope these radicals have got their pound of flesh," he said bitterly. And there was the anonymous phone caller from Little Rock who, when put through to Huntley, requested that harassed gentleman to "Drop dead!"

As the day waned, President Johnson in his first proclamation as President, designated Monday as a na-

The President's body was placed in the White House East Room

(Wide World)

Chief Justice and Mrs. Warren arrive at the White House to offer condolences (UPI)

Former President Harry Truman: "If Mr. Johnson needs any advice, he'll ask . . ." (Wide World)

tional day of mourning. Skitch Henderson, Alfredo Antonini and others were heard in special memorial concerts. The Rutgers University Choir sang a Brahms Requiem with the Philadelphia Orchestra. CBS did a one-hour report on the new President.

For Lee Oswald, the day had begun early. At 11:36 (EST) the networks switched to the Dallas police station as Police Chief Jesse Curry, a chunky, balding man with glasses, explained through the hubbub that he not only had the rifle which did the killing, but the order letter to the mail-order house where it was purchased. The handwriting, Curry said, matched Oswald's.

At that point Oswald was exhibited. The newsmen and the cameras closed in like hunters on the fox. Oswald looked a little weasel-like. He said, "I have been told nothing. . . . I do request someone to come forward to give me legal assistance." To questions of why he did it, he did not respond. As the police led him out, a reporter slipped up close to him, and said, "Oswald, what did you do to your eye?"

"A policeman hit me," whined Oswald for 180,000,000 to hear.

Throughout the day Oswald adamantly insisted he was innocent. As the evidence mounted, the police and District Attorney Henry Wade became surer that they had the case wrapped up, and drew criticism when they said so on TV. At one point on Saturday, Wade told the TV audience: "We have sufficient evidence to convict him."

To which Huntley replied privately: "I'm a TV man, but I hope I'm also a responsible citizen. TV is not a courtroom." And yet the nation's involvement was such that not admitting to opinions would have been like not admitting that your house was on fire.

That, then, was the mood as Saturday drew to a close. The stage was set, but the actors were weary. The nation slept fretfully. If it had known what was in store for the following day it might not have slept at all.

Sunday, November 24

Sunday started quietly with Cardinal Cushing's eulogy, from Boston, to the late President. The President's widow was reported holding up well. She, with other family members, was scheduled to follow the caisson

bearing the flag-draped coffin down Pennsylvania Avenue to the Capitol rotunda, where the body of the President was to lie in state. Before that could happen, however, the nation was to be subjected to yet another shock, one which in some ways was the most jarring of all.

NBC was just concluding a two-minute report from Hyannis Port, when Frank McGee in New York heard Tom Pettit, set up at the Dallas police station, shout, "Give me air! Give me air!" NBC quickly switched to Dallas, just in time for the following, as officially recorded in the NBC log:

> 12:20 P.M. Dallas City Jail—NBC cameras are trained on Lee H. Oswald, the man accused of shooting Pres. Kennedy, he is flanked by detectives, as he stepped onto a garage ramp in the basement of the jail for transfer to an armoured truck—Suddenly out of the lower right corner of the TV screen came the back of a man. We hear a shot & Oswald gasps as he starts to fall grabbing his side. NBC's newsman Tom Pettit on air says "He's been shot! Lee Oswald has been shot! There is absolute panic—pandemonium has broken out."

The shooting of the alleged killer of the President on camera was an event whose deep psychological significance was matched only by its horror. The wielder of the gun, a minor nightclub operator named Jack Ruby, deprived the country of something it needed badly, the chance to formally try Oswald according to law and the oldest traditions of this country. It also served as a reminder that, as CBS's Charles Collingwood put it, "violence had not yet subdued its appetite."

ABC's Edward P. Morgan and Howard K. Smith were to be blunter. "Vengeance is a bludgeon," said Morgan.

"We will never hear this man's story," lamented Smith. "There is something wrong and we do not know what it is."

If NBC's live footage was a kick in the stomach, then CBS's later repeat in slow motion is a kind of grotesque ballet. We see the small figure of Oswald flanked by two detectives. A figure moves out of the group of newsmen, a dark blob in a crouch. He darts forward and toward Oswald. We see the gun. A shot is heard. Os-

Left, a harried Dallas police chief, Jesse Curry, talks to reporters at news conference (Wide World). **Right, The police hold aloft the Italian-made rifle used in the crime** (Wide World)

Caught by TV cameras: Ruby shoots Oswald (Wide World)

Moments after the shooting (Wide World)

Confused and shocked, police seize Ruby (Wide World)

wald cries out and grabs his midsection. There is a split-second for the reflexes to take hold, then a great crush of bodies converges on Ruby. The screen is filled with milling, scuffling bodies, threshing arms and legs.

Perhaps a minute later a stretcher is brought. The camera eye is periodically blocked by arms, bodies, ambulance doors, other newsmen, moving across it. The stretcher is lifted into the ambulance. But the ambulance is blocked by the armored car in which Oswald was to have been removed to the county jail.

Tom Pettit moves about the melee like a sleepwalker, shoving his hand mike into the face of anyone he can get near. The dialog is strangely flat and disassociated, as talk in moments of crisis is likely to be:

PETTIT (to Officer P. T. Dean): How would it have been possible for him to slip in?

OFFICER DEAN: Sir, I can't answer that question.

PETTIT (to Captain Will Fritz): Do you have the man who fired the shot?

CAPTAIN FRITZ: We have a man, yes.

The police, sleepwalking themselves, give out nothing.

The Fates had indeed arranged things strangely. During all this time the procession had been forming at the White House portico to take the body of the President to the Capitol rotunda and the networks had to scramble to get back in time to record the beginning of the solemn, tradition-steeped ritual with which a grieving nation assuages its grief. "Ceremony," remarked Collingwood, "is man's built-in reaction to tragedy."

And it was never more so than on this sunny Sunday afternoon.

The images begin to flood the screen in overwhelming profusion: The caisson so strangely imbalanced with its seven white horses and their four riders; the limousines, long black fish, glutting the curving driveway; the foliage making a tracery as cameras pan up to the flag at half-mast; the chiefs of staff standing nervously on the steps; the three priests who would precede the caisson emerging from the crape-draped White House door, abreast and solemn; a still photographer darting in front of the camera to get a better angle.

The casket emerging, borne by eight enlisted men representing five branches of the service, stiffly inching their way down the steps to the caisson; moments later Mrs. Kennedy, majestic, erect, wan and beautiful, her face a haunting mask of sadness, pausing at the top of the steps where the camera provides one of the memorable pictures—still or moving—of the four days. The children, Caroline and John, seen for the first time, make darting, childlike movements and cling to their mother. The awkward shuffling and whispered words as President Johnson, Robert Kennedy, the family, the myriad Kennedy children, find the right limousines.

At 1:05 (EST) the caisson begins to roll out of the driveway. We hear the hollow clack-clack of horses' hooves, then the muffled drums. Parade-route spectators, some motionless, others moving restlessly across the back of the picture, still others holding children aloft, crane for a better look at Blackjack, the riderless horse, sword strapped to the saddle, boots reversed in the stirrups in the ancient tradition of Tamerlane and Genghis Khan.

Then the camera picks up the long, long shot down toward the Capitol as the cortege turns down Pennsylvania Avenue. Then as quickly the long, long shot the other way, the cortege in the distance with the Washington monument in the background. It is an awesome sight. Edward P. Morgan intones, "History saturates these pavements . . ." And 180,000,000 agree with him.

At the Capitol, the march orders are audible as the military units turn into the plaza. The caisson stops. The high-spirited Blackjack grows skittish, and the tall private who has been leading him has to restrain the animal. The pallbearers remove the coffin as the band plays "Hail to the Chief," in dirge time. A flag bearer precedes the coffin up the steps, dolefully, one step at a time.

Inside the great rotunda the casket rests on the Lincoln catafalque. Mrs. Kennedy, looking straight ahead, takes her place. Caroline's head bobs as a curious child's head will. An aide takes John-John's hand and leads him from the crowded rotunda as the honor guard is posted.

Presently Senate Majority Leader Mike Mansfield begins to speak. In the great rotunda the voices sound hollow, and over all there is an eerie obbligato of nervous coughing which the microphones amplify. The television audience strains to catch what Mansfield is saying:

"He gave us of a good heart from which the laughter

As millions mourn, caisson bearing the coffin moves down Pennsylvania Avenue toward the Capitol (Wide World)

Left, Jacqueline Kennedy and her children on way to Capitol rotunda (Wide World). **Right, mother and daughter kneel to kiss the flag on the coffin** (Wide World)

came . . . of a profound wit from which a great leadership emerged. He gave us of a kindness and a strength fused into a human courage to seek peace without fear."

Caroline's hands fidget and her mother reaches down and stills them as Chief Justice Earl Warren is intoning: "A believer in the dignity and equality of all human beings, a fighter for justice and apostle of peace, has been snatched from our midst by the bullet of an assassin. . . . The whole world is poorer because of his loss."

The camera plays over Robert Kennedy's immobile face. He looks drained, wrung out, hardly hearing House Speaker John McCormack: "Thank God that we were privileged, however briefly, to have had this great man for our President. For he has now taken his place among the great figures of world history."

As the Speaker's voice fades, the new President, face implacable but strong, inches forward toward the catafalque, following a soldier who positions a wreath for him. Mrs. Kennedy stirs and, taking Caroline's hand, comes quickly forward and kneels at the coffin. She kisses the flag, and Caroline follows suit, her little hand fingering the striped silk before they move back to the periphery of the mourners.

Only the coughing and shuffling can be heard as the family goes quickly out. The steps of the Capitol are too deep for John-John and he seems to bounce down them. The President gives Mrs. Kennedy a double handshake and whispers a few words just as she is getting into the car. The line of long, black limousines moves off.

Back inside the rotunda, with its great cavernous dome, the file past the bier is beginning, ABC's cameras have just been playing over the rotunda's statue of Lincoln with Edward P. Morgan's voice over—"It is not the great solemn grandeur but the little human things that are almost too hard to bear," he is saying—when ABC cuts in for a bulletin:

"FLASH . . . LEE HARVEY OSWALD IS DEAD."

In the rotunda a very young couple with a baby, looking very lost, wander aimlessley by the camera. It moves Morgan to comment to his running mate, Howard K. Smith, "You keep thinking, Howard, that this is a dream from which you will awake—but you won't."

Throughout the afternoon and evening the great line outside the rotunda swells. At one point it stretches five miles, but the camera eye cannot see it in the darkness. An announcer later estimates that 250,000 have passed by the catafalque. All evening the pool cameras record their faces—an elderly couple dabbing at their eyes with handkerchiefs, solemn college girls in scarfs, a knot of Marines, a group of nuns, a father with two young sons, a Negro woman, hands folded across her midsection, with a great tear rolling down her cheek. Some wait 10 hours. Some have small children sleeping on their shoulders. As the evening wears on, the pace slows and the guidelines around the coffin are moved inward so that the flow of mourners widens into a great river. Still they come.

It is Morgan who captures the feeling best. It is "the mood of mutinous, somber sadness," he says.

Earlier this morning the cameras have caught a fleeting glimpse of Mrs. Rose Kennedy coming out of church in Hyannis Port. Now at 4:30 (EST) they watch again as the President's mother, her daughter Eunice Shriver, and son Edward leave Hyannis Port for Washington.

Television is at the airport with Secretary of State Rusk about an hour later to greet General de Gaulle. The general emerges briskly from the airplane, declines to say anything for television and strides toward the waiting limousine. Again at 9:30 the special New York Philharmonic concert conducted by Leonard Bernstein is interrupted as cameras go to Dulles airport where Prince Philip and Sir Alec Douglas-Home are arriving from London.

NBC stays on the air. All night long the mourners are still visible, moving past the coffin under the great dome. They are still coming at 9:00 that morning.

Monday, November 25

"This was the day we were restored to sanity," Charles Collingwood said.

The scene at the White House portico at 10:15 A.M. was much the same as the previous day, except that the rhythm had somehow slowed. Six limousines lined the driveway to drive the Kennedy family to the rotunda. Mrs. Kennedy was first out, followed by Pat Lawford, Bobby, Teddy, Eunice Shriver and assorted Kennedy in-laws and children. Notably absent were Caroline and John. Their mother had decided to meet them at St. Matthew's Cathedral after the trip to the rotunda. (Later, at the church, John-John was taken out for most of the Low Pontifical Mass. Neither Caroline nor John went to the cemetery.)

It took just 13 minutes for the procession to make the trip to the Capitol plaza. The widow and the two brothers again took the long walk up the Capitol steps and quickly approached the coffin, knelt, and backed away. As quickly, they turned and walked out of the rotunda.

It took just seven minutes to get the cortege under way—the caisson with the flag-draped casket, the ever-present riderless horse, the three clergymen, the honor guard, the six limousines and the carful of Secret Service men—but, since it was now a full military funeral procession, it was 45 minutes before the cortege again approached the portico, bringing John Fitzgerald Kennedy to the White House for the last time.

At 11:43, the family, the 19 chiefs of state and heads of government, the three reigning monarchs, the dignitaries, President Johnson, Chief Justice Warren, start the long walk behind the caisson from the White House to St. Matthew's. Advancing like a great phalanx, they seem to march right into the television lens. De Gaulle dominates the front line of march. But Queen Frederika of Greece (the only other woman visible besides Mrs. Kennedy) is there, too. And so are Emperor Haile Selassie of Ethiopia, Crown Prince Akihito of Japan, King Baudouin of Belgium, Prime Minister Lester Pearson of Canada, Chancellor Erhard of West Germany, Prime Minister Inonu of Turkey, First Deputy Anastas Mikoyan of the USSR, President Eamon De Valera of Ireland, Prince Philip and Prime Minister Alec Douglas-Home of Britain.

John-John's salute (Wide World)

It is an impressive group of mourners. The emotion tells on the voice of David Brinkley. The camera picks up the shadows thrown by the caisson. The wind takes the edge of the flag as the pallbearers, who seem to be carrying the weight of the world, mount the steps with the coffin. Once inside the church the foreign dignitaries follow De Gaulle to their seats to the right of the family. Again the camera catches the ineffable sadness on the face of Bobby Kennedy, close to his sister-in-law.

The Low Pontifical Mass begins. The flat, nasal voice of Cardinal Cushing is heard praying "for John Fitzgerald Kennedy and also for the redemption of all men." The Mass is said to include all those who are present. So on this day it might be said to include 180,000,000.

"For those who are faithful to You, O Lord, life is not taken away; it is transformed." The Cardinal blesses the casket with holy water. Turning to leave the church, he leans down and kisses Caroline Kennedy on the cheek.

Outside the church John-John stands hard by his mother as the coffin is brought out. In his hand is clasped the pamphlet which he was given while sitting out the main body of the Mass. As the pallbearers place the casket back on the caisson and the procession prepares to leave, John-John fidgets at his mother's side. She leans over—a "majestic" figure, the London papers will say—she whispers something to him, she takes his pamphlet, then he salutes his father. The camera holds on it a full 30 seconds—the small figure and his courageous mother—the camera does a slight shimmy—as if the cameraman, too, were shaking.

Preparing to walk to the funeral services. Among the dignitaries: President Charles de Gaulle of France, Queen Frederika of Greece, King Baudouin of Belgium, Emperor Haile Selassie of Ethiopia (Wide World)

The horse-drawn caisson bears the body across the Potomac to Arlington National Cemetery (Wide World)

As the caisson starts to roll, the heads of state and visiting foreign dignitaries are forced to stand about, waiting for their cars like ordinary men. Ex-Presidents Eisenhower and Truman walk to a car together.

The muffled drums begin. And the hoof-clacks. The family cars fall in behind the caisson and the riderless horse. President Johnson's car is accompanied by the Secret Service men.

A young black-hatted priest peers out of the crowd lining the streets, a woman with hands clasped over her bosom, a handsome soldier in dark glasses, a college boy with a transistor radio at his ear, an older woman with an oversize handbag, a family of five sitting on a curbstone with their lunch.

Ten minutes later the dignitaries are still waiting for their cars and David Brinkley opines that the head of the procession will arrive at the cemetery before the last of it leaves the cathedral.

It is not hard to believe. For it is a procession miles long. As the cortege starts across Arlington Memorial Bridge, the camera captures majestic long shots from Arlington National Cemetery showing the Lincoln Memorial in the background. Over all, the muffled drums.

As the cortege enters the cemetery, the Irish Guard stands at parade rest next to the grave, and the coffin slowly advances to the wail of the bagpipes. As the coffin reaches graveside a flight of 50 jet planes (one for each state) zooms overhead. In keeping with tradition, one plane of the formation is missing. Last to fly over is "Air Force One," the President's personal jet, dipping its wings in tribute to a dead President. The pool camera, panning across the sky, catches it all.

Soon the gently rolling hillside is a sea of somber figures. Cardinal Cushing begins to intone the prayer:

"O God, through Whose mercy souls of the faithful find rest, be pleased to bless this grave and Thy holy angels to keep it . . . the body we bury herein, that of our beloved Jack Kennedy, the 35th President of the United States, that his soul may rejoice in Thee with all the saints, through Christ our Lord. Amen."

The pool camera takes a serene long shot, sweeping over the line of military graves to the Custis-Lee mansion on the hill behind; then, during the 21-gun salute, cuts to Mrs. Kennedy. She seems to start with every shot. Cardinal Cushing asks the Holy Father to grant John Fitzgerald Kennedy eternal rest, and the bugler, lip quivering for humanity, plays taps.

Now the flag folding begins. The camera moves in for close-ups of the white-gloved hands of the honor guard, anxious, eager hands, making triangular folds of the flag that covered the dead President's coffin. There is a poignancy about the image which again recalls the part hands have played in the four days—Mrs. Kennedy's hand in Robert's at the rotunda and at the funeral; the hand of the small boy in a farewell salute to his father; Caroline's hand fingering the flag at the rotunda; the hands of the unseen detective holding aloft the murder weapon in Dallas; the hand of Ruby shooting Oswald.

Now the folded flag passes from hand to hand. The camera follows lovingly. John C. Metzler, superinten-

Jacqueline Kennedy is handed the American flag used to cover the coffin (Wide World)

dent of Arlington National Cemetery, takes the flag, turns and gives it into the hand of the young widow. Finally the hand of Cardinal Cushing sprinkling holy water on the coffin as with voice rising, he says, ". . . the wonderful man we bury here today."

Mrs. Kennedy lights the eternal flame and the funeral is over.

Jackie and Bobby turn and leave the grave together. Jackie's foot catches and she stumbles momentarily.

That evening was a time for recalling little things: Chet Huntley's story about John-John at the rotunda, how at one point an aide took the restless child to the office of Speaker McCormack and gave him a small American flag to play with. And how John-John asked if he could have another one—"for my daddy." How the new President looked, saddened but confident— and confidence-inspiring. How NBC's Bill Ryan could not read the official word of the President's death and had to turn it over to Frank McGee. The sad eyes of Walter Cronkite, the poetic irony of Edward P. Morgan, and the righteous anger of Chet Huntley, and his summation of the Man and the Tragedy: "I didn't always agree with JFK, but I liked his style."

It was also a time of beginning. The nation marveled when the word came through that Mrs. Kennedy would, after 3:30 P.M., receive the visiting dignitaries and heads of state. And, from the news reports, one took away the comforting sense that the new government not only was beginning—it had begun.

For television it was a beginning, too. For if nothing else had happened during the four days, the medium had gained a new sense of what it could do, if pressed. Moreover, it had shown that it did indeed deserve to be called, as Ron Cochran had put it, the window of the world. And that the window was capable of encompassing not just life's trivia, but the deepest of human experience.

As the long vigil ends, the TV cameras pan to the White House flag at halfmast (UPI)

TELEVISION AND THE FEMININE MYSTIQUE

by Betty Friedan
*Psychologist and author of the current best-seller
"The Feminine Mystique"*

PART I

If the image of women on television today reflects—or affects—reality, then American women must be writhing in agonies of self-contempt and unappeasable sexual hunger. For television's image of the American woman, 1964, is a stupid, unattractive, insecure little household drudge who spends her martyred, mindless, boring days dreaming of love—and plotting nasty revenge against her husband. If that image affects men—or reflects, at least, the men who created it—then American men, in their contempt, loathing and fear of that miserable obsessed woman, must be turning in revulsion against love itself.

This is the rather horrifying feeling I had after sitting for several weeks in front of my television set, trying to reconcile the image of woman projected by television commercials and family situation comedies, by soap operas and game shows, with the strangely missing, virtually nonexistent image of woman in all the rest of television: the major dramatic shows, the witty commentary, serious documentary or ordinary reportage of the issues and news of our world.

In fact, the most puzzling thing about the image of woman on television today is an eerie *Twilight Zone* sense that it is fading before one's eyes. In the bulk of television programs today, and even, increasingly, in commercials, one literally sees no image of woman at all. She isn't there. Even when the face and body of a woman are there, one feels a strange vagueness and emptiness, an absence of human identity, a missing sexual aliveness—is it a woman if it doesn't think or act, or talk, or move or love like a person?

Behind that fading image, the nonwoman on the television screen, I found, talking to producers, network decision makers, agency executives, an even more unpleasant image: their image of those millions of American women "out there" watching that television screen, controlling that dial, determining those ratings—the American housewife who, they say, "has taken over television" as she is supposed to have taken over control of her husband, children, home, the U.S. economy and the nation generally. Put the two images together—the woman on the screen and the one watching it—and you

see how television has trapped itself in the feminine mystique.

The feminine mystique is the name I have given to a way of looking at women that has become epidemic in America during the last 15 years. Based on old prejudices disguised in new pseudoscientific dogmas, it defines woman solely in sexual terms, as man's wife, mother, love object, dishwasher and general server of physical needs, and never in human terms, as a person herself. It glorifies woman's only purpose as the fulfillment of her "femininity"—through sexual passivity, loving service of husband and children, and dependence on man for all decisions in the world outside the home: "man's world."

In my book, "The Feminine Mystique," I showed how this sophisticated mishmash of obsolete prejudices (woman's place is in the home; woman is inferior, childlike, animal-like, incapable of thought or action or contribution to society) has been built up, since World War II, by psychologists, sociologists, educators, marriage counselors, magazines, advertising, and by a combination of historical coincidences (depression and war, the bomb, the population explosion, the stepped-up speed of change in the world) and misunderstood needs and frustrations of men and women themselves. The result of the feminine mystique, I maintain, is to stunt the growth of women, robbing them of identity and making them virtually displaced persons in our fantastically growing society. Forcing women to live vicariously through love, husband, children, I submit, is not only making women sick for lack of a self but making love and marriage, husbands and children and our whole society sick.

This whole process is projected on television to such an extreme that the question is not only what the feminine mystique and its stunted, dehumanized, sick image of woman is doing to real women, and their respect for themselves, or men's love and respect for women—but what it is doing to television.

Consider first that drab, repulsive little housewife one sees on the television screen. She is so stupid that she is barely capable of doing the most menial household tasks. Her biggest problem is to get the kitchen sink or floor really clean, and she can't even do that without a kind, wise man to tell her how. ("To think that just a few months ago I was in college and now I'm a wife and mother," she weeps on the television commercial. "I want to be everything Jim wants in a wife and mother. But he says I'm inefficient, I can't cook and clean. I've tried and tried and I just can't get that sink clean.") Her biggest *thrill* is when, with that old man's magic help (which comes in a can), she gets that sink *clean.*

Her other biggest problem is how to keep doing all that cleaning and still keep her hands *"feminine."* She is so unattractive and feels so insecure that she needs all the help and mechanical contrivances modern science and industry can supply to keep her man from leaving her. ("How long has it been since your husband took you dancing . . . brought you flowers . . . really listened to what you said? Could it be that gray in your hair?" Bad breath? Irregular bowels?)

Drawing by Dick Meller

"Television's image of the American woman, 1964, is a stupid, unattractive, insecure little household drudge who spends her martyred, mindless, boring days dreaming of love—and plotting nasty revenge against her husband."

She isn't even adequate as a mother to her children. ("Even the most careful mother can't completely protect her family from household germs," the kind, wise man reassures her. "Is there really more than one vitamin?" she asks him, having never finished fifth grade herself.) In fact, she is barely capable of feeding the dog. (That wise old man has to tell her how to get the mutt out of his "mealtime rut.")

Less than a fifth grader, more like that simple animal in her capacity to understand or take part in modern human society, this television-commercial woman has no interest, purpose or goal beyond cleaning her sink, feeding her kids, and going to bed.

The whole world beyond her home—its politics, art, science, issues, ideas and problems—is evidently beyond her comprehension. For not only is there no television image of a woman acting in the world, but the programming of daytime television and, increasingly, even prime time, assumes she has no interest in it, or ability to understand it. She lives only for love.

But beneath the sacred exaltation of marriage, motherhood and home in the soap operas and the religious tones of the commercials, there is a crude assumption on the part of television decision makers that all those women out there are panting through their boring days of mindless drudgery in a state of permanent unappeased sexual hunger. From a little after 8 in the morning until the late, late hours after midnight, they evidently want from that television screen only the image of a virile male. At least this is the superficial reason given for that disappearing, virtually nonexistent image of woman on the television screen, and the preponderance of male cheesecake ("beefcake" is it called?). "It's women who control the dial, and what a woman wants to look at is a man—a man with sex appeal, a man who's available to her," I was told, over and over again, up through the ranks of television decision makers.

Several years ago, when the networks were under at-

tack from the Federal Communications Commission, CBS put on a daytime news program. The producer, new to daytime, suggested a woman commentator. The network brass said he was out of his mind. In simple four-letter words they explained to him that of all things the dames didn't want to see at 10 A.M., it was a woman. They wanted a man they could jump right back into bed with. But CBS did put a news-oriented show, *Calendar,* into that 10 A.M. time period, and hired actress Mary Fickett to act as Jill-of-all-trades. She did the household commercials, acted as pretty little straight man to commentator Harry Reasoner, and now and then made some forays into the more serious business of the program on her own. The condescension with which he talked down to the women out there may have marred his sexual charm. *Calendar* died.

On the MGM lot, producer Irving Elman explained to me why his show *The Eleventh Hour,* and *Dr. Kildare* and *Mr. Novak* at the same studio, and several other major series, are built around two men—a young bachelor and a middle-aged widower. The bachelors such as Dr. Kildare and Ben Casey are available for a fantasy affair with the younger housewives; the widowers like Dr. Starke in *The Eleventh Hour* are available for the older housewives. In *The Defenders* the older lawyer, Lawrence Preston, is the object of affection for the over-40 crowd; his son, Kenneth Preston, can be embraced by the young mothers. "There is more sex appeal if he is a widower," Elman explained. "It makes him more available. If he were married, his wife would be in the way. And if he were divorced, the women wouldn't like it. It would be too threatening. Marriage is sacred."

The double standard involved here almost seems unfair to men. Madelyn Martin, longtime writer of the *Lucy* shows, explained: "You can't package a dramatic show around a woman, because women want only to look at a man, and they don't want their husbands to look at other women." The housewives "out there" are evidently so insecure that they can't face fantasy competition from a woman on the screen not only for their own husbands, but for their fantasy extramarital amours either. "We have to be very careful to keep Kildare from getting seriously involved with a woman," MGM executive producer Norman Felton said. "Women love stories where there's the suggestion of romantic involvement, but they resent it if he even kisses the girl on the screen. That kiss jars the viewer's fantasy that she is the one with whom he's having the love affair." This, of course, is one of the great advantages of the hospital to television; the romance never has to be consummated because the woman patient neatly dies. "One of the high spots was Kildare's romance with that girl who died of leukemia," Felton reminisced.

If housewives control the dial, why, with no women at all, are Westerns perennially so popular? "Beefcake" of course. *Bonanza,* for instance, really gives the panting women a choice of sizes and ages—four unmarried men: Daddy and his three sons. According to reports, the producer has been toying with the idea of letting one of the four get married but, evidently out of consideration for all those women "out there," hasn't had the nerve to let it happen yet.

If the image makers are right in theorizing that a woman "never wants to look at a woman, only men," is sex really the reason? "Love" is hardly the emotion the television woman seems to feel for that man she clutches so possessively. In the soap operas it is more like a martyred suffering, a noble endurance. ("Get married, stay home, suffer," a high school boy summed up woman's fate, after he had spent a week at home, sick in bed, watching daytime television.) On *I Love Lucy, The Danny Thomas Show,* and other family comedies, that television housewife, far from "loving" or even "liking" her husband, seems positively obsessed with the need to wipe him under the doormat, get revenge against him, control him, manipulate him, show him up for the despicable, miserable worm he really is, and establish once and for all who's really the boss of the house. As if, over and over, she must show herself to be somebody by forcing him to his knees—getting him to admit her unquestioned superiority as the boss of the family.

That warfare is, of course, limited to the family and the house, since the woman is always, and only, a housewife. But sometimes, lately, the woman who gets revenge against the husband isn't actually his wife, but a paid servant or housekeeper like Hazel. (Less competition to those women "out there," since the paid housekeeper doesn't actually go to bed with the husband? Yet, in the essential motif of the family comedy—revenge against the male—Hazel, the housemaid, is indistinguishable from the television wife.)

Since the women in these comedies aren't ever allowed to overreach that definitive level of dullness and unattractiveness (otherwise would they offer too much competition for the supposedly dull, unattractive housewives out there?), the husbands must also be shown as stupid, unattractive boobs for even a semblance of believable suspense or conflict. It is perhaps a tribute to real male vanity, or real male contempt of the female, that television critics often complain of this silly-boob image of the husband, never noticing that the wife in these situation comedies is an even more silly boob. Evidently, in order to retain her "femininity" that wife always has to lose the battle in the end—or rather, demonstrate her true superiority by magnanimously letting the poor fool think he won it. (As on *The Danny Thomas Show* when, after he has subverted her complicated plot to make him give her a mink coat for Christmas, she shames him—by bringing him his rubbers and raincoat in the rain and catching near-pneumonia—into tape-recording abjectly that he loves her, in front of the whole Tuesday afternoon bridge club.)

In the daytime soap operas, the martyred superiority of the wives doesn't even have to be demonstrated; it's just mysteriously, axiomatically *there.* Since the housewives in *As the World Turns* and all the rest must conduct their warfare with men day after day, during the day, the major dramatic problem seems to be to get the men home to be manipulated. It is amazing how often those busy lawyers and doctors and businessmen on television

soap operas come home for lunch! But the neatest trick—which simultaneously accomplishes revenge and keeps the man home permanently to be controlled, or perhaps just to provide the soap-opera housewife with someone to talk at—is to paralyze the husband and put him in a wheelchair.

However it is accomplished, the real emotion played to by this image of woman who supposedly lives for love is hate. As a former network vice president in charge of program development put it: "They [those housewives out there] don't want to look at husbands who are nice or strong. They only want to look at attractive younger men or old codgers out of the battle between the sexes. In the average dame's life the husband is the enemy, the guy you have to manipulate, push around, be happy in spite of. When the daytime serial features a strong husband, and the wife is not the controlling one, the rating is invariably low. The husband becomes acceptable only if he is manipulated by the good, kind, loving, all-wise wife."

But why is there no image of women on television engaged in anything else but that so-called war between the sexes? After all, it is only in the family comedies that men appear as such stupid boobs. The bulk of television features men engaged with more or less valor in action in the world—curing the sick, coping with social problems in *East Side/West Side,* Mr. Novak teaching in the classroom, cowboys in Westerns, supermen zooming into outer space, detectives, and variously engaged individuals in dramas and specials that are concerned with something beyond intramarital warfare, to say nothing of news and documentaries about real issues of the world beyond one woman's house.

Could the very absence of any image of women active or triumphant in the world explain the dream of revenge and domination over the male, the sexual insecurity and self-contempt and even that supposedly unappeasable sexual hunger which television plays to, in its nasty image of the American housewife?

PART II

THE MONSTERS IN THE KITCHEN

They are, says this best-selling author, the millions of mindless, passive housewives who lead empty lives—and TV has created them

Actresses complain, and producers and directors confirm, that there are fewer parts for women on television today. Network brass may say that this is because those sex-obsessed housewives who control the dial only want to look at men. But I submit that television, in its literal embrace of the feminine mystique, has narrowed the

image of women to an emptiness that simply cannot be dramatized in terms of human action.

According to television's image, the only action or dramatic adventure possible for an American woman today is to get sick, preferably with an incurable disease. Virtually the only exceptions are *The Nurses* and the commercial in which a woman plumber fixes the kitchen sink. "Actresses beat down the doors to become our psychiatric patients," says Irving Elman, producer of *The Eleventh Hour*. "They say they're the only parts that give them anything to do. On the other shows, the women just stand in the door, kissing the men good-by."

It's not strange that the unwritten law which permits only the drab "average housewife" image of women on television is causing this fade-out of any image of women at all. For the daily tedium of a life whose biggest challenge is to clean the sink is simply too devoid of human action, involvement with other human beings, or human triumph to provide the basis for drama—or even the basis for a sense of human identity. That's why real housewives who live within that empty image have so little sense of themselves that they need a man to make them feel alive—even a man who talks down to them on television—and why they also are choking with resentment against men, whose lives at least provide enough action to dramatize. Beneath the clichés of the feminine mystique, television plays consciously to this tedium, and to the resentment it engenders—narcotizing woman's very capacity to act and think into a passive, sullen, vengeful impotence.

After all, if it weren't for the real tedium of the so-called average housewife's day, would she ever willingly endure the tedium of daytime television, or the sneering contempt for women explicit in the game shows?

The Price Is Right, Truth or Consequences, Concentration, Queen For a Day seem to assume an average I.Q. of 50 (submoron) in American women; surely, if my psychology doesn't fail me, *most* women are not feebleminded, though years of bombardment by television in that isolated house could make them so. Why else would middle-aged women dress up in children's dresses and hair bows to lumber through an obscene reincarnation of themselves as high school cheerleaders? The suave man at the mike can hardly veil his own contempt at those fat grown-up women making such a public spectacle of themselves ("a siss and a siss and a siss boom bah!").

What does such a denigrating image of real women do to young mothers watching, who are no longer sure who they are, or girls who don't even know who they

can be? What does it do to women, or girls—or the boys and men whose love they want—to see no image at all of a self-respecting woman who thinks, or does, or aims, or dreams large dreams, or is capable of taking even small actions to shape her own life, or her future, or her society?

One hesitates to accuse television of a conspiracy to keep women confined within the limits of that demeaning housewife image, their minds anesthetized by the tedium and lack of challenge of those empty hours, their very confidence in their own abilities to act or think for themselves destroyed so that they meekly buy whatever the kind, wise, authoritative man tells them to. Undoubtedly there are such mindless, passive housewife robots among American women, but why is television doing its best to create more in their image?

Why is there no image at all on television of the millions and millions of self-respecting American women who are not only capable of cleaning the sink, without help, but of *acting* to solve more complex problems of their own lives and their society? That moronic housewife image denies the 24,000,000 women who work today outside the home, in every industry and skilled profession, most of them wives who take care of homes and children too. That image also insults the millions of real American housewives with more and more education who shape U.S. culture, politics, art and education, by their actions in PTA, League of Women Voters and local political parties, and who help to build libraries, art galleries and theaters, from Detroit to Seattle, and even strike for peace.

Why, for instance, isn't one of the leads in a program like *Mr. Novak* a woman teacher? I asked MGM executive producer Norman Felton. He explained: "If you have a woman lead in a television series, she has to be either married or unmarried. If she's unmarried, what's wrong with her? After all, it's housewives we're appealing to, and marriage is their whole life. If she's married, what's her husband doing in the background? He must not be very effective. He should be making the decisions. For drama, there has to be action, conflict. If the action is led by a woman, she has to be in conflict—with men or women or something. She has to make decisions; she has to triumph over opposition. For a woman to make decisions, to triumph over anything, would be unpleasant, dominant, masculine. After all, most women are housewives, at home with children; most women are dominated by men, and they would react against a woman who succeeded at anything."

But that housewife in the family situation comedies is only too unpleasant, dominant and masculine. She is always triumphing, not over forces in the outside world, but in that endless warfare against her own husband or children. "In comedy it's all right," Felton said. "You're not supposed to take her seriously; you laugh at her." Could there be a serious drama about a woman in the home, a housewife? "We couldn't make it dramatic—and honest," he said. "Most of a housewife's life is too humdrum. If you showed it honestly, it would be too dull to watch. Maybe you can get away with it in a hospital. After all, how many dramatic cases does a doctor or lawyer have in a year? But if you tried to do it with a housewife, no one would believe it. Everyone knows how dull the life of a housewife really is."

Thus, if television's only image of women is such a "dull" housewife, there is, in the end, no action or dramatic conflict she can engage in except that warfare with her own husband or children. Unless she gets sick and goes to the hospital, where she can die nobly of a brain tumor. "It makes sense that women are only figures of comedy," said Madelyn Martin, writer of *Lucy*. "When you think of traditional figures of comedy—the short guy, the ugly one, the man with the big nose, the Negro or Jew or member of any minority group—comedy is a way of turning their misfortune into a joke. It's a way of being accepted—'Look at me, I'm funny' and 'Don't anybody laugh at me, I'll laugh first.'"

If women are the one majority in America that resembles an oppressed minority, it's not because of actual deprivation of right, or opportunity, or human dignity, but simply because of that self-ridiculing image—the mystique of the mindless female, the passive housewife, which keeps girls and women from using their rights and opportunities and taking their own lives seriously, in time. In an examination scene in a *Mr. Novak* episode, a high school girl takes the blame for her boy friend's crib sheet to protect his future as a would-be physicist. "It's all right," she says, "let them blame it on me. I'm not going to college or anything. It won't matter to me." Why doesn't it matter to her, her own life and future? Why, in high school, does she already play the martyred, passive wife? No need to work or study in school herself, or plan her own future, the image says. All she has to do is get that boy to marry her—the sooner, the better—and he'll take care of her life.

Do anything you can to hook that man, all those images of women on television say, because you aren't or can't be a person yourself. But without studying, or working, or doing anything yourself, you can be a "housewife" at 18. And get all those expensive things for wedding presents, just like *Queen For a Day*—a lounge chair, a dishwasher, a whole set of china, baby furniture, even a free trip to the beauty parlor every week.

Is it a coincidence that millions of real girls who have grown up watching television—and seeing only that emptily "glamorous" housewife image of women—do not, in high school, have any goal for their own future except being such a passive housewife? Is it partly from lack of any self-respecting image of a woman as a person herself that so many stop their own growth in junior high to start that frantic race to "trap" a man, get pregnant in high school, or quit college to take a "housework" job in industry, to put their husbands through medical or engineering school. By seducing real girls into evading the choices, efforts, goals which would enable them to grow to maturity and full human identity in our society, television's image of women is *creating* millions of unnecessarily mindless, martyred housewives, for whom there may never be a thrill or challenge greater than that dirty kitchen sink.

Thus television's little housewife monster becomes a self-fulfilling prophecy. You can see it happening in the increasingly drab looks, whining voices, and general stupidity of the new young housewives in the commercials. Not very many years ago the average American woman could supposedly identify with a pretty, bright self-confident dame, eager to grow and educate herself and seize any challenge that came along. For instance, Betty Furness. That was *her* image—and it certainly sold refrigerators and stoves to millions of American women, who evidently shared her eager, life-loving self-confidence.

All of a sudden it was decided that Betty Furness's image was making "the average little housewife" uncomfortable. She looked too intelligent or independent or individual, or maybe just too eager and alive. Couldn't she dim herself down somehow, put on a housedress, give off a smell of dirty diapers and unwashed dishes and burned chops in the background to make that "average housewife" feel less inferior? Betty Furness looked "smart" as well as "feminine," and she was proud of it. She had the assured professional air of authority, which is necessary to sell anyone anything: "I try not to open my mouth unless I know what I'm talking about," she said. "I know who I am and I like it. I can't look dumb. I can't dim myself down to that so-called average housewife." [An agency spokesman said there was no attempt to temper the Furness "image."—ED.]

So she moved on, from commercials to daytime television. And then it was decided her image was too "intelligent" for daytime television; she went to radio, like Arlene Francis and the few other intelligent women on TV with whom evidently the new "average" housewives could not identify.

But these new teen-age housewives—the growth-stunted young mothers who quit school to marry and become mothers before they grow out of bobby socks themselves—are the female Frankenstein monsters television helped create. And they may writhe forever in that tedious limbo between the kitchen sink and the television game show, living out their century-long life ahead, in a complex world which requires human purposes, commitment and efforts they never ever glimpsed. How long can even television channel their pent-up energies into vicarious love affairs with Dr. Kildare, vicarious death by leukemia, even vicarious revenge against that husband who is surely not their real enemy?

How long will boys and men love women if this nasty, vengeful martyr is their only public image of woman, and becomes an increasingly vengeful private image? The female Frankenstein monsters, after all, are created by the minds of men. Does the new plethora of widowers, bachelor fathers, and unmarried mature men on television, who pay a maid or houseboy or, soon perhaps, a robot to get the household drudgery done, signify unconscious rebellion against that "housewife" altogether? Do they really want her for a wife? One suddenly realizes that there are no real love stories on the television screen—in the sense of the love stories that one can still see in the old movies, with Ingrid Bergman, Joan Crawford, Norma Shearer, Claudette Colbert and all the rest. No love stories, no heroines— only those housewife drudges, the comic ogres who man the war between the sexes.

Television badly needs some heroines. It needs more images of real women to help girls and women take themselves seriously and grow and love and be loved by men again. And television decision makers need to take real women more seriously—not for women's sake but for their own. Must women only be used as weather girls or "straight men" diaper-and-pot-holders for the male news commentators? Must they be shown only as paid or underpaid dishwashers for fear of making real housewives uncomfortable?

I've had letters from thousands of these real women and, for whatever reasons they tried to settle too soon for this narrow, humiliating "little housewife" image, a lot of them want a second chance to grow. Television could help them get it, not keep cutting them down. Is it a coincidence that daytime network television, which has banished real women with minds like Arlene Francis and Betty Furness to radio, is having less success with that "average housewife" than radio, which feeds their minds with intelligent talk, much of it from women—not only Betty and Arlene but also the Martha Deanes, Ruth Jacobs, and all the bright women on local radio and television.

Women in Seattle have no trouble identifying with a not-so-average housewife named Marty Camp, who runs an extremely successful weekly television show, *New in the Schoolhouse,* based on the idea that intelligent mothers of children want intelligent discussion of the real issues of education. Housewives in Cleveland have no trouble identifying with an intelligent woman named Dorothy Fuldheim, who never talks down to women or men in her commentary on the serious issues of the world. Nor did women all over America have any trouble identifying with the intelligent, resourceful, dignified and courageous image of Jacqueline Kennedy in our national tragedy. If American women are really that stupid and insecure, and if they really control that television dial, what do their husbands do with them while they laugh at the nonfamily satire of *That Was the Week That Was?*

The men who decide the image of women on television could take a tip from a blonde who interviewed me on a local TV show in Los Angeles last summer. She called me at my hotel the day before to ask me some questions, explaining she'd stayed up all night finishing my book. It was refreshing for someone to take the trouble to read my book before interviewing me, and it was a good interview. Over breakfast later she said she liked reading such "tough" books; she hadn't been to college herself. She also said she was taking a pay cut from $750 a week as a nightclub singer to accept this job as television commentator at $250 a week.

"It's the mental challenge of it," she said. "It makes me feel alive. I'm sick of just being a body. I want a chance to be someone myself—and give something of myself—in this world."

(Julian Wasser)

So Who Needs Wall Street?

Danny Thomas put his time and talent into television and has watched his investment grow and grow and grow

by Dwight Whitney

Danny Thomas, the Lebanese confectioner's son from Toledo, Ohio, sat enthroned amid the happy clutter of his office suite at Desilu-Cahuenga one recent day deliberating the past, present and future of Danny Thomas, television actor and business tycoon.

He hardly looked the part of the man worth the $20,000,000 some people say he has, much less the king maker he has undoubtedly become. He wore a nondescript yellow sports shirt, a suede jacket, and he looked as if he needed a shave. Around the office was strewn the tangible evidence of a long and profitable career— awards and plaques, letters from Presidents, a statue of St. Jude, a piano, a picture of himself as a slim Toledo basketball player, a Bible and a sign which proclaims, "I AM THIRD," a typical Thomasonian sentiment referring to the fact that "God and you come first."

All things considered, Thomas had every right to be elated. Instead he bore the unmistakable air of a man just dispossessed. Only a few weeks earlier he had made the final decision to do what he had been threatening to do for a long time: give up the weekly grind of his own *Danny Thomas Show* to enjoy the fruits of his success. "I don't want to be a tycoon," he declared.

Yet he was talking already about taking over the active management of his landlord's studio, Desilu, from its present proprietor Lucille Ball, an action roughly tantamount to a retiring postman taking up long-distance running. Why do it? "Well," says Carl Reiner, the producer of *The Dick Van Dyke Show,* one of the more lucrative Thomas projects, "maybe it's because Danny is an industry to himself. Maybe it titillates him to do so."

The only thing that can be said with assurance is that Danny Thomas is a bundle of paradoxes. He is a self-professed man of leisure who can't stand leisure. He is a would-be entertainer emeritus who can't stand not to entertain. He hates money but loves what it can do. He is the titular head of a production empire which includes *The Dick Van Dyke Show, The Andy Griffith Show, The Bill Dana Show, The Joey Bishop Show* and an "investment" in such things as *My Favorite Martian* and that hardy old evergreen now in rerun, *The Real McCoys.* Recently the daytime rerun rights to his own show and two others were sold to the networks for a grand total of $19,000,000. And yet Danny was able to sit across that desk, smiling benignly at an audience of one, and declare guilelessly, "Me a millionaire, ha! I couldn't write a check for $1200."

The man who thought he had reached his zenith in 1940 when he made $250 a week as a comedian at the old 5100 Club in Chicago took another chomp on his foot-long cigar and added, "Anybody who drives a Cadillac in this business must be crazy. He can't afford it."

This is a pleasant little fiction indulged in by rich men (Danny's bank credit is a cool $1,000,000) who either like to dramatize the fact that they keep their money working or enjoy playing the role of just-one-of-the-boys. With Danny it is both. For the first time in his life he could call himself a success without cross-examining himself first.

"I've done everything I wanted to in show business," he said with an expansive sweep of the hand. "I've done more than I hoped and prayed I could. I don't need to accomplish any more. And yet—I'm an entertainer, pal. I don't want to stop. I must perform as long as I am able."

He doesn't read books, he doesn't fish, he doesn't sculpt, he doesn't do anything except comede. Thus leisure becomes a frightening prospect. The areas in which he can perform are of necessity somewhat limited. To be sure, he will make five specials next season for NBC—three variety shows, one musical version of "Rip Van Winkle," and one straight dramatic show probably to be directed by Frank Capra. "Capra has a thought," he explained, "and I'm not about to quarrel with Capra."

He will appear, as the spirit moves, in Las Vegas or Lake Tahoe nightclubs, but beyond that he has all but priced himself out of the market. He will continue to be the most enthusiastic kibitzer on the lot, sticking his large proboscis into conferences and screening rooms, offering a joke here, a comment there, eating in the commissary with the common people, sending this script back for comedy injections but never really coming to grips with the pick-and-shovel work of producing. He leaves that to his partner Sheldon Leonard.

He can even afford to be philosophical about his failures—which somehow or other usually turn out to be successes. No show, for example, had a worse press over a longer period of time than Joey Bishop's. Its ratings were only fair, Danny recalled, "But I'm not one

who plays the numbers racket," he said. "I was once in 107th place myself."

He is buoyed because *The Bill Dana Show* is coming back next season. Danny said, "Rating-wise he started off where I ended up [with *Make Room For Daddy,* the first version of his own show] four years later. José Jimenez is a great character. Great for the Latin American audience."

He recalled his longtime efforts to groom someone to take over *The Danny Thomas Show.* First it was Pat Harrington, later Pat Carroll and Sid Melton. "Pat and Sid had 16 solo shots at it," Thomas sighed. "But *The Danny Thomas Show* didn't work without Danny Thomas."

Danny is enthusiastic, too, he says, about his new shows for next season. *The Walter Brennan Show,* originally titled *Tycoon,* in the Thomas view is a kind of paean of praise to the geriatric set, a show which Danny says "bawls hell out of the nation for throwing away a man at 65." *Gomer Pyle, USMC* is a hymn to the "child-like simplicity" which Thomas clearly regards as humankind's finest asset.

Yet enthusing and philosophizing are not enough to occupy such a man. Reiner has remarked, "No one thinks of Danny as a boss. He sits around and complains just like everybody else." Sheldon Leonard, his talented partner and chief doer, has added, "Danny is an actor and a comedian and a producer by proxy. But now that he has arrived, he can't see any reason why he shouldn't be a studio operator too."

The reference was to the proposed merger between Desilu and its star boarder, Thomas, whose recent successes have been as spectacular as the landlady's productions (with the exception of her own show) have been so-so. Was it true that the star boarder was going to marry the landlady?

"For a while there the *shadchen* [matchmaker] was working overtime," smiled Thomas. "But somehow negotiations bogged down."

Insiders explain that in the beginning, president Ball made the assumption that Sheldon Leonard would be included in on the deal. When she discovered this was not necessarily the case, her ardor temporarily cooled. "You might say the whole thing is in limbo," Thomas said.

Whatever happens there is always the peculiarly restless, volatile personality of Thomas to deal with. Generous, outgiving, he still loves to indulge a passion for high living. His farm in Cherry Valley near Palm Springs, California, is a 116-acre marvel designed by Paul Williams, furnished (as one visitor has described it) "with the sure conviction that not even the gold plumbing is good enough" and estimated to have cost upward of $500,000. Even the cattle—white-faced Herefords—are "in."

He used to play 10-handicap golf—still does—but hardly in the dedicated manner of a Hope or Crosby. His three children still live at home. Marlo, 26, is an up-and-coming actress; Teresa, 21, is a secretary; and Tony, 15, a sophomore at Loyola High School. Occasionally they will go bowling with their father at night. He never misses Mass on Sunday. Rosemarie, his wife, is domestically oriented, a woman who adjusts to Danny and whose heart and soul is the home—for a man like Thomas, good nourishment but not a total diet.

But Danny has always needed more. His strengths lie in his ability to be himself at all costs, and to project some of this honest intent onto the screen. When he first arrived in Hollywood in the mid-1940s, Louis B. Mayer urged him to have surgery performed on his nose, the same marvelous appendage that he customarily describes as capable of vacuuming lint off the carpet. "People expect to see pretty things, beautiful women, handsome men on the screen," Mayer told him. Thomas didn't agree. "But the world is composed of not-so-beautiful people," he told Mayer. "I would be ashamed to go home to my eight brothers."

He still believes this psychology is what made his show the nonstop success it is. "People rooted for me, the ugly man, to keep that beautiful wife," he said. Indeed, that is the basis for all Thomas projects. "We give reality," he added. "But middle-road, neither too glamorous nor too plain."

Meantime he holds fast to a vision of Utopia in which everyone can dream up beautiful stories about beautiful people. No one will work *too* hard, but just hard enough, and creators will participate, making money by the bushelful.

He says he is tired, and will slow down. No one really believes it, least of all Danny. He says he is "in a hurry not to be in a hurry, watching everybody hurrying to where I've just been."

Review

by Cleveland Amory

OZZIE AND HARRIET

The first dictionary definition of the word "wholesome" is "promoting or conducive to good health or well-being"; the second definition is "tending to improve the mind or morals." We don't know about the mind being improved by *The Adventures of Ozzie and Harriet,* but when it comes to morals, the show could have played old Salem in the days of Cotton Mather. The fact is, it is not only a wholesome show for the whole family, it *is* the whole family. To say there is nepotism here is like saying there is traffic in New York. Practically every member of the cast is a card-carrying nepot—as witness each week's cast of characters:

> "Ozzie" . . . . Ozzie Nelson
> "Harriet" . . . . Harriet Nelson
> "Dave" . . . . Dave Nelson
> "Rick" . . . . .Rick Nelson

And if Kris, wife of Rick, has her billing read "Kristin Nelson appeared as Kris," June, wife of Dave, is still an individual. "June Blair," her billing reads, "appeared as June Nelson." She's a wild one, all right, that June.

Such familiarity might breed, in a lesser critic, contempt. We, however, not only have no contempt for this show, we have a good deal of respect for it. Indeed, we are inclined to believe that these adventures, Miss-adventures and now Mrs.-adventures, which were on radio long before the days of television—and, for all we know, have been going on since before the days of the telephone—still hold the mirage up to nature about as likably as any show on the air; and if you don't like it, it is perhaps less a reflection on the show than it is on the mirage itself—i.e., The American Way of Life.

The wizardry of Ozzie, of course, deserves the lion's share of the credits for this; and, as co-star, producer, director and head writer, he gets them. (His brother Don, incidentally, is also a writer for the series.) Oz is not the world's most exciting actor, but he grows on you. He is a reliable anchor man, and once in a while he actually weighs anchor and lets himself go. We are thinking particularly of one scene where he went over to his neighbor Joe Randolph (Lyle Talbot) to explain why he had to go fishing instead of seeing Joe's home movies and, beforehand, acted out his entire explanation in pantomime outside Joe's front door. He was wonderful.

The rest of the cast grows on you, too—though in the case of Harriet (she once said she had chosen to remain 28 forever), slowly. Dave and Rick are no threat to future Hamlets, but Dave keeps the wholesomeness down to reality (he's at least not wholier than thou), and Rick is always a threat to break up the plot with a song. As for the wives, both June and Kris are, even when they are not right for some particular episode, so obviously right for their husbands that you can easily forgive them. Wally (Skip Young) seems to us less successful, but he has a tremendously difficult role. He's no nepot (he doesn't even go steady with a Nelson) and he is, after all, one of the few regulars on the show who can't just play himself.

(George E. Joseph)

HOW TO MAKE MILLIONS WITHOUT REALLY WORKING

That's the fate of Milton Berle—but he's
not happy about it

by Dwight Whitney

There is an old story about a mule so stubborn no one
could do anything with him. In desperation his owner
hired a mule trainer and the two of them went out to
the bean field to confront the animal. Suddenly the
trainer whipped out a baseball bat and started to beat
the mule on the head.

"Now just a minute!" yelled the mule owner. "I said
to train the mule, not knock his brains out."

"Don't sweat, son," replied the trainer. "First thing
you gotta do is get his *attention.*"

All of which describes Milton Berle's state of mind
today. The millionaire comedian has worn out numerous baseball bats trying to gain the attention of the network that is paying him millions not to work. The
harder he swings, the more frustrated he becomes.
While the network does not use the services of the former Mr. Television and scourge of Tuesday night, it
does not want any of its rivals to have him either. It
would rather keep ebullient Uncle Miltie warming the
bench at $100,000 a year than suddenly have him blast
a homer for somebody else.

This psychology—which, translated into a contract, is
the so-called "pay even if no play" clause—has become
amazingly widespread in recent years. It is a way of
locking up the superstars of television. At the time
(1951) that NBC signed the by-now-famous 30-year
contract with Berle—enough to keep him in Cadillacs
until he is 73—it signed 10- or 15-year contracts with
Sid Caesar, Imogene Coca, Jimmy Durante, Martha
Raye and Max Liebman, all now terminated. (Only
Dinah Shore's and Berle's are still in effect.) CBS, self-
styled "the stars' address," locked up Jack Benny for 15

years in 1949 (his contract ran out this year and he
promptly signed with NBC for next season), and subse-
quently signed long-termers with Lucille Ball, Phil Silvers, Jackie Gleason and Carol Burnett. Garry Moore,
recently deposed from his long-running *Garry Moore
Show,* can collect his $100,000 yearly until 1974. And
earlier this spring Ed Sullivan signed a new contract
which will ensure that old Smiley will be grinning at
somebody for at least the next 10 years, even if it is only
the cashier at the bank.

Crazy? Not at all, says CBS-TV vice president Mike
Dann; just good business. "There are just so many top
TV stars," he says. "So it's essential that you put them
under exclusive contract. You may lose out if one
doesn't work for a while, but the loss is negligible compared to one starring in a hit show for somebody else."

But to Berle, "all pay and no play" has amounted to a
lifetime sentence, leaving him a rich but unhappy man.

Unhappy? At $100,000 per for doing nothing? For
that kind of money who should be so unhappy?

To answer this you must know who Milton Berle is.
He is a complex, highly gifted, likable man who spent
the first 45 years of his life in thrall to his mother. Sandra Berlinger was obsessed with the idea of the youngest of her four sons becoming a star (the others failed to
measure up). When he was a mere infant she commanded him, "Milton, be funny"; at five he won a contest imitating Charlie Chaplin; at 10 he was making silent pictures (with Mary Pickford at the old Biograph
studios at Fort Lee, N.J.); at 12 he made his Broadway
debut (as a juvenile in a revival of "Floradora"); at 18
he tried comedy; and at 22 he played the Palace. His
mother never missed a performance and her piercing
laugh encouraged him in theaters all over America.

In his eagerness to please her, Milton became mimic,
straight actor, singer, dancer, clown, stand-up comedian, movie actor, magician, master of ceremonies,
writer, producer, songwriter and prestidigitator (he is
still a fine card manipulator, a skill he picked up in vaudeville).

He was not so much a man as a cyclone. He dominated TV's formative years. Tuesday was "Berlesday."
He insisted on supervising everything about the *Texaco
Star Theatre* and its successors from costumes to
choreography, thereby contributing to his and its
downfall. He embraced jokes as if they were life itself
and stored 2,000,000 of them in a vault against the time
when he might run out.

King of muggers

When the king of muggers became the prince of
wails, he turned ever more to his Christian Science
practitioner (who had seen him through the dreadful
days after Sandra's death in 1954) to help ease the
wound inflicted by his descent to the ranks of the gain-
fully unemployed.

I found him ensconced in a spacious two-bedroom
suite at the Desert Inn in Las Vegas, where he was appearing for four weeks at $40,000 a week. He came
bounding out of the master bedroom, those beaver
teeth creasing a smile that had lost none of its guile. He

introduced his brother Jack, a silver-haired man who serves as his road manager while doubling as a TV actor on the off weeks; his wife, Ruth, a self-contained young woman who has made a career out of understanding Milton; and their two-year-old adopted son, Billy.

Milton set the child on the coffee table. "Go, Billy," he said. "Ladies and gen'mun, the one and ohnwy awtime gweat, Miwlton Bewle," said Billy in a high piping voice. Berle beamed. "And how does Jack Benny play the violin?"

"Vewy badwy," said Billy solemnly.

"Make Daddy laugh," coaxed Milton.

"No!" said Billy.

"Leave the room," said Milton, adding, as Billy toddled off, "He's only two."

"I have two children," observed Mrs. Berle.

We moved quickly on to the subject of television executives. Milton said he had recently done a *Defenders* for CBS, and that he had had to beg the NBC brass to let him do it.

"I went to Sarnoff," said Milton dramatically. "I said, look, I'll give you the money. Know what the money was? $1500, that's tops on *The Defenders*. I wanted to play the part so much I would have given them the whole contract back—for $1500."

Milton described in detail the life of a man victimized by his own prosperity. His contract states that he shall be "writer, producer, performer and consultant" only for NBC until 1981. Furthermore, it grants him approval of everything. Thus the network is unable to dictate what he does, and a gigantic impasse is reached in which Milton energetically spews forth ideas—and NBC just as energetically spews them right back: ideas like *Bigtime*, a prototype of *The Hollywood Palace; Two Men from Yank*, stories adapted from the famed World War II service newspaper; *Top Banana*, a variety show with a story line; a half-hour situation comedy starring—ready?—Milton Berle.

Cordial to point of insanity

He told of his periodic meetings with "them." "They" are always cordial to the point of insanity, Berle says. "It's, 'Howya, Milton-baby?' Then, 'Sure, we'll talk about it.' We finally meet. They say, 'It sounds marvelous, we'll get back to you.' Hell, they even have trouble deciding to let me do Ed Sullivan.

"I *am* allowed to do nightclubs—which I do 35, 40 weeks a year. And theater." He tapped a script. "This one is [novelist] Saul Bellow's first play. About a TV comedian who feels he's had it and wants to relive his life. And David Merrick wants me for a musical. Last year I did, 'Mad, Mad' for Stanley Kramer and 10 weeks of 'Top Banana' in summer stock.

"I'm also allowed to invest. I own a piece of *My Favorite Martian*. No artistic connection though. For an actor-producer that's very frustrating. Of course, Ruth says she'll leave me if I ever do a show like the old one." He laughed. "But she doesn't mean it."

"I'm not so sure I don't," said Ruth.

Milton lit another cigar. "The funny part is, I haven't made less that $500,000 a year for 20 years. You might say, I'm hung up on money."

Life in Beverly Hills

His wife, Ruth, explained what life was like in their $250,000 Regency house in Beverly Hills. Milton played golf, collected jokes, looked at movies, played benefits, read scripts, made pilots, performed eulogies, met with old cronies, played with Billy, went to church on Sunday, all in an effort to fend off the feeling of creeping uselessness. He's even had an attack of ulcers. "Milton just can't stand having nothing to do," she said.

She—the *Berle* Mesta of Beverly Hills, he calls her—is in charge of parties for his amusement. Otherwise her political activities keep her busy. (She will be a delegate to the Democratic National Convention.) Billy is not a problem; he tours with Milton, Ruth joining them both on weekends. Recently the Berles attended a state dinner at the White House. Ruth danced with the President. Milton told him jokes. In the receiving line, he leaned forward, bared those beaver fangs and said, "Er, I didn't catch the name." The President is said to have laughed.

Milton said, "I have plans for Billy. He can be anything he wants—a doctor. I couldn't. I was too busy fighting for the cue. Now I fight television networks."

Why? More than the pocketbook has been touched here. There are things like pride and the constant need for reassurance to contend with. But still, why not give up the $100,000 and be free? Is it so hard to live on the other $400,000?

"That's a good question," said Milton vaguely. "I guess it's because—well, because it's a lot of money. But that's not what really bugs me. I have a lot to offer creatively and I want to know *reasons*. But there *are* no reasons. Oh, I've tried to make a deal. We'd settle for about half. But *they* are adamant."

"Let them keep the money," Ruth said.

"I can't," said Mr. Television, a faraway look in his eye. "I just can't."

Other side of story

Of course, there's another side to the story. Mort Werner, NBC-TV vice president for programming, says, "We don't like to pay people for not working any more than they like to take the money for nothing. We listened carefully to every one of Milton's ideas; they just didn't seem to work out for one reason or another. And a year ago he told us he wasn't interested in doing a weekly variety show. We let him do a *Defenders* for another network, and he subbed for Ed Sullivan on his show one time that I know of. But we can't let him do too much of that—we're not in this business to help out the competition."

Two hours after he left us, Berle was killing them in the Crystal Room. No one kills in a nightclub with such lethal precision. Jokes may be old, but in the telling he makes them entirely his. Toward the end he confesses to the audience, "This is my life. I love the lights. I love to hear people laugh, and I love to make people laugh."

The applause rises in a shrill crescendo and suddenly the world seems very much the way Milton wants it.

(Jerry Dantzie)

The show is over, but the actor is fuming still

George C. Scott gets some of his frustrations off his chest

George C. Scott launched his series, East Side/West Side, *with high hopes. The hopes were dashed when CBS decided to cancel the show after just one season on the air. In addition to being a talented actor, Scott is an articulate talker, especially when he discusses television acting in general and his frustrating experiences with* East Side/West Side *in particular. Here, in a conversation with a TV Guide reporter, the outspoken actor offers some pungent comments.*

Q. *You once said that television acting was simply "garbaging lines" and not acting at all. What did you mean by that?*
A. In almost every other type of acting there's a considerable amount of time available for study, for projection of a part as to its beginning, middle and end. In television, there is no such luxury. The word "garbaging" was a rather vulgar way of putting the kind of quick, omnivorous process in which a TV actor gets lines in and then spews them out. The luxury of preparation and reflection simply doesn't happen.

Q. *How does that affect the actor?*
A. It makes his acting a form of posturing. In feature films an actor is fortunate if he can get 40 percent of what he'd like to have into the finished product. In a television series film, that percentage has to go down—I would say—to 20 percent, if you want a wild figure. Any kind of emotional involvement is almost nonexistent, and emotionalism is one of the tools of any respectable actor—qualified emotionalism, restrained emotionalism, these are important things. If you happen to be lucky enough to be neurotic and can go to pieces on the spur of the moment and then pick yourself back up and do it four more times, then you should make a fairly good television actor. In a large sense it is not even satisfactory acting.

Q. *What are some of the elements that create this situation?*
A. The nature of the beast. There are so many restrictions, so many difficulties involved, so many mechanical things that beset you that it isn't a question of compromising some great marvelous ideal. It is a question of day-to-day compromise on the most fundamental and mundane kinds of work. And, of course, the large influence of commercialism in the industry.

Q. *How does commercialism affect an actor? How did it affect you specifically on* East Side/West Side?
A. We had a number of sponsors who left us entirely alone, for which we were grateful. That is not what I refer to when I say commercialism. I refer to the need within the industry, within the networks, to produce a salable, marketable product which can be promoted and resold advantageously. This aspect is a strong form of censorship, one which reduces the area an actor can operate in; which acts as a Gestapo and reduces the scope of subjects one can assault. It's an authoritarian, negative, police kind of operation, which most assuredly must finally . . . affect the acting.

Q. *I gather that acting in television is against your better judgment, that you wouldn't do it if it weren't for the money.*
A. I don't think there's any question of that. We must remember through this conversation that we're talking about television *series* work. I believe we've seen good acting on things like *Playhouse 90,* or *Hallmark,* or *Play of the Week.* But even in those cases, how can you measure how much *better* the acting would have been, or how much *better* the production could have been, had they had the time that is available to a Broadway show.

Q. *You reported, before starting* East Side/West Side, *that you wanted the character to grow as the series progressed. Do you no longer feel this is possible in a television series?*
A. It certainly wasn't possible in mine, because they cut it off. But we were on the right track of creating what I call the novelistic concept. For instance, we got Brock out of the rather narrow confines of case work and did something to broaden his horizons by making him a Congressman's adviser. It was one of the steps along that route that would have caused shrapnel-like changes in Brock. Things were happening to him. He became different to an extent—physically, he began to change some of his ways of speech and of dealing with people, and ultimately we would have had him come to a parting of the ways with the Congressman, and Brock would have entered the area of active politics.

Q. *You would have been willing to continue with the series if it had not been canceled?*
A. Say you're willing to complete your commitment to something—you're willing to that extent. I don't say that you're insane to continue it—you know, that you're slavering at the mouth—but you want to finish the job. And we'll never know whether we could have done it, or could have given it that wonderful feeling that a novel has, of a beginning, a growth, a revolutionary process, a change, and then, ultimately, some definite end: a death, a retirement, I don't know. But we would have brought it to a conclusive end.

Q. *And then the series would have been over?*
A. That was our hope, that was the way we had structured it, and we were continuing to structure it.

Q. *In other words, you were prepared to carry on?*
A. Yes.

Q. *In spite of what you say about the restrictions and pressures of television acting?*

A. When you're into something, you do it. And you keep doing it as long as you can stand it.

Q. *Are there any actors in series whose work you admire?*

A. I admire Eedge Marshall; I admire him for his magnificent control of himself, both on and off the screen. I admire him for his perseverance, for his wonderful facility to keep fresh in what must be an extremely taxing role. Yes, I admire what Dick Boone was trying to do; I don't say he achieved it by any means. I admire some of his people: Miss [Laura] Devon, Miss [Bethel] Leslie. I think they're all better actors now, and that's a good thing to say about a TV series. Most actors come out worse.

Q. *Do you think you're a worse actor after your series?*

A. I think there's no question about it. Yes, sir. I think if I had stayed another year, I would have been *that* much worse. Something happens to you psychologically. I don't think it's arty to say that the actor needs nourishment, he needs time and he needs life around him to refresh himself—to refresh his avenues of approach to his work. For instance, we're sitting in this room; I might find something in you that I would steal and use, two years from now, just something you're doing, right now. But I submit to you that if I'm tired, that if I am at war with the network, that if my home life is rotten, let us say, because I'm never home and I don't see my wife and children . . . If I'm a nervous wreck, my sensibilities as an actor become dull—they become blunted—they can't pick up—I just do not have the perception that I had.

Q. *David Susskind, who produced your show, once told you that you ought to get out of television. What did he mean by that?*

A. Yes, David and I spoke about that a number of times. He didn't think I was suitable, that I was right, that I could stand the gaff. He felt that I wanted too much, and it was never going to be delivered, and that I was beating my brains out.

Q. *Recently you said: "I'm going to advise everybody to stay off television." Was that a flippant remark or were you serious?*

A. I was serious about it. Until there is some change in some of the aspects of the industry as we have covered it in this conversation, it is a most unrewarding business, television series acting. Anyone who has any legitimate desires and aspirations should stay out of television. If you want to make a lot of money in a short time, you can do that, and there's not a thing in the world wrong with that. If you're smart, you'll hang on to it because your career is probably through.

Q. *After the cancellation of your show you said that your feelings about television come from "ugly and keen experience." What did that mean?*

A. Keen, I meant sharply felt, cutting. Ugly would characterize the difficult and destructive elements you must deal with in a television series. Mostly my problems were with CBS, and with the restrictions they wished to place on the show, and constantly did. That's what I mean by ugly.

Q. *What were those restrictions?*

A. There was constant blue-penciling of material by the Program Practices Department of CBS, constant interference with the creative efforts of people on the show. It was a policy which was highly restrictive. For example, they never consulted us about the sequence in which the segments would be aired; we'd simply be given a list with the names of the individual shows and the order in which they would be shown. I was highly incensed about this, because it prevented our preserving the novelistic concept.

Repeatedly, we were faced with the excision of lines and scenes from the scripts, and the cutting up of scenes that had been shot. In a segment called "Who Do You Kill?" which dealt with the death of a child in Harlem by rat bites, we were eager to get pictures of the rat in his natural habitat, since he was the villain of the story. We shot some brilliant scenes of rats in action in Harlem. These were all cut out. We had the villain and we couldn't show him. What was their reason? They thought it might be offensive to the sponsor, or to the public, or to someone; I never found out who.

In a segment called "No Hiding Place," a story about blockbusting by unscrupulous real estate operators, there was a scene in which I was to ask a colored woman, a marvelously bright woman—played by Ruby Dee, who is herself a marvelously bright woman—to dance. The scene was edited out of the script by CBS. I insisted that it be put back in. It was, and we shot it. *Then* it was cut out of the footage by the network.

There's nothing anyone can do about these idiocies. The only solution would be for a producer to demand complete artistic control over his show. But that's the most difficult thing in the world to get.

I'll give you a splendid example of how their approach becomes sickeningly comic sometimes. We were doing a show about politics in Greenwich Village and were filming a rally in Washington Square. The young man running for office was characterized as something of a beatnik type. During his speech, a group of Italians in the audience call out insults *"pidocchio,"* which means "louse" in Italian, and other names. Brock jumps up on the platform and makes an impassioned speech, saying, "You like to call names, do you? How about the names your parents were called when they first came to this country, names like 'wop' and 'guinea.'" Then Brock says, sardonically, attempting to prove the stupidity of bigotry: "Everybody knows that all Italians are gangsters and all gangsters are Italians."

Well, the preceding lines, in which the words "wop" and "guinea" were used, were cut because somebody thought they might offend somebody. But the part about Italians being gangsters was left in, which of course *ruined* the entire sardonicism and changed the whole meaning of the speech. As a result, I got hundreds of letters from Italians complaining about what I'd said. And all because some stupid jerk made stupid cuts in the footage.

That's one of the more bizarre and cruelly evil things they did. This kind of harassment was a daily thing.

Q. Has your one ugly and keen experience soured you forever on television acting?

A. I would say just about as well as a person can get soured. One of the many reasons that television is not as good as it may have been nor as good as we'd like it to be is because it is full of hacks, and the really talented and ambitious people go elsewhere.

Q. Do you feel that CBS should not have interfered in any way? They're trying to sell a product, they're producing TV plays for advertisers and for the public.

A. Whenever I hear people talk about products and markets and consumption, a cold chill goes up my back. If you want to be in the meat business, it's a perfectly legitimate way to speak. When you are in the business of contacting through a word or a gesture tens of millions of people and influencing their thinking, influencing their daily lives, as strongly or more strongly than any other avenue of approach to the masses that has ever been devised by man, we are not using the right terminology when we speak of marketing. And when you are speaking about entertainment—if that's what you want to do—you have a perfectly marvelous string of one-right-after-the-other half-hour situation comedies which ostensibly entertain someone. The fact that you can make a social comment, that you can make a spiritual or psychological comment—which may or may not be valuable at some time to millions of people—this apparently is looked at by the networks as being unentertaining. And I submit to you that in that context, Chekhov was unentertaining and Shakespeare was unentertaining, and everybody else who wrote about his times—these people all have no entertainment value. That is the way they think, believe me.

Q. Has anybody ever suggested to you that your feelings about television and television acting may derive from sour grapes, from the fact that your own series was not renewed?

A. Well, that's always a possibility.

Q. Have you heard it from anybody?
A. No.

Q. What would you say if you heard it from somebody?
A. I don't know as I'd say anything. If they feel that's the—emotion I'm speaking from, from a bitter, petulant, soured situation—well, there's nothing in the world I could do to change their minds, so there's no point in bothering.

Q. Can we assume that you categorically will not go back into another television series at any time?

A. I think that those quivering masses waiting for my return can relax and forget it. And those who hated my guts can also relax.

(John Engstead)

They Still Call Her Lucy

The name's the same, the facade's unchanged, but behind them is a woman vastly different from her days with Desi

by Richard Gehman

Lucy—nobody ever calls her Lucille—Ball is a changed lady. The one we will see on her regular CBS series next season is not the same one we see on those seemingly endless reruns of the old series she made with her former husband, Desi Arnaz.

She has not changed demonstrably. That orange-red hair, those huge blue-violet eyes, and that bony-yet-sexy figure all still are the same. She smokes as much as she always has, which is to say compulsively and constantly. She still gives the impression, when talking, of listening to some inner voices that sort out everything she says and load her spoken sentences with a kind of resigned, put-on humor. This is a mind as tough as any man's in a body as pliably feminine as any woman's, and the combination is a delight to all who know her.

Yet there is a difference, a change in her, that anyone, even a casual acquaintance like me, can sense almost as soon as the hand is shaken and the Kissless Kiss, that greeting peculiar to Hollywood, is exchanged.

(The Kissless Kiss consists of an actress pursing her lips as though to kiss someone, and extending her cheek for a kiss, and then forgetting to kiss as she looks around the room to make sure everyone has seen her arrival.)

A few years ago, around 1958, when Desi and Lucy were husband and wife and their show was irrevocably wedded to the affections of millions, Bing Crosby and his writer-producer Bill Morrow one afternoon were watching a screening of one segment. Desi fell down a flight of stairs and soon thereafter Lucy was hit in the face with a huge gooey pie.

Crosby took his pipe out of his mouth and said quietly to Morrow, "This show's got a lot of heart."

Late in 1959 I went to do a magazine story about Desi and Lucy. There were rumors around then to the effect that they were having difficulty. Desi one night was picked up by police who declared that he was drunk.

Despite Lucy's vigorous and seemingly straightforward denials to me, it was plain that all was not well between them. One day he stood in the doorway of her dressing room on the lot they had bought together (the old RKO studios), fatigue bunching and pouching his face into that of a man who plainly was working too hard and seeking release by playing too hard. He was overweight and obviously overburdened.

"You want to eat, dear?" Lucy asked, going through the motions for the visiting reporter.

"No. No time." There was almost hostility in his tone. He flung himself away, back to his desk in another building.

Desilu grossed $20,000,000

She said, inscrutably: "As long as I can work, I'm happy." And then: "I'm too darn busy these days to do anything but work and sleep." Desilu then was producing television shows which, in that year, brought it a gross of $20,470,361. It was the biggest television-producing operation in Hollywood, involved in 27 shows and renting out space to three others.

"The show *has* got a lot of heart," I wrote, not altogether deathlessly, "and some of it is broken."

They were divorced some months later. Soon after that she was in New York, rehearsing a musical comedy called "Wildcat," which she turned into a personal triumph by pretending that the book was worth playing and the songs were worth singing—two notable acts of charity. She also pretended to me, in another interview, that life was worth living. She was fixing a new apartment for her children, Desi IV (now 11) and Lucie (now 13). But there was an odd, strained nervousness about her that was not the same as the sustained jitters that afflict nearly every actress.

It could have been tension over the "Wildcat" rehearsals. More likely it was an awareness that she was, for the first time since 1940, facing life alone. Born in Jamestown, N.Y., in 1911, she had gone off to New York to work as a model in her teens, had been taken to Hollywood to be a Goldwyn Girl, and had married Arnaz in 1940, when he was struggling along with a band which seemed to consist almost entirely of *claves,* maracas, and asses' jawbones.

Their work separated them—he was on the road, she was working in a series of forgettable films. When they were together, they fought. They made the separation official, were parted for three months, and then were back together, finally going as far as to get married in a church. That was in 1949. Two years later they launched *I Love Lucy.* It seems hard to believe, but Lucy Ball now has been on network TV (except for a two-year dropout) for 13 years.

It is harder to believe when one sees her in person. She looks exactly the same as she did when she first went on the air. That difference I mentioned back there is of manner rather than appearance. She keeps the latter unvarying, partly by exercising as hard as a boxer does. She eats normally but sparingly, passing up starches.

All kinds of things happened

"The last time I saw you I told you I wasn't going on this season," she said, anticipating a question, "but that was because my writers, Madelyn Martin and Bob Carroll, were quitting. I was hoping I could talk her out of it—she and Bob had been with me since I was on radio. Fifteen years, it was. She was getting married and keeping it a secret. Then she *told* me she was getting married, and I said, 'Forget the show. I'm done.'

"Then all kinds of things happened. People started leaving CBS, Danny Thomas and Jack Benny and Garry Moore and all, and it looked like we were all storming out of the network, and I thought, 'Well, I'll make a go at it with new writers.' Big challenge."

Lucy lighted a second cigaret; we had not been talking 10 minutes.

"Well, we now have groups of writers, and we're having a ball. We've got five shows in the can already. It's fun—you know, we work in front of three cameras and an audience of 300 and some."

New husband an ingratiating man

Gary Morton came in with a tape recorder. Lucy and Morton, who was a nightclub comedian and whose function now seems mainly to be that of husband, were married a year and a half after she was divorced. He is a handsome, ingratiating man. "Here's the machine for the radio show," he said, setting down the recorder.

"Garry Moore is going off the air—the radio—so they asked me to replace him," Lucy said to me. "I've always had such a big thing about radio. I love it. It's a daily 10-minute show. I can carry this thing with me wherever I go and record on it."

"I'll see you later, honey," Morton said, leaving.

Lucy gazed after him with a look that approached adoration. It was an expression which, if photographed and placed in one of those magazines that always have Elizabeth Taylor on the cover, could have been captioned *Lucy Ball Has Found Happiness At Last.*

Abruptly, she began talking about her marriage to Desi Arnaz. "It wasn't the industry and our working that broke us up," she said, "but the pressure had a lot to do with it. He was a very sick man. I was living with hope for many years.

"When the children got to an age when they were noticing the unhappiness, it was time to move away. That helped me to make up my mind . . . that, and the end of our performing commitments together.

"I didn't intend to get married again. I didn't think I would find a mature, adult person like Gary, a really understanding guy who is wonderful to be around and uncomplicated. He has none of the worrisome characteristics I lived with. I learned from experience. I wasn't going to walk into the same trap.

"One night when I was in 'Wildcat,' Jack Carter and his wife, Paula, said they wanted me to meet a friend. I put it off two or three times. . . . I was too tired, I said. Finally one night I was hungry and I said, 'Well, I'll go for something to eat,' and I met Gary. We had fun. He was going away for a couple of weeks. When he came back we started seeing each other after the theater.

"I found out he was, as I said, uncomplicated, good, sweet, hip, funny, and he appreciated a home, not just the trappings. He knew how to enjoy himself in a home. I got sick during the 'Wildcat' run. Maybe it was emotional, I don't know. I came to the Coast to sell my house and go to Switzerland or somewhere, and he followed me. My friends met him. He knew more people here than I did.

"By the time he was here for a while everybody was saying, 'My Lord, why don't you marry this guy?' Finally I said 'Yes.' It'll be three years on November 19."

Lucy's heart is mended

She glanced toward the door, as though hoping Gary Morton might return. The violet eyes gave me a look that was surprisingly girlish, shy, and demure considering the fact that Lucy Ball is a middle-aged lady who not only is one of the most brilliant comediennes in the business but also runs one of the biggest television factories. She lighted another cigaret—about her 16th in the course of an hour-long interview—as though to hide the little smile of delight that had begun to come across her lovely face.

The show this season probably will have as much heart as it always has had—perhaps, it occurred to me as we exchanged the Kissless Kiss, Lucy Ball's own heart is mended.

Review

by Cleveland Amory

"CANDID CAMERA"

Let us start out by saying that, for pure pleasure, we turn on *Candid Camera* as often as any show on the air—and, unlike some of its Sunday night neighbors, we hope it goes on forever. It is fine art, for it not only holds the mirror up to nature in general but up to our natures in particular and in the end literally gives us Robert Burns's gift to see ourselves as others see us.

It is, in short, the television medium used to its fullest advantage, and everybody on the regular staff—Allen Funt, Durward Kirby, Bob Banner, Elliott Joslin—deserves high credit. As for the irregulars, two of our favorites are Betsy Palmer and the peerless double-talker Al Kelly. Some weeks ago Miss Palmer did a screamingly funny scene as a dentist who lathered her patient. "A little bit of soap around the mouth," she explained, "keeps away the germs." Mr. Kelly did a masterful job on a speech to a group of Macy's clerks who could, of course, understand nothing. Afterward, however, during the question period, a man who had said "I'm not with you 100 percent" was then given a *double* dose of double-talk. "Now," he said, "you're talking."

But the great thing about this show is that it does not belong to the celebrities—it is one show where the public is, literally, the star. As such, of course, not only the joke but the jokee must be good. The most difficult character in comedy, Cervantes once said, is the fool, and he must be no fool who plays the part. No one enjoys the fun when it is cruel, and to this show's credit it is rarely so. At its best, it's terrific. We recall, for example, the woman driving up to a filling station with no engine in her car ("It was there," she said, "a while ago"), the voice that spoke from inside a mailbox ("How do you *think* I got in here? I *fell* in") and the elephant who tried to climb into a phone booth ("Honey, you won't believe this, but there's an elephant trying to get into the booth!" "Well, what does he want, John?").

This season has also had some classics—from the very first show, when some unsuspecting "helpers" of a TV repairman were stunned when baseballs and hot dogs came hurtling through the TV screen, to a recent January show, when a steelworker was exhorted to join a ballet class ("The only thing we insist upon is that you bring your own leotard"). Our only worry is that Mr. Funt lately seems to have given us less of this sort of fun and more of his camera vignettes, which, while interesting, are not what we tuned in to see. We also take a dim view of some other new ideas—such as demonstrations of what happens to jokes when they are repeated. Finally, Mr. Funt is far more fascinated than we are with children's dialogue. We, too, are pushovers for cute faces and cute conversation, but not at the expense of what made this show great.

(Allan Gould)

Jackie Gleason on
SIN, MUSIC, PLATO, PITY AND OTHER SUBJECTS

by Edith Efron

There is respect in their voices when they speak.

Says Ronald Wayne: "He's a unique man. He understands acting, directing, production, writing, music, lighting. He has a high-level intelligence. If you bring a problem to him, you see the thinking process going on right under your eyes. His mind is working while you're talking. And he comes up with the solution."

Says Philip Bruns: "My colleagues at the Old Vic and the Royal Academy of Dramatic Art were Peter O'Toole, Rachel Roberts and Albert Finney. In this country I've worked with stars ranging from Emlyn Williams to Billie Burke. And I'd say that this man is the most creative star I've ever worked with. This man thinks for himself. He has great intellectual, creative power."

Says Frank Bunetta: "He's an amazingly intelligent man. He learns with lightning speed. He's a demanding man. He can't stand stupidity. He's quick, and he expects everybody to be that quick. He thinks what *he* is is normal. He's so intelligent things seem self-evident to him."

These are not speakers at a testimonial dinner. They are, respectively, a producer, an actor and a director. One by one they have sat down beside this reporter in a dark Miami Beach auditorium during rehearsal and have talked extensively about their star. Not one has any idea of what the others have said. The man who is the object of these unusual tributes is Jackie Gleason.

Particularly since he won an Academy Award nomination in 1962 for his role in "The Hustler," people have become increasingly aware that the highly successful Gleason is not only a talented comedian but an amazingly gifted serious actor. Nonetheless, these tributes to his intelligence have a dissonant ring—as if they clash in some profound manner with the Gleason "image." Despite universal acknowledgment of his talent, Jackie Gleason seems still to be seen by most people as a Rabelaisian caricature, a man who swills down liquor by the vatful, who consumes pizza by the ton, who spends money by the bale—a gross, bawdy Pagliacci. Or, as Jackie himself puts it, with a touch of bitterness, "People see me as a fat, flashy fellow, a figure of loquaciousness and rioting. It's true enough. I drink. I make no bones about it. I'm fat because I overeat. And when I get a contract for a lot of money, I'm glad about it. But there's more to me than that."

Controversial ideas

And of course, there *is* more to him than that. For one thing, he is a man with an unusually vivacious intelligence and with a colorful, articulate way of expressing himself. Here is a random sampling of his opinions.

On modern music: "The lives people lead are so limp today that they crave modern music. It seems to give them some stiffness, some rhythm, some beat, some illusion of purpose. But it provides only temporary relief. It goes nowhere. It leaves them with no feeling."

On Plato: "Plato was one of the stupidest men in the world. He thought that if a child was strong he should be made into a soldier; if he was active he should be made into an athlete. He completely forgot human desires in building his system. It was the stupidest thing he could do."

On delinquency: "I hear people say we can erase juvenile delinquency—all we have to do is build another playground. That's ridiculous. What do you do on a playground—shoot a couple of baskets? What's wrong with kids today is mental unemployment."

On educational television: "They say we should have educational programs on TV. Who will select the education? Who will select the philosophy that television will present to the public? That's the guy I want to meet. Once we have that in television, we have what is almost a dictator."

On pity: "I dislike pity in any form. I think it's an excuse for cowardice. The great masochistic tranquilizer is self-pity. If you have a problem and you try to figure it out—that's much more heroic than moaning and groaning and whining."

On sin: "I've always believed that most sins are committed not because of the inability to control them, but because of the ability to perform them."

Jackie Gleason is also an idealist who can speak candidly about his ideals. One sunny morning on a Miami golf course he sat peacefully on a bench with a half-mile of velvety grass rolling away behind him and communicated some of them to us.

"Life is so quick," he said thoughtfully. "If you got to the end and you discovered that you'd accomplished nothing, that would be a terrifying shock. That, I think, is the real fear of death—the fear that you are wasting your life.

"As far back as I can remember, way back when I was five years old, I wanted life to be lovely, warm, thrilling. I wanted life to be beautiful and I wanted to contribute something to its beauty. That's why I became an artist. I escaped from reality into the world of illusion.

"All my life I've had a purpose, a central theme to my existence. People who lack a purpose are unhappy, directionless. They're dissatisfied. Worst of all, they can't do anything well. It frightens them. People give up too easily. They don't accept the necessity of struggle. They don't realize that without obstacles to surmount, without the courage to surmount them, there can be no achievement. Courage, confidence in yourself, is one of the most necessary requisites of any kind of personality."

Jackie himself is a man of astonishing self-confidence in the realm of his work. But when he speaks of his own abilities, he is not boasting. His eyes are serious, his voice is calm, almost impersonal—as though he were evaluating his own artistry from the outside. "I have no use for humility," he says. "I am a fellow with an exceptional talent. In my work, I stand or fall by my own judgment."

Outside the realm of his work, however, Jackie Gleason's imperious certainty collapses. He talks of the world outside of show business as though it were an unknown and unknowable territory. "The world is mystery," he says. "Science gives you proof without certainty. Faith gives you emotional certainty without proof. Intelligence and logic are hazardous, risky instruments. You can't know anything definitely."

He is not a brave man

In this unknowable universe Jackie is not a brave man. In it he does not "stand or fall by his own judgment." He submits to rules devised by others which he does not fully understand. He is engaged in an unending and often anguished struggle to understand and comply with the moral tenets of Catholicism. "You must have rules," he says. "You can sin and rationalize it away, but when you have a set of rules to go by, it makes it a little more difficult to explain away your iniquities."

Gleason is humble, almost childlike in his admiration of men who are "spiritual." Two of his closest friends are actor Jack Haley ("He's a deeply spiritual man. I love a person who has spiritual intentions, spiritual desires and goals") and Bishop Fulton J. Sheen ("I absorb his spirituality, his knowledge, his intelligence"). Even his highly publicized friendship with Toots Shor he describes in essentially moral terms: "Toots and I share our inadequacies. But it's our very knowledge of values that enables us to share our inadequacies."

He accepts the Catholic doctrine of original sin, and his deepest concern is over the issue of moral guilt. His discussions with Bishop Sheen revolve endlessly around one theme: "How do you determine moral responsibility? Is the same act equally immoral if committed with different motives? How guilty *are* you?" He also is given to long discussions about volition with lawyer Edward Bennett Williams: "What is free will? How free is a man to choose his acts? Where exactly does moral responsibility lie? How guilty *are* you?"

He is two distinct people

Jackie Gleason has a foot in two worlds. In the world of "illusion" he is proud, independent, courageous—he is "The Great One." In the world of "reality" he is uncertain, self-castigating, fearful—he is "The Guilty One." He is almost two distinct people, with completely contradictory and warring mental characteristics.

Both "The Great One" and "The Guilty One" are branded into the comedy he purveys on the screen. It is the mentally efficient "Great One" who is the decisive judge, the powerful artist, the practical promoter of his theatrical enterprises. It is the know-nothing "Guilty One" who actually contributes the characterizations that have become so famous over the years. Jackie's characters, he says, reflect his own "view of good and evil." He discusses his sinners: "Reggie," he says, "lets moral inhibitions fly. He drinks. He goes with girls. He kicks his mother in the teeth. Charlie Bratten, the Loud Mouth, is insecure and tries to make his fellow man small so that he can gain some stature—a sin we are all guilty of. Ralph Cramden is a classic example of the inadequate who believes himself adequate but who must face reality."

Even more significant are the characters that embody Jackie's concept of virtue. They are the two helplessly unintelligent buffoons—The Poor Soul and Crazy Guggenham (played by Frank Fontaine). "The Poor Soul is perfect. He's virtue. He's the square. He's a good Christian. Crazy Guggenham, too, is the embodiment of innocence—not very intelligent, childlike, kind." The strange truth is that The Poor Soul and Crazy Guggenham are satires on the Christian virtues: they are Jackie Gleason's versions of Dostoevsky's "The Idiot."

Whatever one may think of Jackie as artist or thinker, one thing is obvious. He is a fascinatingly complex human being and not a caricature. Why has he been seen throughout the years chiefly as a Rabelaisian gimmick? Partly because of the bawdy, ribald, liquor-loving character he assumes on the TV screen; but more than that, because of his off-screen publicizing of this aspect of himself. Why does he do this?

Essentially a shy man

Jackie himself claims that he talks about these matters to the press "because I'm honest about them." His director, Frank Bunetta, says: "I think Jackie talks to the press about fatness and drinking because he thinks that's all they'll understand. It's actually hard for him to talk about the things that matter a lot to him." And Philip Bruns: "Jackie is essentially a shy man. He's inhibited in talking about the things that are most important to him. I think he hides behind all this talk of fatness and drinking. It's a defense."

Whatever the reason, the fact remains that the Gleason image is a distorted oversimplification of a complex human being. There are millions of men who overeat in this world, millions of men who drink too much. But there is only one Jackie Gleason.

THE SOAPS—

ANYTHING BUT 99 $\frac{44}{100}$ PERCENT PURE

With daytime dramas sloshing around in human frailties, authorities contend they merely reflect America's disintegrating morals

by Edith Efron

Some months ago, the sleepy Victorian world of daytime drama made news. The news was that it had ceased to be sleepy and Victorian. In fact, said the reports, the soap operas were doing something no one could quite believe: "peddling sex."

Announced one astounded critic: "Folks squawking about cheap nighttime sex should harken to the sickly sexuality of daytime soap opera. *Love of Life* details frank affairs between married women and men; *Search For Tomorrow* has a single girl in an affair with a married man, result: pregnancy; *The Secret Storm* has another single girl expecting a married man's child."

And, under the headlines "Era of Souped-Up Soapers" and "Torrid Days on TV Serial Front," Variety, the weekly newspaper of the entertainment industry, reported that there was a daytime "race to dredge up the most lurid incidents in sex-based human wretchedness," and cited "a torrid couch scene involving a housewife with gown cleaved to the navel who was sloshed to the gills on martinis, working her wiles on a husband (not hers). The fade to detergent blurb left little doubt as to the ensuing action."

Even a superficial investigation of events in the soap-opera world confirms that these reports are true.

To understand this phenomenon, one must enter the total universe of the soap operas. And if one does, one soon discovers that the central source of drama is not what it used to be in the old days, when the brave housewife, with husband in wheelchair, struggled helplessly against adversity. The soaps have shifted drastically on their axes; the fundamental theme today is, as Roy Winsor, producer of *Secret Storm,* puts it: "the male-female relationship."

More specifically, the theme of nine of the 10 daytime shows on the air when this study was launched * is the mating-marital-reproductive cycle set against a domestic background. The outer world is certainly pres-

---

* *Edge of Night,* the 10th, is not a "soap opera"; it is a serialized melodrama whose hero is a criminal lawyer, and its events bear little resemblance to those described in this article. The two newest daytime dramas, *Flame in the Wind* and *Moment of Truth,* have not been on the air long enough to permit extensive study and are not included in this analysis.

---

ent—one catches glimpses of hospitals, offices, courtrooms, business establishments—but the external events tend to be a foil for the more fundamental drama, which is rooted in the biological life cycle. Almost all dramatic tension and moral conflict emerge from three basic sources: mating, marriage and babies.

The mating process is the cornerstone of this trivalue system. The act of searching for a partner goes on constantly in the world of soap opera. Vacuous teen-age girls have no thought whatever in their heads except hunting for a man. Older women wander about projecting their intense longing to link themselves to unattached males. Heavily made up villainous "career women" prowl, relentlessly seeking and nabbing their prey: the married man. Sad, lonely divorcees hunt for new mates.

This all-consuming, single-minded search for a mate is an absolute good in the soap-opera syndrome. Morality—and dramatic conflict—emerge from *how* the search is conducted. Accordingly, there is sex as approached by "good" people, and sex as it is approached by villains.

"Good" people's sex is a somewhat extraordinary phenomenon, which can best be described as "icky." In *The Doctors,* Dr. Maggie confides, coyly, to her sister: "He kissed me." Her sister asks, even more coyly: "Did you want him to kiss you?" Maggie wriggles, and says: "*He* says I did." Then archly adds: "You know? I *did.*" Maggie has already been married; her sister has had at least one lover. Coyness, not chastity, is the sign of their virtue.

"Good" people's sex is also passive, diffident and apologetic. In *The Doctors,* Sam, after an unendurably long buildup, finally takes Dr. Althea, a troubled divorcee, in his arms, and kisses her once, gently, on the lips. He then looks rueful, says, "I'm sorry," and moves to look mournfully out the window. "I'm not," murmurs Althea softly, and floats out of the room.

The "good" people act like saddened goldfish; the villains, on the other hand, are merely grotesque. One gets the impression that villains, both male and female, have read a lot of Ian Fleming, through several layers of cheesecloth.

To wit: a dinner between villainess Valerie Shaw and Dr. Matt in *The Doctors* in which Valerie leers, ogles and hints ("A smart woman judges a man by his mouth. . . . Yours is strong and sensual. I'm glad I came to dinner"), announces she will be his "playmate" and boasts throatily, "I play hard and seriously—but not necessarily for keeps."

And in *Love of Life* a sinister chap named Ace drinks in a bar with a teen-age girl who used to be his mistress.

"We used to ignite," he breathes insinuatingly. They exchange a kiss—presumably so inflammable that the camera nervously cuts the picture off beneath their chins. "Not bad, baby," he gasps heavily.

This endless mating game, of course, has a purpose: It leads to marriage, the second arch-value in the soap-opera universe. And the dominant view of marriage in the soaps is also worthy of mention. According to the "good" women, it consists of two ingredients: "love" and homemaking.

"Love," in the soaps, tends to be a kind of hospitalization insurance, usually provided by females to male emotional cripples. In these plays, a woman rarely pledges herself to "honor and obey" her husband. She pledges to cure him of his alcoholism, to forgive his criminal record, paranoia, pathological lying, premarital affairs, etc.—and, generally, to give him a shoulder to cry on.

An expression of love, or a marriage proposal, in the daytime shows, often sounds like a sobbing confession to a psychiatrist. In *Search For Tomorrow* Patti's father, a reformed drinker, took time out from brooding over his daughter's illegitimate pregnancy to express his "love" for his wife. It consisted of a thorough—and convincing—rehash of his general worthlessness and former drinking habits. "I need you," he moaned. "That's all I want," she said.

In *General Hospital* Connie's neurotic helplessness proved irresistible some weeks ago; Dr. Doug declared his love. They engaged in a weird verbal competition as to who was more helpless than whom, who was more scared than whom, who "needed" whom more than whom. Doug won. Connie would be his pillar of strength.

Homemaking, the second ingredient of a "good" woman's marriage, is actually a symbolic expression of "love." There is a fantastic amount of discussion of food on these shows, and it is all strangely full of marital meaning. On *The Guiding Light* the audience sat through a detailed preview of the plans for roasting a turkey (the stuffing has raisins in it), which somehow would help get separated Julie and Michael together again. On *The Doctors* one ham was cooked, eaten and remorselessly discussed for three days; it played a critical role in the romance of Sam and Dr. Althea.

If domesticity is a marital "good," aversion to it is a serious evil. On *Secret Storm* a husband's arrival from work was greeted by a violent outburst by his wife, who handed him a list of jobs he had not done around the house. His neglect of the curtain rods was a sure sign that he was in love with a temptress who works in his office. Conversely, if a wife neglects her house, the marriage is rocky.

After mating and marriage, the third crucial value in the soap-opera universe is reproduction. The perpetuation of the species is the ultimate goal toward which almost all "good" people strive. And "The Baby" is the household god.

"Good" people discuss pregnancy endlessly. Young wives are either longing to be pregnant, worried because they are not pregnant, getting pregnant or fighting heroically "not to lose the baby." And at whatever stage of this process they happen to be, it justifies their being inept, irritable, hysterical and irrational.

"Good" men, needless to say, are unfailingly sympathetic to the reproductive process and are apparently fascinated by every detail of it. In *The Doctors* you knew one chap was a "good" husband because he referred to himself as "an expectant father" and earnestly discussed his wife's "whoopsing" with his friends.

The superlative value of "The Baby" is best revealed when he makes his appearance without benefit of a marriage license. He is usually brought into the world by a blank-faced little girl who has been taught to believe that the only valid goal in life is to mate, marry and reproduce, and who has jumped the gun. The social problem caused by this error in timing is solved in different ways. The girl has an abortion (Patricia, *Another World*); she loses the baby in an accident (Patti, *Search For Tomorrow*); she gives the baby up for adoption (Ellen, *As the World Turns*); she has the baby and marries its father (Julie, *Guiding Light*); she has the baby and marries someone else (Amy, *Secret Storm*).

The attitude of the baby-worshipping "good" people to this omnipresent social catastrophe is strangely mixed. The girl is viewed as a helpless victim of male villainy: "She loved the fellow too much," said Angie's father sadly in *General Hospital*. Of course, she has acquired the baby "the wrong way" and must—and does—suffer endlessly because of it. Nonetheless, she is having "The Baby." Thus she receives an enormous amount of sympathy, guidance and help from "good" people.

It seems almost unnecessary to say that only "bad" people in soap operas are anti-baby. The fastest bit of characterization ever accomplished in the history of drama was achieved on *Secret Storm*, when Kip's father recently arrived on the scene. He said: "I can't stand all this talk about babies." This instantly established him as a black-hearted villain.

The worst people of all in the soaps, however, are the "career women," unnatural creatures who actually enjoy some activity other than reproducing the species. With the single exception of *The Doctors*, which features two "good" career women, Drs. Maggie and Althea, even the feeblest flicker of a desire for a career is a symptom of villainy in a woman who has a man to support her. Some weeks ago, we could predict that Ann Reynolds, in *The Young Marrieds*, was heading for dire trouble. She was miserable over her lost career, she had no babies, and she said those most evil of words: "I want a purpose in life."

It is hardly surprising to discover that even when the female characters achieve their stated ideal, they are almost invariably miserable. A man to support them, an empty house to sit in, no mentally demanding work to do and an endless vista of future pregnancies do not seem to satisfy the younger soap-opera ladies. They are chronically bored and hysterical.

They also live in dread of the ever-present threat of adultery, because their husbands go outside every day and meet wicked "career women." They also agonize frequently over the clash between their "needs as a woman" and their "needs as a mother."

The male denizens of this universe are equally miserable for parallel reasons. They suffer quite a bit from unrequited love. They are often sick with jealousy, tortured by their wives' jealousy of their careers and outerworld existence. They, too, have a remarkable amount of trouble reconciling their "needs as men" with their "needs as fathers."

So we find, amid all the gloom in Sudsville, a lot of drinking, epidemic infidelity, and countless cases of acute neurosis, criminality, psychotic breakdowns and postmaternal psychosis.

And this, dear reader, is the "sex" that the soap operas are "peddling" these days. It is a soggy, dreary spectacle of human misery, and is unworthy of all those "torrid" headlines. In fact, if one wants to be soured forever on the male-female relationship, the fastest way to achieve this state is to watch daytime drama.

The real question is not "where did all the sex come from?" but where did this depressing view of the male-female relationship come from?

Hardened observers of TV's manners and mores have claimed that sex is being stressed in the soaps because it "sells." But the producers of soaps retort hotly that this has nothing to do with it. Their story lines, they insist, simply reflect social reality.

Says Frank Dodge, producer of *Search For Tomorrow:* "We always try to do shows that are identifiable to the public. These shows are a recognition of existing emotions and problems. It's not collusion, but a logical coincidence that adultery, illegitimate children and abortions are appearing on many shows. If you read the papers about what's going on in the suburbs—well, it's more startling than what's shown on the air."

"The moral fiber has been shattered in this nation, and nothing has replaced it," says Roy Winsor, producer of *Secret Storm.* "There's a clammy cynicism about life in general. It deeply infects the young. It leads to a generation that sits, passively, and watches the world go by. The major interest is the male-female relationship. That's the direction the daytime shows are going in. Some of the contemporary sickness has rubbed off onto TV."

A consultation with some authorities on feminine and family psychology seems to support these gentlemen's contentions about the soap operas.

"They're realistic," says Dr. Harold Greenwald, training analyst of the National Psychological Association for Psychoanalysis and supervising psychologist of the Community Guidance Service in New York. "I think they're more realistic than many of the evening shows.

They're reflecting the changes taking place in our society. There are fewer taboos. The age of sexual activity in the middle classes has dropped and it has increased in frequency. There is more infidelity. These plays reflect these problems."

Dr. William Menaker, professor of clinical psychology at New York University, says: "The theater, the novel, and the film have always reflected people's concern with the sexual life; and in this sense, what's on the air reflects these realities of life. Increasing frankness in dealing with these problems isn't a symptom of moral decay but rather reflects the confused values of a transitional period of sociosexual change.

"Unfortunately, the vision of sex that seems to emerge on these shows is mechanical and adolescent, immature. The 'love' seems equally childish; it is interacting dependency, rather than a mutual relating between two autonomous adults. As for anti-intellectualism of these shows, it is actually anti-feminine. It shows the resistance of both writers and audience to the development of the total feminine personality. There is no doubt that these shows are a partial reflection of some existing trends in our society; it is not a healthy picture."

Finally, Betty Friedan, author of "The Feminine Mystique," says: "The image of woman that emerges in these soap operas is precisely what I've called 'The Feminine Mystique.' The women are childish and dependent; the men are degraded because they relate to women who are childish and dependent; and the view of sex that emerges is sick.

"These plays reflect an image built up out of the sickest, most dependent, most immature women in our society. They do not reflect all women. In reality there are many who are independent, mature, and who possess identity. The soaps are reflecting the sickest aspect of women."

On the basis of these comments, one can certainly conclude that all this "sex-based human wretchedness" is on the air because it exists in society. And the producers' claims that this is dramatic "realism" appear to have some validity.

But does the fact that a phenomenon exists justify its incessant exploration by the daytime dramas? Two of the three experts consulted actively refrain from making moral judgments. Betty Friedan, however, does not hesitate to condemn the soap operas. "The fact that immature, sick, dependent women exist in our society is no justification for these plays," she says. "The soap operas are playing to this sickness. They are feeding it. They are helping to keep women in this helpless, dependent state."

9:00 ❷ ③ BARBRA STREISAND — Music

(CBS)

'MY NAME IS BARBRA'

Special

Musical-comedy star Barbra Streisand explores the worlds of popular American music and high fashion in this one-woman show.

In the first of three sequences, Barbra portrays a little girl growing to womanhood. The different periods of childhood are represented by a series of impressionistic hallways. Barbra's "playmates" are the musicians who accompany her on this stylized journey.

The second segment was filmed at New York's famed Bergdorf Goodman fashion salon. Barbra romps through a fashion fantasy in which she models outfits created for this show by Bergdorf's designers. During her visit, Barbra provides an ironic musical counterpoint by singing numbers associated with less luxurious surroundings, such as "Brother, Can You Spare a Dime" and "Give Me the Simple Life."

Barbra also performs a medley from her Broadway hit "Funny Girl" and sings "When the Sun Comes Out," "Just Once," and "How Does the Wine Taste?" Peter Matz, who arranged Barbra's numbers, conducts the orchestra. (60 minutes)

(Jim Hardiman/CBS)

PLEADING HIS OWN CASE

After eight years on the air, a weary Raymond Burr tells why he'll continue to shoulder the burden of a weekly television show, as well as a myriad of other responsibilities

by Dwight Whitney

As far as Raymond Burr, the millionaire actor-philanthropist, is concerned, *Perry Mason* has long since ceased to be just a TV show. After eight steady years of playing the part, Mason seems to Burr more like a public trust. And as the self-styled executor of this "trust," Burr is an enormously preoccupied and busy man—busy espousing causes, paying hospital bills for insolvent acquaintances, and promulgating on a worldwide basis "the true meaning of the law" as he sees it.

These responsibilities, growing more awesome all the time, Burr tends to wear like gaily colored hair shirts.

They include the direct support of 12 people, the indirect support of hundreds, including 13 foster children in five foreign countries. He is a director of the Freedom Foundation at Valley Forge, and he is actively involved in the Cerebral Palsy Association, the National Safety Council, the B'nai B'rith and the March of Dimes.

He has arrangements with the Department of Defense and the State Department to take regular trips to entertain American troops abroad—four to Vietnam alone. Since *Perry Mason* began, he has made 68 speeches before bar associations. He contributes heavily in money and time to CARE, the United Jewish Welfare Fund and the Motion Picture Relief Fund. He has his own private Ford Foundation, called the Raymond Burr Foundation, which collects and dispenses funds "for charitable, educational and literary purposes."

Finding Ray Burr, the Canadian hardware merchant's son, actor, art connoisseur, gardener, gourmet and cook, amidst all that compulsive humanism isn't easy. Indeed, finding Perry Mason, a really tough man to misplace, is increasingly difficult. It is obvious that both men—actor and alter ego—have now taken a back seat to the new Ray Burr—doer of good deeds and socially responsible human being.

Why does Ray Burr persist in his killing schedule, living the lonely life of a recluse, holing himself up in his office-bedroom just off the *Perry Mason* set? Why does he get up at 5:30 A.M. to learn those legal speeches? Why does he fight the battle of the calorie to the point where the show closes down while its star takes an enforced rest? It's obvious he doesn't need the money. Is it because Perry Mason is his passport to the council tables of the world?

To find out I met Burr at 6 o'clock of a warm Wednesday night just before his fourth trip to Vietnam. His huge bulk swathed in a green paisley sports shirt, he was making out his will. Behind him stood his lawyer, Donald Leon, a lean gray man given to laughing at Burr's jokes. To one side hovered Bill Swan, his solicitous man Friday whose job is to sort out the urgent from the merely important. Nearby sat three office girls, somewhat nervous witnesses to the signing.

As Burr initialed the final page, he rose from the chair and declared, "The die is cast. Thank you, ladies." Then he moved into his inner office, where the atmosphere changed perceptibly. Gone was the prim sterility of the outer office. Burr's desk was piled with papers, pictures, old scripts and unopened mail. An outsize plaster cast—which he wore when he tore his shoulder tendons in a helicopter accident in Vietnam—lay on the floor evidently exactly where he last stepped out of it weeks before. Through an open door could be seen his king-size bed rumpled and unmade.

Burr leaned back in his chair and said: "With me it is difficult to explain why I do certain things. I have been called a fool. But I try to live my life the way I wish other people would live theirs. I try to honor my agreements. And so I find myself doing things I didn't expect I'd be doing. Like another year of *Perry Mason.*

"I wanted to do a show called *The Power.* In it I

played the governor of a state, and it had some of the same things going for it that *Perry* did. It was the best damn thing I ever read, the best new show presentation anybody in this business had ever seen. What happened was that another show conflicted with *The Power.*"

"*Slattery's People?*"

"I didn't say that!" he replied sharply. "Yes, *Slattery's.* Anyway the heads of CBS decided that with another year of *Perry* in the offing they didn't want to convert at that point. I went along. I'm a paid actor. Once having signed a contract, I had a certain obligation. Last year I still felt it. So we made an eighth year of *Perry Mason.*"

It must be added parenthetically that Burr was and is paid what may be the highest straight salary ever offered any TV actor. He is not and never has been a participant in the profits as are most other superstars. Instead his employers, CBS and Paisano Productions, co-owners of the show, pay him astronomical sums, mostly deferred over what amounts to the rest of his natural lifetime.

Burr explained why he had agreed to do yet another season. "My actors were hurting," he said.

Suddenly I saw him as God's gift to intransigent actors, tender to men's troubles, father of the world. Burr himself was not unaware of the effect.

"I couldn't let go," he continued. "I was concerned. Then there was something else. I've always told myself I'd like to go out on a good year. This year was a bad year. Sometimes the plots got so involved even I couldn't understand them. But next year can be a great one."

I could visualize Burr waiting for that "great year" to go out on until Perry Mason was defending cases from a wheelchair—which at his current rate may not be too far away. "No," Burr said. "You get a kind of a second wind, a different approach, new blood in the writing department. I just have a feeling this can be it."

And yet it was evident—despite the formation of Harbour Productions, Unlimited, Burr's new production company, which, he says, will field two pilots and possibly a movie next year—that it will be a long time before *The Power* or anything else replaces *Perry Mason.* Burr is curiously reluctant to acknowledge that it is still Perry who opens the doors to Burr's larger world.

"No!" he roars, his great beetle brows wrinkling. "Perry presents the image! He is window dressing."

Powerful window dressing. Window dressing enough to make the actor who plays him a big man before the bar associations of the world. Enough to make him a personage in Vietnam, or for that matter anywhere he wants to go. Next year, he says, he will visit 12 countries throughout the world making speeches to universities. Can Gilligan or Jed Clampett do that?

"I speak for world peace through law," he suddenly said. "I'm a kind of one-man lobby for the legal profession. I believe that the world will either destroy itself or learn how to settle things by law. So it becomes the world's most important profession.

"Perry may be a white knight on a horse, but he is accepted. He gives millions of people an awareness of what the law is and the tremendous need for it. It's not

February 1966   115

very often that a person is given the opportunity to use his personal image to do so much good in the world." He paused for a moment. "That's tough to give up regardless," he said.

I said it was my impression he was getting his images mixed.

"No!" he said angrily. "You have to remember I am still me. I sign my checks Ray Burr. I still have six people who do nothing but answer my fan mail, 84 percent of it addressed to me. I am not a 'star'—no one has less temperament. But I *am* aware. I listen. I get things done."

That he does. For example, it has been the custom of the East Coast art galleries to send exhibitions of American works to our embassies in Europe. Burr wanted West Coast galleries to follow suit in the Far East. When they turned a deaf ear, he sweet-talked a gallery in Tucson, Arizona, into setting up such a program. The only catch was there is no money for crating and sending. So Burr simply pays for it himself.

He pushed forward a packet of photographs from the pile of papers on his desk: Ray Burr arriving in Vietnam, Ray Burr landing by helicopter in some remote outpost, Ray Burr, in fatigues, talking to GIs.

"*This* is who I am," he said. "Back in 1951, when I went on my first Korean tour, a general told me, 'We can command men to fight and even to die. But we cannot command laughter and tears. In two seconds you people can supply both needs.' I know what he meant. I have been operated on six times for World War II injuries. I learned that when there is something wrong you don't just stand there!"

Burr does his troop-junketing the hard—Burr—way. While Bob Hope primarily plays major bases with a big brassy show, Burr takes only himself. He spends grueling and physically dangerous weeks hedgehopping by Army helicopter through the brush, going from one tiny Vietnamese outpost to another, often to "play" to a mere handful of men. Last time, he estimates, he shook hands with "13,000 out of 15,000 stationed there."

Sometimes these outposts are surrounded by the Viet Cong and he has dodged bullets on more than one occasion. His painful shoulder injury, incurred on the third trip, and which ultimately hospitalized him, was the result of an emergency helicopter maneuver to avoid Viet Cong gunfire.

Burr has long since given up "entertaining" troops. "I talk," he said. "And I listen. That's the real need."

Burr talked of religion. "I am not a churchgoer," he said, "but I like to say grace in my house. I believe in God—in the efficacy of all religions under a Supreme Being.

"See these hands? They belong to one of the best gardeners in California. They haven't gardened in months. I used to think I could build a wall around my Malibu house and give myself time for these things. Then I found I couldn't. Perry wouldn't let me. One day I *will* get out. If I'm ever going to be the kind of person you would like to be with, I'll have to."

He shuffled the pile of papers again and came up with a mariner's chart of the Fiji Islands. He pointed to a tiny dot. "See that island? I am in the process of trying to buy it. It is two hours by boat from the nearest port of call, and I will have to blast a passage through the coral reef.

"Meantime, I do what I have to do. What is right for me. What I have done may not have brought absolute happiness. But for me it has brought some measure of satisfaction."

It was after 10. Burr's airplane left for Vietnam early in the morning. His eyelids drooped. Just before this lonely man and I shook hands, he said, "If that makes me into a fool, my friend, then that is what I am."

UNCIVILIZED AND UNCIVILIZING

Despite TV's virtues and triumphs, a noted critic contends that there has been nothing too elegant for it to coarsen or too sacred for it to profane

by Louis Kronenberger

The author of this article, the second in TV Guide's series assessing television's effect on our society, is a teacher (Harvard, Princeton, Columbia, Stanford, Oxford, who is currently Professor of Theater Arts at Brandeis), writer (novels, essays) and critic (Time magazine's drama critic, 1938–61).

In approaching the theme of this series—the effects of television on our civilization—what I think must be said first is that television is not just a great new force in modern life, but that it virtually *is* modern life. What, one might ask, doesn't it do? It gives us—be we rich, poor, snowbound, bedridden or slow-witted—the time, the weather, the small news, big news, spot news: now in spoken headlines, now in pictured narrative, now at the very scene of the crime or the coronation itself. It plays, sings, whistles and dances for us; takes us to movies and theaters, concerts and operas, prize fights and ball games, ski jumps and tennis tournaments. It delivers babies, probes adolescents, psychoanalyzes adults. It dramatizes floods, fires, earthquakes; takes you to the top of an alp or the bottom of an ocean or whirling through space; lets you see a tiger killed or a tiger kill.

It becomes a hustings or a house of worship; guesses your age, your weight, your job, your secret; guides you through prisons, orphan asylums, lunatic asylums; introduces you to Presidents, kings, emirs, sultans; lets you see a Winston Churchill buried or a Lee Oswald shot. It teaches you French, rope-dancing, bird calls and first aid; provides debates and seminars and symposiums, quizzes and contests; and it tells you jokes, gags, wheezes, wisecracks, jokes and jokes.

A truly stupendous addition

Television is thus a truly stupendous addition to American life—our supreme cultural opportunity. Nothing approaches it, either in the abundance, variety and immediacy of its offerings, or the vastness, heterogeneity and attendance record of its audiences. It offers a mammoth handout of news, fun, art, sport, information; or of free refrigerators, cars, cruises, honeymoons, second honeymooms—all yours just for turning a knob, writing a letter, answering a phone.

Not too unnaturally, along with the handout there goes a sales talk. For this colossal addition of ours to American life, this supreme cultural opportunity, is also a tremendous segment of American business and our supreme cultural commodity. And not too surprisingly, what with Business paying the piper, Business calls—or cuts short, or calls off—the tune. And since television is Big Business operating with the help of Bigger Business, the two together constitute a form of Biggest Business—a fact we must face, since it makes any other fact about TV and its effect upon our civilization ultimately subsidiary and expendable.

Fresh insights are difficult

It also tends to make any fresh insights and observations about the effect of TV on our civilization hard to come by. Before *we* can have any really new thoughts, TV must itself give proof of really new thinking; before we can find anything notably different to say, television must provide something notably different to say it about. To be sure, there are constantly new craft gadgets, seasonal fashions, technological wrinkles—and there is color television with its promise of greater audience pleasure and fiercer network rivalry. But though these are things that add considerably to our conversation, they add very little to our culture. In providing so vast a menu, television has also—barring lavish Christmas puddings and special treats—pretty much standardized the food, the preparation of it, and the after-dinner speeches as well.

A fair amount on the menu is unexceptionable; and a good deal more has given 100,000,000 people harmless enjoyment. A certain amount of TV is clearly good; a certain further amount—notably in Space Age matters—is both good and unprecedented. But very much else is *not* good, and much beyond that is truly dreadful. Moreover, beyond what television has done, good *or* bad, there is the matter of just how television has done it. The particular nature of what is bad in what TV does, the particular nature of what is bad in

the way it does it, indicate what seems to me the *outstanding* effect of TV upon our civilization—which is that it has made it less civilized. There is a decided exception to this, namely educational television; but educational television, for all the charity and technical help it receives from commercial broadcasting, exists in a condition of virtual poverty, which not only underlines the uncivilized effect elsewhere, it argues no very civilizing *intentions*.

Let us gauge the effect

Let us gauge the effect in various ways. The *programs* themselves are predominantly geared to mediocre tastes and mass reactions—and geared, it would seem, in the hope that neither tastes nor reactions will improve. This doesn't just mean the proportion of sport to art on TV, or of broad comedy to adult humor; it means, even more, the proportion of trite formula to honest experiment, of glib comment to grown-up thinking. Further, the subject matter of countless programs—sex, gossip, violence, material success, cash itself—is uncivilized and uncivilizing both.

Take the most notorious example. The *technical* crime of the big-money quizzes was their being rigged; the technical immorality, that the networks could hardly not know it. But what was really degrading, indecent, uncivilizing, was that, rigged or not, the quizzes pandered to the venality of a whole nation, had multitudes glued to their televisions not at all for the fun of the game, but for the size of the stakes. Knowledge had become the grossest, the most *un*cultural, of commodities. (One can't help wondering whether, if tomorrow playing Russian roulette for huge stakes on TV was declared legal, it too wouldn't become the rage, with wildly mounting remuneration.)

Again, what is more uncivilizing, in fact brutalizing, than all the violence that is offered on TV for sensational and not sociological reasons? What could be less civilized than the endless cheap gags and gossipy wisecracks: what less civilized than TV's flagrant invasion of privacy—not just in terms of outright gossip, but in the way of candid "discussion," or psychiatric "discovery," or photographs of the sick, the unhappy, the doomed? And when the networks do attempt a civilized subject (such as Michelangelo) all too often the treatment makes civilized people squirm.

The *presentation* of the programs is worse, and far more uniform. Whatever the pros and cons for commercial television generally, there can be no argument about how uncivilized, how rife with crudities, timidities, imbecilities, sponsored programs tend to be. The stopwatch technique alone must make a sensitive viewer stop watching. "Men," as Tyrone Guthrie has put it, "stand chalk-white . . . on guard in the studio, charged with the single responsibility of seeing that 'Othello' or Beethoven's 'Eroica' does not run one-tenth of a second over, or under." If the esthetic distortions resulting from this are often appalling, the grotesque and vulgar intrusions and interpolations—the commercials—are worse. There are, to be sure, exceptions; but for the most part the blatancy of the programs' commercialized approach conveys the impression of a cash register in the drawing room, and even right next to a deathbed.

Not merit but mass popularity

As with programs and presentation, so with *procedure*. The "ratings" system, which computes not merit but mass popularity, which queries not those best qualified to judge but those most apt to judge routinely, is more than uncivilized: It is anticivilized. It turns any illiterate into a critic; an entrepreneur into a craven; a defeated contestant into a criminal (punishable by instant banishment). For profits seeker and pleasure seeker alike, there might be point to conducting polls with a view to correcting faults; but here improved quality is no more the issue than intrinsic quality.

Cutthroat tensions

Moreover, the general off-screen *atmosphere* of TV proclaims the lack of accident in how uncivilized the thing as a whole is. Everywhere cutthroat tensions seem mated with back-stabbing tactics. The higher levels of the three great networks suggest a luxury-class Reign of Terror, where the people who live in glass doghouses and the limelighted shake-ups and feuds make TV's administrative life the gossip column's darling. TV doesn't even *wash* its dirty linen in public; it merely waves it. Perhaps the one sure news edge that the press still enjoys over television is the doings and misdoings, the firings and backfirings, of television itself. But though the power side of TV is always agitated and shifting, its money side is solid and stationary. In this the Great Networks are splendidly assisted by the Great Advertising Agencies and the Great Artists' Representatives, so that the alluring daughters and nieces of art—Language and Laughter, Melody and Declamation and Dancing—are constantly bedded and wedded to the paunchy sons and nephews of Mammon. The general effect is often about as civilized as gluttony.

There is, finally, the cultural *irresponsibility* involved in all this. In an empire so vast as television's, in a network hierarchy so unfixed and collapsible, we must look to the very top for the policies that govern it and for the direction it takes. And there we find men known only for their immense wealth and their business power. Whatever their private enjoyments or hobbies, these are not men publicly identified with high culture; indeed, they have made everything in television that *is* so identified, everything that bespeaks artistic experiment, genuine enlightenment, pretty much shift for itself. Where important cultural events are not news already, these men seem to show small interest in making them so.

ETV just a sop

As for educational television, for these men it seems enough to give it a pat on the back and gestures of financial aid. Thus educational television remains a kind of sop that under the present system will never become a sufficient offset. Nor does it constitute a sufficient offset to the bill of complaint raised in this article.

Without at all belittling TV's virtues, its triumphs of news coverage, its operas and concerts, its ability to inform or stimulate or amuse, its serviceability to the many millions of people who use it as a food and not a drug, the glaring fact remains that TV has consistently either imposed uncivilized elements on American life, or aggravated and intensified those it found there. It has helped destroy respect for privacy, it has helped foster a more rackety publicity. There has been nothing too elegant for it to coarsen, too artistic for it to vulgarize, too sacred for it to profane.

Holy horticulture, Batfans, here's how
Batmania bloomed!

by Dwight Whitney

Biljo White, the editor of "Batmania," a mimeographed "fanzine" for Batfans published bimonthly in Columbia, Missouri, never had it so good. Not only is circulation booming, but Biljo, a 35-year-old Columbia fireman, is finding sudden fame as a kind of Bat-Boswell to the comic-book superhero Batman, cartoonist Bob Kane's utterly square and, some say, utterly beguiling "Caped Crusader," whose gaudy exploits have been rattling the pages of Batman comics for 27 years and which are now—ABC hopes—rattling television.

(Sheedy Long)

Biljo owes his present affluence to a number of things, such as the popularization of the terms "in" and "camp," which identifies something so bad that it is good. "*Batman*," says Igor Cassini, the status-conscious editor of Status magazine, whose business it is to determine these earth-shaking matters, "is in—I think. I will have to check with my managing editor."

"Yes, *Batman* is in," says Reg Potterton, his British-accented managing editor. "A most amusing show. It is mass camp. It can be appreciated by the greatest number of people, as opposed to low camp, which is more exclusive and therefore less desirable, or to high camp, which is rarefied camp, so in and restricted that it really—well, it's kind of futile in a way. Mass camp is the best kind of camp."

Camp, shmamp, Batman and his sidekick, Boy Wonder Robin, are with us in a big way. The Batmask, the Batcape, the Batarang, the Batcave, the "atomic-powered" Batmobile, the "secret identities" so dear to the heart of childhood—Batman is "really Bruce Wayne, dedicated millionaire crime fighter" and Robin is "really Dick Grayson, his youthful ward"—have suddenly emerged from their pulpy limbo to become a very hot item on the Pop-culture market.

Batman and Robin were first invented 27 years ago by Bob Kane, a tall, thin New Yorker, for the comic-book firm of National Periodicals, Inc. "Batman" became a best-seller of the genre, then eventually along came the Pop artists like Andy Warhol and Roy Lichtenstein, who began to exhibit their photographically detailed reproductions of comic strips, along with soup cans, in the fashionable salons of America. And Susan Sontag, whose 1964 essay defined "camp." And social satirist and opinion maker Jules Feiffer, who put the comic-book superheroes between the covers of a $9.95 book, along with a nostalgic paean of praise for this "peculiarly indigenous art form."

Then TV caught the bandwagon. In January 1965 Thomas W. Moore, president of the ABC television network, met with Edgar Scherick, then vice president in charge of TV programming, and Douglas Cramer, who was vice president in charge of new TV program development, to discuss some melancholy facts: ratings were low, competition keen, ideas scarce.

"It occurred to us," recalls Cramer, a Batfan in his youth, whose present art collection leans toward Pop, "that Batman might be a possibility. He could operate on two levels. For adults it would be high humor. For kids, high adventure. We began looking around for the man to produce it."

The "right man" turned out to be William Dozier, who made his television reputation as CBS's top West Coast executive during the heyday of *Playhouse 90*. But Dozier was not a Batfan. In fact, as Biljo White was later horrified to learn, he had never even heard of the "Dynamic Duo."

"I was taken aback," Dozier confessed recently. "Batman was simply not in my ken. I have always been associated with loftier projects. [He couldn't have been thinking of *Dennis the Menace, Hazel, The Donna Reed Show* and such, which were turned out while he was

Screen Gems' top West Coast executive.] Moreover, ABC had bought the concept without any idea what to do with it. I bought a dozen comic books and felt like a fool doing it. I read them—if that is the word—and asked myself what do I do with *this?* Then I hit on the idea of camping it."

Dozier called Hollywood screenwriter Lorenzo Semple Jr. into the project. "Lorenzo," explains Dozier, "was the most bizarre thinker I knew." Semple, a thin kinetic chain-smoker who was living in Spain at the time, was also adept at inventing new villains, each more nefarious than the last, to add to the gallery already supplied him by the strip.

Among *Batman*'s villains: Mr. Freeze, a cool-thinker who can live only at 50 below zero; Zelda the Great, a Houdinilike escape artist who commissioned an absolutely escape-proof trap for Batman; The Joker, who plays hideous practical jokes; and The Penguin, a long-nosed fellow whose speciality is fiendish umbrellas.

An impressive gallery

They made an impressive gallery, and Dozier soon had some of the leading character actors in town eager to play his "special guest villains," among them Burgess Meredith, George Sanders, Anne Baxter, Frank Gorshin and Cesar Romero.

Semple invented "camp" situations and dialogue designed to make Batman into the most impossibly square hero ever. When he walks into a discothèque, resplendent in his Batregalia, he explains to the *maître d'* that he doesn't want a table because "I shouldn't wish to attract attention," walks up to the bar and orders a large glass of fresh orange juice. When his "youthful ward" complains about his French lesson, Batman tells him, "I'm surprised at you, Dick. Language is the key to world peace." The Police Commissioner breathes arch put-on speeches into the "hot line" which connects "Wayne Manor, stately home of the scion of the Wayne millions" with the police station: "Whoever he may be behind that mask of his . . . our only hope is the Caped Crusader."

Dozier, meantime, was busily building Batcaves, Batmobiles and other Batparaphernalia. In a Batepisode everything is labeled, the Batpoles down which the Dynamic Duo slides to get to the Batcave (one says "Bruce" and one says "Dick" and on the wall behind them it says, "ACCESS TO THE BATCAVE VIA BATPOLES") and all the Batgadgets.

There is the Intergalactic Recorder, the Terrestrial Scanner, the Interdigital Batsorter, The Hyperspectrographic Analyzer, the Chemo-Electric Secret Writing Detector, the Atomic Batpile, source of power for the Batmobile.

The Batmobile, especially built by a custom-car expert, is strictly Detroit Garish. It cost about $30,000, is built upon a Lincoln chassis, houses a supercharged Lincoln Continental engine and runs in truth on something the existence of which the average Batfan barely acknowledges—gasoline.

Dozier was also building a cinematic style in which, in the words of line producer Howie Horwitz, "all the violence is good clean fun and no one—with the exception of Jill St. John in the pilot—ever gets killed."

Meantime, ABC was the happy inheritor of some unexpected promotional windfalls. Columbia Pictures hauled out of its vaults an old-fashioned Batman movie serial which had been gathering dust since 1943, strung all its 15 chapters together into four hours and 17 minutes of absolute Batheaven, and released it in art houses in 20 cities. Holy barracuda! A smash!

The trade papers reported "booming sales" in all comic books, triggered by the Batman craze. The *Batman* theme by Neal Hefti began climbing on the record charts. A new rock 'n' roll group appeared called "Robin and the Batmen." Three stereo record albums were announced. A New York art gallery pondered an exhibition of the works of Bob Kane, and Macy's took out a full-page ad inviting its customers to meet "Batman's creator" in its men's store.

The afternoon of the premiere, ABC set up a campily posh cocktail party at Harlow's, the "in" New York discothèque, followed by a screening, in the hope of completely capturing the in-crowd. Arthur Murray invented a new dance, the Batusi, for the occasion. Andy Warhol, Sharman Douglas, Mrs. Herbert Bayard Swope, Roy Lichtenstein, Tammy Grimes, Roddy McDowall and about 500 other black-tied guests appeared, "yokking it up," in the words of one seasoned observer, "at every well-oiled cliché."

If the network thinkers were expecting the New York reviewers to dig the camp, they were to be bitterly disappointed. By and large, they thought it was one big yawn, with the possible exception of the New York Times, whose reviewer found the whole camp idea "amusing in spots, though the avant-campists might contend it really wasn't bad enough to be excellent."

Overnight samplings revealed that *Batman* in its early stages was drawing about a 50 percent share of the audience. However, no one knew exactly how well it would do in the long run. For the adults the joke could very quickly run thin, though the children, especially the younger set, seem to be hung up on the fantasy.

A synthetic art form

As one dissenter put it: "Every *Zonk!* is calculated. They are making fun of Batman instead of making him come off in his own terms." To which the chain-smoking Lorenzo Semple replies, sadly: "Things that are really camp were never intended to be. So it is true; ours is a synthetic form of art at best. Perhaps we should have tried to make it *really* atrocious." Some critics think Semple didn't miss by much.

Out on the *Batman* set, such matters seem purely academic these days. Everyone is having a ball, from the "Batleader" (Horwitz) to the "Bat Bard" (Semple) to the "Super Bat Chief" (Dozier). Even the Batactors have a tough time finding anything to complain about. Adam West, the onetime bush pilot who plays the Caped Crusader in what has been described as the Early Deadpan style of acting, can't understand the script. "But who cares?" he says.

The Batleader and the Super Bat Chief have instructed everybody to play absolutely straight, under pain of extinction. This is easy with Robin, played by Burt Ward, who has never acted before and is almost as earnest in real life as he is on the screen.

"But with Adam it's different," the Batleader cautions. "He wants to be Cary Grant. And the first time he gets cute and amusing, the show is dead. I have to tell him, 'Adam, it's Eagle Scout time, sincere and earnest and square as can be.' Thank goodness he gets the message. It's tough when you have a show with lines like 'Which way to the Batroom?' "

TV's Most Engaging Fraud

He's Dean Martin, who talks like a swinger but says he's a square

by Melvin Durslag

Dean Martin warms up his audiences in a television studio with material pretty much culled from his act in Las Vegas. He walks out with a glass half filled. The liquid resembles whiskey but actually is apple juice. He starts to sing.

"Every time it rains, it rains bourbon from heaven."

He looks up at the audience with eyes remarkably glazed for one who hasn't had a slug all day. "How long I been on?" he asks.

He continues, "I got picked up the other night on suspicion of drunk driving. The cop asked me to walk a white line. I said, 'Not unless you put a net under it.' "

Dean then takes a sip from the glass, wincing perceptibly. "What did you think this was, *The Andy Williams Show*? There ain't no ice cream or cookies around here."

While Martin capitalizes on his public image of the convivial boozehound, he expects everyone to understand it's a put-on. He is much too astute a businessman not to know that very few millionaire-singer-actor-idols-of-TV got where they are by really nipping on the sauce. Actually he drinks moderately. Moreover, he would like you to believe, once you penetrate the inner circle, that he is actually a simple kind of fellow leading a conservative almost square, family life in his $600,000 Beverly Hills mansion, seldom taking a drink, and going to bed early so he can get up at the crack of dawn to play golf, which he does six days out of seven.

Will the real Dino please stand up! While he is undoubtedly fond of his wife and large Italian-style family, he has on occasion behaved in a manner to suggest that he is just as susceptible as any other man. As one longtime acquaintance puts it. "Jimmy Stewart he ain't." Moreover, this handy-dandy combination swinger-homebody is as hidden as he is complex. "He's got a wall around him," an associate says. "You never get close to him. In all the years we worked together I never really knew him." So it is all but impossible to tell where the put-on Dean Martin ends and the real one begins.

Meantime it amuses him to be bored with the usual accouterments of the swing life. He insists he rarely attends parties. "I don't dislike them," he says. "I despise them." He seldom is seen in a nightclub. And travel bores him. "I would never travel," he says, "if I didn't have to do it to make pictures." He and Mrs. Martin spent a two-day honeymoon: Dean took her to the races at Del Mar.

To hear him tell it, most of Martin's time is occupied at his impressive mansion, in all reality a two-acre youth center which includes swimming pool, tennis court, billiards room, projection room, recreation room with bandstand, and a motorcycle track. The Martins are a seven-motorbike family.

A rabid television viewer—there are nine sets in the house—Dean spends most of his evenings watching movies on the picture box, flipping to his own show over NBC on Thursdays. Upon awakening each morning, usually at 8:30, he is served breakfast and resumes his TV watching until 11, when it is time to dress for his most serious business—golf. When picture making doesn't interfere, Martin plays golf six days a week. Until he started his TV show, he played seven. He had to give up Sunday, grudgingly, to rehearse the program, which is taped that night at 7.

Meanwhile, guest stars come in days in advance to rehearse. Martin sees them for the first time on Sunday.

While others are busily at work on the program, Dean is meeting his golf companions each weekday at noon. On Saturday, when traffic on the course tends to get heavy, they convene at 8 A.M. He plays in a fivesome, always with the same opponents. They are Nick Hilton, eldest son of Conrad; Fletcher Jones, Los Angeles automobile dealer; Bill Ransom, Beverly Hills realtor; and Bill Bastian, Los Angeles meat packer, known to the others as "The Corned Beef King." It is a blood game, described by Martin as "whip-out" golf. "It's called whip-out," says Dean, "because at the end of each round, you whip out your money."

When publicity sessions began to encroach on his golf time, Martin ordered the public-relations office representing him to limit his press interviews to an hour a week, beginning at 10 each Tuesday morning. They are held in his home.

At 10:30 A.M. on Thursdays, also in his home, his staff meets with him and blocks out his part in the TV program to be taped on Sunday. The conference lasts only an hour, giving him ample time to get to the golf course by noon.

No smash in the ratings, the show has been received reasonably well by critics, some of whom feel that Dean could improve the program by devoting more time to its preparation. He argues the point. "We buck *Thursday Night Movie* on CBS," he says. "When we come on the air, the movie has been running an hour and the plot is just beginning to thicken. This is tough competition for a variety show."

Who needs meetings?

Additional meetings and rehearsals involving himself would be a waste, according to Dean. "I never liked meetings anyway," he says. "They're a drag. Some guys can't live without them. When Milton Berle was a guest on the show, he started calling meetings all over the joint. I said to him, 'Milton, this is my show and we don't make a big thing out of meetings around here.'

"As for rehearsal, how much do I need for the kind of thing I do? The other acts on the show are not my problem. It is my job mostly to introduce people, and anyone can do this who can read. Those big cards are right in front of you."

The jaunty, carefree attitude projected publicly by Dean doesn't necessarily reflect his true nature. A former publicist for Martin appraises the entertainer's pose as "calculated relaxation," pointing out that despite his make-do preparation for his show, he is more serious than he would have strangers believe.

Dean's longtime associate and aide-de-camp, Mack Grey, describes his employer as one who can't function under pressure. "He knows the pace at which he must work and live," says Grey, "and he doesn't want it disrupted. The only time he gets mad is when someone throws him off his pace. For instance, if you were to tell him at five minutes to six that he had to meet someone at six, he would get sore. He doesn't like surprises. He has a timetable all his own and he tries to keep it."

His wife, Jeanne, a former Orange Bowl queen whom he wed 16 years ago in Miami, adds, "He is anything but the drifter he seems to be."

The Martins have three children, and 11 years ago took custody of Martin's four others from his first marriage to Betty McDonald of Morton, Pennsylvania. The match lasted eight years. The seven children range in age from nine to 23, all but the oldest, Craig, residing at home. Completing the household roster of 12 are Mrs. Martin's mother and three in help. Each Monday or Tuesday Dean's mother, Mrs. Angela Crocetti, who lives with her husband in nearby Inglewood, California, comes to the house and prepares a sumptuous Italian spread.

By Martin's appraisal, his life today isn't the most exciting, but it's exactly the way he wants it and it exceeds the fondest dreams of his boyhood, spent in the tough mill town of Steubenville, Ohio. As Dino Paul Crocetti, the son of an immigrant Italian barber, he never endured hardship. "We had a nice home," says Dean. "I had a bicycle and I never missed a meal. But I was just too smart for those teachers in school."

Dropping out at 16, he worked in a service station before graduating to a smoke-shop pool hall where he racked balls in the front—and dealt blackjack and helped run a crap game in the back. Now that he had learned a trade, he moved to the gambling emporiums of Florida, West Virginia and Washington, D.C., earning as much as $8 a day, plus tips.

As a professional singer in the late 1930s, he began as Dino Crocetti, later changing his name to Dino Martini. But he abandoned this, too, when a friend suggested that people would confuse him with Nino Martini, the opera star. Checking the Metropolitan and finding no Dean Martins, Dino settled on the handle he now bears.

A favorite nightclub line of Frank Sinatra's is: "I knew the Dago [Martin] before he had his nose fixed." Dean admits that his organ of smell was beautified at the age of 24. "It cost me $600," he says. "I borrowed the money from a bookmaker."

The colossal success that Martin experienced with his former partner, Jerry Lewis, was, according to Dean, rewarding in one way but dangerous in another. "When we broke up," he says, "people kept whispering behind my back that I was finished . . . that Jerry had been carrying me. This hurt me. It also scared me. I knew I could always make a living as a singer, but I wasn't sure whether I could stay in the big time."

Nor was his confidence bolstered after he made a picture at MGM called "10,000 Bedrooms," co-starring Anna Maria Alberghetti. "It bombed," recalls Dean, "and things looked bad for me. I took a job in a Pittsburgh nightclub. When I finished the engagement, I sat in the hotel with my wife. I said, 'This is it, baby. I've got nothing else lined up now.'

"The next day, I got a call from my agent, Herman Citron. He said he'd found a part for me in a picture called 'The Young Lions,' with Marlon Brando and Montgomery Clift. I was to play a cowardly American GI. Then Herman broke the next piece of news gently. He said that all I was offered was $20,000, which was $230,000 less than I got for '10,000 Bedrooms.' " Martin performed the role so effectively that he vaulted back on top. He calls the picture the pivotal point of his professional existence.

In view of his affluence today, it was surprising to his friends that he would agree to tie himself down to a weekly television show. "When the idea was brought to me," he says, "I thought it was so crazy that I made a farce of it. First, I asked a ridiculous sum. Then I said I wanted to own the package 100 percent after the first showing of the series. I also said I wanted to work Sunday only, and I reserved the right not to sing on the show if I didn't want to. What I asked should have been thrown back into my face, but the network accepted it—and it was lucky for me, because the show has done wonderful things for my records and it has given me a recognition that one doesn't get from movies."

Why he decided on TV

Many who know Martin feel that he embarked upon the TV series not for recognition, nor for money, but to prove that he could make his own television show work, whereas former partner Lewis couldn't. Dean denies this, saying Lewis does not influence his business judgments.

"And what if NBC refuses to renew your contract?"

he was asked. "Then I will try CBS and ABC," he answered. "And if none of them want me, I'll go on with my records and my movies and my nightclubs." Dean was silent a moment, then added seriously, "I'll wind up on a ranch some day. I like cattle and horses."

Which, of course, is beautifully consistent with the inconsistencies of a man accustomed to stepping out on a stage, taking a sip from his highball glass of apple juice, and saying, "I had Thanksgiving dinner in bed. I really didn't plan it that way. It was just that when I woke up I was on the kitchen table."

WALTER CRONKITE

MUST BE DOING SOMETHING RIGHT

After years of struggle, he and his unspectacular brand of newscasting don't have to bow to anybody in the TV news field

by Richard Schickel

Earlier this season the promotion department of the CBS Television Network took a full-page ad in the New York Times to publicize the first of the many minuscule advantages Walter Cronkite and the *CBS Evening News* has lately obtained over NBC's *Huntley-Brinkley Report* in that game of American Roulette known as The Nielsen Ratings.

Around the news division in the network's New York broadcast center on West 57th Street, far from the madding Mad Avenue crowd, reactions were outraged. Fred W. Friendly, who was then president of CBS News, stormed into Cronkite's newsroom and tacked up the offending ad with its boast that CBS was "No. 1" crossed out. "We're not No. 1," he announced to all and sundry, "and I don't want anyone saying we are. We've got a long way to go and let's keep at it."

In a relaxed moment Cronkite and his son Chip repair their slot car race track (George E. Joseph)

Several months later a look of remembered pain crosses Cronkite's face when he is forced to recall that "unfortunate" publicity. "It means we're playing their [NBC's] game," he says. "It may be important in selling the program to advertisers, but it's not important to us." Ratings, he sincerely believes, are a preposterous way to measure the true status of the competition between network news departments and he decries "this constant effort to associate the criteria for entertainment with those for television news."

The two men were not being modest, only accurate. Statistically speaking, there is currently no significant difference between the two major evening news shows. But for Cronkite, that is an improvement. How much a one can be judged by the fact that in 1964, after CBS substituted a two-man team consisting of Bob Trout and Roger Mudd for anchor man Cronkite at the Democratic National Convention, many believed it was only a matter of time before he was replaced or teamed with someone on the news show. Not glamorous enough, they said, not enough of the old pizzazz.

Cronkite never took public note of these speculations or allowed any hurt feelings to show. In retrospect, he finds "no evidence of a deep-dyed plot against me." Instead, he regards the incident as "an honest effort by the network to try something dramatic to enliven a pretty dull convention."

His response at the time was, in effect, no response. No public-relations cosmeticians were called in to alter his image; instead he just kept on doing what he had been doing—reading the news carefully and intelligently.

The tide is with him

The wondrous, faith-restoring result—providing the new management at CBS News does not foul it up somehow—is that no one in his right mind would nowadays predict anything but a long and happy life for Walter Cronkite in his present job. Indeed, the feeling is that, whatever the latest twitches in the ratings, the psychological tide is now running for Cronkite and ever so slightly against Huntley-Brinkley.

It is now clear that square, sober Walter Cronkite, with his muted, singsong delivery and his kindly Old-Uncle-Fred-from-Iowa expression, must be doing something right. But what? In an industry where the notion that you gotta have a gimmick is reverenced as if it were the Sermon on the Mount and the Pledge of Allegiance combined, he remains something of a mystery. After years of being No. 2 and trying harder and all that jazz, how has he finally succeeded in succeeding? Can it be, Charlie, that there is something in those slogans after all?

Alas for cynicism, there appears to be. Walter Cronkite is the man he is today because, if you can believe it, he is pure of heart, true to his ideals and loves his work. Or, as Richard Salant, the present president of CBS News, puts it, "Walter is a newsman who has remained a newsman and has never tried to be a television 'personality.'" Cronkite himself likes to remind interviewers that it was only last year that he passed the point where he had spent more time in broadcasting than he had previously spent foot-soldiering for newspapers and wire services. This is a matter of some importance to him and his voice takes on an edge of defensiveness when he mentions it. Like all members of that dwindling band who pride themselves on being first, last and always newsmen, he appears to harbor a dim suspicion that there is something not quite honorable about electronic journalism or, indeed, the handling of any informational chore that is not "hard," hot and reported under daily deadline pressure.

As if to protect himself from charges of going soft or show-bizzy or selling out, Cronkite has created around him an approximation of the atmosphere in which he learned his trade and his values. He does not broadcast from a studio but from a working newsroom very similar in mood and decor to a provincial wire-service bureau or a small newspaper's city room.

Cronkite bills himself as "Managing Editor" of the *CBS Evening News* and, as one of his colleagues puts it, "guards his title jealously." His office is a cubicle in a corner, a little more gracious and bookish than that of most newspaper M.E.'s, but less grand than most men in the $100,000-plus bracket would deign to accept. Two walls are almost entirely glass, so he can keep an eye on the newsroom, and he spends between nine and 11 hours each day in these environs. Very few of them are devoted to idly tamping his habitual pipe.

"With a lot of television reporters you have the feeling that their work begins when they go on the air," says Friendly. "With Walter you get the impression that his time on the air is the least important part of his job. He acts like he's putting out a daily newspaper."

In short, Cronkite is a working editor. Immediately on arrival in the morning he reads the overnight accumulation of wire-service copy and correspondents' cables, and he stays hooked to the wires all day, even as he gives and receives story suggestions, squabbles with his executive producer, Ernest Leiser, about the lineup for the night's program and generally oversees the operation of his "newspaper."

In midafternoon, when the copy begins to come in from his news writers, Cronkite begins the process of editing and rewriting by which he puts his personal stamp on the items he will deliver on the air. Often this continues straight through the period allotted for rehearsal. Occasionally the show is pulled apart on the air to insert a late-breaking item.

Sometimes there are fluffs

Friendly observes that this devotion to news values over production values "sometimes causes little fluffs on the air. But the audience doesn't mind. They accept them because they sense it's the price you must pay for Walter's total involvement with the news. To him, news is not something he wants to do. He *is* the news."

Cronkite tends to agree with this evaluation of his special appeal. He says, "I happen to like the news. There is not a story on that ticker out there that doesn't interest me." He adds that it's been that way with him since beginning his career as a part-time correspondent while he was a student at the University of Texas. Later, he found he even enjoyed being a press-service "wire filer," a job that involves editing stories from the national trunk wires to fit into a state-wire news budget. "In effect, I was making up the front page for the small dailies," he recalls and he is still retrospectively pleased at the responsibility.

"I never did have any desire to be a pundit"—he grins—"though I do like to think I have always brought a certain compassion to my coverage, whether it was on the police beat in Houston, the agriculture beat in Kansas City or as a wire-service man in World War II."

The theory around CBS is that Cronkite was never intended to cut down his competition in a single swashbuckling stroke. The feeling is that the audience has come slowly to realize the depth of Cronkite's passion for the news and that over the years he has generated a quality of believability no other broadcaster can match. This rapport is just now being translated into rating points.

Praise for Sevareid

Cronkite is quick to point out, however, he did not achieve his admirable place in the hearts of his countrymen all by himself. He enthusiastically joins in the chorus of intra-office praise for Eric Sevareid's graceful handling of the pundit's place on his broadcast. Not only does he admire Sevareid's "batting average," but he thinks freedom from the necessity to interpret enhances his own believability. On those rare occasions when he does express his own opinions, he is always careful to say that he is doing so and then to confine himself to matters of direct concern to him as a newsman—government news management, for instance, or the misuse of the Early Bird satellite.

He also believes that his staff's interest in hard features, ones that tie in closely with the day's events, give him an advantage over the softer Huntley-Brinkley approach to what might be called the back of the show. And he is in complete agreement with Ernest Leiser's evaluation of the two-man news team as "a stunt," leading to a program "that lacks organization and logic."

Emphasis on the stunt, in this view, leads to excessive ping-ponging between Washington and New York and the exclusion of correspondents in the field, where the stories are. According to CBS figures, Huntley and Brinkley are on camera two-thirds of the time, Cronkite only one-third. It is possible, according to the obviously prejudiced analysts, that Chet and David are suffering from overexposure and perhaps from boredom as well. Cronkite believes his format protects him from the former fate, his own attitude from the latter.

Salant, however, thinks such comparisons are invidious. "In my opinion Walter is simply incomparable," he says. "There is no one on the air quite like him." The somewhat more analytically inclined Friendly believed, when he was in power at CBS, that the superiority of the *CBS Evening News* rested not on transitory ratings

advantages or some magic formula, but on the simple fact that "Walter and his staff are better newsmen than the opposition. The difference shows when we have pictures of the Soviet soft landing on the moon at the top of the show and the competition doesn't put them on until they are 16 minutes into it."

As for Cronkite, it seems significant that a man not given to studying his notices should have caused to have framed and hung on his office wall a brief quotation from one of his reviews. It reads: "Viewers rarely recall and relish a Cronkite statement. They believe it instead." To him those words are less a compliment than a credo—very old-fashioned, very unchic but, it would seem, very, very practical.

Review

by Judith Crist

"THE FUGITIVE"

With an Emmy tucked under its belt as the "outstanding dramatic series of 1965," *The Fugitive* is preparing to sprint into its fourth season and its first in color this fall. Meanwhile its summer warm-up (or cool-down) of repeats might provide a clue or two to the series' distinction and durability.

The durability is, actually, part of its distinction. The framework presented to us weekly—offering up Dr. Richard Kimble as an unjustly convicted wife killer on the run to evade the death house and find the real murderer—is enough to try the patience of the most gullible among us (and let's have no real-life analogies with the Dr. Sam Sheppard case, please, now in its 12th year). For even though we're willing to presume that the various arms of the law Kimble almost inevitably encounters in each episode are going to be too stupid to recognize him or, if he is recognized, too inept or kindhearted to capture him in the midst of the good deeds he is almost inevitably involved in, we still want to have the empathic thrill of skirting danger and facing doom along with our hero. And logically, the least logical among us must realize, Kimble cannot be captured until the series is slated to go off the air or have its title changed.

There's no logic either in Kimble's being the nattiest,

best-heeled fugitive on record, never lacking for the price of a drink or the neatly pressed suit the occasion calls for despite his usually hot-footing it out of town empty-handed and with his last odd-job pay check uncollected. So what, then, is the hook?

First, there's David Janssen, whose Kimble emerges as one of the least monotonous of the secret-sorrow, do-gooding, compassionate humanists to have come our way; he's remarkably durable on the eyes, interesting in the performance. And second, there's the freshness of scene, plot and characters that the hero's rootlessness, an able assortment of scriptwriters and directors, and an astute producer provide. Last week (July 12) Kimble served as custodian of a private boys' club run by guest star William Shatner; this week (July 19) he's working for Mickey Rooney in a self-service laundry; next week (July 26) he's having a double load of trouble, courtesy of Melvyn Douglas, as a neuropsychiatrist, and his perennial nemesis, Lieutenant Gerard (Barry Morse).

There are lapses—supercoincidence, irrelevant plot-padding and overcomplexities show up from time to time—but they are rare enough to justify the series' status. The secret of full enjoyment lies in letting the illogic of the format go by and riding with its presumptions. I suspect it's a secret most of us have stumbled on.

HOW DRASTICALLY HAS TELEVISION CHANGED OUR POLITICS?

An eminent historian assesses the influence of the medium on the workings of American democracy

by Arthur Schlesinger Jr.

The time has come for a preliminary assessment of the impact of television on our politics. More and more Americans, it appears, are forming their impressions of the world on the basis of the things they see on the tiny screen. Recent surveys report television as the main source of news for more than 50 percent of our voters, and Broadcasting magazine could plausibly argue in 1964 that television had become the "nation's primary news medium." This widening influence of television over American life raises the question how TV is affecting the basic character of our political system and whether it is strengthening or weakening the workings of our democracy.

Some observers, for example, claim that television is producing a more alert and better-informed electorate; others that it is reducing our politics to a mixture of high-pressure salesmanship and beauty contests. The assessment is bound to be preliminary because the evidence is inadequate, contradictory and inconclusive. But TV Guide is to be commended for posing the question; and I am glad to offer an historian's tentative thoughts on a complex problem.

Television touches politics in a number of ways. For purposes of convenience, one may perhaps distinguish four types of coverage: (1) news programs, (2) pseudo-news programs, (3) interpretation and (4) party programs. It may be well to discuss each category and then attempt a general appraisal.

News

Probably the greatest influence in shaping political judgment is still the reality of events themselves. A depression, a war, a debate over national policy, constitutional rights protected or denied, economic securities enlarged or imperiled, bills passed or defeated: Such facts remain the great determinants of political opinion. And it is in communicating these facts that television has had its most impressive success.

A notable recent example was the coverage of the hearings on Vietnam before the Senate Foreign Relations Committee. I have no doubt that future historians will conclude that these hearings opened a new phase in the Vietnam debate. Before the hearings, most people had suppressed any disquietude they may have felt over the deepening national involvement in Vietnam on the assumption that the President had more information and no doubt knew best. But the hearings had the clear effect, for better or worse, of legitimatizing dissent. If eminent generals, diplomats and Senators were unhappy about our actions in Vietnam, then the ordinary citizen felt free to indulge in his own doubts. And the hearings not only opened up debate over Vietnam; they also ended the taboo which had so long prevented discussion of American relations with Communist China. Would these hearings have had the same effect had they not been on television? I think plainly not—and all the more credit therefore to the NBC network which carried them in full.

Television, through the vivid reporting of actual events, can thus incite new thoughts and emotions in the electorate. It also has the effect in many cases of heightening the sense of popular participation in public matters: Thus the McCarthy-Army hearings undoubtedly made many viewers feel, as they had not before, that the Wisconsin senator was a threat not just to other people but to themselves. When sustained over a long time, this increased sense of popular participation can alter somewhat the workings of political institutions. It seems already, for example, to have reshaped so basic a device in our politics as the Presidential nominating convention.

For most of our history, the convention was a relatively closed powwow for professional politicians, who got chummily together, discussed their candidates, made their deals and presented the results to a passive public. People might have exclaimed, "Who is James K. Polk?" when they heard the outcome of the Democratic Convention of 1844; but they did not feel indignant over the fact that the name of the nominee meant so little to them.

Television has changed all that. The dark-horse candidate, emerging unknown out of smoke-filled rooms for nomination on the 46th ballot, is probably a thing of the past. The tiny screen has made the public an active partner. The feedback is too quick and intense to encourage any convention to risk ditching the favorite of the national audience in favor of a crony of the party professionals. In addition, television has had the happy effect of making conventions shorter. It is safe to assume that the nation will never again have to endure 103 ballots, as it did during the Democratic Convention of 1924.

Conventions, of course, with their inherent drama and suspense, are particularly well adapted to the inquisitive camera. But even television's day-by-day reporting of politics has undoubtedly given the electorate a larger knowledge of public personalities and a greater acquaintance with public issues. News coverage, I think, represents television's best contribution to democratic responsibility.

Pseudo news

By "pseudo news"—a subclassification of Daniel Boorstin's general category of "pseudo event" (in his book "The Image")—I mean the creation of news on the initiative of the medium. Perhaps the term is unnecessarily invidious; for often the news thus elicited is entirely legitimate. Lawrence Spivak's *Meet the Press* and its various imitators, for example, have greatly advanced public enlightenment through the years by their interrogations of national figures.

On the other hand, some pseudo news is mischievous and irresponsible. When President Johnson issued his challenge to the intellectual community some months ago, a television news crew descended on my office in the evident hope that I could be stimulated to denounce the President. This seems a factitious attempt to manufacture conflict (though, in justice to the program, when I said that I considered the President's remarks appropriate, they filmed the interview anyway and put it on the air).

My feeling is that organized shows in a press-conference format serve a useful purpose but that television interviews designed to lure or trap people into sensational statements they would not otherwise make can be dispensed with. It is necessary to add, though, that television did not invent this technique; it is another bad habit it picked up from the press.

Interpretation

Editorialization on television has taken the form of thoughtful personal comment (Howard K. Smith, Eric Sevareid) or, with the recent encouragement of the FCC, of editorials by local stations. Neither form has thus far had very striking results. I do not know whether television has an inhibiting effect on comment; but certainly no television commentator has spoken with the pungency or authority of Elmer Davis on radio, and men like Smith and Sevareid often look more constrained on the screen than they used to sound over the loudspeaker.

In the past, networks have attempted panel discussions, like the NBC series *The Big Issue* a few years back. This is still done a good deal locally and on educational television. Unquestionably these programs have improved the level of political discussion, in part because they permit the suggestion of subtleties and complexities in public problems. But, possibly for this reason, such programs do not seem to have been pursued very diligently by the networks.

What television has done most successfully in the field of interpretation is the analytical documentary—the kind of thing that Murrow and Friendly used to do for CBS, the *NBC White Papers*, the Bell & Howell shows. At their best, such programs have dealt with problems at a reasonable level of complexity and have been a highly effective form of public education.

Party programs

By this I mean time purchased by political parties and leaders, or otherwise made available to them. This, I would say, has been the area of television's most conspicuous failure; and the trouble here begins with the nature of the medium itself. For the effect of television has been to cheapen political discourse, steadily reducing its length, its substance and its rationality.

Sixty years ago an audience which traveled many miles to hear William Jennings Bryan or Robert M. LaFollette hold forth on railroad regulation or the tariff would have felt cheated if the oration lasted less than a couple of hours. The coming of radio set in motion the shrinkage of the political speech, first to 45 minutes, then to half an hour. Then came television. I can recall the insistence of the TV men in Adlai Stevenson's headquarters in 1956 that half an hour was far too long; unless it were a national crisis, 15 minutes, they said, represented the outer limit of the attention span of an American audience.

Now the 15-minute speech is itself almost a thing of the past. The most sinister statistic in political telecasting is the one which records the ominous rise of the spot announcement. H. H. Goldin, a former FCC aide, has estimated that 60 percent of the money spent by candidates on television in recent general elections has gone for spots; the proportion of funds invested in program time has been steadily declining.

This development can only have the worst possible effect in degrading the level and character of our political discourse. If it continues, the result will be the vulgarization of issues, the exaltation of the immediately ingratiating personality and, in general, an orgy of electronic demagoguery. You cannot merchandise political candidates like soap and hope to preserve a rational democracy.

While this drift to spot announcements is in great part the preference of the candidates themselves, the industry cannot be held wholly guiltless, for it would much rather sell spots than program time. Both the candidates and the industry, however, prefer to blame the condition on the audience, which, both claim, will simply not sit still for thoughtful disquisitions on public policy. No doubt a large part of the mass audience could not care less about an intelligent discussion of issues. But there remain a substantial number of viewers, even if less than a majority, who do care. Does not television have an obligation to this important minority, too, as well as to the service of democracy in general?

The ultimate answer to this question lies in the movement which must someday come toward the diversification of the viewing public; UHF and pay-TV will no doubt make it easier for the medium to reach specialized audiences. In the meantime, one wonders whether more free time should not be made available to candidates, especially in Presidential elections. If democracy depends on rational communication, if television is now the dominant communications medium and if television licenses are granted, according to the Communications Act, with a view to the "public interest, convenience and necessity," then it would seem that one of the richest industries in the country might make systematic provision for free time for public debate, at least during Presidential elections.

I recognize that informally the industry has done a considerable amount of this. But I wonder whether it is doing enough to discharge the obligations which come with its highly profitable licenses. Is it not really pretty important to give the electorate a chance to hear a man who wants to be President, even if this outrages people who would prefer to see *The Beverly Hillbillies*? * In addition to lowering the level of the party debate, television may give an initial advantage to the poised, photogenic, other-directed, manipulable candidate.

The rush of professional actors into politics is an obvious consequence of the television age. One shudders a little to think what would have happened, for example, to the Adamses or Jackson or Lincoln if television had existed in the early years of the republic. On the other hand, television is a relatively unsparing medium; it consumes material voraciously, in politics as well as in comedy and drama; and while it may lend itself to slick first impressions, it probably is not hospitable to sustained phoniness and fakery. In the long run, I think, genuine qualities—intelligence, integrity, humor, firmness of purpose—will win out over calculated effects. The Kennedy-Nixon debates of 1960 were a case in point.

The balance sheet

Where do we end up? I do not think that television has wrought a revolution in our political system. American democracy will adapt itself to the tiny box as it has to a series of technological changes from the start of the republic. The effects of television—apart from the nominating convention—have been mostly marginal. It would seem that, through news programs and, to some extent, through pseudo-news programs, television has somewhat widened public acquaintance with issues and personalities; but that, aside from documentaries, its efforts at interpreting the significance of news tend to be

* I would not exclude the possibility of achieving this result in part through a graduated system of federal subsidies, as proposed by broadcaster Stimson Bullitt, or through tax deductions for a portion of lost revenues, as proposed by former FCC Chairman E. William Henry; and I would support researcher Herbert Alexander's suggestion that Section 315 of the Communications Act be amended to permit a policy of "differential equality of access."

superficial; and that its party political programs have encouraged the oversimplification of issues and favored the smooth and bland over the rough-hewn candidate. If voters had to depend on television alone for the information on which they base political judgments, the results would undoubtedly be poor for American democracy.

Yet, so long as television is considered a supplement to newspapers, magazines, political meetings and solitary midnight brooding by individual citizens, and not a substitute for them, it has in certain respects enriched our politics. And it could do so much more. Its power to convey the quality of political leadership is vast; the agony of grief which ran around the world when John F. Kennedy died after a short thousand days as President was obviously in part a result of the way television had made him a cherished figure in remote lands. If television would recognize an affirmative obligation to elevate the level of our politics, and applied as much thought and talent to this as it does to selling detergents, it might play a great role in helping make our democracy more rational and responsible.

Review

by Cleveland Amory

"MISSION: IMPOSSIBLE"

Well, one thing you've got to say for the system—there is one. Take, for example, the Columbia Broadcasting System. When last year they decided, in their infinite idiocy, to take *Secret Agent* off the air—and against, mind you, the specific, utterly systematic advice of this critic—they at least came up, this year, with a reasonable facsimile thereof. And if they can admit their mistakes, so can we—and, we promise you, the first time we ever make one, we will. Anyway, this show has, we readily admit, as much inventiveness and imagination— not to mention as many gadgets and gimmicks—as *Secret Agent* ever did. Furthermore, if they couldn't give us back the peerless Patrick McGoohan—well, look at it this way; it took a whole *team* to replace him. At this rate, when CBS gets around next spring to replacing the Yankees, it ought to take a whole country—and our guess is it'll be Japan.

Quite a team it is in *Mission: Impossible*. First of all, there's the boss, Agent Briggs (Steven Hill). He's very businesslike, but his business, remember, is to make each impossible mission not only possible but also probable and even plausible. Second, there is Cinnamon Carter (Barbara Bain), the kind of girl who, when asked by the man she is with if she can attract the attention of the guards away from him, says quietly, "If they look at you, I'll resign from the sisterhood of women." Third, there is Barney Collier (Greg Morris), the wizard of odds and ends. He can sabotage the TV system of an entire Latin American country without anybody thinking he is anything except an exterminator. Fourth, there is Willy Armitage (Peter Lupus). He never says anything, but you just *know,* if he did, he'd mean every word of it. Once, when he was asked if he could carry 400 pounds, he let loose a torrent. "Sure," he said. Besides all these, there are excellently cast guest stars.

As you've probably gathered, the missions are big stuff, and there's very little time for small talk. What there is is left pretty much to Cinnamon—who's also responsible for pretty much all the humor. It's quite a burden, but she shoulders it womanfully. And the fact

is the very quiet of *Mission: Impossible* adds greatly to its suspense. One week the team has to oust a Balkan dictator. "As usual," Briggs tells them, "assassination is out as a matter of policy." Another week, masquerading as a carnival group, they have to smuggle a cardinal (Cyril Delevanti) out of prison. Here the carnival music in the background was alone worth the price of admission. On top of it all, the show was a two-parter. And, we promise you, it was so exciting that all week long, between those two parts, we could still hear that faint carnival music. And we never thought of *Secret Agent* once.

He's Merv Griffin— PERIOD

This talk-show host hates to talk— about himself

by Robert Higgins

(Ann Zare Shanks)

In Merv Griffin's production offices atop a toy-sized Broadway theater where *The Merv Griffin Show* (an almost Thermo-Faxed copy of *Tonight*) is taped, there's a framed picture of Flash Gordon. Thanks to some paste-up surgery, Flash's face is Merv's and, underneath, a caption reads: "And so Flash *Griffin* sets off on a perilous mission—a daring young man against fearful odds."

In TV's chatterbox derby—where shows traditionally get dumped like dirty ash trays—Griffin (his show is syndicated by Westinghouse Broadcasting Company) is, in fact, something of a boy wonder. The program, now carried in 65 markets, was the fastest-selling of its kind in syndicated history. Not that Griffin could go around licking sci-fi spooks the way Flash used to. But Flash probably couldn't beat Griffin's record in the show-business wars, either. He started out at 19, pulling in a fast $1500 a week as a San Francisco radio singer. That was followed by a road job singing with Freddy Martin's band; a smash hit record ("I've Got a Lovely Bunch of Coconuts"); movies (for Warners); TV game-show emceeing; and his own critically successful, yet low-rated, daytime version of *Tonight* on NBC in 1962.

On the business side, Griffin owns six production companies—and just how much loot that's bringing in is anybody's guess. But when you figure that Griffin is reported to get $150,000 a year for his own show alone, the guessing isn't unpleasant.

All of which adds up to an impressive list of accomplishments. So, upon meeting Griffin, one expects to find if not exactly Flash Gordon, a man justifiably proud of his credits. But one learns instead that Merv putting down Merv professionally is pretty much par for the conversational course. "On my show," Merv says in an unfailingly enthusiastic yet oddly controlled voice, "I'm a traffic cop, that's all. I don't make sparks. I *promote* them. I'm a catalyst. America doesn't want to know what Merv Griffin cares about, feels or thinks."

Truth is, it's almost virtually impossible to find out *what* Merv Griffin "cares about, feels or thinks." He's affable enough, but he answers most questions in two or three sentences punctuated with periods as prohibitive as boulders. No amount of prodding gets much more out of him.

Here's a little of how little you get out of Griffin:

On his childhood: "I was terribly happy and secure." PERIOD. He was also terribly fat, weighing in as a teenager at 250 pounds: "Being fat never affected me emotionally," adding an incredible "*All* fat people are jolly and happy." PERIOD.

On Merv the man: "I don't know and I don't care what makes me tick. I'm not self-analytical. I'm emotionally secure and happy." PERIOD.

On his career (which has been a bit bumpy at times):

"It's been great fun. It still is. It's the great love of my life." PERIOD.

One comes away with a sketch of a man professionally self-negating and socially noncommittal. And it's a little hard to fit that in with the picture of Griffin the successful talk-show host and budding theatrical tycoon. Julann Griffin, Merv's wife, has an answer to Merv the myth: "Merv's always been misplaced as a performer. He tightens up in the limelight. He knows how unimportant it is. Merv finds his greatest joy in producing, in running his companies. He's really a businessman at heart."

There may be some truth in this. San Mateo, California, was the home where Griffin, at age four, was already playing the piano—and not just fooling around, either. By 12 he was so accomplished that he was on his way to becoming a concert pianist. "But I never loved playing," Merv declares. "It was simply an open door to other things."

One of those things was singing. At 19 he was good enough to have a radio show dumped in his lap. "Merv never thought about singing professionally," Julann says. "He merely wandered into the studio to accompany a friend and they hired him." Says Merv: "Singing was a bore to me. I hated saying someone else's words."

Be that as it may, he must have been pretty good at it, because bandleader Freddy Martin offered him a road job. Griffin sang with Martin from 1948 to 1952, during which time he recorded the "Coconuts" song, one of the all-time best sellers. Merv puts himself down there, too. "That thing embarrasses me," he says. "What talent did *that* take. It was all gimmicked up. Phony. Fake."

He downgrades his Hollywood success too. Griffin landed there in 1953 and stayed to make four pictures ("So This Is Love" opposite Kathryn Grayson being a fairly good one). Only, says Griffin, "I just packed my bags one day and left town. I couldn't stand mouthing those inane words in that nowhere town." Griffin got to mouth some better words when he later did a revival of "Finian's Rainbow" in New York. "But even there," Merv says, "I didn't stand out. I had a good chorus behind me. *They* made me look good."

In 1959 Griffin, the man who had successfully launched and rejected careers in music and acting, found himself in the decidedly less demanding (artistically, anyway) world of TV game shows, his first being *Play Your Hunch* on CBS. "At least," Merv rationalizes, "I was speaking my own words—using my *brain*." His brain came in handy because he had more such game-show hosting chores ahead of him (*Keep Talking* and *Word For Word*).

In 1959 Griffin married Julann, an attractive ex-comedienne (they have a son, Tony, six). Even then, says Julann, Griffin was a displaced Rotarian. Says she: "You'd go to one of his parties and be likely to meet the grocery boy. Show people have always bored Merv." They apparently still do. Says Merv: "Standing around a party saying what a nice gal Arlene Francis is, that's not for me. I need more intellectual stimulation than *that*."

Griffin got a taste of "intellectual stimulation" when he sat in for Jack Paar in 1962, before Carson took over *Tonight*. That stint led to his afternoon version of *Tonight*. NBC killed the show, but according to Merv, it was "one of the greatest things" that ever happened to him. "Because of the commotion the cancellation caused," Griffin says, "NBC was desperate to get me back. For a game show. I said, 'OK, I'll go back—but only if I can own the show' [which turned out to be *Word For Word*]. It was blackmail, sure, but let me tell you it made me feel darn happy."

Many Griffin enterprises

Griffin has plenty of productions to take care of nowadays. His enterprises are quite impressive for a couple of years' work. In addition to his own show Griffin has the game show *Jeopardy*, a music-publishing business, two radio stations, a special recording deal with MGM records, and an independent movie company. He keeps 125 people on staff to man all this, along with two separate production centers (on the east and the west side of New York). And although TV game shows and pop records are a long way from classical music and an acting career, Merv maintains he doesn't mind. "I've found what's important to me," he says. "At 41 I'm professionally and personally secure. What more can a man want?"

What more? Well . . . not everybody feels that Griffin is all that crazy about being behind an executive desk—or socially secure, either. As one perceptive acquaintance offered: "Merv is a gifted man in many artistic realms who never quite found himself in any of them. As the years have gone by, he's been locking up the more sensitive, artistic side of him for the more hard-headed, 'practical' side. I could accept his claim that he really wants to be a 'Rotarian' more readily if it weren't accompanied by such an emotional freeze."

Always a con man

As possible as that may be, there are many who feel that Griffin has really found what he wants in life. Associate producer Bob Murphy, who's known Merv since childhood, says: "Merv's always been a promoter—a con man. But not offensively so. He's just a nice, happy guy getting what he wants." Arthur Treacher, Griffin's couch-warming sidekick, agrees. Says he: "Merv's an uncomplicated man who is genuinely happy working his head off at what he loves best. Anyone who says otherwise has his own ax to grind."

Ax-grinders not withstanding, there's still something mysterious about a genuinely talented man dogmatically diminishing his creative past—and turning himself into a noncommittal cipher. Julann Griffin describes him as "The staff of life—sort of like whole-wheat toast." Griffin certainly comes across about as exciting as whole-wheat toast today. That wasn't the old Merv, however. The creative Griffin, though never a major success in any one field, was nevertheless, as one old friend put it, "far more a rich chunk of chocolate cake."

HEY!

Dear Reader,
May we have a word with you?
About commercials.

by Richard K. Doan

Are you no longer swept off your feet by the white tornado? Is that bad-breath routine about to drive you batty?

In short, do you pine for fast, fast relief from those deadly familiar commercials? And does it seem to you that advertisers ought to know it when they're rubbing your fur the wrong way time after time, day after day, night after night, week after week—yes, even year after year?

Relax. They know what they're doing. And—honest!—they don't mind irritating you. Not, at least, as long as they're getting *through* to you. Not as long as you remember their brand, and buy it.

You say you wouldn't buy that brand if you were starving to death and it would save your life? It matters not. You must be in a minority. The experts say it doesn't work that way. Most people will buy a highly competitive product if they think it best even if its TV advertising rubs them raw. Take Madison Avenue's word for it. The boys there aren't laboring to make you love them. All they want to do is sell you.

They have no rules about how long a TV commercial or selling theme shall run. Sometimes a spot's longevity is determined simply by how much the sponsor has, or wants, to spend. Sometimes, as with cold remedies, it's a seasonal pitch. Sometimes, as with the unveiling of new-model cars, it's a passing event.

More often the determining factor is how well a commercial sells. As one Madison Avenue expert put it: "Especially in the drug field, an advertiser may get what he considers a satisfactory commercial and spend against it almost to the end of time."

The Aerowax people, for instance, liked the gimmick of machine-gun bullets spattering off "jet-age plastic" so well that they kept this theme going for four years.

"One reason you'll see a commercial repeated over and over," explained John Bergin of the Batten, Barton, Durstine & Osborn ad agency, who created the successful Dodge Rebellion campaign and who's also involved in selling Pepsi-Cola, "is that the cost of producing commercials has skyrocketed in recent years. It's running up to $50,000 [and sometimes even more] to film a single minute. If Hollywood spent proportionately as much for movies, every one of them would be a 'Cleopatra'!"

But how does an advertiser know when his spot has run its course? Judging by what the agency oracles say, nobody has anything resembling a pat answer.

Suggested Paul Gerhold of the J. Walter Thompson company: "When people stop talking about your commercial, it's time to pull it off."

Sponsors check on spots

Huge sums are regularly spent by the sponsors and their agencies trying to find out whether people are "talking about" their TV spots. This is done by so-called follow-up interviewing of householders, usually by phone or by door-to-door canvassing.

It may come as a shock to many viewers, but these surveys seldom bother to elicit feelings of irritation engendered by a sales pitch. That just isn't considered important.

"Some of the most irritating commercials have been the most successful," says Richard A. R. Pinkham, whose Ted Bates agency has been noted for some of the hardest sells in TV (for Anacin, Carter's Pills, among others). He assured an inquirer that if he and this agency had any such selling job to do over again, "we'd do it just the same way."

Frank Kemp at the Compton agency, who oversees campaigns for such products as Tide, Gleem and Ivory soap, sided with Pinkham's viewpoint. "Nearly everybody supposedly hates those commercials," he remarked regarding a well-known headache remedy's spots, "but they sell. The point is, we're not trying to make people love us; we're only trying to sell."

Pinkham, incidentally, claimed it is more often the sponsor himself rather than the TV audience "who gets bored first with a commercial." "We sometimes have a problem keeping him, not the audience, from getting irritated by it," he reported. He declined to identify any of his clients who have begged for relief from their own ads.

Perhaps the most surprising part of all, however, is the fact that the billion-dollar advertising business has no clear picture yet of the impacts of repetitious selling.

The Schwerin Research Corporation, an outfit that has spent years probing the subject, confessed recently in a report on "The Economics of Wear-Out": "The life cycle of a television commercial is a difficult phenomenon to chart or even to comprehend."

Studies suggest, the firm said, that "the incessant drip" of repeated commercials "evidently splashes off more than it soaks in," possibly because consumer resistance hardens as the pitch gets more familiar or because the commercial has done all the convincing it's going to.

But nobody really knows what massive doses of advertising are doing to TV watchers, according to Schwerin.

"What happens," the researcher wondered, "when the consumer is exposed to a thousand advertising impressions a day—when he may be exposed to the same piece of advertising several times a day—when he is liable to see it again and again for months or even years—and when he is simultaneously exposed to more or less the same competitive claims in the product field?"

Viewers may not have a scientific answer to that one, but they might give Mr. Schwerin some choice opinions.

The Bumbling Barnum of Sunday Night

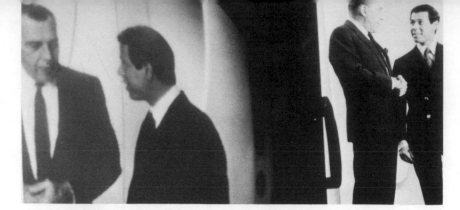

Huge studio monitor picks up Sullivan's chat with comedian London Lee (Dan McCoy)

You have to catch Ed Sullivan off camera to see what's kept him on the air for 19 years

by Robert Higgins

The show bill reads like a psychedelic circus: Mickey Mouse has done his stuff, as well as Helen Hayes, John Gielgud, Charles Laughton and Gertrude Lawrence. Benedictine Sisters have sung. Likewise the Beatles, Joan Sutherland, Ella Fitzgerald and the entire Metropolitan Opera. Chimps chase around on motorcycles while tumblers flip-flop. Bears dance. So do Nureyev and Fonteyn, the Piccoli Puppets and Gene Kelly. Jackie Gleason, Jack Benny, Victor Borge and Bert Lahr have all cracked funnies; so have enough wooden dummies to build a bonfire.

It's *The Ed Sullivan Show,* of course, and it's the most successful program in TV history. This Sunday, June 18, it blithely sails into an unprecedented 20th year on CBS. Like it (and, week in and week out, 30 million Americans do) or lump it (and most critics do from time to time), *The Sullivan Show* is as much a part of America's Sunday nights as cold mashed potatoes and leftover roast.

The success of this marathon mini-Palace rests squarely on the bison-shaped shoulders of Sullivan himself—bwana of TV barkers. Yet years ago nobody would have given you a nickel for his chances of clicking on the Tube. With good reason. Not since radio's fumbling Major Bowes have the airways been subjected to such a bumbling Barnum. Cod-eyed, cement-faced and so scaredy-cat stiff that he's been suspected of harboring a silver plate in his head, Sullivan has yet to complete gracefully the smallest gesture, unravel his vowels ("So letchearit forum"), or conquer a simple introduction ("I'd like to *prevent* Robert Merrill"). Sullivan on-camera has been compared to the "Cardiff Giant," and critic John Crosby once moaned: "What, oh what, is Ed Sullivan doing on the air?" Sullivan has wondered too. He once asked a friend: "What *have* I got?" "I don't know," the friend answered, "but you've got it."

After 19 years, nobody's going to argue with that. Only what *does* Ed Sullivan have? Some answers start to come when you watch him throw his show together. No bumbling Barnum there. *That* Sullivan is a tough-minded, often despotic, brass-knuckled Captain Marvel. He books all the acts himself, but usually doesn't see hide nor hair of them until Sunday afternoon at dress

rehearsal. But he's done his homework: like clipping a comic's 15-minute act down to the required four or five with uncanny editing know-how ("They always look as if I've slapped them in the face, but I'm usually right").

At dress, he screens each act with the protective glare of a duenna ready to snip out blue material ("An audience will forgive a bad act but never bad taste"). He then juggles the show's running order with what he calls "A newspaper make-up man's feel," something Sullivan's 40-some years as a newspaperman and syndicated columnist have taught him something about. And although his "dictatorial attitude," as one aide puts it, hasn't made some actors fall in love with him, Sullivan takes full responsibility for a show's hitting or missing. "No alibis," he says. "If it doesn't work, it's my fault. Only don't tell me how to run *my* show." Few dare. Sullivan once asked Elvis Presley's manager, Colonel Tom Parker, how much Elvis would want for a return engagement. When Parker came up with a couple of do's and don't's Sullivan would have to follow if he wanted Presley, Ed snarled: "Give Elvis my best—and my sympathy," and slammed down the phone.

Get Sullivan away from the klieg lights, however, and another Ed appears. No bumbling Barnum this time. No Captain Marvel either. This one's a warm, often witty, throughly likeable man—a hip David Harum in a lot of ways. Nibbling on his customary chicken leg (just one) and white-wine lunch, Sullivan, 64 now, looks at least 10 years younger. His eyes are a bright, steel blue and the famous bags ("People say they give me character. Who the hell wants *character?*") hardly seem noticeable. His wit is as dry as a good martini (on the harness races he attends most every night: "They start at 8. My horse starts at 8:10"), and his laugh is full and fully enjoyable. More important, however, you're introduced to a man endowed with values which, in show business anyway, sometimes seem to have gone out of style with candlepower footlights. That's the Ed who'll tell you how much he admires professionalism: "I'm absolutely in awe of people who do things *well*"; his deep-felt respect for heroics: "Men who deliver under pressure are the lionhearts of today"; his disdain for the dishonorable: "Dishonor is the most contemptible thing in life";

and his love of kindness: "If people aren't kind, they're nothing. The rest comes out of a machine."

These, in fact, are the two essential Ed Sullivans. First there's the tough, battling Broadway pro and, second, the warm, almost Old World moralist. As Bob Precht, Sullivan's producer and son-in-law, puts it: "I've often wondered how a man with Ed's Old World manners and values has managed to survive in the sniping, murderous world of Broadway." It's a valid question. Tracing Sullivan's life, however, you realize how the two Ed Sullivans fit as perfectly as an old pair of gloves. You also realize how one man nourished the other and made for one of the most rousing success stories in show business.

Sullivan was born one of seven children (Ed had a twin, Daniel, who died in his first year) to Peter and Elizabeth Smith Sullivan in Manhattan's Harlem just about the time the neighborhood started going to pot. His father was a stern, moody man with a $12-a-week job with the Customs Bureau. His mother, Ed remembers, was a "gentle, sensitive" woman given to painting and music. The Sullivans felt Harlem was no place to bring up kids, so when Ed was five the family moved to Port Chester, N.Y.

There Sullivan was to get his first taste of heroes—if slightly on the sly. "My mother would give me money for piano lessons," Sullivan says, "but I'd take the money and go to the movies to see William S. Hart." As influential as such vintage good guys were to be in later years, he should have spent more time in school. He was a poor student ("except in English"). No matter, Sullivan says. In high school he won 10 letters in sports, which interested him more. Sullivan's sister, Helen, now Mrs. Piercy Culyer, says: "As an athlete Ed always came back the hero. A bit battered but always the fighter. It was indicative of things to come."

Indeed. And, back then, Sullivan's admiration for the fighters of the world was intensified through reading the classics, "like 'Ivanhoe.'" Ed says, "I loved the beautiful ladies and romantic heroes." He was an innovator too, Helen says. Once when a snowstorm left Ed and Port Chester High's football team stuck for transportation to a championship game, the imaginative Sullivan bought a car on a small deposit, piled everybody aboard and took off. Sister Helen is still a bit dismayed by that performance. Says she: "Things like *that* just weren't done in our day." Says Ed: "I had to keep that car moving. If I'd ever stopped, they'd have asked me to pay for the damn thing."

The Sullivans never did have money. But Helen says, "We were rich in other ways." They were, too, certainly in the values instilled in them by their parents. Sullivan's admiration for professionalism and quality stems, Helen says, "from our uncles, who'd gather in the parlor on weekends and discuss the important people of the day. We heard about successful people," she goes on, "people of quality, from the time we were able to understand." Sullivan's enthusiasm for "quality" was, in years to come, to establish a bond with his father, to whom he had never really been close. The elder Sullivan was a devotee of opera, and just before he died in

1950 he saw Ed introduce Met singers on *Toast of the Town,* as his show was then called. "All he said was 'That's wonderful, Edward. Wonderful.' I think it pleased him more than anything I ever did."

Television, however, was a long way off during those days in Port Chester. And the Sullivan children were learning other values. "We were taught to respect the rights of others," Ed says. Helen adds: "We never heard mean comments about people being different. A person's blood, color or race was never discussed in the house." But Ed learned to respect the rights of others the hard way. "As a young boy I stole a Tootsie Roll from Mr. Genovese's store," he recalls. "Mother marched me back and told Mr. Genovese, 'Edward *thoughtlessly* picked this up by mistake,' and handed him a penny. I was so embarrassed I never stole anything ever again."

As a teen-ager Sullivan got his first newspaper job with the Port Chester Daily Item. The paper wanted someone to cover local sports and Ed was the natural choice. "Through reading," he says, "I came to love words and language." Although an uncle later offered to send Ed through college, he refused. "I was too interested in becoming a newspaperman by that time," he says. Sister Helen, however, offers: "Ed was too anxious to get into the 'action'"; and the action, of course, was in New York.

During the 1920s Sullivan showed up on New York's Evening Graphic and in 1926 met an attractive brunette through some friends of his. Her name was Sylvia Weinstein, and three and a half years later they were married. Ed's early lesson about "respecting the rights of others" came in handy, and Sylvia says she and Ed "have never had a problem about religion." Sullivan stayed Catholic, Sylvia Jewish, while their daughter, Betty, was raised a Catholic. After 37 years Sylvia, a gracious, still-attractive woman, says their marriage has been so idyllic ("Most important, we've never been bored") that she once playfully suggested that Ed cook up a scandal to take the glitter off the match. "Not that our marriage has been *all* sunshine and roses," she adds. "When Ed first started out, he had his pressures and tensions. He wasn't always the easiest man to live with."

Probably not. Money was a problem, and the problem led Ed right into the greener pastures of vaudeville and eventually TV. Although Sullivan was making $375 a week on the Graphic, there was a child to support ("She would have to go to school somewhere"), and the Sullivans, who were to become habitual swank-hotel dwellers, have never been known to count their pennies. ("We've never believed in hanging on to it for tomorrow," Ed says.) When the Graphic folded in 1932, Sullivan moved to the New York Daily News (where he's been ever since) and used the pressure of his column to front vaudeville shows, and found he could make $3700 for a one-week stand. He was always good to emcee a charity and this led to the News's handing him the job of emceeing its annual Harvest Moon Ball dance contests. Worthington Miner, then CBS-TV general manager, caught Sullivan at this affair in 1947 and signed him to emcee *Toast of the Town.*

"When the first show went on the air," Ray Bloch, Sullivan's longtime bandmaster, remembers, "I can't say I thought very much of it." Neither did the critics. But Sullivan had learned long before how to fight his battles. He didn't take the pans lying down. A chief Sullivan foe was the New York Times's Jack Gould, who did a serious comparison between Ed and, of all people, Milton Berle. Sullivan fired off a scathing letter to Gould, and when Gould called to say, "How dare you!" Ed surlied: "What are you so hot about? I just put my personal opinion of you in a letter. You spread me all over the Sunday Times."

Sullivan can well afford to be haughty. A very conservative guess of his worth is something like five million. And, according to Ray Bloch, he parts with a lot of it much too easily. "He's such a kind man," Bloch says. "He's always handing out money to washed-up fighters." "He worries so about people," Sylvia Sullivan says, "even those he's not always gotten along with. He can't keep a grudge." Ray Bloch agrees: "He'll blow up at somebody and then forget it. After the Jackie Mason blowup on the show, he met Jackie at an airport and said, 'Hi, Jackie. When're you going to be on the show again?'—just as if nothing had happened."

Sullivan associates this generosity with his mother, whom he adored. "Mother was so nice and kind to everybody," he says. "I'm much more like my mother than father. Mother was more loving." So, according to Sullivan's family and close friends, is Ed. Only it's a little hard to tell at times. Sullivan says it's because he's "terribly, almost painfully shy." The shyness, he explains, accounts for the bumbling Barnum on-camera. "I dread that much exposure," he goes on. "Big affairs of any kind. Banquets. I can go out with close friends and not feel shy at all. But if there's one person in the group I don't know, if I feel someone is just a little bit hostile, I clam up. It's a terrible feeling." The stone-face "façade," as Ed calls it, is a defense against this shyness. Ray Bloch agrees. "People think he's cold," Bloch says. "It's only a front. There's an exceptionally warm man underneath." And there is. "I once did my show playing a clown," Ed says. "I loved it. Behind makeup I could always be myself. But without it, I often feel I'm just a baggy-eyed old man."

Sullivan is far more than that. He's still, in many ways, the Irish scrapper from Port Chester whose values the world of show business—to say nothing of the world itself—could profit by. Yet, at 64, the years have taken their toll. "He's mellowed a lot," says daughter Betty. "He used to get angry and feel deeply about things. He doesn't as much any more." She concludes: "He's a nice human being. If you can leave that impression behind, you've accomplished something." Few would disagree. But Sullivan's accomplishments don't end there. "Sometimes when I'm flying over the country," he says, "I realize how many people I reach every week. On the Port Chester Item, I was getting through to maybe 3000. Now it's 30 million. That's quite a jump, isn't it?" It is indeed.

END of the LINE

Why the granddaddy of the TV game shows finally is finished

by Richard K. Doan

You couldn't escape the feeling in talking with that small, select circle of people connected with *What's My Line?* after they had heard the bad news from CBS that they viewed the cancellation decision as a horrible affront to a sacred institution.

True, they all admitted they never dreamed *Line* would last so long. Several years ago co-producer Mark Goodson, who probably holds the 17-year-old series in more reverence than anybody else, confessed he did not understand why *Line* had survived longer than any network evening show except Ed Sullivan's.

Everyone concedes they've had it supergood all these years. Thanks to *Line* (and about 30 other radio and TV series they've created in the past two decades), Goodson and Todman are multimillionaires. They sold *Line* to CBS in 1958, and *I've Got a Secret* to CBS and Garry Moore in 1959, in capital-gains deals, each of which, according to reliable sources, enriched G-T's coffers by about $3 million. Since then the firm has simply produced the shows on a fee basis.

Thanks to *Line,* Bennett Cerf is the country's best-known book publisher, packing 'em in at lectures. Thanks to *Line,* Arlene Francis is a big Broadway box-office draw. As for John Charles Daly, well, how many other people have toted home $4000 a week for half an hour's work for quite a few years?

In a medium that casts off entertainments at the drop of a ratings point, *What's My Line?* has indeed been something unique: It has become as much a part of the American scene as hamburgers. Year after year *Line* has resisted change, a continuing testament to the adage that you don't tamper with a good thing.

But now (or at least as of this writing, for few things are irrevocably final in TV's world) this era is fading. Sunday nights across this land, come September, won't be quite the same.

Why did the curtain have to be dropped on *Line* this year—and on the last two other panel shows in prime time, *I've Got a Secret* and *To Tell the Truth?* *Secret* has been around since 1952, *Truth* since '56; both are Goodson-Todman productions.

The answer is partly the current network rage for entertainment of known young-adult appeal. Surveys

[*What's My Line? reappeared as a syndicated program in the fall of 1968.—Ed.*]

(CBS)

(CBS)

(CBS)

showed that *Line, Secret* and *Truth* had heavy followings among the 50-and-older viewers. But the ratings of the G-T triad had been slipping too. When CBS disclosed the cancellations, *Line* had fallen to 79th, *Truth* to 89th and *Secret* to 95th in popularity among about 100 network shows.

How did the G-T panels survive so long? In hard bookkeeping terms, because they were dirt-cheap to produce, costing around $40,000 per half-hour (plenty of which was G-T gravy), or half the outlay for most other programs of similar length. Aired live rather than on tape or film, and necessarily topical, *Line* has not been stockpiled for rerun purposes. *Truth* and *Secret* have been taped, but only for the convenience of the participants, and aired a few days later. The shows have also had a handy stop-and-start potential for CBS—they could be pulled off without loss from advance production or started up virtually overnight.

More important, the shows wore well with viewers. Goodson says, "For our three shows to have been around for up to 17 years is the greatest kind of compliment. A very substantial part of the public wants this kind of entertainment. There is a sense of incredible danger in a live show."

He insists he isn't bitter about the cancellations except for the way CBS did it in the case of *What's My Line?* The word was leaked to The New York Times. A reporter had Cerf paged at Kennedy International Airport as he waited to fly on vacation. "How do you feel about *What's My Line?* being dropped?" he was asked. He knew nothing of it. When the Times man had hung up, Cerf phoned Goodson. That was the first Goodson heard of it. Reflecting on the incident later, the producer sighed, "It's the arrogance of power, I guess."

Bitter or not, everybody connected with the show closed ranks on hearing CBS's death sentence and tried to fight off the inevitable talk about burying the series. They all hoped CBS would change its mind. Nobody was going to consider *Line* dead, not right away anyway.

The members of the *Line* clan are a small, exclusive club. In the days following Dorothy Kilgallen's tragic death in 1965, Daly likened the hunt for a panelist to replace her to the storybook search for Cinderella. "We have to be sure her foot fits the glass slipper," he was quoted as saying. "If she doesn't fit into our family, we'll just freeze her out." No Cinderella was ever found.

The program was born sometime in 1949 or early 1950. Mark Goodson and Bill Todman, a couple of enterprising young radio-TV producers, had a quiz show on CBS-TV, *Winner Take All,* and a CBS Radio quiz, "Spin to Win." Records were played and listeners were phoned and asked to identify the tunes. The music was picked by a young fellow named Bob Bach. Bach had a propensity for trying to guess people's occupations. Sometimes he would get Goodson and Todman to "play the game" while lunching, focusing on some fellow diner. Often they'd lay bets. Then Bach would get up and ask the unwitting subject what he did for a living.

Exactly who got the idea of transforming this bar game into a TV series, nobody recalls. Then Mark and Bill assembled a bunch of people in an empty CBS studio and had them test format ideas. Among those participating were Daly, critic Gilbert Seldes, novelist Kathleen Winsor and author Jan Struther, who is credited with the idea of having contestants "sign in" on the blackboard.

When the producers took the idea to Charles Underhill, then a CBS program executive, they called the show *Occupation Unknown.* "That's dull as hell," Underhill reacted. "You need something with more life. What do fellows say on the commuter train when they meet? One'll say, 'I'm in socks. What's *your* line?'" Goodson lighted up. "That's it! Only 'What's *My* Line?' would be better." And so the title was born.

The first show was aired February 2, 1950. Daly was quizmaster. He had recently quit CBS News for ABC and was appearing as a panelist on a game show called *Celebrity Time*. "We picked him," Goodson recalls, "because he had great dignity and was a great ad-libber." One of the original panelists was Hearst columnist Dorothy Kilgallen, who had been appearing on an all-femme gab show called *Leave It to the Girls*. Her co-panelists were a former governor of New Jersey, Harold Hoffman; a psychiatrist, Dr. Richard Hoffman; and a poet, Louis Untermeyer. The show, one interested onlooker remembers, "was dull as dishwater."

Mark and Bill realized their brainchild needed some mirth. Next time they brought on Arlene Francis. On the fourth show they added comedy writer–comedian Hal Block, who began deliberately injecting gags into the questioning. (Sample: If the contestant was a girdle manufacturer, Block would be cued to ask questions about kitchen items. "Will it make ice cubes?" he'd inquire innocently.) It got laughs, but the producers decided spontaneous humor was better and dropped this approach.

About a year later Bennett Cerf pinch-hit for absent panelists several times, then joined the cast. The fourth panel seat came to have such regular occupants as the late Fred Allen and Steve Allen. Finally it became a guest spot, as it is today.

The mystery guest has been part of the routine from the beginning. Ballplayer Phil Rizzuto was the first, Elliott Roosevelt was the second. While virtually every big name in show business has done this stint, *Line* has not succeeded in luring the really big politicos before its blindfolded quizzers. Daly says Secretary of State Dean Rusk is a *Line* enthusiast and has promised to be a mystery guest. But he never has gone on. The Duchess of Windsor came to see the show twice (without the Duke), and associate producer Bob Bach, who has been chief mystery-guest and panelist auditioner all these years, tried to induce her to come on the show. She demurred, suggesting he ought instead to get Garbo and Mrs. Woodrow Wilson. (He didn't get them, either.) Bach, who was a Riverdale, N.Y., schoolmate of Jack Kennedy's, also buttonholed the late President when he was a Senator, but to no avail.

Even so, *Line*'s panel has had some important identities to probe for, such as Eleanor Roosevelt, Carl Sandburg, Sister Kenny, Admiral Halsey, Chief Justice Warren (before Daly married his eldest daughter), Frank Lloyd Wright, Marian Anderson and General Van Fleet. Among movie idols, perhaps the most often remembered is Liz Taylor, the first time as a sweet 17, the second time with Mike Todd.

Dorothy Kilgallen, everybody agrees, was *Line*'s most determined player of the game, and probably most adept at it. Not long before her death she strode off the show one night in tears, sobbing to Cerf that she hadn't been able to guess a contestant's occupation "in three whole weeks."

It amazes Cerf how little the viewers are aware how often the panel strikes out. "Some nights we don't guess anybody," he says. "But nobody seems to notice."

One guest panelist never got invited back. He was a famous personality. "He guessed everyone, even the mystery guest," Goodson relates. "We didn't know how, but we knew it wasn't on the level. Later we found out he had a confederate in the audience who read the occupations off the monitor and signaled him in sign language!"

Once Arthur Godfrey was undressing for bed on a Sunday night when he remembered he was booked as the mystery guest. He threw on his clothes and got there just in time. Several times Mark Goodson has stood in the wings, chalk in perspiring hand, ready to sign in as mystery guest because it appeared a scheduled celebrity would not be there. Just a few months ago Judy Garland, sitting in her dressing room with curlers in her hair five minutes before she was to walk on, told Bach, who reminded her of the hour, to get lost. Forty seconds before her cue she walked up to Goodson in the wings and wanted to know what all the excitement was about.

Several years ago Bob Hope had been all over New York guesting on shows and plugging a new movie. The panel, as Cerf tells it, agreed among themselves that if they sensed from the applause that Hope was the guest, they'd deliberately fail to identify him. "We guessed everybody else we could think of—Groucho Marx, Harpo Marx, Zeppo Marx," Cerf chuckles. "When John told us to take our blindfolds off and meet Bob Hope, the show was ready to sign off and Hope was furious. He had no time to plug his picture!"

There was the time an elephant trainer appearing on the show was recognized by a Michigan viewer as a wanted car thief; he walked off the show into the arms of the law.

The most oft-told blooper, of course, is about Sam Goldwyn. He confided to Miss Kilgallen that he was going to be mystery guest on *Line*. "Oh, you shouldn't have told me that!" she scolded him. That night he dined with Cerf. "What a dope I am!" he told the publisher. "Today I told Dorothy Kilgallen I was going to be on her show." Both Cerf and Miss Kilgallen had to disqualify themselves.

Line has had distinguished watchers. The Eisenhowers were such fans during White House days that at their request tapes of the show were flown down to Augusta, Georgia, several times when they missed the show on the air. The Hubert Humphreys are fans, Daly reports. President Johnson phoned the *Line* studio the night his secretary appeared as a contestant.

Some months ago, when Cerf's Random House publishing firm became a subsidiary of RCA, General David Sarnoff tried to coax Cerf into quitting the show on the grounds it represented a conflict of interest, *Line* being on CBS and Cerf now being a director of RCA, which owns NBC. "Let it be," he told Sarnoff. "It won't last forever." The General acquiesced. "I didn't realize," Cerf added recently, "that it would in fact be over so soon!"

(Frances McLaughlin-Gill)

HOW TO MANUFACTURE A CELEBRITY

Take the case of Barbara Walters,
who's one-third of the way through
the assembly line

by Edith Efron

There is a peculiar machine at work in this culture. It was conceived by public-relations men and it is a cross between a vacuum cleaner and a sausage maker. It sucks people in—it processes them uniformly—it ships them briskly along a mechanical assembly line—and it pops them out at the other end, stuffed tight into a shiny casing stamped "U.S. Celebrity."

Most people are perfectly aware that the machine exists—but they don't know exactly how it works. For those who are curious about the details of the process, a good case history is available these days—that of Barbara Walters.

The young, attractive reporter on the *Today* show is already on the assembly line—in its early stages. To wit: She's shown up once on the Johnny Carson show, in full glamor regalia; she has received one telegram from Mrs. Johnson inviting her to a White House breakfast; the Father's Day Committee of America has just named her "The Woman of the Year," etc., etc. All of which are exactly the kinds of things that happen to people who are being slowly stuffed into the celebrity casing.

Why Barbara Walters was ever sucked into the machine is hard to say. "I never expected anything like this to happen to me," she says—and one can readily believe her.

Four years ago Barbara Walters was buried in the ranks of The Invisibles—those hard-working and talented people who often take the pictures and write the words that on-screen "stars" point at and speak. Specifically, she prepared "women's interest" feature stories and interviews for the *Today* show—hiding modestly behind the scenes while female celebrities, each known as "The Today Girl," mouthed her lines and graciously cashed in on her work. "The Today Girl" kept changing over the years—Lee Meriwether, Helen O'Connell, Florence Henderson, Betsy Palmer, Pat Fontaine and Maureen O'Sullivan have held the job. But in varying degrees all were chosen to satisfy the TV axiom: that too great a display of brains and competence in a woman would shrivel the mass audience. Says one *Today* executive off the record: "Most of these women had personality and charm but they didn't seem to be quite right for the job. A number of them—Pat Fontaine and Maureen O'Sullivan in particular—were downright sirupy. They lacked an intellectual approach. Frankly we got fed up with the sirup."

During the endless behind-the-scenes discussions about the hypothetically ideal "Today Girl," Barbara Walters sat like a quiet mouse, listening. "I'd say to myself, 'Hey fellas, look at me, I'm right here, how about me?' but I couldn't bring myself to say it out loud." Then one day the same idea hit producer Al Morgan. Fresh from the failure with Maureen O'Sullivan, he and Hugh Downs finally decided to give·Barbara Walters a chance and put her on the air a few times a week to present her own work. The experiment was successful. The mass audience didn't shrivel. In fact, it actually liked the earnest, hard-working, unpretentious girl, a little brusque, a little shy, who did her own homework and acted like a reporter, not a feather-headed hostess.

She has now beaten all records for female durability on the show. Variety, the show-business trade publication, thus summed up the reasons for her success: "Barbara Walters has been able to make meaningful, believable conversation and at the same time maintain her sex appeal, albeit in a low key. Hers is a victory of brains over mannequin beauty . . . her very lack of slickness has worked to her advantage. . . . Even minor imperfections of speech have somehow added to her personal attractiveness."

Sometime during the first year of Barbara Walters' on-screen work, the celebrity machine began to purr softly in her direction.

The cycle began very modestly, with the discovery of Barbara by the press. A flurry of little feature stories about her, her show-biz background (her father, Lou Walters, is a nightclub operator), her Sarah Lawrence education, her marriage to theatrical producer Lee Guber, appeared in newspapers. Her first formal profile appeared in TV Guide. Life did a slightly cheese-cakey story about her. "All you can see is legs!" she says.

The next step of the cycle took the form of professional recognition. She was asked to do radio "Monitor" shows, "Emphasis" shows five days a week, and a monthly article for the Ladies' Home Journal. "It was exciting," she reports. "Suddenly people were giving me the opportunity to do other kinds of work. At first I said yes to everything, but I couldn't keep up with it. Now I do only three features a week for 'Emphasis.' "

As her sphere of action widened, she was piped into the lecture circuit and was deluged with invitations to lecture to colleges, to women's clubs.

Then a totally new element entered the picture: commercials. Once considered degrading "hucksterism," the delivery of commercials today is considered chic and slides the person being processed for celebritydom into the next big stage of the cycle. She did commercials for Citgo and assorted commercials for the Today show, and by virtue of appearing publicly in a nonreportorial capacity she suddenly became something called a "personality."

Thereupon certain characteristic things began to happen to her—none of which had anything to do with her professional skills. She was now being courted as a "name." The details of her wardrobe appeared in feature stories on women's pages. Vogue asked her for "25 beauty secrets." Cosmopolitan asked her to pose in Pucci towels. Interior Design magazine did a feature story on the decor of her apartment. A Boston newspaper invited her to give advice to career girls. Her name started showing up in theatrical tidbit columns. Charitable organizations asked her to send them personal articles to put up for auction. Her face appeared on a few covers of little magazines. She was asked to do roles in summer stock. And she has made appearances on talk shows with Virginia Graham, Mike Douglas and Johnny Carson. She grins as she talks about her appearance on the Carson show: "I looked glamorous! I had the dress, the earrings, the whole bit."

With her status as a "personality" jelling nicely, the next step mechanically occurred: Her name began to appear on a variety of fancy guest lists, compiled by people with a litmus-paper sensitivity to status. She was invited to functions she had never been invited to before. Telegrams arrived saying such things as: "Invite you to be our guest for Gordon MacRae opening at Empire Room, the Waldorf." An engraved invitation arrived asking her to attend Governor Rockefeller's inaugural ball. "I get invited to openings, to previews of movies, to publishers' cocktail parties, to all kinds of fashion shows," she reports. "They used to sit me on the press side of the Paris fashion show at Ohrbach's. This year they sat me on the celebrity side." To cap the climax came the inevitable invitation to the White House on March 13, 1967, an automatic tribute to a sufficiently processed personality:

"MRS. JOHNSON INVITES YOU TO A CEREMONY-RECEPTION AT THE WHITE HOUSE TO SALUTE THE HEAD START PROGRAM . . . PLEASE PRESENT THIS TELEGRAM AT THE SOUTHWEST GATE. THE SOCIAL SECRETARY. THE WHITE HOUSE."

Barbara was moving along the assembly line now at a nice clip—ready for the next mechanically bestowed honors to fall upon her. The celebrity machine now started to feed her name onto the lists of candidates for awards. Quite abruptly, as if a button had been pushed, a variety of different organizations simultaneously discovered staggering virtues of character in her. The Fragrance Foundation held its fifth annual luncheon on the theme "Give Thanks For Women" and honored Barbara Walters, along with such women as Bonnie Cashin, Bette Davis and Fannie Hurst. Brandeis University and Albert Einstein College of Medicine gave her awards for achievement. The National Father's Day Committee gave her a medal designating her "Woman of the Year." Harper's Bazaar is including her in its list of "100 American Women of Accomplishment." And, as might be expected, she has been given the key to a city—Fort Worth.

She is now becoming ripe for a new and more sophisticated stage of the processing. Where her work on the Today show went quite unnoticed four years ago, it is now receiving vocal applause from other celebrities, who are always willing to acknowledge the shiny casing. A startled Barbara recently learned from Hubert Humphrey that he was her "fan." She received a copy of a fan letter addressed to an NBC executive written on Executive Mansion stationery from Mrs. John Connally, wife of the governor of Texas. Not to be outdone by Texas, Mrs. John V. Lindsay, wife of the mayor of New York, also wrote her a little note thanking her for "a very enjoyable introduction to television interviews."

Needless to say, there is a steady feedback of Barbara's growing fame right into the executive offices of NBC itself. Quiveringly sensitive to all signs of success on the part of its personnel, NBC has come to realize that it has a baby celebrity on its hands and has been acting accordingly—giving Barbara Walters a touch of the red carpet treatment in her own bailiwick. "I now have an office with a window," Barbara announces jubilantly. "I've got a black-and-white TV set. I have a full-time secretary—I don't have to share her with anyone. And my *picture* is on the *wall* of the corridor leading to the *Today* office! They've put my picture in ads for the *Today* show. NBC chose me and Chet Huntley to talk to the NBC Radio affiliates. The president of the company gives a party for returning foreign correspondents every year—I'm invited to that party now. *And the chairman of the board and executives say hello to me in elevators!*"

All of which leaves Barbara Walters where? Strangely enough the answer is: approximately where she was when she started. She's only about a third of the way through the assembly line. She's still nowhere near the big leagues, inhabited by women like Zsa Zsa or even by Arlene Francis. Her features are by no means engraved on every mind in the country. "My day-by-day life has not changed at all in the past four years," she reports. "I'm a sort of second-class celebrity. I'm not one of New York's beautiful people. I'm not in the columns. In fact, I'm not a celebrity at all in New York. When I go out of New York, people come up to me and say they watch the show. But I can and do go everywhere in New York without being recognized. If I'm introduced at a dinner party by my married name, nobody knows who I am. I met an old boss at a party recently. He didn't know who I was. The truth is, if somebody recognizes me in New York I'm thrilled to death."

The slowly grinding machine has left a few marks on Barbara. "I'm more secure," she says. And she also looks much more like a glamor girl than she used to.

"When I first went on the air I looked boyish, like Barbara Walters, Girl Reporter. I looked a little tough. Now my makeup is different. I wear false eyelashes, much lighter lipstick. My hair is softer. Altogether I have a softer look. And I'm a little more daring in my clothes. I have prettier clothes—brighter, gayer clothes now."

But she is remarkably unimpressed with the machine that is processing her. She chats candidly about the meaningless mechanics of fabricated fame. "They ask you to lecture and write books. But they don't care what you lecture on or write books about. All that matters is being a celebrity, and you can lecture and write books on anything you want. As for awards—it often means they just need a celebrity to sell a ticket to a luncheon."

Her personality has not changed by an iota since the processing began. She is as unpretentious as ever. Her secretary says: "She's not temperamental or pretentious. She didn't strive for this. She started from the bottom and made it of her own accord. She has no agent. She's not out for publicity." Says Barbara's husband, Lee Guber: "She's terribly realistic. Her friends are still her friends. You can't corrupt anyone that's incorruptible."

But this doesn't mean that Barbara Walters isn't enjoying the process of being turned into a star. She *is* enjoying it, vastly. "It's *terribly* nice. I always feel like saying, 'Who, me?' It's a great pleasure. It does make life a little cushier. It's chic to say these things don't matter, but it's *terribly* nice to have the recognition."

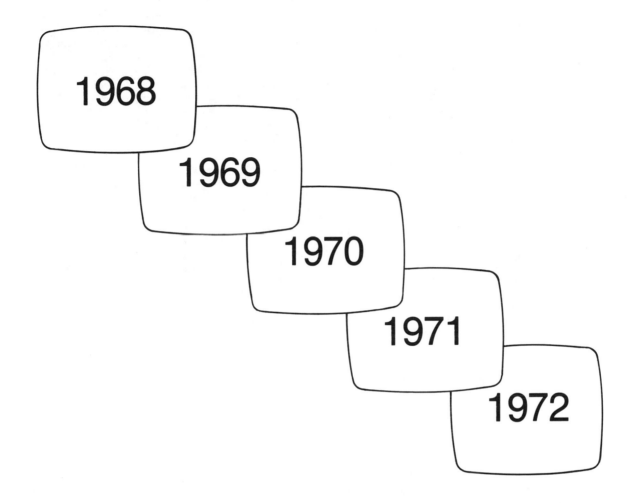

What the Negro Wants from TV

Sculpture by Ernie Lauser (Talone/LaBrasca)

A considered discussion at a time when some contend that the medium is enraging and frustrating black viewers

by Art Peters

There was a time, 15 years ago, even 10 years ago, when Negroes were a rarity in television and the inclusion of a colored actor or actress in drama or situation comedy in anything other than a menial servant's role was guaranteed to produce controversy, raging debate, angry reaction from Southern viewers and possible sponsor withdrawal.

Today, in this the enlightened age of civil rights, the barriers of race have been lowered and Negroes are gaining acceptance in television.

Unfortunately, they are gaining acceptance as *Negroes,* not as human beings. That is, they are seldom shown as rounded, breathing, living characters with whom the audience can become *really* involved.

Part of the problem is, of course, that television to a large extent mirrors American society, in which, despite substantial gains, the Negro still plays only a limited role.

This raises the key question of whether television should not make an effort to lead rather than just to keep up with the parade.

George Norford, high-ranking Negro executive with the Westinghouse Broadcasting Company, has this perceptive observation: "Television is doing a lot to improve the Negro image, but not nearly enough. When all of television's good deeds for Negroes are lumped together, they are still so infinitesimal they are almost lost in the over-all big picture.

"It's not enough for television merely to reflect the existing Negro subculture in its drama programs. Television can and must use its persuasiveness and power to create a new acceptance among whites of the Negro and a new awareness on the part of the Negro himself of his own ability and potential. Television could be the catalyst, the force that creates and promotes racial understanding. By merely keeping step with current social trends instead of taking the lead in seeking new horizons in race relations, television is missing out on a signal opportunity to contribute."

P. Jay Sidney, veteran Negro actor who has appeared in more than 200 television dramas, takes this position: "Negroes rarely get the opportunity to portray human beings on television. They are usually cast in the role of auxiliaries to white people. Their only reason for existence on the screen, their *raison d'être,* is for the benefit of white people in the story."

Bill Cosby, star of the espionage series *I Spy* and television's most celebrated Negro actor, has this to say: "Writers and producers seem to think you need a special reason for a role to be played by a Negro—that he has to pounce on someone or be pounced upon. Because of this, Hollywood has helped to promote a negative image of the black man. When a Negro comes on the screen, the audience immediately tenses up. They know they are about to witness some violence, whether physical, verbal or emotional. If someone were to make a film about a Negro who didn't have any great conflict because of his color, who loved and was loved by a black girl and raised a black family, the audience would come back to see it again, looking for some hidden meaning."

In this way two Negro actors, intimate with television and the movies, sum up not only the plight of Negro actors and actresses, but the problems of their flesh-and-blood counterparts in real life as well.

The fact is that many Negroes feel that only grudging desegregation has been achieved and that the real goal of integration remains tortuously beyond reach.

Walter Carroll, sales manager for KDIA, the San Francisco area's largest Negro radio station, has this to say: "There have been three civil-rights acts passed in the last 10 years, but it has not made *that* much difference."

What difference there *is,* and there is a difference, comes in the *number* of roles awarded to Negroes, a growth reflecting the growth in civil rights.

Negroes are, in fact, seen in a variety of dramatic roles on network programs. However, Norford is right when he says TV's acceptance of Negroes parallels that of society at large but doesn't blaze any new paths.

Unless they are cast as servants or entertainers, Negroes are rarely involved in dramatic scenes which show America at play, be they at country club dances or church socials.

Negroes are almost never cast as judges, airline pilots, boat captains, college presidents, cowboys, bank executives, salesmen, editors or engineers. Negroes are generally accepted in television dramas these days as policemen, teachers, FBI agents, soldiers, doctors, espionage agents, radio-and-electronics workers and detectives.

There are notable exceptions of course, as there are to most rules, but even when a Negro is cast in the role of an executive or professional man, his demeanor by necessity is usually servile or compliant, seldom domineering, harsh or superior.

And, ironically, the same ground rules which forbid Negroes to be cast as domineering executives usually prevent them from portraying criminals, unless, of course, they are penitent or remorseful.

In discussing these problems, actor Sidney referred to his testimony before a Congressional committee which, five years ago, was investigating charges of discrimination in the TV industry.

"It's been five long years," he declares, "but things haven't changed much for the black man in television. Casting directors have now latched onto the idea of placating civil-rights groups by placing a Negro in a key role here and there, perhaps as a policeman or a nurse. Earlier, the Negro was portrayed in films as a maid or a teeth-chattering, knee-knocking, 'Feet-don't-fail-me-now' flunky. But, even today, the Negro remains a servant, at least psychologically, in the movies and on television. His roles are a little more sophisticated, to be sure, but he is nevertheless a servant, a type of auxiliary to white people."

Sidney cites his own experience last spring when he was hired as a regular in an important supporting role on the popular daytime soap opera *As the World Turns.*

"I was supposed to be a research physician in that series," he says, "and yet, emotionally and dramatically, I did not exist as a person. My whole function in those 14 segments was getting a white boy out of jail. I was a nonperson in the plot, a one-dimensional figure with no life of my own. I didn't have any problems. There were no things about which I was personally glad or sad, nothing toward which I personally aspired. I had no past, no future, no family. I existed only for that white boy. I was, in other words, an auxiliary, not a human being."

His tone suddenly becomes vehement. "Hell!" he explodes. "Life is not just going to your laboratory every day."

Unlike most of his contemporaries, Sidney has not been content merely to voice his concern about the status quo. During the past five years he has launched a one-man crusade against the industry, picketing television studios which don't hire Negro actors and actresses in representative numbers and buying ads in trade publications excoriating advertising agencies and sponsors for failure to use Negroes in televised commercials.

Despite his militancy, Sidney is one of the milder voices in the growing clamor against discrimination in television programming.

Fifty-one-year-old Florynce Kennedy, outspoken Negro woman lawyer, who for many years has been active in civil-rights endeavors in New York City, says, "Let's face it, the situation has reached the crisis stage."

She believes that millions of black Americans subconsciously regard television in the same manner as the downtrodden peasants in some foreign country might regard a ruthless dictator who flaunts his power and wealth while his subjects grovel in poverty and destitution.

"Television," she declares, "feeds the frustrations and angers of the black masses by showing them a way of life they may never enjoy, a world from which they are forever barred. Although the ambitious Negro through sheer perseverance may rise above his circumstances and attain a position and money enabling him to buy the luxuries of life—a new car, a boat, a fancy home with swimming pool—he remains an outcast from the mainstream of society, unable, because of his color, to actually belong. Television, by excluding the Negro from most of its programs, helps to reinforce this image of rejection."

Paradoxically, the sound and fury are mounting against television at a time when the industry appears to be doing more than ever before in the Negro interest. Television's highest-ranking executives, convinced that most of the verbal brickbats are being thrown by a few misguided, uninformed and possibly envious persons, speak in wounded, exasperated tones of continuing Negro protests.

"There are five times as many Negroes appearing on television in feature roles today as there were only a few years ago," points out one well-known producer. "Frankly," he declares, "most of this fuss is being kicked up by Black Power groups. I think that the responsible Negro leaders are aware of the tremendous strides that Negroes have made on television."

The "responsible" Negro leaders are indeed aware of *some* progress, but they are not at all happy about it. Whitney Young, executive director of the National Urban League and a recognized moderate on civil rights, made this observation several weeks ago: "Perhaps stations would be more aware of their responsibility if they employed more Negroes. Federal law requires that any business holding a government contract must furnish proof of fair employment practices. Yet the Federal Communications Commission regularly grants valuable licenses to television and radio stations without such requirement, even though there are some notorious violations."

George Norford, who, in addition to his position at Westinghouse, coordinates the activities of the Broadcast Skills Bank, an agency developed by the networks in conjunction with the Urban League to recruit, train and employ Negroes for the broadcast industry, contends that progress is being made behind the cameras. He says: "Negroes on TV cannot all be Bill Cosbys or Sammy Davises or Nichelle Nicholses. Some have got to be just plain Joe Smith, technician; Harry Brown, accountant; Bob Jackson, writer. This is where roughly 92 percent of Negroes employed in TV are. Indeed, this is where most people employed in the industry are."

Another hopeful note is sounded by Mike Dann, vice president of programming for CBS-TV. "The Negro has achieved status and he has attained the highest responsible positions in American life," Dann declares, "and if we in television are accurate writers and producers, we will show the Negro in various occupations and endeavors, not for the sake of recognition, but for the sake of accuracy."

Although Dann believes that television is slowly but surely getting around to fairly representing Negroes in dramatic roles, he agrees with Sidney that television continually fails to portray the Negro as a flesh-and-blood human being. "I think the real problem is creating dramas which really make you care about the Negro as a person," he says. "We do not have enough dramas in which the Negro portrays the kind of character with whom you can really identify. I think it is because the Negro is cast all too frequently in the role of a helpful person in solving someone else's problem, a type of person whom you don't really care about as a human being and who functions solely in support of the hero in the play."

The subject is obviously a sensitive one at the networks. At NBC, Mort Werner, vice president in charge of programming, declined to discuss it at all, sending word down through an aide, Charles Smith, that the network prefers to stand on its record.

Smith, in turn, pointed out that NBC has "pioneered" in developing such Negro television stars as Leslie Uggams, Nichelle Nichols, Bill Cosby and Don Mitchell. Next year, Smith said, Diahann Carroll may be the first Negro woman star of a weekly television drama series, if present plans jell and a pilot film she recently made is picked up by NBC.

Significantly, neither Cosby, who already is an NBC star, nor Miss Carroll, who soon may be, is satisfied with television's treatment of the Negro in drama roles.

In a recent first-person newspaper article, Cosby declared that Negro children in big-city ghettos have few black heroes to pattern their lives after other than the dope peddlers and pimps who wear diamond rings and drive flashy cars and who are impressive because they have found a way to beat the system.

Noting that most Negro doctors, lawyers and other professional men move out of the ghettos once they attain a measure of success, Cosby feels that the image of these hard-working, ambitious, successful black men is lost to Negro children.

"It is the responsibility of TV and films to build a better image for the Negro," Cosby insists. "I see no reason why there can't be films with Negro cowboys who can shoot and ride and do all these things that people respect in a cowboy. Why can't there be black pilots in war stories?"

Miss Carroll echoes Cosby's sentiments. "It is important that Negro children have symbols with which they can identify," she declares. "They must be taught to have pride in their blackness, and television can help them establish this identity."

Civil-rights leaders and performers in the industry agree that as long as television continues—by ignoring the credentials of Negroes as human beings—to emulate the white society it serves, the medium will remain a negative force operating against the interests of the black man. The dilemma is perhaps best summed up in the words of actor P. Jay Sidney:

"The image that Negroes have had since they were first dragged off of slave ships has been that they are something less than human. As long as this image persists, it will be impossible for any civil-rights laws that are passed to be enforced. When a Negro applies for a job, he not only has to qualify, he has to get past the image the white interviewer has of him. That image may have been reinforced only last night on TV."

IRREVERENT
is the word for the Smothers Brothers

The hip, exuberant pair has created
good ratings and severe headaches
for its network

by Dwight Whitney

There's Tommy Smothers. What a gas! There's his one blue eye and his one green eye leering out in glorious CBS color. There's the familiar flat-footed stance, the impish little-boy look known and loved by millions. There's that goofily ingratiating expression which audiences so often mistake for underthink. Underthink? Tommy is no underthinker. He is consciously playing

out what surely must be, in a thousand variations throughout history, the oldest of the anti-Establishment jokes. He is Adam in the Adam and Eve sketch. The serpent sorely tempts him with the apple. Suddenly a thunderous voice is heard off-stage. "That's a no-no!" it booms.

The "no-no" came within a silly millimeter of not

(Ken Whitmore)

making it to the air, just as Tommy and Dick Smothers suspected it would. The weekly dictum from Program Practices known by the Smothers as "the Big Daddy memo"—which holds absolute dominion over what can and can't be seen on CBS—came down from upstairs right on schedule.

"The line, 'stared into her vestibule,' is suggestive and should be deleted," it read in part. "The Apple sketch . . . will be acceptable only after deletion of 'That's a no-no' delivered by the disembodied voice. It can only be interpreted as the Voice of God and as such must be considered irreverent."

Irreverent! That is the name for the Smotherses, exuberant young proprietors of *The Smothers Brothers Comedy Hour*. Theirs is the hip, youthful, where-it's-at, anti-Daddy Cartwright TV show, the antidote for the folksy, old-shoe type of entertainment currently dominating the charts. "We're what's happening," Tommy says flatly. "We were always what's happening." "Yeah," says Dickie. "Even in that old series—the one that flopped—we were happening. We just made the mistake of listening to people who *thought* they knew what our comedy was all about."

Last spring, when their new variety show temporarily knocked off the theretofore invulnerable *Bonanza*, which competes in the same time slot, the network was astonished and delighted. But traumatized. The bosses had not quite realized what they were getting into. Their boyishly charming new ratings champions upended everything near and dear to the Establishment, challenging long-established taboos all the way from hippies to heroes, sex to civil rights, censorship to religion, the war on poverty to Smokey the Bear.

An old-fashioned minstrel show got in some groovy licks on draft-dodging: "Why does a chicken cross the border?" "To avoid the draft, Mr. Bones!" One sketch, cancelled out on several Texas stations, depicted the President as moving his ranch to Washington in a kind of "One Man's Country" concept of the Presidency, complete with mammoth barbecues and 10-gallon hats. George Washington's chat with Betsy Ross became "mindblowing"—a word Program Practices invariably blue-pencils out of the script. "It's OK to satirize the President," said the Big Daddy memo, "as long as you do so with respect."

The boys take particular delight in their weekly "editorial," delivered dead-pan by their second banana, Pat Paulsen. The one on censorship was especially wicked and might just as well have been addressed to the Program Practices department.

"We are not against censorship because we realize that there is always the danger of something being said," it read. "And even worse, of it being heard. . . . They have the right to censor what you hear. The Bill of Rights says nothing about Freedom of Hearing. This, of course, takes a lot of the fun out of Freedom of Speech. Ha, ha, ha. Without the censors we would all be at the mercy of the warped minds of the television industry."

Young audiences relished the put-on. More conservative folk tended to take it straight, even when written in double-talk. One such editorial, on gun laws, drew 10,000 requests for copies. Always the boys are careful to maintain what Saul Ilson and Ernie Chambers, their producers, call "the Nice Nephews image." They come at each joke ("Not really a joke, but an attitude," says Chambers) as innocently as lambs. Tommy comes off as the befuddled but well-meaning man-child, hopelessly hung-up over the complexities of modern life, and thus beyond reproach.

Unhappily, the network bosses don't always see it that way. There have been a few letters—10 times as many complaints, the brass notes gloomily, as Red Skelton receives in a week, all blaming the network, never those "nice boys." No good to say this is infinitesimal considering the 30,000,000-odd who watch the show every week. "Around here," says Dick, "150 letters is a catastrophe." The network has the audiences, the agencies, the sponsors, the stockholders, the pressure groups to think about. "When we wanted to support Mothers For Peace last Mother's Day," says Dick, "Program Practices said we mustn't 'influence legislation.' "

Diplomatic mediator in disputed matters is the vice president in charge of West Coast programming, Perry Lafferty—known as "the Smothers Brothers' U Thant." Lafferty, along with programming chief Mike Dann, had thought the boys were "miscast" in their first series and that they could make a dent in *Bonanza* by going after the young (15–30) audience. "We were sure they would like the irreverence of these apple-cheeked fellows," Lafferty explains. "But they turned out to be a little more topical than we had envisioned. The network is for what they are doing. It merely becomes a matter of degree."

The brothers won some and they lost some. They won the battle of the no-no. They won the battle of Tommy's zipper caught in the tablecloth, an intensely human predicament that drew some frowns in the Bible Belt. They lost the battle of Elaine May, in which she and Tommy had planned to play censors who become too enamored of what they're censoring. Sometimes, it was a dead heat. In one instance, Barbara Eden and Tommy set out to play, as Dickie was careful to explain, two "sexually enlightened" college students. The joke was that at no point was anything said about sex at all, much less anything sexy. Still the letters poured in: "Don't let the boys talk about sex!" Sometimes they played a little game with the network, deliberately writing naughty words and situations into scripts knowing they would be cut but giving them a bargaining point later on.

Ironically, they never intended their comedy to take

this turn. While they considered themselves groovy cats as college entertainers at San Jose State, in the coffee houses, and later as recording artists and nightclub entertainers, they avoided topical comedy. "We prided ourselves on *not* taking any political stands," explains Tommy. "Then two years ago I began to get upset every time I read the paper."

"When we began this show, we didn't know what a Smothers comedy hour was supposed to be," Ilson adds. "I don't think Tommy did either. It just sort of grew."

Tommy remembers not being able to resist the LBJ jokes—"those little picky Bob Hope–type jokes which aren't really daring but just seem that way." Then one day the whole style of comedy came to full fruition in a number called "McNamara's Integrated Band." The brothers created a situation in which they set out to sing the most uncontroversial, inoffensive numbers they could think of, because, after all, they were "just entertainers." They began with "Potatoes Are Cheaper," but it turned out that it is entirely possible to interpret this grand old song as a politically loaded ode to the Depression. Likewise "Chicago," which they discovered to be a thinly disguised social comment on "the shame of the slums." Bilked and frustrated, they tried "McNamara's Band," certain it couldn't possibly offend anyone. But it turned out there was nobody Jewish in the band.

As their success snowballed, so did their aspirations. They took pains to pack the operation with turned-on Smothers-type talent. Pat Paulsen came from the coffee houses. So did an endless parade of rock groups and folk singers. So did an increasing number of writers. Soon the young Turks began to outnumber the old guard, and the management was discomfited to find that its high-priced writing staff included an ex-night-club comic, an ex-half of a comedy singing duo, and an ex–social worker.

Tommy was off on a new kick. He believed that old-line TV people weren't using what they had. "They say they're stifled," he said to me one morning. "Can't do this, can't do that. Why not blow their minds? It's the ultimate goal." Tommy pushed for the extended use of fast zooms, quick cuts, overlays, reversed polarities, and the chroma-key process, for that instant psychedelic effect. He met instant resistance from nonpsychedelic technicians and went through three soundmen in his search for "that subliminal thing that makes a show a little better." He installed a monitor facing the stage so he could check the rehearsal action, and a tape machine in the dressing room so he could do the same for the dress.

This brought him into friendly disagreement with Ilson and Chambers. "We've been at odds a lot," Tommy says. "We want to do this thing totally. Saul and Ernie are not as far behind as the Establishment, but they're not where we are." It also brought about the firing last summer of Stan Harris, the show's first director.

They are now working on their third director and next year will have a new producer. Ilson and Chambers will leave at the end of this season. The boys left no question what the trouble was. "We could be more effective as [full-time] producers," Tommy says. "Right now our energies are split. So we're doing only half a job, and end up being only about two-thirds as effective as we should be."

"We control the show," says Dick. "We have less garbage than most shows. We spend the bread. We see that it's written six, eight minutes short to take care of the groovy ad-libs. We insist on the uniqueness of our comedy."

Tommy says merely, "Performers should reflect the times they live in. Why shouldn't TV do wild things? Because producers work in fear. Fear of losing their jobs. We are not as afraid as they are, and that's where it's at."

Tommy's only fears are that he is getting too slick, that he is losing the character which, he says, "grew out of that awkward age around 15 when a kid just doesn't know what to do and tries to cover." No such fears assail Dick. He is much more the pragmatist and homebody. Married to his college sweetheart, his family is of consuming importance to him. He often spends an hour washing his favorite car—a 1956 Porsche Speedster, "the groovy flower model"—before coming to the studio. While Tommy worries, Dick naps.

Tommy, recently divorced, is a swinger with the bachelor apartment, the house at the beach, and the blondes to go with them. Dick recently moved out of a $120,000 Beverly Hills house and into a $55,000 one in Woodland Hills so his three kids would have a neighborhood to play in. Tommy is more likely to involve himself in intellectual or political activism. Last November, for instance, he was scheduled to make a benefit appearance in San Francisco in behalf of Edward Keating, the anti-war candidate for Congress in the Shirley Temple Black district of San Mateo. However, because of his heavy schedule, he had to bow out.

Generally speaking, it is Tommy who gets the play in the press. This is because Dick can give the impression of being bland and sometimes a little distant, and because Tommy is forever doing the talking. Tommy is fiercely protective of his brother and calls him "the most underrated man in TV." Yet Dick is all there, and is considered by the professionals as one of the best straight men in the business. "Dick listens more eloquently than most people talk," says Ilson.

The brothers remain fiercely loyal to each other. "Tommy and I," sighs Dick, "we could produce one helluva groovy show together."

They already have produced a "helluva groovy" show. It is a suspense story. Will a couple of cutups from Redondo Beach, California, really succeed in making the world safe from the Big Daddy memo? Or will they overplay their hand and let all that beautiful talent slide off onto some remote psychedelic nowheresville? The answer may be a long time coming. Meanwhile, one thing is certain. TV comedy is more alive for their presence.

[*The Smothers Brothers Comedy Hour was cancelled by CBS on June 8, 1969.—Ed.*]

Review   by Cleveland Amory

"ROWAN AND MARTIN'S LAUGH-IN"

This show is what *That Was the Week That Was* wasn't. Where the latter was generally too cute and smug, and often too labored as well, *Rowan and Martin's Laugh-In* is a genuine, ingenuous breath of fresh fare. And this despite the fact that there are two real drawbacks here. One is that the show is too long. Unlike so many half-hour shows on the air, particularly the taut, dramatic ones, which should either not be on at all or should be on for a full hour, this one is a half-hour too long. With humor, an hour is—well, an hour. And the same jokes which in the first half-hour might have turned us on, in the second all too often turn us, and the set, off.

The other drawback is that the show stars the Messrs. Dan Rowan and Dick Martin and yet their spots are, curiously, the least successful. While put-down man Dan wears well, put-on man Dick is more often than not a bit much with which to put up. Take, for instance, his John Wayne hang-up. We like running gags as much as the next man, but we demand that they keep, if not running, at least moving. Or take Dick telling Dan about his trip to Rome and standing on the spot where Caesar killed Brutus. "Caesar didn't kill Brutus," says Dan. "Oh," says Dick, "I'm glad he pulled through." "No, no," Dan goes on, "you're historically incorrect. Brutus killed Caesar." "I heard it," says Dick, "the other way around." "You heard," says Dan, "that Caesar killed Brutus?" "That's funny," ends Dick, "so did I."

This, actually, is a fairly typical sample of their routines, and the trouble was, as a put-on, it was just not well enough—well, put on. Nonetheless, outside of these criticisms, there is so much to be commended here we hardly know where to begin. The pace is wonderfully fast and the mixtures are deft—particularly those of seemingly live stuff with taped spots, the cameos with the crossovers, as well as the celebrities with the civilians. Even the music is worth mentioning—it's excellent. As for the various features (New Talent Showcase, Mod Mod World, *Laugh-In* news, etc.) they are always fresh—and frequently hilarious. And if, in the blackouts, we sometimes get one too many De Gaulle or British jokes, still the level is extraordinarily high. We like all the regulars—Judy Carne, Eileen Brennan, Goldie Hawn, Henry Gibson, Gary Owens, Jack Riley, Roddy Maude-Roxby, Joanne Worley, et al.—but if we have to name our favorite, it's Miss Worley. "Boris," she says, "says capitalism doesn't work. But then, neither does Boris." Finally, even when *Laugh-In* does an oldie, it is so well done you love it all over again—witness the wonderful marriage bit: "If Dinah Shore married John Byner, she'd be Dinah Byner," "If Ida Lupino married Don Ho, she'd be Ida Ho," "If Sybil Burton married Ish Kabbible, she'd be Sybil Kabbible," etc.

All in all, A for effort, B for performance and C for—see it.

"THERE NEED BE NO APOLOGY, NO LAMENT"

Television, says an FCC Commissioner, is performing a great service in helping us achieve a common culture

by Lee Loevinger

IN DEFENSE OF TELEVISION
Third of a Series

TV Guide has published numerous articles critical of television and will continue to do so whenever criticism is warranted. The purpose of this current series, however, is to analyze the beneficial effects television has had on our world and its citizens. The authors, therefore, have been asked expressly to limit themselves to a discussion of these positive aspects, even though they may also have some negative attitudes about television and its performance.

Maybe television really isn't very important—it doesn't necessarily influence people just because they watch it for hours on end. That is about the most charitable opinion expressed by six eminent intellectuals writing in TV Guide in 1966. Similar derogatory views appear almost daily in newspapers and magazines.

Meanwhile millions of people, a large part of the population, spend every evening watching the tube. A recent survey disclosed that only 14 percent of slum homes in one large Eastern city took newspapers, but 100 percent had television sets.

What's going on, and is it good or bad? A rational approach recognizes two separate questions here. The first: What is television actually doing? The second: What should it be doing?

In the voluminous writing on the subject, there has been little effort to separate these questions. Most critics are so anxious to tell us what they think television should be that they neglect to examine what it actually is.

A fairly comprehensive review of what has been written shows five general theories of broadcasting:

First was the hobby theory. When we were winding wire coils on old cereal boxes, making condensers (capacitors) out of tinfoil and waxed paper, using "crystals" and "cat whiskers," and listening on earphones, the real joy of radio was getting the most distant stations. A boy in St. Paul, Minnesota, thrilled to hear KDKA simply because it was in Pittsburgh. After World War II, much of the interest in television was the novelty of getting a picture in your own home. In those days people enjoyed manipulation of the device as much as programs, and broadcasting was more a hobby than a means of mass communication. Radio is still a hobby for more than a quarter-million licensed amateurs; but most of us have long since become more interested in programs.

When broadcasting declined as a hobby, it grew as a news medium. In the early 1930s newspaper publishers tried to prevent broadcasting of news. A separate radio news service was established, but finally publishers conceded the rights of broadcasters, and news wire services were offered to radio stations. Public reliance on broadcasting has grown since then until now a Roper survey indicates more people look to television as a primary news source than to newspapers. This had led numerous observers to the view that the journalistic function is the principal and proper role of broadcasting.

Others see the journalistic theory as emphasizing mere news reporting too much, while neglecting social influence. They point to the vast audience of broadcasting, larger than any other medium in history both in numbers and percentage of population, and claim this offers a chance for great social influence. Since social problems are now so urgent, this leads to the conclusion that broadcasting is, or should be, an instrument of social reform. This view sees television as a means of doing quickly and easily what home, school, church and state have been struggling to do slowly and painfully for years. A similar view is official in some countries, especially communist ones, which subject broadcasting to strict government control because of its supposed social and political influence.

Recently some philosophers and scientists have rejected the journalistic and social-reform theories in an effort to discover what broadcasting actually is, rather than starting with their own ideas of what it ought to be. The best-known of these is Marshall McLuhan, a Canadian professor now at Fordham, who has become the Billy Rose, or perhaps the P. T. Barnum, of the academic world.

McLuhan's thesis and slogan is, "The medium is the message." This means that each medium changes the environment or creates a new environment, and consequences of this change are more significant than the messages carried. McLuhan regards all media as extensions of human senses, and points to effects of such sense extensions through printing, radio and television. McLuhan says mass media created "the public," and argues that this fact is more important than any particular message.

Most recently William Stephenson, a social scientist at the University of Missouri, has suggested "the play theory of mass communications," based on novel, technical and ingenious methods of investigating and measuring attitudes. Stephenson says play is activity that is self-sufficient and pursued for the pleasure in it, while work involves effort undertaken for some ulterior purpose, such as production of goods, ideas or profit.

Mass communication is engaged in for pleasure, not for information or improvement. For example, people look first in the newspaper to read about events they have been involved in and already know about, as a football game they have seen. This shows they read newspapers not for information but as play. The "fill," the ordinary content, of mass communications is neither debasing nor escapism, but a buffer against anxieties and tensions of modern conditions. Culture and national character are formed by songs, gossip, sports, dances, competition and other forms of communications pleasure. The role of mass communications is to maximize communications pleasure and individual freedom in a world of increasing social controls.

Each of these theories has some useful and accurate observations, but none is wholly adequate to explain obvious facts about television and radio. These are:

First, that broadcasting, especially television, is the most popular communications medium in history. It is the first truly mass medium reaching all classes and groups in society.

Second, American-type broadcasting has universal appeal. Even such typically American programs as Westerns are popular throughout the world, as is American popular music. Public demand has forced even government-operated broadcasting systems to present such programming.

Third, broadcasting is increasingly performing the journalistic function of news reporting for a growing segment of the public, while literacy and prosperity are increasing.

Fourth, television arouses strong emotional reactions in both critics and public. Strangely, those who say they dislike television seem to be as regular in their watching and passionate in their views as those who like it.

Fifth, television is largely disdained by intellectuals, both genuine and would-be. Some publications do not consider it respectable to write about television without disparaging it.

Sixth, broadcasting has become more a part of ordinary life than any other means of communication, except possibly talking. It is clearly a component of our common culture.

Testing the five theories we have described against these facts requires a more detailed analysis than is possible here, but such analysis shows that each is consistent with some but not all of the facts. The difficulty is that each theory has focused on one or a few aspects rather than the whole complex picture. We can better understand broadcasting in modern society if we regard it as an electronic mirror that reflects a vague or ambiguous image. As society is complex and many-faceted, broadcasting reflects a variety of images. These are never precisely focused and completely clear.

Society is reflected in the media mainly as an organized group or groups. But the audience watches as individuals. Looking at a blurred or vague image, different individuals see different things. This is because everyone engages in some projection, a common psychological process which consists of attributing our own attitudes, ideas or feelings to perceptions we get from the environment.

Psychologists use projection in the Rorschach "ink-blot" test by showing a series of ink blots to different persons and asking each to say what they mean. The different things people "see" in ink blots indicate ideas, attitudes and feelings of the observers.

All of us interpret observations according to our attitudes. To a child, "Alice in Wonderland" and "Gulliver's Travels" are stories of adventure; to an adult they are charming and fanciful allegories. Similarly, television programs mean different things to different people, and mean different things to one person at different times, depending upon attitude and mood.

Regarding television as an ambiguous mirror reflecting a slightly blurred image of society in which each viewer sees, by projection, his own vision of society and self, explains the observable facts. Television is popular because, as a reflection of society, it is responsive and adapted to mass attitudes and tastes. It increasingly performs the journalistic function because it is immediate, personal and comprehensive. Television is often better than personal observation, as it can go further, faster and see more, yet conveys a sense of personal presence and participation.

There is emotional reaction to television because by projection each person sees some of his ego in his perception, so he reacts as though statements about television were about himself—which they are so far as they involve his impression of television.

A simple test shows how projection involves ego and emotion. Hide and watch people passing a mirror. Almost no one can resist looking at his own image, and few fail to show some reaction. Or try taking pictures and showing them to the subject. People love to see pictures of themselves but never say they are flattered.

The intellectuals are alienated by television because they want to see images of themselves, as they think they are, and instead they see images of the common man and the mass of society. But television is an element of our culture because it shows things of common and universal interest. National culture is not found in museums or formed by graduate schools or universities. It is composed of common habits and patterns of living of people in daily activities, and of the common interest in entertainment, sports, news, and even advertising. The "fill" or ordinary run of material in everyday broadcasting is a more important part of common culture than the occasional artistic triumph or esthetic masterpiece. Whether or not anyone thinks this is the way things should be, observation shows that this is the way things are. The "reflective-projective theory" which regards television as an ambiguous mirror in which each viewer sees an image of both society and self is simply descriptive of known facts.

This view does suggest the role television is best adapted to serve. One of our most pressing needs today is to strengthen our common culture and sense of national unity and purpose. The only media that reach enough people or touch people intimately enough to achieve this are radio and television. Whether television lifts us to esthetic or intellectual heights or elevates our artistic standards is less important than whether it helps us achieve a common culture and sense of national unity and purpose.

It is more likely to do this by responding day after day to the wants and tastes of the million-strong masses than by straining for approval of scornful intellectuals. There need be no apology and should be no lament for a broadcasting industry which provides the mass of people with programs they watch and enjoy daily. Disdainful talk about television seeking "the lowest common denominator" misses the important point. Culture is not arithmetic, and the cultural denominator of popular programs may be the highest, not the lowest, that is truly common. The important point is television does achieve a *common* denominator in society.

If there were less programming it might be of better quality. But the character of life depends upon everyday experience more than upon great infrequent ceremonial occasions. Amiability at the breakfast table is more important to a happy marriage than design of the wedding gown.

As television lets us share daily a common reflection of society and helps us see a similar vision of our relationship to society, it builds a common culture to unite our country. This now appears to be its natural function and highest ideal. It is enough.

Drawing by John Huehnergarth

by Dick Hobson

Southerners watch Westerns.
Eggheads dig Gleason.
Literates prefer Don Adams.
Less-literates go for Jim Nabors.
Blue collar workers choose countrified situation comedies.
Affluents prefer movies to anything else.
Lawrence Welk is boss with the Geritol Tribe.
Sophisticates pick specials.
Everybody likes Tennessee Ernie Ford.

If it sounds like plain common sense, it is that and more. It all derives from highly sophisticated demographic surveys designed to show just *who* watches *what*. Gone are the days when it's enough to say that a program rates in the Top 10 or 20 or Top 40. Today's sponsors want to know the "demographics."

These elaborate sampling surveys would never have been undertaken were it not for the insistent demands of TV merchandising. Yet the facts themselves remain uncontaminated by commercialism. The findings are sound sociology. We can forget consumer products for the moment and focus on the Sociology of Viewing Preferences—who watches what.

The following "demographics," determined by the A. C. Nielsen Co. and excluding specials, reflect the tastes of America over a six-week period from October 23 to December 3, 1967.

First, consider the U.S. as a whole*:

U.S. TOP 10

1. Lucy Show
2. Andy Griffith
3. Bonanza
4. Red Skelton
5. Gunsmoke
6. Family Affair
7. Jackie Gleason
8. Gomer Pyle
9. Saturday Movies
10. { Beverly Hillbillies / Friday Movies

Here we see that there are three "countrified" comedies (*Griffith*, *Pyle* and *Hillbillies*), two Westerns (*Bonanza* and *Gunsmoke*), two variety shows (one "countrified"—*Skelton;* one "citified"—*Gleason*), two family comedies (*Lucy* and *Family Affair*), and two movie nights. This is just a start. Industry wants to know the viewer's age, sex, geographical location, income, education, occupation and a lot more.

Nielsen begins by breaking down viewing preferences by geographical region. For contrast, consider the Top 10 ranking shows for the South and the Northeast:

TOP 10 IN SOUTH	TOP 10 IN NORTHEAST
1. Gunsmoke	1. Jackie Gleason
2. Bonanza	2. Smothers Bros.
3. Andy Griffith	3. Dean Martin
4. Lucy Show	4. Ed Sullivan
5. Gomer Pyle	5. Friday Movies
6. Red Skelton	6. Saturday Movies
7. Family Affair	7. Lucy Show
8. Virginian	8. Thursday Movies
9. Daniel Boone	9. Tuesday Movies
10. Beverly Hillbillies	10. My Three Sons

The South's Top 10 is similar to the U.S. as a whole, with eight shows in common. Conspicuously absent are movies, originally made for a more sophisticated thea-

---

* All data and rankings on pages 148–149 (left) of this article are copyrighted by A. C. Nielsen Company, 1968; all data and rankings on page 149 (right) are copyrighted by Home Testing Institute/TvQ Inc., 1968.

---

ter audience. Also missing is *Gleason*, an urban taste. In their place are two more Westerns.

The Top 10 in the Northeast has only four shows in common with the U.S. nationally. *Out* are all the countrified situation comedies and Westerns. *In* are the citified variety shows which occupy the top four places. *Gleason* leads the pack. The Northeast has two more movie nights.

Comparing Northeast and South, the two regions have only one show in common: *Lucy*. For the rest, their tastes are dissimilar. In movies, it's 4 to 0. In variety shows it's 4 to 1.

So much for geography. Breakdowns by income give us a new look:

TOP 10 FOR INCOMES UNDER $5000	TOP 10 FOR INCOMES $10,000 & OVER
1. Lucy Show	1. Saturday Movies
2. Gunsmoke	2. Dean Martin
3. Andy Griffith	3. Friday Movies
4. Red Skelton	4. Andy Griffith
5. Lawrence Welk	5. Thursday Movies
6. Bonanza	6. Smothers Bros.
7. Gomer Pyle	7. Family Affair
8. Family Affair	8. Jackie Gleason
9. { Ed Sullivan / Virginian	9. Tuesday Movies
	10. FBI

Tastes of the lower income group are similar to the U.S. as a whole except that movies are out, *Gleason* is out, and *Welk* and *Sullivan* are in.

The most conspicuous feature of the upper income group is the prominence of movies—four of the Top 10, including the No. 1 show. The upper income groups have three citified variety shows and the first dramatic show to appear in these ratings, *The F.B.I.*

In comparing the two income groups, the uppers prefer movies and drama, the lowers prefer Westerns and situation comedies. In the variety field, the uppers prefer *Gleason, Martin* and *Smothers,* the lowers prefer *Skelton*, *Welk* and *Sullivan*.

Education changes the picture again:

TOP 10: GRADE SCHOOL EDUCATION	TOP 10: 1+ YEARS OF COLLEGE
1. Lucy Show	1. Saturday Movies
2. Andy Griffith	2. Mission: Impossible
3. Gunsmoke	3. Smothers Bros.
4. Red Skelton	4. Dean Martin
5. Bonanza	5. Jackie Gleason
6. Gomer Pyle	6. Tuesday Movies
7. Family Affair	7. Bewitched
8. Lawrence Welk	8. NFL Football
9. Virginian	9. Thursday Movies
10. Jackie Gleason	10. Get Smart

The Top 10 for the grade school educated mostly follows the national rankings except for the exclusion of movies and the addition of *Lawrence Welk* and a Western.

The Top 10 for the college educated, however, is dissimilar. *Gleason* and movies are all they have in common with the U.S. as a whole. Next to *Saturday Movies,* the highest rated show is a drama, *Mission: Impossible.* Their two situation comedies, *Bewitched* and *Get Smart,* are considered more sophisticated than *Lucy* or *Pyle.*

Classifying TV households by education of the head of the household, the Nielsen Company estimates there are 15.3 million homes in the grade school category and 12.7 million in the one-plus years of college. Grade school types prefer Andy Griffith and Jim Nabors; college types prefer Elizabeth Montgomery and Don Adams. The grade school educated go for *Skelton* and *Welk;* collegers like the *Smothers Brothers* and *Dean Martin.*

The blue collar Top 10 generally goes along with the U.S. as a whole, but the white collar Top 10 has more movies, citified variety shows, and a drama, *Mission: Impossible.* Blue collars comprise 48 percent of all TV households; white collars 36 percent.

TOP 10: BLUE COLLAR	TOP 10: WHITE COLLAR
1. Andy Griffith	1. Saturday Movies
2. Lucy Show	2. Dean Martin
3. Bonanza	3. Andy Griffith
4. Red Skelton	4. Smothers Bros.
5. Beverly Hillbillies	5. Mission: Impossible
6. Gunsmoke	6. Jackie Gleason
7. Gomer Pyle	7. Tuesday Movies
8. Bewitched	8. Family Affair
9. Green Acres	9. Thursday Movies
10. {Family Affair / Sat. Movies}	10. {Friday Movies / Lucy Show}

The blues have two Westerns in their Top 10 to the whites' none, four country comedies to the whites' one. Both like *Lucy* and *Andy Griffith.*

There is strikingly little overlap between the Top 10s of the South and of the Northeast (one show), between those of the Under $5000 and the Over $10,000 (two shows), between the Grade School Only and the One-Plus Years of College (one show), and between the Blue Collar and the White Collar (four shows). The next time one hears the phrase "Top 10," it is fair to ask *which* Top 10.

On the other hand, there is a great deal of overlap in the Top 10s of the South, the Under-$5000 income group, the Grade School educated, and the Blue Collar workers, which we shall consider together under the heading "Just Plain Folks." Almost as much overlap is found among the Northeast, Over-$10,000 income group, One-Plus Years of College, and White Collar workers, an aggregation which some advertisers call "Sophisticates."

A goodly number of "specials" were aired during the six-week period under study. They were excluded. Were these taken into account, the Top 10s of the Sophisticates would include between five and eight specials; the Top 10s of Just Plain Folks would include only one or two. The Tennessee Ernie Ford special is the only one that consistently scored as well with both.

Further demographic breakdowns are regularly conducted by the Home Testing Institute of Manhasset, Long Island, and expressed as numerical "TvQ" scores. Whereas the *Nielsen* ratings are based on a sample of 1155 homes and show merely whether the household TV set is switched on and, if so, which channel the set is tuned to, *TvQ* scores are based on a survey of 2000 individuals in 750 families and go further to measure attentiveness and degree of enthusiasm for programs.

The shows in TvQ's Top 10s are generally more sophisticated than those in Nielsen's because they are programs the viewers are interested in rather than possibly just the best of a bad lot—the least bad at the time period. Significantly, Nielsen's two big rating leaders, *Andy Griffith* and *Lucy,* are entirely absent from TvQ's Top 10s. In fact, *The Lucy Show* fails to appear on a single TvQ *Top 20* breakdown.

The following demographics, supplied by HTI, reflect the tastes of selected age and sex categories in November 1967, during the period under discussion:

TOP 10 AMONG CHILDREN 6–11	TOP 10 AMONG TEENAGERS 12–17
1. Flying Nun	1. Guns of Will Sonnett
2. Second Hundred Years	2. Second Hundred Years
3. Family Affair	3. Monkees
4. Monkees	4. Star Trek
5. Gomer Pyle	5. Smothers Brothers
6. Bewitched	6. Flying Nun
7. Beverly Hillbillies	7. Saturday Movies
8. Gentle Ben	8. I Spy
9. Off to See the Wizard	9. Dragnet
10. Walt Disney	10. Family Affair

TOP 10 FOR ADULTS 18–34	TOP 10 FOR ADULTS OVER 50
1. Saturday Movies	1. Lawrence Welk
2. Friday Movies	2. CBS News
3. Thursday Movies	3. Bonanza
4. Wed. Movies	4. Walt Disney
5. Mission: Impossible	5. Virginian
6. Tuesday Movies	6. Family Affair
7. Dean Martin	7. Gunsmoke
8. I Spy	8. Dean Martin
9. Sunday Movies	9. Gomer Pyle
10. High Chaparral	10. Daniel Boone

From these Top 10s, as well as from other HTI Top 10s that fill out the total age and sex picture, some new sociological perspectives emerge:

Family Affair appeals to children, teen-agers, women, and middle-aged and old people—everybody, in fact, but young adults.

Westerns are most liked by men of all ages and old people. There are no Westerns in the Top 10s of children or women.

Movies are the Top 10 choice of young adults but not of children (it's bedtime) or the elderly.

The Flying Nun is No. 1 with children and No. 6 with teen-agers, and appears on no Top 10 for older folks.

It should be no surprise that the No. 1 show for the age group 50 and older is *Lawrence Welk.* Other shows in the Top 10 of the Over 50s—and for no younger age group—are *The Virginian, Gunsmoke* and *Daniel Boone.*

Shows that are Top 10 choices of husbands but not of housewives are Westerns and action-adventure series. Housewives prefer movies.

Gentle Ben, of course, is strictly a kiddy passion, and *The Smothers Brothers* a prime teen taste, but *Gomer Pyle* is something of an anomaly, appearing only on the two Top 10s at either end of the age spectrum: children and adults over 50. Certainly something to ponder.

"I'LL TAKE MY CHANCES HERE, ANY TIME"

Johnny Carson opens up on subjects he doesn't discuss on the air
by Robert Higgins

John William Carson is as synonymous with Slumbertime U.S.A. as curlers and cracker crumbs between the sheets. From the first brassy bars of "Johnny's Theme" to the final fade on what has to be the busiest couch this side of a Harold Robbins novel, some 10 million viewers gladly flood their eyes with Murine to stay up late, even too late, with Johnny.

No matter. Viewed horizontally or vertically, Johnny Carson is television's undisputed Captain Midnight. Squirming into the *Tonight* hot seat vacated by a pouty Jack Paar in 1962, Carson today is—to put it mildly—sitting pretty. For sewing up the witching hour for NBC—Carson has squelched a gaggle of late-night chatterboxes (Les Crane, Merv Griffin, Regis Philbin)

over the years—the network pays Carson over a million per annum. Fun City visitors ranging from Vice President Humphrey to the Scotch-slugging king and queen of Brooklyn gypsies vie for a tête-à-tête with Johnny. The rewards are obvious. Marveled thorny Britisher Kenneth Tynan: "Anyone seen on *The Tonight Show* is automatically famous." Even the already famous, like Zsa Zsa Gabor, risk Carson's incredibly quick wit for the exposure. When wordy Zsa Zsa refused to button her pretty lip, Carson sassed: "Any girl who owns a drip-dry wedding dress can't be all bad."

Yet, as any Carson buff knows, Johnny's television manners are usually as impeccable as a parson's. Not only is he genuinely interested in treating his visitors with respect but to Johnny, one well-placed look is worth a thousand gags. The Carson takes are predictable. If a guest mutters something off-color, Carson becomes an Eagle Scout who's inadvertently heard a dirty joke. Let somebody put him down and he freezes into a Jack Benny gaze of utter indignation. Funky jokes don't faze him either. He'll let the line clunk to the floor, gaze at the klieg lights, and then hum a chagrined "Ho-o-o-kay."

Not that Carson's style is all dumb show. Essentially a comedian who reacts to events and people around him, Carson is a past master at turning a sexy situation into a palatable (for NBC's censors) laugh. Samples: A blatantly shapely chorine is greeted with a mock "I suppose you're on the way to a 4-H Club meeting?" Joining physical education expert Debbie Drake on a mat for a demonstration, Carson cracks, "Would you like to phone the desk and leave a call?"

No one has ever confused *The Tonight Show* with *Lamp unto My Feet.* Carson's Little Boy Blueness—usually double entendres, he says—are par for the 90-minute course. Getting titters for a sex-loaded line in his monologue, Carson rebuked the crowd with "This isn't Captain Kangaroo, you know. I'm not going to stand here and tell you how the camel got the extra hump." That's Johnny, like a swig of Schweppes: cool, bubbly and a little tart. He's likable too. "Johnny comes into the bedroom," Walter Kempley, Carson's head writer, says. "You have to like him or you wouldn't invite him in in the first place."

It's all Johnny Carson, bona fide *BIG* star, and it's all as familiar to most Americans as "The Star-Spangled Banner." The private Johnny Carson, however, is the best-kept secret since the Coca-Cola formula. Adamant about playing *The Tonight Show* strictly for laughs, Carson is inordinately reluctant to air controversy or take sides on issues. (Of late, however, he's been campaign-

Johnny Carson chatting with Judy Garland

ing for stronger gun-control laws.) And although he hosts the country's most successful "talk" show, Carson, in fact, is the least talkative host around. After his opening monologue, and maybe an Aunt Blabby bit, Carson's job is primarily that of a catalyst. Ninety-nine and forty-four one-hundredths percent of the time he is pure performer, seldom giving the viewer a hint as to what he would talk about without a countryful of customers waiting for the next funny line, next guest or next bleep in the tape.

The press hasn't gotten Carson to talk much either. First of all, Carson hates interviews. Second, he can get uppity and blow the whole story. Reporters are briefed on some of the danger signals; for instance, if Johnny drums his fingers on the table, he's bored—a sure sign the reporter is taking his last look around. And pushy writers get the back of his hand. When one aggressive fourth estater snapped, "What made you a star?" Carson slapped him with "I started out in a gaseous state, then cooled."

So up we trudged to Carson's Rockefeller Center retreat, hoping to experience what a private talk with Carson would be like. He works out of an isolated, deadly quiet office on the seventh floor, which, on the hour of our arrival, also happened to be deadly hot. "The air conditioner's broken down," Carson starts out, crisply apologizing for the sweaty tee shirt he's been forced to strip to, as he stiffly settles on the couch. Right off we think of roughly 200 more congenial locales in which to interview television's talkiest nontalker.

Unfortunately, the first question we put to Carson—about what he considers *The Tonight Show* highlights over the years—turns out to be the finger-drumming query of all time. "I don't know," he says vaguely. "Five and a half years is a hell of a long time. I can't remember who was on *last night.*" *Drum Drum Drum Go the Fingers.* "I had Janet Leigh on once, and I mentioned how nice it was to finally have her on the show. She told me she had been on twice before. I'd completely forgotten." *Drum-Drum-Drum.* "And Janet Leigh isn't exactly a fry cook at Riker's."

Ho-o-o-kay, we say to ourselves.

Q: Well, does the fact that the show's been called "blue" bug you?

A (A bit uptight): What's "blue" mean? No one has ever been able to define it for me. What does prurient interest mean? The courts can't even define pornography.

Carson grabs for a cigaret. "I've been called a foul mouth," he says tensely. "Well, some four-letter words I could mention [and he mentions them] never corrupted

anyone. My kids once asked me what words I considered to be bad. I told them, 'nigger, kike, greaseball, wop.' Those words are *fraught* with meaning. But, as Lenny Bruce said, 'No one has ever been hurt by a pillow.'"

Suddenly, Carson is up and pacing the rug. "I've been accused of spouting 'blueness.' So was Paar. It goes with the territory. I stripped down to my pants to do a stunt, and you should have seen the letters I got. They *poured* in. You can wear bathing suits on the beach and no one objects. But because we go into the home, everyone is up in arms. I can't say what that means about the letter writers. If some little old lady gets her jollies seeing me stripped to the waist, that's her problem."

He is back on the couch, arms on his knees, and going great guns. "I've been out with some of the columnists who've called me 'blue.' They told me some of the foulest jokes I'd ever heard. And not just between two men, but in public places where everyone could hear them. Then they turn around and call me 'blue.' It's like newspapers writing editorials about pornography. Then on the amusement pages you find an ad for 'Orgy at Lil's Place.' Well, I don't want newspapers lecturing me about *morality.*

"The hypocrisy bugs me," Carson continues. "The networks are just as hypocritical. They'll censor me and then put on a prime-time movie like 'Palm Springs Weekend,' which is nothing less than a sex romp in Palm Springs. But on my show, if a cleavage is too low the netting goes up. And we're being shown at *midnight.*"

There seem to be an awful lot of midnights when Johnny isn't on. In other words, all those vacations he takes. We bring this up and it opens a whole new can of words.

"I'm on 39 weeks," bristles Carson, "and off 13. I know people complain about my taking time off to play concerts and clubs. They don't understand mine isn't a 9-to-5 job. It's a different bag. My club act is set. I know exactly what I'm going to do. I relax. I enjoy it. It's a vacation. On the show I never know where I'm going. Whether I'll have to go out there and fight to get it moving, get it cooking. But I can't take three minutes to explain to people that I need time off. If they don't understand, I can't worry about it. I don't *care* if they don't understand.

"I suppose they think I'm doing it for the money," Carson goes on. "People resent it when they learn I'm going to Las Vegas to make $50,000 a week. I can't help the fact that I make money. No one seems to remember

(All photos Paul Wilson)

the time I was making $40 a week and working just as hard for it. And I make my money *honestly*. No one seems to acknowledge that. O'Brian [columnist Jack O'Brian] calls my money 'loot.' Do you know what loot means? Stolen money. Bounty. He actually sees it as *stolen money*. And when I worked out my last contract with NBC, I read how I was holding up the network for more money. Not in one story did I see that NBC makes 26 million a year on my show. When I took over, they were making 13½ to 14 million. I wasn't exactly holding them up."

We come up for air and fumble around our person for a fresh pencil when, by gosh, Carson's at the starting gate again. The subject this time is his well-known reluctance to side with issues, especially this year when celebrities are falling over themselves to jump on political bandwagons. "It's not my job to get into the political wars," Carson says. "I can't use seven hours of air time as a platform. It's OK for actors to get involved. It's fine for Paul Newman. People go to see him in a movie and he's a character—not Paul Newman. It's the same with John Wayne, and we all know where he stands. But I'm always Johnny Carson. There I am in the living room every night. The audience has a personal relationship with me. It's a totally different bag. Hope and Benny don't get politically involved. I can't either. I have some strong opinions on Vietnam. But it wouldn't do any good to air them on the show. However, I'm in a position to voice my opinions, privately, to people who can do something about the situation."

In the wake of Robert Kennedy's assassination, television's alleged role in glorifying violence has become a hotly debated subject. Carson considers the controversy and says, "There are network meetings going on now about violence. I'd like to know why they think there is too much violence *now* and didn't to begin with. After the rioting, all sorts of studies were made to discover the cause of rioting. I could have told them the cause *before* the rioting: racism, lack of job opportunities, a need for educational facilities, rats . . ."

A decidedly somber Carson returns to the subject of TV violence. "I don't know if TV violence has an influence," he says. "I'm not a psychiatrist. But pointless violence has to be unsettling to the young. They have to become immune to it. And something is wrong when they take off shows like *Exploring* and *Mr. Wizard* to put on those ——— cartoons. They're easier to sell, of course. It's the old give-'em-what-they-want theory. How will we know *what* they want until we try giving them something different? After three assassinations, something's wrong somewhere."

The somber Carson suddenly switches to a markedly confident Carson. "We're being told that we're a sick society, a violent society. I don't think we are. No more than any other, certainly. *We* didn't kill six million Jews. *We* had nothing to do with the mass murders in Russia. And Duvalier, in Haiti. That butcher. I'll take my chances here *any time*."

This is Johnny Carson . . . off the air.

CHICAGO
A POST-MORTEM
The head of NBC News defends his
network's coverage of the
Democratic Convention
by Reuven Frank

A new love-hate relationship has suddenly burst forth between television and its basic audience. Not between television and the intellectuals and upper-middlebrows, the ones who talk about boob tubes and finally break down and buy one for the kids; the ones who up to 1960 bemoaned the passing of conversation in America (as though they ever listened); the ones who at cocktail parties were always importuning you to do subjects no one would watch—including them. But between television and the basic American audience, the most middle-class majority in the history of man.

They don't watch any less, but after several years of telling poll-takers they trust television above other media of news and information, they are now saying that the era of trust is over. Network mail has reached surprising volume, and the letters which approve are treasured. Politicians hint at punitive actions. Appointed officials and big-name Washington newspaper writers participate in a swelling chorus of rejection, conspiracy-hunting and abuse.

The one crystallizing event which brought this about was television's coverage of peace demonstrators meeting Chicago policemen during the Democratic National Convention. The Federal Communications Commission itself has received enough letters on this one event to prompt it to take the ominous step of directing the networks to evaluate FCC mail and, in effect, justify that coverage. The networks are caught between principle—refusing to participate in what seems to be a clear violation of the First Amendment by the FCC—and practicality—the need to get on the record what really happened.

The details of what happened in Chicago are already fading into memory, but the impressions, the memory of the emotions, will remain. What happened in Chicago seems to be this: several thousand people, mostly but not all young, came there to make their anti-war protest heard. The City of Chicago tried in every possible way to assure that they got no attention. They therefore got more attention, in the country and around the world, than they deserved or dared expect.

The reason was television: not what anybody in television did but the *fact* of television, the existence of television. It demonstrated the shortsightedness of planning any public event these days without taking television truly into account, because it is just plain there, and its absence would be even more obvious than its presence.

Another thing happened in Chicago that almost dis-

(UPI)

appeared from public discussion the day the convention ended. The convention was a disunited one, and its disunity was patent. Controls imposed on delegates and others entitled to be there may or may not have been unusual but they seemed harsh to the delegates themselves and to the people watching at home. At the center of this storm, also, was Mayor Richard J. Daley of Chicago, delaying and then ordering adjournments, cuing and cutting off band music. The fuss over the peace demonstrators and the police has driven the troubles of the convention itself from memory.

The letters make almost no mention of what happened inside the convention hall; and the polls, which show 70 or 60 or 50 percent of Americans siding with the Chicago police against the demonstrators, have not even bothered to poll the country about what they thought of the convention.

Immediately following the convention, the criticism seemed to be concentrated on charges that we had spent undue time in showing the demonstrations and the police actions in suppressing them, and that our reporters and commentators had made statements about the police action which directly or indirectly criticized the police. This was easy to answer because it was simply not true.

The time NBC devoted to direct network coverage of the convention totaled more than 35 hours. The time devoted to the pictures of the demonstrations was 65 minutes, less than 3 percent of the total time. Of these 65 minutes, 30 were in prime time. (The consideration of prime time is important because Mayor Daley raised it when he demanded network time for his "reply.") Also of these 65 minutes, 12 were a resume of scenes already shown, a late-night summary of events, and clearly labeled as such. The other networks had similar experience.

I have reviewed the NBC transcript of the 65 minutes in question. To me, it is notable among other reasons for its brevity. The transcript is unusually short for 65 minutes of pictures. It showed no statement critical of the police; it showed almost no value judgments at all. It was simple descriptive material accompanying pictures. Most of the time our reporters said nothing at all, merely letting the pictures be shown.

The regularly scheduled programs which NBC News produces reused some of these pictures; and the reporters gave their analyses as they often do with news events whether they have been covered live or not. Hugh Downs and others carried on a long discussion during the *Today* program.

From implying that we had shown too much, the criticism shifted in the week after Labor Day to the implication that we had not shown enough. The new and larger wave of letters, stimulated, at least in part, by Mayor Daley's public statements, were to the point that we did not show the provocation of the police which led to the action we did show; and then, to a lesser degree, that we did not describe adequately the organization and history of the demonstrations as they were developed over the months preceding the conventions. It was criticism of too little rather than too much coverage.

We have only the word of Mayor Daley and official Chicago police spokesmen as to the degree of provocation. No one denies that there was some. The transcript of our own 65 minutes mentions it prominently To accept uncritically the evaluations of various Chicago officials about the high degree of provocation is no more justified than accepting uncritically the statements of various people in relatively high public position that there was no provocation at all. Blair Clark and Richard Goodwin, in behalf of Senator McCarthy's campaign organization, sent telegrams to the networks asking to answer Mr. Daley if he were given time on television. They detail what they consider and state was the entirely unprovoked attack by Chicago policemen on young McCarthy workers after Thursday midnight of convention week.

The point of all this is that the statements by Mayor Daley and his associates about the extent to which the demonstrators provoked the police cannot be accepted without much more information and documentation.

Up until the violence, it was our conscious policy to avoid covering too much of the activities of demonstrators lest we fall into the trap of doing their advertising for them. Months of "underground newspaper" ads organizing two streams of the demonstrators were known to everyone in the news field, and little was done about it for this reason. During the actual convention coverage, little attention was paid to the demonstrations Monday and Tuesday night for the same reason. When open clashes occurred within range of our cameras, which were relatively stationary, there was no longer any responsible reason for withholding coverage.

But all this begs much more important questions. The tone of the criticism is a lack or loss of faith in television reporting itself. There is implication after implication, in the letters, in certain newspaper accounts and comments, that all this came about because of in-

(UPI)

tent, because the networks wanted it this way as a sort of revenge. Revenge that the two national conventions were in different cities, revenge that floor credentials were allotted below what we considered minimum needs, revenge against a catalogue of greedy motives and mythic presences. And if the answer is no, why haven't we stopped beating our wives?

What did this? The nature of the coverage was not substantially different from the nature of the coverage in 1964, 1960 and 1956. Nor for that matter from the nature of the coverage of the Republican Convention this year. There was some criticism of what we did that week, but of manageable and expectable volume. It was more than counterbalanced by open expressions of approval and appreciation.

But in Chicago, the event itself was different, and the coverage is blamed for that. There is no logical answer available other than this one.

Since 1956 it has been our pattern to rely on four floor reporters for reporting events inside the convention hall. By interviews and by statements they explain proceedings, expected developments and also currents of thought and action which otherwise would not reach the public. It is our position that the official proceedings of a convention are only a part of the journalistic record of that convention, and this has been the best method we could devise of fulfilling journalistic responsibility to find and report the rest of the story. These four floor men are augmented by reporters and mobile electronic equipment at many locations away from the convention hall, at the convention headquarters hotel, at candidates' headquarters and at other locations.

Our equipment has improved over the years and our men have grown more experienced. But the basic structure has not changed since 1956.

A third element in that basic structure, the least-known element, is a body of reporters covering each principal candidate and as many as 40 of the principal delegations.

The degree to which this entire reporting system was called on to present news material other than the official proceedings was not substantially different from 1964, although many of the letters express criticism of it in a tone which implies 1968 was something brand-new. This is just one more instance where the criticism cannot be taken to mean what its words say. There is no doubt the critics are disaffected or hostile. But they give reasons which were just as valid in previous situations which they did not see fit to criticize.

Lately, when I have had to reply to criticism of our covering more than the official proceedings, I have often gone beyond the simple statement that there is more news at a convention than takes place at the podium and that it is our responsibility as journalists to find it and report it. We spend a great deal of time and effort every fourth year reporting that world-shaking event, the choice of the American President by the American electorate. We cover primary campaigns, the important primary elections, the election campaigns, Election Night, all in detail and depth, deploying all our men and expending network time which sheer business

considerations would not necessarily justify. The national nominating conventions are not only themselves important events in this process, but they are the locales of many other events bearing upon this process, some important, some minor.

The managers of the convention have not yet learned well enough to realize what it means that television is there. They know it as a fact, but they do not appreciate it. Television is there and will always be there. Individuals working in television organizations do not make the decisive difference; the fact that television is there makes the difference. Television has been invented and developed and it exists. The politician tends to see this as giving him access to the public. Now the public has access to him. It may be, as has been said, that there were conventions in the past which were even more rigidly managed. But not when people could watch it as it happened, feel that it was they being managed.

There have also been many references, in letters and in print, to the fact that the first pictures of the Michigan Avenue demonstrations interrupted Mayor Carl Stokes of Cleveland, who was seconding the Presidential nomination of Vice President Humphrey. Usually there is an implication of some sinister purpose. Again, the explanation is far longer and more complicated than the original charge.

First of all, it is our practice to try to present the entire nominating speech of every serious nominee, unless truly major news events intervene, but to consider seconding speeches subject to much less stringent criteria for interruption. Mayor Stokes, as I say, was seconding Mr. Humphrey's nomination.

Secondly, when it became apparent that events outside the convention hall would not be available for live television broadcast because of the circumstances of the telephone-equipment installers' strike, I set down the rule that if we could not cover live, we would cover with television tape as soon as it became available; if tape was ruled out, we should do it with film; and if film was out of the question, we might try the sound signal from walkie-talkies, and show still pictures on the television screen. But we would do what we could, as we could, to discharge our responsibility to the television audience to cover the entire story in the manner it had come to expect. That first piece of television tape was rushed by motorcycle courier from Michigan Avenue to the Merchandise Mart; screened there on a spot-check basis for technical reliability; an editor evaluated it and chose less than four minutes, which was all we could handle; and as soon as it became available, we were ready to use it. Since the speech placing Vice President Humphrey's name in nomination was still being made, we deferred the tape until the nominating speech ended, and used it instead of Mayor Stokes's seconding speech. (Later that night a video-tape excerpt from the speech was used.)

I want to return to the point I made earlier, that the coverage is blamed for the event. I have no competence as a social scientist, and the explanation I suggest impinges on those disciplines.

Between 1964, the last convention year, and 1968,

the average middle-class American has gone through many wrenching experiences. His tranquility has been shattered. He has been exposed to realities of war in a way no previous generation of Americans has had to face its war. He has seen ghetto riots in his living room. He has watched with horror young people of good background expressing contempt for his dearest values in the way they dress and act and what they say. Berkeley and Hough and Hue; Columbia and Newark and Tet; what he has seen on television has shaken him physically and morally, made him fear for his safety, his savings, his children, his status. The world as reported by television threatens him. It is a short and understandable step for him to conclude that television threatens him. Television has become the object of what psychoanalysts call transference.

This, not any event, nor anything any or all of us working in television organizations did, accounts for the extent and depth of feeling which followed the Chicago convention coverage. Nowhere is this clearer than in the case of the demonstrators who clashed with the police. Since, unlike black demonstrators, their protest is not against being excluded from the fruits of current America but against the very premises of current America, they are particularly hated. They are verbal and symbolic. They don't throw rocks at trains; they lie down in front of cars. They don't carry firearms, but Vietcong flags. They know the words that shock and the words that anger and how and when to use them. They know what cleanliness is considered next to, and some of them intentionally remain dirty. (There is no doubt in my mind that a few came to Chicago hoping for the kind of police treatment they got.)

This unease, this frustrated hankering for tranquility, this complex of fears and hates greater than any within living memory underlies this political year, the campaigns, the polls, the emphasis on repression. Minorities who are willing to disrupt can be very disruptive. Our society and our law are supposedly dedicated to the protection of minorities, but the price of disruption of the majority seems too high. This frustration keeps bursting forth and will until there is some solution. Repression is in most cases the conditioned answer, but that seems to too many to be going too far, especially if it happens where they can see it.

If such young protesters are as unpopular as I think in the United States today, it seems to me worth suggesting that by showing their confrontation with the police without at the same time denouncing them, we may have appeared, to those who loathed them, to be supporting them. This was made worse by showing them being beaten. The normal reaction of most Americans is sympathy with victims, any victims in any situations. People who hated the victims were revolted by their own sympathetic reactions. This revulsion was transferred to the medium, television. Knowingly or instinctively, Democratic politicians who felt their cause damaged by what happened in Chicago and because it was seen, used this revulsion as justification.

What is even more interesting is that so many of the letters about Chicago went on to all the other underlying concerns of contemporary America. Many, even most, Americans consider themselves individually threatened these days. There are three sources of threat: racial conflict, the Vietnam War, and dirty young people with long hair. (It is very often pointed out that many of this last group are not young. No letter I have read points out that many of them are not dirty, or that many of them have short hair.) All three threats run through the letters, and therefore presumably through public attitudes, as a single refrain. And yet only the last one is relevant to the event itself. All three are relevant to current attitudes, and especially to the real world as seen on the face of a television set.

Television allows no respite, no selectivity. The newspaper reader's eye can skip what bores him, ignore what disturbs him. If he has had enough of black militants, he need go no farther than the headline. If he has special distaste for stories about child molesters or Biafran starvation, he can turn to the ball scores without forcing the editor to give up what he thinks are his responsibilities. Not on television.

If the *Huntley-Brinkley Report* shows the Vietnam War five days one week and the viewer always watches the *Huntley-Brinkley Report,* he will see the Vietnam War five days that week. He can't skip it or ignore it. So why don't you show some good news? Why don't you say some nice things? Why must we always be faced with aggressive minorities, riots, looting, killing? The fact is we do show good news and say nice things, but not enough to erase the afterimage of the inescapable. The only other answer must be a new kind of journalism.

It's the kind of journalism the French have on their television. And when the crowds went into the streets last May, the television reporting was one of the bigger targets. It had betrayed them and fooled them and lied about them, and everybody knew it. Even that might not be so bad. But if you don't believe a medium of journalism, can you believe it when it gives good news?

As for the news we put out, we put it out because we think it ought to be put out. We are the current stage in the centuries of evolution of our kind of free journalism, governed by tastes and ethics passed on through what is essentially oral tradition, reacting to conditioned criteria of importance and public interest, hemmed in by some law but not much, consciously or subconsciously always responding to the need to be current, relevant and involving. Relevant to what? To the public and what it cares about. Entertainment is a part of all journalism in all media at all times of history. Being interesting is very much a part of why journalists do what they do.

But American journalism as an institution is never venal. (Specific exceptions prove nothing.) It never does things purely for its own gains. Although it is always the product of many subjective decisions, these are made according to some image of what the public wants and the conditioned impulses of journalists of how they should act and conduct themselves. They do not act from self-interest.

This, which is true of newspapers in this country, is just as true of journalism on television. It is in the nature of American network television today that even its most economically successful activity could be easily replaced with something outside journalism which could make more money. And the biggest, most difficult, most controversial activities in news, such as covering national political conventions and space launchings, go on at huge money losses.

This system of journalism being impelled by internal needs and supervised by internal controls is what we call free journalism. It exists in very few countries. It is the system under which the reporter demands access to facts and events for no other reason than that he is who he is, and his argument is always accepted.

That is our system. It is so ingrained, nobody thinks about it very much, and it takes more words to describe than merely to sense. We grew up with it, and that's the way it is. It moved over to television journalism automatically, without conscious decision or open debate, although it's full of debatable propositions. These are the propositions being debated most these days, although so far the challengers are mostly emotional and the rational shape of useful debate is not yet evident.

In most countries in the world today, in most societies, at most times of history, this journalism without a social purpose is abhorrent. The social purpose varies with the time and place, but none at all seems like one of those vacuums that we are told nature always fills. In Spain, journalists are expected to advance established religion and government; in China, to rally the people; in the Soviet Union, to avoid the frivolous and contribute to the progress of socialism. These purposes exist in constitutions and Organic Press Laws promulgated by people who believe them intensely and unselfishly. Our rationalizations about a public entitled to information freely obtained, about a press which checks on government, about the right of journalists to be free even when outrageous, run counter, in those countries, to moral fundamentals.

And here, today, in the United States, facing a frightening jigsaw of crises for which we are unprepared, many people seem to think that American journalism, and above all American television journalism, should be governed by ennobling purposes. We are castigated for not promoting unity, for not opening channels of interracial communication, for not building an edifice of support for our fighting men, for not ignoring dissent, for not showing good news.

Our system does not now provide for working toward social good. Let us even postulate that there is a unanimously accepted social good which television journalism should set itself to achieve or promote. And the decision would be made by five Albert Schweitzers sitting around a table. Whoever put them there could, in time—perhaps far, far off in the future—replace the five Albert Schweitzers with five Joseph Goebbelses, or five Joseph Stalins, or five George Lincoln Rockwells. You see, it's not the five Albert Schweitzers who are important, but the table.

I say the table itself is evil. To those who worry about television, or television news, being too powerful, I say there is no doubt that there is great potential power here, but only if used. The only safeguard is free journalism, journalism without directed purpose, because whether that purpose represents good or evil depends on who you are.

Television is an institution, but its functions are performed by people, by individuals, by citizens, by mature men and women, by parents, by householders, by wage earners, by patriots. Each of these as individuals may support the purposes people urge on us. I think most do. We try to keep them out of our work as well as we can, being only mortal, frail and otherwise human. Because, as a colleague puts it, the choice is between the truth imperfectly perceived and the social good dogmatically formulated.

If you tell a medium of journalism what to put in and what to leave out, even if you know in your own heart you are promoting the public welfare, even if most people agree with you, then you are changing journalism as it exists in America. Whatever you call it, censorship is censorship, and all censorship is aimed not at the transmitter but at the receiver.

APOLLO 11

Details of the manned lunar landing and TV coverage

On October 4, 1957, the Soviet Union successfully placed man's first artificial satellite in an orbit around the earth. Preceded by rocket research conducted decades earlier (notably by U.S. physicist Robert Goddard), Sputnik I nevertheless signaled for the public the beginning of the space age.

Sputnik also signaled something else: the beginning of a race between the USSR and the United States to land a man on the moon and bring him safely home. Several weeks ago, the Soviet Union, having witnessed the rapid progress of our Apollo program, informed its citizens that the first man on the moon would probably be an American. As we went to press, that prediction seemed about to come true.

The mission

Apollo 11, the eight-day lunar-landing mission, was set for a launch this Wednesday at 9:32 A.M. (EDT) from pad 39-A at Florida's Kennedy Space Center. If the flight goes on schedule, the Apollo capsule will leave its earth parking orbit and head out for the moon shortly after 12 noon.

For the next 72 hours, the flight should be pretty much routine. Then, at about 1 P.M. next Saturday, July 19, the spaceship enters lunar orbit and the astronauts prepare for what must be considered history's most dramatic adventure: landing on the moon (set for next Sunday) and a walk on its surface (Monday) lasting nearly two and a half hours. Concluding the mission: lunar module (LEM) liftoff from the moon and docking

A TV Guide Close-Up

3:00 **4** **20** Super Bowl

Drawing by Schmidt

Special/Color

The AFL's New York Jets meet the NFL's Baltimore Colts in the third annual Super Bowl. Curt Gowdy, Kyle Rote and Al DeRogatis report from Miami. (Live)

Jets.

A heart-stopping 27–23 win over Oakland brought superstatus and the long-awaited league title to New York. AFL Player of the Year Joe Namath passed less but won more in '68. The receivers are led by George Sauer (66 catches for second in the league), Don Maynard (all-time pro yardage leader) and tough Pete Lammons. The running game gets straight-ahead power from Matt Snell (sixth in the league) and fancy stepping from Emerson Boozer. Aggressive pass rushers Gerry Philbin and Verlon Biggs are standouts on the fine defensive unit.

Colts.

Earl Morrall starred as the Cinderella quarterback, leading the league in passing and winning the MVP award as the Colts marched to the title. Top receivers are tough John Mackey and fleet Willie Richardson. Tom Matte, a tenacious, hard-bitten runner (10th in the league), leads the ground game. The defense is stubborn and stingier than Scrooge. Teamwork was the word as the defense turned in three regular-season shutouts, and then picked up another one in the NFL championship game, handing the Browns their first shutout in 143 games.

NEW YORK JETS

11	Turner, J.	K-QB	50 McAdams	....LB
12	Namath	QB	51 Baker	LB
13	Maynard	FL	52 Schmitt	C
15	Parilli	QB	56 Crane	LB-C
22	Hudson	DB	60 Grantham	LB
23	Rademacher	DB	61 Talamini	G
24	Sample	DB	62 Atkinson	LB
26	Richards	DB-FL	63 Neidert	LB
29	Turner, B.	E	66 Rasmussen	G
30	Smolinski	B	67 Herman	G
31	Mathis	B	71 Walton	T
32	Boozer	B	72 Rochester	T
33	Johnson	K-E	74 Richardson	G
41	Snell	B	75 Hill	T
42	Beverly	DB	80 Elliott	T-LB
43	Dockery	DB	81 Philbin	DE
45	Christy	DB	83 Sauer	E
46	Baird	DB	85 Thompson	DE
47	D'Amato	DB	86 Biggs	DE
48	Gordon	DB	87 Lammons	E

BALTIMORE COLTS

2	Brown	B	53 Gaubatz	LB
15	Morrall	QB	55 Porter	LB
16	Ward	QB	61 Johnson	G
19	Unitas	QB	62 Ressler	G
20	Logan	DB	64 Williams, S.	LB
21	Volk	DB	66 Shinnick	LB
26	Pearson	DB	71 Sullivan	G
27	Perkins	E	72 Vogel	T
28	Orr	FL	73 Ball	T
32	Curtis	LB	74 Smith, B.R.	T
34	Cole	B	75 Williams, J.	G
37	Austin	DB	76 Miller	T
40	Boyd	DB	78 Smith, B.	DE
41	Matte	B	79 Michaels	DE-K
43	Lyles	DB	80 Cogdill	E
47	Stukes	DB	81 Braase	DE
49	Lee	K	84 Mitchell	E
50	Curry	LB-C	85 Hilton	DE
51	Grant	LB	87 Richardson	FL
52	Szymanski	C	88 Mackey	E

with the command module (also on Monday); transearth injection, beginning the homeward journey (Tuesday); and splashdown and recovery in the Pacific (Thursday, July 24).

The astronauts

Neil A. Armstrong: a civilian, the Ohio-born astronaut has been picked as the Apollo 11 command pilot—and the man who will first step out onto the moon. During the Korean War, Armstrong flew 78 combat missions and later joined NASA as a test pilot. Becoming an astronaut in 1962, he flew the Gemini 8 flight (March 1966) and performed the first docking of two vehicles in space.

Edwin E. Aldrin Jr.: an Air Force colonel, he graduated third in his class at West Point, flew combat in Korea and spent five and a half hours in space during the Gemini 12 flight (November 1966). He is the LEM pilot for Apollo 11, and will be with Armstrong on the lunar surface.

Michael Collins: an Air Force lieutenant colonel, he has logged more than 3200 hours in jet aircraft. A pilot on the Gemini 10 flight (July 1966), he, too, has performed extravehicular activity. For Apollo 11, he's been chosen as command-module pilot.

TV coverage

If the mission goes as planned, this week's TV coverage will include liftoff and color telecasts from Apollo (Thursday and Friday) en route to the moon. Next Monday (July 21), viewers will be treated to an unparalleled TV program: a live telecast of the astronauts on the moon, using a black-and-white camera taken from the LEM and set up on the lunar surface.

All of the networks plan extensive coverage from launch to splashdown, with continuous reporting beginning next Sunday morning (July 20) and running for at least 31 hours.

LIVE—FROM THE MOON

For two and a half hours, the world will watch the most awesome show ever

by Neil Hickey

In television, the word "special" is applied haphazardly to pre-emptive programming no matter how pallid or pointless. The most truly "special" television program in the medium's history, however, will begin when a 38-year-old civilian named Neil Armstrong climbs down a ladder from a spiderlike space vessel and gingerly places his foot upon the surface of the moon.

That precise instant—if a great deal of elaborate planning goes on schedule—will be visible to television audiences here on earth, making them participants in the crowning moment of man's utmost adventure of discovery.

TV's most special special—a live program from the surface of the moon—will last roughly two and a half hours. Armstrong and his colleague. Lieutenant Colonel Edwin E. Aldrin, will produce and direct it, as well as be its only performers. Costumes and additional dialogue are by the Manned Spacecraft Center in Hous-

ton, Texas. The stars of the show will act their parts on the barest of stages: a tiny, barren patch of the inhospitable lunar surface.

Let us now peruse the script for this most remarkable of dramas. Recall that by the time the show begins, three astronauts (Lieutenant Colonel Michael Collins is the third) will have traversed the quarter-million miles from the earth, orbited the moon and divided their space vehicle into two parts: a lunar landing module (the LEM) and a command module, which stays in orbit around the moon with Collins at the controls. The LEM has descended to the moon's surface, and Armstrong and Aldrin have remained inside it for almost 10 hours—checking their equipment, eating, donning their pressure suits and even sleeping to store up energy for the ordeal ahead.

Finally, the emotional moment arrives—the two men throw open the LEM's door and stare outward at the

Neil Armstrong sitting in the lunar module on the moon (NASA)

(NASA)

moon's lonely wasteland. Armstrong, who is commander of the expedition, crouches and then backs out the doorway, easing himself and his bulky, 185-pound spacesuit through the narrow opening. (The suit weighs just over 30 pounds to Armstrong, since the moon's gravity is only one-sixth of earth's.) He stands on the LEM's "front porch" for a moment and then reaches to his left and pulls a lanyard which opens an external compartment near the spacecraft's base, exposing a small specially designed black-and-white television camera aimed at the LEM's ladder and the moon surface beyond.

The show has begun.

Tens of millions of television screens on earth are alight for the first close-up of an extraterrestrial body. All is still for a moment, and then Armstrong begins backing down the ladder—slowly, slowly, slowly—the white suit with its bubble top and strange hoofed galoshes retarding his movement. We see him reach the bottom, stand for a moment on the LEM's round landing pod, and then step to the surface of the moon.

His actions for the next several hours will be as scrupulously choreographed as a production of "Swan Lake." Armstrong takes a few cautious steps to establish that he can indeed walk on the surface without danger, and then makes a brief check of his spacesuit to be sure it's operating as expected. He then commences the single most important task of the entire moon-walk period: the collection of a sample of the moon's surface.

Armstrong detaches from his suit a metal stick with a small bag at the end of it. Using it like a golf club, Armstrong scoops up a bit of the lunar surface (his pressure suit makes it impossible for him to bend down), detaches the bag from the stick and places it in a thigh pocket of his suit. (Now, even if some misfortune terminates the mission abruptly and Armstrong is forced to hurry back to the LEM and blast off, the moon sample is secure.)

Aldrin, inside the LEM, passes down, via a simple clothesline-like device, a still camera which Armstrong affixes to his chest plate. (He can now take still pictures simply by aiming his body and tripping the shutter.) Moments later, Aldrin comes down the ladder and joins Armstrong on the lunar surface. As Aldrin orients himself and checks out his pressure suit, Armstrong is having a look at the outside of the LEM to determine if there is any damage caused by the landing. He then approaches the live TV camera in its stowage box near the ladder, removes a small tripod, picks up the camera itself, and walks away from the LEM.

With slow Frankensteinian pace (caused by the restrictions of his pressure suit), Armstrong carries tripod and camera—which is still transmitting live pictures back to earth—to a point roughly 40–50 feet from the spacecraft. He raises the camera and slowly aims it about the lunar landscape, giving earthlings their first panoramic TV pictures of the moon.

Armstrong then places the camera on its tripod and points it back toward the spacecraft. The camera's wide-angle lens will henceforth observe the astronauts' activities as they go about their carefully prescribed duties during the rest of the lunar exploration.

While Armstrong was setting up the TV camera, Aldrin has been busy preparing the equipment they'll need to conduct further geological sampling. He also props up and unrolls what appears to be a window shade made of aluminum foil. This is a gadget designed to trap invisible particles of the so-called solar wind which passes over the moon. It will remain in place until the astronauts are ready to leave the moon, then be rolled up and placed on board the LEM to be brought back to earth for study.

Now Aldrin takes the still camera from his colleague and begins extensive photo coverage of the landscape and the LEM, while Armstrong—with tongs and a scoop which allow him to work in an upright posture—collects rocks and gravel and other loose geological specimens and stows them in boxes for the trip home. He then makes an elaborate examination of the LEM's exterior and reports what he sees via radio to earth as Aldrin takes still pictures of the entire inspection and the TV camera grinds on.

Now it is time to unload from another compartment of the LEM a pair of scientific devices which will be set out on the moon's surface and left behind as a kind of unmanned space station. One is a seismometer to measure the structure, strain and physical properties of the moon's interior, as well as meteor impacts and movement of the crust. The other is simply a reflector to serve as a target, in the years ahead, for laser beams from earth which will be the most accurate measuring tape yet devised of earth-moon distances and fluctuations. This laser reflector also will help scientists develop a large body of new information about the structure and origin of the moon, about the nature of gravity and even about the size of the earth.

There follows another period of photographing and rock-sample collecting, including the taking of a core sample from just under the moon's surface. The astronauts also put down a gnomon—a small tripodal rod that will provide both a color scale and a standard of measurement for the teams of photoanalysts who will later pore over the moon pictures.

Soon it is time to begin the small "housekeeping" chores before drawing to a close history's first moon TV special. Armstrong and Aldrin weigh their geological specimens and pack them up for the trip home. Aldrin climbs back into the LEM and Armstrong starts hoisting up to him, via the "clothesline," the rock boxes and still camera. Armstrong takes a last look around the bleak moon landscape—at the seismometer and the laser reflector, at the television camera which is staring back at

him from its tripod a few score feet away—and then slowly mounts the ladder and disappears into the LEM's doorway.

The first moon TV special is over.

The LEM will remain on the moon's surface for another 10 hours while the astronauts check out all their systems, jettison unneeded equipment, eat and sleep, and chat with their earth colleagues and Colonel Collins, who is still orbiting in the command module.

When it comes time for the astronauts to leave the lunar surface, the base of the LEM—with its landing pods, empty stowage closets and television-cable connections—will remain behind. There will be no TV pictures of the actual liftoff from the moon (even though the camera is still in place on its tripod) because the TV transmitter is in the LEM's upper compartment (called the ascent stage), which simply will separate from the lower stage at the time of departure and be on its way to rendezvous with the orbiting command module. The TV camera will be switched off shortly after the astronauts re-enter the LEM.

The TV camera that will be abandoned on the moon was specially designed by Westinghouse's aerospace division to withstand the most horrendous physical conditions. It must, for example, survive the terrible vibrations of the Saturn V launching rocket, the shock of the moon landing, extremes of pressure and temperature, as well as possible meteoroid bombardment and particle radiation.

Its TV signals will be transmitted to earth via antennae on the LEM, or if that proves unsatisfactory, by means of a special antenna (designed by RCA) which looks like a transparent umbrella in a windstorm. The signals are picked up on earth by a worldwide communications network which has three receiving stations located strategically 120 longitudinal degrees apart (to give full 360-degree coverage)—in the Mojave Desert, in Australia and in Spain. The signal is then sent to the Manned Spacecraft Center in Houston, where it is relayed to the commercial television networks for transmission to your home screen.

Aside from the black-and-white TV pictures we'll get from the lunar surface itself, there's also a chance we'll be seeing some candid color TV transmissions from inside the command module during its journey to and from the moon—just as on earlier Apollo flights. Neil Armstrong's reputation as a spaceman, however, is that of a single-minded, nerveless, businesslike operator who has little patience for what he considers the public-relations folderol of unnecessary TV transmissions. So the betting is that we'll be seeing far less TV during this journey than we did when Colonel Tom Stafford was piloting Apollo 10 last May.

But the live 2½-hour television program from the lunar surface is a built-in and important facet of the Apollo 11 mission itself. Thus, American taxpayers are assured of a front-row seat for the most emotion-packed moment of a drama which has so far cost them $24 billion—the most expensive TV special in history.

Desi Arnaz Jr.

Ralph Edwards

Queen Elizabeth II

Perry Como

Dave Garroway & J. Fred Muggs

Ray Milland

George Reeves

Red Skelton

Bishop Fulton J. Sheen

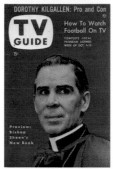

Kukla, Fran & Ollie

Warren Hull

Jimmy Durante

Loretta Young

Jack Webb

Bing Crosby

Robert Montgomery

Red Buttons

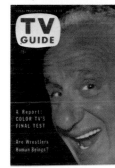

Groucho Marx

Eve Arden

Harriet, Ricky & David Nelson

Frank Sinatra

Patricia Benoit & Wally Cox

Gale Storm

Ben Blue & Alan Young

Howdy Doody & Bob Smith

Joan Davis & Jim Backus

Arlene Francis

Roy Rogers

William Bendix

Jerry Lewis & Dean Martin

Jayne Meadows & Steve Allen

Betty Hutton

Lucille Ball

Barry Nelson & Joan Caulfield

Gracie Allen & George Burns

Marion Marlowe

1955

Arthur Godfrey

Cast of ''I've Got A Secret''

Ed Sullivan

Martha Raye

Edward R. Murrow

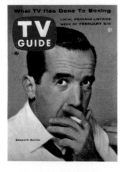

Cast of ''Your Hit Parade''

Sid Caesar

Art Carney

Buddy Ebsen & Fess Parker

Robin Morgan & Peggy Wood

Audrey Meadows & Jackie Gleason

Eddie Fisher

Danny Thomas

Cast of ''Lassie''

Patti Page

Julius LaRosa

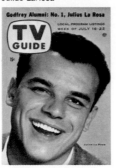

Art Linkletter

Roxanne & Bud Collyer

Hal March

Richard Boone

Phil Silvers

Liberace

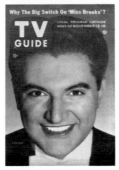

Jack Benny

Mary Healy &
Peter Lind Hayes

Lawrence Welk

Janis Paige

Frances Rafferty &
Spring Byington

Dave Garroway

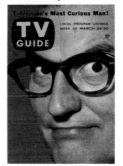

Grace Kelly

Bernadette O'Farrell &
Richard Greene

Cast of "Father Knows Best"

Steve Allen

Bob Cummings

Bill Lundigan & Mary Costa

Gail Davis

Jackie Cooper

Elvis Presley

Alfred Hitchcock

Edward R. Murrow

Buddy Hackett

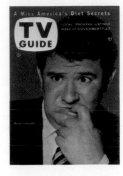

Victor Borge

Dinah Shore

Jerry Lewis

Bob Hope

Jane Wyman

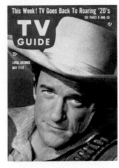

Hugh O'Brian

Jane Wyatt & Robert Young

Charles Van Doren

Nanette Fabray

James Arness

Esther Williams

Ida Lupino & Howard Duff

Lassie

Cast of "What's My Line?"

Loretta Young

Peter Lawford & Phyllis Kirk

James Garner

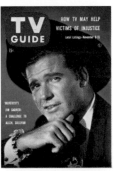

Mary Martin

Walt Disney

Ricky Nelson

Gisele MacKenzie

Imogene Coca & Sid Caesar

Walter Winchell

Tennessee Ernie Ford

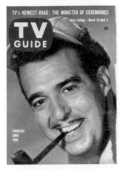

Polly Bergen

Guy Williams as ''Zorro''

Shirley Temple

Richard Boone

Pat Boone

Bill Cullen

Steve Lawrence &
Eydie Gorme

Dick Clark

Barrie Chase & Fred Astaire

Jack Paar

Ronald and Nancy Reagan

1959

Lola Albright & Craig Stevens

Milton Berle

George Gobel

Walter Brennan

Dinah Shore

Dick Powell

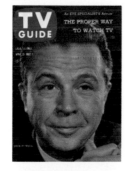

Edd Byrnes

Steve McQueen

Lloyd Bridges

Janet Blair

Arthur Godfrey

June Allyson

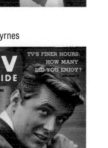

Robert Taylor

Ingrid Bergman

Jay North

Jack Benny

Clint Walker

Art Carney
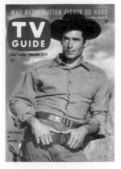

Cliff Arquette
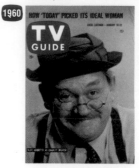

Garry Moore

Chuck Connors

Raymond Burr &
Barbara Hale

Ann Sothern

Ernie Kovacs & Edie Adams

Gene Barry

Darren McGavin

Cast of "Bachelor Father"

Gardner McKay

David Brinkley &
Chet Huntley

Nick Adams

Betsy Palmer

Arlene Francis

Debbie Reynolds

Danny Kaye

Ward Bond
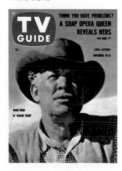

Cast of "Checkmate"

Perry Como

Barbara Stanwyck

Eric Fleming &
Clint Eastwood

Robert Stack

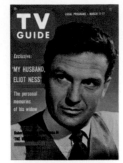

Roger Smith

Mitch Miller

Rod Taylor

Donna Reed

Walter Brennan &
Richard Crenna

John McIntire &
Robert Horton

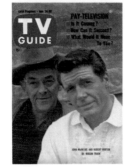

Bob Keeshan

Hugh Downs

Dwayne Hickman &
Bob Denver

Carol Burnett

Red Skelton

Joe E. Ross &
Fred Gwynne

Dorothy Provine

Mary Tyler Moore &
Dick Van Dyke

1962

Shirley Booth

Jacqueline Kennedy

Troy Donahue

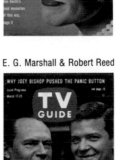

E. G. Marshall & Robert Reed

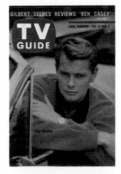

Alan Young & Mr. Ed

Connie Stevens

Don Knotts

Efrem Zimbalist Jr.

Raymond Massey &
Richard Chamberlain

Jackie Gleason

Richard Rust &
Edmond O'Brien

Jack Lord

Jacqueline Kennedy

Edie Adams

George Maharis &
Martin Milner

1963

Princess Grace

Richard Chamberlain

Cast of "Bonanza"

Johnny Carson

Judy Garland

Bill Bixby & Ray Walston

George C. Scott

Patty Duke

1964

Mary Tyler Moore, Dick
Van Dyke & Carl Reiner

Claudine Longet &
Andy Williams

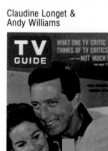

Shirl Conway & Zena Bethune

Vincent Edwards

Dean Jagger &
James Franciscus

William Windom &
Inger Stevens

Vic Morrow & Rick Jason

Mary Tyler Moore

Cast of "McHale's Navy"

Amanda Blake

Fred Flintstone

Fred MacMurray

Gene Barry & Gary Conway

Mia Farrow

Gig Young, Charles Boyer & David Niven

Robert Vaughan

Cara Williams

Jim Nabors

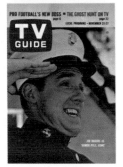

Julie Newmar

Andy Williams

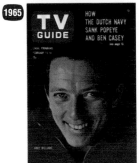

David Janssen

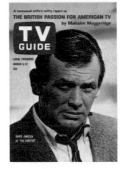

Andy Griffith

Bob Denver & Tina Louise

Flipper

Raymond Burr

Fess Parker & Patricia Blair

Anne Francis

Cast of ''The Addams Family''

Cynthia Lynne & Bob Crane

Eva Gabor & Eddie Albert

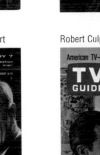

Robert Culp & Bill Cosby

Barbara Eden & Larry Hagman

Ben Gazzara

Barbara Feldon

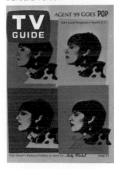

Cast of ''The Beverly Hillbillies''

Adam West

Lucille Ball

Frank Sinatra

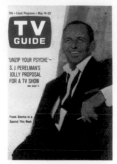

Sally Field

Walter Cronkite

The Vietnam War

Robert Vaughn & David McCallum

Marlo Thomas

Ron Ely

James Arness

1967

Diana Rigg & Patrick Macnee

Dale Robertson

Phyllis Diller

William Shatner & Leonard Nimoy

Dorothy Malone

Dick Van Dyke

Elizabeth Montgomery

Barbara Feldon & Don Adams

Chet Huntley & David Brinkley

Raymond Burr

Sally Field

Kaye Ballard & Eve Arden

Dick and Tom Smothers

1968

Joey Bishop

Mike Connors

Robert Wagner

Barbara Eden

Dan Rowan & Dick Martin

Dean Martin

Cast of "The Mod Squad"

Frank Sinatra

Ann-Margret

E. J. Peaker & Robert Morse

Diahann Carroll

1969

Cast of "Mission: Impossible"

Cast of "Laugh-In"

Tony Franciosa, Gene Barry & Robert Stack

Jack Paar

Moon Landing

Merv Griffin

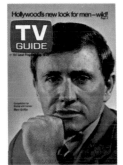

Linda Cristal & Leif Erickson

Cast of "Room 222"

Andy Williams

Doris Day

1970

Diahann Carroll

Jackie Gleason

Carol Burnett

Glen Campbell

David Frost

Johnny Cash

Liza Minelli

Red Skelton

Herschel Bernardi

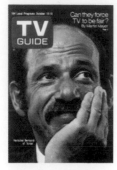

Dick Cavett

James Arness

Tony Randall & Jack Klugman

Goldie Hawn

Broderick Crawford

Harry Reasoner

Paul Newman

Henry Fonda

David Cassidy

Cast of "All in the Family"

Cookie Monster

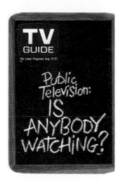

Howard Cosell, Don Meredith & Frank Gifford

Jack Lord

Shirley MacLaine

James Franciscus

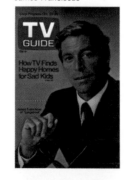

James Garner

Flip Wilson

Arthur Hill

Richard Nixon & Mao Tse-tung

Mary Tyler Moore

Johnny Carson

James Brolin & Robert Young

Peter Falk

Glenn Ford

Don Rickles

Sandy Duncan

Rod Serling

Julie London

Jack Webb, Martin Milner & Kent McCord

George Peppard

Meredith Baxter & David Birney

John Wayne

Alistair Cooke

Beatrice Arthur

Mike Douglas

Julie Andrews

The Duke & Duchess of Windsor

Barbara Walters

Bob Newhart & Suzanne Pleshette

Bill Cosby

William Conrad

Karl Malden & Michael Douglas

Richard Widmark

David Carradine

Dennis Weaver

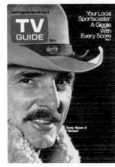

Telly Savalas

Blythe Danner & Ken Howard

Frank Sinatra

Katharine Hepburn

Mason Reese

Bob Hope

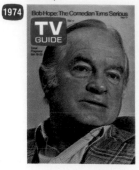

Dom De Luise

Richard Boone

James Stewart

James Franciscus

Tony Musante & Susan Strasberg

Cast of "The Rookies"

John Chancellor

Lucille Ball

Johnny Carson

Telly Savalas

Freddie Prinze & Jack Albertson

Cast of "The Waltons"

Sophia Loren

Cast of "Good Times"

Angie Dickinson

James Garner

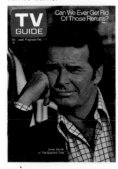

Chad Everett

Cher

Muhammad Ali

Barry Newman

Jason Robards &
Colleen Dewhurst

Bicentennial

Howard K. Smith &
Harry Reasoner

Mike Douglas

Carroll O'Connor

Cloris Leachman

Lloyd Bridges

David Soul &
Paul Michael Glaser

Robert Wagner & Eddie Albert

Robert Blake

1976

Ron Howard & Henry Winkler

Angie Dickinson &
Earl Holliman

Cast of "M*A*S*H"

Redd Foxx
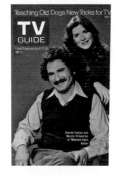

William Conrad

Bob Hope

Danny Thomas

Jack Palance
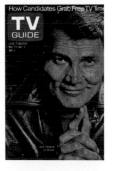

Gabriel Kaplan and
Marcia Strassman

Beatrice Arthur

George Kennedy

Cindy Williams &
Penny Marshall

Sonny & Cher

Louise Lasser

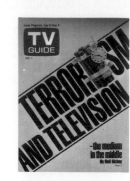

Bob Dylan

Farrah Fawcett-Majors,
Jaclyn Smith & Kate Jackson

Linda Lavin

Vivien Leigh & Clark Gable

Tony Randall

Valerie Harper

David Brinkley &
John Chancellor

1977

John Travolta

Superbowl

''Roots''

Barbara Walters

Telly & George Savalas

Martha Raye & Rock Hudson

Liv Ullmann

Jack Klugman

David Frost & Richard Nixon

Cast of ''One Day at a Time''

Tom Brokaw

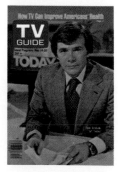

Robert Blake

Alan Alda

Marie & Donny Osmond

Ed Asner

WHAT IS TV DOING TO THEM?

Last of an eight-part series
What television should be doing to
safeguard our greatest natural resource—
our children
by Neil Hickey

"For some children under some conditions, some television is harmful. For other children under the same conditions, or for the same children under other conditions, it may be beneficial. For most children, under most conditions, most television is probably neither particularly harmful nor particularly beneficial."

That famous quotation from the 1961 study by Schramm, Lyle and Parker ("Television in the Lives of Our Children") encapsulates all that we know—some say all that we will ever know—about the effects of television upon children.

And what, indeed, does it tell us?

Very little, obviously. Human beings, including children, are simply too complex, and the influences upon them too diverse, to allow any more precise conclusions about how a single factor in our lives—in this case television—alters our thinking and our behavior.

All of which is not to say that we know *nothing* about television in relation to children. A tiny residue of certain knowledge settles at the bottom of the great murky vat which contains all the studies, experiments, polls, graphs, essays and sudden hunches about children vis-à-vis the little box called television. For example:

• The most potent single influence upon what a child watches on television is what his parents watch.

• In homes where parents take the trouble to offer attractive alternatives to TV, the children watch less TV.

• A child who watches "too much" television usually is suffering some emotional distress which is causing him to retreat into TV-watching. It's not that he's fascinated with the programs. He's unhappy—consciously or not—with his home life, his school life, or his relations with his friends.

• Bright children discover television early, use it heavily, then drift away to other pursuits around age 12, less intelligent children remain enthusiastic viewers for longer.

• The quality of most network TV designed specifically for children is limited by the networks' competitive desire to attract maximum audiences for advertisers—usually the makers of toys and breakfast foods.

* * *

Such truths, scarce though they may be, can lead perceptive and concerned parents to some conclusions of their own about how television can best relate to their family life. For example, many child experts have pointed out that parents who tune in spontaneously to TV's discussion programs, concerts, documentaries and drama specials invariably induce similar tastes and appetites in their children—especially when the program becomes a jumping-off point for a simple discussion at home of what it all meant.

For example, a family watching a TV version of "Death of a Salesman" might be led to ask their children how they felt about Willie Loman's kind of traveling life, whether they thought the two sons acted properly toward their parents, and if the mother reminded them of their own.

In such ways, tiny ideational seeds are planted in the child's mind that will grow blossoms later on. At certain ages, children benefit from such small probes and questions which pique them. Answers will come aplenty in time. The prior problem, however, is: What are the right questions?

Dr. Leon Eisenberg, chief of psychiatry at Massachusetts General Hospital, told TV Guide: "There is some good material on television right now—*Captain Kangaroo* and *Misterogers,* for example. The value of such programs can be increased if parents join the children in watching, and ask questions, and carry over some of the activities into the rest of the day. Too many parents use television as a cheap baby sitter, and that's bad in two ways: first, the child may be exposed to material which is confusing and harmful to him, and second, it may cut him off from his peers, reading and other activities."

"There's a socialization process that goes on," says Dr. Edward L. Palmer, research director of the Children's Television Workshop. "Children come to like what their parents impart value to. In subtle ways, parents wield great influence on what their children watch."

Example is by far the best persuader. It is hard, claims Schramm, to make a river rise above its source. If public affairs, ethics, science, nature and other such topics are not discussed in the home, "is the child easily convinced that they are important enough to view on television?"

This crucial influence of parents and their life styles upon their offspring's habits—including TV-usage patterns—can scarcely be overestimated. That opinion was unanimous among all the experts TV Guide interviewed.

In homes where a parent reads to the child and is reasonably attentive to his natural curiosity and desire for actual experience rather than vicarious experience, the child automatically watches television less.

Of course, it's just as possible that insensitive parents, rather than attracting their children into real-life pursuits, can drive them into TV-watching as a refuge. Dr. Lawrence Zelic Freedman, of the Center For Advanced Study in the Behavioral Sciences, has written: "When televiewing is, in fact, excessive . . . it is reasonable to assume that the behavior is symptomatic of intolerable stress in [the child's] environment—whether conflicts in the home, frustrations at school, or among his peers—or of brewing anxiety or emotional instability within him."

Schramm puts it a slightly different way: no child is likely to be harmed very much by television if he has warm and secure social relationships and has no serious psychological troubles. Dr. Eisenberg says: "Prolonged and exclusive watching of television is most sharply seen as an indication of something wrong with the child's social adjustment. A child who is a poor reader or whose parents are not available to him may fall into this. *If TV were filled with the most wonderful content, it would still be detrimental if it kept the child from playing with other children, from studying and so forth.*"

Most children in their early years benefit intellectually from television—in vocabulary-building, in absorbing a general set of cultural values, in stocking their minds with concepts and facts which otherwise they wouldn't have learned that early. "I suspect that TV informs and instructs in its own way as much as colleges do," says Dr. Palmer. "TV has a greater educational influence than all the formal establishments devoted to education. *So for a parent to say, 'I don't let my child watch television' is to relegate him to cultural deprivation.*"

Palmer surmises that TV "just must have a lot to do" with a child's acquisition of simple, basic knowledge about his country and his world; the fact that there are such things as Presidents and policemen and soldiers and that they perform certain functions. As children approach adolescence, however, the brighter ones decide spontaneously that TV has taught them all it can, and turn to books, magazines, records, movies and social activities. The less bright children tend to remain heavy users of TV.

Part of this decline in usage by brighter children seems attributable to the high content of fantasy—instead of reality—in children's TV. The more imaginative child, as he grows older, is hungrier for information than for pure entertainment. Child psychologists have suggested that a medium so potent in the transmission of information—about nature, science, ethics—is derelict when it opts instead for the wispy, fragile world of fantasy, whether live or animated.

Schramm says this: "Do we consider our children so slight a resource that we can afford to bring them up on an intellectual diet of such a kind? Do we really believe that this is the way to make leaders and thinkers?"

In addition, it is a fact that most adults—including television programmers—chronically underestimate how much a child can absorb and understand. One psychologist told us that he believed *any* principle could be taught to *any* child, as long as it was translated into terms familiar to the child.

Says Dr. Eisenberg: "Children often are simply not treated seriously enough. I don't mean that first-graders should be reading 'War and Peace.' But some of the truths about life contained in 'War and Peace' certainly *can* be taught to children."

Children's programs are afraid to talk about death, says Eisenberg, but many children already have been privy to the deaths of relatives and friends. "They'll have confused ideas [about it] unless we bring some clarity to the subject," he says.

But all such altruistic concerns are simply not the principal preoccupation—nor can they be—of TV programmers in the American system of commercial television: the networking structure which places the advertiser's interests first and the audience's second. "What has held back children's television . . . for 20 years is the commercial interests of the broadcasters," says Dr. Gerald Lesser, Bigelow professor of education and developmental psychology at Harvard University's Graduate School of Education.

"I have faith in kids. I'm not saying that the programs produced for children have terrible, harmful consequences. But it's meaningless junk that can be put on for little expense and makes a lot of money. The quality of most of it is abysmally bad. Not enough thought has gone into it. Commercial exploitation has produced an endless, grubby bag of cartoons."

Lesser and a number of other psychologists we talked to lament this fixation by children's programmers with "winning the ratings battle." As long ago as 1961, Schramm and his colleagues were concerned about it, and all the same factors are still operative today:

"We sympathize with television broadcasters for the competitive pressure of the sponsor system. . . . Because of this competition, the networks also are forced to be tough-minded about program ratings—for example, even to discard some lower-rating and higher-quality programs because they influence the rating of programs next to them. It is necessary to maximize the drawing power of the schedule at the cost of experimentation with 'quality.' This undoubtedly represents a severe problem to commercial broadcasters. We consider that it also represented a shortsighted attitude which may produce immediate profits, but will ultimately result in harm to both sponsor and broadcaster."

Occasional specials sprinkled into the children's TV schedule mitigate this condition somewhat, but not sufficiently to satisfy most child experts, who feel that the networks produce quality specials almost against their better judgment and only to keep the critics at bay.

"Children's television gets by on good intentions," Lesser says. "They'll frequently take a classic children's book and destroy it. But those programs are rarely subjected to critical analysis in the press, and the networks automatically get a high mark just for effort. But if we ever get beyond this stage of applauding them for merely being well-intentioned, then we can make progress."

He thinks that television has never truly captured the imaginations of children, nor moved them, as much as a handful of authors—Lewis Carroll, E. B. White and illustrator Maurice Sendak, among others—whose special genius has been in touching the minds of children. And that's due partly to the fact that writing TV programs for children has never been the highly prestigious undertaking that would attract the best creative minds.

But what *should* children's television be? That is the

pertinent question since (1) children watch so much television (an average of 50 hours a week), and (2) about two-thirds of intellectual development occurs before a child even starts his formal education (according to University of Chicago psychologist Benjamin Bloom).

What kinds of programs *would* satisfy the social scientists and psychologists and educators who are unhappy about the current state of "kidvid" in the United States? We asked that question of a dozen or more specialists while researching this series of articles, and discovered a surprising consistency in their recommendations.

Principally, they favor "reality" as opposed to "fantasy"—stories and essays and mini-documentaries about the real world, meticulously produced with young people in mind. Eisenberg, for example, would like to see programs with "role models" for children to pattern themselves after. "Let them see what doctors do, and what astronauts, writers and poets do. That way they can form career ambitions."

Nobody says that slapstick should be eliminated from children's TV schedules. In small doses it's a pleasing and helpful satire of all the silliness that goes on in the adult world, and children understand it as such. Similarly, children are quick to perceive the essential foolishness of an adult who is "talking down" to them in patronizing fashion.

But television's chief task ought to be to create a variety of options, a "cafeteria" (in the words of one psychologist) of program types so that children would have at least the *chance* of browsing among reasonable alternatives and picking the best. "Right now, we have no decent range of options," says Dr. Lesser. "There are a few good programs like *Misterogers* and *Captain Kangaroo*, and after that it's mostly cartoons and things like *Romper Room* and *Bozo the Clown*, which are purely exploitive."

Dr. Sheldon White, professor of psychology at Harvard's Graduate School of Education, says it would be most beneficial to "put before children organized essays on the life around them," with special attention to the needs of children who prefer more serious TV fare. Networks should give at least as much thought, he believes, to what will be good for the children as to what will be good for the ratings. "They have found out that fast slapstick will draw the maximum audiences. Maybe all attempts to break that mold will meet with defeat."

The value of the medium to children is to show them places and events they otherwise wouldn't see, since children, obviously, don't have the chance to get around very much. *The ultimate accomplishment—according to TV Guide's sampling of experts—is to catch the child's imagination by showing him the world, what its possibilities are, how people get along in it, how they interract with each other, and what his place in it might be.* This can be done either through fiction or fact.

TV can also provide the child with information on "folk heroes"—such as Thomas Jefferson, Charles Lindbergh, Daniel Webster, Jonas Salk, Mark Twain, the astronauts, among thousands of others—whose achievements might spur the child to study these lives further and perhaps even say to himself, "Maybe *I*

could do something like that." At the moment such a question forms itself in the mind of a child, television has performed a true and lasting service to the nation's health and future.

Such goals require a cadre of creative people in the ranks of TV programmers—writers, producers and directors, as well as sociologists and psychologists—which has not materialized thus far in the 25-year life of television in America: creators in sufficient numbers and of sufficient dedication to employ the medium of television to its highst potential in speaking to children.

The National Commission on the Causes and Prevention of Violence stated in part in its report released September 23: "Although all of the networks say that they are keeping abreast of current research on the effects of violence on viewers, until recently . . . each has taken the position that the research . . . is *wholly inconclusive. . . .* We believe that the television networks, network affiliates, independent stations, and other members of the broadcasting industry should recognize the strong probability that a high incidence of violence in entertainment programs is contributing to undesirable attitudes and even to violence in American society. It is time for them *to stop asserting* 'not proved' to charges of adverse effects from pervasive violence in television programming . . . when they should instead be accepting the burden of proof that such programs are not harmful to the public interest. Much remains to be learned about media violence and its effects, but enough is known to require that constructive action be taken at once to reduce the amount and alter the kind of violent programs which have pervaded television."

The networks were quick to reply that they had already eliminated the largest bulk of "violence" from their new programs during the many months in which the Commission was preparing its study. Chairman Milton S. Eisenhower acknowledged this but pointed out that the old, violent network programming was now being syndicated as reruns and that it would probably take a decade for the stations to work these shows out of their programming. That put the case up to the individual stations' managements.

It is patently inadequate, however, for TV programmers merely to create shows which do *not* display violence and which do *not* flaunt sex. What is required is the more positive action of fashioning shows which utilize, to best advantage, television's vast potential for reaching the minds of children—of touching them and moving them and enlarging them.

The constant questioning about the effects of sex and violence on children—questions which, to date, are unanswerable—has left many with the illusion that this is the only aspect of TV to be concerned with. This is not true. What is required quite as urgently is for broadcasters—both commercial and noncommercial—to marshal the effort and the money and the will to create children's programs which ·have point and pith and imagination.

When that happens, we will know that American television is taking its responsibilities to children seriously.

The Oldest Living Teen-ager

At 40, Dick Clark is still capitalizing on
his remarkable appeal to youth
by Digby Diehl

(Bruce McBroom)

Dominating the coffee table in Dick Clark's Sunset Strip office sits a large sturdily encased Ant Farm. And within those confines intended for numbers of instinctively obedient *Formicidae Hymenoptera* is contained a secret philosophy concerning *Adolescentes Americani*. Why, you can almost see those tiny teen-agers crawling around busily between the two sheets of glass when Dick says . . .

"I see no sin in being commercial. I've had a lot of interesting arguments with hippies about this. My 'thing' is being commercial. There can't be anything *wrong* with that, as long as this is a capitalistic country."

The World's Oldest Living Teen-ager smiled capitalistically and ticked off the provinces of his Youth Empire. "We own 16 companies in Los Angeles alone," he explained. "The television arm has two regular shows on the air right now, *American Bandstand* and *Get It Together*, which made its debut January 3, as well as my 'Music Bag' special, which is still in syndication. We have completed three motion pictures, and another is scheduled for immediate production. We have the largest production-promotion company for concerts anywhere, and we own three radio stations." That's not even mentioning the teen publication ("The Dick Clark Newsletter"), drive-in restaurants, radio commercials, CATV programming, promotion for soda and guitars, and hot-rod racetrack interests that Dick is involved in. He notes, and probably correctly, " that we have one of the best organizations in the country for reaching the youth market." Truly a thought to thrill an Ant Farmer's heart.

At 40, Dick Clark still has the sincere, well-scrubbed good looks of an emissary from the Campus Crusade For Christ. His pleasing DJ's voice has not altered with success, and, perhaps more than ever, he exudes oceans of likability. In the midst of his Teen Kingdom a bit of business briskness is added to the on-camera relaxed charm, but the man is very much like his television image. In his role as a teen tycoon, however, "Clahk" is held in awe as a manipulator with much power. Power, alas, that might have been greater if not for those Congressional investigations which brought on the payola scandal—alleged gifts to disc jockeys—in 1959.

"At the time," Dick recalls, "I was the only nationally

known figure playing recorded music. As the guy out front, I got asked a lot of questions, and the Senators were surprised to find out that there was so much money in pop music I didn't need to be paid to play records. It was a shock to the political mind that I could accumulate great wealth in a short length of time without stealing. They're not used to that sort of thing." After seven months of hide-and-seek, the investigating committee exonerated Dick of payola charges, but left ABC with the embarrassing feeling that there might be a minor conflict-of-interest problem.

"ABC asked me to divest myself of my recording and publishing interests, which I did. Probably now that complex would be in excess of $12 million. I had 33 music companies (domestic and foreign) involved in everything from publishing to record pressing, distribution, artist management, label-making . . . there wasn't anything we didn't cover." Although he now refers to the investigations sardonically as "a very *maturing* experience," Dick emerged with popularity higher than ever, riding *American Bandstand* on the crest of a rock-and-roll television wave that hasn't stopped yet.

The *Bandstand* is one of the dinosaurs of television, along with Lawrence Welk and Ed Sullivan, with only two to go to make it 20 years on the air. The Saturday afternoon show no longer has its former influence as a make-or-break record outlet ("No, but it would if we were on every day again," says Clark with a twinkle), yet the same low-budget format continues to draw audiences, year after year. "When I first entered the national TV scene, rock-and-roll was a 'fringe quantity' to most adults. Radio had already created a thing called Top 40 music, and *Bandstand* had been on the air since 1952, so when it went network in 1957, it became the TV Top 40 outlet automatically."

The *Bandstand* show was originally created because it was less expensive than old English movies for daytime programming, but its rapid ascent brought prestige and a host of imitators. "*Shindig!, Hullabaloo, West Ninth Street, Hollywood à Go Go, Shivaree, Where the Action Is* and *Happening '68* all followed and failed," he points out. "They all just went to the Top 100 sheet and booked the acts. Even our own show, *Where the Action Is*, which was probably the most expensive, ambitious daytime show ever put on, couldn't touch the *Bandstand* ratings."

Can anyone really look at a TV screen writhing with *American Bandstand* youth and not be reminded of ants busily tunneling over and under each other? There is a certain parallelism, according to Dick. Like people-watching. "People-watching! You just can't beat it! It's been going on since folks just sat in the railroad station. All it needs is a personality to head it up who will subjugate himself to the audience, and that's me."

Over the years Dick has evolved smoothly from his role as the reassuring Big Brother chaperon into that missing link of American life: the Good Father. Appropriately 52 percent of the present *Bandstand* audience is composed of women over 18, hungrily reminding themselves that *Dick Clark is 40 and still looks young!* "I

don't try to fake the teen mannerisms," he says. "I *act* 20 years older than the kids because I *am*. I dress the part—I don't affect the clothing or the hairstyle or the language of youth, because it changes all the time. I'm the only constant factor of the show."

Clark's *Happening '68* and its indistinguishable sequel, *Happening,* heaped records, personalities, contests, fashions, and "anything we thought might have appeal" on top of superclean Paul Revere, Mark Lindsay, and the schlock-rock Raiders, attempting to tap that subteen audience. They had all the Nielsen allure of a stale bottle of soda. *Get It Together,* with Sam Riddle as continuing co-host, presents pop groups live, in-concert in the slot just before *Bandstand.* "But I still don't expect it to be another *Bandstand,*" he admits. "Let's face it; kids have turned to movies."

So has Dick, running in tandem with American International Pictures, producers of "Beach Party Bingo," "I Was a Teenage Werewolf" and "The Wild Angels." The first film, "Psych-out," followed the classic DeMille formula: nine reels of blood, horror, violence and sex; one reel of redemption. When pressed concerning his "Psych-out" cast of "teen-agers" who are nearly 30, he pleads "artistic license"; as for the rest: "I can't defend it. There are a lot of goofs in it, things you could correct if you had more time."

His second, "The Savage Seven," is a "contemporary Western" with motorcycle cowboys. According to Dick, "It's laughingly called the 'Gone With the Wind' of motorcycle pictures," and has music by a British pop group, the Cream.

His recent contribution to cinematic art is last year's "Killers Three," a teen version of "Bonnie and Clyde" (how's *that* for an original idea?). "This is a black comedy of the anti-hero type," says Dick. "The story of three young people who are trying to do no more than young people today: get out of the rut, be different, succeed in the way they want to."

Dick sees these films as informational community services. Concerning "Psych-out," he says: "Everybody has said this is a picture that kids ought to take their parents to see, so that they'll know what a very influential minority is causing to happen." Right. But which minority, the hippies or Dick Clark Productions?

All of these gems have zoomed into the profit margin thus far, which makes one wonder why Clark's next effort will be a full-length animated cartoon version of "Robinson Crusoe." Dick is quick to answer: "I see it as a sort of 'Yellow Submarine,' complete, of course, with a rock-music score." Of course. For that musical silver lining makes everything fit into the ecology of the Ant Farm.

When his promotional machinery swings into high gear on those movie score tunes, it is a marvel to watch. For example, a few years ago, the Cream's "Tennis, Anyone?" was transmogrified into "Theme from the 'Savage Seven'" and made a hit when Atco Records made an "error in labeling"; it failed to place "Savage Seven" in large letters in the title, Dick claimed. Incredibly, this became the focus for a publicity campaign, an excuse for dozens of calls to DJ's, a hundred telegrams to station managers, 300 telephone calls by his staff to record pluggers across the country, memos to distributors, press releases wholesale, immediate items in the trade papers, a hard push on the now-chagrined employees of Atco. All this directed almost completely from memory by Dick.

After the hit single comes the personal appearance tour, which he also handles with remarkable energy. His booking and promotion unit, which skyrocketed to success with the *American Bandstand* tours, began in 1956, and last year grossed $5 million. He has arranged one-nighters for the Monkees, the Raiders, Tom Jones, Miriam Makeba, Bill Cosby, Engelbert Humperdinck, the Supremes, the Four Tops, Marvin Gaye, and hordes of lesser-knowns, totaling over 300 last year. And new businesses keep popping up like teen boat cruises, campus film festivals, circuses, and even, shudder, adult entertainments.

Meanwhile, Dick's heart is still in televisionland. His documentary special, "Years of Rock," culled from past Clark productions is presently being negotiated. As Dick sees it, this capsule survey of pop music from 1950 to the present is a way to cash in on "the nostalgic yearnings of young people. With the oldies-but-goodies being revived, sometimes I feel like a history teacher." Typically, the ol' history teacher has placed at least one bet on the future by shooting a TV pilot of a popular music show featuring Roger Williams for CBS.

Let the country boys have evening shows, for Dick is being considered for one of those early-morning 90-minute shows with absolutely no teen interest. He likes the idea. "I have a whole host of *Bandstand* graduates who remember me when—and would still watch. I'd like to play something other than a teen idol, which I've never really been anyway." If he does it, he may not corner just the teens but all of us.

Of course, he abhors such cynicism. "I've always been the front man for things writers don't like. Initially, they didn't like rock-and-roll. It was always, 'Dick Clark, interesting fellow who knows what he's doing, but how can he push this garbage on youth?'" Alas, writers— and Dick Clarks—never change. "Not everybody enjoys filet," insists the cultivator of youthful taste, "they often prefer hot dogs—or if not 'prefer,' then that's the way their taste has been cultivated."

Oh yes, one other thing about the Ant Farm on Dick Clark's coffee table that isn't true of his bustling teen kingdom—

All the ants are dead.

A TV Guide Close-Up   **Movie** © **6:00** **4** **⑳**

Ray Bolger, Judy Garland and Jack Haley (MGM)

"THE WIZARD OF OZ"

Special

This excursion into delightful fantasy is telecast for the 12th time.

L. Frank Baum's story follows a young girl from Kansas named Dorothy. Caught in a tornado, she's whisked out of the Midwest and dumped smack into magic Munchkin Land.

Traveling on the Yellow Brick Road, Dorothy meets the Scarecrow, the Tin Woodman and the Cowardly Lion, who join her to seek the Emerald City and the wonderful Wizard of Oz.

The opulently mounted Mervyn LeRoy production was filmed with special effects and dozens of sets. Victor Fleming directed. The songs are by Harold Arlen and E. Y. "Yip" Harburg, who won an Oscar for "Over the Rainbow." Judy Garland won a special juvenile Oscar for her performance.

Cast . . . Dorothy: *Judy Garland.* Scarecrow: *Ray Bolger.* Cowardly Lion: *Bert Lahr.* Tin Woodman: *Jack Haley.* Wicked Witch: *Margaret Hamilton.* Wizard of Oz: *Frank Morgan.* Good Witch: *Billie Burke.* Highlights . . . *Judy:* "Over the Rainbow." *Ray, Bert, Jack:* "If I Only Had a Brain, the Nerve, a Heart." *Judy, Ray, Jack, Bert:* "We're Off to See the Wizard." (Rerun)

ASTAIRE

He's hung up his dancing shoes, but he can't shed that special magic
by Leslie Raddatz

He announced his retirement in 1945. Three years and three pictures later Hedda Hopper wrote, "He will probably be doing his final scenes from a wheelchair." The following year he received a special Oscar for his contributions to musical motion pictures. In 1953, after still more high-flying films, The New York Times referred to him as "the ageless Astaire." By 1957 he was saying, "When they review my pictures, they don't say whether they're good or bad—they just write about how old I am." In 1958, when his first television special won nine Emmy Awards, Time called him "the slim little light-foot guy with his ageless grace."

Today, Anno Domini 1970, Fred Astaire—at what he refers to sardonically as "a notable 70"—is co-starring as Robert Wagner's superthief father in four episodes of *It Takes a Thief* this season. And the old magic is still there. After his first appearance in the ABC series, Variety's critic wrote, "His *élan* steals the show from 'Thief' Robert Wagner." Another critic said, "When the younger star looks up at the older, there is such unabashed admiration in him that it's like a glow."

Wagner does not mind being upstaged by Astaire, and the glow goes back a long time—to the days years ago when Wagner, then a boy living near the Bel Air golf course, would watch Astaire playing and say, "Good morning, Mr. Astaire," and Astaire would answer, "Good morning, Mr. Wagner." Someone who knows Wagner says, "Bob adores him." It was Wagner who called Astaire to ask him to play his father in *It Takes a Thief*. When Astaire, after debating the matter for six months, agreed to take the role, Wagner said, "The shows you're in will be *your* shows." Astaire doesn't admit to caring about that. Basically a shy man, according to a friend, he says, "I don't think I'm the greatest actor in the world—I don't even know whether I'm any good. I consider myself in semiretirement. I don't have to work—I do what *I* like."

What he likes to do no longer includes dancing. Although 15 years ago he was saying, "I don't believe the public would accept me in a nondancing role," he has in recent years played many dramatic parts, the first in the old *GE Theater*, which he refers to as "Ronnie Reagan's show." Today he says flatly, "I'm not going to dance any more, with anybody." But the dancer's grace and flow are still in every move he makes, whether entering a TV scene or running—not walking—to answer the phone in his spacious Beverly Hills home. It could

Astaire (left) on the set with Robert Wagner (Gene Trindl)

hardly be otherwise. He has been dancing since he was four, when he was Fred Austerlitz in his native Omaha, Nebraska. Soon afterward his mother took him and his sister Adele to New York and put them in Ned Wayburn's dancing school. When they entered vaudeville, the name became Astaire ("Austerlitz sounded too much like a battle," Fred said later). Although a Jersey City theater manager once said, "The girl seems to have talent, but the boy can do nothing," the Astaires became vaudeville headliners and by 1916 were on Broadway in "Over the Top," starring Ed Wynn.

Other top musicals followed—"Apple Blossoms," "Passing Show of 1918," "Lady Be Good," "Funny Face," "The Band Wagon." The team broke up in 1932, when Adele married Lord Charles Cavendish, whom she had met during the London run of "The Band Wagon." Fred continued on his own in "The Gay Divorcee." He came to Hollywood in 1933—the year he married socialite Phyllis Potter—and scored his first movie hit in "Flying Down to Rio." It starred Dolores Del Rio and Gene Raymond, but Fred Astaire and Ginger Rogers stole the picture. The rest, as they say, is history—the succession of Astaire-Rogers musicals, followed by 20-odd more with such dancing partners as Rita Hayworth, Judy Garland, Vera-Ellen, Cyd Charisse, Eleanor Powell, Paulette Goddard and Leslie Caron, and four TV specials with partner Barrie Chase.

Over the years Astaire has been characteristically tactful in refusing to name his favorite dancing partner, but hints surface in conversation with him: "Adele was right for me at the time." . . . "Ginger was a great personality. She may have faked it a little, but we knew we had a great thing going." . . . "Rita Hayworth and Cyd Charisse were probably a little tall for me—I'm 5 feet 10, and by the time they got those high heels on . . ." But of Barrie Chase he says, "She was the inspiration for the TV specials. I don't think I would have done them without her."

But Fred Astaire has always been more than a dancer. There have been other popular movie dancers—Gene Kelly, Dan Dailey, Donald O'Connor—but none of them had the charisma, the aura of the superstar which Astaire has had for so many years. A veteran Hollywood reporter once said that there were only five superstars—Greta Garbo, Clark Gable, Humphrey Bogart, John Wayne and Fred Astaire. Robert Wagner says, "He's got it going all the way—his clothes, his house, his automobiles, his whole movement and the energy he generates. There's not a false note struck by him. It's a feeling, a rhythm—it's all of those things." On the set of *It Takes a Thief,* he is treated with dignity and respect, partly because of his longtime high standing in the Hollywood pecking order, but also because, despite his affability and unfailing courtesy, he has an innate dignity of his own which inspires dignity in return. In an area where first names are usually *de rigueur,* he is almost always addressed as "Mr. Astaire"—only old friends call him Fred. A co-worker on *It Takes a Thief* says, "Some of them treat him as if he were fragile as an egg. Others are blasé. But they all flip."

Unlike many stars, Astaire has managed to retain his unique position in Hollywood and throughout the world without playing roles that were romantic *per se.* Director Rouben Mamoulian once said, "He acts like an uncle in love scenes, but the women seem to go for him anyway." And Astaire admits, "I never even kissed Ginger Rogers in most of our pictures, not only because I didn't want to, but my wife didn't want me to." Astaire *is* a romantic figure, however, whether in white tie and tails twirling around a dance floor in an old movie or now, at 70, in open-collared shirt and Apache tie. Many of his fans did not approve of him in "Finian's Rainbow" because he was not the suave, impeccably dressed, dashing personality they had grown to know. In *It Takes a Thief,* there is a *marchesa* waiting impatiently and believably for him to keep their date.

The white tie and tails are gone now. In fact, in his autobiography, "Steps in Time," Astaire says, "At the risk of disillusionment, I must admit that I don't like top hats, white ties or tails." But on- and off-screen, Fred Astaire is still as suave, impeccable and dashing as ever. He still races horses, as he has for many years, and often goes to the track. Unlike many horse fanciers, though, he says, "The game has paid for itself." Concerning the racetrack, he adds emphatically, "It's like a missionary center compared to the theater today!"

He still plays golf, but he does not go out dancing ("I'm not the discothèque type"), but then he rarely ever did. However, if he hears a record he likes, he may "move with it." In the center of his library is a pool table ("I've been accused of building the house around the pool table. I guess maybe I did"). Nearby is a set of drums ("I play them whenever the mood strikes me"). On the walls are pictures of race horses, with the most prominent spot reserved for Astaire's all-time money winner, Triplicate, which cost $6000 and won $250,000. Astaire speaks familiarly of such wealthy racing figures as Jock Whitney and, despite only two years of formal education in a New Jersey elementary school, has been at ease for decades in high social circles everywhere.

His home, even by Beverly Hills standards, is impressive—marble-paved entryway leading into high-ceilinged, richly decorated rooms with large windows overlooking the swimming pool and handsomely landscaped grounds. Astaire's 92-year-old mother lives in a wing of the house originally built for his daughter, Ava. Mrs. Austerlitz came to California to be with her son when his wife died in 1954. The Astaire nonchalance cracks only when he speaks of his wife's death. "I still can't quite realize it happened," he says. "That may sound strange after 16 years." Daughter Ava, recently separated, lives in an apartment in Beverly Hills. Her older brother, Fred Astaire Jr., is a charter pilot in northern California and the father of Astaire's only grandchild. Sister Adele divides her time among New York, Ireland and Jamaica.

Unlike most men his age, Astaire prefers not to talk of the past. "I've had my kicks." He shrugs. "I have lots of things to be pleased about." But, after 66 years as a performer, he has definite ideas about what he feels constitutes entertainment: "The shows I have done are a lot of fun. They aren't pretentious or trying to prove anything. They are for entertainment—period. If people don't like it, that's *their* problem. It definitely is not mine. This has been my show business attitude for many years. It's the only way." Concerning present movie and theater trends, he says, "They've forgotten a seven-letter word—decency." Angry about sexual scenes that were added to a movie after he had completed his work in it, he says, "They weren't in the script, or I wouldn't have done the film. People wrote and said they were surprised I would appear in such a film. I was as surprised as they were. I will not be part of anything crummy. I couldn't go to work if I had to do something distasteful to me."

How long will he keep on doing what he is doing? Although Robert Wagner said, "I want him to do as many shows as he can," unfortunately for Wagner and the fans of Fred Astaire, *It Takes a Thief* will leave the air after the summer rerun season.

True, this particular program may be over and Astaire may insist that he is semiretired, but you can be sure he'll be around, as nimble and debonair as ever.

A hit--in any language

The glowing account of how a noted author became involved with
"The Forsyte Saga," which has captivated audiences in 55 nations

by James A. Michener

I had been invited to Sweden on official business and time was pressing. I suggested that we meet on Wednesday, but the government men protested, "Impossible! In Sweden everyone spends Wednesday night with the Forsytes."

"Who are they?" I asked.

"*The Forsyte Saga*. John Galsworthy's nine novels made into a brilliant television series by the BBC."

And that was my introduction to a madness which has gripped a large part of the world. In Holland whole families stayed home to watch the 26 episodes. In Malta, which had recently gained independence from England, everyone stayed glued to the telly to follow the Forsytes, an upper-middle-class English family who thrived from 1879 to the mid-'20s. It was a notable hit in Zambia.

The series was shown in 55 different countries (either with subtitles or dubbed dialogue depending on the country), including Russia, and wherever it went it captivated the citizenry. When one of the stars, Susan Hampshire, visited Oslo, Norway, during the run there, 40,000 jammed the stadium to see her, and another 20,000 lined the streets.

Last October the series was finally aired on NET stations across America and the results were stunning. Jacob Hay, TV writer for the Baltimore News American, summarized critical opinion: "This series is absolutely superb, utterly compelling and unnervingly believable."

TV Guide's Cleveland Amory called it "entertainment—prime, rare, rib-roast, Kansas City–cut enter-

tainment." John Beaufort of the Christian Science Monitor checked 30 stations that were showing the series and found these responses: "absolutely staggering, immense, one of the best."

As the episodes unfolded and America had a chance to meet the fascinating members of the sprawling Forsyte family, the mania that had overtaken other nations hit. In Moorhead, Minnesota, Professor Herbert Abraham and his wife built their entertaining plans around the Forsytes. "We invited only people who were watching regularly, and at 9 o'clock we moved to the television room and conversation halted."

The Jack Bilers of Toledo, Ohio, like many families, watched as a group. "What a thrill it was to be entertained instead of insulted. We find ourselves, after an episode is over, discussing the Forsytes just as if we knew them."

Helen Hayes, who was visiting lecturer at the University of Illinois when the series was being shown, got back to Chicago each Sunday night just as the *Saga* came on the screen. Going directly to the television set, she sat enraptured and allowed no one to speak until the episode was over.

If NET was uncertain whether it had a hit or not, they found out when some of their stations interrupted scheduled episodes. KERA of Dallas, Texas, ran into transmission troubles one Sunday night and had to cancel. The switchboard was swamped with more than 400 protests that night, 100 the next day and 60 on Tuesday. KWSC in Pullman, Washington, made a real miscalculation: "We blew it December 23. Foolishly we sub-

The battling cousins, Jolyon the artist (Kenneth More, left) and Soames the lawyer (Eric Porter), at the start of the feud whose consequences last nearly half a century (NET)

The star-crossed lovers, Jon (Martin Jarvis) and Fleur (Susan Hampshire), cannot marry because of the Forsyte feud. This role propelled Miss Hampshire into instant stardom (NET)

stituted an evening of Christmas offerings and turned our viewers into Scrooges. Bah, humbug, how dare you pre-empt the Forsytes?"

In Miami, the NET outlet received a constant chain of phone calls: "We've just arrived from the North on our vacation and we daren't miss the Forsytes. When do you show them?" Numerous stations received calls of a special kind: "We were traveling and missed the last two chapters of *The Forsyte Saga*. If we came down to the station, could you screen them for us?" Station WGBH in Boston handled this rather neatly: "So many viewers wrote of their great sadness at having missed one episode or another that we ran two 'Forsyte Catch-up Weeks,' with episodes 1–5 running Monday to Friday the first week and 6–10 the second."

The *Saga* pretty well determined my life for the next half-year. Come Sunday night at 8:30 my wife would say to our guests, "You'll have to go home now." When I visited the University of Texas on a tight schedule I ducked out of one meeting so that I could catch the *Saga* on the local station. In a dark room I found about half the professors sharing the television screen with me.

In the middle of the series I experienced a crisis. I was invited to an exciting trip to Tromso in northern Europe, the Serengeti Plain in Africa and Angkor Wat in Asia. I declined, explaining to my hosts, "I can't miss the central episodes of the series." They asked, "What series?" and I said, "Fleur's getting married," and when they asked me who Fleur was, I knew they were hopeless. But they arranged a schedule whereby I could fly out of New York right after the Sunday night screening and return late on a Tuesday in time to catch the rerun that night. In this way I had to miss only two episodes.

My most instructive experience came in Tromso, a small Norwegian town more than 200 miles north of the Arctic Circle. In winter, of course, there was no daylight, and as I wandered the streets hungry for something to read, I happened to find a bookstore, where I asked, "Would you by chance have any volumes of 'The Forsyte Saga'?"

"Any?" the man said. "We have them all." And he showed me a shelf containing many copies. He explained that the television series had been the most popular ever screened in Norway. "It was in English, of course, but we bought the books and followed the story." I told him that I had missed two of the central episodes, and when I told him which two, he reconstructed them from memory. "Seeing that series was one of the top adventures of my life," he told me.

To anyone interested in television the question naturally arises, "Did the excellence of the *Saga* come about because it was built upon excellent books?" No.

Galsworthy's first novel in the series, "A Man of Property," appeared in 1906 and was quickly recognized as a fine piece of work. It was built upon a set of stalwart characters—the famous Forsyte aunts and uncles—and it depicted a mid-Victorian style of family life that had long since vanished. What was not noticed at the time was something which became apparent in the later novels: whole sections of the book were written almost as if they were passages from a play.

Galsworthy was a highly skilled dramatist and at this time was more famous for his plays than for his novels. Notable dramas like "The Silver Box" and "Justice" proved his interest in social themes and enjoyed long runs in London theaters. It is instructive, if one has the time, to read the nine novels as the series unfolds, for then one will see how much of Galsworthy can be lifted from the printed page right onto the screen. In fact, almost every good line in the series comes directly from Galsworthy, shortened sometimes but always with his stamp.

On the whole, however, the novels were ordinary. The last four seemed appallingly bad when I first read them and even worse when I reread them in Norway. When Galsworthy published them, there must have been at least two dozen men and women writing in English who could have done better (Ernest Hemingway, Edith Wharton, Thomas Hardy to name three).

The brilliance of this series does not stem from the books. The early volumes were good, but the series was better.

Why? First, it was not afraid to take time. Robin Hill and Mapledurham became real places. The episode "Dinner at Swithin's" showed in leisurely fashion how the Forsytes gathered for a ritual meal which of itself was unimportant except that when it was finished you knew the family better. Twenty-six hour-long episodes are the equivalent of about 10 full-length movies, and in that time real characters can be depicted.

Second, it was done seriously. In the first episode the characters caught exactly the right mood of gentle sarcasm plus intense preoccupation with their petty problems, and this mood was sustained throughout the series. Since the characters cared, the audience cared; but since the characters had a sense of self-amusement, the audience viewed them charitably and with frequent glimpses of recognition. They were real people, and if their problems were self-centered and petty, they were nevertheless problems in which we became involved. Care was taken with sets, with costumes, with the selection of old newsreels inserted to lend authenticity, and with scripts which preserved Galsworthy's dialogue.

Third, it was cast to perfection. Among the scores of characters there were almost none who were not top flight. Since the budget had to be kept low (the entire series cost only $700,000 to make), great names were not used, but great actors were. The five or six principal leads were flawless. I don't see how they could have been better.

Eric Porter, as Soames Forsyte, found himself with one of the top dramatic roles of this century. Imagine playing the lead in 10 movies, progressing from an obnoxious young lawyer in the first to a splendid old fighter in the last: great confrontations in court, rape, divorce, betrayal, hatreds that continue to the grave, love for a confused daughter. If Porter never got another role—and he ought to get dozens on the strength of this performance—he could retire happily.

Kenneth More, as his cousin Jolyon, will be most people's choice as the male star of the series. He was unbelievably good, a Dickens-type character with whom one intuitively identified.

Nyree Dawn Porter, a beautiful New Zealand girl and no relation to Eric Porter, had the principal female role, Irene, and filled it with distinction. She was tortured, bitter and, in the end, something of a witch. She is perhaps the character most interesting to watch in her development.

The surprise of the series was a marvelous young actress, Susan Hampshire, whose body is as supple as a reed, whose face is a mirror for transparent emotions. For her role as principal female lead in what amounted to five full-length movies, Miss Hampshire was paid minimum scale. It was the best deal she ever made, for it projected her into instant stardom. In fact, she could have afforded to pay the BBC for the privilege of appearing as Fleur.

But it was in the casting of the 116 subsidiary characters that the BBC outdid itself. Watch John Welsh, as Soames's father; he could not be improved upon. Or Derek Francis, as the corrupted manager who brings disgrace upon Soames's company. I thought Lana Morris, as the Austrian governess for whom Jolyon abandons his wife, was excellent. And Margaret Tyzack, as Winifred, was one of the luminous spots in the series, growing better with each episode.

Had the BBC taken these 26 scripts and filled them with hack actors, they'd have had a hack series. But with this cast, the series almost had to be a success.

Much of the success was due to the nostalgia with which the world looks back on the relative stability of the Victorian Age. I was fascinated by glimpses into family life when even the most moderate household contained three or four servants. Twice in the *Saga* women are shown living in near penury. Each has her servant in proper costume.

English critics have suggested that we enjoy looking at the Forsytes because we can feel so superior to them. It is true that they live within their own little fortresses, oblivious to the problems of the world; but they are not trivial people. The fact that they control their society rather than allowing it to control them makes them enviable to those of us who are submerged by the world. I'd like to see a gang of hippies tangle with Soames Forsyte!

Finally, one of the most charming aspects of the series was the short interviews following each episode. They were conducted by James Day, president of NET, and allowed the viewer to meet at first hand the principal actors, the writers, the designers, the BBC directors. The high seriousness with which everyone approached the subject enticed the viewer into doing the same. Only one interview was disappointing, the one with Susan Hampshire, for she came on unnecessarily flippant. The rest were like visits with well-informed friends.

Many critics have asked, "Isn't the *Saga* really a soap opera?" That's easy. Of course it was soap opera—at its glowing best. In structure it was remarkably similar to *Peyton Place:* a large number of interrelated characters is set down in a constricted setting and things happen, with each episode containing glimpses of three or four continuing stories. The difference is this: in *The Forsyte Saga* the characters are differentiated, well rounded and with universal application; the dialogue is literate; the problems dealt with are substantial; and over all there is a high seriousness.

In the Bible the Book of Ruth is a soap opera saved by these same qualities. "Ethan Frome," one of the best short novels ever written, is pure soap opera, but with what magnificent control and impact! I have never objected to soap opera if it attained the quality of "Romeo and Juliet," and I am not ashamed to confess that I fell completely under the spell of this one. The Saturday Review was correct when, in giving the *Saga* an award, it said in the citation, "A sustained level of excellence demonstrating that the lowly art of the soap opera can be elevated to new heights."

Part of the success stemmed from the fact that the series was long. It lasted half a year, so that you lived with the characters and came to know them. Had it consisted of 13 half-hour episodes, I believe it would have been a failure. The human mind sometimes wants substantial statements, long books, powerful motion pictures.

This leads me to wonder what television can do next to keep the worldwide audience which the Forsytes commanded. The Jalna books from Canada would be a natural and the Canadian Broadcasting Corporation ought to get on that job right away. Here too the television series would be better than the books. Thomas Mann's great novel of 19th-century Germany, "Buddenbrooks," would yield a powerful series. Honoré de Balzac's Parisian novels would require some whipping into shape, but the characters are unbeatable. And Thackeray's "Vanity Fair" could be stunning. At the moment I can think of no American novels that could be so used, but there must be some in hiding which dedicated professionals could bring to life.

The Forstye Saga on television was one of the significant cultural events of this century. Not only was it a joy of itself; it also demonstrated those things which television can do better than any other medium.

As for the millions who will meet the Forsytes during the current NET rerun, I can only say, "You lucky people." I'm waiting for the two episodes I missed first time around. They should hit the screen about mid-July, and this time I shall allow nothing to sidetrack me from seeing them, so don't invite me anywhere during midsummer unless you provide me with a television set and keep silent when 9 o'clock rolls around. I think I'll see the whole series over again. Most of my friends are doing so, because it's the best thing on the box.

Series creator Joan Ganz Cooney and three friends from *Sesame Street* (Robert Fuhring)

Kindergarten May Never Be the Same Again

The impact of "Sesame Street" has been enormous

by Richard K. Doan

The *Sesame Street* anecdotes are just about endless.

In New Jersey a three-year-old boy burst into his parents' bedroom in the middle of the night clutching his pillow. "Mommy! Daddy!" he cried. "My pillow—it's a rectangle!"

In London a British TV program showed a sequence from *Sesame Street* picturing life on a dairy farm. Afterward a newsman asked his son, four, if he had learned where milk comes from. "Of course," the lad replied. "From America."

In Pennsylvania a youngster nagged his mother until she bought him a trash can. He just wanted it to sit on—the way they do on the show—while he watched *Sesame Street.*

Some of the stories are poignant.

In New Orleans a teacher, close to tears, reported she had worked fruitlessly with a retarded 2½-year-old boy trying to teach him to count. After watching *Sesame Street* for one week, he could count to 10.

A New Jersey mother said her four-year-old daughter, after watching *Sesame Street* a few times, remarked, "Susan and Gordon [two black regulars in the cast] are *bad* people. They're different from us. Their hair and skin are all funny." Some days later the child reported, "Mommy, Susan and Gordon aren't *really* funny or bad. Now I know them, and every day they make me feel happy inside."

The racial understanding *Sesame Street* seems to be promoting is an added bonus. "We get lots of letters from parents," says *Sesame Street*'s creator, Joan Ganz Cooney, "telling us things like 'I foresee a world in which there's racial harmony in 20 years, because you're bringing it to our children in this show'."

All across the country, it seems, there have been waves of such ecstasy every day this past year. But a more significant result is that *Sesame Street*, an $8-million experiment in televised education, has unquestionably made its point: that the programming techniques of commercial TV, so long known to have captured young minds to simply entertain or sell to them, can be employed just as effectively to teach them their ABCs.

Indeed, measuring *Sesame Street*'s achievement is impossible at this moment, not only because new evidence of its impact emerges daily, but because its ultimate effect on American education may not be fully known for *years*. For instance, it is widely suspected in education circles that the series has so preschooled the preschoolers that kindergarten may never be the same again. "After *Sesame Street*," fears David R. Cook, professor of education at Northeastern University, "the kids will probably find school dull and stifling in the extreme."

But for the moment such concerns aren't fretting most mothers of *Sesame Street*'s fans.

"The two major events of the century," a Canoga Park, California, mother proclaimed, "are a man on the moon and *Sesame Street!*"

"I think," mused a black mother in Brooklyn's Bedford-Stuyvesant slum, "if my son had been able to watch *Sesame Street* when he was two, he'd be a genius."

Everywhere, if thousands of letters to the Children's Television Workshop, producer of the series, are to be believed, the story is the same: millions of three- to five-year-olds—and younger—have discovered the joys of counting from 1 to 10, of knowing A from Z, and of knowing the distinction between a triangle and a rectangle. They go about the house, mothers testify, pointing out squares in waffles and Xs in linoleum patterns. And when the family goes out for a ride, they sing out letters and numbers on street signs.

Nevertheless, *Sesame Street* does have some detractors.

A Boston University professor of education, Frank Garfunkel, attacked the series in the Boston Globe, charging it taught "rote memorization" and "put a noose" around children's ability to ever "engage in sustained and developed thought." (Dr. Gerald S. Lesser of Harvard University and others quickly disputed this view.)

In the magazine Childhood Education, Minnie P. Berson, director of a nursery-through-third-grade experimental program at the State University College at Fredonia, N.Y., demanded, "Why debase the art form of teaching with phony pedagogy, vulgar sideshows, bad acting, and layers of smoke and fog to clog the eager minds of small children?" She thought it would be better to "tap some of the marvelous artist-teachers in nursery schools and kindergartens" for TV teaching.

Some mothers and other adults have expressed fears that *Sesame Street* is "brainwashing" children, "spoiling" them for formal schooling, "assaulting" their senses with its "frenetic pace" and "psyched-up music." A Kentucky mother branded it "a St. Vitus's Dance nightmare." A Glendale, California, man thought the whole thing "positively destructive" to children.

Such objections are all but lost, however, in the din of praise. And the only complaint known to have moved *Sesame Street*'s producers to alter the show in any respect came from militant feminists. They protested the "menial" role played by Loretta Long as Susan, the young housewife. Next fall, to make everybody happy, Susan will have a job as a nurse.

Since well before *Sesame Street*'s debut last November, the project has enjoyed an abundance of helping hands. The commercial networks and stations have aired news specials and spot announcements plugging the series. VISTA workers helped form local viewing groups. The National Council of Negro Women and National Council of Jewish Women pitched in to promote the show in ghettos, as did countless other organizations. RCA donated 150 TV sets, and New York's Bergdorf Goodman store, Monsanto Co., Creative Playthings and Ruth Scharf clothes gave 27 more to day-care centers.

Several months ago, when word got around that *Sesame Street*'s underwriters had not yet renewed the series for a second year, alarmed parents raised a howl.

That brought quick assurance from the U.S. Office of Education, which had put up half the initial $8 million, and the Ford, Carnegie and Markle foundations and Operation Head Start, which had put up the balance, that funds would be forthcoming for a second season beginning this fall.

Children's Television Workshop staffers can only guess at *Sesame Street*'s total audience, but there is abundant evidence that Nielsen ratings putting the in-home total at five to six million viewers far underestimates it. Some kindergarten classes have been watching, even though *Sesame Street* is not designed for in-school viewing.

A door-to-door survey in Bedford-Stuyvesant—the kind of low-income area CTW wants most to reach—found 90 percent of the preschoolers watching in homes having working TV sets.

Looking back, Mrs. Cooney, CTW's attractive and dynamic executive director, says she never feared "monumental failure" for the series, but did think the response would be far more mixed.

"I expected TV critics and parents to like it and dig it," she recalls, "but I thought educators would get on it. Instead—publicly at least—they've been as enthusiastic as the parents and critics."

Kindergarten teachers may feel less kindly, Mrs. Cooney imagines, when *Sesame Street*'s pupils arrive at school this fall. But if it does start a revolution in the classroom, she won't mind. She *hopes* for it. And she thinks *Sesame Street* has the clout to do it.

"The 200,000 disadvantaged children in Head Start weren't enough to turn the school situation around," she observes. "You can't turn the American education system around unless you go for the *millions*. But we've got *troops* going in. We've got *divisions* going in!"

Specifically, what Mrs. Cooney hopes *Sesame Street* will do is "make kindergarten and first-grade teachers take a harder look at their curriculums" and possibly decide to "start teaching reading *right away*. In other words, get the children reading earlier."

This fall *Sesame Street* not only will be covering the same learning ground it did in the first year, but will be going on to more advanced teaching: mathematics, such as addition and subtraction; reading preparations; maybe some dabs of Spanish. "Our four-year-olds are going to create havoc when they reach the first grade," Mrs. Cooney predicts. "And we *want* it that way."

She is flattered that *Sesame Street* seems to have helped trigger a movement in commercial TV toward better children's programs. "I think," she adds, "this country is getting ready to insist on the networks' dropping commercials from children's shows. I feel it in the atmosphere." She finds it significant, among other things, that President Nixon, "out of the blue," wrote *Sesame Street* a fan letter.

Taped repeats of this season's shows started June 1 on most of the 185 public-TV stations that carried the series during the school year. These reruns will continue through September 11, then there will be a short hiatus. A 30-week series of new programs will be launched November 9.

This fall, *Sesame Street* will have the biggest network any regular series has ever enjoyed: more than 300 stations, 50 or so of them commercial outlets in communities with no public-TV stations. That is, if the commercial stations are eager enough for the series to pay for it. CTW wants to realize some income from this source.

In addition, the Canadian Broadcasting Corporation has bought this past year's series and will begin showing it September 28, at 11 A.M. daily. British, Australian and other foreign TV systems have shown interest in running *Sesame Street* too.

In the year ahead, CTW's big push will be to step up utilization of the program in inner-city areas. Full-time workers for this purpose will be trained in New York in late summer and dispatched to about 12 major cities to set up storefront offices in ghettos.

Steps are afoot to incorporate CTW as a permanent program-producing agency, with Mrs. Cooney as president, and already plans are under way to launch a second series, this one aimed at seven- to 10-year-olds and stressing reading skills. Soon CTW hopes to license books, record albums and other products, which, in Mrs. Cooney's words, "would increase the educational impact" of *Sesame Street.*

Not surprisingly, *Sesame Street*'s bounding success has brought glory to its creator. CTW staffers describe Mrs. Cooney as "canonized" since the show-business paper Variety hailed her as "Saint Joan." Last month she added another title: an honorary Ph.D., conferred by Boston College.

And, finally, Mrs. Cooney feels she has won a bet with Madison Avenue. "Two-year-olds," she says, "who can't even say the show's name—they call it *Tet-a-mee Tweet*—have watched our alphabet commercials and called out, 'Mama—X! X!'

"You know, we bet that these abstractions would be just as meaningful as products to children, and a lot of Madison Avenue-ites doubted it. They thought the efficacy of commercials was in their being about concrete products you could see on supermarket shelves.

"But we've shown that 'X' can be *just as meaningful* to a child as a box of cereal!"

WHAT IS TELEVISION'S WORLD
OF THE SINGLE PARENT
DOING TO YOUR FAMILY?

Despite differing opinions, there is no denying its importance to adults and children alike
by Dr. George Weinberg

Dr. Weinberg, clinical psychologist and therapist, is the author of "The Action Approach: How Your Personality Developed and How You Can Change It."

The TV ratings strongly suggest a startling fact: on television, one parent may be better than two. On about a dozen shows this fall you will be able to watch the way a man alone, or a woman alone, raises a family.

These light situation comedies feature widows, widowers and adoptive parents—but never divorcees. Among the widows are Doris Martin (*Doris Day*), Julia (*Diahann Carroll*), and of course Lucy (*Lucille Ball*), who has been going it alone for many years now.

Shows featuring widowers are even more numerous. They include *The Courtship of Eddie's Father, Nanny and the Professor, To Rome with Love, Mayberry R.F.D.* and *The Governor and J.J.* Add to this list *Family Affair,* which depicts an adoptive father of three, and it seems that the public wants to see men alone even more than women.

The creation of these shows was a natural. Ed Vane, vice president of nighttime programming production for ABC, put it this way: "With one parent absent, the remaining parent is free either to embark on romantic endeavors or else to attend to the children."

James Komack, producer of the highly successful *Courtship of Eddie's Father,* who is also a writer and occasional actor on the show, considers the one-parent format necessary for delving into the parent-child relationship. He said, "A woman would interfere—would take away half the time, half the affection, half the moment."

Perhaps in real life, love is not diminished by the presence of a second parent. But on television it is. And thus some of the power of these shows lies in their ability to convey an adult-child love relationship better than the ordinary format could.

It seems clear that the essence of these shows lies in their ability to do this. Probably this is why their audiences overwhelmingly want the parent to stay single. An incident that occurred while *The Courtship of Eddie's Father* was being tested reveals this. About 350 people were seated in an auditorium, each equipped with a dial to indicate enjoyment on a scale from one to five. The moment Eddie's father expressed genuine interest in an eligible female, the audience turned its dials down to express disapproval. They wanted their widower to remain one. He never came that close again.

When you consider the multimillions of people who watch these single-parent shows, you get an idea of their importance as models and sources of learning for parents and children alike. Never before has so great a mul-

Drawing by Dill Cole

titude watched a handful of parents in action at close range. Naturally, the aim of these shows is entertainment. But, whether we like it or not, they are also providing important models for us as parents and as children.

The most common complaint against these shows is that they are unrealistic. The fathers tend to be downright rich. Secretary Lucy lives lavishly, and nurse Julia enjoys a spacious walk-up apartment with an enviable kitchen. Though marriage and serious romance have been denied to these TV parents, at least they are comfortable. "Too comfortable to be realistic," say the critics of these shows.

Said Judge Beatrice Burstein of the Nassau County Family Court: "Because the parents on these shows are affluent, they do not encounter many of the basic problems we expect in such families. In actuality, the pressures caused by money difficulties are nearly always present in single-parent homes."

Some say the children themselves are too well behaved and are reasonable beyond their years. All the children pop in with exceptional insights. Jody and Buffy of *Family Affair* repeatedly demonstrate uncanny sensitivity to adult problems. On many of the shows the children's insights are apt to be unexpectedly philosophical. The message seems to be "Listen to little children carefully, and you will learn great truths."

As a group, these TV children are certainly unusual. Little Eddie of *Courtship* struggles to replace his deceased mother by finding a mate for his father. Children in such straits are apt to be more territorial than this. Only when a potential replacement for a deceased parent comes along does the real trouble begin.

The case for unreality was put well by June Aiken, youthful office manager of the national organization Parents Without Partners. "In real life, even among children who love each other, there is a degree of selfishness—and there isn't on these shows." Miss Aiken summed up the position of a number of leaders in family reconstruction. As she put it, "The parents cater unduly, and the children too often come across as impossible little sweetie-pies."

It is certainly true that the children are unreal in always responding to reason. In part this is due to dramatic considerations. For instance, you couldn't waste 10 minutes of national TV time telling an obstinate child the same thing over and over again. Certain of the real dilemmas faced by single parents are never brought to light.

And what about the blatant avoidance of divorce? In real life, divorce is more than a hundred times more often the cause of such situations than is the premature death of a mate. Yet on these TV comedies none of the single parents has a former mate alive and kicking. Even Lucy, who portrayed much of her life on her show, abandoned reality when she switched to the single-parent format. She plays a widow—not a divorcee.

The decision to avoid divorce on these shows is lamentable. As we all know, divorce is a fact of life for many people, and by now I think most people in the United States are capable of rooting for a divorced person who is trying to make a new life.

In spite of these limitations, the experts I canvassed felt overwhelmingly that our one-parent family shows are doing a very worthwhile job.

Said Dr. Louise Ames, chief psychologist and associate director of the Gesell Institute: "If I were a person alone, bringing up a child, and were feeling swamped by the responsibility, I'd get some support from them."

Granted, the composure of the characters portrayed is sometimes almost too good to be true. But a good model is worth seeing even if it is unusual. When, on *Family Affair,* Uncle Bill discovers that Cissy, who is 18, has decided to get married simply to keep up with her girl friends, he controls himself and hears her out. Later, after making it his business to talk with her fiancé, he tells the two of them together that he does not think they love each other. "Gregg's a nice boy," he says to Cissy. "But you are getting married for the wrong reason."

Whether or not you agree with the tactic isn't critical. It is straightforward and decent, and therefore, like much of what we see on these shows, it is worth considering. Was Uncle Bill unrealistic not to go beserk? Perhaps. But the presentation was valuable to viewers for that very reason.

When, on *Mayberry R.F.D.,* Sam Jones discovers from small signs that his son is removing himself and losing zest for their relationship, he sets out systematically to recover the boy. The story is the father's ·struggle to make contact again—perhaps a struggle that should be more familiar to us than it is.

If these programs seem unrealistic because they show us an abundance of well-intentioned and ethical people, this can hardly be called a fault. They stand in contrast to shows that thrive on depicting neurosis and violence.

As child-psychologist Dr. Elizabeth Barker put it, "They take seriously the handling of small problems— the kind that really do arise in life. The very importance given to a relationship between a parent and child, or to a tiny event with meaning in that relationship, cannot help but heighten our sensitivity to other people's needs."

It may not matter whether you agree with a father's reply to his son. The main message is that the father *did reply* and took his son seriously. If the chief fault of these shows is that they exaggerate the attentiveness of parents and the judgment of children, perhaps this is not harmful. On the other hand, they may incline people in directions that will allow them to find more intimacy and pleasure.

One can look at it this way. Most of us tend to reenact with our children what we saw in our childhood homes. The person whose father never picked him up or kissed him is apt to treat his children the same way, not out of considered coldness but out of our natural tendency to do the familiar. These new and influential models of family life make new experiences familiar. They can wedge into long-standing unconsidered attitudes.

The psychologist Dr. Ruth Hartley, who has defended TV against censorship, points out that these shows stress a valuable "role reversal." The father is in the kitchen, or the mother is trying to fix the plumbing. In this simple example, a freedom is being suggested to great numbers of people. If the very same needs arise in their lives, the possibility of their handling them in new ways without embarrassment is brought closer by such examples.

Statistics suggest all these one-parent family shows are watched by men, women and children in approximately equal division. Why are they so successful? To many of us, the promise of daily life as we once envisioned it seems gone and irretrievable. The honest ethic of the characters on these shows, their devotion to value, their ability to express affection and love for one another, are reassuring to us. There is seldom a half-hour show on which kindness is not the chief motive of one of the characters. Admit it or not, it is important to us to see people, even on the screen, who meet our childhood hopes.

Perhaps these shows can do something to reduce the estrangement between the generations. Today's alienated youth too often were presented with TV families in the recent past that did not have to struggle for social harmony. Today's family shows could be medicine to our troubled times.

These shows are much more important than they might seem at first glance. They have become TV's golden chance to educate us where we all agree we need education most—in our parent-child relationships. Many agree that, despite their shortcomings, the programs are already giving us much of value. It will be interesting to keep an eye on their progress. They have suddenly increased in number. Our next generation will have had them as an important childhood influence.

Honest –
she loves the movies

TV Guide's critic tells why her judgments are severe as she explains her philosophy of criticism
by Judith Crist

One thing a critic has is critics—and mine include a quartet of perennial—nay, eternal—letter writers who make the whole critic business worthwhile. I think of them as teen-agers of all ages who write to me with reg-

ularity under a number of pseudonyms, claiming a variety of occupations for themselves and mailing their letters from all parts of the country. It's their constancy that endears them to me, but it has also convinced me it's time to resort to form letters for the replies that I've hitherto kept personal or to open the whole wormy can of movies-on-television criticism in public.

The first writer goes in for the Critique Oblique, or possibly subliminal. "I am x-teen years old," this letter begins, "and I want to be a movie critic like you. Do I have to finish high school?" The next, who frequently pretends to be an irate housewife or an angry old man, demands, "Why don't you keep your opinions to yourself and just tell us about the movies?" The third is outspoken: "You must be a pretty rotten person, you —— —— ——, not liking Elvis Presley movies. He is decent and fine and pure." And the fourth is declarative: "You'd probably drop dead if you saw a movie you liked. I know I'd drop dead if I ever read a kind word about a movie from you."

Well, over and over I've gone through the biographical bit about the years of college and graduate school, the teaching and newspaper work that led to theater and film reviewing; I've explained that my job as critic requires the expression of opinion; I've declared my admiration for Elvis, if not his movies, and suggested that as the embodiment of the decent, the fine and the pure he might not enjoy his fans labeling even imperfect strangers —— —— ——; and I have listed and relisted all the perfect, perfectly good and even perfectly awful movies I have lavished love on—and survived. And over and over comes the quartet's cacophony of complaints—to be met on the other side of the sound barrier by the cant of *cinéaste* and critical colleagues who insist that there's small point in reviewing movies on television, because any movie lover knows that movies aren't for TV, and TV watchers watch anything that moves.

Nonsense—and stuff. First of all, anyone who is a movie critic can't "hate" movies. He has, in fact, not merely to "like" movies but to love them with a fanatic's passion. A New York City–based film critic like myself has to see nearly all of the more than 400 new films that open annually in that city; add to that score—thanks to a couple of imaginative movie-minded local channels— about 10 to 15 movies worth rewatching or that I had never seen before. And obviously, to subject yourself to film after film at this rate, you either have to be the world's foremost masochist—or else you have to be the movie lover that any film critic worth the label is.

If you're not a passionate devotee of film—or, in plainer language, a movie nut—you can't really function as critic. Why bother to criticize if you don't care? The analogy is simple if carried on to human relations. When as children we'd accuse our mother of "picking" on us, she'd say, "Of course a stranger wouldn't. Only someone who loves you would." It is, after all, only the person who cares, who demands an adherence to standard, who dreams of the perfectibility of the beloved—

and who refuses the easy out, who won't settle for cheap and who will recognize sincerity and integrity and cherish these, while scorning the specious and denouncing the cheap-jack.

So much, then, for the nonsensical notion that the severe critic "hates" movies. And should one be less than severe? We've seen what parental permissiveness produces; what about critical permissiveness? And here the critic is caught fore and aft. On one side there are the television programmers who are, after all, in a catbird seat: what they show will be watched, so why not settle for the easy out, the favorable deal, the "package" that might contain one high-level Hollywood product and include five other flops that certainly didn't hit the big-city houses? The public's getting it all for free and if you don't like it—switch off, buster. And the critic's a spoilsport and a carper—and obviously just a voice crying in the video wilderness, judging from our peachy old ratings.

That's the fore—and for the aft there's the audience watching whatever moves on the small screen. They are, after all, getting it for free—the only payment is the chop-up presentation with random cutting (not really for censorship and with small heed for coherence) so that 10, 15, 20 different products can be touted during and in between station breaks that are really not required under the rules. And they are, even with the least Hollywood product—albeit not with the tailored-for-television cheapies—getting better production values than they get in the average television presentation; they're getting to see big-name stars who don't show up on every talkie-talk or game show—and they are, for the most part, getting something a bit different from the usual run-of-the-situation-comedy-or-serial-mill product. And television in general has conditioned its audience to be grateful for small and even dubious favors. So why does a critic have to come along and look at the whole thing "objectively" and suggest that maybe there are better ways (by switching channels or just switching off and doing something else, like talking to humans or reading a book or taking a walk) of spending the hours of our lives?

I hope you caught that "objectively" up there—because I hope you realize that no matter what critics pretend to, there will be objective criticism only when the ultimate computer starts spewing out film reviews. Critics are people; their opinions are personal. But their subjectivity is, hopefully, tempered by a background, an experience, a knowledge that broadens the value of their viewpoint. And that viewpoint, it seems to me, is one for the layman to come up against—and, hopefully, try out for size against his own.

We're all critics—but what separates us from the other animals is that our discriminatory reactions go beyond taste, smell and instinct and involve a bit of gray matter. And what separates the professional critic from the other reactors is essentially that he articulates the reactions that the layman is, alas, prone to put in a succinct "Wow!" or "Yuch!"

The critic, oddly enough, is not out to rule the world, egomaniac though he must seem by his choice of profession. And I think only the pretentious among us would lay claim to trying to "elevate the public taste." I have a sneaking suspicion that the public can elevate its own taste, given half a chance; that anyone will enjoy a good movie more than a bad one, let a fine actor affect him more deeply than a ham can, see that a great director has more to tell him than a hack has. But they won't reach all of us in the same way; what we are qualifies what we see—and we are all very different people, with our own likes and dislikes, our own irrational preference and our equally fallible prejudices. Thank goodness. I dread the day when we are standardized in mind and emotion, when we lose the capacity to honor our individuality and refuse to have the courage of our singular conviction or stand as a vocal minority.

The critic's job is to put forth an individual viewpoint for his readers to evaluate and react to. That, I think, is his function—to stimulate a response, hopefully favorable or very possibly negative—but a response. For in responding we are forced to think for ourselves, probe, discover the whys of our agreement or disagreement and therefore formulate our own standards, test them and live by them.

Unlike most of my colleagues, I think movies can endure the fragmentation of television. Good movies remain good movies no matter how they are chopped up; bad movies are often improved when consumed in small disconnected doses. Mediocre movies suffer most, perhaps; their faults are enlarged by segmentation and their virtues fade as the momentum of the movie-as-a-whole is lost. But what a "bad," "mediocre" or "good" movie is remains a matter of taste.

We each have a standard. Mine, for a "good" movie, requires that the movie fulfill its aspiration and that in the course of that fulfillment it illuminate some facet of experience for me, provide some sort of emotional empathy or tell me something about somebody or something. A film might aspire to do nothing but make one realize that people are funny or life is a ball or that surfing is exciting—or it might strive to encapsulate the fate of man in the story of a cowboy encountering civilization, or a philosophy of life in a family relationship. If the aspiration is honest, a film has virtue even if it does not quite succeed. I think honesty of approach, an assumption that the audience has intelligence, a dash of inspiration and a bit of style are the least I demand of a film. If one gets more than that—hallelujah. I don't think anyone who is willing to devote his time to watching should settle for less—and he has not only the right but also the duty to demand more.

We are too prone to settle for little these days, accepting the banal, the cheap and the degrading because we are paying for it only with our attention. With awareness, you would realize that there is more art, inspiration and style to at least half the "station break" commercials than there is to 80 percent of the films that are flooding television's prime time. But too many of us slide into stupefaction before the set and let ourselves get caught up in the sloppily constructed twice-ten-thousand-times-told tales that are slickly unrolled in front of us, without a critical pause before, during or after. And two precious hours slip by.

The critic's practical function, in effect, is to act as an advance agent, as the previewer who has been there and hands on an opinion to a friend. No need, of course, to follow a friend's advice blindly. You learn, after a while, what your friend's hang-ups and tastes are—and you act accordingly. You may agree from start to finish on everything. Your tastes may be completely opposite—and that's fine. You may differ on your evaluation of performances; you may agree about everything except Westerns; you may disagree about everything except Elvis, or part company when it comes to comedies, or have nothing in common but your reactions to war movies. You learn these things about your friend; you ought also to latch on in the same way to your friendly neighborhood critic, learn where you stand in relation to each other—and view—and review—for yourself. You have to be your own critic, when all is said—but you have to be critical. You don't sit back in a restaurant and let the waitress heap your plate according to her whim, simply because you can't possibly like everything and anything that's put in front of you. You ask for the menu—and don't you on occasion ask what the day's special is or what the waitress might recommend?

Hard to believe, but a critic's major goal is to share the good things, to advocate what he considers quality stuff, to urge others to see what has pleasured or enriched him. There's little joy in negativism, even though, alas, it attracts the most attention. Certainly it is rampant during the doldrum months for most of the network movie season, when trite trash is rerun and rerun and rerun, while the goodies—like "The African Queen" or "The Innocents"—are held out; if we're really good kiddies, and sit through the fourth rerun of a creaky Jerry Lewis or Bob Hope oldie, maybe we'll get to see a Class A movie every five or six weeks and see it again in nine months or a year! We seem to spend months on end plodding along—and the carrots just dangle at the end of the stick. Golly, mums, one network has acquired "West Side Story" for next season— and lots of C movies to supplement it.

Well, this critic's notion is that we don't really have to watch a great deal of drivel to get to the goody at the end of the stick. Where are the other "West Side Story"–level movies? Wouldn't we rather see six reruns of a classic than sit through the 90th brand-new tailored-for-television how-to-slaughter-your-wife or reluctant-spy or jet-set-slime nonsense? Or would you? Why not think about it, about what you've really liked, about what was worth those two hours out of your life—and what wasn't? Just because it's allegedly for free, are you going to settle for cheap?

Don't just sit there. Think something. Hopefully, say something. At very least, react, A critic does. But why should I do all the work?

(Larry Raphael)

You've come a long way, baby

Happy Hotpoint is now Mary Tyler Moviestar
by Dwight Whitney

If it's Mary Tyler Moore, the last of the lace-curtain romantics, you're talking about, forget all that big-domed stuff about learning how to act. Actors Studio? Acting has nothing to do with it. Our girl operates on good old Irish "instinct" and "feeling"—never had a lesson in her life.

"I never went the Actors Studio route," Mary confided a few weeks ago. "I'm not an actress who can create a character. I play *me*. I was scared if I tampered with it I might ruin it. I've always identified with the '30s—Ruby, Ginger, Fred, Mitzi, all those people. To me, a Brooklyn girl, show business meant singing and dancing. The sun rose and set on that Golden Girl dancing her way to stardom."

Today, despite everything, the sun still rises in approximately the same location as far as Mary is concerned. During the bumpy period after her great TV success, as middle-class America's zingiest housewife in *The Dick Van Dyke Show*, she tried vainly to make it in the movies. Her co-workers had a name for her: "Mary Tyler Moviestar." This did not indicate an ego trip; it was merely a tribute to the old-fashioned romanticism which is the essence of the girl. Mary wants very badly to make it, despite protestations that her family—"I am cursed with a happy marriage"—comes first.

"Don't be misled," cautions Richard Deacon, her longtime colleague on *Van Dyke*. "There is an inner determination there. It puts up a kind of plastic shield. You love Mary, everybody does; you may even know her, but never beyond a certain point."

So it happened just the way it did to ambitious girls in those grand old Keeler musicals with all the traditional bumps and bruises along the way. Mary had a positive flair for bruises. Even her triumphs were marred by aggravating little frustrations. The Happy Hotpoint commercial, for instance. Mary first made the TV scene at 18 as a dancing pixie popping out of an ice tray. "Hi, Harriet," she would pipe. "Aren't you glad you bought a Hotpoint?" Happy was only three inches high and so heavily corseted and made up that she was hardly recognizable as a woman at all.

Mary pluckily ignored this indignity and went on to become famous as Sam, the telephone operator in *Richard Diamond*. There was just one catch. Only her legs appeared on screen. Everybody talked about Sam, but they had difficulty recalling Mary Tyler Moore.

When all of her finally made it to *The Dick Van Dyke Show*, one of the most admired comedies ever to grace TV, even this had a bittersweet flavor. Van Dyke, as the star, was making all the money. (Mary Tyler Moore, who she?) When it became evident that her contribution was, some thought, as great as or greater than his, Mary doggedly remained her modest, long-suffering self.

"Saying how I feel about the *Van Dyke Show* is like saying how I feel about my family," she muses today. "It was my childhood in the business, my growing-up time, the happiest period of my life." Dick was the most giving performer. He really cared about you and wanted you to be funny—and comfortable. He was, well, he was *my* Actors Studio. Dick—and Deac and Carl Reiner and Shelly Leonard—taught me what I know."

In the end she emerged as a star in her own right. "It takes no giant brain," sniffed Hedda Hopper, "to see that Mary will be TNT on the screen." But Hedda hadn't counted on the stubborn inability of some producers to see what Mary was all about. After promising her "a Doris Day buildup" (right away she was in trouble), Universal cast her as Julie Andrews' overly prim, birdlike roommate in "Thoroughly Modern Millie."

The picture was a success for everyone but Mary. "It did her great harm," claims Arthur Price, her business manager and one of the brains behind her present career. "All that sweetness and light scared people."

Things quickly deteriorated. Universal put her in what she calls "afterthoughts." Like that "optimistic comedy" with George Peppard about a toucan bird with the miraculous ability to make everybody love everybody. The critics gave it their own kind of bird.

Then she was cast as a nun in "Change of Habit" opposite Elvis Presley—Elvis Presley?—which amused Mary some, but not much. "He was a Teddy Bear, a very physical, loving person who hugged a lot, and a perfect gentleman. If you don't watch yourself, he calls you 'ma'am.' " The movie didn't help her career.

However, nothing happened to her that was quite as shattering as "Breakfast at Tiffany's." Mary had to pick up the pieces of her ego in a sack. It all began like the plot of a Ruby Keeler musical. The most powerful stage producer in America, David Merrick, planned to do an important musical based on the Truman Capote book. So he reached out across 3000 miles and asked Mary to star as Holly Golightly, an adorable if loose-living lady who rated as one of contemporary literature's most engaging antiheroines. Dick Chamberlain, another TV expatriate, was to play the male lead.

Mary, every nerve quivering, arrived in New York in September 1966 to begin rehearsals with only one act on paper. "A script? Who needed it?" recalls Mary. "With Merrick producing, Abe Burrows directing and writing, Bob Merrill doing the music, Michael Kidd the choreography? Everything spelled winner."

Trouble began to develop immediately. Burrows couldn't decide who Holly was, a tough little tramp or a sentimental floozy. Broadway theater people, who tend to hold TV people suspect anyway, developed a show-me attitude. "They hang around to see if you can stand up without two or three people helping you," observes an actor with the scars to prove it. When it became evident that "Breakfast" (then called "Holly Golightly") wasn't working, Mary tended to shoulder the blame.

"I'd never done a Broadway show before," she says, "so I didn't know how I was supposed to feel. I thought maybe some magic happened when the curtain went up. Perhaps it would all come together in Philadelphia."

Mary opened in Philadelphia with bronchial pneumonia, a temperature of 102, and a range of "about two notes." The critics were merciless. Among other things they said she couldn't sing—which on that particular night happened to be true. Burrows began frantically rewriting, which meant that Mary was frequently up until 3 A.M. learning a new scene.

The nightmare intensified in Boston. Audiences hooted her scenes with Dick Chamberlain. At one point in the show he had to ask her, "Where did I go wrong? How can I help?" "Try operating on the script, Dr. Kildare," roared a heckler.

Mary was very stiff-upper-lip, very Ruby Keeler, throughout the whole ordeal. "I wanted to prove that TV could do it," she recalls. "But after the show I'd fling myself into the arms of my husband and cry."

Soon Edward Albee was commissioned to do a whole new script. The author of "Who's Afraid of Virginia Woolf?" proceeded to write Holly as a much more vulnerable and poetic heroine. Mary loved the script so much it brought tears to her eyes. "It was beautiful, *really* beautiful," she recalls. "If we had just had the luxury of three weeks' rehearsal! It would have worked, I *know* it would have worked. As it was, there was Albee running around saying, 'But I just don't *understand* musicals!', David Merrick hitting the panic button, and . . ."

When the show limped into New York for previews, the press described the audience as "alternately bored and shocked." Hecklers shouted derision. Walkouts occurred in midact. Merrick closed the show before it ever had an official opening night. He and his backers took a loss estimated in excess of $500,000.

As for Mary, she was left with a lot of headlines reading "America's Pluckiest Loser," which were nice but didn't help much when she tried to pick up the already frayed ends of her movie career. Television, to which she yearned to return, was out of the question. The industry now found it all too easy to believe that Mary wasn't really all that zingy but had merely ridden to her Emmys on the coattails of Van Dyke.

The turning point occurred in the spring of 1969 when she and Van Dyke were "reunited"—to use that cloying press-agent word—in a special. The ratings were surprisingly strong. Since Van Dyke had recently teamed with Leslie Uggams amid great fanfare, and no sparks had been generated, the town decided maybe Mary had had something to do with it after all.

Networks began waving fistfuls of the green. CBS offered her carte blanche to do "anything she wanted," as well as an ownership arrangement whereby, if the show went, she could become the wealthiest ex-hoofer in town. Mary and Arthur Price got together the initial concept: she would play neither a married woman (she didn't want to compete with people's memories of the *Van Dyke Show*) nor a widow (TV had enough of these already). What TV comedy lacked was a good divorcee. So Mary would play a divorcee.

In September 1969 the "multimillion-dollar" CBS deal was signed. Mary felt vindicated and renewed, like a kid who finds that her bicycle wasn't stolen after all.

Mary and her producers, the bright young team of Allan Burns and Jim Brooks, who scored heavily with *Room 222* last season, went immediately to work on *The Mary Tyler Moore Show*. "What a joy," Mary didn't mind saying, "to see a script that doesn't have to be memorized. It's *all me*." It was about this zingy 30-year-old divorcee named Mary Richards whose problems are very *relevant*, see, and she has to start life all over again so she gets this job with the news department of a small TV station.

But hey, what's this? CBS is complaining that the public will never accept a divorcee as a funny heroine, no matter how relevant. So how about a compromise? She's not divorced, only jilted. She's been going with this guy—well, actually they've been living together, but we don't talk about that. He takes a walk, leaving our girl to fend for herself. Why, it's even better than a divorcee. *Everybody* will be able to identify, yes?

Yes, Mary told herself. So Burns and Brooks invented an irascible, Spencer Tracy–type producer of the news (Ed Asner), a gorgeous but dumb anchor man (Ted Knight), a cynical newswriter (Gavin MacLeod) and, best of all, Rhoda, a rasping, opinionated, but funny neighbor (Valerie Harper). The trouble was that Miss Harper threatened to steal the show. That was Mary's cue. "I hope she does," said Mary stoutly. "It will only be good for the show."

To which Allan Burns replies: "Nobody steals *anything* from Mary Tyler Moore."

Not that life hasn't been kind to Mary. For an "instinctual" woman who "adores informality," she leads an uncommonly well ordered existence. She is still married to her own Mr. Right, a personable, immaculately groomed comer in the 20th Century-Fox executive suite named Grant Tinker. He is a corporate vice president whose connections make it awkward for him to mix in his wife's career. But without his presence, Mary says, "I do not function."

The Tinkers live on palm-lined Beverly Drive in the stately part of Beverly Hills with Mary's 14-year-old son, Richie (by a previous marriage), a bumptious trio of dogs named Maud, Diswilliam and Maxim de Winter (after the hero of "Rebecca"), and a modest but correct art collection. He drives a Cadillac. She drives an XKE. They tend to socialize with the right people, including Herb Schlosser, who heads up NBC's West Coast programming. And the *au courant* restaurants are not as strange to them as Mary would sometimes have you believe.

"We're barefoot people," she keeps insisting. "It's silly to fight it. We plan to move to the beach. Grant is happier in sweat shirt and Levi's than anybody."

This fall Mary is back in the "intimate" medium, cozying up to the live audience in the kind of TV she loves, doing "my thing," giving the lie to all those Broadway and Hollywood types who said she couldn't do it, and just plain enjoying.

Of course, being Mary, she is prepared for any eventuality—critics, ratings and all. As Truman Capote himself told her during the darkest days of "Breakfast at Tiffany's," "The true philosopher welcomes adversity."

She'll buy that. After all, look what it did for Ruby.

The league that TV built

Behind the AFL's spectacular success lies a story of money and muscle
by Stanley Frank

On any given play in pro football, the prime function of 21 of the 22 hulks on the field is to knock somebody on the large of his back. If you will disabuse yourself of foolish notions about football and keep firmly in mind that it is a bruising game usually won by the team with the biggest, strongest studs, you will understand in a flash how the derided AFL gained superiority over the NFL in four years.

Yes, we know the AFL had been operating for nine years when the New York Jets stunned one and all by winning the 1969 Super Bowl. Then the Kansas City Chiefs made the comeuppance of the arrogant NFL stick last January. But the whole thing really began at 3:40 P.M. on January 24, 1964.

At that precise instant Carl Lindemann, vice president of NBC Sports, burst into his office in a fury and barked at his secretary, "Get me Joe Foss." He had just come from NFL headquarters, where bids for the league's TV rights in 1964 and '65 were opened.

Pro football was booming and NFL games were the hottest property since the loot from the Brinks robbery. Fans throughout the country had rented motel rooms beyond the 75-mile TV blackout of home games to catch their heroes on the tube. CBS's two-year $9.3 million contract with the NFL had expired and NBC was determined to outbid its arch rival for the prize package.

Lindemann had more than doubled the ante with an offer of $20.3 million and was confident he had a lock on the new contract. Imagine his shock when CBS submitted a bid of $28.2 million.

Now Lindemann, still wearing his overcoat, was on the phone setting up a meeting with Foss, president of the AFL, whose five-year contract with ABC also had terminated. It was for $1,785,000 a year— a figure that was contingent upon time sold to sponsors. The audiences were so small—one-third the NFL's—that the league had received less than a million dollars in some seasons.

On January 29, 1964, NBC announced it had signed a five-year contract with the AFL for $36 million. A deal of that magnitude often takes at least five months to negotiate. NBC had college football then, but it was so desperate to compete against CBS for the pro audience that it went overboard to wrap up the AFL in five days.

"The TV contract with NBC was the key to achieving parity with the NFL," confides Milt Woodward, who re-cently retired as Foss's successor. "MCA, a talent agency that handled our contract with ABC, got 10 percent off the top, and poor sales to sponsors left our eight teams with less than $100,000 apiece in some years. Suddenly, each team was guaranteed $750,000 a year. NBC also advanced five teams $250,000 to bid against the NFL for college stars. That put us in business. Signing players was the name of the game."

People with a proper respect for money recall with a reminiscent shudder the insane "war" that enriched scores of strapping youths beyond the dreams of ava-rice during the next two years. Donny Anderson was given a bonus of $600,000 for signing with the Packers. Joe Namath got $400,000 from the Jets, Dick Butkus $300,000 from the Bears, Tommy Nobis $250,000 from the Falcons. A marginal player who was drafted by both leagues and did not demand a bonus of $10,000 to $100,000 for his meat, muscle and gristle was either tongue-tied or a certifiable cretin.

The AFL, brushed off as a bush-league outfit by the opposition, signed half its first-round draft choices. "An important angle was overlooked at the time," says Tom Landry, Dallas coach.

"The AFL then had only eight teams competing for players against our 14 teams. The colleges send up about 60 real pro prospects a year; after that the talent runs thin. That meant each AFL team was selecting seven men while we were getting only four picks on the first four rounds of the draft."

So the AFL wound up well stocked with large, vibrant bodies when a truce was called in 1967 and the two leagues agreed to merge and draft from a common pool of college players.

Let's go back to the proposition that football is a physical game demanding a modicum of deep thinking only by the quarterback—and many of his crucial deci-sions are made by coaches on the sidelines. With the possible exception of the wide receiver, who runs downfield like a striped ape for long passes, the princi-pal duty of the other players is to butt heads with the foe. The text for today's sermon is taken from the com-mentaries of Jim Marshall, Minnesota defensive end: "This is a punishing game and you have to punish peo-ple to win."

Sports experts possess one trait that has endeared them to generations of coaches. Every one has 20-20 hindsight. It was perfectly obvious, when the war for players ended, that the AFL presently would be the dominant league. Listen to Weeb Ewbank, coach of the Jets, who inaugurated the new era by beating the quiv-ering daylights out of the Baltimore Colts in the Super Bowl two short seasons after the merger.

"A football player reaches his peak at the age of 26 after four seasons of pro ball, stays on that plateau for a year or two, then starts to lose his speed and effective-ness. Everybody in the business knows this and goes through life saying veterans must be replaced to stay on top. After I won NFL championships at Baltimore in '58 and '59, Don Kellett, the general manager, went

Drawing by Rowland Wilson

into a huddle with me and asked why no team ever had won three straight. Both of us knew the answer. Veterans had been kept after they began to slip."

Ewbank smiled ruefully. "Although I was aware of that common failing, I fell into the trap the following year. Several vets had been below par in '59, but I wanted to believe they'd just had off-seasons. You feel loyal to men who have knocked their brains out for you and you want to see them earn big money for a few more years. So I kept my fading old-timers in the starting line-up in '60 and it was midseason before I realized they were over the hill. By that time younger players had lost almost two years of valuable experience."

The NFL unquestionably was much stronger when the AFL, fortified by NBC's money, began making passes at Grade-A prospects in 1965. Paradoxically, the NFL's chief asset, experienced personnel, was a liability. Rookies had a tough time breaking into veteran line-ups.

Take Donny Anderson, the hotshot voted most likely to succeed in the Class of '66. Had he gone with an AFL team, he would have been thrown into the arena immediately to get his lumps—and savvy. He signed with the champion Packers, who were so loaded with vets that he was used mainly as a punter. Even in his second season Anderson averaged only seven carries from scrimmage a game.

Remember what Ewbank said: A player reaches his peak after four years of pro ball. It happened right on schedule in the last two Super Bowls. In 1969, the Jets' and Colts' line-ups were identical in weight. But the Jets' offensive and defensive units averaged 5.3 pro seasons compared to the Colts' 7.1, a difference of nearly two years.

That's a significant difference in physical resiliency and the response to those emotional appeals to go out there and bust a gut for the greater glory of the club. Pros have been hearing such harangues since high school, and the longer they are exposed to the exhortations, the more cynical they become.

In the 1970 Super Bowl the Chiefs and Vikings again were evenly matched in beef on the hoof. Again, the AFL entry was closer to the peak. The Chiefs averaged 5.7 pro seasons, the Vikings 6.1.

There is reason to suspect that celebrated NFL brutes had made their reputations beating up on slightly elderly opponents. Carl Eller, the 265-pound ringleader of the Vikings' Purple People Eaters, was outmuscled in the last Super Bowl by Dave Hill, hardly recognized in the AFL as the incarnation of Attila the Hun. The previous year the Colts' John Mackey, recently chosen as tight end on the all-time NFL team, was cooled off by Dave Herman, an obscure Jet.

Two incidents involving the same man in successive play-off games last season underscored the AFL's coming of age, which means getting mean, tough and nasty. TV viewers of the Minnesota-Cleveland game for the NFL title saw Joe Kapp, the Vikings' hard-nosed quarterback, belt Jim Houston into unconsciousness with a head-on collision. In the Super Bowl, Kapp made the mistake of trying to run over Kansas City's Aaron Brown. He was knocked out of the game.

Chagrined NFL moguls did not have to look beyond their own ranks for proof of the age-old law of nature that young, aggressive animals continually claw their way to the leadership of the herd. Dallas entered the league in 1960 and didn't win a game. The team presently was two yards, then 13 seconds, away from beating mighty Green Bay for two titles. Minnesota, the defending champion, is another expansion team that was in last place in the Western Conference only three years ago.

Then there was the remarkable record forged at Cleveland by Paul Brown, who started from scratch with rookies he coached in the service during World War II. Brown won four straight titles in the All-America Conference and, after it was disbanded, promptly captured the NFL championship. In all, Cleveland led its division for 10 consecutive years, a dynasty that was more notable in some respects than the Packers, the Yankees in baseball and the Celtics in basketball.

The All-America Conference was forced to the wall by the well-established NFL, but the AFL survived because it had two added assets: (1) TV revenue; (2) Lamar Hunt. His father is H. L. Hunt, who is reputed to be the richest man in America. All right; maybe two people have more money. In 1959, young (27) Hunt made a pitch for the NFL franchise in Dallas and was turned down. He was so miffed that he bought a ball and started his own league. He was joined by three other well-heeled football addicts—Bud Adams, a Houston oil man; Ralph Wilson, a trucking tycoon; and Barron Hilton, of the hotel family.

All their money and zeal would have gone down the drain without NBC's $36 million, plus $6,700,000 for the league's Championship and All-Star games. The network never will break even on the investment, but it derived enormous satisfaction gloating over the shaft it gave CBS when the AFL picked up all the marbles in the Super Bowl.

Carl Lindemann was asked whether he was surprised it happened so quickly. "Not really. It was obvious our league had a lot of top talent," he said, giving it the smooth executive sell. Then he grinned sheepishly. "Surprised? Hell, I was in shock at the end of the Jets' victory. It was unbelievable. Two weeks before the game Howard Cosell told me, 'I feel sorry for you. The AFL will be killed.' After the first period of the game Cosell said, 'I was wrong. You'll win it big.' I was so emotionally wrapped up in NBC's rivalry with CBS, I was afraid the dream would blow up in my face if I looked at the field."

You will note that there has been no reference here to strategy, tactics and other technical matters dear to the hearts of experts with newspaper space or air time to fill. For a good reason: it's strictly gobbledygook. The side with the strongest, most belligerent tigers who are "up" for a game will win it every time. If a team is outmanned, data fed into all the computers at MIT by geniuses will be futile.

People with fanciful ideas speak of Kansas City's "multiple offense" in terms generally used to describe the calculations behind Neil Armstrong's moon walk. The champion Chiefs are supposed to have a repertory of 300 plays that can be sprung from 66 different formations.

"Nonsense," says coach Hank Stram. "We have 18 basic running plays and 10 pass patterns, about the same number as every team in the business. If players are overloaded with too much detail, they can't carry out blocking and tackling assignments. That's the payoff. Deception is worthless without execution."

Although the leagues are operating officially as one organization for the first time this season, the AFL will retain its identity in the minds of players and fans for a long time, particularly when the two conference leaders collide in the Super Bowl.

"I think the AFL will win it for two more years," Milt Woodward says. "Then the common draft will equalize competition, but right now we have the edge in big, strong players."

Woodward may be biased, but one thing is certain. The AFL never again will be an automatic 17-point underdog in the Super Bowl,.

Producer Norman Lear with Carroll O'Connor and Jean Stapleton   (Gene Trindl)

Bellowing, half-baked, fire-breathing bigotry

has made "All in the Family" a hit and may make Archie Bunker a permanent part of the English language
by Rowland Barber

Where were you on the night of January 12, 1971? Specifically, at 9:30 P.M. (8:30 Central Time)?

If you were a programming executive of CBS Television, you were battening down against the tempest you knew would be unleashed against the network sometime within the next 31 minutes.

If you were a switchboard operator for CBS or one of the network's affiliates, you were likely on special night duty—figuring out your overtime while waiting for the board to light up like panic time at Mission Control.

If you were Norman Lear, producer, writer, and fomenter of the imminent uproar, you were pacing the floor of a viewing room in Television City, Hollywood, like an expectant father—which in many ways you indeed were.

If you were watching CBS on your home screen, you had just seen *Hee Haw* trundle its raucous way, buckety-buckety, into fadeout. Your station identified itself, then withdrew, as expected, for 60 seconds of commerce.

Then a disembodied voice launched into an unexpected kind of pitch: a disclaimer: "The program you are about to see is *All in the Family*. It seeks to throw a humorous spotlight on our frailties, prejudices and concerns. By making them a source of laughter we hope to show—in a mature fashion—just how absurd they are."

The gist of the *caveat* was that the following show could be hazardous to the emotional health of the sensitive viewer.

And you might well have been wondering, at that moment, What the hell's coming *on* next—a topless salute to the Vietcong?

What came on next was the first episode of *All in the Family*. If you stayed with it, you were surprised—and delighted. Or you were shocked—and offended. It was a startling show, one that allowed for no middle ground. Things were said, for laughs, that had never been heard before on an American television comedy. They were said mostly by Archie Bunker (played by Carroll O'Connor), a 50-year-old star-spangled, red, white and blue-collar bigot.

Bellowing, snorting, mocking, insinuating, Archie Bunker tilted nonstop at the enemies of his own particular state—i.e., anybody who is not white, Anglo-Saxon and Protestant. ("Fein*berg*, Fein*stein*—it all comes to the same thing, and I know *that* tribe." Or, "Let the spades and spics go out and hustle, just like I done.") Archie let go with equal gusto at alien institutions such as the mini-skirt, the humanitarian pulpit ("That Reverend Bleedin' Heart . . . up there in his ivory shower"), Sunday brunch (Archie was innately suspicious of any food he couldn't put ketchup on), and sex during daylight hours.

The verbal gunplay in that first episode didn't end there. Archie's favorite target—even if it was a moving target that shot back—was his son-in-law Mike. Mike was a prepackaged anathema to Archie: a young liberal, complete with long hair, who clung as obstinately to his end of the political spectrum as Archie clung to his. Mike (Rob Reiner) and Gloria (Sally Struthers) were living with Gloria's parents, Archie and Edith, until Mike finished college ("learnin' how to be a subversive").

While Archie's ammunition was the home-baked epithet ("dumb Polack" . . . "the laziest white man I ever seen"), Mike's was an arsenal of causes (poverty, rights of minorities, equal opportunity). The two of them were organically unable to pass each other without flaring into argument. When Gloria got caught in the cross fire she took her lumps from her father, too (his "flesh and blood," Archie observed, was a "weepin' Nellie, pinko and atheist," like her "meathead," her husband).

Archie considered his wife Edith (Jean Stapleton) unworthy of attack—serious discussion being a strictly male province—except for the order *"Stifle yourself!"* whenever she managed to make one of her foggy pronouncements. Edith is a virtuoso of the misconstrual. Her mind, blissfully attuned to the rosy side of life, operates on the principle that a stopped clock tells the right time twice a day. When Archie made reference to "black beauties," Edith reflected, with a little glow of pride, "Well, it's nicer than when he called 'em coons."

Only once did Archie Bunker acknowledge the brotherhood of man. That was in his pay-off line at the end of Act Two: "I hate a smart-ass kid no matter what his color is!"

Well. Fade out *All in the Family*, Episode One. Now it was CBS's turn to be surprised—and delighted. The storm warnings had been unfounded. There was no tempest, no tidal wave of righteous indignation. At affiliated stations across the country switchboard operators were puzzled as to why they'd been summoned to extra duty.

In New York City (the Bunker menage was located somewhere in the Borough of Queens) 400 phone calls—"not an extraordinary number"—were logged. Callers' comments were split down the middle between "terrific" and "disgusting." Chicago: 214 for, 90 against. Philadelphia: 90 for, 52 against. Cleveland: 2–1 in favor; Los Angeles: 3–1; Denver: 50–50. Detroit wired in: "Unusual so little response, even from Hamtramck [a predominantly Polish-American suburb]" Indianapolis: "Most unusual thing that's happened is that there hasn't been a *flood* of adverse reaction." Huntsville, Alabama: "Surprisingly few complaints."

Only two stations reported a record telephone response, New Orleans and Minneapolis. In each city favorable callers were in the majority. What was most astonishing, all along the network, was that there were any favorable callers at all. A spokesman for WCAU in Philadelphia summed it up later in the week: "We never heard from the Pros until this show. In the past, the Antis always made all the noise."

One prediction did prove to be correct: the initial airing of *Family* got a dismal rating on the Nielsen scale. Producer Lear admits that he expected nothing more. "We were a brand-new show, practically unheralded, and you can imagine how our uncensored dialogue sounded to people who'd just been snickering over *Hee Haw*. If we baffled them, they had a choice of powerhouse movies to switch to on NBC and ABC. But I knew we were going to be talked about. When word-of-mouth began to spread, we'd begin to climb."

Lear was right. Ratings went up steadily, week by week. By midpoint in the series (the seventh of 13 episodes), the Nielsens had already more than doubled. Just as heartening were critics' reviews and the unceasing flow of mail from the public. The latter, according to Lear's partner Bud Yorkin, has been "so far, our biggest satisfaction in doing the show."

As the season was coming to an end, the Yorkin-Lear office was still receiving between 100 and 200 letters a week from viewers, eight out of nine of them notes of gratitude. A browse amongst the letter files is revealing. Four connecting threads run through the patchwork fabric of the mail:

1. A lot of people are thrilled by the recognition, in a comedy series, of life as it is really lived. ("Great bit— Mom looking on the back of the greeting card to see if it was a Hallmark. My mother always did that." And *mine*. "Most of today's shows make an average middle-class person feel shabby and unhappy because we haven't got 'mink' rugs, etc., but the Bunkers' house looked like mine after 24 years—lived in.")

2. There is a widespread desire, which includes a grain of personal guilt, to see the Archies and the Mikes among us exposed and put under a comic spotlight. ("You are embarrassed to hear yourself or someone you know in almost every line of dialogue." "These are people that are all around you in real life, and it's fun to bust their bubbles." "Great! We could see a couple of our relatives in it." "Even though our daughter's husband is a lawyer it doesn't make him any less of a meathead." "I live with such people. Archie Bunker LIVES!")

3. There is a growing weariness over the predictable fare served up endlessly in situation comedies. ("What a surprise! I always thought you people were capable only of shows like *My Three Sons* and *Green Acres*." "What a delightful change from the pabulum offered most of the time." "Makes all the other plastic series look and sound like what they are—so much hard-pore cornography.")

4. There is abroad in the U.S. a cynical conviction that the law of the TV jungle—Survival of the

Fatuous—is irrevocable. This was the stoutest of all the threads that ran through the *Family* mail. ("One of the best things that ever happened to television, so I guess it'll be canceled." "My fear is that your honesty will not serve you well, and before you begin you will fade into oblivion." "I'm afraid to say I like it because so many good programs don't stay on the air.")

The "Antis," of course, had other words for *Family*. Their favorite ones were, in order: disgusting, vulgar, revolting and trashy. A few of the dissenting minority were more specific. A Texas viewer: "Too much like life. All the women in my family are liberals and all of the men are conservative, and I get all the liberal garbage I need without having to watch it on television." From a thoughtful lady in California: "My grandchildren had never heard such words as 'hebe' or 'coon' or 'spic' until I let them watch your program. They liked the character of Archie and laughed at him. . . . Really, I think you are popularizing the very things we want to get rid of in our world."

The CBS hierarchy was well aware of the show's fringe pollution. Nonetheless, after a careful study of the balance sheet, the network decided to bring the Bunkers back next season.

The fact that *All in the Family* got on the air in the first place may be victory enough for now. It certainly is for Norman Lear, who is happy about the whole thing. He is also tired: a 70-hour workweek can do that to you. He had given much of himself, including 30 pounds of weight, to bring his *Family* to life on the tube.

The project was born three years ago after Lear read an item about a series that was enjoying quite a vogue on BBC television, *Till Death Do Us Part*. The series dealt with a squabbling lower-middle-class English family and depicted them unretouched, warts, biases, stupidities and all. Lear checked with a friend who had just returned from London. The friend said yes, it was a marvelous show, and yes, it could be just as relevant and just as funny if it were transplanted to America. But of course it was too hot for any U.S. network to handle. It would wind up as a half-hour of pantomime set to bleeps and station breaks.

Lear was then in New York editing his movie "The Night They Raided Minsky's," an opus which also let it all hang out. Convinced that America was ready for mature-audience television as well, he sought and acquired the U.S. rights to *Till Death Do Us Part*. Between cutting-room stints, Lear wrote a pilot script in which he Americanized his acquisition, resettling the family in a blue-collar quarter of New York City, and titling the re-creation *Those Were the Days*.

ABC was entranced by the script, and agreed to finance the filming of the pilot episode. In a brilliant stroke of casting, Carroll O'Connor and Jean Stapleton were signed for the leads, everybody fell down laughing at the finished film, and hosannas were sounded all around. Even as the echoes died, however, network feet began to chill.

"ABC didn't quite have the guts to put the show on," Lear recalls. "So they decided we had to shoot a second pilot, claiming they weren't happy with 'the kids.' So we recast the Mike and Gloria parts and reshot the same script. A network says '*Ahem!*' by spending money.

"This time the film went on the shelf. ABC forgot about it and lost their option. Fade to limbo. Then last summer, while I was editing our movie 'Cold Turkey,' our agents called and said that CBS wanted to view the pilot. Well, *Those Were the Days* went through CBS like wildfire, and they agreed to put it on the air in the first available slot. Under its third name—*All in the Family*.

"The episode that kicked off the series in January," Lear continued, "was *still* the same script I'd written two and a half years ago. Except of course it was given a fresh production—taped with a live audience while four cameras rolled around picking up the nonstop action. We wanted to convey the *spontaneity* of family life. Has anybody ever recaptured that feel since the classic old radio show 'Vic and Sade'?

"There were three other big differences. We were lucky enough to get John Rich as director. John's a master of the 'instant-theater' art of directing live television. And we found two kids who were perfect matches for Carroll and Jean—Rob Reiner and Sally Struthers."

The kick-off episode didn't have much of a story, admittedly so. "I used the excuse of the Bunkers' wedding anniversary to go pot-shotting around," Lear says, "just to establish the people and the mood." Subsequent episodes, however, have had solid plots, without a decibel's loss of laughter. Archie has had to cope with such bile-roiling issues as interracial blood transfusions, unlicensed hippie marriages, homosexuality and the incursion of a black family into the Bunkers' block. Edith had her day as a murder-jury holdout who becomes an overnight celebrity, and that rankled Archie too.

There was a segment in which Gloria became pregnant, then miscarried. The father-daughter confrontation at the end was touching, leaving many of the studio audience in tears. In a later episode Archie was further humanized when he confessed that *he* had just been crying—while watching the movie "Love Story."

For all his rant and cant, Archie Bunker is, basically, lovable. He is just plain dumb sometimes, but vicious never. "That's because Archie is the bigger-than-life epitome of something that's in all of us, like it or not," said Lear. "Remember the line, 'You're the laziest white man I ever seen'? That line was my father's—addressed to me, more than once. And I used to accuse him of making racial slurs, and we'd get into real Mike-and-Archie shouting matches. And we were a middle-class *Jewish* family.

"Tell you something else. About myself. Recently I met for the first time one of my daughter's favorite teachers. I'd talked to her on the phone, and had been very impressed by her. Then I saw her for the first time. She was black, and I was shocked. I knew, intellectually, that I had outgrown all that emotional nonsense, but I couldn't help my reaction. Looking back on the scene now, I'm laughing at myself. And I guess that's what *All in the Family* is all about."

WHY YOU WATCH WHAT YOU WATCH WHEN YOU WATCH

The answer is to be found in "The Theory of the Least Objectionable Program"

by Paul L. Klein

It is about time that you all stop lying to each other and face up to your problems: you love television and you view too much.

I used to be the guy in charge of the ratings at NBC, and my waking hours were filled with people either complaining about how inaccurate the ratings were or, without my asking them, volunteering that they "never watch TV, because the programs stink, particularly this season."

Let's look at the facts, because only by examining the nature of the disease can we cure it, or at least make peace with it.

The Census Bureau tells us that 96 percent of U.S. homes have a television set (and over a third of those have two or more sets, with the number of homes and sets growing each day). The Census Bureau also shows that TV penetration is highest among the more affluent and better-educated segment of the population. In fact, 99 percent of the homes with over $15,000 annual income have at least one TV set—the majority of them have more than one—and most of them have a color set. And also we all know how they complain about the programs and how they say they never watch the stuff.

The truth is that you buy extra sets, color sets, and even pay a monthly charge for CATV to view television. Yet when you view an evening's worth of TV you are full of complaints about what you have viewed. But the next night you're right back there, hoping against hope for satisfying content, never really learning from experience, and another night is shot. Instead of turning the set off and doing something else, you persist in exercising the medium.

With more TV sets and clearer, more colorful pictures on those sets, you are tuned to TV *more* this year than last, and last year more than the previous year, etc.

The fact is that you view TV regardless of its content. Because of the nature of the limited spectrum (only a few channels in each city) and the economic need of the networks to attract an audience large enough to attain advertising dollars which will cover the cost of production of the TV program, pay the station carrying the program, and also make a profit, you are viewing programs which by necessity must appeal to the rich and poor, smart and stupid, tall and short, wild and tame, together. Therefore, you are in the vast majority of cases viewing something that is not to your taste. From the time you bought a set to now, you have viewed thousands of programs which were not to your taste. The result is the hiding of, and lying about, all that viewing. Because of the hiding and lying, you are guilty. The guilt is expressed in the feeling that "I should have been reading instead of viewing."

It is of course much more difficult to read than to view, even for people making over $15,000 a year—and certainly for Uncle Fud, whom I'll get to later. Reading requires a process called *decoding*, which causes a slowdown in the information taken in by the user. TV viewing is very simple to do—kids do it better than adults because they are unencumbered by guilt—and the amount of information derived from an hour's viewing is infinitely more than is derived from an hour's reading.

But print has been around for a long time and it has attracted people who have learned to express themselves in this medium, so the printed content, on the whole, is superior to the TV content. Still, most of us prefer television.

Despite the lack of quality content, the visual medium is so compelling that it attracts the vast majority of adults each day to a progression of shows that most of these people would ignore in printed form.

The process of viewing works like this:

A family has just finished dinner and one member says, "Let's see what's on TV tonight." The set gets turned on or TV Guide gets pulled out. If it's TV Guide, then the list of programs (most of which are repeats) is so unappealing that each member of the family says to himself that he remembers when TV Guide made an awful error in its program listings back in 1967 and maybe it has happened again.

The set is turned on whether a good program is listed or not at that time. Chances are over 100 to 1 that there is nothing on that meets this or any family's taste at that moment. But the medium meets their taste.

The viewer(s) then slowly turns the channel selector, grumbling at each image he sees on the screen. Perhaps he'll go around the dial two or three times before settling on one channel whose program is *least objectionable*.

"Well, let's watch this," someone in the family says. "There's nothing better on." So they watch. No one thinks of jogging a couple of laps around the block or getting out the old Parcheesi board. They watch whatever is least objectionable.

The programmers for the networks have argued that this is a "most satisfying" choice—not LOP (least objectionable program). But if it were, then why would everybody be complaining and lying about TV viewing? I don't deny that in some rare time periods, "least objectionable" is actually most satisfying, but the bulk of the time people are viewing programs they don't particularly consider good, and *that* is why the medium is so powerful and rich.

Readers of this magazine will complain to me, even after admitting they practice LOP more than they should, that their LOP is usually not represented among the "Top 10" or, another way of looking at it, that the Top 10 Nielsen programs contain so many shows *they* never view.

The ratings are not inaccurate. Nielsen ratings measure whether the homes in the United States have TV sets that are on or off, and if on, what channel (program) is on the screen. It happens to be a very accurate measure of TV set and program usage. Inaccuracy is not its problem. Rather, the problem is irrelevancy. It's as if we lined up a bunch of schoolboys and measured their height to determine their weight. While we have a very accurate measure of height, it has only a partial relationship to the attribute we want measured. The ratings that you are familiar with are what I call "homes ratings" which give all homes an equal vote, regardless of how many people are in the home and who is actually viewing. Therefore they have only a partial relationship to the attribute we want measured.

All "homes ratings" techniques equate a home with one old man who lives in one room with an outhouse (Uncle Fud) viewing *Gunsmoke,* with a family of four in a Great Neck, N.Y., Tudor, viewing *Laugh-In.* One home, one vote. If more Uncle Fuds are viewing *Gunsmoke* than Tudors are viewing *Laugh-In, Gunsmoke* is said to be "beating" *Laugh-In* in the ratings. Nonsense!

"Top 10" is a measure of set tuning. Uncle Fud's set (and he can't read, so he gets no satisfaction out of seeing *his* program in the Top 10) is worth the same as your set. It seems fair, but it isn't. Uncle Fud and his cohorts have nothing else to do (no other media competition) and therefore their weight in the home population and their consistency of viewing can yield an illusion of popularity that is irrelevant and bad for the medium.

Before advertisers became sophisticated, they purchased advertising, and paid the most money for advertising time, on the programs with the highest ratings. Almost always these programs were loaded with Uncle Fuds, people who could not buy enough of the advertised product to pay for the advertising time. Yet these high-rated programs made the program opposite them low-rated—because high-rated and low-rated are relative in the kind of TV system we have. Uncle Fud's choice then stayed on and was imitated by other producers looking for "hits" or Top 10 programs and the low-rated shows were dropped.

As the irrelevancy of these measures began to be understood, particularly in the past year, we saw for the first time high-rated programs being dropped and low-rated programs being kept on.

For instance, *Mayberry R.F.D.,* a Top 10 program, will be dropped after this season because its audience contained too many people who could not afford to buy the advertised products; same goes for *Green Acres, The Beverly Hillbillies, The Jim Nabors Show, Family Affair, The Men from Shiloh,* etc. The concept of hits has changed. A hit is a program that reaches a mass of young adults, preferably those who live in the big cities.

The operation of LOP dictates that small-town families who used to love *Family Affair* will now be forced to view a Least Objectionable Program from three urban-appeal offerings, just as in the past the urban audience was forced to pick between three rural-appeal programs in many time periods.

When two networks played rural-appeal offerings in a time period, the third network would find it advisable to play an urban-appeal program to "counterprogram" the time period. If the rural-appeal program had its traditional slant it would, particularly in the early evening, cream off the kids and old ladies (I call this bimodal) in the urban centers as well, and this unbeatable cartel (kids and old ladies, who have remarkably similar tastes) would beat the urban-appeal program in audience *size.*

Marcus Welby, M.D. was the season's big hit and it is *not* rural-appeal, but urban-appeal. And it is not bimodal, just the opposite—strong young adult. Why does this show succeed in the face of my previously stated theories behind high ratings? The reason is that *Marcus Welby* always plays against at least one public-affairs program and on some weeks it plays against two (*CBS News Hour* every week and *First Tuesday* once a month).

The lying and the guilt are all wrapped up in this time period. We view too much TV, we view content we dislike, content that is frivolous, unsatisfying, unrewarding. We state that what we want from TV is more important content—like public affairs. Well, when public affairs is on, we really want to see it, we really should see it, but it's too objectionable compared to the entertainment programs opposite it.

Welby is constructed public affairs. Someone gets sick, near death in fact, on *Welby* and it all comes out well. On *CBS News Hour,* they die.

It is very rare that viewing in any time period is lower than normal. It is very difficult to either raise or lower the "sets-in-use" in a time period, indicating once and for all that viewing has little to do with content. When "Bridge on the River Kwai" was on (first time), sets-in-use rose five points—and when *Laugh-In* was a national phenomenon sets-in-use were up somewhat. But recently *Welby* was pre-empted for a public affairs–type program (but starring Robert Young) on a week when both *CBS News Hour* and *First Tuesday* were on.

A few things happened. First off, more people saw public affairs that night than had seen that kind of beloved program since this happened many years ago in the same time period. (I remember the letters we got back in 1967 or '68, when this first happened, complaining that the networks never took the viewer into account by their vicious scheduling of three quality programs opposite each other.) Actually all three enjoyed greater viewing in the *forced* viewing situation—you either watched public affairs or you did not watch anything—than they would have had each program been opposite entertainment.

In addition, all three of the programs were repeated later and they got very small audiences. Apparently no one felt so bad about missing the two he didn't see that he searched them out when they were repeated.

Secondly, with *Marcus Welby* out of the time period, the sets-in-use viewing network TV in New York dropped 14 percent from the average of the week before and week after (when a repeat *Welby* was on)—indicating that quality may be one way to drive set usage down. Or, that public-affairs programming, as now constructed, is not the quality we like to think it is.

Things are going to change in TV. The medium itself will change. People love TV. They love the ease of viewing and the ease of distribution; video pictures delivered right to the home. Somebody's going to figure out how to give this medium more satisfying content—not remove the guilt completely, but reduce the guilt as we head toward a completely visual culture.

PUBLIC TELEVISION: IS ANYBODY WATCHING?

by Richard K. Doan

Funny thing happened to public TV, so called, on the way to . . . well, wherever it was going:

It became upper-class TV.

Darling of TV's disenchanted. Pet of TV's critics. All but ignored by TV's masses. That's public TV.

Nearly everybody (or so it seems) *talks* about public TV. Boy, how they warm over *Sesame Street, The Forsyte Saga, Civilisation, The First Churchills* and all that!

But do many of them *watch* it? Not so you can notice.

Or, at any rate, not so those nose-counters of mass viewing habits, the A. C. Nielsen people, can find out.

And when public TV's own forces cast about for evi-

dence of who's watching, what do they find? Why, not only that it is a tiny minority, but a very special one: the affluent, the college-bred and, quite often, the politically liberal.

Evidence: an independent survey of public-TV viewing in Syracuse, N.Y.; Jacksonville, Florida; St. Louis and San Francisco discovered that "public television is perceived not as a medium for 'the people' but rather as a segregated vehicle for the higher-educated segment of the population, and a little left of center." Interviewers found that 37 percent of those who donated money to public TV in the four cities rated themselves as liberals (as against 32 percent middle-of-the-road and 21 percent conservative); 60 percent were college graduates and nearly 45 percent had incomes over $20,000.

The findings didn't surprise Richard O. Moore, president and general manager of KQED, San Francisco's public-TV station. "Many people, both inside and outside of public television, have been saying this for a long time," Moore noted.

Evidence: KQED itself admitted in May that a study it characterized as "the largest, most comprehensive" ever made of a local station's audience (21,465 phone calls by 244 volunteer interviewers) had shown that while KQED occupies very viewable Channel 9 and is one of the country's more imaginative public-TV outlets, only 1.7 percent of San Francisco area TV households watched it on an average evening. Another finding, according to the study: the more educated a household, the more it watched KQED while watching commercial TV less frequently.

Evidence: Boston's WGBH-TV, another enterprising public-TV operation with the best air facility of all, Channel 2, scored its highest prime-time rating in history last summer: a 19 percent share of the local audience for a Sunday night Boston Pops Concert, an attraction only a shade lower than highbrow.

For public TV, a 19 percent share is sensational. In commercial TV it represents disaster.

Indeed, by commercial standards, public TV's solidest hits wouldn't survive a second round of Nielsens.

Most public-TV fare, in fact, attracts something like a *tenth* the size of audience picked up by the *least* popular network evening show.

Sesame Street, public TV's prize exhibit to date, has, to be sure, been right in the running in the daytime, grabbing as high as 40 percent of the audience in Boston, for example.

But try as they may, the best the public-TV people can muster in seemingly impressive figures are so-called cumulative statistics like one the Corporation For Public Broadcasting regularly bandies about: that 33 million Americans have a look at public TV "at least once a week."

Privately, many public-TV officials are puzzled and frustrated over the seeming rejection of their best programming efforts by the great mass of viewers, despite widespread critical acclaim.

If public TV can win Emmys and Peabody awards, why is it still shunned by 95 percent of the audience? "I don't know. I just don't know," one of public TV's top programmers shrugged abjectly.

Does all this mean public TV is a bust?

Has it been proven that John Q. Viewer really couldn't care less about a "meaningful alternative" (as public TV has been called) to commercial TV's programs?

Is Congress apt to go on stepping up Federal funding of the noncommercial system ($30 million plus $5 million in matching funds for fiscal 1971–72) if public TV mainly serves a small elite?

The answers depend entirely on how you look at it.

And how you look at it depends on who you are.

Take the commercial broadcasters. They can—and do—handily put down public TV as a minor medium hardly anybody looks at. And they have the ratings to prove it.

Take the TV critics. They worship at public TV's shrine. Why, even attempting to review *Civilisation* seemed "almost sacrilegious" to TV GUIDE's Cleveland Amory. And what does it matter whether *many* people are watching? "If only 20 people are watching an ecology show and they happen to be presidents of chemical companies polluting the environment," exploded Long Island's Newsday critic Marvin Kitman, "that carries more weight than a network show which has 20 million viewers, half of whom are under nine."

Take random samples of public response:

Early this year a businessman presented New York City's WNET with 5000 shares of stock worth $40,000. He had broken his leg, and in the ensuing enforced idleness had discovered the joys of noncommercial TV, he said, and just wanted to show his appreciation.

Tens of thousands of viewers "vote" by mail on the issues debated weekly on PBS's *The Advocates*.

Conservative William F. Buckley Jr. thought enough of public TV's reach (and the opportunity to sway some of its left-leaning fans rightward?) to switch over to it from commercial syndication.

President Nixon congratulated Mobil Oil Company on spending $1 million to underwrite PBS's *Masterpiece Theatre* and to promote *Sesame Street*.

There are signs aplenty like these that public TV is catching on.

In public TV's own high places, the defensive argument is that PBS shows may not be capturing big audiences in ABC, CBS and NBC terms—but if you add all those viewers up, they'd fill a lot of ball parks!

"Sure, we'd like to get bigger numbers," admits John Macy Jr., president of CPB, the top corporate entity in public TV. "But if you use other measures than the usual TV yardsticks, you see we are reaching very respectable numbers of people."

To both Macy and Hartford Gunn Jr., president of Public Broadcasting Service, which supplies national programming to more than 200 PTV stations across the country, the most agonizing handicap is their lack of

VHF (low band) facilities in many of the nation's biggest cities, including Washington, D.C.; Los Angeles and Cleveland. What can you expect, a public-TV official grumbled, when, in Washington, even FCC Chairman Dean Burch's children can't watch *Sesame Street*?

How this shortcoming is to be surmounted has not been fathomed, but Gunn does foresee continued growth in *number* of stations, perhaps to 300 by 1980, and he thinks PBS will pick up steam as it gets enough money to add a sixth night of programming weekly, possibly in 1972. He laments the fact that many PTV stations aren't even on the air seven nights a week.

At the same time Gunn confesses he feels public TV has for too long "ignored some of the great verities of television" such as the proven appeal of series as opposed to "anthology" programming, and the need to feature continuing personalities to build audience.

PBS, as Gunn and his staff are acutely aware, is not so much a "fourth network" as it is half of a fourth network. The big commercial chains, even under the FCC's new prime-time limitations this fall, will each deliver 21 hours a week of evening fare, plus their newscasts, late-night talk shows and daytime series. PBS will muster a mere 13 hours a week, spread over five nights, plus daytime feeds for *Sesame Street, Mister Rogers' Neighborhood* and the new *Electric Company* reading show.

The most encouraging find to date, perhaps, in public TV's search for viewers is an unpublicized analysis of Nielsen ratings made for the Ford Foundation by Paul Klein, a former NBC vice president. Klein reported that more than 16 million TV homes—27 percent of them—watched some part of PBS's programming over an eight-week period last fall-winter. "Not too bad," the analyst observed, considering that "in a big portion of the country" PBS is seen only on a "deprived" UHF outlet.

In New York City, where PBS enjoys Channel 13 exposure and where viewers tend more "to prefer the arts and drama," 54 percent of the TV homes tasted PBS's fare.

The Ford Foundation, public TV's single biggest benefactor (over $200 million in grants since 1951), hopes, however, to unearth something more refined than Nielsen's head count as a gauge of public TV's impact. Under a $50,000 project "drawing on some major social scientists both here and abroad," the foundation has begun a search for "some new instrumentality."

"Nobody here wants to get into the ratings game," explained David Davis, Ford's overseer of public-broadcasting activities. "You might destroy public broadcasting if you tried."

But frankly, Davis added, the foundation wouldn't mind finding out how, among other things, public TV might at least *sometimes* reach *some* of those viewers who now studiously ignore it.

A good many other people in public TV wouldn't mind learning how, too.

The voice you love to hate

It belongs to Howard Cosell, who doesn't need to be loved
by Saul Braun

(Ken Regan)

Howard Cosell rises from behind his desk on the sixth floor at ABC headquarters in New York and starts upstairs to broadcast one of his daily five-minute radio shows, which he does live, without scripts or (apparent) preparation.

He is a tall man with a sunken chest and a pronounced slouch, which is a tall man's way of letting you know he really is modest and unaggressive. This is in marked contrast to his attention-getting voice, which for some reason puts me in mind of Bill Stern.

In the elevator, he pretends not to notice Sam De-Luca, the former New York Jets' captain, now an ABC radio account executive. "Never in pro football history," Cosell orates, "has a player attempted—as many infractions of the rules—and been discovered at it—as frequently—as Sam DeLuca." The door slides open and Cosell leaves without so much as a glance backward. These impromptu insults are (I soon realize) Howard Cosell's way of conversing with people he likes.

In the press room he rips several feet of tape off the ticker and scans it rapidly. In the studio he pulls out a stopwatch and sets it alongside the mike. He discards the wire services with one scornful raised eyebrow and sits patiently building concentration. In repose his eyebrows arch. So do three forehead lines. Cosell wears a permanent mask of reportorial skepticism.

On signal he leans forward, fingering his modernistic sunglasses: "Hello again, everyone. This is Howard Cosell—Speaking of Sports." For approximately five minutes he delivers himself of some opinions (among them that Earl the Pearl Monroe of the Baltimore Bullets is the most exciting sports personality after Muhammad Ali and Joe Namath) and some thick farinose rhetoric with the stamp of Cosell imbedded, as Cosell might say, therein.

"Dick Barnett," says Cosell, "is a pro who treats with a contest for what it is to him. Something that must be won for his continuity of income, with him playing an important role therein."

When he has concluded, the stopwatch records that Howard Cosell has hit his time perfectly. It is an amazing thing to watch. Some of the sentences have the consistency of aging quicksand, true, but they all parse and have development and pace and, unlike the output of most sportscasters, they generally make good sense. I imagine the concentration needed to accomplish this must be great, and the pressure overwhelming.

"Howard is unique," says ABC Sports president Roone Arledge, "a great talent at what he does. He has a great mind and great technical ability. If you need four minutes and 20 seconds with a commercial in between, he will ad-lib sentences and paragraphs and come to a meaningful conclusion and it will be four minutes and 20 seconds. As you know, there was a lot of controversy about Howard last year, but it is not true that we ever considered not rehiring him. We wanted to feature the personalities of Howard and Don Meredith and not just caption pictures. I thought people were tired of the religious approach to football, treating everything like the Second Coming."

Last year's *NFL Monday Night Football* line-up—Cosell, Meredith and Keith Jackson—went up against some very stiff competition from the other networks, yet held, Arledge says, almost a 32 percent share of the audience for the full three hours. He credits the interaction between Meredith and Cosell, the one casual, drawling, light-handed, a loping plainsman; the other hard-hitting, portentous, slouching and scuffling along Eastern Seaboard pavements.

Meredith's wry irreverent style is visible in his account of how the labors will be divided, now that Frank Gifford is replacing Jackson to do the play-by-play: "This fall Frank will provide the polish, and he's so good-looking he'll entertain the ladies. Howard will entertain the pseudo intellects. That leaves me with Middle America."

Meredith got an Emmy for his work. Cosell got a mountain of irate mail. The reaction resembled the response a district attorney would get after announcing the indictment of Mother for Apple Pie in the Third Degree.

In this case Mother is American sports. On this subject Cosell says, provocatively, "Sports is maybe the primary means in the United States for sustaining illusion and delusion. How else can you account for so much indignation over the books by Bouton, Meggysey, Flood and Sample? Of *course* I believe books like that should be written. They help puncture the myth that sports is a privileged sanctuary from real life.

"If you take a stand on issues in any walk of life, you've got to face adversity," Cosell says with a sigh. "Especially if you do it in an area where there has been a history of Establishment pabulum, mass mythology and illusion. Kennedy didn't write 'Profiles in Courage' about men who were overwhelmingly popular. He wrote it about men who were right."

A profile in courage of Cosell would list among his adversaries such glittering sports names as Casey Stengel, Weeb Ewbank (Cosell later changed his mind and said so publicly) and most recently Wellington Mara, who, Cosell says, "hasn't played to an empty seat in 15 years, yet is playing off the City of New York against the State of New Jersey in a crass ploy for either a new stadium or a greater seating capacity than the 65,000 that Yankee Stadium affords him."

It does undeniably take courage to speak out as candidly as Cosell does. His six-figure income is susceptible to all sorts of subtle but unmistakable pressures. Herb Granath, ABC director of sales, has to reassure advertisers that they are buying viewer attention and that Cosell means increased attention. ABC bills more than 70 million dollars for sports attractions, so the stakes are high. "I have had nothing but support from the network," Cosell says, "but I still consider my greatest feat simply my survival."

Why, then, I asked, does he trouble with it?

"Look, my constituency is blacks, kids who are sick and tired of all the nonsense, and intelligent people everywhere. Nowadays the sports beat is everywhere. The most important things happening in sports are transcendental to sports. Do I like to have my fanny ripped by people who I feel are a) not qualified and b) motivated by personal considerations such as envy or so on, and c) not honest? I don't like that, no. But if it's honest contention, I'm not averse to that, and I've had moments of enjoyment in what I do. And I believe I'm having an effect. I believe I am."

It should come as no surprise to viewers familiar with his authoritative, penetrating, pertinent style (or, depending on your point of view, his caustic, egotistical, verbose style) to discover that Howard Cosell was meant by family calculation, by training, and probably by innate temperament, to be a lawyer. He was born in Winston-Salem, N.C., in 1920, and raised in Brooklyn, N.Y., where, he says, "I grew up Howard Cohen on Eastern Parkway, and my father's dream and my mother's dream was to have a son who was a lawyer." Cosell accomplished that handily (graduating with honors from NYU and then NYU Law School and passing the state bar at the age of 21), but before he actually began a practice, World War II intervened. During the war he rose to the rank of major and met and married Mary-Edith Abrams. They now have two daughters: Jill, married and the mother of a small son; and Hilary, a student at Sarah Lawrence.

"When I came out of the Army I had a wife and a daughter and I had to make a living," Cosell recalls. He engaged in a law-firm partnership, but his heart was elsewhere. "In college I was in summer stock. Ogunquit. Stockbridge. I'm a frustrated actor, *sure!*"

He entered broadcasting in 1953 through a side door, after receiving a call asking for permission to use a legal client's name—Little League—for a summer replacement radio show. Better yet, asked the caller, would he consent to host the six-week show by getting kids to ask provocative sports questions? He would and he did—so successfully that the show lasted five and a half years.

In the meantime ABC had offered him a five-minute show at $25 a shot, 10 shows a week (which he accepted happily, although it was below scale wages). Eventually he became manager of ABC Radio Sports.

In his long broadcasting career, Cosell has rarely been far from controversy. In the '60s he was doing incisive sports documentaries, including one on predominantly black Grambling College that is his special pride. Racism in what he calls "this distorted sociology of ours" incenses him whenever the topic arises, and he takes every opportunity to be heard on the subject. His support of Muhammad Ali's right to fight incurred the wrath of many viewers. Cosell further incensed some viewers by doing a show on the Masters golf tournament in which he compared the venerable but lily-white tournament to Scarlett O'Hara's legendary mansion:

"You walk the fairways—and suddenly—even as you smell the magnolia—the wisteria—you see it there—Tara."

"Oh"—he laughs recalling it—"I had a ball with the thing." He takes even more pleasure recalling what happened after he held an interview during the '68 Summer Olympics with Tommie Smith, the black track star who had given a black-power salute when accepting his medal. "A man in Ohio took out an ad in the local paper calling me a traitor for putting that 'traitor' on the air. First of all, Arledge wanted it. Secondly, the point is to let the man explain what he's doing. That's *news.*"

A result of all these contentions was that Cosell himself began to be news. He got a lot of attention, which some peevish critics insist was the point of it all. One writer describes him as "the Martha Mitchell of the sports world." Another says, "He'd be a fabulous sportswriter if he'd come down with laryngitis." Even comedians like David Frye and Bill Cosby have Cosell routines, like this one: "Flash floods in Iowa killed 300 people yesterday. They all deserved it."

Last fall, on *NFL Monday Night Football*, Cosell was still asking provocative questions and incurring the wrath of so many viewers that mail was running as high as 9 to 1 against him during the first few games. Some ABC executives believe the volume of mail was more the product of residual anti-Cosell feelings than with anything he actually said on the air. Arledge and Chet Forte, the series' director and producer, spent the first four or five Tuesdays of the season avidly watching re-runs.

"We looked at the entire tape," Forte recalls with wonderment, "because we just couldn't figure it out. What did he *say?* Every week I'd call Howard and say, 'Howard, you didn't say a *thing* wrong.' Well, after a few weeks, it began to straighten out and there were as many pro letters as con."

What Howard said would have passed totally unnoticed in some other medium or if said some other way or in some different tone of voice or if he wasn't known to be the staunchest defender in sports of Muhammad Ali's right to his title or if the entire field of sports weren't devoted to presenting itself for public appreciation as the last unsullied American institution, one that embodies all our beloved virtues and (unlike politics, say) none of our equally traditional and equally beloved vices.

Cosell managed to create copy and discord with such sensational ripostes as the information that Len Dawson has a high completion percentage because he throws many short passes, or the disclosure that George Sauer was not making the right cuts, or that they're going right over so-and-so's middle guard as though he were made of ricotta cheese. Most sportscasters avoid comments like these as though they were actionable, particularly the former ballplayers.

"Sometimes what appears to be obvious, isn't," explains Gifford. "A defensive team will hide it from the offensive team and if they can hide it from them they can hide it from me. Maybe the player you've been critical of is covering for the guy who really made the mistake. Which way do you go? I happen to admire the players enormously. If they're out there they're great athletes, period. But," he concedes, "maybe we are seeing it in a more positive way than we should."

This year, with Gifford joining the package, lines of jurisdiction between the three sportscasters are being further blurred. Gifford will do the play-by-play and Dandy Don Meredith will supply color and amusing commentary. As for Cosell, he will be . . . well, Cosell. Contentious, outspoken, caustic when the occasion demands.

Last season, when the criticism was coming hot and heavy, Cosell admits he wasn't sure he wanted to come back. "I went through hell during the football season. The turning point for me was Philadelphia, our ninth game. I was struck by a bug in the middle ear, producing a violent form of vertigo. I thought I was getting a stroke. I was terrified. I had trouble with words and when I did the lead-in to the half-time films, I appeared drunk. With all that, it was probably the most beautiful thing that ever happened to me, because of press criticism. Psychologically, I said to myself, it's ridiculous to take that seriously. To overreact. So, after Philly I matured."

The day that Howard said all that, he was under attack in the press for his coverage of the Benvenuti-Monzon fight in Monte Carlo, and he was in a high state of excitement, so much so that he began shadow boxing with me in the elevator. "You've come on just the right day," he exulted. "For today Howard Cosell answers back."

And so he did, on the evening news. It had been a long day for him: putting together a piece on Joe Namath, making the rounds of the sports beat, bringing fight judge Arthur Mercante home for a drink, and winding up drooping, near midnight, over a Chinese dinner at Dewey Wong's.

"I relish the battle," he said, with a wan smile, "but I'm wearied by it."

Background

"'S WONDERFUL,
'S MARVELOUS,
'S GERSHWIN"

A musical genius is recalled
by a famous wit and pianist
who knew him well
by Oscar Levant

[*Jack Lemmon in* 'S Wonderful, 'S Marvelous, 'S Gershwin *is being shown January 17 on most NBC stations. To add to your enjoyment of the special, we are providing this background information.—Ed.*]

Once upon a time, in a fabulous era in American musical history, there lived an astonishing young man—brilliant, handsome and gifted. The time was the '20s and '30s; the man was George Gershwin.

That there is now in the '70s a brand-new generation of people who know little or nothing about the life and works of George Gershwin comes to me as a painful shock. Can it be possible that this musical genius (about whom the eminent composer Arnold Schoenberg said, "There is no doubt that he was a great composer. What he achieved was not only to the benefit of a national American music but also a contribution to the music of the whole world") is becoming forgotten?

Nostalgia for the '20s and '30s is now upon us. George Gershwin was a vital voice of those years, a magician who electrified the musical world with his originality and inventiveness. He was, and still is, the only composer to bring the American jazz idiom not only to Broadway and the screen, but to Carnegie Hall and the opera house.

His talent was enormous—his wonderful songs, his dazzling orchestral works, his virtuoso pianistic ability, his conducting, his painting—he even excelled in golf, tennis and Ping-Pong! And all with great vitality and style.

Although he was multitalented, Gershwin had little formal education. Born in Brooklyn, September 26, 1898, raised on Manhattan's Lower East Side, he left high school at the age of 15 to become a song plugger for a music publishing firm, Remick's, in Tin Pan Alley. But his musical studies, begun at the age of 12, continued throughout his career. According to his devoted brother Ira, the brilliant lyricist, there was rarely a period in George's life when he was not studying.

His collection of paintings, wherein he displayed unusual acuity and selectivity, led to his own participation as a painter of genuine talent. Among his portraits was one of Jerome Kern, the dean of musical comedies, and his last was of Arnold Schoenberg. To demonstrate that he was not unaware of himself, he did a self-portrait, dressed in a top hat, white tie and tails, gazing at himself in a contrivance of mirrors which produced multiple reproductions of himself on canvas.

Long before I ever heard of the name Gershwin, he had made a distinct impression on me. I was 12 at the time, a child pianist, and had been taken to see a show called "Ladies First," starring Nora Bayes. I was there because the show was conducted by my uncle, Oscar Radin, but the only memory I have of the event was the skillful playing of the unknown (to me) pianist who accompanied Miss Bayes in her songs.

A few years later, when I had to go to work in dance bands, the songs that aroused my interest were "Fascinating Rhythm," "The Half of It, Dearie, Blues" and several others. I took note of the composer's name—George Gershwin.

My first encounter with Gershwin came in 1925, after I had recorded "Rhapsody in Blue" for Brunswick Records. That engagement had been an unexpected opportunity—the regular pianist with the orchestra had failed to show up and I was called in as a last-minute substitute. When I completed the recording in one take (I was 18 and nerveless), it occurred to me they could pay me whatever they wanted for the job, even union scale, which they did.

This, I reflected later, would not have happened had I not been so fond of Gershwin's music and so eager to make the recording. I thought there might be consolation in a word of praise from the composer and, in my youthful bumptiousness, I called him up for approbation. I didn't get much. Gershwin was quite firm in his preference for his own recording on Victor Records. He did have a high opinion of his own worth, but his was a just and accurate estimate—he was well aware of his great gifts.

My friendship with Gershwin began in 1930, when his show "Strike Up the Band" was playing the Selwyn Theater in New York and I had written the music for a concurrent show called "Ripples." Thus began a relationship in which I was accepted as a constant guest of George and his brother Ira, whose wife Leonore reigned as hostess over their adjoining penthouses on Riverside Drive.

The two pianos in George's apartment made it possible for us to play his music together as it was written. He had such fluency at the piano and so steady a surge of ideas that anytime he sat down just to amuse himself, something came out of it.

George and I would sometimes play Bach's Passacaglia in C Minor for two pianos. But George preferred generally to play his own music, delightfully—and not necessarily at someone's request. George S. Kaufman once said that George could get to a piano faster than any Olympic runner.

I used to kid him. I'd say, "He has himself in the palm of his hand." And when someone asked me if I thought George Gershwin's music would be played 50 years hence, I am reported to have replied, "If he's still alive, it will be."

In addition to collaborating with George in private performances of his music, I also had the opportunity occasionally to play his works in public. In the summer of 1932, Lewisohn Stadium was presenting an all-Gershwin concert, and George suggested that I play the "Concerto in F." This was conditioned by the fact that he was playing both the "Rhapsody" and the "Second Rhapsody" and finally decided that he could not undertake the "Concerto" also.

The pleasure I had in appearing on the program was only exceeded by the gift that George presented to me a few days following the concert. I came up to his apartment, and he greeted me with a small-boy smile, his hands clasped behind his back. "What would you rather have," he said, "money or a watch?"—simultaneously handing me a handsome wristwatch inscribed with an affecting simplicity: *From George to Oscar, Lewisohn Stadium, August 15, 1932.*

I'm grateful now that I didn't get what I would have preferred then—the money.

The most ambitious undertaking of Gershwin's life was the writing of the folk opera "Porgy and Bess." During the three-year work period he referred constantly to the score of Wagner's "Die Meistersinger" as a guide, presumably, to the plotting of the vocal parts. No two works could be more dissimilar.

"Porgy and Bess" has become one of the greatest musical ironies of modern times. The Negro race was enthralled and thrilled when it was first performed in 1935; now they look on it as an Uncle Tom horror. However, it has been performed in most opera houses throughout the world; in the third revival with the great Leontyne Price.

Gershwin's curiosity about things was translated into a curiosity about himself, a need to know himself better, which propelled him into psychoanalysis. He had been advised by his devoted friend Kay Swift to be analyzed, and it was his analysis that broke up their friendship.

He was extremely gregarious by nature, loved parties and was the toast of elegant society; they loved him and he in turn adored them. He also had an instinct for good manners and at least the normal quotient of girls.

I tried to arrange a match between him and Jerome Kern's attractive daughter Betty. "If you marry her, you'll have the biggest amalgamation of copyrights in American history," I said happily. He did take her out, but nothing came of it.

I recall another girl who played the piano. She would play a Gershwin song, "Isn't It a Pity?," which had chord changes in almost every bar. This nice girl always played the wrong chord changes and the wrong bass notes. George laughingly said to me, "I just cannot see that girl any more." Those wrong bass notes were too much.

Once when George was speaking about a girl he'd been in love with who had married someone else, he remarked ruefully, "If I wasn't so busy, I'd be upset."

When George and Ira came to Hollywood in 1936 to write the score for two Astaire movies and the "Goldwyn Follies," he entertained many beauties of the town, but the one he fell madly in love with was the fascinating Paulette Goddard. She intrigued him with remarks like "George, why don't you write music that people will hiss?"

He could not be seen with her publicly because she was married to Charlie Chaplin. He overcame this by escorting his mother and Lillian Hellman, the playwright, to the Trocadero, a Sunset Strip nightclub. Then he'd leave them and join Paulette at her table. Lillian Hellman was quite annoyed at being made a shill for George.

Of his escapades someone once remarked, "He's trying to prove he's a man." "What a wonderful way to prove it," I observed.

I was often lightheartedly acrimonious or sarcastic with him but my real feeling for him was undiluted idolatry.

He did not live to see the three movies for which he and his brother Ira had written such marvelous songs: "They All Laughed," "They Can't Take That Away from Me," "Love Walked In," "A Foggy Day," "Nice Work If You Can Get It," "Let's Call the Whole Thing Off," and many more.

George Gershwin died in Los Angeles July 11, 1937, of a brain tumor. He was 38. His tragic death provoked expressions of disbelief and sorrow from friends and strangers alike who, until then, had not realized how deeply and to what extent they had held him in their affections. If there was any consolation, it was that he had loved his life, he had fulfilled his dreams.

"IT LOOKS LIKE MY UNCLE OSCAR!"

How a certain trophy got its name, and other tales of a Hollywood institution
by Leslie Raddatz

Irony—never a hot commodity in Hollywood—abounds in the 45-year history of the Academy of Motion Picture Arts and Sciences.

The Academy began as an elite group set up to circumvent the rise of craft and trade unions in the movie industry, and for years the major studios were its principal means of support. Today, members of Hollywood guilds and unions run the Academy. The major studios are no longer a power, their function as entertainer of the masses usurped by television. And television, which puts up $1,000,000 to air the annual Oscar Awards, has become the financial angel of the Academy.

Oscar was a nameless afterthought when the Academy was founded back in 1927, after a dinner of film notables at Louis B. Mayer's beach house at which the late movie mogul suggested "a wonderful idea"—an organization to represent not one group or faction but "the industry as a whole." Two years later, an Award of Merit was proposed, and art director Cedric Gibbons sketched the now-familiar figure. Molded by sculptor George Stanley, Oscar is 13½ inches tall, weighs 6¾ pounds, is made of gold plate over a combination of base metals, and costs approximately $100 to make.

How Oscar got his name is a matter of legend and disagreement. The official version is that in 1931 Margaret Herrick, longtime executive director of the Academy but then a newly hired librarian, said, "Why, it looks like my Uncle Oscar!" Other Academy employees took up the name and were overheard by Sidney Skolsky, who began using it in his column. Skolsky does not deny his part in the legend but says he made up the name himself after he became weary of referring to "the stat-

Janet Gaynor with Charles Farrell in "Seventh Heaven." She won first Oscar (Museum of Modern Art/Film Stills Archive)

uette." And finally, Bette Davis, who won her first Academy Award in 1935 and is the only woman ever to be president of the organization, insists that she named it after her husband at the time, Harmon Oscar Nelson.

The then anonymous Oscar made his debut at a banquet at the Hollywood Roosevelt Hotel on May 16, 1929. It took 15 years for the Awards ceremony to move from hotel ballrooms to theaters and auditoriums. In 1945 it went on network radio for the first time; in 1953 on network television. Today an estimated 250,000,000 persons watch the festivities in the United States, Canada and Mexico, and in some 40 countries overseas via communications satellite. Two hundred and fifty saw that first presentation back in 1929.

In the years since, some Award ceremonies have become legend:

☐ Ten-year-old Jackie Cooper, nominated for "Skippy," falling asleep on Marie Dressler's shoulder in 1931;

☐ Director Frank Capra's premature start for the podium in 1934 when emcee Will Rogers called out, "Come and get it, Frank," only to find that Rogers meant director Frank Lloyd;

☐ Claudette Colbert's 1935 dash from the railroad station to accept the award for "It Happened One Night." She had not expected to win and was boarding a train for the East;

☐ Greer Garson's 20-minute-long "thank you" speech in 1943, which inspired an Academy "suggestion" that winners keep acknowledgments brief;

☐ Olivia de Havilland's snubbing of her sister, Joan Fontaine, when the latter came up to congratulate her in 1947 for "To Each His Own";

☐ Elizabeth Taylor's halting walk to the stage on the arm of Eddie Fisher after a critical illness in 1961 to accept the Oscar for "Butterfield 8";

☐ George C. Scott's victory for "Patton" in 1971 after spurning the nomination.

The late Walt Disney is the all-time Oscar record holder. By the time of his death in 1966, he had received 26 Oscars, plus three Honorary Awards and the Thalberg Award, voted by the Academy's Board of Governors to "creative producers whose records reflect a consistent high quality of motion-picture production." Among performers, the leaders, with three Oscars each, are Katharine Hepburn and Walter Brennan, the latter in the Supporting category which was added in 1937. "Ben-Hur" won more Oscars than any other picture— 11 in 1960.

Some great names and great movies have been passed over by the Academy and then given belated recognition through Special Awards. Charlie Chaplin will return for a Special Award this year, after being ignored by the Academy since that first dinner in 1929, when he received a Special Award for "The Circus." Other Special Awards have gone to Greta Garbo and Cary Grant, who somehow never managed to win the annual sweepstakes. "Citizen Kane" received only a Best Screenplay Oscar in 1942, but Orson Welles was finally given a Special Award in 1970.

Winners of the Oscar are chosen by vote of the Academy members, more than 3000 of them. Up to five nominations are made in 20-odd categories. Balloting on nomination is restricted to members of the Academy branch concerned; i.e., directors nominate directors, actors nominate actors, etc. But in the final balloting, all members vote in all categories to choose the winners.

The Academy Awards have been denigrated for years. Raymond Chandler once wrote, "The Oscar ceremony is Hollywood's frantic effort to kiss itself on the back of the neck." Truman Capote said, "It's outrageous—all politics and sentiment and nothing to do with merit." Even such an industry stalwart as the late David O. Selznick admitted that "there has been inadequately expressed appreciation by an electorate influenced unduly by transient tastes, by commercial success, by studio log-rolling and by personal popularity in the community of Hollywood."

Although the decline of the major studios has eliminated most of the log-rolling and bloc voting, the Hollywood trade papers are still fat at balloting time with advertisements for pictures and performers seeking the accolade—a practice the Academy unsuccessfully attempts to discourage. But what was probably the biggest advertising campaign ever, for "The Alamo" in 1960, failed to produce more than an award for, appropriately, Sound.

It remains a fact, however, that other factors besides merit can influence the final outcome. In 1961, Hollywood's sympathy after Elizabeth Taylor's near-fatal illness, rather than her performance in "Butterfield 8," got her the Oscar. It was probably personal popularity which made John Wayne the winner in 1970 for "True Grit" over such better actors—as he would be the first to admit—as Richard Burton, Dustin Hoffman, Peter O'Toole and Jon Voight. Yet Laurence Olivier ("Hamlet," in 1949) and George C. Scott ("Patton," 1971) could hardly be considered popular or sentimental favorites. Blockbusters like "Ben-Hur," "West Side Story" and "Gone With the Wind" can sweep the Oscar race, but "little" pictures like "Marty," "It Happened One Night" and "All the King's Men" proved that Academy members do not necessarily have their eyes on the budget or the box office.

The Academy of Motion Picture Arts and Sciences ("What art? What science?" said D. W. Griffith) is a nonprofit organization with a considerable income. Its 3700 members each pay $48 annual dues; it rents its theater for screenings of new films; and its Players Directory, "the casting director's Bible," published three times a year, carries some 7200 listings at $8 each. But the Academy Awards are its principal source of revenue, although part of the $1,000,000 TV fee goes to put on the annual show and pay the performers and musicians who take part in it. The Academy has its own building in West Hollywood, which houses a full-time staff of 35, a 1000-seat theater, a film archive and a library of technical and historical information which is invaluable to movie historians, students and journalists. The Academy annually awards college scholarships to students of the motion-picture crafts, and sponsors a series of films about film-making used by schools and civic and technical organizations.

Although the Oscar winners are chosen by only 3000 people, all within the industry, they have an impact which translates into dollars at the box office and in future contracts for a winning player. It is estimated that an Academy Award can add at least a million dollars to a picture's box-office take, and Elizabeth Taylor's price went to a million dollars a picture after she won hers.

But Oscar means more than mere dollars and cents. Among all the awards—from critics' groups, film festivals, magazines—somehow Oscar is the only one with charisma. As a pundit has said, "What Pulitzer is to literature, what Nobel is to science, Oscar is to Hollywood."

OSCAR WINNERS YEAR BY YEAR

in the three most important categories— Best Picture, Best Actor, Best Actress

1927–28: "Wings"; Emil Jannings ("The Last Command," "The Way of All Flesh"); Janet Gaynor ("Seventh Heaven," "Street Angel," "Sunrise").

1928–29: "The Broadway Melody"; Warner Baxter ("In Old Arizona"); Mary Pickford ("Coquette").

1929–30: "All Quiet on the Western Front"; George Arliss ("Disraeli"); Norma Shearer ("The Divorcee").

***

1930–31: "Cimarron"; Lionel Barrymore ("A Free Soul"); Marie Dressler ("Min and Bill").

1931–32: "Grand Hotel"; Fredric March ("Dr. Jekyll and Mr. Hyde") and Wallace Beery ("The Champ"); Helen Hayes ("The Sin of Madelon Claudet").

1932–33: "Cavalcade"; Charles Laughton ("The Private Life of Henry VIII"); Katharine Hepburn ("Morning Glory").

1934: "It Happened One Night"; Clark Gable ("It Happened One Night"); Claudette Colbert ("It Happened One Night").

1935: "Mutiny on the Bounty"; Victor McLaglen ("The Informer"); Bette Davis ("Dangerous").

1936: "The Great Ziegfeld"; Paul Muni ("The Story of Louis Pasteur"); Luise Rainer ("The Great Ziegfeld").

1937: "The Life of Emile Zola"; Spencer Tracy ("Captains Courageous"); Luise Rainer ("The Good Earth").

1938: "You Can't Take It with You"; Spencer Tracy ("Boys Town"); Bette Davis ("Jezebel").

1939: "Gone With the Wind"; Robert Donat ("Goodbye, Mr. Chips"); Vivien Leigh ("Gone With the Wind").

***

1940: "Rebecca"; James Stewart ("The Philadelphia Story"); Ginger Rogers ("Kitty Foyle").

1941: "How Green Was My Valley"; Gary Cooper ("Sergeant York"); Joan Fontaine ("Suspicion").

1942: "Mrs. Miniver"; James Cagney ("Yankee Doodle Dandy"); Greer Garson ("Mrs. Miniver").

1943: "Casablanca"; Paul Lukas ("Watch on the Rhine"); Jennifer Jones ("The Song of Bernadette").

1944: "Going My Way"; Bing Crosby ("Going My Way"); Ingrid Bergman ("Gaslight").

1945: "The Lost Weekend"; Ray Milland ("The Lost Weekend"); Joan Crawford ("Mildred Pierce").

1946: "The Best Years of Our Lives"; Fredric March ("The Best Years of Our Lives"); Olivia de Havilland ("To Each His Own").

1947: "Gentleman's Agreement"; Ronald Colman ("A Double Life"); Loretta Young ("The Farmer's Daughter").

1948: "Hamlet"; Laurence Olivier ("Hamlet"); Jane Wyman ("Johnny Belinda").

1949: "All the King's Men"; Broderick Crawford ("All the King's Men"); Olivia de Havilland ("The Heiress").

1950: "All About Eve"; Jose Ferrer ("Cyrano de Bergerac"); Judy Holliday ("Born Yesterday").

1951: "An American in Paris"; Humphrey Bogart ("The African Queen"); Vivien Leigh ("A Streetcar Named Desire").

1952: "The Greatest Show on Earth"; Gary Cooper ("High Noon"); Shirley Booth ("Come Back, Little Sheba").

1953: "From Here to Eternity"; William Holden ("Stalag 17"); Audrey Hepburn ("Roman Holiday").

1954: "On the Waterfront"; Marlon Brando ("On the Waterfront"); Grace Kelly ("The Country Girl").

1955: "Marty"; Ernest Borgnine ("Marty"); Anna Magnani ("The Rose Tattoo").

1956: "Around the World in 80 Days"; Yul Brynner ("The King and I"); Ingrid Bergman ("Anastasia").

1957: "The Bridge on the River Kwai"; Alec Guinness ("The Bridge on the River Kwai"); Joanne Woodward ("The Three Faces of Eve").

1958: "Gigi"; David Niven ("Separate Tables"); Susan Hayward ("I Want to Live!").

1959: "Ben-Hur"; Charlton Heston ("Ben-Hur"); Simone Signoret ("Room at the Top").

***

1960: "The Apartment"; Burt Lancaster ("Elmer Gantry"); Elizabeth Taylor ("Butterfield 8").

1961: "West Side Story"; Maximilian Schell ("Judgment at Nuremberg"); Sophia Loren ("Two Women").

1962: "Lawrence of Arabia"; Gregory Peck ("To Kill a Mockingbird"); Anne Bancroft ("The Miracle Worker").

1963: "Tom Jones"; Sidney Poitier ("Lilies of the Field"); Patricia Neal ("Hud").

1964: "My Fair Lady"; Rex Harrison ("My Fair Lady"); Julie Andrews ("Mary Poppins").

1965: "The Sound of Music"; Lee Marvin ("Cat Ballou"); Julie Christie ("Darling").

1966: "A Man for All Seasons"; Paul Scofield ("A Man For All Seasons"); Elizabeth Taylor ("Who's Afraid of Virginia Woolf?").

1967: "In the Heat of the Night"; Rod Steiger ("In the Heat of the Night"); Katharine Hepburn ("Guess Who's Coming to Dinner").

1968: "Oliver!"; Cliff Robertson ("Charly"); Katharine Hepburn ("The Lion in Winter") and Barbra Streisand ("Funny Girl").

1969: "Midnight Cowboy"; John Wayne ("True Grit"); Maggie Smith ("The Prime of Miss Jean Brodie").

***

1970: "Patton"; George C. Scott ("Patton"); Glenda Jackson ("Women in Love").

(Dennis Brack/Black Star)

BRINKLEY ON BRINKLEY

—and other topics
by Saul Braun

David Brinkley's three sons don't take his high celebrity very seriously, even though surveys have indicated that he is familiar to more Americans even than the Beatles or John Wayne. The reason the Brinkley boys don't take it seriously is, simply enough, that their father doesn't. More than that. He finds it annoying and embarrassing and it prevents him from doing some of the work he likes best to do. He hasn't for some time been able to go out and cover Presidential campaigns. Back in 1960 he was in the field with Hubert Humphrey in the West Virginia primary and discovered, to his dismay, that the voters were less interested in the candidate than they were in getting Brinkley's autograph.

"It was just . . . embarrassing. What I think is that you could put a baboon on television every night for 15 years and he'd become some sort of celebrity. I'm a newsman, a reporter. I don't like the term anchor man and I never use it. It's just one of those clichés that

evolved out of the atmosphere. Never have used it, never will.

"When Huntley left the show, we went from six days a week to seven. That's when we had McGee, Chancellor and Brinkley rotating all the time. It was obviously bad programming because there never was any familiar character or pair of characters people could get used to, so then we changed to what we have now, and we plan to stay with it. The changes didn't make much difference in the ratings. We were second to Cronkite before Huntley left—two, three years before Huntley left. Nationally, CBS is now 15, NBC is 13 and ABC is at 10.

"Frankly, I've never paid that much attention to the ratings. I never really think about them. I think ratings are a legitimate concern but we shouldn't be obsessed with them. If they're low, then you have to do something to get them up. As on a newspaper, if your circulation is low, then obviously there's something wrong, and there's no doubt people would rather have the news in an attractive, relaxed package than have it delivered to them in a box wrapped in black paper."

By 1967 The Huntley-Brinkley Report had embedded itself so deeply in the American consciousness that some newscasters tended to reproduce the distinctive Brinkley cadences without necessarily intending to. Brinkley spoke that June at the commencement exercises of Knox College in Illinois and told with dry pleasure the tale of an encounter at the Washington airport.

"When I was there waiting for an airplane, a lady came up to me and said, 'Aren't you Chet Huntley?' And I said, 'Yes.' Actually, that is the polite answer, because first of all it doesn't make any difference. People confuse us all the time; nothing could be less important, so if I had said, 'No, I'm Brinkley,' then she would have been embarrassed and would have felt it necessary to apologize, which was not necessary, and this would have taken some time and I would have missed my airplane. So I said, 'Yes,' and she said, 'Well, I want to say I think you're pretty good, but I don't know how you put up with that idiot in Washington.' "

In 1969 Brinkley left Washington and moved to New York, but he didn't much like it. So he went back.

"Since I didn't have to do it, I didn't want to do it. I found myself spending too much time messing around with the mechanics of living. One of a hundred examples is that I like opera and instead of doing my work, I found myself wondering, How am I going to get across to the West Side and the Met, because it looks as if it might rain, and things like that. That's no way to live.

"Now I live in town in a small house and I have a farm, you might call it, but it's not farmed. A big piece of land out in Virginia in the mountains, where I like to go when I can.

"Most of my friends are people that I've known for 20-odd years. Friends of long standing. One is a professor of English at Georgetown University. One is a guy who lives out in Maryland in the country and writes books, Doug Wallop. Art Buchwald is a good friend.

And a lot of newspaper people. And a number of politicians, remnants of the Johnson years and the Kennedy years.

"Mostly we talk. Serious talk. Once in a while somebody will get fancy and have a dance or something and put on some rock music, but it's mostly talking. I read more than I watch TV."

Reading is not the only solitary pursuit he enjoys—he is also an expert woodworker. These are not unnatural developments out of a lonely childhood. He was born in 1920 in Wilmington, N.C., into a strict Southern Episcopalian family that had produced lots of ministers and a doctor or two. There were two older brothers and two sisters and then after a hiatus of 10 years, David.

"It was just taken for granted that everyone was going to work and behave himself. Pampering of children was not done. We were anything but pampered. Children obeyed and they said *sir* to their fathers and *ma'am* to their mothers. My father died when I was a baby. Everybody starts out with some sort of mother thing, whether it's a hang-up or a fear or whatever it is, it's something. And my mother was very ungiving, in terms of affection. I have always liked to write, all my life, and I remember writing a story, which I think I thought was funny. I took it to her, and she read it and handed it back and said, 'Why are you wasting your time with that kind of nonsense?' And it was a long time afterward before I understood the cruelty of it, so I might in fact have spent all these years trying to prove her wrong. It's quite possible.

"I think there are some interesting parallels between journalists and politicians, their motives and needs and drives. In the case of the politicians, it's a seeking of approval and a seeking for power. In journalism it may be more of the first and less of the latter, because there's no real power in journalism. People say you have it, but you don't. You may write about them, talk about them, watch them, follow them, chronicle their doings, but *they* have the power."

Some years back, when Brinkley was beginning a half-hour documentary news program titled David Brinkley's Journal, *he approached a young film editor to work with him, and, surprisingly, the young man refused. "Don't you want to work on the best news show in television?" Brinkley asked. "Sure," the film editor replied, "it'll be the best show. And I'll be making hundreds of dollars in overtime because, David, anybody who works with you is going to work plenty of overtime until the show is exactly right. But, David, I'd never see my family again."*

"When I leave here at the end of a day I'm like a squeezed lemon. Any time I get an idea I have to use it immediately. I read the papers, I read the wires, I talk to people, I circulate around town some. I do five radio shows a week, they're about 500 words long, and I do five TV shows a week. They run whatever they run. There's no set time. It varies. Some nights just a little short essay kind of thing that I hope is interesting. Sometimes it's a little film story about some aspect of American society that I hope tells something of how we live and how we don't. I have no format. I have always been opposed to formats of all kinds. To an extent, though, it's essential, one reason being that before I do anything, there are about 30 people that have to know what I'm going to do, because they have to push buttons and this and that.

"Ours is the only human activity whatsoever that is punctual. I don't mean 6:29:20 or 6:31:15. I mean 6:30 period. And just that little fact alone is grinding, the fact that you can't be one second late or one second early. We're the only people on earth who are always on time. It is a burden, because you may say, 'I'm not ready. I could use another 15 minutes.' Well, you can't *get* another 15 minutes, you just can't. It is a grind. It'll drive most anybody crazy, and it requires the kind of temperament that will enable you to put up with it. I think over a period of time it probably has some effect on your personality. It has on mine. I'm very impatient with delay and stalling and fooling around.

"I used to do a weekly half-hour documentary program which at times was pretty good. But it was in addition to the news and it was damn near killing me, just the sheer volume of work and time it took. And so after a while I tried very hard to get two or three ahead so I could get a couple of weeks off from this extra work, and I did all the work to get a couple of weeks ahead, but I could not get anyone *else* to get two or three weeks ahead. So I could never get ahead and it irritated the hell out of me. I've often not made it very well. Very often you just have to slap something together to fill the time.

"I like what I do, but I don't much like the way I have to do it. I would like to be able to write something when I have something I want to write, rather than having to write something when I have to write something. One thing I'm not sure about—if I didn't have to work and if I didn't have to write, I don't know how much writing I'd do. I don't know how lazy I am because I've never had a chance to find out."

David Brinkley began his career in journalism in his home town. He was then 17, a high school columnist for a weekly newspaper, the Wilmington Star-News, owned by a relative. Among other assignments, he covered the meetings of the men's civic clubs in town. He remembers one speech that ran an hour that was entitled "The Romance of Cast Iron Pipe." After acquiring eminence in his profession, he spoke before one of those groups. They gave him a plaster statue of General Douglas MacArthur with a clock in his belly. He more frequently speaks before college audiences these days. After his speeches on campus, he generally retires to an informal bull session with students that runs for hours.

"I love it. It's great fun. And I have a very clear sense of an evolved consciousness that is very often, not always but very often, doubtful, questioning, but of not yet having been convinced, not destructive, quite often creative. I'm not talking about the East Village crowd, I'm talking about young people who are still willing to try. In colleges and out. I find them heartening, attractive, often wrong but for good reasons. Hell, everybody who's 19 years old is wrong about a lot of things, because in most cases he doesn't know what he's talking about. But nevertheless they do talk and they do care about it and they think about it and they ask about it and they read about it. And I think if about five previous generations, including mine, had done the same things, this country would be in much better shape now than it is.

"Of course, the technology for getting those answers wasn't available. With a television news program we reach people who have never been reached by serious news before, people who might or might not subscribe to or buy a newspaper, but who, even if they do, don't generally read much of it.

"We have access to the opinions of an awful lot of people whose opinions are not otherwise available, and over the years I have heard from hundreds of thousands of them, and I read many of those letters. And answer them. I would say yes, their development has been that of the species, in some respects. For one example, the disenchantment with war as a device of national policy now runs very strong and very deep in people of all types and of all ages, whereas through much of human history it has been glorified and regarded as a patriotic enterprise to be admired, supported, respected and even loved. I think that is changing, profoundly, in this country."

His special place was the skeptical, ironic voice that was perhaps the first expression many people had ever heard of their own suspicions that they weren't always being leveled with. He was the special voice for those with an eye (or a nose) for foolishness in high places. Foolishness and perhaps worse.

Brinkley's view of things hasn't much changed, but deepened. Something has settled in his face. He has grown puffier. The delicacy and lightness have gone out of his prospect of humanity and its foibles. There is a gravity and distance, and the wry has aged. It is mellower, yet heavier. Easier to swallow, harder to keep down. It is almost as if he has grown rigid and weary asking the same question with that raised eyebrow: Haven't you had enough?

"The federal government is marvelously equipped to start things and totally ill equipped to stop them. It never stops anything. Everything that was started in the '30s to deal with the Depression and unemployment is still thriving and booming. Government as an instrument of social reform is an idea I used to hold but don't much any longer. Very often it tramples to death whatever problem it was supposed to solve. It usually manages to succeed in spending the money on itself instead of the problem.

"We hear, for example, the cry that our prisons have never been properly built or maintained or designed or operated because people refuse to pay the taxes to support them and so on. This is utter nonsense. *Utter nonsense.* The people in this country have paid more than enough taxes to gold-plate every prison in 50 states.

"The main problem of prisons is that for about a generation we have been spending our money for battleships and bombers and aircraft carriers and air bases

and that sort of thing, while the civilian aspects of American society, including prisons and one hundred others, have gone into a decline. That is the truth that we have to face, sooner or later. I think we may slowly be coming to it now.

"Power is very much apart from the people. The people in this country have no power. There are a great number of members of Congress who were elected by a figure that I'm taking out of the air, but it's somewhere close, who were elected by something like one-hundredth of one percent of the people in the country. They tend to be the older members who are very senior and very established and who are lightly challenged if at all, such as, for example, although he is now dead, Mendel Rivers of South Carolina, who could (and in fact did) simply on his own authority decide the U.S. Navy needed another 450 million dollars which it hadn't even asked for, and he just threw it in as a sort of tip. Just threw it in. That's the kind of power he had.

"And there is no outside force that can do anything about the structure of Congress, so the result is that the reformers and the reformed are the same people, and that's a very difficult condition. Also, you have to remember that Washington is always somewhere around half a generation behind the rest of the country.

"I have an idea I think is pretty good and I'm going to do a television program about it. That is, say twice a year, we take a national referendum. An essential part of it would be two or three weeks of a great national splurge of discussion. Have the President go on TV and say, 'Folks, I think that Question 5 is terrible, and you really should say no, because if you say yes it's going to do this and that.' And let everybody have his say, so people will know what the alternatives are.

"I think it would be sort of a neat idea. It wouldn't solve everything, but it would give people a genuine feeling of participating that they don't have now. Congressmen could still vote as they pleased, but if they voted against the officially measured views of their constituents, they would have a hard time defending it."

David Brinkley has never been much of a one to suffer fools gladly. And he feels that often those who criticize television, whether from the liberal or conservative viewpoint, don't know what they're talking about.

"We reach a lot of people who don't really understand what news is. They don't understand what journalism is. They don't understand what a reporter is. They have the idea that when we put something on the air, it means we like it. It means we advocate it, support it, believe in it. They simply don't understand that our job is to tell what happened, whether we like it or not.

"In all these attacks on the news media, there's one fact that tends to be forgotten. And that is that in numerous countries in the world the politicians have seized power and muzzled the press. But there is no country in the world where the press has seized power and muzzled the politicians. So if people are concerned about dangers to their liberties, they ought to know where these dangers come from, and they do not come from the press."

"No, No, Nanette," starring Ruby Keeler, is featured on the Tony Awards telecast (ABC)

Boost for Broadway

A famous producer discusses the Tony
show and what it means to the theater
by Ross Drake

Swilling a stomach-settling concoction straight from the bottle, like whiskey, stabbing an assertive finger at his intercom, already cradling the telephone, Alexander H. Cohen hardly misses a beat in his monologue. "What are those repertory companies performing all over the place?" he is demanding. "Where does Minneapolis get 'Death of a Salesman'? What's the biggest *film* ever made? 'The Sound of Music'? What are some of the others? 'My Fair Lady'? 'West Side Story'? 'The King and I'? Where do they come from? It's all *Broadway!*"

Cohen saying "Broadway!" is like Kipling saying "England!" In the mind's ear, one hears it tolling like the Rank Organisation gong. Cohen is a major theatrical producer, and knows the troubles Broadway is heir to, but he has faith in the theater's vitality and a hardheaded sense that it will sell. By way of proving the point, he took charge of the American Theater Wing's annual Tony Awards program six years ago, put it on national television, and watched it grow from an hour-long special in 1967 to a two-hour 25th-anniversary spectacular last year that was a critical and ratings bonanza. And

now he's ready with another two-hour Tony show, which ABC will telecast this Sunday night (April 23).

Cohen is a seasoned promoter—of plays, theater tours, and once, as Bulova's advertising director, of a multimillion-dollar line of Academy Award watches—and he understands how badly the theater needs a life-giving jolt of publicity. In his view, Broadway is the world's No. 1 tourist attraction, and anyone who can afford the price of a plane ticket is a potential recruit to the box office. The glamor of the Tony telecasts, he believes, is a compelling form of enticement.

The other major award shows, the Oscars and the Emmys, have been bruised and abused by the critics, but Cohen feels bound to defend them. Movies and television are unwieldy international industries, he points out, whereas the theater is more intimate and clannish, tucked away in a few square blocks of midtown Manhattan, and easier to deal with creatively. "I probably know everybody in the business on a personal or first-name basis," he says, "so it makes it easier for me to do my show. I suppose I should be saying, 'Yes, I'm a great genius, and I do things the other guys can't.' But that's a lot of nonsense."

Cohen's program at least isn't encumbered, like the Oscar telecast, with a tedious succession of technical awards. There are only about 20 Tonys presented each year; it doesn't take a master's degree to figure out what they're for, and they don't get in the way of the entertainment, which this year includes people like Alfred Drake, Lisa Kirk, Desi Arnaz, Larry Blyden, Constance Towers, Janet Blair, Ruby Keeler, Helen Gallagher, Bobby Van and Patsy Kelly—all doing the things that made them famous instead of standing around shredding envelopes. Above all, it isn't *de rigueur* for stars to cop out on the ceremony.

"At last year's Tony Awards," declares Cohen, "nearly every person nominated in every category was present. We do not *tolerate* people coming on stage and saying [in piping falsetto], 'Mr. Ross Hudson is in the west of Africa shooting big game and I am his maid and he told me to come and say thank you and therefore I have come to say thank you.' We won't put up with that." It isn't a matter of cracking the whip, he implies—the theater is a proud institution, with a wholesome regard for tradition. If, by chance, fewer than half the nominees in any category are on hand, the award is withdrawn from the ceremony and presented after the show.

Once the Tonys were a cozy intramural affair, with a tenuous grasp on survival. Founded in 1947 as a memorial to Antoinette Perry, the late executive director of the American Theater Wing, they seemed headed for oblivion in 1966, when the Wing turned them over to the League of New York Theaters. Cohen dusted them off, set them up in style on ABC, and briskly refurbished the concept. Now the show is a glossy Broadway spectacular, featuring scenes from the season's top musicals, the best entertainment the theater can offer, and, finally, somewhat dwarfed in perspective, the awards.

Cohen realizes Broadway doesn't command the teeming constituency of TV or the movies, and that viewers take only a cursory interest in who wins most of the hardware. "What the audience cares about," he perceives, "is that it's going to see 'Jesus Christ Superstar' or 'No, No, Nanette.'" Cohen counts on presenting some electric moments from each this Sunday, plus a selection from Melvin Van Peebles' abrasive all-black musical, "Ain't Supposed to Die a Natural Death."

"Superstar" and "Nanette" represent the current extremities of the commercial musical—one a new-wave pop-rock opera, with hyperthyroid staging by Tom O'Horgan, director of "Hair"; the other a Busby Berkeley nostalgia trip. The Van Peebles show is in another vein entirely—a raw slice of life from the ghetto. "You won't see anything like it anywhere else on telvision," claims a Cohen aide, and that, in Cohen's estimation, may be reason enough for presenting it. People ought to care what's going on in the black theater, he maintains, and if they don't—well, he's going to show them anyway.

Cohen doesn't consider himself tyrannical about the Tony telecast—he is a willing audience for suggestions, he says—but the controlling judgment is his. After the sponsor and the ad agency and the network have spoken, Cohen sifts and ponders, then does exactly as he chooses. Compromise is enfeebling in the theater, he believes, and he likes to take responsibility for anything he produces, whether a hit or a disaster.

Apart from the habitual absenteeism, one of the prime embarrassments of Oscar night is the dazed incoherence of some of the winners. Healthy egos all, they must at least *suspect* they could win, but when the hour of decision arrives they come reeling on stage as glassy-eyed and breathless as if they'd just been clipped with a brick. Cohen expects something better of the Tony nominees—"By and large, they are imaginative people," he says—but ground rules exist just in case.

Nominees are seated strategically, all on the aisles, so they don't have to go clawing over each other in a windmilling dash to the stage. They are encouraged to get to the microphone quickly, accept their medallions, and swiftly retreat to their seats. There is an unofficial 15-second limit on thank yous, and no one has ever abused it, though Cohen's recurring nightmare is of someone droning on interminably while dawn slowly cracks.

Nominees are chosen by committee, and winners by a coalition of heavy theatrical types—producers, directors, playwrights, actors, choreographers, scenic artists, critics, et al. Sometimes there are special awards, and for Cohen's purposes, this year's choices are a windfall—actress Ethel Merman, composer Richard Rodgers, and the Babe Ruth of long-running Broadway musicals, Harold Prince's production of "Fiddler on the Roof."

Merman will dig into her scrapbook for a medley of sturdy perennials from "Anything Goes," "Annie Get Your Gun," "Call Me Madam," and "Gypsy," while Rodgers' tribute will be a musical salute—selections from his 50 years of Broadway hits.

For Cohen, the Tonys are a celebration of Broadway, but a point of departure as well. Obviously, his growing attachment to television is a way of taking up slack in a dwindling theatrical career. His only Broadway adventure this season, Joan Rivers' "Fun City," collapsed in a week and expired, and more angels could dance on the head of Jim Brady's diamond stickpin than are crowding producers' offices waving fistfuls of cash.

In his optimism, Cohen believes that television could give the theater a reviving jab of adrenalin. The home audience is restive, he feels, and wearily turning away from the Monday-through-Sunday sameness of timeworn formula programming. "Quality appears to be having its day," he observes hopefully. "Public Broadcasting is beginning to gain an audience." He expects the networks to counterattack, with fresh ideas of their own.

Where should they turn for material? "Well," beams Cohen expansively, "I don't like to give the simple answer: they call *me*—but I think they will say, 'Listen, if we're going to get people who haven't worked in television before, what about some of those guys in the theater? What about David Merrick? What about Harold Prince? What about Alex Cohen?'"

Drawing by Jack Davis

In the beginning there was Groucho Marx, miles of film and a car named De Soto
by Bob Foreman

Groucho Marx and his brother Gummo, who was his personal manager, and I were being shown around an old movie studio just outside Hollywood. This was where Groucho's new television show, *You Bet Your Life*, was to be filmed. It was a big barn of a building, unused for years and very seedy.

Dr. Ferenz Fodor, in charge of filming the show, had selected the place and was having trouble finding something nice to say about it. Finally he came up with, "Groucho, it's completely fireproof!" Groucho raised his (real) eyebrows and replied, "No self-respecting fire would come into the joint."

That was in 1949. I had flown from New York to California to get Groucho to film the commercials I had

written for our client, his sponsor, De Soto. Our advertising agency had sold the De Soto division of Chrysler a year of *You Bet Your Life* on NBC radio and television, and I had been assured Groucho *loved* doing commercials. Without charge.

I stepped out of my $99 berth on the prop-driven Constellation after the all-night flight and was driven to a bungalow at the Beverly Hills Hotel. Such style befitted a writer for Groucho even though I was only writing car commercials. One week later I was still cooling my suntanned heels at the hotel pool.

Groucho refused to see me. Gummo was the only Marx brother who'd talk to me and he was available every day, all day, at his home or at the pool. Not having been in the brother act for many years gave Gummo a complex. The quality of his humor was strained, especially since he couldn't produce Groucho and I could lose my job.

On the seventh day, a Sunday, Gummo had me paged at the pool and said Groucho would see me. I drove around the block to Groucho's house and met Gummo in the front hall. We were soon joined by a platoon of agents and network characters. For half an hour all paced up and down. Then Groucho appeared, wearing a cerise cap with oversize visor and a purple shirt. The crowd melted away. I advanced, hand extended, and said, "I'm pleased to meet you, Mr. Marx."

Groucho said, "You won't be when I get through with you."

I stammered that I had some very funny De Soto commercials for him to film. Also a camera crew, a De Soto borrowed from a local dealer, and we had to get started if we expected to have the commercials ready on time.

"We don't expect to," he said. "Besides, I get $25,000 for a day's shooting."

I looked for help. The others were pretending not to be there. "That's for making features," Groucho added. "I wouldn't do commercials for twice that."

The silence was broken by Gummo, the agents, and station people saying good-by. This left me alone with Groucho. Minus an audience, he changed. He invited me into the house. We sat and had a drink. He asked questions about television advertising, about car advertising, about Madison Avenue. Two hours later he had agreed to tomorrow's shooting and every piece of copy I'd shown him. Free.

When *You Bet Your Life* was devised, television was radio's stepchild. The Groucho Marx series our ad agency had induced De Soto to sponsor on NBC was to be a "simulcast"; that is, a radio show with cameras on it. The radio portion cost $12,500 a week, the television $2500. At the end, 1961, TV was $40,000 and there was no radio.

The show's format was a loose kind of game, with three pairs of contestants vying for money and a jackpot. Also there was a gimmick called "the secret word," which a contestant might inadvertently mention, causing a wooden duck to fly down from the ceiling. Then the lucky couple split $100. Actually the game was nothing but a way to get Groucho to be funny with people, raise his eyebrows, finger his cigar and be himself. When I say "himself," I mean himself. He refused to wear the frock-coat or paint on his eyebrows and mustache, as he'd done when portraying Wolf J. Flywheel or S. Quentin Quale in movies. Our De Soto sponsors learned Groucho would be in mufti only when I had flown out there—*after* they'd signed the contract. They wanted out—but their legal eagles couldn't find anything in the contract saying Groucho had to wear a frockcoat.

Then Detroit begged me to beg Groucho to dress up. In a pepper-and-salt business suit he looked like a Midwest bank president and they were sure no one would recognize him. I tried to argue with Groucho, but he shut me up with "If I can't be funny on television without funny clothes and makeup, to hell with it." He turned out to be right; *You Bet Your Life* was in the Top 10 for years, and Groucho, without a funny costume, made heroes of the De Soto division, their ad agency and me.

You Bet Your Life had to be prerecorded on film because Groucho was used to working from a script. He couldn't be expected to ad-lib funny—or clean—week after week. So the show was scripted, leaving plenty of room for his ad-libs. This meant we had to film an hour and a half's worth of Groucho and cut out whatever was too dirty or unfunny.

We had technical problems, too. No camera held more than 10 minutes of 35-mm film. It was unthinkable to stop twice while Groucho was performing in front of 500 people (in the fireproof studio) and reload the camera. Groucho and the audience would cool off; the show would grind to a halt.

Enter Dr. "Two-Door" Fodor, as Groucho called him in deference to his new sponsor. The Doctor, who resembled a mad scientist in a B picture, had developed a camera that held *20 minutes of film*. We anchored eight cameras in four different positions and filled each with film; Camera 1 took close-ups and ran for 20 minutes, then Camera 2, right beside it, was switched on. The same thing in the other positions. The amount of film to be developed and pasted together to make 30 minutes of clean fun was monumental. Also expensive, which meant less take-home for Groucho and caused him to say, "We could be making 'Gone With the Wind' every week and I could be playing with Scarlett O'Hara instead of George Fenneman [our announcer]."

Producing the show created some peculiar jobs. Bob Dwan was billed as director but spent most of his life in the laboratory cutting out and pasting together pieces of negative. Bernie Smith, also billed as director, was really the writer. However, we didn't want the people to know Groucho's comments weren't ad-lib. You folks at home never saw the large squares of cardboard onto which Bernie's script had been lettered. They were cue cards composed after talking to the preselected contestants. But Groucho could see them and his sly grin, with eyes averted, meant he was looking for the next cue.

While a great deal of the pure-Grou was too blue for the average American family, I figured it was just right for the De Soto dealers of America. So I gathered a reel

of no-nos from the cutting-room floor, and they were the highlight of a big meeting in Detroit. Our agency account executive thought they were too dirty even for car dealers. He said Groucho and I would lose us the De Soto account.

Writing commercials to be filmed in Hollywood was a new experience for me. I'd write them in New York, have storyboards drawn, and take the train to Detroit for approval. There I'd act out each scene in front of the group. I got by the first commercials by larding them with girls whom the artist made look sexy. For example, I had a girl hidden in the trunk of the car to be discovered by Groucho. Then George Fenneman made the point De Sotos have roomy trunks. But I had a bad time getting the Detroiters to agree to what I thought was my greatest stroke of genius—the show's tag. I showed them a drawing of Groucho sticking his head through a De Soto-Plymouth dealer sign, saying, "Go to see your nearest De Soto-Plymouth dealer and tell him Groucho sent you." Then I attempted Groucho's bit with the eyebrows and cigar. Though this became the best-known show signature of its era, it almost didn't get on the air. After my poor Groucho imitation, I stood back awaiting their applause. There wasn't any. Our dealer signs are oblong, one executive said. The sign in my drawing was round. "You can't stick your head through an oblong," I said. They discussed this for a while, and then a vice president finally said, "Oh well, if *you* like it, Bob, put it in."

In 1958 I wrote a novel with a television background and the publisher asked me who might do a blurb for the dust jacket and for advertising. I sent the galleys to Groucho and a week later got a letter with this postscript: "I just read 'The Hot Half Hour' by Bob Foreman. It's clairvoyant. It's revealing. It's even sexy. Go to your nearest bookstore and tell 'em Groucho sent you!"

IT STARTED
AS A GREETING CARD
TO MILLIONS

Now with its 100th telecast at hand, "Hall of Fame" can look back on a distinguished, innovative history
by Terrence O'Flaherty

In the fall of 1951, when the young medium of television was still teething contentedly on *Howdy Doody* and *Broadway Open House,* NBC set its sights a little higher and engaged Gian Carlo Menotti to compose a Christmas Eve opera that told the story of a crippled boy named Amahl who lived on the road to Bethlehem. But no advertiser was willing to hum the $150,000 tune it would take to put it on the air, and Christmas Eve approached without a sponsor.

Although Hallmark was impressed with the heartwarming production, December 24 is a poor time to sell

Christmas cards. By then they've all been bought. But the company's president had an unusual idea: Why not sponsor it as a thank-you to all the people who *did* send Hallmark cards?

And that's the way "Amahl and the Night Visitors" first went on the air—with a brief thank-you voiced by Sarah Churchill and no commercials. Viewers responded to Hallmark's gallantry by swamping the NBC switchboard with congratulatory calls all through the night.

It was the beginning of *Hallmark Hall of Fame* as we know it today—undisputably television's finest series and probably the only one in history where the slogan for the sponsor's product ("When you care enough to send the very best") can be applied, as well, to the entertainment displayed in his name.

On November 17 *Hall of Fame* is sending us its 100th telecast, "The Hands of Cormac Joyce." It is an opportunity for viewers to pause and look back with astonishment and appreciation on 21 years of "first nights."

No matter what avenue you use to approach the series, eventually it leads back to Joyce Hall, the tall, spare plainsman from Kansas City, now 81, who had, single-handedly, invented the everyday greeting card. He had been thinking about a new kind of television series, and the success of "Amahl" convinced him that only quality entertainment can sell a quality product. He thought Shakespeare might be a good place to start. "I don't think you can do much better than Shakespeare," he said simply.

Maurice Evans agreed. If Hall had invented the greeting card, surely Evans had invented Shakespeare for a whole generation of American audiences. He was willing to do a two-hour "Hamlet" and Hall was happy to sponsor it. The trouble was getting a network to interrupt its regular programming to air it. No one had ever put on a two-hour television drama before.

All the networks were approached, but only NBC's Pat Weaver was interested enough to make room for the melancholy prince of Denmark. As a result "Hamlet" hit the air April 26, 1953. It was not only TV's first full-length Shakespeare, it was TV's first two-hour drama and, because Evans substituted Edwardian trousers for the traditional Tudor tights, it was also the first "Hamlet" that didn't wrinkle at the knees or bag at the seat.

The production introduced stage director George Schaefer to television and it was produced by a little live wire named Mildred Freed Alberg who had succeeded in getting everyone together in the first place. Schaefer quickly became known as a director who respected the playwright, the actors and the audience and realized all three were linked in the success of any drama. After "Hamlet" he raced through a succession of dramatic gems for Hallmark that would take a theater-lover's breath away: "King Richard II," "Macbeth," "The Devil's Disciple," "The Corn Is Green," "The Taming of the Shrew," "Man and Superman," "On Borrowed Time," "Kiss Me, Kate," "Winterset," "Time Remembered," "The Teahouse of the August Moon," "Cyrano de Bergerac," "Abe Lincoln in Illinois," "Blithe Spirit,"

"The Fantasticks," "Elizabeth the Queen"—and 45 others . . . just refer to any list of the best plays and *Hallmark* has done most of them.

In the process of getting them on the air, Schaefer formed television's most elegant repertory company. For its lucky members *Hallmark Hall of Fame* was a romp through actors' paradise led by Evans, the precise Welshman, in 11 major roles. A list of all of the participants would read like an honor roll of the best performers of our time, from Katharine Cornell in "There Shall Be No Night" and Sir John Gielgud in a 1970 "Hamlet" to Mary Martin in "Born Yesterday" and George C. Scott in "The Price."

Dame Judith Anderson—petite in person but a giant on stage—played a variety of *Hallmark* leads, including Lady Macbeth twice. She recalls the original live production in 1954 as a two-hour grind in a jungle of scenery braces and camera cables, using every inch of floor space in NBC's enormous Brooklyn studio: "We'd race from one set to another, changing costumes and throwing off crowns as we went. I have no sense of direction whatsoever and I remember one awful moment in the second act when Maurice and I bumped into each other in the dark behind scenes. I whispered, 'Where do we go next?' and he answered, 'My God, I don't know. I'm following *you!*' "

Elfin Julie Harris appeared so often that a leading role for her seemed to be a prerequisite for any drama produced by Schaefer between 1956 and 1967, during which she played 10 parts any actress would love to sink her teeth into, including the Queen in "Victoria Regina"; Joan of Arc in "The Lark"; the missing Russian princess in "Anastasia" (opposite Lynn Fontanne); a deaf mute named "Johnny Belinda"; Eliza Doolittle in Shaw's "Pygmalion"; Nora, the original fem-libber, in "A Doll's House"; and the love-torn nun in "Little Moon of Alban," a role which was written for her by James Costigan, one of *Hallmark Hall of Fame*'s playwrights-in-residence. "Alban" was the first of 20 original dramas in the series.

Audience ratings for the first years were small, but the 1960 production of Shakespeare's "The Tempest" became the first classic drama of any sort to hit the Top 10 in TV audience ratings, with an estimated 21 million viewers. Hollywood and Madison Avenue were astonished. The Bard had outdrawn even *Ozzie and Harriet*, a jellylike confection considered at that time to be what viewers liked best! The presence of Richard Burton in the cast might have been responsible for the popularity, had it not been for the fact that it was produced in 1960 B.C. (Before "Cleopatra" and his liaison with the Queen of the Nile.)

Hall has no interest in ratings. "Just because people watch your show doesn't mean they are buying your product," he has said. "I'd rather make eight million good impressions than 28 million bad ones." The ratings are available, however, and they are interesting.

Hallmark hit its biggest audience in 1958 with a live production of "Hans Brinker or the Silver Skates" with Tab Hunter, Basil Rathbone and 50,000 pounds of real ice. It held the *Hallmark* audience record for the next 11 years until 1969, when it was broken by another children's story, "The Littlest Angel."

The lowest-rated single show was "A Cry of Angels," based on Handel's problems in composing "Messiah," with Walter Slezak struggling mightily among the sharps and flats as the composer.

If at first they don't succeed, *Hallmark* has been known to try them again. Take "The Green Pastures," for example. Of all the explanations of the Creation, none is more satisfying than the Sunday school version pictured in Marc Connelly's play: "Now you and Eve will have the run of this here garden," says De Lawd. "But take it easy because you're a new kind of experiment with me and I ain't sure you'll work out yet."

The *Hallmark* adaptation was a delight, but no one saw it, because it ran opposite a more contemporary recitation of the Adam and Eve story: a circus party thrown by Mike Todd and his wife, Elizabeth Taylor, in Madison Square Garden to celebrate the first birthday of Todd's movie "Around the World in 80 Days." It had dancing elephants, 1000 tons of ice cream, 4000 pizzas and 18,000 celebrity guests, including Elsa Maxwell looking like a giant Pekinese.

When the audience count came in, the evening might have been called "Around De Lawd in 90 Minutes." Almost no one had seen "Green Pastures." But when it was rerun two years later, Miss Taylor was no longer appearing with the circus, the competition was light and the show attracted one of the biggest audiences in *Hallmark* history.

Four years ago the series strayed from its traditional romanticism to explore the contemporary scene and came up with three winners: "Teacher, Teacher," the study of a retarded child; "A Storm in Summer," based on the uneasy friendship of a Jewish delicatessen owner (Peter Ustinov) and a black youngster (N'Gai Dixon); and "The Price," with George C. Scott, Colleen Dewhurst and Barry Sullivan.

Not all of the shows in the series have been outstanding. There was that time in October 1960, for instance, when Schaefer set out to find "Shangri-La" in the Mountains of the Blue Moon, accompanied by several of the original "Lost Horizon" characters plus an American ballroom dance team and some awful songs reminiscent of Tin Pan Alley. They didn't make it.

But most of them *have* made it. "The Magnificent Yankee" in 1965 was a proud occasion because it starred Alfred Lunt and Lynn Fontanne, whose dignity and craftmanship are unique in the theater. During rehearsals in a grim hall on New York's Lower East Side, the Lunts charmed the rest of the cast by bringing their lunch in a wicker basket. Schaefer described it this way:

"At the noon break Miss Fontanne would find a table somewhere in the room and spread out a fresh cloth and silver. The two of them would lunch graciously, then put everything back into the hamper and take out a Scrabble set, entirely oblivious of the people scurrying around them. They always looked marvelous. Instead of the usual slacks, Miss Fontanne wore a Dior dress and a mink hat. Lunt wore a sport shirt with matching ascot. When I gave the cast a day off, Lunt asked if the two of them could come back anyway to work some things out."

After watching the Lunts in rehearsal for several days, playwright Emmet Lavery said: "I felt as though I were watching a Rolls-Royce being assembled."

In a way, that's what the *Hallmark Hall of Fame* has always been—the Rolls-Royce of television entertainment, a handcrafted vehicle of comfort, style and precision. The very best.

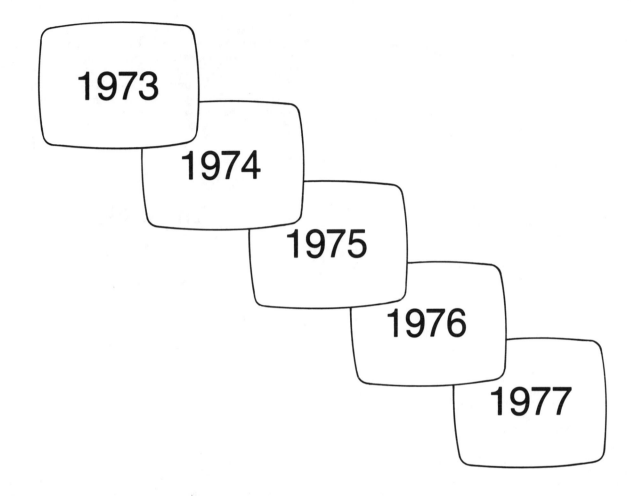

Review

by Cleveland Amory

"AN AMERICAN FAMILY"

This is the show you may have heard about— the public-television documentary series about the tribal tribulations of an American family. Margaret Mead has declared that this program is "as new and significant as the invention of drama or the novel." With all due respect to Dr. Mead, we think this is a touch much. So, for that matter, is her explanation that the reason the viewer was told at the beginning that the parents of the family are now separated was "to make the suspense bearable." In our opinion, if the viewer hadn't been told a separation was coming, he would have engineered a split of his own.

In a word, the producer was lucky. With the separation, which he didn't know would happen, the show works. Without it, the idea of spending an hour a week for 12 weeks with Mr. and Mrs. William C. Loud of Santa Barbara, California, their five children, their ranch house, their swimming pool and their four foreign cars would have all the appeal of watching 12 hours of— well, Mr. and Mrs. William C. Loud's home movies. The Louds now claim that anything good about them ended up on the cutting-room floor. Maybe it did—but then again, maybe it didn't.

"These people touch without meeting," says writer Fredelle Maynard, "meet without touching." This is a pretty rounded sentence for such squares as you have here. But from the viewers' point of view, equally important is the fact that it takes so long for us to meet them. Whether this was because the producers didn't have enough cameras or because, when they did, the Louds either froze or spent the time showing off, the fact remains that we get seemingly endless events like a New Year's Eve party, horseplay with spray cans, and a dancing-school ballet, with precious few individual moments. We ourselves sat through three episodes of *An American Family* without ever learning enough about either of the two younger sons or the two daughters, to be able, on a dark night (and the lighting wasn't too good either) to tell them apart. And we do get awfully tired, where teen-agers are concerned, of not having an interpreter who speaks Mumble.

Still, as we told you, because of the separation, the show does work. It's boring and banal, but it's supposed to be boring and banal. A show can, after all, be so boring it's fascinating, so banal it's intriguing. And this one, despite its shortcomings, is. There's something about the father's desperate college try, the mother's desperate control, the whole family's desperate with-it-ness, that makes you watch to the bitter—and bitter it is—end.

The most arresting episode so far was the one in which Mrs. Loud visited Lance, the 20-year-old eldest son who lives in New York's Chelsea Hotel. To entertain her, Lance and his roommate, a young man named Soren Ingenue, take her to a transvestite variety show. "I was amused some of the time," she says afterwards, "and I was bored some of the time, but a great deal of the time I was just embarrassed." And that might be an epitaph for *An American Family.*

"I Think ABC Dropped the Ball"

Dick Cavett talks about where he is and where he's going
by Leticia Kent

On a fair, gray day in New York, Dick Cavett peers across the giant-sized, walnut desk in his tiny office and, with characteristic deadpan, says, "I realize that a network television talk show that was supposed to stay on five nights a week and now isn't on five nights a week may be construed to be a failure."

At 36, Cavett somehow conveys the impression of a precocious child whose manly voice is permanently wired to a microphone. But his wit is grown-up—and so is his cool. You have to admire his cool. ABC has cut back *The Dick Cavett Show* to one week each month because of low ratings. They've given one-third of the leftover time to Cavett's old mentor, Jack Paar, for a rival talk show and they've allotted the remainder to various "late-night specials." Yet Cavett appears unperturbed (except that he *is* chewing gum) as he explains, "I don't feel that my show is a failure. I just feel that the mechanisms of the business didn't accommodate it perfectly."

ABC never figured out how to promote *The Dick Cavett Show,* he claims, nor did they promote it enough; and too few—about 141 out of 175—of its affiliates carried the show. Of these, some 25 stations delayed telecasting it until the wee hours of the morning. He sees ABC as "a network recovering from severe disequilibrium." And so he reckons that if he had been on another network, "say, NBC, which is more fully subscribed by its affiliates, the whole picture might have been different." (*The Tonight Show,* he points out, is carried on 212 of NBC's 219 affiliates with no delayed transmissions.)

"Mechanisms of the business." "Disequilibrium." Evasions, yes, but literate evasions, even when delivered with comic authority in flat Nebraska tones. Is it possible that Cavett's show is in trouble because the great viewing public is turned off by his literacy?

"Oh, I expect that the 'great viewing public' *is* antiliterate," he concedes, "but I think there's enough viewing public that isn't. And I never really set out to do a reforming kind of television program. I hate the fact that I ever got labeled as an intellectual, particularly as it's clearly demonstrable that I'm not one. It strikes me as odd that people consider me something more than just an entertainer. The show fulfills my ambition to be an entertainer, that's all. Sure, I've asked myself, 'To whom am I playing?' 'Do I have an image of somebody out there?' Well, I don't. But the show has found an audience appropriate to it without my ever having pictured a group of typical Cavett viewers."

However "appropriate," ABC did not consider that Cavett's weekly audience (then some 14,450,000 viewers) was large enough, and in April 1972, according to Cavett, the network advised him somewhat ambiguously to "substantially improve" his ratings. "So I did," he says blandly, as if he were talking about someone else. "I improved by more than 30 percent. And then they redefined 'substantial improvement of ratings' and cut back the show anyway. You can't fight that. But I think that an enormous number of people watch the show who don't get counted. A man who used to work for Nielsen once told me that the people who like the 'better programs' are often those who don't want to be surveyed or interviewed or to have devices placed in their homes—which makes them unmeasurable as an audience.

"Can you imagine ratings hardware," he asks incredulously, "in the homes of such guests on my show as [writers] Norman Mailer, Gore Vidal and Janet Flanner? Or in the homes of the college students and young professionals who would tune in? In the sense that these viewers are not measured, my show may indeed be, as FCC Commissioner Nicholas Johnson has said, 'for people who don't watch television.'"

On the other hand, some people don't see all that much difference in the various brands of talk show. Is it possible that Cavett's ratings are middling because his music, intro, monologue, ads and guests blend into everyone else's music, intros, monologues, ads and guests?

"Not unless Carson is the exception that proves the rule," Cavett retorts, chewing without a sound.

"I think my show has been damn good," he says. "In its way, it has been the best of the talk shows, attracting a good audience and good guests." He ticks off some of the good guests: Groucho Marx, Orson Welles, Lieutenant Colonel Anthony Herbert, the Lunts and Noel Coward, Barry Goldwater, Laurence Olivier . . . "If you can produce a show that turns out this well, that's widely acclaimed, and ABC can't figure out a way to keep it on

the air, nuts to them." He is cool and expressionless but, somehow, you get the idea that there may be a passionate believer behind the facade.

If *The Dick Cavett Show* is the "best of the talk shows," why is *The Tonight Show* apparently twice as popular?

It's one of those awful if-you're-so-smart-why-aren't-you-rich questions, and Cavett moves uneasily in his chair. Then, very quickly, the best-but-not-the-most-popular of the talk-show hosts removes the gum from his mouth, pushes back the chair and stands up. "Because of the factors, station line-up and so on, that I mentioned earlier, and because," he says surprisingly, "a long time ago Jack Paar made watching the 11:30 P.M. slot on NBC a national ritual—which is not to put Johnny Carson down. Carson's very good."

Then is it possible that Paar may repeat his feat on ABC and knock off Cavett? Silence. "I wouldn't care to predict that," he says dryly. "Paar gave me my start in TV. I gave him his restart. The situation is symmetrical."

Then would he care to comment on Paar's show?

(Harry Benson)

Cavett demurs. "Not in print," he says. It's a rule he maintains throughout the interview. But he manages, without actually saying it, to convey the impression that he thinks there is something familiar about the show ("There is a lot of pressure on Paar to do what he used to do"). And he can damn Paar with faint praise. "Most performers hide their feelings," he remarks, with art that seems like relish—"Paar is as exposed as a lobster without a shell."

Cavett has a year's contract with ABC. But that is no assurance he will stay on the tube. Considering the small difference, thus far, between their national Nielsen ratings (Cavett: 4.3; Paar: 4.2), it seems unlikely that Cavett will be pre-empted by Paar. The contest could be with late movies, which, on CBS, sometimes have outpulled even Carson (whose rating is 8.4).

"I was a celebrity worshipper as a kid," Cavett likes to say. And one of his thrills in his present role is in being a kind of midwife to famous guests who panic on camera. "For 90 minutes," he confides, "someone I've always admired is totally in my hands and it's up to me to help that person get through the show. There's a sense of power in that, but there's also a sense of 'When am I going to grow up and do whatever it is that this is preparing me for?' The thought of doing this for the rest of my life is just unthinkable."

He is sitting again and smiling. His boyish face is brightening more and more as if he had just had an idea that was brilliant. "I guess I could go out to the colleges and, like Norman Mailer, read from my published works"—the voice heavy with sarcasm—"from my 'Playboy' interview. I can act some. I'd like to be a movie star. But I can't decide which roles are mine. In high school and college, I was doomed by my d-e-e-p voice to play character roles, and so I tend to imagine myself in the same parts as Dustin Hoffman or"—he whispers hoarsely—"George C. Scott or"—a low growl—"Lee J. Cobb. Probably none of these is appropriate. My favorite Walter Mittyism is that Dustin Hoffman and I change places. He takes over my job and I get to star in 'The Graduate' and 'Little Big Man.' My God, this is going to look *preposterous* in print! Just say I'm not dying to get out of what I'm doing into the thing I've always wanted to do."

Cavett's face leans over the desk. "You're disappointed, aren't you?" he says. "You want me to be a social critic. Don't lay that on me. It's like calling me an intellectual. It's not a role that I'm very good at, fond of or interested in. I guess I could say again what I said before: I think ABC dropped the ball—the show has been so good that it ought to be on five nights *every* week. You may think me a twisted egotist for saying this: I'm sorrier for some of the viewers than I am for myself. It's nice for me to get some time off, to be able to do other things. But there are people out there who say mine is the *only* show they watch on television—and they mean that."

The reporter may have imagined it, but at the end, Cavett seemed to have dropped his neutral expression. He looked engaged, present, even as if he cared.

SEPTEMBER 20, 1973

A TV Guide Close-Up

BILLIE JEAN KING VS. BOBBY RIGGS
8:00   **7**   **8**

Special

Women's Lob vs. The Hustler, Part 2.

Bobby Riggs, at 55, has played tennis in a dress and bonnet, with chairs on the service lines and while dragging a dog around the court. Last May, playing for real, he won the infamous Mother's Day Ms.-match against Australia's Margaret Court. Tonight, he meets Billie Jean King in a $100,000, winner-take-all, five-set match at Houston's Astrodome.

Says Riggs with his customary swagger: "She likes to come in close to the net and put away those easy shoulder-high shots. She won't see anything like that from me. I can lob it 300 feet at the Astrodome."

Maybe so, but Mrs. King, 29, is not to be taken lightly. She's a five-time Wimbledon champion and, despite falling victim to heat exhaustion two weeks ago at the U.S. Open, she is at the top of her form.

Howard Cosell, Jack Kramer and Rosemary Casals report. (Live; 2 hrs.)

(ABC)

Oliver J. Dragon of *Kukla, Fran and Ollie*

"IT WAS NEW AND WE WERE VERY INNOCENT"

A famed TV critic recalls television in the '50s with admiration and affection

by John Crosby

"Patterns" was an original hour-long TV drama about life in the upper reaches of very big business that *Kraft TV Theater* put on the air January 12, 1955, conceivably TV's greatest vintage year. The next day the author, Rod Serling, woke up famous—just like Lord Byron after "Childe Harold." Within two weeks Serling, a struggling author up to then, got 23 offers of TV assignments, three movie offers and 14 requests for interviews from newspapers and magazines.

Does TV generate that kind of excitement any more? Maybe over quarterbacks. Or Mark Spitz. Certainly not over the author of a TV play. In the '50s everyone was *interested* in TV—the educated and the featherbrains alike. It was new and we were very innocent.

I remember walking into "21," a fairly sophisticated beanery, one day in the 1950s and finding the whole restaurant buzzing with talk about another Rod Serling TV play, "Requiem For a Heavyweight." This was a *Playhouse 90* drama (directed by Ralph Nelson, produced by Martin Manulis) about the wreckage of a once-great heavyweight, very moving, maybe a little sentimental by today's standards. There were stunning performances by Jack Palance, Keenan Wynn, Ed Wynn and Edgar Stehli.

The important thing was that "Requiem" set the whole town talking in much the same way Al Jolson used to do when he'd walk out on the stage of the Winter Garden and knock 'em dead in the 1920s. Television was *the* medium of the moment and it attracted all the brilliant young kids, as moviemaking (unquestionably *the* medium of right now) does today.

Talent seemed to gush right out of the cement—brilliant young directors like Arthur Penn, John Frankenheimer, Franklin Schaffner, Sidney Lumet, Robert Mulligan, Fielder Cook, Jack Smight; writers like Gore Vidal, Paddy Chayefsky, Horton Foote, Reginald Rose; actors like Paul Newman, Rod Steiger, Geraldine Page.

Probably the most celebrated of all TV dramas—and the most typical of the 1950s—was "Marty," Paddy Chayefsky's gentle story of a lonely Bronx butcher (Rod Steiger) who finds a lonely, homely girl to love at a dance. It was full of wry, pungent humor, dialogue so good you could taste the Bronx air and smell the back alleys, the delicatessens. This was the ash-can school of TV drama; there was a lot of it and it still, 20 years later, reads very well.

I hope we may yet realize one of Gore Vidal's great dreams of a TV repertory theater that would revive the best TV dramas. It would certainly include Vidal's own "Visit to a Small Planet," the wittiest and most iconoclastic of all the TV dramas. In it Cyril Ritchard played a highly styled visitor from outer space who takes over the earth as a sort of prank.

Ken Tynan once asked me which was my all-time favorite TV play and I unhesitatingly picked "Old Man," a *Playhouse 90* drama produced by Fred Coe, the best producer of all. This was an adaptation by Horton Foote of a harrowing William Faulkner story about a Mississippi chain-gang convict (played with inarticulate anguish by Sterling Hayden, whom no one had ever before suspected of being an actor) sent on a rescue mission during a Mississippi flood. He gets lost and rescues a pregnant woman (Geraldine Page) who gives birth in flood and storm. Oh, it was shattering in its extremity of situation, its laconic talk, and its savage ironies.

Television was the feeding ground then of both the Broadway stage and the movies. "The Miracle Worker," another *Playhouse 90* drama, produced by Martin Manulis, directed by Arthur Penn, was the story of how a great teacher makes a human being out of the blind, deaf and dumb little Helen Keller. It later became a play and a movie and, frankly, it lost a little of its original impact and honesty with each change of medium.

I felt the same about others that wound up on Broadway or on film. "Twelve Angry Men," a great *Studio One* original, starring Franchot Tone, became a film starring Henry Fonda; it was shorter, sharper, crisper as a TV show. J. P. Miller's "The Days of Wine and Roses," a

Mary Martin as Peter Pan (NBC)

great teleplay on *Playhouse 90,* made a popular movie—but it didn't have the clout it had on TV.

There were a half-dozen hour- or 90-minute-long dramatic shows on every *week* in the '50s—*Kraft, Studio One, Philco, Goodyear, Celanese* (which did only Broadway hits) and, best of the lot, *Playhouse 90*—and the best and the most memorable of all were live.

Something went out of the game when TV drama, if you can call it that any more, moved to film and to Hollywood. The difference between the 1950s and the 1970s is the difference between "Marty" and *Mission: Impossible.* One *Mission: Impossible* I saw not too long ago was about a world-famous scientist whom those nonactors who were regulars on that thing had to wrest from the combined clutches of the army, air force and police of the enemy. Oh yes, he was locked behind 14-inch solid-steel doors, 12 stories underground. They got him, too. Marty got the girl and they got their scientist.

In the early '50s TV had no money and it was full of conversation and puppets. Faye Emerson was there, with her plunging neckline, telling us about the divine parties she'd been to the night before. Arthur Godfrey strummed his ukulele and told folksy jokes.

Kukla, Fran and Ollie was an enchanting puppet show all the intellectuals raved about, much as they later raved about *Sesame Street. Kukla* came from Chicago, as did Dave Garroway, the very embodiment of the bop movement, the original cool cat who talked a language of his own. In its sight gags and puckish humor, you might call his *Garroway at Large* a forerunner of *Laugh-In.* It was way ahead of its time.

The 1950s comedians were giants. Sid Caesar on *Your Show of Shows* was a comic genius, much adored by the intellectuals and the unwashed alike. He could wrench laughter out of you with the violence of his great eyes and hands and the sheer immensity of his parody. The original battle of the sexes on TV was Jackie Gleason as a bus driver and, as his wife, Audrey Meadows, the two circling each other like prize fighters. I'm afraid custom has staled and age has withered Lucille Ball, but, brothers, you should have seen our Lucy back in the '50s. She was touched with the divine fire, an inspired clown.

There are no comic giants today, but what TV comedy *has* got that it certainly didn't in the 1950s is honesty, bite and relevance. I was dumbfounded when I watched my first *Laugh-In* in England. Jokes about homosexuality, about Negroes, about Vice President Spiro Agnew (pretty nasty ones) and extremely nasty jokes about the U.S. Army; not one of those jokes would have been permitted in the 1950s, so complete was the censorship. About the most pointed joke you could make then was how hard it was to get a taxi in the rain, because the rain didn't advertise, had no political affiliations and fell on black and white impartially.

I don't want to spread the impression TV was all marvelous back in the '50s. There were some perfectly awful shows: Lawrence Welk and his damned Champagne Music (Is he still around?). Liberace tinkling on the piano, flashing his dimples, waving his posterior, and talking about Mom—all pretty sick-making. There was Mrs. Arthur Murray, the most determined female since Lady Macbeth, trying to teach us—the girls in long bouffant dresses, the men in white tie and tails—how to waltz as if we were all becalmed in 1905.

Then there were the big-money quizzes on TV, one of the all-time American insanities, ranking well up there with dance marathons and flagpole sitting. There were half a dozen of these shows—*$64,000 Question* and *Challenge, The $100,000 Big Surprise, Twenty-One*—which gave away bigger and bigger sums of money (up to a quarter of a million dollars eventually) if you could recite, say, the name of the Tudor Kings of England in a minute and a half. Then the whole thing blew up in a shower of sparks when a disgruntled quiz contestant revealed that he had been coached and given the answers in advance.

The most towering figure on TV was not an entertainer or a quiz contestant, but a newsman—Edward R. Murrow. No one since Pericles in ancient Athens has tried so hard to instill political wisdom in the whole community. In *See It Now* Murrow and his producer, Fred Friendly, tried quite simply to tackle the momentous issues of the day—segregation, poverty, witch hunting, the Cold War. The most important people on earth—Presidents, scientists, writers, everyone from Harry Truman to Louis Armstrong to J. Robert Oppenheimer—all appeared on *See It Now.* The talk was simple, honest, courageous—and it had that virtue of all the greatest shows of being understandable to the common folk as well as the intellectuals.

In 1954, when Senator Joseph McCarthy was still a bogeyman to frighten little children with, Murrow tackled him head on in *See It Now,* which showed McCarthy for what he was—sneering, truculent, a liar, more than a little mad, wholly evil. Afterwards Murrow faced his viewers and told them McCarthy was *their* fault. "This is no time for men who oppose Senator McCarthy's methods to keep silent. There is no way for a citizen to abdicate his responsibility." That was the show that started McCarthy on his way to oblivion, one of the great TV shows of all time.

At this writing, we have The Sam Ervin Show, and a very good show it is (we get it over here in England), but the audience seems bored. We were more wide-eyed in the '50s, when Virginia Hill, a gangster's moll right out of Damon Runyon, won the nation's heart on the Kefauver crime-investigation hearings, the first televised Congressional hearings. For sheer drama Sam Ervin will have to go some to top the impact of the gentle Boston lawyer Joseph Welch, during the McCarthy hearings, who demolished Senator McCarthy with a single question: "Have you no sense of decency, sir? At long last, have you left no sense of decency?"

Today television seems, curiously enough, to be returning to its original virtue, that of actuality. There is far more sport on it now, and this is not a bad thing; television was always best when you didn't know the ending. The news shows are far longer, and far more expert, and far bloodier and more cynical and searching. Even the best of the more cerebral shows seem to be about prior actuality—shows like *The Six Wives of Henry*

VIII, Search For the Nile, Elizabeth R., and an alarming number come from England, including even Alistair Cooke's *America*—a BBC show.

Ours was an age of innocence, and in retrospect some of the great stars—Jimmy Durante making those great exits in pools of light, Fred Astaire with his puckish grin on "An Evening with . . . ," and above all Mary Martin, who was perhaps the greatest TV star of all—seemed bathed in original innocence.

Mary Martin was on a lot of shows—"Ford 50th Anniversary Show," "The Skin of Our Teeth"—but her greatest triumph was as Peter Pan. Superbly directed by Jerome Robbins, "Peter Pan" was the most polished, finished and enchanting TV show of the '50s and, with an audience of 65 million, the most successful.

It's the story of a little boy who wouldn't grow up. That was the '50s all over.

John Crosby, who now lives in London, was for many years the radio and television critic of the New York Herald Tribune.

What Makes <u>60 Minutes</u> Tick?

It starts with the producer's credo: "When the viewer gets bored, I get bored"
by Saul Braun

"People identify with people. Television is best not when imparting information but when you let people share an experience."

So says Don Hewitt, executive producer of *60 Minutes,* CBS News' award-winning magazine-style show. Hewitt, a thin, tanned, cigar-smoking man in his early 50s, is one of the important people in the media, one of the "Eastern news Establishment." If he doesn't want you to see something, you won't see it on *60 Minutes.*

"Being the executive producer of *60 Minutes,*" says Hewitt, "is like being the managing editor of a magazine. I have 14 producers. They're like contributing editors. I pick good guys, and once we determine a story, they go, and I don't see it again until what we call a rough cut. Then I go in and look at it. I figure what's kind of talky, what's got good pictures, what's got sex appeal. And that's how I put together the line-up."

Rumors of news management notwithstanding, says Hewitt, he has never been stopped from doing a story he wanted to do. Among his favorites is one they called "An Enemy of the People," about a worker at Lockheed who blew the whistle on record faking and mismanagement on government contracts, and got ostracized by his co-workers for his pains. He is proudest of those stories that have themselves made news, like the Colonel Anthony Herbert piece. Herbert had been given wide media exposure for his claims that the Army had covered up atrocities in Vietnam. Herbert was confronted, in the *60 Minutes* studio, with an Army officer whose actions he had described, and who disputed Herbert. It was a powerful television event.

Hewitt calls himself a "liberal" but says it without much conviction. You do not have to spend much time with him to realize that his allegiance is to the higher politics of communications. He says that he doesn't let politics interfere with his primary goal, which is disseminating information (with no taboos except those imposed by "taste") in an interesting and exciting way. "I want to package reality as attractively as Hollywood producers package fiction," says Hewitt. "I don't like to process the news. I like to make news."

Hewitt made news with the Herbert piece, and interviews with ITT lobbyist Dita Beard, writer Clifford Irving, and others. Flashy news breaks aside, however, the show has won more than its share of awards for its ability to come up, week after week, with pieces that hold the

On the set, producer Hewitt is bracketed by correspondents Wallace (left) and Safer (Ken Regan/Camera 5)

viewer. "If I've had any success in this business," says Hewitt, "the principal reason is this: when the viewer gets bored, I get bored."

The basic format of *60 Minutes* (which will return on Sunday evenings for its sixth year after the football season ends) is artfully designed to prevent viewer boredom. The hour is broken by teasers, headlines, a ticking clock and studio monologues by the star correspondents, all wrapped around (usually) three pieces of varying tone, running seven to 20 minutes or so apiece. The week I visited, the line-up included an interview by Mike Wallace with the Palestinian guerrilla Kamal Nasser, who was assassinated shortly after the interview had been taped; a surprisingly peppy report on soybeans and the price of meat; and a friendly but lackadaisical look at life in Australia under its new prime minister. These pieces were followed by a debate between conservative commentator James J. Kilpatrick and liberal Nicholas von Hoffman.

The two star correspondents, Mike Wallace and Morley Safer, have vastly different personalities. The Wallace trademark, developed over a long, award-filled career in journalism, is the tough, probing interview. His busy, stern, hard-working face has evoked anxiety in numberless bureaucratic miscreants, and his favorite pieces are, he says, investigative stories and profiles. Safer, in contrast, is relaxed, somewhat detached, maintaining a philosophical perspective. A Wallace interview will disclose some of the tax loopholes that benefit wealthy investors. A Safer interview will introduce you to the delights of Countess Innocente, who stays at the Ritz Hotel in Paris with her pet boa constrictor.

"We called that one 'Ritz, Ritzy, Ritziest,'" Safer recalls. "Marvelous place and people. It's the kind of piece I like to do because it's a writing piece. It's difficult in the sense there's no story. There's no event. But history is one of the things we cover, and nothing like the Ritz will be built again."

Safer says that spending five consecutive days at the Ritz, as he did, was an atypical luxury. More often, he finds himself traveling to three cities in three days to cover three stories. Asked to estimate how many miles a year he travels, he said, "It's something crazy. Something in excess of 100,000 miles."

He appears none the worse for it. Canadian-born, he's a small square-shaped man with curly, dark hair, who wears modish suits with colorful shirts. His conversation is studded with all sorts of arcane worldly lore. "There's no way to get good caviar in a restaurant. The best is always eaten in the kitchen. Do you want to know what makes the show work?" he goes on, shifting gears. "The fact that we do not have a rule book. There's nothing we can't cover."

In addition to Hewitt and the correspondents, there is a fourth key man: Palmer Williams, whose title is senior producer. Williams maintains the show's story file, a blue flexible folder with almost 200 ideas in it waiting for development.

"Ideas come in to us by mail, from our own reading, every conceivable source," says Williams. "We have ideas

sitting there for six months or a year, which we may eventually get to."

Once approved, developed, filmed and edited (a process that takes anywhere from a week to several months), a story may or may not be put into the earliest line-up. The primary consideration, says Hewitt, is the possibility of hanging the piece on a news peg: "We'll keep a piece until it's ready to make news, have it all edited and slick and good, and put it on the shelf. Example. There's going to be a Black September incident any week now. And that'll be our peg for our Black September story. The Kamal Nasser interview was originally part of that story."

Wallace was in Beirut for an interview with Nasser in the downtown offices of the Palestine Liberation Organization and then—in an itinerary calculated to disorient the most stable of body clocks—Amman, Tel Aviv, Frankfurt and New York within a week. In the interim Nasser was assassinated and Hewitt decided to rush together a piece entitled "Conversation with a Dead Guerrilla."

On Saturday, shortly before the air date, Wallace was in the editing room at *60 Minutes,* looking over the shoulder of Alan Wegman, the film editor, who was seated at an expensive electronic console cutting film with the skill and nonchalance of a surgeon.

Usually, Wegman explained, the stories are edited during the week, and on the day of the telecast the material is transferred from film to tape. Then Wallace and Safer add their live bridges and introductions to the various stories, and the entire package is rolled onto a single master tape. The Nasser story meant weekend overtime, as well as seemingly endless changes certain to be changed again—and the certainty that Hewitt would make more changes when he arrived. "When that happens," said Wegman, "I take my nice pills."

Wallace spent some time identifying locations with Wegman, and with Palmer Williams, who had wandered in, and then he ambled down the hall to his own office to write his commentary, which he then took into an isolation booth to record for sound-man Joel Dulberg: "Three days after that interview, Kamal Nasser was shot dead in his Beirut apartment . . ."

The next day—air day—the cameramen hung over their cameras and the correspondents sat patiently in orange chairs before a bright green backdrop while Hewitt bounded back and forth between the studio and the control room, shouting and prodding and losing his temper when things went wrong. "You know what makes good television shows?" he asked rhetorically. "Attention to detail."

By 5 o'clock or so, Hewitt had paid attention to a number of details and was satisfied with the show. People began to gather in his office to watch the air tape. Hewitt turned on his set and watched his show's logo come up. Despite a grueling, energy-depleting day, and despite having watched the show numerous times, he leaned forward as it began. He said, matter-of-factly, "This is one of the few areas of television where there's still pride of authorship."

(Gene Trindl)

Tales of Telly

He drove a bus when he was 12½, he won $125,000 at baccarat, and then there was the time he . . .

by Al Stump

In the French resort of Biarritz one morning not many months ago, Telly Savalas awoke and discovered he'd overslept. He leaped into action. Telly had an appointment in Bilbao, Spain, 80 miles across the border, in less than two hours.

Friends of this big, burly and bald performer claim that he's the wildest automobile driver in Europe. Racing south in his 300-h.p. Mercedes, Savalas sped through village stop lights, burned rubber in 80-m.p.h. skids, scattered pedestrians, chickens and goats, and even drove on sidewalks in order to save time. A passenger, actor Paul Picerni, says, "I wasn't just nervous—I was terrified."

Having been a regular in *The Untouchables,* Picerni is an authority on auto wrecks, and he expected the climactic crash sequence at any moment.

Reaching the Bilbao docks in a dust cloud, Telly pulled up in time to greet his wife, Lynn, and their two children, arriving by steamship from London.

"For great events," declared Savalas, beaming, "Telly is never late!"

Tales told of Aristotle "Telly" Savalas—a burly, 6-foot-1 Greek-American whose bullet-slick bald head and menacing mien are his trademarks—often strain belief.

One night in a Mayfair, London, gambling club, his friends relate, Telly won $125,000 at baccarat. Urged to quit, he replied, "What, spoil a hot streak?" He then lost $117,000. Savalas left the club arguing, "But I made a clear profit of $8000."

When he was 12½ years old, says his mother, Christina, he drove a Greyhound bus from Brooklyn to Philadelphia—with passengers aboard. "He'd gone through bus driver school posing as 20," she explains, "and without telling the family. He was a very large boy and passed all the tests."

Adds Telly: "The bus cops only caught me because they noticed my voice was squeaky."

Free-swinging it through life, making 32 movies in 11 countries since 1961—and until now not much involved with the small screen—he's been difficult for TV producers to pin down. This season the 49-year-old Savalas stars in CBS's new detective series *Kojak.* The series came close to not happening, because Savalas was bored with playing hard-case cops and not much interested in confining himself to a single sustained job. Universal Studio executives pursued him hither and yon. "I chased him from Madrid to Rome to Paris to London," says Universal's Tom Tannenbaum. "He wasn't indifferent to the idea that became *Kojak,* but he wouldn't sign anything except the dinner check."

Writer Abby Mann, creator and executive producer of the project, insisted that Savalas and no one else be hired to fill the role of Lieutenant Theo Kojak of the New York police. "He's exciting, enormously talented, one of the most sensitive performers around," Mann believes. "He has brute power, which he releases with no seeming effort. Yet gentleness and compassion underscore his style. And Telly's perfect for TV—he needs no preparation.

"He can spend 15 minutes phoning in horse bets, then walk on and instantly do the most delicate type of acting."

Capturing Telly became an all-out effort in mid-1972, when CBS chairman Bill Paley and supervising producer Matt Rapf agreed with Mann that they had to have him. Jack Gilardi, Telly's agent, found himself with a client who wasn't yet a major star but who was offered, in Gilardi's words, "a remarkably high dollar."

Privately, Gilardi doubted that Telly could be signed for *Kojak.* To Savalas, the best things in life are found by adventuring in strange places. He speaks four languages and doesn't like to be tied down in one spot.

Finally, however, and as he says "with trepidation," he accepted the deal. Savalas makes the point: "I don't dislike television. My objection is that I'm always thought of as tough and sinister, and I've been unable to get away from a police badge or killer's knife. The interrogation rooms, the sirens, the whole stereotype were endangering my career." Even his much-hailed '72 portrayal of a cynical detective in the network movie "Visions" didn't please him. In "Mongo's Back in Town," another 90-minute TV film, he found the old themes repeated.

A character actor, Savalas may have agreed to do *Kojak*—although again he plays a cop—because he now advances into the lead role. Another reason: he majored in psychology at Columbia U and is much concerned with crime in America. "There's a stench in the precincts, streets, courts, parole boards and prisons," he says with intensity. "If our show can catch hard truths, it'll be worthwhile. If it doesn't—if certain promises made me concerning the somewhat documentarized script aren't kept—then they'll hear from me. I've already insisted that we focus on the New York scene and away from synthetic sets in the San Fernando Valley."

Lasting three hours, Abby Mann's "The Marcus-Nelson Murders" of last March was the pilot for *Kojak*, and Savalas won an Emmy nomination for it.

Regarding his baldness, he concedes, "Certainly it's my identification. But it wasn't until after 'Marcus-Nelson' I was seen as a total performer. I was at the racetrack and the crowd mobbed me, almost trampled me."

Many critics wonder how CBS can gamble on a hairless hero with big ears and a swooping nose. Savalas isn't worried. Caesar, Cyrano and Rasputin weren't handsome, but fought off women, right? "Anyway, I've got hair," he goes on. "Quite a bit of it."

Telly Savalas *has hair?*

Yes, indeed. The explanation goes back a decade to the time he played Pontius Pilate in "The Greatest Story Ever Told." Director George Stevens asked Savalas to shave his head as a role-aiding device. "But I was afraid it'd scare my children if I suddenly came home bald. We brought them onto the set and they watched it happen. I liked the effect—it makes me look more Greek, or something."

Each morning, lathering up, he shaves what, if allowed to grow, would be an adequate amount of dark brown wavy hair.

His rather brutal visage is nature's joke, says his brother, George Demosthenes Savalas. "Outside of some Golden Gloves fights when he was a kid, Telly's never hurt anyone," says George. "He abhors violence. When he's very angry, he gets quiet. He'll tell the other party, 'Walk away from me for 15 minutes, then let's talk and settle this.'"

The acting fraternity regards anyone who succeeds without an apprenticeship as a freak. Savalas is a superfreak. At age 35 he had never acted or faced a camera. He had written and directed radio shows and had been director of the Stamford (Connecticut) Playhouse when, in 1959, David Susskind noticed him and felt his suggestion of power, menace and sexuality was a rare thing. Savalas began acting on *Armstrong Circle Theater* and as Lucky Luciano in a series, *The Witness*. He was a natural. "It all seemed freak circumstance to me," he says. "But then Lancaster—Burt—brought me to Hollywood.

"Next thing I knew, there I was in Alcatraz prison in a cell next to Burt, getting fast expert coaching"—in "Birdman of Alcatraz," for which Savalas won an Academy Award nomination in his first screen role.

In recent years Savalas has overcome a fear of air travel, a fear so acute that he literally froze at the boarding ramp. One day, friend Paul Picerni drove him to the Los Angeles airport. "Unless *you* go too, I don't go," said Telly. Picerni, who was due elsewhere, flew to New York with him, holding his hand. Savalas: "The stories that Lancaster had to get me loaded with drink—and I'm mostly just a casual wine drinker—to get me on a plane to Alcatraz, unfortunately are true."

Will power overcame the problem. Yet Savalas still occasionally drives, rather than flies, from his Beverly Hills home to Manhattan in one of seven cars he owns. It's a 70-odd-hour trip. He travels nonstop, with brother George sharing the driving while Telly snuggles up in the back seat and watches TV on a special built-in set.

Another side of this son of a Sparta-born businessman is his generosity. He's a check-grabber and a happy-go-lucky spender. Example: In a Madrid hotel shop, he bought a shirt which was too small for him. He phoned the shop, asking that a few others be sent to his room. A boy arrived with 32 shirts of all colors. Telly bought all 32, for $710. Why? "Did you see the look on the kid's face?" said Savalas to a traveling companion. "He's ecstatic."

Yet Telly regards himself as a pretty crafty negotiator. At one point he heard that some Hollywood stars had pried automobiles out of studios as a bonus for signing. Soon after that, he was approached in London by Britishers to co-star in "Crooks and Coronets." The money offer was good, but Telly sadly rolled his eyes and sighed, "I have this recurring dream of owning a Rolls-Royce, the Silver Cloud model . . . and next week I'm due back in the U.S.A."

The Silver Cloud is now parked in the garage of Telly's home in Beverly Hills, a house he bought from Paul Newman some years ago.

In his early ventures into TV, he was the guest-artist heavy who was killed off quickly—as in *Cimarron Strip* and *Garrison's Gorillas*. Since then, Savalas has acquired considerable international fame, chiefly from such movies as "The Battle of the Bulge," "Beau Geste," "The Dirty Dozen," "Cape Fear," "Genghis Khan" and "The Scalphunters." This body of work led to another of those tales of Telly. It happened on a plane bound for Rome.

Savalas: "There was this stranger aboard who kept bothering me with compliments. He insisted that I was his favorite actor. I tried to get rid of him, diplomatically, without luck. He hung around my seat for much of the trip.

"Finally, I hid in the rest room. When we reached Rome, this chap was waiting for me at the departure door with more flattery about how he was the world's No. 1 Savalas fan. By now I hated the sight of him.

"The plane was met by an honor guard, many dignitaries and a cheering crowd. For a moment, I thought the turnout was for me."

Then the stranger—not Telly—was escorted off the plane to a gala reception.

Annoyed, Savalas asked who he might be.

"King Constantine," said an official, "of Greece."

Savalas maintains a flat in London and a home in Garden City, N.Y., but his base is a colonnaded two-story manse in the film colony which he shares with his young wife, Lynn, and daughters Christina, 22, Penelope, 12, and Candace, 10. The walls are hung with paintings executed by Telly's mother, Christina, a noted American artist. "My mother," says Telly, "is the notable one of our family. She's a fine painter. She also speaks her mind."

At the premiere of "The Dirty Dozen," an earthy war movie, Mother Savalas stood in the theater lobby and denounced the film as "beastly" and "horrible." She told the producer and his staff they should be ashamed of themselves. "I was slightly embarrassed," says Savalas, "but I kept my mouth shut. In my family, you don't talk back to Mother."

From her he inherited a bold tongue and independence. From his late father, Nicholas, he learned about fun and the unpredictability of life. "My father made a million or two as a businessman and inventor and lost it all in the '29 crash . . . and told his five kids to laugh with him about it."

Another fun-lover of Telly's ancestry, Jimmy the Greek, the Las Vegas odds-maker, sums him up with "He's a romantic, going through life like a craps player. He shoots for his point and, win or lose, he comes up smiling. If *Kojak* makes it big, or if TV takes its number down and scratches out, it won't change Telly. He's indestructible."

And he can grow hair any day he feels like it.

BOB HOPE

THE COMEDIAN TURNS SERIOUS

By Neil Hickey

PART I

"About seven years ago," Bob Hope is saying, "a few people felt me out about running for the Presidency. But I have no ambitions that way, really no ambitions. If I did, I'd say yes, and go. I don't think I'm qualified."

A few years before that, Jack Warner had suggested that Hope run for the United States Senate from California. "But that's not my bag—although politics is a lot like show biz."

Being funny has been Bob Hope's bag for 45 years. Last May he turned 70 with no deceleration of the breakneck pace that has marked his life for far longer than most of his fans can recall. "But I'm not really 70," he said the other day. "That's just on paper. I'm really about 50 in the way I feel and think, and in my physical condition. I couldn't possibly ever think of retiring."

At close range during a three-hour chat, Bob Hope's demeanor supports that judgment: the flinty voice is still firm and well modulated; the eye is keen and watchful; the stride still has that fluid balls-of-the-feet grace. And with little urging, he lets you know that his schedule is as packed as ever: seven TV specials for NBC; a book called "The Road to Hollywood," to be published in February; another book called "The Last Christmas Show," which he's still writing; a couple of TV pilots which he's producing. He expects to star in a movie next year about the late Walter Winchell; he may star in a Broadway musical and appear for the first time at Las Vegas. Then there are the shows at military hospitals, the benefits, the TV guest appearances, the speeches.

Why? Why does such an extremely wealthy 70-year-old man drive himself so relentlessly? Hope is ready for that one, and leans into it eagerly. "Because I need the money!"

You need the money?

"*I need the money. I seriously need the money.* I'll have my tax man tell you that. It's true. I need the money!" And, after a pause for that to sink in: "All my money is in property, and it has kept me very broke paying the taxes."

He owns 12,000 acres of California land, most of it in the San Fernando Valley ("Oh, it's awful good property. Beautiful. A lot of it's on the ocean"), and the property tax on it last year was $900,000. When you add to that

Bob Hope during his 1966 Christmas tour in Vietnam (NBC)

federal, state and local taxes, plus assorted operating expenses, Hope's "nut"—his basic annual upkeep—totes up to a disquieting sum. How much?

The comedian holds up two fingers. "Two large ones," he tells you. Two million dollars must be earned each year before he pockets a cent for himself. "Sounds a little silly, doesn't it?" he asks. "But it's absolutely true."

Yes, but what about all those reports that you're the richest man in the history of show business? Are they a little overblown? "Not a little! They're out of sight! They're fictionized!" he says, his voice rising. "I wish I *did* have that kind of money."

One magazine, he recalls, claimed he was worth a half-billion dollars. Look magazine decided his wealth was $225 million. "Fortune said I was one of the richest men in the world—without any basis, without checking with me! You wouldn't believe a thing like that could happen! I would say today that my property is worth $27 million."

He pauses and smooths his hair with the heel of his hand. "Nobody realizes all that," he adds reflectively. "They think, This guy is loaded. But it's not true." He has a Palm Springs home and a "big place" in North Hollywood to support.

"But don't feel sorry for me," he says, at length. "I'll make it."

It's difficult to feel sorry for Bob Hope in any circumstances, although he's been criticized hotly in some circles lately for his outspoken stand in support of the Vietnam War. Has his consistent candor on that subject hurt him professionally?

"Oh, I don't really know," he says pensively. "I think it might. But all you can judge on is your popularity. I still play all the places I always did, and do as good or better than ever. My TV shows are still one-two-three in the ratings, and I'm getting offers that are unbelievable. So I can only judge it on that."

Has the press—many of whom are liberals—been hostile to you in recent years? Hope is asked. He thinks that over and says, "No, I don't think so. Even if you're a liberal, you still live in this country, and this country will be here long after us. I've said many times that everybody is allowed to do their own thinking. As long as we don't destroy the system that makes it all work."

A few newsmen reported that Hope had received an unfriendly reception from some troops on a recent tour of Vietnam. "No way. No way," says Hope. "They are so great in Vietnam they want to kiss you. Men come up, say God bless you and squeeze your hand. They are the greatest audience ever known, and they are so grateful. When you fly that long to see them, man they love you. They don't *like* you, they *love* you!"

But wasn't he booed by some soldiers during a performance at a place called Lai Khe? Hope denies it. He had visited the White House before traveling to Vietnam, he recalls, and told his audience that the President had a plan for ending the war. There were 15,000 men in the audience, and "two or three of them" voiced loud incredulity at that news. "And it was reported that I was booed at Lai Khe. It wasn't true."

Ever since May 6, 1941, when he agreed to do a show at March Field, California ("The biggest 'yes' I ever gave"), Hope has entertained more military men than any performer in history, and has traveled (he estimates) six million miles doing it. Starting in 1948, with a request from the State Department to entertain Berlin airlift forces, he has done Christmas tours of U.S. bases abroad. Since 1954 those tours have been filmed and edited into sponsored television shows.

A lot of criticism of yet another sort has attended those Christmas shows. Don't Hope and his large troupe travel at government expense to produce a TV program for which he is paid handsomely by big TV sponsors? The huge military audiences at those bases, say a few of Hope's nonadmirers, are convenient window dressing for a wholly commercial and very profitable TV production.

Hope is impatient with that kind of talk. "Again, it's a criticism by groups that are anti-fun." People who say those things are, for some reason, "against the Administration," he feels, "or are trying to get at me for some reason I can't understand." He always mounted a 2¼-hour show at every stop along the way during his overseas Christmas tours (they ended in 1972), and constructed the TV shows from snippets of film from each. "We went to the trouble of going over there and running into situations that aren't exactly good for your health."

As regards the money, he claims it would be the same for himself and the cast if they simply sat in Burbank and created a Christmas show. "It makes me mad when I have to explain these things," says Hope. "It burns me up. These performers, out of the goodness of their hearts, volunteered to go and do these things. Nobody goes to Vietnam and lays their life on the line unless they *want* to do it. You see? It's that simple." And anybody who maligns those motives, says Hope, "you've got to worry about a little. You want to study them. Study those people."

Study them for what? he is asked. What are you suggesting?

"I'm not suggesting anything," Hope says, earnestly. "Just study them and see what they're doing for their country. Do that. I don't want to imply to you that everybody shouldn't be able to say anything they please. I don't want you to think I'm picking on any particular group. I just want to say I can't understand the reason for those people, and I wonder what they've got in mind."

It is a fact that Bob Hope has received every manner of decoration and encomium from both Democratic and Republican leaders for his military tours and fund-raisings. (He is constructing a museum in Burbank to house the thousands of plaques, scrolls, trophies, honorary degrees and civic awards he has collected over the years.) The late President Kennedy presented him a Congressional medal in 1963, an honor afforded only two other entertainers in the country's history: George M. Cohan and Irving Berlin.

Hope is especially proud of that distinction. "It answers all the questions, really," he says. "Every Congressman—the leaders of our country who represent the people—voted on that award: liberals and Democrats, guys on the left and guys on the right. They voted, and I got it. This answers all the questions about anything, as far as I'm concerned. It's silly for me to stand up here and try to defend myself."

Hope has been personally acquainted with every President since Roosevelt, but with none so closely as with President Nixon. "I've known the man for 20 years, I've always liked him and the family. We played golf when he was Vice President, and I got an honorary degree from Whittier College."

In the late 1960s, Hope began expressing himself candidly on the matter of pressing the Vietnam War to a successful military conclusion. "I didn't like what was happening," he recalls. "The protests and demonstrations, I thought, helped the enemy. I became very concerned for one reason: I wanted to help the Vietnam situation come to an end, and I didn't see any other way but to stick with the people who could bring it to an end. As soon as we convinced the North Vietnamese they could not win, our guys could get home."

He remembers going into burn wards in Vietnam and seeing the maimed soldiers there. "I tell you, if you ever see that scene, you want to get that war over with. And so I could only figure out one thing. In talking with the leaders who really knew about this war—the *big* people, you know—I decided there was only one way we could end this war, and that was by sticking with the people who had the power to do it. And, luckily, it did end."

He's not at all certain that the loose ends have been tied up, however. The absence of a clear-cut military victory for the U.S. "could bring on a problem that maybe we have to face later. You never know if they're going to get another foothold there."

Hope toys with the lapels of his pale blue sports jacket, and emits a sigh. "We're all sick of war—everybody. I had a big argument with my daughter a couple of years ago. She said, 'Where are we going in Vietnam?' You know. That's a young person's thinking. I *know* what we were doing in Vietnam. I'd been around it for nine years. A lot of young people don't know what's going on. I know that our mission was to help the country, and I knew that we had to resolve it and get out. And we could have been out seven years ago and saved half a million lives if it was handled the right way."

The right way, he says, is what the United States did at the end. "We bombed the North Vietnamese until they said yes. We'd convinced them that we weren't just going to slap them and step back, which we did for a long time. You know, Harry Truman won't go down in history as a slaughterer of people because he ended a war with Hiroshima and Nagasaki."

Hope ponders a moment, and adds, "I sound like a hawk, talking like that. I sit here now and say we should have bombed them. Bombing means killing. It's a harsh word, isn't it? But it's one of those things. When you're fighting . . ." The sentence trails off.

Hope is compared occasionally to the late Will Rogers, since they both found humor in news columns and poli-

tics, and in their association with politicians. "He was marvelous," says Hope, "the only one of his kind. But I don't think you can compare us. I'm another kind of fella, a fast one-liner man. Not that I'm any better, or as good, as he."

Hope has been called the Jester to the Establishment, he is reminded: a "safe" comedian whose humor bumps but never bruises. "I think that's true," he says. "I think a long time before using a joke that's on the borderline of hurting somebody." He isn't really an extrovert, he claims. "You won't believe this, but I'm basically shy. I think a lot of people are. I do have confidence in what I do, so I go forward. But I've never been the loud kind of guy."

He has only the dimmest recollections of his childhood in Eltham, England, where he was born. More vivid are the rough-and-tumble vaudeville days of Cleveland in the early 1920s. He had a song-and-dance act then with a girl named Mildred, his first sweetheart. One day in 1924 he went to his partner's mother and asked permission to take Mildred on the road to play other vaudeville houses in the Midwest. The mother said she'd have to see the act first.

"So one day she came to the theater and saw the show," Hope recalls, "and said to me afterwards, 'You're not taking *my* daughter on the road with *that* act.' " A few years ago, Mildred—long since married to somebody else—visited Hope at the Burbank studio and mused upon the long and glittering road that her former partner has traveled since 1924.

"If my mother were alive today," said Mildred, "I'd smack her in the mouth."

And how does Bob Hope feel about his life and times, as he nears a 50th anniversary in show business? "I'm happy with my image now," he says, "happy that people laugh and feel bright when they see me."

How would he like to be remembered? "I don't care—just so they don't say, 'Who was he?' "

PART II

One of these days, he says, he'll write a book called "Thanks For the Memories" and that will be the coda, the kicker, the final wrap-up on a half-century show-biz career. And it has been an unparalleled career, irrespective of how much or how little one responds to Bob Hope as a performer or as a man: 71 feature films, almost 300 television specials (plus innumerable guest appearances), more than 1000 radio shows dating back to 1934, a half-dozen Broadway shows, too many live appearances and benefits to count, and a quantity of world travel that ranks him with Marco Polo and Henry Kissinger.

He was in comparative repose one day recently in a Waldorf Towers suite in New York when a visitor asked him to reflect upon his long life (he'd reached 70 on May 29) and event-packed times. Leslie Townes Hope is that rare bird: a middle-class Wasp who has, as a comedian, attained show-biz heights customarily reserved exclusively for Jews and Catholics of threadbare origins.

(L to r) Lynne Overman, Martha Raye, W. C. Fields, Shirley Ross, Bob Hope and Ben Blue as they appeared in the movie "The Big Broadcast of 1938" (Springer/Bettmann Film Archive)

He's even a Briton, born in Eltham, England, and transplanted to this country at the age of four, when his stonemason father settled in Cleveland and helped build the Euclid Avenue Presbyterian Church. ("He was so proud of the job he'd done, we moved close to the church and changed from Episcopalian to Presbyterian.")

Hope's earliest recollection is of getting zonked on the head with a rock in England while protecting his dog. "I still have the scar. That's why I remember it." The only other thing he recalls about England is that his family lived on a block with a park behind it. "From there on, I black out."

A streak of show biz ran in the family. "Mother was a concert singer; my father was an amateur comedian. He was pretty cute around the house, making jokes all the time." (His mother died in 1933 "when I was in 'Roberta,'" and his father in 1936, "when I was in 'Red, Hot and Blue.'")

He gravitated to vaudeville houses around Cleveland and soon was doing blackface comedy and softshoe routines, first with partners and then as a single. The great comedian Frank Fay once played Cleveland, and Hope's mother took young Leslie to the show. Halfway through it, Hope recalls, she said in a loud voice, "He's not *half* as good as you are." Everybody in the theater turned around, and Hope dove under the seat in embarrassment. "Fay lived long enough to see me play that same theater," says Hope, "and I told that story on the night he came."

Hope got himself hired for a Broadway show called "Sidewalks of New York" in 1927. "Ruby Keeler was in it, and Al Jolson used to come and pick her up every night. Broadway in the 1920s was a glamorous place. There were so many shows going on and so much show business around, a fellow could come to New York and never have to leave the area: every nearby town had a vaudeville house. In Jersey alone you could play two or three months: Paterson, Elizabeth, Jersey City. Now, I don't know where you could play."

During the run of "Roberta," an actor in the show named George Murphy (later Senator from California) took Hope to a cabaret to hear a singer named Dolores Reade. Hope was smitten instantly. "I invited her to see the show, but she didn't come backstage afterward because she was embarrassed. She had thought I was a chorus boy, but really I was a featured player."

He tracked her down, however ("I had been chased, so it was a refreshing switch when I turned to chase somebody else"), and they were married in 1934.

Hope was spotted by film director Mitchell Leisen in "The Ziegfeld Follies of 1935" (singing "I Can't Get Started with You") and was whisked off to Hollywood for a movie called "The Big Broadcast of 1938," which contained a song called "Thanks For the Memory."

"Leisen told me, 'Remember, pictures are different from the stage,'" Hope recalls. "'In pictures, you act with your eyes.' If you ever see that picture, you'll see me rolling my eyes all over the place."

Even though Hope has made 71 feature films, his stature as an entertainer has always derived mostly from radio and television. (He has been under contract to NBC continuously since 1938.) He has never made a memorable film, and only die-hard movie buffs can name more than a handful of them ("My Favorite Blonde," "Louisiana Purchase," "The Lemon Drop Kid," "Beau James").

Better remembered are the seven zany "Road" pictures he made with Bing Crosby between 1940 and 1962: "The Road to Singapore," "Zanzibar," "Morocco," "Utopia," "Rio," "Bali" and "Hong Kong." Crosby always got the girl, but Hope got most of the laughs. His comedic style had been hammered into form on the anvil of vaudeville; it was distinctly and unmistakably his own.

He considers, belatedly, that the late Broadway columnist Walter Winchell had an influence on that style. "Winchell knew that a long column item bored people, so he wrote a lot of fast, short ones. When I started out, people said I talked the way Winchell wrote. It was the smarter, more sophisticated way to go. You know, 'Good evening, ladies and gentlemen, this is Bob Pepsodent Hope, living by the skin of my teeth. And I want to tell you . . .' I used to let them catch up with me. First I'd run away from them, they'd laugh, and then I'd pause for them. It was an overlapping runaway style." And it still is.

That style, and the content it enshrouds, have caused some observers to conclude that Bob Hope's chief appeal is to people over 50; that he has lost the younger audiences who know him mostly as a politicized friend of the mighty, and court jester to the status quo. Hope denies it vehemently.

"That's not true," he tells you. "No way, no way. I play more colleges now that I ever did. Just travel with me and see what happens with young people. And just ask NBC for the surveys on the makeup of my audience."

In those well-publicized travels, has he made any assessment about the current mood of the nation? "Well, I think people were elated that the Vietnam War ended, and now they're confused again with all the counter-charges about Watergate. I just hate to see them dig up all that past dirt and fling it around. I think it kind of confuses the American people and it's a shame they have to go into that. We've just been through five or six rough years with Vietnam. But I think we'll get this over with and bounce back."

The talk turns to his off-stage family life. Yes, he sees his four adopted children regularly, says Hope: Linda, 34; Anthony, 33; Kelly and Nora, both 27. (So far, there are three grandchildren.) They were all brought up as Catholics because Dolores is "a great Catholic, you know, a devout Catholic." Did they ever try to convert you? "No, not really. But I'm religious in my own way. Religion is a wonderful thing for people. I know, when we've been close to disaster a couple of times on our trips . . . you think about it."

About those trips: how has his wife managed all these years to bear up under his prolonged absences, especially at Christmastime? "Well she has . . . what shall I say? . . . grown accustomed to it. She was on the first two Christmas trips, so she knew what it meant. She's been on five altogether. She still sings very well. We get her up at parties. Yes, she's kind of sad that she doesn't go on every trip. But she's gotten used to it."

His own health is splendid, "outside of a little knee wrench now and again. I play golf all the time—a 12 handicap." An eye ailment that afflicted him several years ago has cleared up. "That had a lot to do with making me feel good today. It made me conscious of what I was doing. It was sort of my barometer." He exercises every day and keeps careful watch on his food intake.

At 70, Bob Hope is a proud man—proud of the more than "1000 awards and citations for humanitarian and professional efforts" (as his official biography puts it) that soon will reside in the museum he is building for them; proud of the 23 honorary degrees from places like Wilberforce University, Pepperdine University, Ohio Dominican College and Pace College; proud of the high ratings his TV specials invariably attract; proud of his association with dignitaries outside the world of show business; and proud that an English kid from Cleveland got to meet those people and have such a good time in the world telling jokes.

So far, Bob Hope has a lot of memories to be thankful for.

"I'LL TELL YOU WHO JOE MANNIX REALLY IS"

But first, a few words about Muggerditch Muggerditchian, Krekor Ohanian and a judge named Denver Peckinpah by William Saroyan

The readers of TV Guide might like to know how some of the articles find their way into the magazine. I have here before me at my hangout in Paris (that's France, although I am very partial also to Paris, Texas—if you've never been there, plan to go first chance you get), I have here a letter forwarded from my Fresno address, which starts out: "We'd like to have you do a piece for us, if you're so inclined. Mike Connors, star of *Mannix*, is a former Fresnoan and is also, I'm told, of Armenian stock."

It's from one of the editors of TV Guide.

Fresnoan is not acceptable, to begin with.

When I sold the Evening Herald from 1916 through 1919, and Mike Connors had not yet been born, his father, Krekor Ohanian, attorney at law, with an office in the Bank of Italy Building, which opened for business in the late summer of 1917, was frequently seen passing my corner on his way to the Court House, to try another little misdemeanor case of some kind—not infrequently the illegal possession and operation of a still (for the manufacture of firewater, made of raisins, and

Drawing by George Price

called most appropriately *rahkhi,* since that is the name of this particular booze).

A farmer who liked to drink with his friends while they played backgammon or cards (called *tavlie* and *scambile*) during the off-season manufactured his own good stuff because he had the raw material and the simple machinery to do it with, and he didn't have anywhere near enough English to know that there was a certain Mr. Volstead who had flimflammed the nation, with the help of a kind of reverse Women's Lib, a kind of No Lib, Women *or* Men, into a voted and legal condition called Prohibition (which in turn brought into American life the real Chicago, the real Al Capone, the real speakeasy, the real rumrunner, and the phony gin that was the most popular drink smart people drank all during Prohibition).

And this farmer could barely have been restrained from murdering the eight Internal Revenue agents who fell upon him and his still with hatchets and began to chop up his barrels with good stuff mellowing in them.

The farmer was put in jail, and soon word reached Joe Mannix's father, Krekor Ohanian, that Muggerditch Muggerditchian of the noble Muggerditchians of Moush, just below Sassoun, a little north of Bitlis, a little west of Van, was in the county hoosegow and didn't know what for.

The lawyer explained to the farmer that even if you do have an extra ton of good muscat raisins and a perfectly good still, you are not allowed to make your own firewater for wintertime home consumption and the entertainment of good friends, all of whom cherish such warmth, because they know "there is such a thing as dying," a favorite saying of farmers.

And so one day at the Court House the judge was Denver Peckinpah, or Denver's father, or Denver's uncle, and 30 years later along came Sam, who went into moviemaking; and there was Krekor Ohanian, born in Harpoot, or Van, or Dikranagert, or somewhere in Armenia (in *Armenia,* not Turkey, as the immigration department's illiterates put it in the records), to defend the vineyardist Muggerditch Muggerditchian.

And, if I may say so, there also was this writer, although scarcely 11 years old at the time.

The judge was stern.

The district attorney, a man with the improbable name of Lovejoy (that's the kind of place Fresno always has been), was stern.

But the defense attorney was *not* bullied by their sternness, and as for the defendant, he was ready to break up the place—after four days and five nights in jail without a drop of good stuff and no satisfactory explanation for the preposterous situation.

The trying of the case took exactly 11 minutes, and is forever unforgettable for the defense attorney's series of statements, questions and answers: "Look at that man, your honor," he said. "Muggerditch Muggerditchian, 54 years old, the father of four sons, two daughters, the owner of 10 acres of muscat vines. Does he look like a bootlegger? Does he look like a bartender? Does he look like a gangster? Does he look like a criminal? Your

honor, does he even look like a man who could *become* any of those things? No, your honor, because the man is a farmer. The revenuers did their duty. It is not for me to say that they were stupid and had taken their instructions from moving pictures at the Liberty Theatre. Eight big men fell on Muggerditch Muggerditchian and wrecked his still and spilled his winter's whiskey. Brave men, there they sit, ready to testify that the defendant was not easy to subdue and apprehend. Now, I ask you to look at *them,* your honor. Do *they* look like farmers with 10 acres and a houseful of kids, or do they look more like Lon Chaney in the movies?"

"Objection," District Attorney Lovejoy shouted.

And Judge Peckinpah said, "Sustained. Mr. Defense Attorney, would you please confine your thoughts to the law and let the poetry go?"

"I want this man sent home," Krekor Ohanian said.

And old Denver Peckinpah said very softly, "I'm *sending* him home, but we *do* want the District Attorney to have his turn, too, don't we?"

Thus it was that this writer came to admire both the Ohanian tribe and the Peckinpah tribe, and never again heard about the Lovejoys, although it is not unlikely that they moved to Pasadena and are rich.

In the Evening Herald, people of Fresno were referred to as Fresnans. This was unacceptable then and is unacceptable now. Sometimes it is both desirable and necessary to use two or three words instead of one nonword like Fresnoan or Fresnan.

As for being a former man of Fresno, that also is not true—Joe Mannix, Mike Connors or Krekor Ohanian is no more a former man of Fresno than I am for being at this moment in Paris.

I just don't happen to be in Fresno, that's all, just as Joe-Mike-Krekor doesn't either, too, because he's working long hours five days a week getting out new chapters of the big television hit, which is seen around the world and loved by everybody.

Why?

Because Joe Mannix is actually Muggerditch Muggerditchian, the muscat vineyardist.

Joe Mannix in several of the chapters, speaking as Joe Mannix, has let it be known that he is an Armenian, and at least in one chapter he exchanged a rather interesting assortment of Armenian words with his old pal and my cousin, Sipan Rostom Bagdasarian—thus we have a rather refreshing if confusing situation: the producers of the show must have humored Mike Connors to let him make of Mannix an Armenian, but then why not?

As the old saying is, everybody's got to be something, and there are only about 22 people left in America who *look* Armenian, Jewish, black, Indian, Mexican, or unmistakably Anglo-Saxon.

Mannix has a secretary who is very beautiful inside and outside, and it has been pointed out that this talented young woman is one of the first black players to perform a major part in a television series—for how many years is it now? Six?

Everybody looks like everybody else, not because the

melting pot is working, but because snobbism isn't.

Anybody who has talent has talent; anybody who hasn't talent is not put into any kind of category on that account—he is safe at home with everybody else.

And that's the end of the matter.

I was in the bar of the Californian Hotel in Fresno about 40 years ago, drinking Courvoisier brandy at half a buck a shot, when Joe Mannix's father, Krekor Ohanian, came and sat beside me and told the bartender Grogorty to draw one, received the tall glass with the foaming head, and drained it, just as I finished the snifter of brandy and held out the glass for another, which Grogorty poured. Whereupon the defender of farmers and other innocents held out the beer glass and in Armenian said to Grogorty. *"Bootmi ossdekh leets,"* which translated means "Pour a little in here." And it is to the glory of all of us, I suppose, that Grogorty slowly and neatly put about a third of a shot of brandy into Krekor Ohanian's enormous beer glass.

Fresnoan? How would you identify a great man whose fame went no farther than Muggerditch Muggerditchian's vineyard, who happened also to die?

A former humaneo? Or what?

I'll tell you who Joe Mannix really is.

He is Krekor Ohanian's smiling son, and damned proud of his dad.

DOES TV VIOLENCE AFFECT OUR SOCIETY?
YES
by Neil Hickey

The jury is in. After hundreds of formal scientific studies and decades of contentious debate, reasonable men are obliged to agree that televised violence does indeed have harmful effects on human character and attitudes, and that something ought to be done about it.

"There comes a time when the data are sufficient to justify action," said the U.S. Surgeon General as long ago as 1972, delivering to Congress one of the most exhaustive ($1 million, three-year) research projects ever undertaken by social scientists. "The overwhelming consensus [is] that televised violence does have an adverse effect on certain members of society." The evidence was "sufficient to warrant appropriate and immediate remedial action," said the nation's chief health officer, and he

added: "These conclusions are based on solid scientific data and not on the opinion of one or another scientist."

In the three years since that ringing and unequivocal declaration, TV watchers have been treated to uncounted thousands of brutal homicides, rapes, robberies, fist fights, muggings, maimings and all-out mayhem. TV networks continue their reliance on violence as a staple of their action-adventure series and regularly air theatrical movies like "Bonnie and Clyde," "The Godfather" and "In Cold Blood." In addition, local stations daily offer old gangster, Western and war films, reruns of rampageous prime-time melodramas, and old cartoons now considered too violent for network use.

Thus, it is virtually impossible for Americans, of any age, to avoid the depiction of violence on their TV screens. (One scientist estimates that by the age of 15 the average child will have witnessed 13,400 televised killings.) Also, many local stations have adopted "tabloid" news formats in which they compete for ratings by emphasizing homicides, riots and catastrophes.

As a result, the whole angry debate about blood-and-guts TV continues, as private citizens complain to Congress and the FCC, and those bodies in turn demand that the TV industry rid itself of gratuitous violence. A so-called family viewing hour will commence on the networks in September; and the National Institute of Mental Health is supporting research to develop a "violence index" to quantify and categorize TV violence.

Meanwhile, violent crime has been increasing at six to 10 times the rate of population growth in the United States. (Obviously, nobody blames all of that on television.) Our homicide rate is roughly 10 times that of the Scandinavian countries; more murders are committed yearly in Manhattan (population 1.5 million) than in the entire United Kingdom (population 60 million); from 1960 to 1973, violent crime in the U.S. jumped 203.8 percent.

Proof that levels of TV violence have remained unacceptably high—even after the Surgeon General's report, and subsequent supportive studies—is easily at hand. In the 1973–74 viewing period, for example, violence occurred in 73 percent of all TV programs and in 54 percent of adult prime-time TV plays, according to the most recent Violence Profile, published in December, by Dean George Gerbner and Professor Larry Gross of the Annenberg School of Communications at the University of Pennsylvania.

While the actual "incidence" of violence is somewhat lower than in past years, say Gerbner and Gross, the current profile shows the highest rate of "victimization"—a ratio of those who commit violent acts to those victimized—in the seven-year history of the study. And perhaps even more important, their experiments now indicate that heavy TV watchers tend to overestimate the danger of physical violence in real life. (Such unreasonable fear was found most acute among young watchers, and in particular among young women. Significantly, women are frequently portrayed as "victims" in televised mayhem.)

Yet another recent study (by University of Utah researchers) appears to prove that children who are heavy TV watchers can become "habituated or 'desensitized' to violence" in the real world. Normal emotional responses to human suffering become blunted, the researchers conclude, and this desensitization may easily cause "not only major increases in our society of acts of personal aggression but also a growing attitude of indifference and nonconcern for the victims" of real-life violence.

Dr. Robert M. Liebert, a psychologist at the State University of New York (and a principal investigator for the Surgeon General's report), says unequivocally: "The more violence and aggression a youngster sees on television, regardless of his age, sex or social background, the more aggressive he is likely to be in his own attitudes and behavior. The effects are not limited to youngsters who are in some way abnormal, but rather were found for large numbers of perfectly normal American children." That conclusion arises from analysis of more than 50 studies covering the behavior of 10,000 children between the ages of three and 19.

Liebert added that one significant study showed that "it was not a boy's home life, not his school performance, not his family background, but the amount of TV violence he viewed at age nine which was the single most important determinant of how aggressive he was 10 years later, at age 19."

So incontrovertible is the case against televised violence that most high network executives no longer bother to dispute it. CBS president Arthur Taylor confesses that "TV is increasingly one of the probable determinants" of anti-social behavior. At hearings in April 1974, before Senator Pastore's subcommittee (convened to assess recent progress in reducing television violence), network officers contented themselves with recitations of their good deeds and good intentions toward reform. NBC chairman Julian Goodman, for example, admitted that the Surgeon General's study "told us more than we had ever known before about the relationship between viewing violence on television and subsequent behavior," and agreed that "that relationship is now generally recognized."

That tableau—network bosses in the dock—has become a familiar sight. As long ago as 1954, Senator Estes Kefauver was demanding hard answers to questions about televised violence. He never got them. In 1961, Senator Thomas Dodd heard testimony that TV's utilization of violence had remained (as one observer put it) "both rampant and opportunistic." (One independent producer told of being asked to "inject an 'adequate' diet of violence into scripts." A network official told another program supplier: "I like the idea of sadism.") Dodd held follow-up hearings in 1964.

Following the 1968 assassinations of Senator Robert F. Kennedy and the Reverend Martin Luther King, as well as bitter rioting on campuses and at political conventions, President Lyndon Johnson established the National Commission on the Causes and Prevention of Violence (headed by Dr. Milton Eisenhower), to undertake a "penetrating search into our national life" in the attempt to get at the roots of our seeming lawlessness.

The commission, while pointing out that TV is not the sole culprit, concluded that "Violence on television encourages violent forms of behavior, and fosters moral and social values about violence in daily life which are unacceptable in a civilized society . . . it is a matter for grave concern that at a time when the value and the influence of traditional institutions . . . are in question, television is emphasizing violent, anti-social styles of life."

The commission further complained that, despite repeated promises over the previous 15 years, the TV industry had failed to reduce violence levels and failed also to conduct research into the effects of televised violence.

An incredible 94.3 percent of cartoon shows contained violent episodes in 1967 (according to data developed for the commission by Dean George Gerbner), and in 1968 there were 23.5 violent episodes per hour in cartoons. That same year, 81.6 percent of all prime-time entertainment shows contained violence. Said the commission: "If television is compared to a meal, programming containing violence clearly is the main course."

Enter Senator Pastore. In 1969 he set in motion the Surgeon General's investigation, which produced the toughest and best-documented indictment yet on televised violence. During hearings on the completed report in 1972, Senator Pastore labored to cut through scientific jargon and elicit unequivocal testimony on the report's root meaning. He ultimately succeeded.

PASTORE: You, Dr. [Jesse] Steinfeld, as the chief health officer of the United States of America, have said, "There comes a time when the data are sufficient to justify action. That time has come." Is that your unequivocal opinion?

STEINFELD: Yes, sir.

Political scientist Ithiel de Sola Pool, a member of the Surgeon General's Advisory Committee, voiced the consensus: "Twelve scientists of widely different views unanimously agreed that scientific evidence indicates that the viewing of violence by young people causes them to behave more aggressively."

Even network representatives on the advisory committee, under dogged questioning by Pastore, confessed their general agreement with the findings. CBS's Dr. Joseph Klapper, for example, admitted that "there are certainly indications of a causal relationship" between TV violence and aggression by children. And NBC's Dr. Thomas Coffin agreed that the time had come for some remedial action.

Even so, a number of network operatives and partisans chose to misinterpret the report in the mischievous hope of blunting its effect. A few network spokesmen, emphasizing its cautious tone (normal for such social-science documents), insisted to friendly journalists that the report was inconclusive and largely meaningless. Similarly, a few ideologues focused their own disagreement on the conviction (unrelated to TV violence's effects or the lack thereof) that government has no business even studying the content of TV programs. That pincers movement was short-lived and unsuccessful. The report easily outlived its critics.

In the heightened glare of public attention, the networks then took a long hard look at the violence quotient of their programs and did, in fact, significantly reduce the senseless mayhem on Saturday morning cartoon shows. (Those deposed violence-ridden cartoons are, nonetheless, seen every afternoon on hundreds of local TV stations.) The industry's effort to reduce violence in its prime-time series and movies was less successful.

Or, at least, the effort didn't satisfy Congress, which last year demanded of the FCC some concrete proposals on how to mitigate, once and for all, the wearisome problem. FCC Chairman Richard Wiley summoned the network chieftains to Washington, and after several powwows there emerged the "family viewing time" concept: a nightly no man's land (7–9 P.M. ET) sanitized of violent and sexy incidents and guaranteed "OK" for the whole family to watch. The plan also provided for "advisories" to warn viewers (both during and after the "family hour") of material that might be harmful or offensive.

While Chairman Wiley called the concept a "landmark" and Senator Pastore said it was "a wonderful idea," hardly anybody, privately, considered it anything but a gentlemen's agreement between Congress, the FCC, the networks and the NAB to take the heat off all of them. (Variety called it the "biggest public relations hype" since Evel Knievel fell into the Snake River Canyon.)

Framers of the scheme conveniently chose to overlook data proving that televised violence can have deleterious effects on adults as well as children; and that kids by the millions are glued to their television sets at *all* hours of the day, not just between 7 and 9. Thus, the "family hour"—ratified this April by the NAB and slated to be unveiled in September—is perceived by most experts as a subtle carte blanche for "business as usual," or, as one writer put it, "gore as before."

Others take it as final proof that self-regulation of the TV industry can't work, that networks will always place self-interest above the public interest when profits are jeopardized. As Robert Liebert put it: "A significant conflict of interest has existed between people concerned about children and people concerned about profit." So far, that conflict remains unresolved.

Traditionally, TV people have invoked the First Amendment at the mere hint of any government meddling with their right to air violent programs. Lately, however, that argument has been challenged by a growing body of media theorists and civil libertarians who—weary of the television industry's chronic inability to police itself—are saying, in effect, "Bunk!" Says Liebert: "It is a pseudo issue for broadcasters to claim that they have a right, by reason of Constitutional guarantees of freedom of speech, to give kids any sort of junk they want to on the argument that if the broadcaster isn't free and unmonitored, then democracy will be endangered. That isn't so. There is no precedent whatever for believing that adults' freedoms are endangered because a society enforces policies that are necessary for the welfare of its youth."

No society can be indifferent to the ways its citizens publicly entertain themselves, argues Professor Irving Kristol of New York University. Bearbaiting and cockfighting were prohibited by law, not so much out of compassion for the animals, he points out, but mostly because such spectacles "debased and brutalized" the audiences who flocked to see them. That prohibition (among many others) has been counted an acceptable formal limitation upon people's constitutional rights.

The case for controls in the area of television is debated in a new book called "Where Do You Draw the Line? An Exploration into Media Violence, Pornography, and Censorship" (edited by Victor B. Cline, Brigham Young University Press). "The battle for civil liberties should not be fought on the backs of children," writes psychiatrist Fredric Wertham. The argument that protecting children from harmful media exposure is an infringement of civil liberties "has no historical foundation," he says.

"It has never happened in the history of the world that regulations to protect children—be they with regard to child labor, food, drink, arms, sex, publications, entertainment or plastic toys—have played any role whatsoever in the abridgment of political or civil liberties for adults."

A growing number of legislators are inclined to agree. Representative Torbert Macdonald, chairman of the House Communications Subcommittee, has chided the FCC for putting its "seal of approval on the manner in which self-regulation has worked." In his view, said Macdonald: Self-regulation "has been and continues to be a dismal failure," and he threatened controls "that the networks won't like" if they continue to pursue ratings and profits at the public's expense.

Representative John M. Murphy (D., N.Y.), sponsor of a pending bill that would drastically delimit network control over TV programs, says, "After 18 years, I think it is safe to conclude that we cannot rely on the industry to police itself." TV programmers have enforced only "token reduction" in violence, he maintains, and used a "system of phony euphemisms and cosmetic language" to cover up what are "still the most violent programs in history."

In March, after reviewing the "family hour" plan and calling it a "snow job," Murphy inquired of the FCC: "How can you possibly ask that we give the TV industry another chance to clean up its own house?" (A few critics suggest getting at the networks through their affiliates by requiring all local stations to specify at license-renewal time how much violence they have purveyed. If the level is too high, the license might be withheld.)

Thus, the specter of censorship wafts into view like an unwelcome visitor. It's a solution nobody claims to want, but it may become less unthinkable in the current atmosphere of dismay over televised violence and the industry's stewardship of the public's airwaves.

DOES TV VIOLENCE AFFECT OUR SOCIETY?

NO

by Edith Efron

Some 29 cops-and-robbers shows have been on the network air during the past year, and the "sex and violence" pack is out again baying with full throat, blaming crime on network plays and generally inspiring jaw-cracking yawns in people with a sense of history.

It is a tiresome fact that crime antedates network television—Cain and Abel being the archsymbolic case in point. One of the earliest remnants of man lies in state with clear evidence that a primitive ax had been buried in his skull. Bluebeard, Jack the Ripper and Lizzie Borden have acquired a certain renown as small-scale free-lance murderers. As for torture and murder on a grand scale, Attila the Hun, the Inquisition and, in our own century, Stalin, Hitler and Mao cannot be surpassed. And, to my certain knowledge, none of these was inspired by television.

It's another tiresome fact that every new technological development in the history of human communications has always brought the "sex and violence" ministry out of its lairs to cry out dolorous warnings about the threat to public morality. It is never the ministry's morality that is in the slightest danger—only that of the great unwashed. As any history of censorship will tell you, this claque has carried on with an identical frenzy in every era, uttering identical warnings about: the printing press, the nickelodeon, the silent movies, the talkies, comic books, radio and TV. Rarely has it carried on about communications forms primarily enjoyed by the upper classes—such as books or the theater.

There is only one reason today to pay the slightest attention to this claque, and that is: it is now brandishing "scientific" studies at us which allegedly "prove" that the sight of TV "violence" can indeed "cause" real-life violence. And, to complicate matters, a batch of journalists has fallen for these claims, a group of politicians and HEW bureaucrats see glory in endorsing them, a coalition of what Variety calls "liberal intelligentsia" and "the blue-collar class" ("Archie Bunker and the professor") has climbed on the bandwagon, and what should have been dismissed as unscientific trash is fast acquiring the luminous aura of revealed "truth"—a "truth" that can lead directly to government censorship.

So there is nothing for it but to argue the case against trash posturing as science. In one article, the analysis must necessarily be restricted to the essentials. But any reader who wants more extensive information on the point I raise is invited to consult two series of articles already published in TV Guide. ["A Million-Dollar Misunderstanding," November 1972, and "The Children's Crusade That Failed," April 1973.]

The first thing you should know is that the "TV violence" controversy is merely one of the typically ugly quarrels raging in the social-science community. To understand why, you need merely remember that the social sciences are not true sciences. Although sociology and psychology use statistical measurements, what they choose to measure and what their measurements mean once they've got them are always open to question, generating acute and frequently vicious controversies, particularly as they affect public policy.

The "TV violence" issue has become just such a controversy. Intimidation is in the air, and we are principally hearing the voices of one aggressive pressure group—the group that holds TV as "proven" guilty. Psychologist Ruth Hartley, who has subjected many of the "TV violence" studies to scathing analysis, told me, speaking of her colleagues: "You can't imagine what they do to you if you dare to say that TV *doesn't* hurt children."

You get a full sense of the gutter level of the debate when you know that a few years ago former FCC Commissioner Nicholas Johnson denounced all network programming executives as "evil men" and "child molesters." Few today, however scornful they may be of the "violence" studies, care to subject themselves to such invective. Ironically, the networks have themselves silenced some of the most brilliant men in the field by the simple act of hiring them to do research. "We are all routinely called prostitutes now, unless we play along," one of them said to me.

All this is sufficient reason to approach the "violence" controversy with immense skepticism and, above all, to use one's own judgment.

Now, with this as background—what about the "violence" studies—in particular the batch of 23 different research projects and experiments conducted for the Surgeon General? What do they actually prove? The hardheaded answer is: Nothing. And the fastest way to tell you why is to quote from the Report to the Surgeon General itself, written by a jury of 12 social scientists who evaluated this body of research. The jury was, and remains, torn into bitterly hostile factions, which is what makes any statements all have signed quite significant. They all agree that the very problem of analyzing TV's "impact" on viewers is almost unsolvable by its very nature, and they cite a list of reasons. The language is a bit heavy, but plow through it:

• The authors tell us that "the complexities of developmental processes in childhood and adolescence and the variations from one individual to another make it difficult to predict the effects" of any single stimulus, let alone the tremendous barrage of stimuli coming from TV.

• They tell us that "each person in the audience perceives and . . . interprets the stimuli through his own patterns of ideas, values and responses," thus that generalizations about all people or all children cannot be made.

• They tell us that "the impact of television viewing can only be fully understood when we know something about a young person's own nature, his family, his neighborhood, his school and other major influences in his life."

• They tell us: "It is difficult to design studies which isolate the effects of television content from these other variables. As a result, generalizing from laboratory experiments, surveys, or short-term studies to the long-term, real-time world can be risky."

• And they tell us: "Understanding the relationship between research results and free-ranging human behavior has been a persistent difficulty in attempts to apply scientific findings to the problems of daily life."

To translate this into ordinary English, it says: We don't know very much, yet, about how people work. . . . Every child and adult in America is different. . . . TV content is complex and is perceived differently by every individual. . . . TV is just one of innumerable influences in any individual's life. . . . We don't know how to test its effects. . . . And when we try to do so, we usually don't understand our own findings.

It should be obvious that even *one* of these objections is enough to kill the whole kit and caboodle of such studies. And *all* of them, taken together, make the project a lost cause. In fact, the jury says as much. They all confess that "it would be easy and scientifically justifiable to abandon the search for real-world causal relationships with the declaration, 'nondemonstrable.' "

But TV "violence" researchers are stouthearted types, and the fact that they know something to be rationally impossible doesn't stop them from trying to do it. Even the networks, in their desperate desire to prove to bullying Congressmen that they are concerned about America's children, rush in where angels would fear to tread. And all that happens, of course, is that the impossible becomes more impossible yet, because if you can't "demonstrate" something by rational means . . . well, you resort to irrational means! And there are so many irrational aspects to these studies that it is puzzling to know which ones to isolate in a single article. A few illustrations will have to do.

One pertains to the ostensibly dry and dusty realm of definitions. As the Surgeon General's jury—again, all of them—put it: "For scientific investigation, terms must be defined precisely and unambiguously." Well, the definitions in this group of studies would make Funk and Wagnalls weep. "Violence" in these studies means such things as: physical attack . . . self-defense . . . the destruction of property . . . racist stereotypes . . . and playing football! "Aggression" is even more startling. It means everything that "violence" means, plus: "anti-social conduct," a concept that covers everything from small-fry belligerence at the sand pile to mass murder

. . . *and the energetic pursuit of any goal, whether pro- or anti-social, creative or destructive!*

Here's the effect of using words so wildly: By such standards, a TV comedy featuring a stereotyped Aunt Jemima mother, with a pushy two-year-old who's always first at the jam pot, and an ambitious, hard-working son who is putting himself through college by playing football, can now be classed as an extremely "violent" film! And among "aggressive" characters, we can now lump: Hitler, cooking millions in ovens . . . Solzhenitsyn, defying a succession of Soviet dictators to write "The Gulag Archipelago" . . . Martin Luther King, leading a nonviolent demonstration to gain voting rights for blacks . . . Helen Reddy, self-assertively belting out "I Am Woman" . . . and Snoopy, trying to shoot down the Red Baron!

So what common phenomenon, what common misbehavior are all these studies investigating? None. Taken as a group, they are resplendently meaningless. And the failure to make moral differentiations between the "violence" of attack and the "violence" of self-defense, between creative self-assertion and murder, is stupefying.

With this kind of conceptual and moral chaos lying concealed at the very base of the project, what kind of "findings" did it produce? They were chaotic and weirdly contradictory: Some testees become more "aggressive" after seeing TV "violence." The majority of testees do not. Some testees become more cooperative and "pro-social" afterwards. Some testees become more "aggressive" after watching comedies and erotic material than after watching "violent" material. And so forth. The jury—again, all of them—concluded politely from all of this that you can produce either "anti-social" or "pro-social" responses, depending on "the opportunities offered in the experiment." Which is a scholar's way of saying you can manufacture any results you like.

Now, sensible people, facing this kind of intellectual nonsense, will simply put on their hats, go home, and settle down to a jolly evening with *Kojak, Mannix, Cannon* and Co., who, if they have any virtue in common, it is the capacity for lucid deduction. But if your colleagues have just blown one million dollars in tax money, if a U.S. Senator demands an accounting, and if you have private or professional reasons for not walking out, you can do one of two things: You can say, loudly, "A causal connection between TV violence and crime has been proved," and then hastily admit that there's a chaotic situation here. Or you can say, loudly, "This is a hopelessly chaotic situation," and then hastily add that some sort of tenuous connection may have been shown.

That's what the Surgeon General's jury said. After describing the chaotic "findings" with such words as "tentative and limited," "not wholly consistent or conclusive," etc., their bottom-line conclusion read: "We have noted in the studies at hand a modest association between viewing of violence and aggression, among at least some children, and we have noted some data which are consonant with the interpretation that violence-viewing produces the aggression; this evidence is not conclusive however, and some of the data are also consonant with other interpretations."

What does *that* mean? Nothing. A cartoon in the American Psychological Association Monitor for March 1972 satirized the report with a caption reading: "Our studies show conclusively that TV does not cause violence—except when it does."

As far as I can tell, after spending almost a full year of my professional life reading such studies and discussing them with social scientists, there are only two "links" between the watching of TV and crime—*real* crime, as defined by the law—and both warrant close inspection, mainly for what they tell you about the "violence" researchers.

The first "link" lies in a batch of surveys, done both in America and in England, showing that delinquent-type adolescents watch much more TV, and TV "violence," than their stabler nondelinquent peers. Similarly, studies of prison populations indicate unusually heavy watching of TV, and of TV "violence." This "proves," according to some researchers, that the sight of TV "violence" causes crime.

Only it doesn't. Other Anglo-American studies also show, with great consistency, that the group in society that does the heaviest watching of TV "violence" shows is the group that is least intelligent, least educated, poorest, *and most unstable*. But this is precisely the group that has always been the chief reservoir of violent crime, and it was so well *before* the invention of TV, and of televised cops-and-robbers shows.

Further: other Anglo-American studies show with great consistency that normal adolescents not only watch less TV and less TV violence than delinquents, but start getting bored by the set at age 10, if unusually bright, and at age 12, if they're normally intelligent. This, postulates Britain's Hilde Himmelweit, indicates that for stable youngsters, living itself is a more satisfying experience than watching television. Which again suggests that the dividing issue is that of emotional stability, not televised cops-and-robbers.

Finally, in America, a large chunk of adolescent crime, and of the prison population, comes from the black world. And, whatever the individual differences in this world, it is known to suffer acutely from the problems of institutionalized poverty and racism. It is heavily loaded with hostile, fear-ridden, unstable people. Has any sociologist ever had the sheer gall to suggest that black looting, rioting and stealing can be pinned on TV's cops-and-robbers shows? That the crimes of people such as Eldridge Cleaver, Rap Brown and George Jackson, that the crimes of Black Panthers, of the Symbionese Liberation Army, can be pinned on the likes of *The Untouchables, Mission: Impossible, Mannix* and *Kojak?* No. But if one cannot pin black crime on cops-and-robbers shows, one has just disposed of a large chunk of real-life criminals!

Is one then to conclude that TV's power to "cause" crime applies only to *whites?* Are TV "stimuli," perhaps as a gesture of racial expiation, out to punish the honkies?

It is perfectly obvious, when you put all these facts together, that only one generalization is possible: that acutely disturbed, anxious and unstable people, whether black or white, criminal or not, are watching more TV, and more TV good-vs.-evil plays, as an escape from the misery of their lives. That is a "link" if you like—but it's not a "causal" link. TV isn't *creating* criminals; criminals, along with the wider unstable population, are *using* TV for their own psychological purposes.

The second "link" is the deranged person who sees a violent act on the air and copies it. And this, to some TV "violence" researchers, along with the most ignorant of the censorious groups, "proves" that TV "causes" crime. Does it? We certainly know that from time to time some sick being sees depictions of crimes in the news, the movies and on TV, and then re-enacts them. We know that a scattering of disturbed, often politically alienated, people have imitated kidnappings, bombings, skyjackings and terrorist acts reported in the news. We know that a deranged 15-year-old girl led a gang rape of a nine-year-old girl with a bottle, after seeing a similar scene in an NBC film. We know that when a report of a suicide is covered on the front page of the newspapers, a rash of suicides—violence directed at *self*—occurs. This kind of thing happens. It will happen again. People do walk among us who can blow sky high at any moment. But they are statistically rare, and the diverse media of communication are not the "cause" of their dangerous psychic instability. Libraries full of studies of the genesis of crime all over the world attest to the fact that the roots of such psychic instability lie deeply buried in their past.

The plain fact is that TV films, like news or movies, cannot turn otherwise normal people or children into predators or self-destroyers overnight, let alone in 10 minutes or two seconds. What's more, the "violence" researchers know this perfectly well. They *claim* that the reason they don't set up experiments to study TV's direct capacity to make people commit crimes is that such experiments would be unethical. That, they say, is why they are obliged to study the alleged substitute, "aggression." But this is plain poppycock.

For many years now, "violence" researchers have been calmly playing miles of "violent" film to hundreds, possibly thousands, of adults and children, and never has one violent crime been committed by a soul, adult or child, after "exposure" to these allegedly dangerous "stimuli." *What's more, the TV researchers never expected this to happen. That is the secret premise of all their studies. TV researchers know perfectly well that in the real world TV "violence" just simply does not do what they charge it with doing.*

Since, for years, no one bothered to pay the slightest attention to researchers as they warned us against what we all *knew* to be untrue, they have invented a mysterious explanation that we cannot check simply by looking around us. They've come up with the scary concept of "cumulative" effects—i.e., that we are all sitting around, year after year, subconsciously storing up violent "stimuli" that are gradually making us "insensitive" to crime and can culminate by "causing" even *normal* people to act criminally. And, of course, they've already come up with studies "proving" a growing insensitivity.

Well, I can't read the subconscious processes of

200,000,000 people. But I can read ratings, I can read sales figures, I can read salary lists and profit reports. And they tell me a strangely different story about possible "cumulative" effects.

What they tell me is this: that the success of the cops-and-robbers shows, like that of all the good-vs.-evil shows on the air, is exclusively a function of the *continuing heroes*. It is the heroes, the pure-hearted men with the dedicated, courageous, indomitable characters, who generate the ratings; whom the people, old and young, tune in faithfully to see every week; and to whom they are loyal year after year.

By contrast, it is not the discontinuous villains who pull in the ratings. These are not the drawing cards, nor do they command the high salaries. They are eminently forgettable props whose sole function is to serve as foils for the heroic virtues. (Do *you* remember the villain of last week's *Mannix?*)

It is precisely because the heroes are absolutely reliable emotional magnets that the networks schedule so many heroic series. Network TV's economic existence, and an enormous number of its technical calculations, are totally based on the certain, *proved* knowledge that the overwhelming majority of the U.S. public and its kids are fixated on the simple, continuous vision of good,

just men. To a striking degree, network TV's profits flourish in the loam of hero worship.

To ignore this *proved* evidence that the overwhelming majority of viewers identify emotionally with the good, and have so identified "cumulatively" for decades—while concocting unprovable scare stories about the collective unconscious and its alleged "cumulative" absorption of evil—is about as intellectually nasty a phenomenon as I know. If, indeed, the "cumulative" watching of evil is turning us all gradually into depraved beings, then the "cumulative" watching of good must be turning us all gradually into saints! You cannot have one without the other. That is, unless you can demonstrate that evil is something like cholesterol—something that slowly accumulates and clogs the system while good is something like spinach, easily digested and quickly excreted.

This scare story about "cumulative" effects in normal people is all that stands between the "violence" researchers and a good gusty laugh from the American public that would blow them all away into the dustbin where they belong—the archaic dustbin from which censors of the entertainment of "the people" have always sprung. Our contemporary censors are not one whit more rational than their predecessors throughout the ages Just inconceivably more devious.

Why We Won't Win the 1976 Olympics

One big reason is spelled AAU
by Melvin Durslag

Drawing by Rowland B. Wilson

The television bombardment trumpeting the 1976 Winter and Summer Olympic Games has begun. ABC, which owns the TV rights, is promising extraordinary coverage of the Games.

Indeed, the coverage could be colossal. America's teams may not be. Those expecting great American heroics and wide-scale collecting of gold ornaments had better hibernate during next year's Games, or turn their dials to happier shows, such as soap operas.

Winning in the Winter Olympics, of course, hasn't been a U.S. habit for a long time now. And the Summer Games, once America's long suit, have found this nation lagging. Even in track and field, traditionally a U.S. power sport, there was a slippage at the Munich Olympics in '72. Experts assaying the picture see a further decline in 1976.

It is argued by some that winning isn't essential in an international event whose primary purpose is good fel-

lowship. But an all-out effort *is;* anything less runs against the grain of a sports-minded people.

What seems to upset most athletes is the watery effort we organize. It was the contention of Steve Prefontaine, holder of eight U.S. distance-running records, that amateur sports programs in the U.S. have fallen scandalously behind those of many other countries.

"In international competition," said Prefontaine, "people don't realize the disadvantages the Americans have. Training camps of the Iron Curtain countries and many of the democracies are superior. Their coaching is superior. Their building program is superior. Their government backing is superior." Prefontaine, tragically, will not be competing in 1976; he was killed in an automobile accident last month.

The decline by the U.S. is generally ascribed to two

factors. First, we gradually are becoming a pro-oriented sports people. Amateur games are being suffocated by the professionals, who gobble up newspaper and magazine space and flood the television screens. Viewers and athletes alike are becoming indifferent to amateur sports. Now it isn't even possible for the U.S. to send its best amateur basketball players to the Olympics—the lads don't want the Games to encroach on their upcoming pro careers, which pay off like the Irish Sweepstakes.

The other reason is weak leadership. The U.S. Olympic Committee is ranked as little more than a travel agency, commissioned to arrange transportation and lodging for our teams.

And charged with the everyday responsibility of running the major segment of amateur sports in this country is a mountain of ineffectuality called the Amateur Athletic Union, known on Broadway as the AAU.

Embattled for years with one force or another, the AAU had a major falling out in 1963 with the NCAA—the ruler of college sports—which then formed its own track group, the U.S. Track and Field Federation. It was and is the charge of the USTFF that the AAU is so inept that a substantial national program can't get airborne in this country. (Those in a few other sports have also put together their own associations.)

But, for better or for worse, the AAU remains the kingpin, franchised (since 1912) as the governing body of U.S. amateur sports by the International Amateur Athletic Federation.

Operating out of a small office in Indianapolis, the AAU exists partly on revenue derived from television, most of it from a contract with CBS.

The AAU also collects dues from athlete members and fees paid by the meets it sanctions.

Athletes, coaches, leaders of private clubs and meet promoters may disagree on a variety of matters, but almost all are linked by a common contempt for the AAU. As one club director explains: "The AAU isn't Hitler. It's more like the Marx Brothers."

Guarding the ramparts of puritanism in this country, the AAU is your friendly watchdog, protecting the populace against the evils of athletic corruption. One time, for instance, an Olympic champion hurdler accepted an invitation to get married on the former TV show *Bride and Groom.*

Less than affluent, the athlete welcomed the stove, refrigerator and other household items he and his wife received. But for prostituting his good amateur name, he was suspended by the AAU for a year.

Not long ago, world high-jump champion Dwight Stones netted $296 for appearing on *The Tonight Show.* Rising seven feet from their chairs, shocked AAU leaders balked, demanding that the athlete turn over at least two-thirds of the money to the AAU. Stones ignored the order. Instead, he turned over all the money to the Pacific Coast Club (of Long Beach, California), for which he competes.

Stones then rejected the opportunity to tour with the U.S. team in China. He told a reporter, "What would a guy do over there? You can't talk to the people. That

means for 24 hours a day you would be totally dependent on the AAU. I'd go berserk."

Athletes also charge that the AAU operates a poverty program in which entrants in a track meet, for example, are usually allowed $25 a day for hotel, food and other expenses. (Major-league baseball allows players $23 a day for meals alone.)

When food and lodging are provided for track athletes, the AAU grants them incidental money in the grand sum of $3 a day. Even visiting foreign athletes are subject to the AAU's stinginess. Debarking in New York, where he learned the amount of his pocket cash, a Belgian runner caught the next plane back to Brussels. Today that fellow works for Interpol, investigating, no doubt, how one can maneuver in New York on $3.

To make their feelings known about those who govern them, a group of U.S. athletes appeared at the AAU meet in New York last winter attired in tops bearing the likeness of Mickey Mouse. "We're dressing to fit the occasion," one of them explained.

Conditions have reached the point where the AAU is no longer able to muster its best team for the annual track meet with the Soviet Union—athletes find excuses not to go. The U.S. squad in Moscow in 1974 was so unrepresentative that the Russians were insulted.

"The AAU isn't a corrupt organization," says Dick Bank, a formidable authority on track who has served for years as a TV commentator on the sport. "It just gets so bogged down in nit-picking and in trying to assert its muscle that it doesn't get much accomplished. Some of its capers are a roar. I remember an AAU meeting one time to discuss some bad checks issued by a club director. The meeting droned on for three and a half hours. When the time finally came to vote, it was discovered that of the 14 officials who had opened the meeting, fewer than eight remained. There wasn't enough for a quorum."

Al Franken, director of the Sunkist Invitational, a major meet in Los Angeles, contends that the AAU discourages competition by the grief it causes sponsors.

"They drive promoters nuts," says Franken. "If you want to invite top foreign stars to your meet to hype up the show, you can't do it directly, but must go through the AAU. At the pace at which the AAU moves, your meet can be long over by the time the AAU makes contact with the athletes."

A tendency to overcriticize the AAU is noted by Jim Bush, coach of national championship track teams at UCLA.

"The AAU may lack strong organization," says Bush, "but a lot of the members in it are fine people who volunteer their services and work for nothing more than love of sport. They'll stand in the rain and measure high jumps and discus throws and they'll want nothing in return. Only a handful will get to make the glamorous foreign trips."

Bush argues, as do most athletes, that the well-meaning volunteers now assisting the AAU should be enlisted by a government-backed national sports ministry, which would become the nation's central amateur-sports agency. It would unify and strengthen the amateur-sports program as similar agencies have done in other countries.

Not long ago, California's Senator John V. Tunney backed a bill that would establish such a sports ministry, but it was tabled—for a reason explained by Dick Bank.

"Some very important people in this country are honorary officials of the AAU," he says. "Knowing little about sports, they see the organization as a fine American institution. They don't understand the roadblock the AAU is causing. But these people, nonetheless, have political influence—enough to prevent the AAU from being legislated out."

And so the argument lingers, as it has now for decades. And our international sports effort continues to lose altitude. Depending upon your viewpoint, this may or may not be important. The purpose here merely is to offer cold compresses to those television viewers working up a temperature over U.S. chances in '76.

AS WE SEE IT [ROD SERLING —A EULOGY]

On hearing of Rod Serling's death, one recalls that he was eminent among his colleagues in capturing and expressing the pure wonderment and awe that spring from contemplation of the mysteries of life and death.

There was no missing, either, Serling's fascination with the sweep of time and space, but he could sharp-focus down to his own planet with a keen contemporary eye and take long hard looks at the society around him. "Patterns," about the tough demands of business and what they did to executives, won him an Emmy.

His compassionate study of a broken-down pugilist, "Requiem For a Heavyweight," gained him another. "A Town Has Turned to Dust" won nomination, and "In the Presence of Mine Enemies" was hailed as a memorable chronicle of the Warsaw ghetto. The prolific Serling's works also received Sylvania, Christopher and Peabody awards.

As a writer, producer, narrator and self-taught dramatist, he gave his work to the TV audience in an abundant stream for a quarter of a century. Radio was already using his scripts while he was still a student at Antioch College, which he had entered on the GI bill after his Army service as a paratrooper.

During much of his career, Serling was an angry crusader, pleading the cause of quality television. And in recent years he chose to expound his views as a teacher of creative writing and TV appreciation and criticism at Ithaca College.

Although a comparatively young man—he died at 50—Serling was nevertheless one of television's pioneers. For he was one of the skilled and impassioned young playwrights who made possible TV's Golden Age and the likes of *Studio One* and *Playhouse 90*.

He was a charming man—involved, concerned, restless—and he made a great contribution to television. We are all in his debt.

PAY-TV: POISED FOR A GIANT LEAP?

A satellite in the sky may be the thing that will finally get toll viewing off the ground
by Richard K. Doan

Out in the Hollywood hills and in nearby Beverly Hills and Santa Monica, film and TV celebrities such as Cary Grant, Telly Savalas, Gene Hackman, Don Rickles and producer Norman Lear don't go out to the movies as much as they once did. Instead they lounge at home, watching nearly current pictures on a closed circuit called Channel Z. Sometimes Channel Z's star subscribers pop down to a TV studio and tape interviews to be tagged onto the showing of pictures they're in, especially around Oscar time. There's some thought this helps influence Academy voters among Z's audiences.

Drawing by Bill Charmatz

Meanwhile, back East in Long Island's populous Nassau County, where the reception of New York City's seven major TV outlets is clear and sharp, thousands of households are frequently switching off ABC, CBS and NBC shows to watch uncut movies and live sports events from Madison Square Garden, all piped into their living rooms on a pay-TV channel without commercial interruptions.

What all this means is that pay-cable (as pay-TV via CATV is coming to be known) has begun to make interesting, if not yet significant, inroads.

To be sure, pay-cable's under 200,000 subscribers nationwide is still a very small number. And even the most optimistic of cable enthusiasts agree that "feevee" isn't going to rob broadcast television of any sizable number of viewers for perhaps years to come. Recently the standard prediction has been that somewhere between a million and two million U.S. homes might be watching pay-cable programs by 1980. That would leave a projected 75 million other homes still tuning in only free over-the-air TV.

The Federal Communications Commission has put some curbs on pay-TV's attractions, dictating that it may not "siphon" (from broadcast TV) movies between three and 10 years old and certain sports events that have been carried on conventional over-the-air channels. There are also complex other FCC restrictions that the cable industry charges are designed to protect the broadcasting establishment.

On the other hand, there are growing indications that subscription TV, a long-frustrated dream, is poised for a giant leap: Time Inc. last April committed $7.5 million to ambitious plans to set up a satellite-fed national pay-TV network and, within a month, three of the major cable-system owners, including TelePrompTer Corp., biggest of them all, jumped in to affiliate with the new entity. Indeed, there were early signs that a rush could soon be on among the nation's cable operators to sign up for the 80 hours a week of movies, sports and other fare to be offered by Home Box Office, Inc., a fully owned Time subsidiary. Such a development, of course, could knock out all the modest-growth predictions.

Until it came up with the satellite-network plan, HBO had been growing by inches, reaching some 115,000 cable subscribers via microwave and land lines in New York, New Jersey, Pennsylvania and Delaware. Teleprompter, in joining the HBO network fold, made its Northeastern systems available for immediate linkup, jumping HBO's reach to nearly 300,000 homes.

Barring unforeseen delays, earth stations costing about $75,000 each, with 32-foot receiving dishes, will be erected this fall in Florida, to begin picking up HBO fare beamed from New York via RCA-leased satellite.

HBO's initial network affiliate, UA-Columbia Cablevision, which has Fort Pierce and Vero Beach cable systems, also expects next year to put up earth stations at its cable sites in Fort Smith, Arkansas; Laredo, Texas; Yuma, Arizona; El Centro, California; and Pasco/Kennewick, Washington. Another cable operator, American Television and Communications, expects to feed HBO programs to 250,000 cable homes from an Orlando, Florida, earth station.

But it's the TelePrompTer plunge into pay programming that will give HBO its biggest shot in the arm. TPT said it expected ultimately to put up 24 earth stations, at a total cost of perhaps $5 million for these and home-reception gear, to deliver HBO's shows to 82 cable systems in 21 states with a total of 870,000 homes.

All of TelePrompTer's biggest systems will be in the pay network except half-owned (with Hughes Aircraft Co.) Theta Cable in Los Angeles, the Z Channel originator, which will go on programming its own pay movies.

Exuberantly, TelePrompTer president Russell Karp told a reporter, "Everything that cable has promised—the television of abundance—is starting to happen."

Not only that, but it appeared that Time's pioneering Home Box Office had such a long head start in pay-TV networking that any late-arriving competition would be hard pressed to catch up. Robert Weisberg, whose TeleMation Program Services is a major buyer of movies and other programs for cable, supplying some 25 pay-TV systems at recent count, has said he was exploring satellite and microwave networking prospects. Paramount and one or two other film studios have toyed with getting into the business. But most cable experts see no HBO competitor in sight.

Satellites or no satellites, pay-cable of course can go only where CATV has gone before, and cable's growth has been seriously slowed in recent years, owing in part to the recession, which has dried up venture capital. Even so, more than 10 million U.S. homes are hooked into cable systems and at the moment, less than a fifth of these are receiving pay channels. That leaves considerable room for "feevee" growth where cable already is. (It costs a cable system anywhere from $15 to $50 per home to gear up for pay-TV depending on equipment used.)

Not to be totally overlooked, too, is the possibility of revival of the original concept of pay-TV—over the air. But that approach is conceded by most to be farther away, since satisfactory hardware is yet to be developed.

So far, pay-cable is mainly going the per-channel route, with subscribing homes paying a monthly fee of $5 to $9 for the pay channel on top of their basic service fee of $5 or $6. Most cable people agree a day will come, some years hence, when the industry will switch over to a per-program formula—a clear implication that viewers will be paying more for their cable entertainment in the future. At the moment, the country's only going per-program experiment, located in Columbus, Ohio, pipes movies to about 1000 homes. As in the case of over-the-air pay-TV, a satisfactory set-side "box" for sophisticated cable-program selection is yet to be developed.

It's the momentum pay-cable is picking up in a few urban areas that is now attracting notice. Originally cable was conceived as a device for extending the reach of TV signals into localities with poor or no reception—and indeed that's where most cable is. Its second function has been to "import" distant-city signals into communities with only one to three local channels.

But suddenly it is the places with a plethora of over-the-air choices that are experiencing significant growth of pay-cable. Theta Cable, the one feeding double features nightly to the Hollywood colony, started up its Z Channel in April 1974 with just 500 homes on the line. In a year it jumped to 30,000, making it the country's largest pay-TV system.

"People are calling other systems around here, asking, 'When can we get Z movies?'" reports John Atwood, Theta's president. By this year's end, Atwood said, Theta will be offering its pay channel via microwave to neighboring systems.

In the East, Charles F. Dolan, president of Long Island's Cablevision, took over a system in late '73 with just 50 miles of cable. By this year it had grown to 800 miles of lines, and Dolan was pushing for 2000 miles by year-end.

Remarkably, of 32,000 homes taking his basic Cablevision service as of last summer, more than 99 percent were paying $11 to $14 a month to get the pay channel and added features.

Dolan believes he could have 175,000 Long Island homes signed up by the end of 1977. That was about the number of pay-TV homes in all the U.S. several months ago. And Nassau County, Dolan recalls, was an area "nobody wanted for cable service because TV reception was so good there."

In all, a few more than 60 cable systems around the country recently were offering pay channels. The third-largest of them, in San Diego, had about 20,000 homes. Most had somewhere between 200 and 2000 subscribers.

Paul Kagan, publisher of the authoritative Pay TV Newsletter, thinks cablers have been slow to awaken to where the CATV pot of gold is. "It has taken CATV, as an industry, about three years to discover that its economic destiny is attached to the living-room box office," Kagan asserts. Until the HBO satellite was announced, he feels, pay-TV was "literally plodding along."

The upsurge in pay-cable's fortunes ironically comes at a time when the big broadcast networks have begun tapering off on prime-time movies. It's unlikely ABC, CBS and NBC are reverting to TV series because they see pay-TV on the rise as a purveyor of movies-at-home. But it's worth noting that cable lately has been getting the jump on the networks in airing some big theatrical attractions such as "The Sting," "American Graffiti" and "Harry and Tonto," not to mention such no-nos for over-the-air TV as "The Night Porter."

Pornography, incidentally, isn't cable's come-on. X-rated movies are generally eschewed. Home Box Office books R-rated films only after 9 P.M., and some systems are putting "key-lock converters" into homes where parents are concerned about the R-rated fare. HBO cautiously ran "Night Porter" after 11 o'clock recently and claims it got few complaints. TeleMation's Bob Weisberg says only one picture he handled was edited: some "Deliverance" scenes were snipped out for one market. Viewers who'd seen the picture in theaters crabbed about the deletions.

"It's the convenience of watching at home that's crucial," Weisberg feels. "Pay-cable watchers are people who don't go to the movies. Surveys show they typically have been out to only one movie in the last year. Yet they'll watch them regularly at home. They're mostly the 30-, 40-, 50-year-olds, not the young marrieds."

The one thing there's no doubt about is that movies are what makes the mare go. The problem is that while the movie producers are glad to pick up the extra change the pay-cable business can bring them, the broadcasters are putting the squeeze on the infant competitor by lobbying for even more restrictive curbs on cable than the Federal Communications Commission already has imposed and are pushing the studios into "exclusivity" deals under which movies are "warehoused" by the networks to keep them from being shown on cable.

Despite such measures, pay-cable obviously is on the march toward an ever larger role in living-room entertainment. Admonishing broadcasters to give "top priority" to campaigning in the halls of Congress and the FCC against pay-cable inroads, a high-ranking network official, senior vice president and general counsel for ABC, Inc., Everett H. Erlick, warned recently: "People are shortly going to have to pay for at least some of the television programs they now see free over the air."

The big scare the networks have frequently sought to throw into TV viewer ranks, to arouse opposition to pay-TV, is that it eventually might rob watchers (except at a price) of such sports events as the Super Bowl and the World Series. The cable people scoff at this claim, insisting it would be "political suicide" for them to try to lock up such attractions.

Still, the haunting possibility of it exists, if pay-TV grows into a massive box office. And growing it is.

THE
FAIRNESS DOCTRINE

Is it a "fickle affront to the First Amendment"?
Or
Would its elimination be "the worst single thing to happen in the history of U.S. journalism"?
by Chris Welles

A doctrine that requires broadcasters to present important public issues "fairly" sounds, on the face of it, like a simple and straightforward affair, about as controversial as *Little House on the Prairie* and almost as American. But, in fact, the FCC's Fairness Doctrine has, in the past year or so, become an explosive issue. Arthur Taylor, president of CBS, calls it "a potentially destructive tool." Former Senator Sam Ervin says it is a "fickle affront to the First Amendment."

On the other hand, the Committee for Economic Development, a prestigious business-supported research group, has come out strongly in favor of the Fairness Doctrine, and the chairman of the FCC, Richard Wiley, argues that elimination of it would be "the worst single thing to happen in the whole history of U.S. journalism."

So the debate is on. And it's a hot one, sharply dividing people who usually agree with each other. Broadcasters are pitted against broadcasters, liberals against liberals, and conservatives against conservatives. Wisconsin Senator William Proxmire has introduced a bill to abolish the Doctrine, while Rhode Island's John Pastore is fighting to retain it. Both are liberal Democrats.

The problem with the Doctrine is that, while everybody is in favor of being "fair," few people can agree on what fairness means in practice or how it should be achieved and guaranteed. "Even those of us who approve of it agree that the Fairness Doctrine has been a bloody mess," says Thomas Asher, former executive director of the Media Access Project, a Washington public-interest law firm. "It doesn't lend itself to precision and is hard to enforce. It leads to a high volume of litigation and a low volume of public understanding."

The root of the controversy, however, is rather simple: to what extent should the federal government exercise control over the way news and public issues are presented on radio and television? It all boils down pretty much to a question of whom do you trust or, at least, whom do you distrust less, the government or the networks.

Those who favor the Doctrine fear that the networks will abuse their predominant and privileged position in the nation's news flow. Therefore, they say, broadcasting must be checked by limited federal supervision. Those who oppose the Doctrine fear that federal supervision could easily become unreasonable censorship. They find the networks quite capable of fulfilling their public-interest responsibilities without government regulation. The present debate over the Fairness Doctrine could importantly affect the nature of broadcasting for years to come.

Though the Fairness Doctrine essentially is a philosophical issue, it derives from a technological fact: there is a limited number of frequencies on which radio and TV programs can be broadcast over the air. While there is no practical limit to the number of people who can exercise their right of free speech by publishing newspapers and magazines, only a relative few can transmit over the airwaves, particularly on the heavily watched VHF channels, without causing electronic interference.

A series of laws beginning with the Radio Act of 1927 has developed the idea that, since some people necessarily must be denied the right to use the airwaves, the few who are permitted to use them must be prohibited from monopolizing the viewpoints expressed. In return for the privilege of using the airwaves, broadcasters must adhere to standards of "public convenience, interest or necessity" and broadcast a variety of viewpoints in addition to their own. The public's right to be informed thus justifies limits on the broadcaster's right to free speech. Through its power to issue broadcast licenses, the FCC is supposed to ensure that broadcasters live up to these obligations.

The Fairness Doctrine itself was laid down in a 1949 FCC report that was later upheld by Congress and the courts. It decreed that a broadcaster must spend a reasonable amount of time discussing controversial issues of public importance, and do so in a way that fairly reflects opposing points of view. Unlike the Equal Time Rule, which requires broadcasters to grant equal time to competing candidates for political office, the Fairness Doctrine permits the broadcaster to take as strong an editorial stand as he desires—as long as he also reasonably presents the opinions of those with contrary positions.

The scope of the Doctrine's use has been determined by a variety of FCC and court decisions. Its constitutionality was established in the famous Red Lion case, which concerned an attack on a journalist, Fred J. Cook, broadcast over WGCB, a conservative radio station in Red Lion, Pennsylvania. When Cook complained, the FCC ordered WGCB to give him air time to reply. The station refused and filed suit. In 1969, the Supreme Court unanimously upheld the FCC. A frequency licensee, the Court said, is a "fiduciary with obligations to present those views and voices which are representative of his community and which would otherwise, by necessity, be barred from the airwaves."

Applying this principle to paid commercials is a tricky problem. A 1973 Supreme Court decision, in a case concerning attempts by private groups to buy air time to advocate political views, helped ease that problem by ruling that broadcasters do not have to sell time to such groups; that a station is not obliged to grant access to the airwaves to every group that demands to purchase time.

In 1967, the FCC forced TV stations to put anti-smoking commercials on the air to counterbalance cigaret advertising, but last year the Commission decided that the Fairness Doctrine cannot be applied to ordinary commercials promoting the sale of a product. That applies even if the advertising is false or misleading or the use of the product is a matter of controversy. However, the FCC made it clear that the Doctrine does apply to ads that consist of "direct and substantial commentary on important issues." For that reason the networks have, generally speaking, refused to accept ideological advertising.

By and large, the courts and the FCC have strengthened the Fairness Doctrine. Most rulings have been favorable. But that hasn't deterred an increasingly vocal group of critics, particularly NBC and CBS, who argue that broadcasters should have the same unfettered First Amendment rights as newspapers and magazines. They point out that broadcasting is no longer the restricted medium it once was. The nation's 8760 broadcasting outlets now outnumber daily newspapers by more than four to one. And cable television may soon dramatically expand the number of broadcasters.

Those who oppose the Doctrine are most aroused by its sanction of government involvement in news broadcasting. Fairness in covering controversial issues, NBC chairman Julian Goodman recently told Congress, "is an essential professional standard for any responsible journalist. But when it becomes a government-enforced doctrine, it automatically gives the government authority to second-guess news judgments and threatens to make it a supereditor for broadcasting." CBS's Arthur Taylor said the Doctrine is "a potential tool for determined and unscrupulous public officials to destroy what is, in effect, the only national daily press that this diverse nation has."

As an example of this potential, many Fairness Doctrine foes cite incidents recently revealed by former CBS News executive Fred Friendly: According to Friendly, White House and other Democratic politicians during the Kennedy and Johnson Administrations covertly engaged in "an unsavory project of political censorship" that consisted of using the Fairness Doctrine to harass right-wing radio commentators. Part of that campaign, Friendly alleged, was Fred Cook's challenge in the Red Lion case, which Friendly said was backed by the Democratic National Committee. (Cook has denied the charge.)

Foes of the Doctrine claim that even without specific government pressure, the potential has been enough to inhibit broadcasters, especially at local stations, from putting hard-hitting public-affairs programs on the air. NBC News correspondent Bill Monroe told Congress that when he left a newspaper for a TV news job he was surprised to find "a consciousness of government, an anxiety about it, that robbed TV executives of the same quality of journalistic zest and readiness to take initiatives displayed by newspaper executives." In return for the "limited and sometimes dubious benefits" of the Fairness Doctrine, Monroe said, "we suffer the imposition of blandness, timidity and don't-rock-the-boat fear of government" on the nation's radio and TV stations.

Proponents of the Fairness Doctrine have not been quite as visible as its opponents, but their views are no less firmly held. Exclusive rights to use broadcast frequencies, they point out, remain a government-conferred privilege, and public-interest criteria remain the only means to determine who should be granted that privilege.

Another argument offered by proponents of the Doctrine is that statistics on how many radio and TV stations there are, as opposed to the number of newspapers and magazines, are misleading; that much of the print media consists of small weekly newspapers, trade journals and limited-circulation publications; that they are no match for the concentrated power of the TV networks; that lumping TV in with radio simply confuses the issue; that the vast majority of radio stations provide a steady diet of popular music and pay almost no attention to controversial public issues. They also point out that cable-TV is still in its infancy and its long-term effect is hard to foresee; and that its growth has been hindered by understandable opposition from the networks.

Fairness Doctrine supporters worry that television has a much stronger economic motivation, because of advertiser preferences, to broadcast bland entertainment and sports shows than to present controversial public-affairs programs. "I see myself as a libertarian," says Ned Schnurman, associate director of the National News Council, an independent watchdog of press fairness, "but I think the Fairness Doctrine is the only existing assurance that the networks will responsibly discharge their responsibilities regarding news and public affairs."

The Doctrine provides an important guarantee of access to the airwaves by contrary and minority opinions, its adherents argue. "It's a hell of a big stick for us," says Russell Hemenway, director of the National Committee For an Effective Congress, which assists political candidates in challenging incumbents.

Proponents admit the potential for government misuse of its power, but point to the lack of evidence that the power has been used unfairly. None of the incidents related by Fred Friendly alleged irresponsibility by the FCC. "We're not trying to set ourselves up as the national arbiter of truth and objectivity," says FCC Chairman Richard Wiley. He points out that even when challenged successfully on fairness, broadcasters cannot be compelled by the FCC to change or delete programming. They retain almost complete discretion over how, when, and in what form contrasting views are to be presented. (CBS's *60 Minutes* recently dealt with a rash of fairness complaints about a segment last February on Jews in Syria by presenting a brief commentary by Mike Wallace summarizing the criticism and giving CBS's rebuttal.)

ABC News president William Sheehan, who favors the Fairness Doctrine, feels that the FCC has behaved quite judiciously in applying it. "I don't think they have any appetite for becoming the editor of last resort," he says. Some observers suggest that, if anything, the FCC has been lax in the Doctrine's application. Of 4300 fairness complaints filed with the Commission during 1973 and 1974, 97 percent were dismissed out of hand. In only 19 cases did the FCC take action against broadcasters. And during the Doctrine's 26 years, only two stations have had licenses revoked for fairness reasons.

While some broadcast newsmen agree with Bill Monroe, most questioned for this article did not. William Sheehan says the Fairness Doctrine "has not been an inhibiting factor" in ABC's news coverage. Despite the statements of his superiors, CBS's Mike Wallace, who on *60 Minutes* often tackles controversial issues, says "it hasn't troubled me." Edwin Newman, who narrated and co-authored a 1972 NBC documentary critical of corporate pension plans—which, the FCC ruled, violated the Fairness Doctrine—refused to join the network in what was to be a successful challenge of the ruling. "Providing it is reasonably administered," Newman says, "I find nothing in the Fairness Doctrine to object to." To Donald McGannon, chairman of Westinghouse Broadcasting, which owns seven radio stations and five TV stations, the Doctrine is, if anything, "a goad and an incentive to us to do what we're supposed to do effectively and well."

FCC Chairman Wiley thinks some broadcasters use the Fairness Doctrine as a "shield." That TV broadcasts a paucity of controversial public-affairs shows, he says, "is more due to its own timidity than any kind of regulation. If a newsman is letting the Fairness Doctrine inhibit him, then I suggest he might be in the wrong business."

Clearly, the notion of the federal government as overseer of the nation's radio and TV news and public-affairs programming is an ominous one. Yet, as Fred Friendly has noted, "the power of the major broadcasters is so awesome that the thought of their exercising it totally unchecked is hard to accept." Though the exercise of federal power is relatively visible and under continual outside scrutiny, network power is exercised largely invisibly.

Opinions differ, but it seems to many that the Fairness Doctrine doesn't need to have an inhibiting effect on the honest pursuit of news and public affairs by radio and TV stations. "If you want to go out and report," says Edwin Newman, "you go out and report." And some observers regard the Doctrine as a useful reminder to broadcasters of their public accountability as beneficiaries of federally sanctioned monopolies. From that point of view, it would appear to be a small price to pay for a mechanism that guarantees to outsiders at least a modicum of access to the nation's airwaves.

From another point of view, any infringement of the First Amendment rights of any newsman seems a very high price to pay for what may be a doubtful benefit. The Fairness Doctrine, from this angle, appears to contain at least the seed of government control of the news.

Keep the Fairness Doctrine or dump it? There are problems—and dangers—either way. Americans will eventually have to decide which course seems less risky.

Background

THE MISS AMERICA PAGEANT

A distinguished author explains its
perennial appeal for millions of men
and women
by Isaac Asimov

Every year the Miss America pageant (NBC, September 6) glues an incredible number of men and women to the seats in front of the television set.

Why?

I can't believe it's through an abstract interest in beauty. It isn't the fascination of watching well-proportioned girls in bathing suits. Nor (in the case of the women who watch) is it an absorption in the vast array of intellectual talents displayed by the contestants.

Do I know this because I have studied the situation deeply? Have I delved into sociological theory? Am I an expert on human reactions? Have I interviewed a well-chosen sampling of the viewing public?

No, to all these things. What I have done is to perform what the physicists call a "thought experiment." I have imagined something that will never happen except in the imagination and I have seen whether there is some obvious conclusion I can come to.

Suppose all those pretty girls come out, just as they always do, smiling and dimpling, demure in their bathing suits, walking regally, pirouetting daintily, making little speeches, answering little questions—everything exactly as is, with two exceptions: (1) None of them wears an identifying sash, so that you don't know who any of them are. (2) No winners are announced.

Please ask yourself how much of the fun would be gone, if you didn't know who was who, or who won. How much would you watch? I think you would watch very little, if at all, and what you did watch you would find very dull.

Any contest in which you are interested is one in which *you* are involved, and what you want to prove is that *you* are better than the other person. Whomever you root for represents *you;* and when he wins, *you* win.

The identification might be very straightforward, since you might root for your fellow countryman to beat the foreigner, without knowing the actual merits of the case otherwise. All things being equal, you root for your own sex, your own culture, your own locality. *You* are in the ring or on the field or at the chessboard or before the judges, and you rely on the contestant to represent *you* with greater skill than the real you has and to make it possible for *you* to win.

If the nature of the case makes it difficult to identify with one contestant over another (how do you see one horse rather than another representing *you?*), you set up artificial criteria. You bet money on one particular horse or another, making your choice for any of a number of reasons (a careful consideration of form, the colors of the jockey, the dream you had last night). After that, that horse is *you*. It carries *your* money (and with what do you identify more closely than with *your* money?) on its nose.

Of course, any contest in which you begin by identifying with a contestant for patriotic, ideological, local or trivial reasons can be made still more interesting, if you sharpen the identification by risking money.

All this applies to the Miss America contest, where each contestant is identified by a state. There can't help but be a bit of personal satisfaction for a native of Bismarck to see Miss North Dakota looking pretty and doing well.

But looking pretty and doing well is not enough; mere identification does not in itself satisfy. There has to be victory as well. If Bert Parks ever said, "All you contestants are so pretty and so talented, you all tie for first prize," he'd be run out of town.

It isn't, after all, how you play the game that counts in those contests where *you* are participating vicariously. It's whether you win or lose.

Granted that the Miss America contest provides identification plus the suspense of perhaps winning and the possible glory of actually winning, why is it more popular than another kind of contest could be?

In my opinion, this is because it offers a kind of identification that is both more intimate and more universal than almost anything else can conceivably be. The contest carries with it, therefore, our most subtle and important hopes for victory.

Our society places great stress on beauty as the road to a woman's success in snagging a man. Women are conditioned to displaying and accentuating their physical assets unmercifully, and men are conditioned to being affected by them.

The Miss America contest becomes the drama of the universal marketplace of sexual success, with the contestants representing the most choice offerings one can find. (Put that way, it sounds demeaning to women and, as a matter of fact, feminists do find beauty contests demeaning.)

And we all participate in that kind of marketplace.

Each male viewer can pick the girl whose sales display appeals to him, if he is not irrevocably bound to state patriotism. He can make a mental purchase, and then see if the official judges are wise enough to agree that he is a shrewd buyer and has made a bargain.

Each female viewer is watching the "professionals" of their group, so to speak, the ones that look best in the marketplace. Each woman viewer can identify with the one contestant who represents her own particular style brought closer to perfection (or the style she wishes she had).

Each victory then is an affirmation of the desperate need of everyone to do well in the marketplace of the sexes—in the game of the Miss America contest, if not in real life.

Background

"FEAR ON TRIAL"
The case that ended blacklisting on television is recalled by the lawyer who won it
by Louis Nizer

[*On Thursday, October 2, CBS presents "Fear on Trial," a drama special based on the successful lawsuit by John Henry Faulk against Aware, Inc., for falsely labeling him pro-communist and thus ruining his broadcasting career. To supplement your viewing of the program, we are providing the following background information. Ed.*]

Sincerity and inner conviction are the lubricants of persuasion. Therefore, I have never thought of trial lawyers as actors who merely simulate emotions.

Yet two great actors have played me in trials that were turned into plays and television specials. Van Heflin played my role in "A Case of Libel," based on the Quentin Reynolds-Westbrook Pegler case. At the end of the show's run on Broadway, he and the cast suggested I play myself on the last night. I declined, saying, "I can't. I'm not the type!"

How true. Van Heflin had sat in my office (when clients were not there) and studied my mannerisms. He had come to court to observe me. He had made notes. But when he played the part, it was all Van Heflin. I discovered nothing of myself in it. And good that was; *he* was the type.

I am sure the same applies to George C. Scott, who plays me in the Faulk case, a CBS special called "Fear on Trial." He too will live up to the image far better than I could.

No matter how brilliant the television presentation of this case, which put an end to blacklisting on television, a subtle point cannot be depicted. It involves an important principle that I will explain here, to supplement the drama.

Blacklisters justified their conduct by asserting their right not to hire communists. They turned the table on "liberals" by asking, "Would you hire a Nazi to appear on your station if you owned one?"

This caused some stuttering—then an attempt to find a fallacy. "No, but the trouble is you weren't sure he *was* a communist." This argument was quickly batted down. "It is libelous, in law, to call someone a communist who isn't. Just as it is to call someone a Nazi who isn't. Don't set up a falsehood as a straw man. *Assume* that the performer is a communist or a Nazi. Won't you concede our right to blacklist him? Must we hire him though we detest his principles? Must we afford him moneys that, because of his fanaticism, may flow into the coffers of his party and undermine our government?"

John Henry Faulk (left) and his counsel Louis Nizer outside New York's State Supreme Court in 1962. Faulk was awarded $3.5 million in damages, but the award was later reduced to $550,000 (Wide World)

The blind spot in this argument is that, as an individual, you have a right not to hire anyone even for illogical reasons. It is enough that you do not like his hair, his clothes, even the color of his tie, or that he wears none. When you hire a woman, even her size or high-pitched voice may be enough to reject her. She has no legal grievance because you exercised discretion, no matter how arbitrarily.

But if you arrange with other potential employers not to hire her—that is an illegal boycott. You may not close the door to her employment by combining with others to go along with your judgment, whether your judgment is sound or whether it is arbitrary. What is an absolute private right of decision becomes illegal when you give it the power of collective action.

This is not a new principle. It is true in other areas of law. For example, the corner grocer may raise his prices outrageously, if he wishes. We depend on competition to bring him to his senses. The customer will simply patronize some other grocer. But suppose all the grocers in the neighborhood get together and agree to raise prices. That becomes a violation of the anti-trust laws. It becomes illegal price fixing.

The law considers this so evil that it makes such conduct a crime, punishable by fines and/or jail.

So what an individual may do—that's benign. It turns cancerous when his conduct metastasizes by his conspiring with others to join the boycott.

This was the situation in the John Henry Faulk case. A number of "patriots" banded together to prevent talent agencies, sponsors and TV stations from employing certain performers.

An organization called Aware, Inc., combined with an owner of a supermarket chain to punish any producer, agent or network that used, on any program, a performer who was listed as pro-communist. The supermarket barred the product of the sponsor. The network was deluged with organized postcard protests. A booklet called "Red Channels" was a directory of the political "record" of each performer, director or other talent engaged in radio and TV production. A secret list of names resided in critical desk drawers. All on it were mysteriously ineligible. Advertising agencies, sponsors and television executives were disgusted with the pressure upon them. But economic realities prevented them from becoming martyrs to principle. The pacifier of conscience was: "Why borrow trouble by hiring a listed actor or actress?"

Of course, so evil an enterprise produced corrupt by-products: individuals who checked and cleared a suspect actor for a fee; sloppy accusations so that noncommunists were put on the blacklist and suddenly found that all doors were closed to them; on several occasions, the only exit was suicide.

How one courageous man, Faulk, fought this conspiracy for six years against forbidding odds and exposed it is the story of "Fear on Trial." But independent of that suit is the subtle principle that an individual's precious right of choice may be forfeited if he enlarges his power by collective action.

(Gene Trindl)

This Dropout Has an M.A. from Yale

College didn't prepare Henry Winkler for the role of Fonzie
by Arnold Hano

In a phone booth on the Paramount lot in Hollywood, Henry Winkler is bargaining with Playboy magazine. Playboy wants to shoot a photo story of Winkler in his role as Fonzie, in the ABC nostalgia series *Happy Days*.

"I am flattered as can be," Henry Winkler says over the phone, "but if you want to do 'Fonzie,' I will have to pass. The story will have to be me, not the character." Playboy agrees, and Winkler hangs up triumphantly. He wants to be treated like a star.

It is barely possible that you know neither Henry Winkler nor the character he plays, Fonzie (full name Arthur Fonzarelli), the tough-talking, motorcycle-riding high school dropout on *Happy Days*. *Happy Days* has suddenly become a genuine hit in its second full year, possibly because of the beefing up of the role of Fonzie. Winkler now receives co-star billing, just behind Ron Howard and Tom Bosley, and it is to Winkler that much of the show's fan mail comes.

"Women want to marry me," he says. "People name dogs, cats, birds after Fonzie. I was asked to join Hell's Angels. Fans send me gifts."

Not that he needs gifts. Winkler's salary has grown from several hundred dollars a week two years ago to several thousand a week today. "I love the fact I can go into a restaurant and I don't have to order the $3.95 special."

On personal-appearance tours, he is mobbed by young people. The first time he went on tour, he arrived at the Little Rock airport at 11:30 at night, and 2000 screaming people greeted him.

"A woman pasted herself to me, and I had to carry her like baggage."

Winkler asked the woman, "You want to let go?"

"No," she said. "I'll never get this opportunity again."

The crowds no longer number 2000. Winkler claims that more than 70,000 were on hand in Milwaukee. Whether there were actually that many or not, "It is a heightening experience," he says.

Perhaps he needs heightening experiences. Winkler is 5 feet 6½ inches tall and weighs 134 pounds. At Dallas he got out of the studio-rented limousine and a girl said, "Oh, you're so short." Winkler related the incident to a fan magazine, which promptly ran an article entitled "Is Fonzie Too Short For You?" Six thousand fans assured the editors he wasn't.

There's one more odd sign of stardom: rumors of his death. His sister, Beatrice, received a phone call last summer from Boston telling her that Henry had been killed. Later Winkler received articles from Australian magazines reporting his death in a car crash. An Omaha radio station had him dead from an overdose of drugs. Both AP and UPI recently phoned ABC-TV looking into rumors of his death. Winkler finds it all pretty funny. "It's great. If people want to spend that much time on my death, I'm flattered."

Actually, fame is not all that great, nor always funny. "Stardom is not easy to handle," he says. "If you start thinking you're more than you are, the cockiness will kill you."

Winkler's problem is that he thinks he's less than he is. "Somewhere along the way, I decided I'm second rate. I'm not good enough. I'd like to be as self-confident as Fonzie."

But he is not Fonzie and he understands the difference. "I know nothing about motorcycles. I have an education. Fonzie is a dropout. I refuse to be that *macho* in my life. Fonzie is afraid of nothing."

Winkler is afraid of many things. When his New York agent said to him on September 1, 1973, "All right, Henry, it's time for you to go to Hollywood," Henry Winkler was terrified.

"What do they want with a short Jewish kid with a big nose?" he asked.

Henry Winkler is short and Jewish, but he's not really a kid. He was 30 years old on October 30.

He was born in 1945, the only son of Harry and Ilse Winkler. Harry Winkler, with his wife, left Nazi Germany in 1939 and went to New York. The Winklers have always been reasonably wealthy. The family car was a Packard. Henry attended a private prep school when he wasn't in school in Lausanne, Switzerland. Henry was supposed to follow in his father's footsteps. Do well in school. Take over the family lumber business.

Henry turned out to be a sensitive youngster, easily teased by friends. "I cried myself to sleep many nights. I'd think of killing myself, so they'd all be sorry."

His decision to become an actor triggered a family fuss. "My father and I re-created all the great wars of history," he says. "My mother was more subtle. She'd fix breakfast for me—eggs, toast and guilt."

As a result, doubt plagued him. "In college I knew I wasn't good enough. When I auditioned for Yale to get my master's in drama, I knew I wasn't going to be accepted. The first day at Yale they told us. 'A lot of you aren't going to make it.' I packed my bags."

He was graduated from Yale in 1970 and immediately joined the Yale Repertory Theatre company, earning $175 a week. Later he did New York theater and made two films, which he describes as terrible. Radio and television commercials kept him alive.

But it all began to change when his agent suggested he go to Hollywood. At first he balked.

"Every day for 16 days my agent would say 'Go' and I would say 'No.'" He finally flew out on September 18, 1973, with a thousand dollars to last him a month. He lived on the cushions of a couch in a friend's room. When the friend moved her boy friend in, Henry slept in the bathroom. But 17 days after he'd arrived, he went to work in a *Mary Tyler Moore Show* episode. Then came a *Bob Newhart* episode and the pilot of *Friends and Lovers*.

On October 29, 1973, his agent, Joan Scott, sent him over to Paramount to read for *Happy Days*.

"I sat, waiting to be called. Micky Dolenz, from *The Monkees*, went in, his hair greased back like the '50s. He was taller than I. Finally it was my turn. They said, 'How are you?' and I said, 'See that sweat stain? That's how scared I am. What am I doing here? You don't want me. You want a big shot.'"

The next day—his 28th birthday—he was hired as Fonzie.

He took quick control of the role. In costume they wanted him to wear a cloth jacket and penny loafers.

"How can I play a tough with penny loafers?" he asked.

"Oh," they said, "we'll raise the heel half an inch."

He flew back to New York and got his black boots. The cloth jacket became a leather jacket.

Fonzie's success has given Winkler a springboard. He made a TV film, "Katherine," and won critical acclaim. He has turned down two series offers, one an ABC-Paramount spinoff of the Fonzie character, and the other based on the New York cop Serpico. He says he'll work two more years on *Happy Days,* then turn to feature films.

He is not always an easy actor to work with. In the *Newhart* episode, he didn't like his lines, found he could not get the director to change them, and stormed off to one of the show's producers, who told him to play them any way he wanted to. "The director hates me to this day," Winkler says.

Recently, on the *Happy Days* set, he discovered that some of his lines had been chopped out. Angered, he flung his script down and shouted, "They cut me out of the scene!" Ron Howard—who is a Winkler admirer—pulled Henry aside and told him to cool it.

Marion Ross, who plays the *Happy Days* mother, has also witnessed Winkler's temperament. "When Henry feels crowded, he'll make cutting, rude, sarcastic, remarks. When he directs them to me, I say, 'I don't like that. I don't like you, Henry.' "

Most of the time Marion Ross likes and admires Henry very much. "I'm watching a young actor who's going to be famous."

Adulation—from his fans, from his peers—has come to Henry Winkler. Is this why he acts?

"Part of it is adulation. But when I'm doing the work, I don't think about the adulation. I think about creating the perfect character in the sky. About creating the perfect energy. What an artist can do with his paintbrush and his imagination and his eyes, I can do. My whole body is the paintbrush. I must do it all. I'm driven."

Winkler lives in a bare one-bedroom apartment in West Los Angeles, with his stereo equipment and his 11 plants. He talks and plays music to them. The plants are all healthy and thriving.

He wishes he could say the same for himself. He dates women and often ends up in what he calls "love/anguish," an unrequited passion for an indifferent girl. He writes "the worst poetry you ever read," which he sends to women who don't want to read it.

"I get so confused I start to freak out sometimes. I feel very alone in a crowd. I want someone to say it's OK. Except it can't come from someone. It has to come from me. *I* have to say, 'You're OK, Henry.' "

And he remembers what Stella Adler told his class at Yale: "There is a little devil inside you who wants to destroy you." The thing inside, says Winkler, is self-doubt.

The battle goes on.

FACT
OR
FICTION?

Truth may be the first victim when
television "docudramas" rewrite history
by Bill Davidson

I have long since reformed, but I began my career in journalism as a writer of lies for a sportscaster named Bill Stern, who, in renown at least, was the Howard Cosell of his day. Every week, another writer and I—on Stern's direction—would unabashedly make up so-called

true sports stories, mostly about historical characters who were dead and could not protest. One of my classics was about Abraham Lincoln, who, having been assassinated at Ford's Theater in Washington, regained consciousness just long enough to say to Secretary of War Stanton, "Tell General Abner Doubleday not to let baseball die." After that whopper, NBC ordered Stern to label his dramatizations "sports *legends*," but his weekly radio show continued to prosper.

Now, with the age of "docudrama," "actuality drama," or whatever it may be called, the broadcasting industry seems to have come full cycle. There it was again, the word "legend," as in "The Legend of Valentino" on ABC-TV last fall. Rudolph Valentino was introduced as a starving house burglar (actually he began as a fairly successful hustler and movie bit player); his benefactress, June Mathis, was portrayed as a beautiful minor writer who went back to obscurity in Brooklyn to suffer her unrequited love for Valentino (actually she was fat and ugly, one of the most powerful screenwriters in the history of the movies, and much more influential than Valentino); etc., etc., etc.

But ABC at least had the good grace and honesty to label its Valentino picture "a romantic fiction." The problem is that too many other blockbuster network docudramas *also* are tainted with romantic fiction, but, just as with Bill Stern's tall tales, they are presented to the public as essentially true stories.

Last November, for example, NBC gave us "Eric," about a real-life young man who died after a courageous struggle against leukemia. The two-hour film began with the flat-out statement that "this is a true story," yet the boy's name was changed, the locale of his battle for life was transposed from Connecticut and New York to the State of Washington, chronology was altered, the unpleasant but most inspiring facts of Eric's ordeal were excised, his athletic prowess as a soccer player was blatantly exaggerated in a scene just before his death, and—most inexcusable of all—there was a tender love story between Eric and a nurse named Mary Lou, which according to the boy's mother, Doris Lund, didn't happen as it was portrayed.

Earlier came "I Will Fight No More Forever" on ABC, which at first viewing seemed to be a noble, historically accurate look at the persecution of Chief Joseph and the Nez Percé Indians by the U.S. Army in the late 1870s. The show's sponsor, the Xerox Corporation, even sent out printed classroom guides for use by schoolchildren throughout the country. But then the historians were heard from. They complained that not only were there incorrect juxtapositions of time and place in the docudrama, but that even attitudes and recorded events had been distorted. For one thing, Chief Joseph's pursuer, General Oliver O. Howard, was shown as a liberal in his thinking toward Indians; but actually, at the time of the events depicted, he was one of the Army's hardliners, dedicated to the use of all means to defeat the Nez Percé. Another typical historian's complaint: the show opened with the murder of an Indian by a white settler, who later was killed in an act of vengeance by the Indian's

James Whitmore and Ned Romero (as Chief Joseph) in "I Will Fight No More Forever" (ABC)

son. Historically, a Nez Percé Indian *was* murdered, but his son's revenge was exacted not on the actual malefactor but on 19 other innocent settlers in the area.

How about "Babe" on CBS, the "true story" of the great woman athlete Babe Didrikson and her valiant losing fight against cancer with the help of her wrestler husband, George Zaharias? As CBS vice president Steve Mills told me, "We frankly set out to make this a warm, idyllic, unusual love story, from the facts as supplied by Zaharias himself. I guess he can't be blamed for remembering only the good things of the marriage." Unfortunately, too many sportswriters were witness to the frequent storminess of the Didrikson-Zaharias relationship and they complained, in effect, that Hollywood had made a sugar-coated Disneyized version of what essentially was an *All in the Family* conflict, with tragic overtones.

Similar accusations of truth-bending have been leveled against nearly all of this season's docudramas, among them "The Silence," "Fear on Trial," "Foster and Laurie," "The Deadly Tower," "Collision Course," and "Guilty or Innocent: The Sam Sheppard Murder Case." Swipes have been taken in advance at "Helter Skelter" (the dramatization of Vincent Bugliosi's book about the Charles Manson murders) and "Return to Earth" (the story of astronaut Buzz Aldrin's emotional breakdown after walking on the moon) and "Farewell to Manzanar" (a personal reminiscence of our controversial concentration camps for Japanese-American citizens during World War II).

Does this mean that the docudrama is more drama than docu? Probably yes.

Are facts sometimes distorted to make a better story? Probably yes.

Is the American public deliberately being misled by representations that these films are in fact true stories? Probably yes.

My answers to all three questions are qualified because there are some extenuating circumstances in what is an ages-old conflict between hard fact and dramatic license in all forms of theater, dating back to William Shakespeare and beyond. There are no better illustrations of this problem than the two most challenged docudramas of the season: "Fear on Trial" and "Guilty or Innocent: The Sam Sheppard Murder Case," which, incidentally, has the highest Nielsen rating of any TV movie so far this season.

"Fear on Trial," you will recall, was CBS's *mea culpa* about how it contributed to the anti-communist blacklisting of radio-TV personality John Henry Faulk in 1956, and his long court fight for vindication. The show, though generally praised, has been accused of selective condensation to the point where important CBS witnesses against Faulk (and on the side of the blacklisters) were eliminated. Also, there has been considerable criticism of the not-quite-accurate handling, in the docudrama, of Faulk's estranged wife, who drops out of sight midway through the script, whereas she was in fact in the courtroom for at least part of the trial.

David Rintels is the writer of "Fear on Trial." He also is the respected president of the Writers Guild West. Rintels told me, "It's been a bitter, galling experience for me to be accused of falsifying facts. I had to tell a story condensing six or seven years into a little less than two hours, which means I could just barely hit the major highlights. I did what I think all writers should do—present the *essence* of the facts and capture the truth of the general story. As it was, CBS didn't come out looking too good, even though I couldn't include all the details. Attorney Louis Nizer's summation to the jury took more than 12 hours. I had to do it in three minutes.

"As for Faulk's wife, the divorce was so messy that I made the judgment call that it would be better to eliminate her from the latter stages of the story, rather than dredge up painful problems for a lot of people. I stuck to the record, except in intimate scenes for which there was no record—and that's what writers are paid to do. I'll go to my grave believing I dealt honestly with the overall facts."

The defenders of NBC's Sam Sheppard docudrama also claimed the right to winnow out the truth as they saw it, in the interests of necessarily compressed storytelling. The main beef against the film was that it overexaggerated newsmen's outrageous behavior in the courtroom *during* the trial, whereas the U.S. Supreme Court's landmark Sheppard decision had also cited "massive pretrial publicity" as an important factor bearing on the inability of the defendant to get a fair trial.

Lesley Warren and Franco Nero in "The Legend of Valentino" (ABC)

To Louis Rudolph (who wrote the story and developed the project), it made more sense dramatically to play up visible courtroom disturbances by the press rather than concentrating on the difficult-to-photograph pretrial transgressions by late columnist Bob Considine and others. "It all amounts to the same thing," he told me, "and every word we used in the disturbance sequences came out of the transcript of the trial." He admitted some exaggeration for dramatic effect, and executive producer Harve Bennett added, "We *did* select only certain scenes from the transcript for emphasis—but they were all true."

The truth. There indeed are varying versions of it, as writer Ernest Kinoy found when he wrote the script of ABC's "Collision Course," in which Henry Fonda plays Douglas MacArthur and E. G. Marshall is a credible Harry Truman. Kinoy says he faithfully followed both the MacArthur and Truman memoirs in depicting the events before and after the fateful meeting of the General and the President on Wake Island at the height of the Korean War. "But then," said Kinoy before the program was telecast, "I was faced with the meeting itself, which took place inside a Quonset hut on the island with absolutely no one else present, not even a military secretary. I made up that intrinsic key scene, based on what I knew had happened afterwards when Truman fired MacArthur. The Truman partisans have one idea of the truth of that meeting in the Quonset hut and the MacArthur admirers have their version—so undoubtedly I'll be slammed by both." He was, and apparently with good reason, because the version of the meeting that Truman developed later strayed a good distance from the facts.

John Henry Faulk loved "Fear on Trial." After all, it was his version of what had happened. Astronaut Edwin (Buzz) Aldrin isn't quite so sure about ABC's interpretation of his inability to cope with life after leaving the space program, even though the film "Return to Earth" is a dramatization of his own book and he served as consultant to the TV project. (The movie has not yet been shown on TV.) Aldrin said, "On the whole, I'm satisfied with the picture, but condensation sometimes alters the truth. For example, you're left at the end thinking I'm still a mixed-up guy emotionally, when by now I'm actually recovered and coping quite well. Also, there's a romantic scene at the end in which I'm walking down a beach hand in hand with my ex-wife. It never happened that way. In fact, I'd already told her I wanted a divorce and was going to marry someone else."

Brandon Stoddard, vice president in charge of TV movies at ABC, has his own version of the facts in the Aldrin docudrama. He told me, "In normal film structure, we'd show a man slowly falling apart, destroying his family, but fighting back and recovering. But we didn't do it that way because it didn't happen that way at that time. Aldrin then was a man suffering deep depression and I felt we *had* to show a depressive as he actually is. It doesn't help the film but it is accurate."

Of all the docudrama experts I spoke with, Stoddard made the most sense. He frankly admitted that his network does "actuality" movies because they're easier to sell to a potential audience during pre-broadcast promotion "if there are actual names and events that are familiar to people to begin with." He said. "We should not be held to the absolute truth of pure documentaries, because we're in the business of making *movies,* and audiences watch movies to be moved, to get involved with characters who live and breathe and whom you like and don't like. I'm not a reporter. If it's pure documentary you're looking for, the news department does it better. Docudramas get much higher ratings. I consider them to be historical fiction as opposed to history—and historical fiction always far outsells history at the bookstores."

Stoddard added, "On the other hand, we are very aware of the terrible danger and responsibility involved in doing our kind of historical fiction. By using dramatic license, we can take a point of view that could affect the attitudes of millions of people. For example, we have '21 Hours at Munich' in development. It's about the massacre of the Israeli athletes by Arab terrorists at the 1972 Olympics. Since we have to tell at least part of the story from the point of view of one of the Arabs, we can't create sympathy for him. We *must* get the message across that with acts of terrorism, no one wins in the end. I'm not sure it will work, and if it doesn't, we'll yank it as a docudrama."

The problem is that, given the success of the docudramas, no one in the industry is ready yet to openly label their product "historical fiction"—except possibly in the rare case of a "Legend of Valentino," in which the truth was *so* distorted that to do otherwise would have been ridiculous. Thus, CBS's "Helter Skelter" (an upcoming film about the Charles Manson murders) begins with actor George DiCenzo saying, "You are about to see a dramatization of actual facts in which certain names have been changed. But the story is ture." The story is *not* all true. At the very least, because of pending lawsuits, certain fictional adjustments had to be made.

What with possible docudramas coming up on Senator Joseph McCarthy, the Attica prison riots and Martin Luther King Jr., television experts in the academic community are justifiably disturbed. One such expert is psychologist Dr. Victor B. Cline of the University of Utah, who pioneered in studies of the effect of TV violence on children. Dr. Cline told me, "The very real danger of these docudrama films is that people take it for granted that they're true and—unlike similar fictionalized history in movies and the theater—they are seen on a medium which also presents straight news. No matter how much they call these movies 'drama,' they're really advocacy journalism. They can't help reflecting the point of view of the writer or the studio or the network. I think they should carry a disclaimer to the effect that the story is not totally true but based on some of the *elements* of what actually occurred."

But, as we learned from Orson Welles's panicking the country with his radio version of "War of the Worlds" in 1938 (and recently done in semifictional docudrama form on ABC-TV), even that won't prevent people from believing what they see on television.

The Lives and Loves of Salvatore and Cherilyn, Part IV

by Rowland Barber

What has happened so far: In Part I, you remember, our hero and heroine, having long since changed their names to Sonny and Cher, toured Middle America hand-in-hand to dispel the rumors that they were "the battling Bonos." When they returned to Hollywood to launch the third season of *The Sonny & Cher Comedy Hour,* Cher said: "There is truly magic in our act." Sonny said: "What I really want to be is a movie actor." He was turned down for the part he wanted in "The Godfather Part II."

In Part II their act came apart, magic and all, along with their 10-year marriage. Cher sued Sonny for divorce. Sonny sued Cher for $24 million for breach of contract. CBS didn't sue anybody, just heaved a corporate sigh and announced the termination of the show. Cher went to Europe. Sonny went to ABC. Cher said: "I love Son very much, but I had to leave him." Sonny said: "What I really want to be is a movie actor." He was turned down for the part he wanted in "Earthquake."

Part III. Next year, 1975. CBS unveiled the *Cher* show, with Cher facing an audience alone for the first time in her life. "The closer I got to going on," she said, "the more I missed Sonny and the scareder I got." Sonny called to wish her luck. He had plenty of time to watch *Cher* because ABC had canceled *The Sonny Comedy Revue.* Cher missed Sonny so much she parted with her interim consort, record tycoon David Geffen, and married rock singer Gregg Allman. Cher left Gregg Allman. *Cher* began to slip in the ratings. Cher went back to Gregg Allman. That did not help the ratings. CBS emitted a corporate chortle and announced the final solution: Sonny would come back to Cher and they would star in *The Sonny & Cher Show.*

Their reunion was strictly professional, not personal. Conditions of the reunion included (1) Sonny's dropping his lawsuit against Cher and (2) Cher's agreeing to

(Frank Teti)

make a personal-appearance tour with Sonny during the summer of '76. Shortly afterward, condition (2) was tabled when Cher announced that she was pregnant. The Allmans expect their firstborn this summer. "I can wait," said Sonny. He did not mention being a movie actor.

And now (for those persevering souls who are still with us), we turn to our next installment—Part IV, subtitled "The Sanctity of Divorce," the episode that dares to ask the question "Is that old magic really back?"

Cher is back in her Television City dressing room, seven hours before she and Sonny will face an audience "together again for the first time." Swaddled in a pink terrycloth robe, she is curled up on a corner of a recessed divan. The dressing room is heavily mirrored and carpeted and heavy with the scent of roses, with a scattering of tropical and Amerind motifs.

Exactly how did the idea of the CBS reunion originate? I ask her. Who started the ball rolling? Network programmer? Agent? Manager? Lawyer? Or Salvatore "Svengali" Bono, the little old image creator?

"None of the above," said Cher. "It was me. My idea. I made the decision after I'd done four *Cher* shows, last fall. Nothing to do with the ratings. Doing a show alone was more than I could handle. I had to be into everything, from helping on scripts to picking the music. And they had me doing a monologue. That's not like me, to be out there alone making with the jokes.

"I have to have fun working. Well, I wasn't having any fun.

"For example, I had this guest—it wouldn't be fair to give his name—a real star: movies, stage, TV series, the whole shot. I was playing like a hippie and he was a very straight guy. I threw him an ad-lib and he got uptight, really ticked off. He said, 'You can't say that because I don't have a line to come back with, so unless you write me a line, I'd appreciate it if you'd just cut that out.'

"After he said that, I was so nervous I felt really yucky. Now, if it had been Son, it would have been a funny bit *because* of the ad-lib! From that time on, no matter how much we rehearsed—and I was really busting my butt— I could never get to where I felt confident in what I was doing, you know?

"So Paulette [her secretary] and I were in New York on a quick trip, between taping shows four and five. All of a sudden I knew what I had to do. I picked up the phone and tracked down Sonny, who was out doing one-nighters, in Denver, and I said, 'Son, I've got this crazy idea. . . .'"

"What was his reaction?"

"Why don't you go ask Sonny? His dressing room is next door."

I went next door. Shuttle diplomacy. It was indeed like going from Little Egypt, sultry with the sweet murk of roses, to Tel Aviv, cool, pragmatic, starkly contemporary. Sonny had just changed from a Charlie Brown costume to his accustomed blue jeans. Susie Coelho, his current companion, a slim, quiet girl of dazzling dark beauty, is on the phone with somebody at their house; perhaps, she says aside to Sonny, they should go home and feed Scruffy during the lunch break. "Nah," says Sonny, "let's stay and talk."

Salvatore Bono may have the hair and mustache of a raunchy Mafioso, a history of record-plugging and rock-and-rolling, and the credentials of a canny dealmaker. But when he talks, with that undisguisable gosharoony voice of his, he is the apotheosis of Henry Aldrich and Andy Hardy.

What was his reaction when Cher reached him in Denver last fall with her "crazy idea"? "I thought—and I said, 'As long as I know you, Cher, I will never cease to be amazed by you.' Then I said, 'Well, why not?' Doing a show together made a lot of sense. I wasn't having any fun by myself, and I knew the terrible demands on Cher of doing a single. I saw her going down. They were trying to make a producer out of her. Cher is an intuitive performer and terribly insecure if she's made to do anything else.

"Even her singing was affected. She was putting herself into a key that was right on the fringe of her range, forcing her power. Now she's back where she belongs. Her solo today was terrific."

Earlier, I had watched the taping of her solo, "Breaking Up Is Hard to Do," with uncommon interest. In the run-through, Sonny was close at her side, coaching her, coaxing her, supporting her. When the tape rolled, he stood between cameras 2 and 3 conducting her performance with the loving ferocity of a Leonard Bernstein. Is this any way to run a divorce? "The important thing is," Sonny continued, "Cher is having fun again."

Back west, all the way next door, to the hothouse. Cher, indulging herself in a toothpick lunch of cold shrimp and chunks of papaya, was saying: "I've been looking at some of the old *Sonny & Cher* shows. Do you know that in the monologues, the openings and closings, I never talked? I said like three words to Sonny's 25, and then only to Son, never to the audience. Now I feel comfortable about talking. For one thing, I don't have to be so bitchy any more. That was a character write-in so I could have something to hide behind.

"We have nothing to hide. We can be different now and show how we've grown—not by our wishes, but by the fact that it's really happened. You know what? I really love papaya." She laughed. "No I mean, I have to say that my life right now is just perfect. Gregory's coming home from North Carolina tomorrow. The burdens of the show are out of my hands. I can do stupid things and laugh again."

Shuttling east, Little Egypt to Tel Aviv. Sonny: "There's been just one insulting comment on Cher and me being back together. People like Johnny Carson who say we've done it only for the money. What the hell is *he* doing? Sure we work for money, I can't deny that. Cher and I want to make a good living at our trade, which happens to be television. We weren't making it alone, so we'll try it together. Professional integrity is our first concern, not money.

"I'm enjoying myself because this time around I'm just a hired hand. No partnership, no ownership position. I lost a bundle on *The Sonny Comedy Revue* because of deficit financing. But this is terrific, here."

Once again, equal time in the other dressing room. Cher: "I try to take everything in my stride. People are entitled to their opinions. But a thing I read last night really hurt my feelings. An article in the London Observer. The *Cher* show is starting to run in England, and I guess they figure a piece like this, about me, will stir up interest. What rotten stuff! Like—'This woman lives in a two-million-dollar house, spends 500 bucks a week on manicures, drives one of her three Ferraris when she's not using her Rolls-Royce or Mercedes, has 600 pairs of shoes, and 1000 beaded dresses, and she's not happy, and isn't it a shame?' I sure as hell wouldn't like anybody like that. Thank God she doesn't resemble anybody I know. But why do they do it to me? First I wanted to throw the paper in the trash, then burn it, then I just sat and cried.

"But too many good things are happening to let that bug me. Do you realize that Chastity will be seven years old in a couple of months? She's so happy that her mom and dad are working together again."

Twenty feet away, in the other country, Sonny made a final observation. "You know why Cher and I are so interesting? Our lives are laid wide open for the public. We have no secrets. When we go out there in front of our first audience tonight, we'll be telling them everything they already knew about Sonny and Cher but were afraid to say."

That night the delays seemed endless. The 300-odd people in the audience remained remarkably patient while crews fiddled with the set and the lights and ran test after test with stand-ins. Behind the cyclorama that enclosed the stage, in the dark passageway by the dressing-room doors, I waited for the stars to emerge. Sonny popped out of his door, alone. He was probably nervous. I said something inanely reassuring like, "Well, here we go again." He gave me a strained grin, then disappeared back into his dressing room. Five minutes later Cher came out, alone, knocked on Sonny's door. He came out. "Good luck, Son," she said. "Good luck, Cher," said Sonny. They shook hands, then retreated to their respective hiding places.

The studio rocked with applause, cheers, whistles, when Sonny and Cher came out in the dazzling light at the top of the show. Then the odd thing happened. Sonny said, following the cue card, "Well, folks . . . I don't know if any of you have heard about it, but Cher and I are not married any more." It was a throwaway line, geared for a chuckle of recognition. Instead, there was a beat of silence. Then, out of the audience, on a dying wave, came a many-throated moan. "A-w-w-w—"

Sonny looked sharply out beyond the cameras and the cue cards, stunned by the reaction. Cher's mouth was agape. Sonny stammered: "You—you mean you haven't *heard*? No—no—it's *true!*" He recovered quickly and got back to the script, but nothing was quite the same from that moment on.

It was a deep puzzlement. Did it mean that "national publicity" was not truly national, not all-pervasive, and that in spite of it most people still didn't know about the Bonos? Or did it mean that people did know but refused to accept the truth, and chose instead to nourish the fantasy of the way things used to be? Were they saying, "Please—take us back to Camelot, because if you don't, we won't go with you"?

Only time held the answer. It began to relinquish the answer sooner than anybody expected. The first *Sonny & Cher Show* was reported a lofty No. 7 in the Nielsen ratings. The second show was No. 9, sharing the heights with the Winter Olympics. Then came the reading on their third Sunday outing: Sonny and Cher were in 38th place. *A-w-w-w-w-w-w.*

Since then the ratings have been picking up and the show has been renewed for next year. It looks like installment V is almost inevitable.

(Steven Schapiro)

"Music Changes, But I Don't"

And so, after 26 years on TV, Lawrence Welk has more stations (and more money) than ever
by Dwight Whitney

It is taping day on Stage 54 and not a day on which Lawrence Welk, 73, the North Dakota farm boy who rode to glory on an accordion, normally feels like talking. As Les Kaufman, his press agent of 24 years, is quick to explain, Welk can get very nervous, even testy, on a day like this. It seems that the milk of human kindness, an important component of the Welk personality, tends to curdle under stress. OK to talk to the troops on taping day; interview the wunnerful Champagne Lady if you must; chat with Joe Feeney, the Irish tenor; or find out from Arthur Duncan, the tap dancer, what it's like to be the only black face in the 50-person Welk troupe; but Lawrence? Leave the boss alone unless you want to get your head taken off.

But here I am, below decks in Welk's splendiferous subterranean dressing room, a mahogany-paneled suite inherited from Sonny Bono, and the man is a pussycat. One would have thought he had spent 50 years preparing for this afternoon's chat.

Almost 50 years have gone by since Lawrence and his five-piece band made their debut on that new thing called radio in Yankton, S.D., in 1927, and he is now in his 26th uninterrupted season on TV. He has acquired 10 grandchildren. No wonder he is sweet-dispositioned, full of little jokes, and obviously enjoying himself even though the morning has been ominously slow: director Jim Hobson (23 years with Welk) has barely managed to get through rehearsal on seven of 19 production numbers, leaving a pressure-packed 12 for the afternoon session.

By this time, Lawrence chuckles, he should be used to it. He is particularly chuckley about the dressing-room decor. ABC, the network from whom he rents the facilities with which to tape his syndicated show, is forever doing it over at a cost of thousands just to suit the whim of some star. When, several months later, the star's show is cancelled, Lawrence inherits the space. Some of the ex-tenants have been Tom Jones, Julie Andrews and the Lennon Sisters—during the days when his darling former singers had grown up and, alas, defected to Jimmy Durante.

"I don't feel bad when they build other stars fancy dressing rooms," Welk chortles. "It's just a matter of time before I take them over."

The world is full of what he calls "true believers," folks who contend that when the last viewer has risen up in his wrath and smitten the last temperamental no-talent, can't-sing-the-melody TV star, Lawrence will still be there waving his baton at his "musical family" and pronouncing everything "wunnerful, wunnerful."

Even at 73. Lawrence, how *do* you do it? He smiles gratefully at the question. "I take good care of myself. I play golf. I watch my diet. I swim every day in my heated pool. I love my work." He smiles again. "I guess I must be the only man in TV whose show is seen 52 weeks a year. I still make 32 live [on tape] a year and rerun 20 of them in the summer."

There is enormous pride here. "Only missed twice in 26 years. When the Kennedys were assassinated. My whole life, you might say, is based on longevity. Music changes, but I don't. Most of the people who star with me—my musical family—find they can't get away from me. I'm the father, they're my children. I think we produce a better product that way. . . . When you keep people together for a long time, the work becomes just a little finer."

As he talks, the built-in television screen that monitors what is happening on the stage above keeps flickering. Musical director George Cates is putting the band and the "featured performers" through their paces under the watchful eye of Jim Hobson in the booth, leaving Lawrence free to reminisce.

There is the matter of ABC's having the temerity to drop his show, back in 1971. The very idea of this is

good for a chuckle because it turned out to be such a bonanza for him. With some help from his old friend and syndicator, Don Fedderson, he simply packaged and sold the show himself. Within a year he had a larger audience and was collecting a larger share of the profits than he ever did under the auspices of the network. Today he has a record 261 stations, the overwhelming majority of which are network affiliates, and a long waiting list.

An almost equally happy thought today is the manner in which the "father" has the "children" provided for. Back in 1957 Welk instituted his "profit-sharing" plan. This calls for his company, Teleklew, to contribute a sum equal to 15 percent of the earnings of each member of the musical family into a fund, which is in turn invested in other companies. This year the money is in insurance. The longer a featured performer stays (there are no stars except Lawrence), the more substantial his potential income becomes. This makes it progressively harder for a performer to escape from the "family" into a career of his own.

The catch is that Lawrence pays everybody (with almost no exceptions) union minimum wages. Norma Zimmer, who has been his Champagne Lady for 16 years, still calls him Mr. Welk, still makes union scale (which is $294.50 a week) and considers herself lucky, or so she says. What this means in a less sentimental context is that the cost of talent has been cut to the bone. Teleklew can produce an hour show for less than half what it might cost another supplier, while asking advertising rates comparable to what the networks are asking. Welk's syndicator, Don Fedderson, distributes the show, along with some commercials sold at $50,000 per minute, on the barter system—instead of the stations being paid to broadcast it, they settle for the privilege of peddling some of the spots to their own advertisers.

Upstairs, Joe Feeney, the Irish tenor, is rehearsing his number, "Without a Song," and out-Dennising Dennis Day. Suddenly Lawrence is all ears, behaving as if he were hearing Joe for the first time.

"If I could have gotten this boy when he was young, I could have made him into the world's greatest tenor," he says, sighing. He picks up the phone. "Ask Joe to come down." When Feeney, a small, somewhat stocky, open-faced Irishman, arrives, Lawrence sits him down on the couch and proceeds to give him a singing lesson. It seems that the phrasing on "Without a Song" leaves something to be desired. Joe is attentive and contrite, the small boy vying for Brownie points.

"You are singing it like this," Lawrence says paternally. He demonstrates. "Now I want you to try it like this. *Without—a song—the day will—never end. . . .*" Feeney tries it. "See what I mean?" beams Lawrence. "Wunnerful, wunnerful."

"Not the easiest man to develop into a strong personality," Lawrence says when Feeney has gone. "Came to me 20 years ago from Lincoln, Nebraska. Didn't have any training. Or any money. But I took him on. Now he's got nine kids and a ranch in the Simi Valley. You know, there are some people who just don't have a natural inborn sense of rhythm. I have to give it to them."

Tom Netherton, all 6 feet 5 of him, is doing his thing on the monitor. No problem developing *him* into a strong personality. Tom is young (27), with a big Robert Goulet-like voice, and is Lawrence's current favorite. Lawrence's favorites are as variable as the wind. A few years ago it was Ken Delo and before that Bobby Burgess, the dancer. Among the ladies, no one ever quite came up to the Lennon Sisters, not Norma the Champagne Lady, not even Tanya, who married Larry Welk Jr. The Lennons were special. They embodied everything Lawrence believed entertainment should be, and when they left him, it hurt, despite vigorous and frequent denials. "All that giggling, wriggling supertalent," says one veteran Welkite. "When they left—mostly to have babies—it was almost more than Lawrence could bear."

For his part, Lawrence keeps reaffirming his faith. "Kathy Lennon told me, 'We're not mad at anybody.' They are good girls. Their uncles Ted and Jack are still important parts of our business organization. For me there is no greater joy than taking someone everybody says doesn't stand a chance and making a winner out of them.

"Like the Semonskis. I was in Florida playing a golf tournament when I spotted them. Six little Polish girls from New Jersey. They were terrible, just terrible. Somebody had taught them all wrong. But I saw potential there. I moved them out to my mobile-home-park–restaurant in Escondido and made the older ones singing hostesses. That would give us time to work."

He gives a signal and suddenly the dressing room is alive with Semonskis, giggling, wriggling and ranging in age from 8½ to 19. They are all over him queuing up for the ceremonial kiss. Welk beams. They bow to the press as if on cue, fasten their smiles in place, Welk supplies the pitch, and they tear into "I've Got a Never-Ending Love For You," sung *a capella.*

It is difficult to tell who is more pleased, the girls or Welk. They may have been "terrible" once, but today they look, sound and feel exactly like the Lennon Sisters except that there are more of them. The littlest and most beguiling, Michelle, is even younger than Janet Lennon, the littlest and most beguiling Lennon, was the year she started. Lawrence can see it now, a never-ending supply of Lennons and Semonskis strung out into a musical eternity. Already they are established members of the "family."

"I put them on at first even though they weren't quite ready," he confesses. "I got by by letting the little one dance with me."

What he is working for with the Semonskis, he explains, is "the sound that is exactly right for them, something to hang their hats on. I think they are ready. I think you will see the day when these girls will be able to command $25,000 a night."

Upstairs, the monitor reveals, the Champagne Lady—"to whom I didn't have to teach anything," Lawrence says—is running over a Beatles song: *Love was such an easy game to play / Now I need a place to hide away . . .* Or

the song is running over her. With Norma it is sometimes hard to tell. No matter; it pleases Lawrence. "She has taken wunnerful care of herself," he says. "She is the complete artist. That's the thing with all the members of the musical family. We have a strong in with our viewers. They like this sort of thing."

The run-through finishes with Ken Delo's Jolson medley and Guy Hovis' Elvis imitation. Suddenly the dressing room is full of people. Don Fedderson and his longtime press agent, Les Kaufman, arrive. Fedderson has missed only two Welk tapings in 20 years, he firmly states. Sam Lutz, Welk's executive producer and longtime booker, is in and out. So are Bernice McGeehan, the fan-magazine writer who put together the two best-selling Welk biographies ("Wunnerful, Wunnerful" and "Ah One, Ah Two! Life with My Musical Family"; a third is coming out soon); Rose Weiss, his costume designer; and Lois Lamont, Welk's longtime secretary, who is doing quite a lot of twittering today. Lois is married to a Welk bass player, Russ Klein—which pleases Lawrence. He thinks back to that day in 1945 in Milwaukee when he first tried to hire her. Lois' parents were not about to let their little girl go off on the road with a bunch of crazy musicians.

"I didn't interview Lois," chuckles Lawrence. "Her parents interviewed me. She insisted. They relented. And I had a secretary."

While in a reminiscing mood, he acknowledges that he never really knew what to expect when KTLA, Channel 5 in Los Angeles, invited him to perform on infant television in 1951.

"We were playing at the Aragon Ballroom in Ocean Park at the time," Lawrence says. " 'What's involved?' I asked the station manager. 'Nothing. We just come out and pick you up, that's all.' 'And me?' 'You just *play,*' he said. Well, I just played. And the first thing I knew, 26 years had gone by."

The years have made some dramatic changes, not the least of which is that Welk, the son of a poor German farmer, is many times a millionaire. He used to be self-conscious about his speech and the fact that he never did (as he put it to Joe Feeney) "bother" to learn to speak without an accent. "I decided," he says, "it was an advantage. People appreciate you being exactly what you are."

If Lawrence does not pay his people well, he makes it possible for them to make a few bucks moonlighting. Myron Floren, the accordionist who was once regarded as Welk's heir apparent, can take the band out to, say, the Atlantic City Steel Pier any time he feels like it and draw $25,000 a night. The only catch is in the billing: "Myron Floren and His Orchestra Featuring Members of the Lawrence Welk Orchestra." Consequently they all (with the possible exception of the Semonskis) augment their salaries by moonlighting somewhere (just the Welk name will do it in most cases). Sam Lutz handles the bookings.

"It is good for everyone. They get the money. I get the good will," says Lawrence without batting an eyelash.

But mostly there is that good feeling that he is "helping my musical family." There's Arthur Duncan, for instance, the tap dancer. The thought of this now-not-so-young man and what "a real great natural delivery" he has makes Welk feel mellow and, in this instance, sad.

"You know any place I can buy jokes?" Welk says suddenly. "I mean, is there a collection, is there a book? You see, Arthur has this funny way of saying things. If he won't find himself material, I have to do it for him. . . . Hire a comedy writer?" Lawrence says, frowning. "Well, no, I couldn't do that. It takes away from the homey way

we operate. We like to pick our *own* material and songs."

Lawrence gets up and disappears into the bathroom. The sound of an electric shaver. Showtime approaches. In a minute he emerges, wearing a white-and-brown windowpane jacket and a red tie. Director Hobson's voice comes over the monitor: "Ready, Lawrence?"

Welk is very ready. "I have much to be grateful for," he says. "Everything a man could want in this world." He smiles and is up the circular staircase to work.

A TV Guide Close-Up   SEPTEMBER 23, 1976

PRESIDENTIAL DEBATE   9:30 ABC, CBS, NBC, PBS

President Ford
(Wide World)

Governor Carter
(Wide World)

"Inflation has been cut in half. Payrolls are up, profits are up, production is up, purchases are up . . . we are in the full surge of a sound recovery to steady prosperity"—President Gerald R. Ford in his acceptance speech at the Republican National Convention.

"While inflation has declined from its previous levels, it still remains unacceptably high. The major economic problem, however, is unacceptably high unemployment"—Former Georgia governor Jimmy Carter in an economic position paper, April 1976.

Special

President Ford and Governor Carter debate the economy and other domestic issues in the first of three confrontations. (Republican Vice Presidential candidate Robert Dole and his Democratic counterpart, Walter Mondale, will participate in a single debate at a time and place as yet unspecified.)

The networks are providing live coverage of the debates, which are being sponsored by the League of Women Voters. The site for tonight's is the Walnut Street Theater in Philadelphia.

The format is question-and-answer. A panel of newsmen (unnamed at press time) asks the questions; the candidates have three minutes to answer them, and an additional two minutes to respond to any follow-up questions. Each candidate is allowed to comment briefly

on his opponent's replies, and has three minutes to make a closing statement. There will be no opening remarks.

This is the first debate between Presidential candidates since 1960, when Massachusetts Senator John F. Kennedy challenged Vice President Richard M. Nixon. It is being staged by the League of Women Voters and is eligible for telecasting because of a new interpretation of the equal-time rule by the Federal Communications Commission. The rule, obliging television and radio stations to make their facilities available to all qualified candidates for office, was simply suspended by Congress in 1960. But in this election year, the FCC has said that a debate may be aired so long as it is a legitimate news event rather than a studio confrontation arranged by the broadcasters themselves. (Live)

A TV Guide Close-Up

Clark Gable and Vivien Leigh (Jerry Vermilye)

MOVIE 8:00 ④ ⑳
"GONE WITH THE WIND," PART 1

Hollywood's best-remembered film.

Set during and after the Civil War, "Gone With the Wind" chronicles the devastation of the South and tells of a romance that has become one of the screen's most famous—between fiery Scarlett O'Hara (Vivien Leigh) and dashing Rhett Butler (Clark Gable).

The 1939 movie is also memorable for its vivid moments of wartime spectacle, especially the burning of Atlanta and the panorama of thousands of soldiers lying wounded in a railroad station.

"Gone With the Wind" won eight Oscars, including Best Picture, Actress (Leigh), Supporting Actress (Hattie McDaniel) and Director (Victor Fleming).

The film concludes tomorrow at this time.

Ashley: *Leslie Howard.* Melanie: *Olivia de Havilland.* Mammy: *Hattie McDaniel.* Gerald: *Thomas Mitchell.* Ellen: *Barbara O'Neil.* Frank: *Carroll Nye.* Aunt Pittypat: *Laura Hope Crews.* Dr. Meade: *Harry Davenport.* Charles: *Rand Brooks.* Belle: *Ona Munson.* Prissy: *Butterfly McQueen.* Careen: *Ann Rutherford.* Brent: *George Reeves.* Pork: *Oscar Polk.* Suellen: *Evelyn Keyes.* (3 hours)

A TV Guide Close-Up

Edward Asner and LeVar Burton (ABC)

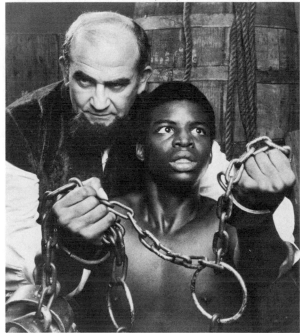

ROOTS 9:00 ❼ ⑧

Debut

The saga of a black-American family.

Adapted from Alex Haley's best-seller, "Roots" dramatizes a century in Haley's family history—from his ancestors' life in 18th-century tribal Africa to their emancipation in the post-Civil War South.

The eight-part drama begins in Africa with the birth of Kunta Kinte, Haley's great-great-great-great-grandfather. For Kunta, village life is carefree in its simplicity and rich in tradition and, at 17, he undergoes the grueling rite of manhood. But soon after his initiation, the slavers arrive—and put Kunta in chains aboard a ship bound for America.

The series will be shown over the next seven evenings.

Cast (Part 1) . . . Kunta: *LeVar Burton.* Kunta's Mother: *Cicely Tyson.* Kunta's Father: *Thalmus Rasulala.* Davies: *Edward Asner.* Slater: *Ralph Waite.* Wrestler: *Ji-Tu Cumbuka.* Brima Cesay: *Hari Rhodes.* Fanta: *Ren Woods.* Nyo Boto: *Maya Angelou.* Kintango: *Moses Gunn.* (2 hours)

In an era of frantic muckraking
in the press . . .

Is Television Doing Its Investigative Reporting Job?

by Neil Hickey

PART I

"Investigative reporting is the sacred cow of journalism in our time," says ABC newsman Brit Hume. American journalists are off on a muckraking binge the like of which hasn't been seen since the century's first decade, when writers like Ida Tarbell, Lincoln Steffens and Upton Sinclair were bending to their task of rooting out malfeasance and malpractice in government and big business.

America is in "the age of the great exaltation of the investigative reporter," said The New York Times's ace investigator, Seymour Hersh, in accepting the Drew Pearson Foundation award for uncovering CIA meddling in Chile. The search for scandal in high places "has become almost obsessive since Watergate," says Newsweek. Journalism schools are crowded with students avid for their own crack at stories like the Pentagon Papers, My Lai, sex in Congress and consumer fraud.

By far the biggest part of this muckraking glut is showing up in newspapers, magazines and books. Television, for whatever reasons (and some of them are valid, say the medium's defenders), is far off the pace in uncovering official villainy. "The state of investigative reporting on television is pitiful," says a network staff producer. "Everybody pays it lip service but practically nothing ever appears on the air. I defy you to name more than a handful of true investigative reports in the whole 30-year history of television."

"Our job is to comfort the afflicted and afflict the comfortable," says Steve Bauman, an investigative newsman at New York's WNEW. "The trouble is, television doesn't do enough of either."

Many local stations, some observers claim, are more involved in undercover reporting than the networks are. In Des Moines, for example, station WHO-TV filmed decoys exchanging food stamps illegally in a four-part series that resulted in federal scrutiny of food-stamp abuse. New York's WABC-TV mounted an elaborate and prolonged exposé of a state school for the mentally retarded called Willowbrook, causing public outcry and

official redress. Elsewhere, stations have hammered away at petty fraud, collusion and conflict of interest among county and municipal officeholders.

But even at the local level, there's less muckraking than meets the eye. "Very few stations are really participating in true investigative reporting," says Gene Strul, news director of WCKT in Miami, which has won Peabody Awards two years in a row for investigative reporting. "Stations set up investigative units with the best of intentions and then, for whatever reasons, they fall into disuse. The investigative reporting that does get done receives a lot of promotion, which misleads people into believing it's far more extensive on television than it really is."

Some network newsmen argue hotly that TV has been as bold and as active as any other medium in producing tough exposés—CBS's "The Selling of the Pentagon," for example; NBC's "Pensions: The Broken Promise"; and ABC's "Fire!" They submit that series like *60 Minutes, ABC News Closeup* and NBC's *Weekend* are doing creative and original reporting on behind-the-scenes stories; that hard-hitting mini-documentaries (e.g., NBC's five-parter on the Teamsters' union, and CBS's three-part study of the Russian wheat deal) have appeared on network nightly news programs from time to time; and that network television, overall, is the possessor of an impressive tradition of robust documentaries going back to "Harvest of Shame" (Edward R. Murrow's 1960 study of migrant workers), "Who Killed Lake Erie?" "The Banks and the Poor" (on public television), "Biography of a Bookie Joint," "The Business of Heroin" and others.

But it's clear that the actual volume of investigative reports on television—week by week—is minuscule in view of the legendary resources, riches and far-flung news-gathering potential of TV journalism; in view also of the fertile plain that stretches before any energetic reporter looking for misdeeds—government, the courts, the military, big business, big labor, the professions.

Critics detect a subtle, pervasive self-censorship at work, growing out of network television's genetic relationship to three important constituencies: the U.S. Government, the affiliated stations and advertisers.

It's the government, the argument goes, that is the benevolent landlord that allows television to graze in such green pastures and produce such brawny profits. And while TV's chieftains may be craven, they are not stupid. They are sensitive to the weapons the government can bring into play against them should an exposé touch the wrong nerves.

The powerful affiliates, for their part, are presumptively more conservative, both temperamentally and politically, than network newsmen and are thus uncomfortable with tough anti-Establishment journalism. So influential indeed are the affiliates that their collective disfavor caused the networks recently to junk their enthusiastic plans for an expansion of the evening news programs to one hour—a move that could have paved the way for more frequent investigative reports.

TV advertisers—many of them multinational corporations and conglomerates—are imagined by critics to take a dim view of reportage that cavils about price-fixing, collusion with regulatory agencies and influence-peddling in the U.S. Congress and abroad.

Some of those accusations are just plain bum raps, say TV's defenders. "We've done reports on every important subject you can possibly mention," says CBS's veteran documentarist Jay McMullen. "And I for one have never been aware of any pressures from advertisers or affiliates or the FCC." Still, there's a whole laundry list of reasons—invoked regularly by TV people and outside observers alike—why the television medium is *not* fully competitive in the muckraking game:

• TV needs pictures, but investigative stories often tend to be encyclopedic and nonvisual affairs with a "talking head" spouting hard-to-follow facts in front of a few incomprehensible graphs and charts.

• An important TV exposé might take six to 12 months of research and undercover legwork, then fail to produce a "smoking pistol" or an airtight case. It could then be junked as too risky or too inconclusive to be put on the air.

• TV, unlike the print media, has an obligation under the Fairness Doctrine to provide opposing views when treating matters of public importance, or when engaging in anything that might be broadly construed as a "personal attack." As a result, tough investigative stories sometimes get "balanced out of existence" and lose their bite. ("The FCC says, 'You have nothing to worry about from us. All we want is fairness, and what's wrong with fairness?' " explains Gene Strul. "What's wrong with it is that a government agency ought not to be able to tell a news organization what it can and cannot do. In a sense, they're serving as censors and they have the weapons to do it.")

• A decent investigative story on the nightly news programs needs four or five minutes (out of 22) to lay out the facts with any clarity or completeness. That's more than networks are willing to commit except for exceptional stories.

• TV has nagging logistical problems that almost defeat the best efforts of undercover reporters. Says documentarist Peter Davis ("The Selling of the Pentagon," "Hearts and Minds"): "If Woodward and Bernstein had shown up at their rendezvous with Deep Throat lugging a camera, lights and sound equipment, the whole Watergate exposé might never have happened. People who want to remain anonymous simply are not going to have their pictures taken, even in disguise."

Underlying all such rationales, of course, lurks the guiding principle that inspirits (or dispirits) the entire television medium: ratings. "There simply is no great appetite for this kind of programming," says a TV executive. "People get bored to tears with corruption stories unless they relate either to the White House or to some sex bomb in a Congressman's office."

Steve Bauman of New York's WNEW agrees: "A few years ago, we did a lengthy series on the city's Municipal Loan Program, a scheme by which low-cost mortgages and construction loans were granted to private devel-opers to rehabilitate slum dwellings. It was a most sophisticated real estate transaction we were taking apart to show how the city was being ripped off, and as a result it was very technical and dry."

The station telecast 84 reports on its news show over six months. Bauman's producer once told him, during that period: "The Municipal Loan scandal is the best thing that ever happened to New York's beer companies." How come? asked the reporter. "Every time we say, 'Here's more on the Municipal Loan scandal,' " replied the producer, "half the audience gets up for a beer." Still, at the series' end, 28 persons were indicted and the loan program abolished.

In sum, the whole practice of investigative reporting on television is so expensive, risky, time-consuming, potentially litigious, speculative and unmarketable that it's a wonder *any* ever gets on the medium. Furthermore, nobody ever got in trouble with the FCC for *not* exposing scandal, so why should a station or network walk willingly into that Sargasso Sea? Still, it *is* done, and sometimes quite effectively.

NBC's investigative unit, for example, points with pride to its reports that Howard "Bo" Callaway, as Secretary of the Army (he later was President Ford's campaign manager), had met with Department of Agriculture officials to pressure them toward favorable action on the expansion of his Colorado ski resort; that Congressman Robert Sikes of Florida had been involved in conflict of interest on some Florida business dealings (he was reprimanded by the House and stripped of his subcommittee chairmanship; *60 Minutes* also broadcast a Sikes exposé); that about half the members of the House and Senate have the same kind of unvouchered expense funds that Vice Presidential candidate Richard Nixon had in 1952—which brought on the famous Checkers speech.

CBS's Don Hewitt, producer of *60 Minutes* ("We do *plenty* of investigative reporting"), recalls several features fondly: an Emmy Award-winning study of what really happened in the Gulf of Tonkin; a report on how easy it is for anyone to acquire fake passports, credit cards and bank accounts; an exposé of medical laboratories that were offering kickbacks to Medicaid clinics in return for business.

And ABC's Marlene Sanders, boss of the *Closeup* unit, cites such hour-long shows as "West Virginia: Life, Liberty and the Pursuit of Coal," "Food: Green Grow the Profits" and "The Paper Prison: Your Government Records."

In spite of all such claims, TV's news executives recognize that the really big corruption stories of recent years have all been broken by "pencil" reporters. Watergate, for example, was arguably the most parlous intramural crisis since the Civil War, but television had no part in its exposure, although the day-by-day TV-news coverage had a telling cumulative effect on the public mind, as did the live televised hearings of the House Judiciary Committee.

One big problem with so-called investigative reporting on television is figuring out a definition that suits everybody. "I think it's a bumper-sticker phrase," says Don

Hewitt. "I'm not sure I know what it means," says Jay McMullen: "Everybody talks about investigative reporting, but few can agree as to precisely what it is. All good reporting is investigative in some sense." The strict constructionists claim that investigative journalism must consist of original, creative reporting that exposes wrongdoing and results in official action: an indictment, a Congressional hearing, new legislation, dismissals. Others say that a TV documentary or news report can be "investigative" if it simply rounds up little-known or hard-to-get facts about a subject of public importance (not necessarily involving illegality) and dramatizes them in such a way that they provide a fresh, and perhaps startling, perspective on the matter.

Obviously, the great mass of television's investigative work—even such efforts as "The Selling of the Pentagon" and "Harvest of Shame"—fall into the second category. And so powerful is television's effect that those reports, too, strike the viewer with the force of new information, moving him to wonder: "How long has *this* been going on?"

Other questions remain: Are TV-news executives genuinely committed to investigative journalism or only to the appearance of it? Is there *too much* irresponsible muckraking going on in this country, to the detriment of our institutions and our good opinion of ourselves? They are troubling to those TV reporters who are genuinely committed to digging out and exposing unpleasant facts.

PART II

BEHIND TV'S CAUTIOUS PURSUIT OF WRONGDOING

Critics wonder whether the medium is really suited for hard-nosed journalism

In John Bunyan's 17th-century allegory, "The Pilgrim's Progress," there appears the Man with the Muckrake, a witless drudge who "could look no way but downward." Offered a celestial crown in return for his rake, he would "neither look up nor regard the crown he was offered," but went right on with his dreary task.

In an angry speech, President Theodore Roosevelt used that fable to flay the "reckless journalists" who were busy publishing (in such magazines as McClure's, Collier's, Everybody's and Cosmopolitan) revelations of bribery, conflict of interest, stock fraud, monopolistic practices, vote-buying, child-labor abuse and hazards to public health.

While we shouldn't "flinch from seeing what's vile and debasing," bellowed Teddy, the journalist who never does anything else, who "never thinks, speaks or writes" about the positive side of American life, "speedily becomes, not a help to society, not an incitement to good, but one of the potent forces of evil."

That speech helped hasten the end of the first great age of American investigative reporting (indeed, the public was already tiring of such bad news), and more than 60 years went by before Watergate ushered in the second. And now, right on schedule, we are again hearing admonitory voices suggesting that the whole thing may have gone too far. The press is on an "investigative-reporting binge," said retired Associated Press general manager Wes Gallagher last spring, causing the public to look upon it as "a multivoiced shrew, nit-picking through the debris of government decisions for scandals, but not solutions. . . . Readers and viewers are being turned off."

In a similar vein, former UN Ambassador John Scali (now an ABC News senior correspondent) warned that "the pendulum has swung too far in the journalistic zeal to rout out evil" and that "there is almost a tendency not to treat the government as an adversary but as the enemy." He worried about the "unbelievable numbers of bright-eyed, energetic would-be crusaders" who, having observed the deification of newsmen like Robert Woodward, Carl Bernstein and Seymour Hersh, are "furiously searching for the Pulitzer Prize and the big story that will catapult them to fame."

Predictably, most newsmen say "Nonsense!" to such cautionary finger-wagging. "Endless investigative reporting would still not begin to catch up with the things that government and business are doing to us," says Stanhope Gould, who headed investigative units at CBS and NBC (and is, for the moment, out of television). There are enough "totally unresolved questions," Gould says, "to keep investigative reporters busy from now until forever."

Many newsmen do agree, however, that scandalmongering, as such, need not be the main ingredient of investigative reports. CBS's Jay McMullen, for example, says, "I'd hate to see us get involved in the scandal business on a regular basis. I hope the quick and easy exposé will not replace the more serious attempt to deal with the things that are wrong with our society. Our job should be something more than turning up crime."

Newsweek recently suggested that the main interest of investigative reporting should be "to enlighten and not just to indict"; to explain why government works the way it does and not merely to "ferret out wrongdoers."

What's really needed, says one TV newsman, is for the networks to make the same kind of commitment to investigative reporting as they did to the coverage of space shots and Vietnam—an organic long-term investment.

It takes time. "You can't say, 'Zap! You've got an investigative unit!'" says Stanhope Gould. "It's got to grow. You've got to figure out how it integrates into your news organization and how much air time will be made available on the various broadcasts."

Gould feels that the networks have begun to be serious about such a commitment, even though television "can't be as tough as newspapers" because of Fairness Doctrine requirements, which have a kind of "chilling effect." The real inhibition, however, derives not from government or advertisers (says Gould) but is an institutional self-censorship "that results from working for a large corporation and knowing in your head what can get on the air, what's acceptable. There's too much of that, and not enough people who try to push the boundaries back."

TV has what Gould calls "print envy"—a nagging (and well-founded) conviction that newspapers are chiefly in the business of publishing news, while TV news operations are a poor (and perhaps unwanted) relative of the television-entertainment industry.

If TV's muckrakers sometimes envy their print brethren, the opposite is rarely true. Says Seymour Hersh of The New York Times: "I think most respected reporters, really good reporters, wouldn't touch television with a 10-foot pole." Why? "Too much show biz," too many technical problems, too little time to tell the story. "I think television *can* do an excellent job," Hersh says, "a better job than it does."

CBS's special on the F-14 fighter-bomber was "first-rate," he says, and "The Selling of the Pentagon" was basically "very good" in spite of angry complaints ("some of which were legitimate, by the way") from official quarters. He thinks that *60 Minutes* is "the best, as far as I can tell. But even so, their stuff often isn't as tough as I want it to be."

Another full-time investigative reporter in the print medium is the Village Voice's Jack Newfield, who claims that TV isn't serious enough about muckraking and has been "too cautious rather than too zealous in this area." He also thinks that TV needs to start hiring "real journalists" instead of "corporate, homogenized, pretty faces" who read their lines like actors.

Although Newfield is exclusively a print journalist, he once worked in loose collaboration with WNEW-TV investigative reporter Steve Bauman on an exposé of a nursing-home scandal in New York City. Their combined efforts resulted in the appointment of a special prosecutor and the ultimate conviction of a nursing-home tycoon who was preying on the elderly and their families. "It was a uniquely visual story because there were real victims whom Bauman was able to put on camera," Newfield recalls. "What he did on television was an incredibly powerful supplement to what I was doing in the Voice."

More recently, Bauman—one of New York's most energetic young TV investigators—and other members of WNEW's investigative crew broadcast a major exposé of bribe-taking among New York's welfare administrators. Using hidden cameras and tape recorders, the newsmen managed to film three of their own crewmen (plus a member of the district attorney's office) successfully buying their way onto the welfare rolls with payments of $200 each to welfare workers. As a result of the mini-series, the U.S. Department of Health, Education and Welfare has begun a large-scale scrutiny of New York's welfare practices.

Says WNEW news director Mark Monsky: "This story is almost a textbook case, not only of good, basic investigative digging. But we actually captured the whole thing on film."

Bauman, discussing TV's track record in investigative journalism, says: "I don't think it's doing much of a job at all, and neither is the print medium." He scoffs at the suggestion that a regular diet of investigative reporting may be too expensive for most TV stations to maintain. "There are no money problems in television," he says. "Television stations make a fortune; any news program that is reasonably successful is making huge profits. It's a matter of prying it loose from them."

Most TV stations don't muckrake, because it "draws heat," says Bauman. "They're so fat and sassy that they don't have to worry about doing original work, because everybody is comfortable and why make waves? If you're a TV reporter and you're making a lot of money doing silly jokes on the air and treating even serious matters with superficiality day after day—why create problems for yourself? That's the philosophy, and I can understand it." Investigative work can be "truly dangerous," says Bauman, and he and other TV investigators have been threatened with physical harm.

Another WNEW newsman, Gabe Pressman, sees "great timidity" at the network level, partly because upper-echelon TV-news executives "don't have the kind of aggressive journalistic background" that old-line newspapermen have. They got where they are, he says, "not by putting some crooked official in jail" but because they are, for the most part, "corporate politicians" who have shown themselves to be capable administrators. Those men are motivated more by the needs of the "company" than "the spirit of John Peter Zenger."

TV newsmen in Washington are especially lackadaisical with regard to muckraking, says Pressman. "You go to a White House press conference and you meet a lot of reporters who just feel it's a great honor to be there. There's a lack of guts in Washington by the networks. They don't know their own strength."

The suspicion persists among TV theorists that, no matter how much muckraking the medium does or how well it does it, television simply is not a hospitable place for this kind of fare. TV viewers are used to the steady drip-drip-drip of game shows, situation comedies, melodramas and variety shows that require little but semi-attentive passivity. The intrusion of a sober and accusatory documentary, requiring one's full attention, is too jarring to be effective—or so the argument goes.

Says ABC's Brit Hume, once an aide to Jack Anderson: "An investigative report requires that the viewer concentrate on what he's being told. It's usually complicated stuff, and sophisticated in the sense that it involves judgments about what should and shouldn't be. But TV makes you lazy mentally. It may be in the nature of the medium. We are not used to thinking while watching TV—so we won't and don't."

Nonetheless, the second age of muckraking proceeds and doubtless will be with us for a time. And television clearly is something less than a full partner in making that age flower. One suspects that, had Lincoln Steffens and Ida Tarbell and Upton Sinclair lived in the TV era, they would have reveled in the prospect of telling their stories in color and sound. And Theodore Roosevelt would have had that much more to bellow about.

Hardly the Retiring Kind

Even as he reminisces
about his storied past,
Frank Sinatra, at 61, is busy
planning concerts, movies and a book
by Neil Hickey

(John Bryson)

Frank Sinatra is sipping tea with honey. The face, at 61, is unlined except for small pockets under the famous blue eyes. He cocks his head suddenly and points through the window of his Waldorf Towers apartment (the same suite he has occupied, off and on, since he emerged as a pop-culture idol in the 1940s) toward the twilight sky over his home town of Hoboken, N.J.

"Look at that fantastic color!" he says. "You don't often see the sky that deeply blue, especially around here." He ponders the deepening azure silently. The Sinatra stomach is now flat and the face has regained its old angularity; gone is the paunchiness and shapelessness of recent years. He's down to 157 pounds (from over 180), he tells you, and sports a 33-inch waist, thanks to "eating only a third of my food, cutting down on the booze and exercising every day."

Thanks also to retiring from his retirement. In 1971 Frank Sinatra announced he was through with saloon singing, movies, television. "Excuse me while I disappear," he had sung to a packed house of celebrities at the Los Angeles Music Center during an emotional concert that was his abdication rite. But he quickly unabdicated and resumed his throne as Entertainer of the Century.

And now he was relaxing in the security of his Waldorf aerie (an armed guard outside the door), making plans for his next television special, "Sinatra and Friends," to be seen this Thursday night (April 21) on the ABC network. In a few days he'd go on to London for eight concerts at Royal Albert Hall (and a meeting with Princess Margaret). Then to Caesars Palace in Las Vegas and Harrah's in Lake Tahoe, Nevada, for some saloon singing. There'd be a one-nighter in Palm Springs, California, for the benefit of the Eisenhower Medical Center and another (on April 27) at Carnegie Hall in New York for Lenox Hill Hospital (top ticket price for the latter: $5000 per seat; honorary chairman: Mrs. Aristotle Onassis). And then on to engagements at the Latin Casino in Cherry Hill, N.J. (April 29–May 8) and the Westchester Premier Theatre in Tarrytown,

N.Y., for two weeks (May 17–29) with Dean Martin. And on June 6 he'd commence 2½ months of filming in New York for his first made-for-television movie, "Contract on Cherry Street," to be seen on NBC next season.

"That sounds like an awfully rough schedule," says Frank Sinatra, "but last year's was tougher." Why does a 61-year-old man of considerable wealth need that much activity? "I don't know. I'm singing well. I feel marvelous. I vocalize at least 45 minutes a day. Barbara [his wife of nine months, the former Barbara Marx] chases me around the tennis court. When I'm at home, I punch a sandbag. That's great for the breathing." With his fingertips, he taps the chest that produced the tones that reduced several generations of female fans to pudding. "Gotta keep the bellows nice and big," he says.

Frank Sinatra puffs his pipe, descends to an easy chair and stretches his legs. A visitor is moved to remark that he appears at peace with himself after 35 years of a public life that's been more eventful than most and frequently stormy. "I really have found some kind of wonderful tranquility," he says. "What the hell, it's about time. I'm at a very happy point in life. Barbara is a marvelous woman, a great gal. I have a different kind of life now altogether—and two marvelous grandchildren."

And no more of that retirement stuff, at least not for now. "I had a discussion recently with Mickey Rudin [his lawyer, who handles his business affairs], and I said, 'Where are we going? What's our plan? I'm 61 years old, what do I want to do with myself?' I decided I'll continue doing what I'm doing for another five or six years and then get the hell out before becoming a bore. Some people will say, 'He should have gotten out 10 years ago.'" Sinatra laughs heartily. "But that's a matter of taste. I'll pick up my Social Security and go home when the time comes."

When that happens and Frank Sinatra does indeed pack it in for good, it'll be the end of a professional career that—no matter what one thinks of the man personally, and opinions vary widely—has no parallel in the American entertainment business. The Sinatra story has become an American folk tale.

Most of the tale was told in banner headlines: the tempestuous courtship and marriage to Ava Gardner after divorcing Nancy Sinatra, the mother of his three children; the short-lived marriage to Mia Farrow, 30 years his junior; rows with the press; speculation about his alleged acquaintanceships with underworld figures; his celebrated friendships with (and political support of) Presidents John F. Kennedy and Richard M. Nixon, Vice President Spiro Agnew, Governor Ronald Reagan.

And along the way there were 50 movies ("The Manchurian Candidate," "The Joker Is Wild," "Pal Joey," "Anchors Aweigh," "Guys and Dolls"), including two of the best performances ever laid down on film by an American actor: Maggio in "From Here to Eternity," for which he won an Academy Award; and the dope addict Frankie Machine in Nelson Algren's story "The Man with the Golden Arm."

And yes, there were albums by the score and single records from "I'll Never Smile Again" and "There Are Such Things" to "Love and Marriage" and "Send in the Clowns." There were unbuttoned performances in Las Vegas in the 1960s with cronies Dean Martin, Sammy Davis and Joey Bishop.

It's a baroque tale that soon will get an authoritative telling. "I'm now doing the book," says Sinatra. "I'm well into it. It should be ready by the end of 1978." And he's doing it alone, he insists, working in longhand and with a tape recorder, spending long sessions fleshing out the story piece by piece as half-forgotten incidents occur to him.

"Right now, I'm trying to dig back in my head. I find I can only remember to about three or 3½ years of age. I was ready recently to sit down with my mother and a tape recorder. But I waited too long. I wanted her to tell me what kind of boy I was." (Last January 6, Sinatra's 82-year-old mother died in the crash of a private plane en route from Palm Springs to Las Vegas to attend her son's opening.) "Her death was a shame, a blow. Especially because of the manner in which she died. She was a woman who flew maybe five times a year. I could understand if it happened to me."

Sinatra shifts in his chair and leans forward, elbows on knees. "My birth was a disaster. I never had it clear. My mother was hurt terribly—physically. She couldn't have any more children after that. They set me aside to save my mother, thinking there wasn't much hope I'd live. I waited too long to ask her about it. I thought I'd title one of the chapters of the book 'The Day I Was Born I Nearly Died.' "

He laments that his father ("He could neither read nor write") wanted him to go to college, but Sinatra dropped out of high school after 2½ years and never went further. "That's one of the biggest regrets I ever had. Through street knowledge, though, I learned a hell of a lot in my lifetime—meeting people. I always had the tendency to migrate toward older people. I came from a jungle. It was as bad as Hell's Kitchen. Sometimes I see people I went to school with. Some of them look like they're 90 years old."

The prospect of a movie based on his autobiography intrigues him. "I'd like to put down the vocal tracks myself, like they did in 'The Jolson Story.' " Then "we'd get a Larry Parks" (the actor who played Al Jolson and lip-synched his songs) to impersonate the adult Sinatra and a second actor ("some kid of 16 or 17") for the early years. He has no views at the moment about who should be cast to impersonate him in the film.

Sinatra is somewhat rankled by the recent biography of him written by gossip columnist Earl Wilson. "I asked him not to do it," says the singer. "He stood in my dressing room at Lake Tahoe and I specifically asked him not to write the book because I was doing my own and I didn't want him to jump in ahead. But he went to the newspaper morgues and dug out a lot of old news clips and strung them together. I've only skimmed it, but I can see it's a dull book. It's not the content I object to. I'm disappointed in Wilson. As a friend of 30 years, I thought he wouldn't do it."

Things like that happen to the man whom many people are fond of calling the Greatest Entertainer of the Century. How does he feel about such labels? "It's a tremendous exaggeration. I don't believe that. To give anybody that title makes him the fastest gun in town, and he becomes a mark. There's plenty of room for everybody. There are a lot of people who are great performers. I saw Jolson once when I was a kid. He was dynamite. He *exuded* electricity. And these days there are people like Wayne Newton. Also Sammy Davis. His rhythm, his mimicry, his whole demeanor on stage is tremendously exciting."

Still, it's Frank Sinatra who is, by the consensus of his peers, the best pop singer (he'd prefer "saloon singer") of all time—the flamboyant Chairman of the Board.

"Flamboyant? That's in the mind of the beholder. I am not flamboyant. I don't wear funny clothes. I am not demonstrative. I do my job and I go home." Yes, he gets angry at times, Sinatra admits. If a co-worker is unprofessional or inefficient, "I don't have much tolerance for that."

He sighs and shifts in his chair. "There are personal things too. I've been hurt many times. When I'm in public, people are sometimes crude toward me and make silly remarks. They want to prove something, I guess. They want to take on the fastest gun in town. You know: 'Who is this guy who goes around in his own jet plane? Why does *he* have all this adoration? He's just a singer.'

"Others come right up to me in restaurants and shoot 25 pictures. I say, 'May I finish my dinner?' They become nasty, so I tell them. 'Take a walk. You've shot a couple of rolls of film. That's enough.' " But those occasions have been rare, says Frank Sinatra.

And even rarer, he insists, have been the much publicized bouts with newspaper photographers. "There's been very little of that in recent years. And the public, generally, has been very considerate toward me. These days, I can walk around New York. People say, 'Hi, Frank.' I sign autographs. People take pictures with their cameras. I enjoy that."

He denies that he's always been hostile toward the press. "That's an unfair statement—a generalization. But when they treated me unfairly, I struck back. I've turned the other cheek. Hell, I've turned all four cheeks and I still get the short end." His reputation as an enemy of the press derives, in part, from an incident in 1947, says Sinatra, when he was "physically rough on one man"—Hearst columnist Lee Mortimer. Sinatra shakes his head pensively. "If he was alive today, I'd knock him down again. He was a————."

Press criticism? "Most of the time it's fiction. I find it makes my life easier if I ignore it." He did holler, though, about an incident in London not long ago. "I was watching a TV interview on the BBC, and suddenly I heard the interviewer saying that I got the Maggio role in 'From Here to Eternity' through the Mob. Well—that's so far from the truth! It was an out-and-out libel, and the producers of the movie could have told them that. We threatened to sue England, in effect, since the BBC is government-owned. They came up with a prompt apology, and I'm pleased to say that our own press here printed it in full."

The Maggio story had gained credence because novelist Mario Puzo had used a fictionalized version of it in "The Godfather." "He'd heard that myth somewhere and just said to himself, 'I think I'll use that in the book.' "

Still, over most of his professional career, Sinatra has been parrying accusations about his alleged acquaintanceships with Mafia figures. He waves his arm expansively. "I know a lot of those guys. People have said to me: 'Why did you have friends in the Mob?' I say, 'I was *not* friends with them.' They say, 'Do you know so-and-so?' I say, 'No, but I've met him.' When the Copacabana was open, there wasn't one guy in show business who didn't meet them there. Let them buy you a drink. So I've stopped trying to explain that to people. I was having dinner with Rosalind Russell once, and I said, 'Why don't they get off my back about this thing?' She said, 'Forget it. If they had anything to go on, you'd have been indicted years ago.' "

But not much really gets under the Sinatra skin any more—except maybe rock-and-roll lyrics. "I've never really been bothered by the music itself. I live with it. But the lyrics . . ."

He cocks his shoulders and gestures with upturned palms. "I'm not a prude. Please understand that. But they're sex songs, out and out. I *loathe* what they're doing in many of these lyrics. If disc jockeys had any class, they wouldn't play them. Same with magazines. Kids can wander in and read them. I'm not implying that we should become book burners. But we need decency somehow."

It was his Italian-Catholic upbringing speaking. "I was an altar boy. I still practice my religion quite dutifully. I go regularly to Mass, although sometimes I might miss several Sundays in a row. That 40 minutes of serenity is very important in one's life."

West of the Waldorf Towers, where Frank Sinatra sat smoking his pipe, the sun was going down behind Hoboken.

(Christopher Little/Camera 5)

ABC'S QUARTER-MILLION-DOLLAR MAN PERFORMS HEROICS TOO

How programming whiz Fred Silverman helped his network become a big winner in the ratings race
by Dick Hobson

PART I

"He's a speeding bullet! A flywheel in a motor! He's 220 volts through a 110 wire! A master antenna! A one-man band! He could catch lightning in a bottle!"

Gosh, a new ABC-TV superhero?

In a sense. These are the words used by one dazzled admirer to describe ABC's $250,000 Man, programming whiz, ratings wizard, and prime promulgator of superheroics both on and behind the tube—Fred Silverman.

Remember when ABC was an object of scorn and contumely? ("Wanna end the Vietnam War? Put it on ABC and it'll be cancelled in 13 weeks.") Today those pitiable also-rans are sporting buttons proclaiming: "We're No. 1!" A. C. Nielsen reported that 130,000,000 Americans watched at least part of ABC's *Roots*—the last episode was the most-watched TV show of all time.

One day two years ago, the young (then 37), hypertensive, flash-tempered, unpredictable and fiercely competitive Fred Silverman ("Freddie" in the business) moved over from CBS (where he was vice president in charge of programming) to ABC Entertainment (as president in charge of same)—and ABC's stock instantly shot up two points. It continued climbing—doubling in one year. And another doubling is considered likely.

Building on solid groundwork already laid by network president Fred Pierce, who hired him, Silverman and his colleagues boosted ABC from third place to first, winning the Neilsen Sweepstakes for 1975–76 by half a rating point and raising ABC's ratings average by two points (for estimated additional corporate profits of $40,000,000). Then ABC took the calendar year 1976 by 1½ points (increasing corporate net earnings by almost 320 percent). The network is leading in the 1976–77 season by more than three points, and the money hasn't stopped rolling in. With prime-time minutes going for as much as $130,000, total ABC broadcasting revenues last year exceeded *one billion dollars* for the first time. ABC-TV's profit-spread over nearest rival CBS could reach $100,000,000 this season.

"Does anyone question whether Silverman is worth $250,000 a year?" asks Variety rhetorically.

As of early April, Silverman had zapped both rival networks 23 out of 29 weeks in the ratings. The *Roots* episodes were the top seven programs of "*Roots* Week," making it the highest-rated week any network has ever had.

He has driven the other two networks frantic by, among other stratagems, raiding their star rosters—Harvey Korman from CBS, Redd Foxx from NBC, both for next season. He set off the worst spate of series cancellations in recent memory, triggering a chain of executive-suite upheavals along New York's Broadcast Row. Said Norman Lear, the man with the most (nine) shows on the air: "Freddie's in quite a unique position of leadership. They're all watching now."

And imitating. Snapped one rattled network rival: "What Freddie is doing is exactly what we will be doing, so let's cut through all the horse [bleep] and get down to business!"

What is Freddie doing exactly? To find out, I caught the Speeding Bullet in his digs at ABC's West Coast headquarters, dominated by a 30-foot rust suede sofa with enough seating space for an Osmond family reunion.

Contrary to impressions fostered by trendy reportage, Freddie was nattily accoutred (not "rumpled and out of fashion," as The New York Times Magazine would have it), his voice emanating from nature's chosen orifice (not via his nose, as New Times would have one believe), his manner civilized (not "innocent of the finer social graces," as Time trumpeted), his decorum decorous (no hint of the "kicker-over of wastebaskets" described by People). In short, just your average upper-echelon six-figure corporate executive whose only deficiency, it seems, is a good press agent.

On this January morning he was expostulating on the failure of a visiting contingent of 52 TV editors and columnists to comprehend the audience appeal of *Laverne & Shirley*—providing our first ingredient in what might be called "Freddie's Formula":

Maxim 1: "Make people laugh. There's enough tragedy in the world." Or, as he was saying: "The primary purpose of putting a comedy show on the air is to entertain people. And anybody who approaches half-hour comedy or television entertainment of any kind in any other manner is stupid! You must first get the people into the store."

Maxim 2: "People tune in to see a star." Silverman is always telling the creators of new shows: "Stop inventing these wonderful characters that are impossible to cast. Television is a personality medium. Start out with a piece of talent." If writers' intentions get bent out of shape by Freddie's Formula, they're expendable. Take *Kojak*, initially based on Abby Mann's Emmy-winning TV-movie. "The Marcus-Nelson Murders," in which the writer said he "wanted people to understand that cops are human beings like everybody else." But Silverman's "people over premises" maxim required that *Kojak* be tailored to fit its stolid star, Telly Savalas. The result, according to Mann: "Kojak is imperturbable; he's always right. He has become exactly the reverse of what I intended."

Maxim 3: "Stress the positive, not the negative." Like MGM's Louis B. Mayer, Silverman cloaks himself in the good old apple-pie values. "God knows, somebody's got to do it! Pick up any newspaper these days and it's just terrible! The new programs on television dwell on crime. I think we should provide positive models for the audiences that we serve. I feel strongly that there should be many different places in the schedule where the family unit is presented in a positive way."

Maxim 4: "The common man is more appealing." Silverman has a predilection for shows with an earthy ambience, possibly reflecting his "blue-collar" childhood (his father was a TV repairman). "I think Freddie always felt that characters in the blue-collar or lower-class TV series were more appealing to America in a lot of ways," *Happy Days* producer Garry Marshall says. "That's the whole Fonzie character. He's uneducated; he's got nothing; but he's not giving up. It's the whole thing of *Laverne & Shirley*—two lower-class bimbos who work in a brewery and struggle and try to get in love and get hurt and who nevertheless are happy and full of dreams. These are real people to Freddie."

Maxim 5: "It's up to me to find new stars." TV stars are a rare and special breed, Silverman contends, and he is constantly prowling around unlikely places looking for new ones. There was the famous night he called an old friend, producer Fred Baum, from Las Vegas: "I just saw an act I'm going to make a star—Sonny and Cher." Baum reacted: "Are you nuts? They're on the downslide!" And the rainy night Freddie drove out to the end of Long Island for a look at a record act in a leaky tent and signed Tony Orlando & Dawn to a CBS contract. "Nobody in his right mind would do that!" was the consensus—even after he pulled it off. Over at ABC he persevered, and when *Donny & Marie* clicked, there were still the nervous jokes: "At least they won't get a divorce."

Maxim 6: "Familiarity breeds acceptability." Producer Marshall airily gives away the secret of Silverman's success: "Fred's theory, which I agree with, is that if you go to a cocktail party and you don't know anybody, which is an uncomfortable situation, your tendency always will be to gravitate to somebody you know rather than to this terribly exciting, wonderful person over here whom you don't know and you're a little afraid to go up to and try to start a conversation with."

Ergo: give the viewers somebody they know. Which explains Freddie's "spinoffs," "crossovers" and "cross-promotions." It's all part of Freddie's Formula to make "The ABC Family" seem just like kissin' cousins.

Maxim 7: "Take chances and run scared." For all his hot rolls of 7s and 11s, Silverman regards hit-picking as the biggest throw of the dice ever. "The shows that are the riskiest are also the shows that have got the potential to be the biggest hits." There are those who say that he's not really that good a gambler when it comes to picking programs; that he left the CBS schedule a shambles; that he inherited a brilliant development slate at ABC.

His megagamble—*Roots*—was not in program-picking (its inception is credited to his predecessor, Martin Starger, and programming executive Brandon Stoddard), but in serializing it on an unprecedented eight successive nights. Insiders say that Silverman and other ABC executives were so skeptical of the genealogical epic's pulling power that they ordered it "aired and over with" one week prior to the crucial "sweep week"—when viewer ratings determine ad rates for local stations.

Maxim 8: "It's not only the show but how the audience is told about the show." Silverman's canny concept of "audience expectation" helped him decipher the inner workings of The Viewer Mind, which he now manipulates shamelessly. His victory in some "very bitter fights" at CBS unleashed a blizzard of promotional blurbs, leading to the usual jokes: "Tony Orlando is on two hours a week, one hour for the show and one hour for the promos." At ABC, where he calls all the shots, Freddie's promos are pandemic.

"Grabbers" are a Silverman trademark. As MTM Enterprises' Grant Tinker recalls: "When Fred heard about *Rhoda*'s wedding, he said, 'Let's clear an hour and make it like Lucy's baby!' And it got a hell of an audience."

Maxim 9: "Work the viewer mind." Freddie became the Dr. Strangelove of program tactics last fall when he unleashed a form of Orwellian warfare—with unexpected results. NBC started it by suddenly announcing a blockbuster movie, "Airport 1975," starring Charlton Heston, to kick off the new season on a Monday night, threatening to eclipse ABC's *The Captain & Tennille* debut. What could he do to take the sock out of "Airport"?

He could schedule a couple of air-disaster movies— "Murder on Flight 502" and "Sky Terror"—over the preceding weekend, specifically to mislead viewers into thinking they'd *already seen* "Airport 1975." "Now that really is a form of genius, you know," marveled one of Hollywood's Freddie-watchers, "for him to think that he could work the viewer mind that way." His ploy wasn't entirely successful—"Airport's" draw proved too powerful—but his disaster flicks over the final weekend of the old season pulled enough viewers to help give ABC the overall ratings title for 1975–76.

Maxim 10: "Keep a hard-action line." As bad money drives out good, according to Freddie's Formula, "hard" shows drive out "soft." At one point last year, *The Bionic*

Woman had in work an episode, "Claws," about a mountain lion jeopardizing schoolchildren. "You can't do this episode!" he told the puzzled producer. "You're competing with *Little House on the Prairie* and you've got to keep a hard-action line or the viewers will switch over."

It was too late to change the story line, and when "Claws" aired, true to Freddie's warning, the series dipped from fourth to nineteenth in the ratings. Executive producer Harve Bennett got Silverman on the phone: "I salute your instinct! We won't do that kind of show again." How did Freddie know that "Claws" would be perceived by the viewers as too soft? Because the "audience expectation," as implanted by program announcements, would perforce invoke the innocuous images of "kids and cuddly animals."

Maxim 11: "Cartoons aren't only for kids." For Freddie, the much-bruited-about "family hour" came as a lucky break. As Filmways TV chief Perry Lafferty tells it: "Most comedy has gotten too sophisticated now for 8 P.M., so you're limited to things like *Happy Days* and *Laverne & Shirley,* which are Freddie's. And you can't do shows with violence, so there you have Freddie's *Six Million Dollar Man* and *Bionic Woman*—a lot of flying around and derring-do but no shooting. See how clever it was to think of that solution? He has lined up shows that have almost cartoon overtones."

But it's not only kids who are watching these programs, according to Silverman: "I have to say that the shows with 'cartoon overtones' are among the most popular television programming for adults in the whole country."

Maxim 12: "Grab 'em while they're young." There have been jibes about Silverman's "Saturday morning mentality," but that infamous "daypart" is where he learned how to attract audiences. *Shazzan! The Herculoids! The New Adventures of Superman!* For seven years he fired off such a barrage of "hard-action" shows for kids that alarmed parents finally got together to protest.

Silverman feels he's gotten a bum rap: "Well, it's just better copy to say, 'He brought the monsters to Saturday morning,' because that's provocative. But I was also the first to move into live action. I put *Children's Film Festival* on the air, which won a Peabody Award. I was the one who put the *CBS Children's Hour* on. I was the one who brought Dr. Seuss to CBS."

There are perhaps other ingredients to "Freddie's Formula," but by the time they're articulated, the prodigious programmer will be someplace else, chortling yet another maxim: *"Don't copy yourself."*

Yet, isn't Silverman's game, when you get to the bottom line, simply a prescription for maximizing viewers, maximizing ratings, maximizing revenues? Is it all that hard to picture Silverman delivering Faye Dunaway's bravura speech in the movie "Network"? "I'm talking about a $6 cost-per-thousand show! I'm talking about a $130,000 minute! Figure out the revenues of a strip show that sells for 130,000 bucks a minute!"

Bob Wood, the former CBS president who made Fred Silverman his programming chief, who fought the rating battles alongside him for five years, and whose extravagant encomiums opened this article, said it all: "If you consider the system as a given, then Freddie is merely one helluva practitioner."

PART II

"HIS WHOLE SCENE IS WINNING, WINNING, WINNING"
But master programmer Fred Silverman denies that he is obsessed with ratings

Prime mover of ABC to No. 1 in the Ratings Race! Unmaker of competing networks! Toppler of rival programmers! Orchestrator of ABC broadcasting's first billion-dollar revenue year! Zounds! What makes Freddie run?

"The money is not a primary factor," said Fred Silverman, president of ABC Entertainment, one January morning at his West Coast headquarters in Century City. "Like my move over here—although there was substantially more money, that was not the motivation. I just thought that for two or three years it would be fun. It's fun to go from a meeting on *Roots* to a meeting on a new cartoon show."

He did not say: "I'm not somebody who likes to lose!" or "I want to win every time, period!" This was certainly not the Silverman of old, as described by those who know him best: "His whole scene is winning, winning, winning!"

Compulsively driven to be No. 1 in TV's Ratings Race, Freddie had made television his entire life. "It was to him more real than the world," concluded Les Brown of Silverman in his 1971 book, "Television: The Business Behind the Box." Just how totally the tube had taken over his existence has been attested to by others: "I've been to his apartment many times and he literally has three TV sets side-by-side all going at once." "He goes to bed only when *Sermonette* comes on."

Confronted with this testimony, the New Silverman exploded: "I sound like a dingbat! I hate to destroy the myth, but it's not true. You know, when you're working in television all day long, there are better things to do when you come home than put the TV set on."

Fred Silverman has been called "today's version of Harry Cohn, Louis B. Mayer, Darryl Zanuck—a showman through and through." But in a period of increasing public concern about network influence on the quality of American life, social-activist-cum-TV-tycoon Norman Lear discerns more contemporary, if disquieting, implications in Silverman's brand of showmanship:

"We're living at a time when the corporation dominates, and I think Freddie would have to get the prize as the best 'corporate showman.' That's not the same thing as the personal flair of a Mike Todd, who staged that enormous shindig at Madison Square Garden for his wife. Or a Louis B. Mayer, who wept real tears when he negotiated a deal. They had a flair for personalizing."

(Christopher Little/Camera 5)

It's a different phenomenon at the TV networks these days, says Lear: "The flair they execute is a corporate flair. Living ratings 24 hours a day is a corporate thing to do."

Asked if he would own up to the appellation "corporate showman," Silverman replied: "I think that in most instances there is a mutuality of objectives." Veteran Freddie-watchers like Lorimar's president Lee Rich (*The Waltons*) know their man: "The name of the game is numbers and Freddie's smart enough to recognize that this is the way you live."

Yet the New Silverman, incredible as it may seem, pooh-poohs the ratings race: "Many, many decisions—most of the decisions—aren't made for ratings. There are people who run each of the three TV networks who have a sense of responsibility, who feel that it is a gigantic medium, who generally want to make it a better medium. I know it sounds crazy, but nevertheless it's the truth." Sounds crazy, all right, coming from the fiercest competitor the Grand Nielsen Prix has ever known.

This is how today's Silverman talks: "The world is a lot larger than the television business. The older you get, the more you realize that there's a whole world out there, that there are things more important. And that is a great concern when you have children. The birth of my second child a few months ago has driven the point home even more."

Lately concerned about demythologizing his image, Silverman told a contingent of TV editors: "Don't believe all those stories you read in People and Time. It's ridiculous to think that somebody is going to read the 40th episode of *Starsky & Hutch*!" Yet the evidence of his "superhuman" attention to detail ("Oh, by the way, you're running the crawl over plastic flowers—change them to fresh") is incontrovertible. "Freddie's imprint," insiders say, "is on everything."

Silverman simply never takes his eye off the ball—the corporate objective. "This is really the first interview I have had in quite a while," he told this writer. "But somehow I'm thinking, and I'm still not sure, that these articles will be productive for ABC—and I'm just a company man."

He was still smarting from that all-too-candid Life magazine story nearly six years ago that so embarrassed the corporate brass at CBS. "That was terrible! The article came out, as luck would have it, a week before the start of the television season, and I'll never forget, poor Sandy Duncan—this poor girl—and we're quoted about bets being made on the survival of her show!" The "company man" in Freddie was horrified, and he has kept writers at arm's length ever since.

Silverman claims that he *never* was the Freddie of legend, that it was all a myth of the media. This is how he prefers to picture himself:

• "I was one of the very few people at CBS who championed the continuation of *Captain Kangaroo* where there were a lot more commercial forces at play that said: 'Take it off the air. It's losing money.'"

• "I take a lot of pride in the fact that during my tenure as program head CBS won an impressive number of Emmys. And the Emmys have historically been a benchmark of quality."

• "The greatest contribution I can make to the industry and to the audiences who look at our programs is to try to put programs on the air that represent a high level of quality."

There's an irony in Silverman's being considered the ultimate "company man." Actually, he was, at CBS, more the Henry Kissinger of programming—the lone decision maker—impatient with bureaucratic strictures. "He used to pick up the phone and go right over the heads of his own people," said one producer. "Today he's getting better at doing things within channels."

His style and pace tend toward the strongly personal as well. "He used to run around in his eagerness to have all the best of everything, and he would grab and buy and spin," remembers a leading program supplier. "He was frantic, almost a little mad, always doing something abrupt. He's a better executive today, getting almost statesmanlike."

His staff people are dedicated to him on a personal rather than organizational basis. "He wants to win so badly," says former CBS-TV president Bob Wood, "that he's in there pushing, pushing, pushing and pretty soon he develops a psychology among the people he works with that if something fails, Freddie'll be terribly disappointed, so everybody works very hard."

He's modest about his achievements, magnanimous about spreading the credit around. "The top management here really deserves the lion's share of credit for whatever success ABC has enjoyed this past calendar year," says Silverman. "I think it's been Fred Pierce, who is really a first-rate executive; and Leonard Goldenson and Elton Rule, who are two of the most supportive, dear people I've ever worked for."

For Silverman at CBS the corporate climate had been frustrating. He had "made millions" for the network by keeping it No. 1 in the ratings all through his five years as programming chief. Yet the corporate perquisites were minimal. After 12 years with the company, he was a vice president (at $150,000) with no security, no contract and little corporate recognition for his efforts. No fewer than three presidents reportedly wanted to fire him.

ABC's offer was irresistible: the title of president, $250,000 a year for the first three years, a fourth year at $350,000, stock options, $750,000 worth of life insurance, a four-year production deal if he ever chose to leave, habitations and autos on both coasts. ABC has

fewer layers of management, giving him a much freer hand. And he would be working with Fred Pierce, president of the network, an old buddy since 1958, when they were both reaching for the bottom rung of the corporate ladder.

At ABC, Freddie relaxed, got happy, and lost 40 pounds of tension-induced avoirdupois. He had confided to a friend that he wanted to help make ABC No. 1 without making any personnel changes—and he did. It took less than a year.

Silverman is one of the few network programming executives with a knack for working with the "Hollywood crazies." Producer Leonard Stern (*McMillan*) speaks for the majority: "What Freddie manages to do is to personalize an impersonal business. You're dealing with an individual 'somebody' who lives and breathes and doesn't just spew statistics."

Says John Mitchell, president of Columbia Pictures Television: "Freddie's a very warm, emotional guy underneath it all. He can be reached; he can be touched. I know he can cry."

Says *Happy Days* producer Garry Marshall: "The man laughs! It's strange, but other network executives don't laugh. I've taken comedy pilots into screening rooms where they say, 'That looks as if it's going to be funny.' Freddie goes ha-ha!"

Just about every Hollywood producer has witnessed Freddie's terrible temper tantrums when a project isn't going the way he would like. "I saw him go cuckoo in the halls of ABC. I saw the rage that in a personality like Freddie's is the core of what he is. You don't see it until somebody crosses him," one of them said. Many producers are afraid of him.

But at least they know exactly where Silverman stands: "He's one of the very few executives to give you a yes or no answer. The other guys lie: 'Oh, how wonderful! I'll get back to you.'" "This is a great business for kidding yourself. Freddie's the only one with the guts to say, 'Let's fix it or get it off the air.'"

Having only lately reordered the priorities in his life, Silverman must look back at his former self with some incredulity. His "telemania" was contracted at an impressionable age. He remembers when his father, a TV repairman for Sears in New York City, brought home a Trans-Vision kit with an oversize chassis and a four-inch picture tube. It took four months to assemble. "See, he's always been at this thing in his mind," Bob Wood explains. "At 14, he was running up and down the halls of the RCA building, looking in wastepaper baskets for discarded scripts."

Most TV wives consider themselves virtually "widowed" by the tube and resent all the time their dedicated husbands put into it. Luckily for Silverman, his wife, Cathy, loves the broadcasting business and shares in his career. It's a *Bridget Loves Bernie*–style marriage, à la the CBS Catholic/Jewish situation comedy that Silverman reluctantly pulled off the air after protests from some religious groups. Up from the CBS stenographic pool, Cathy was his secretary for several years before their 1971 nuptials, performed by both priest and rabbi. They have two children: Melissa, four, whom Freddie constantly quizzes about her TV preferences, and an infant son, William, born last December.

Silverman is not caught up in the status-symbol steeplechase; his tastes are unpretentious. He once bought a Jaguar XKE, which only gathered dust in the garage. He wears semi–Ivy League, off-the-rack suits— even to Beverly Hills parties where Dorso bush jackets and Gucci loafers are the mode. By his program purchases he has made men millionaires, yet he remains unimpressed by wealth. Invited to *Starsky & Hutch* producer Aaron Spelling's luxurious Holmby Hills estate with private road, electric gates, heated pool and tennis court, Silverman only remarked, "Some house, Aaron."

One of the rewards of his job, Freddie feels, is that "I've gotten to meet an awful lot of very nice people and very talented people who I really think will be friends regardless of whether I'm working in a network." Yet even his friends sense a certain distance: "He's a very guarded man." According to Universal Television's Tom Tannenbaum: "I've seen guys who have wronged him, unfair players, hucksters who've pulled some fast ones, and it takes a long time for them to get back in the door."

Has Silverman any detractors? "I've met people who don't like him, can't stand him, think he's crazy, think he's unpredictable and a lot of other things," says one studio head, "but they are probably also admirers."

"Hollywood is really terrible!" says Filmways TV chief Perry Lafferty. "It's not enough that you succeed, but the other person should also fail miserably! They can't stand it when Freddie says, 'Let's do *Donny & Marie*,' and it's a hit; 'Let's do *Charlie's Angels*,' and it's a hit. But that's the way this town is—everybody goes nuts because Freddie's succeeding!"

While Silverman was at CBS, something happened that shook up his fond notion of himself as a company man. Network president Frank Stanton, who had expected to move up to the chairmanship of the company on William Paley's retirement at age 65, was himself sidelined. Paley decided not to retire and forced Stanton to leave.

"See, the three networks are still going to be here in some form when we're all gone," Freddie said. "Life goes on. I think I saw it clearest when Frank Stanton left CBS. And, to me, Frank Stanton has always been—will always be—the heart and soul of CBS. I think he is a great man. There will never be another leader like him in the industry. His personality shaped that corporation.

"And he left one day and—surprise of all surprises— it just went right on. So, you know, with that in mind— we're all on this earth for a short period of time. As Perry Lafferty used to say, 'You're not fighting a religious crusade.' It's something that really is the truth."

At 39, Fred Silverman is already looking outside the television industry. "The world has got some severe problems," he said in January, "and there aren't too many capable people in positions to solve them. I might just surprise everyone in a couple of years and leave the business. How do you like that?"

The Farrah Phenomenon

While American sex symbols come and go, none has ever risen so fast as the 30-year-old blonde with all that hair
by Bill Davidson

It was a big day in the short happy history of the Farrah Phenomenon. The early-morning hours were enlivened by a news item to the effect that two million copies of a Farrah Fawcett-Majors poster had been sold in less than four months by Pro Arts, Inc. of Medina, Ohio, thus breaking poster-sales speed records previously held by Fonzie, Marilyn Monroe and the shark from "Jaws."

At 10 A.M., Barbara Walters called about the possibility of a TV interview—at home with Farrah and her husband, Lee Majors—à la Miss Walters' interviews with the Jimmy Carters and the Gerald Fords.

At 10:17 A.M., there was a $40,000 offer for Farrah to appear at a Seattle auto show, merely to sign autographs for three hours.

Just before noon, a famous designer proposed a million-dollar deal to manufacture a line of Farrah clothes.

After lunch, there were discussions with Farrah's agents about a suggested biography by Grosset & Dunlap, a New York book publisher; a deal was closed to flood the toy market with a Farrah doll; a deal was rejected to permit a line of Farrah wigs to be licensed; Farrah T-shirts were approved; a line of Farrah cosmetics received favorable consideration; but bed sheets featuring a full-length life-sized imprinted likeness of Farrah were turned down on the grounds that they might appeal to the prurient interests of teen-agers and others.

But then, at nightfall, came the most exhilarating news of all for Farrah's large retinue of publicists and merchandisers. Scholastic Magazines, Inc., announced the results of its poll of more than 14,000 junior and senior high school students. Their No. 1 personal hero: Farrah Fawcett-Majors. Just one national or international leader made the Top 20. That was the President of the United States, Jimmy Carter, in 16th place.

In addition to what this says about the psyches of America's young, it also solidifies the rapidly growing belief that—in emotional appeal, at least—this year's Fonz is a smallish 30-year-old blonde with rumpled-looking hair who receives only second billing in the season's smash-hit new television series, ABC's *Charlie's Angels*. Based on the volume sales of Farrah posters and merchandise, she also must be considered this year's version of Betty Grable, Lana Turner and other pinup queens of the past.

Which is surprising, since along with Farrah's obvious assets—good legs; striking wide-set aquamarine-colored eyes—she is considered by many experts to rank third among Charlie's three angels by the accepted standards of classic beauty. In profile, her nose is slightly bent. When closed, her mouth is thin-lipped and somewhat pouty; when open, by her own admission, it shows "too many teeth." Her figure has been described by some as "scrawny," by others as "flat."

Nevertheless, the Farrah Phenomenon is in full swing, and no one knows how far it will go or how long it will last. The one acknowledged fact is that no one ever attained this kind of super-stardom so fast. Betty Grable, Marilyn Monroe, even the Fonz, took at least two years to build. Two years ago, Farrah was just another Hollywood hopeful. She had kicked around the town rather aimlessly for six years after graduating from W. B. Ray High School in Corpus Christi and studying art and sculpture at the University of Texas. She was known mostly as Lee Majors' constant companion (becoming his wife two and a half years ago), and as the girl in the Wella Balsam and Mercury Cougar TV commercials. Her acting skills were rudimentary and were displayed mostly in bit parts and TV movies like "The Girl Who Came Gift Wrapped" and "The Great American Beauty Contest."

All this changed for Farrah when *Charlie's Angels* was created last year. Producers Aaron Spelling and Leonard Goldberg (*The Rookies, Starsky & Hutch, Family*) had developed the series idea about three beautiful girls working in a dream-world detective agency for a never-seen male private eye, and they quickly sold the concept to ABC's Fred Silverman. The show was built around Kate Jackson, who had co-starred for Spelling-Goldberg in *The Rookies.*

Spelling told me, "We were completely taken by surprise by Fred's instant acceptance of Kate. Things usu-

ally don't go that fast in TV. We had a second brunette in mind, Jaclyn Smith, but we figured we'd better throw a blonde at Fred for contrast. I knew Farrah from when I double-dated with her and Lee Majors. Len knew her from when he was the head of production at Screen Gems. We put our heads together and tentatively said to Silverman, 'How about Farrah Fawcett?' Once again he amazed us by saying, 'Great. Who's next?' We later found out he was aware of Farrah from three TV movies she had done for us, especially 'Murder on Flight 502.' "

Kate Jackson was signed for $10,000 per show, the lesser-known Farrah and Jaclyn Smith for $5000 each. Says Goldberg, "It was then that the *Charlie's Angels* phenomenon began and it was as startling to us as the Farrah Phenomenon that grew out of it. We thought it was a nice little show, nothing more, and we were totally unprepared for what happened. It was a hit from the start."

From nearly the very first week, the Farrah Phenomenon *also* was under way. Spelling and Goldberg strove mightily to keep the three angels equal (each received an identical motor home as a dressing room, for example), but Farrah soon forged ahead of the other two in fan mail and media attention. Little boys began to phone the studio by the thousands asking for Farrah's photograph. The ABC publicity department was deluged with requests for Farrah interviews from publications all over the U.S.—and from European countries where *Charlie's Angels* had not yet been shown. The ultimate fan magazine, People, on its personalities-of-the-year cover, gave Farrah's photo more space than Jimmy Carter's, Robert Redford's and King Kong's combined.

Although Spelling-Goldberg manfully set about making merchandising deals for the three angels, the deals and subsequent sales were dwarfed by those made for Farrah alone by Marge Schicktanz, her agent for TV commercials and merchandise-licensing at the William

Morris Agency. When I visited Mrs. Schicktanz one day, she was barely visible behind folders of proposed Farrah deals piled up on her desk.

One question about all this has still not been satisfactorily answered: *Why?* The success of the show itself has been explained by labeling it as a throwback to the simpler times of *The Man from U.N.C.L.E.,* when audiences craved pure comic-strip fantasy in their cop shows. Another theory is that it's basically a prime-time girlie show in the guise of action-adventure. Farrah partially confirms this latter possibility, saying, "When the show was No. 3, I figured it was our acting. When we got to be No. 1, I decided it could only be because none of us wears a bra."

But what about the incredible emergence of Farrah, as against the comparatively routine stardom of the other two angels? This is a subject of great puzzlement and controversy among psychologists and other experts. One Ohio college professor attributes it to her hair: "That mussed-up blond mane looks as if she just got out of bed and is immediately ready to get back into it." A Los Angeles psychiatrist told me, "The key to the whole thing is that men think of her as a sexpot and women invariably describe her as 'adorable.' When women call another woman 'adorable,' that means she poses no threat to them in terms of seducing their husbands. Maybe that's because they read about this girl's happy marriage to Lee Majors and that she even hyphenated her last name with his."

Another psychiatric opinion: "She's a throwback to Lana Turner and Brigitte Bardot. She seems to have skipped the whole unpleasant decade of the 1960s, which people want to forget."

Jay Bernstein, her personal publicist, says: "All I can think is that with her and her husband, I've got another Lombard-Gable combination on my hands." Then, he soberly adds, "The only thing she still has to prove is that she can act."

My wife thinks, "She has the look of 'I'm very happy and full of life today, and tomorrow is going to be even better.' She radiates a *wholesome* sexiness. There also seems to be a sweetness—almost a tinge of Mary Tyler Moore beneath that mop of hair."

Take your choice.

Farrah herself, not given to philosophizing, merely repeats the old saw that she "just happened to be in the right place at the right time."

And Spelling-Goldberg, gloomily looking at the soaring Farrah merchandising figures (in which they do *not* participate), say: "Who knows how long this will last? But if we'd go out of the television business and into the Farrah business, we'd be one helluva lot richer."

At the time, neither Spelling nor Goldberg realized the full extent of their Farrah Phenomenon problem. Shortly thereafter, Farrah announced she would not be returning to the show next season, as she now visualized herself a movie star. Spelling-Goldberg said, "But you have a contract with us." Farrah replied, "No I haven't."

We'll see—when the show resumes production this week.

TV'S
$$$$-RATED MOVIES
What are the most popular old films on television? The answers may surprise you
by Joe Walders

Movies have always been a staple of TV programming. Today your local station can choose from more than 20,000 feature films to play on its late movie or early show. But have you ever felt that "Godzilla vs. the Smog Monster" and "Attack of the 50-Foot Woman" are the only pictures your local station owns?

Does it just *seem* that way? Or do stations in fact play the same movies over and over again?

TV stations do favor specific titles—not so much to save on film rentals, but because audiences want to watch certain movies again and again. So if you were a station's program director, the task would appear simple enough: show the movies your viewers want.

But how on earth do you know which ones they like?

For starters, most TV stations look to the TV Feature Film Source Book, published by a New York City firm called Broadcast Information Bureau (BIB). BIB's Source Book rates just about every sound feature film ever made for its appeal to TV audiences. Like the star rating system (****) some newspapers use to evaluate current movies, the Source Book rates old movies similarly—only instead of stars, it awards dollar signs ($$$$).

What makes a $$$$-rated movie? Avra Fliegelman, editor-in-chief of the Source Book, discusses what goes into her ratings. First of all, she explains, a movie's performance in theaters has no hard and fast relationship to its television performance.

For example, the Cecil B. DeMille circus drama "The Greatest Show on Earth" (1952—with Charlton Heston, Betty Hutton, James Stewart) not only was the top moneymaker of the year, but it also won the Academy Award for Best Picture. Yet it has rarely done well on television.

Other films that have failed to duplicate on television their impressive theatrical successes include: "Easter Parade" (1948—with Judy Garland, Fred Astaire), "Magnificent Obsession" (1954—with Jane Wyman, Rock Hudson) and "Strategic Air Command" (1955—with James Stewart, June Allyson).

Conversely, as Avra Fliegelman states, there are other pictures that are very popular today on TV although they never set any box-office records. Movies in this category include almost all science-fiction and horror pictures and certain movie series like the Sherlock Holmes and Charlie Chan pictures.

Besides a movie's box-office record, BIB's ratings consider a picture's reputation with critics, its age and its cast. "Stars are important on television, as they are in the theaters," Fliegelman points out, "but it's a different type of star."

"King Kong" with Fay Wray
(Museum of Modern Art/Film Stills Archive)

**"Casablanca"
with Humphrey Bogart
and Ingrid Bergman**
(Museum of Modern Art/Film Stills Archive)

"High Noon" with Gary Cooper and Grace Kelly
(Museum of Modern Art/Film Stills Archive)

Gene Barry, for instance, was never a big *movie* star; however, *Bat Masterson* and *Burke's Law* made him a big *television* star. Thus his early movies, like "Atomic City" (1952), draw more audience interest today on TV than they did when they were first released. Likewise, viewers today will loyally watch the early movies of such TV stars as Raymond Burr, Robert Stack and Efrem Zimbalist Jr.

This is not to say only TV stars attract viewers to old movies. The presence of movie superstars like James Cagney, Humphrey Bogart, Bette Davis, Steve McQueen, Paul Newman and John Wayne in any picture almost guarantees good ratings time and again.

Walt Baker is program director of KHJ-TV, an independent (no network affiliation) station in Los Angeles, and has been programming movies for 20 years. He adds his own judgments to BIB's ratings. What makes a movie popular with KHJ's viewers?

"The age of the picture is important," Baker replies. "We want the newer pictures whenever we can find them. That, of course, doesn't hold true with classics." By "classics" Baker means pictures like "King Kong" (the 1933 version) and "High Noon" (1952).

Baker's second criterion is the picture's genre. "Action formats really work better for us than almost anything else," he says. "Action formats" means war films ("To Hell and Back," 1955—with Audie Murphy), crime melodramas ("Al Capone," 1959—with Rod Steiger), Westerns ("The Magnificent Seven," 1960—with Yul Brynner) and horror and science-fiction pictures ("Them," 1954—with James Arness).

Viewers will watch these pictures repeatedly. "The number of times [a picture is shown] doesn't seem to diminish the success of the picture's ratings. What can hurt it," Baker explains, "is if you show it too close to the last showing. We attempt to maintain a six-month separation [between showings]."

Like Los Angeles, New York has several independent stations that depend on movies as the mainstay of their programming. Larry Casey is manager of film and program services at WOR-TV, a New York independent. Casey agrees with Walt Baker's assessment of the kinds of pictures that work on TV. Science-fiction and horror films are big in New York. Why? "They're very exploitable," Casey says. "I think they appeal to a diverse audience, including viewers who might enjoy these films just because some of them are so ludicrous."

There are a few quality sci-fi pictures such as "The Day the Earth Stood Still" and "The Time Machine." However, most fit into Casey's "exploitable/ludicrous" description: how about "I Was a Teenage Frankenstein," "The Beast with a Million Eyes" and "Billy the Kid vs. Dracula"? Pictures like these are rerun often, not only because they are popular, but because Hollywood has produced only a few hundred of them.

What about classier nonaction films?

"Musicals in general do not pull very good ratings," Casey says. "We run Fred Astaire Weeks once or twice a year. We get a lot of mail on it, but the ratings aren't as good as you would think. These films appeal to a very limited audience."

"That's absolutely right," agrees Robert Morin, vice president of MGM's syndicated television sales division. "The public, in spite of what they say, would rather see pictures like 'White Heat' [1949—with James Cagney, Virginia Mayo] and 'Force of Evil' [1948—with John Garfield] than 'Meet Me in St. Louis' [1944—with Judy Garland, Margaret O'Brien], which is a terrific MGM musical."

Of course, as Morin and others point out, there are exceptions. "If you give them a really *great* musical like 'The Wizard of Oz' [1939—with Judy Garland], they'll watch it," Morin notes. And although viewers are also disinclined toward romantic drama, "Casablanca" (1943—with Humphrey Bogart, Ingrid Bergman and Claude Rains) is the notable exception here.

Program directors do monitor viewer mail and phone calls. But there's a built-in problem in relying on viewers' direct response.

WCCO-TV in Minneapolis is one of a number of stations that have asked viewers to vote for the movies they'd like to see. While such proven ratings powerhouses as "High Sierra" (1941—with Humphrey Bogart, Ida Lupino) and "Public Enemy" (1931—with James Cagney and Jean Harlow) registered as favorites, so did such musicals as "Top Hat" (1935—with Fred Astaire, Ginger Rogers) and "High Society" (1956—with Frank Sinatra, Grace Kelly and Bing Crosby). But when these musicals were shown, their ratings did not match their voted popularity, although the action pictures' ratings did. This is why WCCO-TV film director Harry Jones concludes that the calls, letters and even the votes don't provide a representative sample of what movies his viewers really want to watch.

WCCO did turn up a Marx Brothers cult in the Minneapolis–St. Paul market. Other markets have other "cults"—exceptionally loyal fans who will watch their favorite performer or genre of movie ceaselessly. There are cults for Bogart, W. C. Fields, Charlie Chan, Sherlock Holmes, Tarzan and science-fiction and horror—to name a few. Because the cults are relatively small, their films are usually scheduled in marginal time periods.

And then there are certain kinds of films that audiences simply won't watch. KHJ's Walt Baker describes them as old black-and-white dramas and romances or musicals whose stars are no longer well known or popular. There are thousands of 1930s and 1940s pictures that sit on TV distributors' shelves just gathering dust.

However, there are times when a distributor will intentionally take films out of circulation. Right now, United Artists Television is "resting" some titles, the theory being that after a number of years audiences will be eager to see these pictures again.

But viewer preference and distributor's whims are not the only reasons you are seeing fewer titles more frequently these days: there are fewer movie time slots on local stations' schedules. A decade ago, ABC and CBS affiliates ran late-night movies because the networks didn't provide programming at 11:30 as they now do (the networks do schedule some movies at 11:30). Talk shows and game shows, dirt cheap for stations to buy, have further cut into movie showcases. Today an affiliate can supply its movie needs with a few hundred titles whereas previously a thousand or more weren't too many.

These trends have made the movies-for-TV business a buyer's market (except in the largest markets like New York, Los Angeles, Chicago). Even so, TV sales are still profitable. The current movie prices in New York, for example, range from $100 for one run of a black-and-white oldie to a high of $7500 for something like "The Battle of Britain" (1969—with Laurence Olivier, Michael Caine). These are *average* New York prices for a number of pictures in a package; individual pictures may be priced substantially higher or lower.

Multiply these per-showing rates by the typical 10-showings-per-station contract and then by the 100 major TV markets, and you'll see how lucrative the movies-for-TV business can be.

If this makes you envious of actors for their movie residuals, it shouldn't. Most of the movies shown on television pay royalties only to owners of the studios.

The most intriguing question about old movies on TV is the one that's impossible to answer positively: Which picture has been shown the most times on American television?

Although there is some disagreement on this score, many program directors point to "Casablanca" as the movie most frequently seen on home screens.

However, even the owners of "Casablanca," United Artists, aren't sure of its status. Erwin Ezzes, chairman of United Artists Television, tried to calculate how many times "Casablanca" has been shown, but he found that the booking records for 1956–60 have been discarded. He does state that "Casablanca" has never stopped playing in at least one major market since 1956.

So while it's impossible to be completely certain, "Casablanca" seems a reasonable choice for the movie most often shown on TV. Indeed it may be the very ubiquity of "Casablanca" that has given rise to a widely held but erroneous bit of movie lore: that classic line of dialogue, "Play it again, Sam," was never spoken in "Casablanca"! Humphrey Bogart and Ingrid Bergman each tell piano player Dooley Wilson to "Play it, Sam"—but not to "Play it *again,* Sam."

No matter though. Even if Rick doesn't tell Sam literally to play "As Time Goes By" *again,* Sam will play it again for Rick and Ilsa, and for us viewers. And you can bet it won't be the last time either.

PLAY THEM AGAIN . . . AND AGAIN . . . AGAIN

In a straw poll, with no pretense of being scientifically accurate, we asked program directors around the country to name the 10 most popular, most often shown movies in their markets. These are the titles that they named most frequently:

1. "Casablanca" (1943—with Humphrey Bogart, Ingrid Bergman)
2. "King Kong" (1933—with Bruce Cabot, Fay Wray)
3. "The Magnificent Seven" (1960—with Yul Brynner)
4. "The Maltese Falcon" (1941—with Humphrey Bogart, Mary Astor)
5. "The Adventures of Robin Hood" (1938—with Errol Flynn)
6. "The African Queen" (1951—with Humphrey Bogart, Katharine Hepburn)
7. "The Birds" (1963—with Rod Taylor, Tippi Hedren)
8. "Citizen Kane" (1941—with Orson Welles)
9. "Miracle on 34th Street" (1947—with Maureen O'Hara, Edmund Gwenn)
10. "Girls! Girls! Girls!" (1962—with Elvis Presley)
11. "King Solomon's Mines" (1950—with Stewart Granger, Deborah Kerr)
12. "The Treasure of the Sierra Madre" (1948—with Humphrey Bogart, Walter Huston)
13. "The War of the Worlds" (1953—with Gene Barry)

The same poll revealed the most popular *series* of movies to be the Sherlock Holmes pictures starring Basil Rathbone and Nigel Bruce.

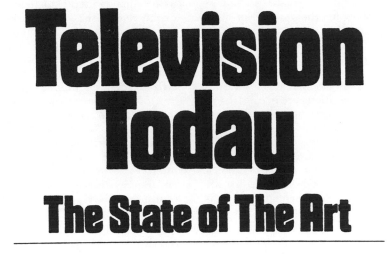

Television Today
The State of The Art

A thorough examination of why the American TV system is what it is
by Merrill Panitt

PART 1

NEWS REPORTING

On the surface, television is doing beautifully.

The audience is watching more than ever—about six hours and 18 minutes a day in the average home.

Networks and stations posted record highs in profits last year on income of about $6 billion. Income of $14.1 billion is projected for 1985.

Television has become not only the most effective communications medium but also the strongest social force in America today. It is, for better or worse, dissolving our geographical differences in speech, dress and life styles.

Most observers agree that it played a significant part in the success of the civil-rights movement, in the youth revolution of the '60s, in turning public opinion against America's military involvement in Southeast Asia, in forcing Presidents Johnson and Nixon out of office.

President Jimmy Carter attributes his victory in an extremely close election to the exposure he gained during last year's televised debates.

The medium has power beyond the dreams of conquerors. It has achieved economic success unprecedented in the history of communications. It has gained audience devotion never before attained by a form of entertainment.

Nothing—not even business recessions—seems to affect the growth of network profits. Cigaret advertising, once worth some $200 million a year to the networks, was banned from the air. A half hour of network prime time each evening was given back to the stations, reducing network potential advertising income by one-seventh. A federal law prohibited the premium prices once

demanded from political candidates. The FCC restricted network ownership of television programs, putting an end to their profitable rights to syndicate programs in the United States. Pressure from citizens' groups forced them to reduce the number of commercials on children's shows. Still, network profits kept rising.

Yet television is a nervous, defensive, ambivalent medium, its extravagantly paid but insecure network executives fearful of change, its programming under constant attack, its relationship with government

Drawing by Bill Charmatz

schizophrenic. "Government interference!" is the standard cry whenever Federal Communications commissioners or congressmen jawbone about television's excesses, but the industry is quick to demand government protection from possible inroads into its territory by cable and pay-TV operators.

At the local level, station owners are quite aware that they are in what one leading broadcaster terms "A comfortable business." In fact, the stations are becoming less affiliates than appendages of the networks. Some owners resent having up to two-thirds of their broadcast time controlled by a network. More resent being paid by the network as little as a fifth of what they might get if they were able to sell the time locally. There are occasional rumbles of discontent among network affiliates, but for the most part their resentment is outweighed by the bottom-line figures the network-station relationship produces.

No one—station or network—wants to make waves. The system works too well, the business is too profitable for taking chances. Security lies in keeping things as they are, in a state close to stagnation, in making only enough change to give the appearance of change.

Perhaps, considering the nature of television, its dependence upon advertising and therefore upon the obvious, if simplistic, solution of trying to reach most of the people nearly all of the time, Americans are fortunate that the quality the medium offers them is as high as it is. Perhaps the fact that, after 30 years of television, the efforts of broadcasters are directed far more to reaching the largest audience than to presenting the finest programs is a cause for national concern.

It may be that both propositions are true, that we are seeing reasonably good television, but that it isn't good enough, isn't varied enough, isn't worthy enough of such a pervasive and powerful means of communication.

This series of articles is an attempt to assess the state of the art/business today, to tell how and why the American television system works, for this system has a crucial effect upon the personal lives and attitudes of those who watch it (and those who don't), and upon the society and the world they live in.

Since television is the chief source of news information for nearly two-thirds of all Americans—and since news is the basis of television's strength as a force for social change—news is a logical starting point.

Network news is a headline service with some pictorial coverage. It is an effortless way for the viewer to find out what's going on in the world without having to bother reading through a mass of details. In the process of distilling the news to its essence for television, a great deal must be omitted and oversimplified. The complex society we live in is affected by concepts of government and foreign affairs, by theories of economics and geopolitics. Since concepts and theories do not lend themselves easily to pictures—or to brevity—network news must concentrate more on *what* happened (or at least what happened that can be photographed) than *why* it happened.

Still, more people today than ever before are aware of what happened, and for this, television can take credit. Coverage of breaking news—fires, battles, civil disturbances—is immediate and impressive. Meetings of world leaders, space shots, news conferences are reported as they happen, and the networks spend huge sums to bring the important events of our time to viewers in an effective manner. Not yet, though, have they learned to be as effective in making the great thoughts of our time interesting to viewers.

Television's need for pictures is easily exploited by protestors, picketers and politicians. Although the excesses of the '60s (when street or campus demonstrations often began when television-news cameras arrived, and ended when they left) are no longer commonplace, demonstrators still do their loudest slogan-chanting when cameras and microphones are pointed at them. The intent, of course, is to impress and influence people watching the evening news. By now viewers are well aware of the game, and it takes more than routine cheering and slogans to impress them. Violence helps. Anti-busing demonstrations in Boston held the nation's attention on television effectively when demonstrators were battling police and banging the sides of buses. Interest lagged when the dispute became less physical.

In what may be more a characteristic of democracy than the fault of the medium, a candidate for public office stands a better chance of attracting television coverage while consuming ethnic foods than while delivering a speech on economic issues. In the recent Presidential campaign, television was guilty, but no more guilty than newspapers and magazines, of appearing to devote more coverage to trivialities than to the candidates' differences on basic issues. Mr. Carter's thoughts on lust in Playboy and Mr. Ford's slip of the tongue on Poland's independence from the Soviet Union prompted more intensive press coverage than the candidates' views on nuclear energy, multipurpose missiles or détente. Unfortunately, more voters saw or heard about the trivialities on television than read about them in print.

Network television has only a few minutes—22 minutes plus commercials and other interruptions during a half-hour news show—to cover the events of the day. The number of words employed would fill three columns of a newspaper page. Yet, in those few minutes the newscast must present not only the obvious headlines of the day but, when possible, a story the other networks do not have, a "special" or "investigative report" to prove Network A is doing a better job of reporting than Networks B and C.

Generally the news is just about the same on all three networks, the chief difference being the person or persons who sit behind the anchor desk, read the news and introduce the picture coverage. All three networks work desperately to attain the prestige and money that go with first-place position in news ratings. The prestige helps build audience (and higher advertising income) for the winning network's other news and public-affairs shows and enhances the network's public image.

To the viewer deciding which network news show to

watch, the determining factor is not the news, but who is delivering it. At this point, capable and experienced Walter Cronkite appeals to more viewers than capable and experienced John Chancellor and David Brinkley or capable and experienced Harry Reasoner and Barbara Walters. All of them—and the reporters, writers and editors who work with them—are under tremendous pressure to be fair, for most members of the audience belong to some minority, whether it be ethnic, racial, religious, political or professional; and they all are alert to real or imagined slights. Perhaps the most remarkable achievement of network news is, considering the pressures, its success in avoiding blandness, its ability to present the news as objectively as possible.

What is needed, all agree, is more time to relate the major news of the day, time to explain and interpret what is behind a news event and what may result from it. In order to do this, the three networks have been trying for several years to expand their nightly half-hour news periods to an hour, by pre-empting 30 minutes of time now allocated to the stations. But the local stations that carry network news won't let them. Like everything else in television, it's a matter of money.

With 725 commercial stations on the air (93 of them independent), each network has about 200 affiliates that agree to carry network programs for a number of hours each day. (In cities with only one or two stations, a station may be affiliated with more than one network.) In return, the network reimburses each affiliate with a small percentage of the station's normal time charges. Because station income is greater if the time is sold locally, the stations are unwilling to sacrifice one more minute, much less a half hour, to the networks, for the admirable cause of expanded news. Expand your news if you like, they tell the networks, but do it in network time, not in station time.

Network attempts to soften the blow by permitting the stations to sell—at full rate—some of the commercials in an early-evening hour-long network news show failed. The station owners are as competent in arithmetic as the network executives, and the plans for another half-hour of network news in station time adds up to less income for stations.

A number of stations in large cities are offering as much as two hours of local news leading into the network news. It is expensive programming, but it is profitable, and the news competition among stations is so heated that the news itself frequently plays only an incidental role in the rush for ratings.

The local race for first position in news has spawned a new kind of professional—the television-news consultant. These experts at audience building have found that viewers of local newscasts like handsome anchor people, a dramatic opening story, many brief news items rather than fewer and longer ones, pictures of fires and other disasters, and bantering among the anchor man, weatherman and sportscaster. With many stations hiring consultants, it was inevitable that local news would be glutted with handsome anchor people, dramatic opening stories, et cetera. When ratings fall off, stations rush to

hire a consultant or, if they've already had a consultant, to hire an even better-looking anchor person, increase the number of news items, step up the bantering.

News becomes entertainment, with the objective being to hold the viewer's attention so that he'll sit through the commercials. Before each commercial break—and this happens on some network newscasts too—the anchor man delivers a teaser for a story that will be revealed *after* the commercial break. If the story is sexy enough, it may be used as a teaser before several breaks and finally delivered near the end of the newscast.

For the most part, this mechanical approach to local news has led to stations paying more attention to the form than to the substance of the news. It has been worse. For a time it was believed that a majority of viewers wanted more comedy with their local news, and jokes became the order of the day in what critics labeled the "Happy News" format. Stations that indulged in slapstick found the audience jarred by the juxtaposition of floods, famines and funnies and were forced to tone down the comedy.

Technological advances have resulted in miniature television cameras that can be used for live coverage of breaking news, and the development of electronic news gathering (ENG) for local newscasts. ENG offers stations an opportunity for extraordinary live pictures of fires, demonstrations, meetings and similar events. (It also, unfortunately, sometimes offers viewers pictures of an event before the reporter has had time to gather the facts of the story to accompany the pictures.)

Another encouraging aspect of local news is the increased number of stations that have hired investigative reporters and allocated the necessary time, effort and money to permit them to develop original reports.

The networks bear the expense of bureaus throughout the world, of transmission costs and of huge headquarters staffs. They also transmit pictorial coverage of national and international events to their affiliated stations to be taped and used on local news shows.

The news operation generally appears on network books as a loss item, although there certainly is no shortage of advertisers willing to pay up to $28,000 for a 30-second commercial.

Local news is definitely profitable. That is why no local station wants to risk cutting into those profits by relinquishing local news time—or any other local time—so that network news can be expanded.

The viewer has little to say in all this. He may or may not be satisfied with 30 or 35 short news bits and a flock of commercials as his daily measure of local news. And he may or may not be satisfied with what the networks are able to do in their present news broadcasts. But he apparently must accept what the majority of his fellow viewers seem to want to see, and what the economic structure of television permits him to see.

Television news, then, is the same as nearly everything else on television—directed to the mass audience, programmed to provide maximum income, with minimum thought given to improving either the cultural level of the audience or the stature of the medium.

Drawing by Bill Charmatz

PART II

NETWORK POWER—IS IT ABSOLUTE?
How advertisers, affiliates and producers fare in their struggles with the Big Three

At the heart of most of the achievements—and the failures—of the communications medium that pervades nearly every aspect of American life is the television network.

Once a convenient arrangement that permitted stations to broadcast quality programming they could not afford individually, and permitted advertisers to reach across the country with their programs and commercial messages, the networks now stand in absolute control of the medium. They determine what programs Americans will see, who will make them, who will perform in them and what their content will be.

In the final analysis, network executives say, the public determines what will be on the air. In truth, what the public determines is what will *not* be on the air. If the audience refuses to watch one network offering, another is submitted. The same men who selected the original program decide upon its replacement. The same thinking that brought about the first decision brings about the second. And, if necessary, the third and fourth and fifth.

The power of the networks brings them into conflict with other segments of the television business—with advertisers and agencies that buy commercial time from the networks; with local station affiliates that carry network programs; with producers who sell programs to the networks.

There was a time when advertisers selected programs, had them made and sponsored them on the air. Then,

in 1958, the quiz scandals broke. A number of sponsored big-money quiz shows were caught playing hanky-panky to boost ratings, indulging in such practices as giving contestants answers to questions. The networks pleaded innocence, blamed it all on sponsors and announced firmly that they would now take charge of the programs they put on the air.

In short order it was all but impossible for a sponsor to buy a show from a producer. Instead he had his pick of several programs offered to him by the network. These programs, as it happened, were partly owned by the network. It had provided funds to make the pilot show and in return had an interest in the program. Before long, networks owned, at least in part, nearly every show they telecast. They thus received money from advertisers not only for the air time but also for the programs themselves. As prices rose, fewer and fewer advertisers could afford to sponsor programs. They found it more expedient, and profitable, to spread their commercials among a number of programs and thus reach more viewers.

Eventually, however, the Federal Communications Commission forced the networks out of major involvement in entertainment-program ownership.

Instead of sponsoring programs, most network advertisers now buy one-minute or 30-second commercials in various programs. The one-minute spots usually amount to two 30-second commercials devoted to different products owned by the same advertiser. These are called "piggyback" commercials, and there has been some experimenting with 15-second "piggybacks."

Television is a seller's market now. Available time—the six network minutes allotted for commercials each hour in prime time—now sells at an average rate of $100,000 a minute but is so scarce that a number of advertising agencies and production companies are speaking seriously about trying to form a fourth network. A network solution, sent up as a trial balloon and then shot down as adverse reaction from agencies and stations thundered in, was to increase the number of network commercial minutes per hour from six to seven. Added to the number of local-station minutes sold by stations each hour, that would increase viewers' exposure to commercials and promotions in prime time from about 7½ minutes to 8½ or nine minutes. (Outside of prime time the TV Code permits 16 minutes of nonprogram material per hour—but only two-thirds of the stations subscribe to the Code. The others are free to run as much advertising as the traffic will bear.)

Some national commercials are placed directly on local stations, and, of course, the local stations sell commercial time to local advertisers. Estimates for 1976 have network income from advertising up 22 percent from 1975 to $2.8 billion, national commercials placed on local stations up 37 percent to $2.2 billion and local advertising up 27 percent to $1.7 billion.

Business is good. Advertisers who used to wait until Friday of each week to buy next week's unsold time from the networks at distress rates are now committing millions of dollars for commercial time months in advance.

Advertisers are generally unhappy because they have little to say about the kinds of programs on the air. They want their commercials on popular shows, but some express discomfort about being associated with programs that feature violence. A number of them, including General Foods, have refused to buy time in such programs.

Other advertisers are eager to sponsor documentaries, dramas or other programs of superior quality but find little of such programming available on the networks. These advertisers—Exxon, IBM, Mobil, Xerox, Gulf and others—contribute money to public broadcasting to get such programs on the air, to relatively small audiences, even though on public broadcasting they are not permitted to advertise.

Another sore point with advertisers is the number of commercials the networks lump together during commercial breaks. Advertisers prefer more interruptions in a program and few commercials during each interruption. Viewers apparently prefer fewer interruptions. The networks try to offer a compromise, but the results for viewers are chopped-up programs and a bombardment of hard sell; for advertisers, skyrocketing costs at a time when their commercials are all but lost in the cacophony of other commercials.

There are complaints from Madison Avenue, but not much more than that. The three networks are in the driver's seat. Their chief problem now is to try to allocate what commercial time is still available to advertisers who will be back when business may not be so good. Procter & Gamble, which spends nearly $350 million a year on television, has little difficulty picking up a few more minutes for commercials. An advertiser who spends less than a million a year is less likely to be favored.

Viewers are being subjected to more and more television advertising. In 1967 they saw an estimated 100,000 commercial minutes on the networks: 94 percent of the commercials were a minute long (the rest 30 seconds) for a total of 103,000 commercials. In 1974 they watched 105,622 commercial minutes; 76 percent of the commercials were 30 seconds in length (the rest a minute) for a total of 170,400 commercials. Thus the number of network commercials alone increased 65 percent in eight years, and undoubtedly has increased since 1974.

Among the effects of so many commercials are the restrictions on writers. An hour-long program must have four breaks and must be written so that action reaches a high point before each commercial break. Producer-writer Richard Alan Simmons said of series writing: "There's no such thing as sitting down to a blank piece of paper. You start with characters probably invented by someone else, whose background and reactions are set in previous episodes. You've got to fill in the plot around these characters—and see to it that the action peaks every 15 minutes to provide a lead-in to the commercials."

The station conflict with networks is a quiet one, attracting attention usually when the networks appear to be ready to encroach on station time, as was the case in the networks' campaign to expand their news shows to an hour.

But one station group, Westinghouse's Group W (which owns stations affiliated with each of the three networks), recently petitioned the FCC to conduct an investigation into the network-station relationship. Some 100 stations have written Don McGannon, Group W president, that they support his position, although most of them will not risk saying so publicly. The Justice Department *has* said so publicly. Its anti-trust division filed a petition with the FCC supporting a broad inquiry into network practices. Justice went even further, in suggesting that the FCC consider whether the networks shouldn't be required to divest themselves of some or all of the stations they own. The FCC has agreed to conduct an investigation.

McGannon's position is that the networks treat the stations cavalierly, that networks reimburse stations for carrying network shows at what now amounts to about 13.8 percent of the station's regular rate, that the networks increased their programming on local stations 22 percent between 1960 and 1976, that their sales increased 92 percent between 1964 and 1974 but payments to stations increased only 15 percent.

The Group W chief, an outspoken critic of sex and violence on network programs, also wants the networks to provide station operators an opportunity to see programs well in advance of air date so that they can decide whether to carry the shows. (NBC recently announced it would improve its prescreening arrangements with its affiliates.)

While McGannon, whose company owns stations in large cities, is publicly critical of the networks, his fellow broadcasters are, if not entirely satisfied with the healthy profits their network affiliations bring them, hardly willing to endanger those profits by indulging in intramural squabbling.

The money, in brief, is good. For the stations it could, and possibly should, be better, but most of them are not complaining—out loud. The networks say the stations are well paid for what amounts to using some electricity to keep the station on the air. McGannon says his company spends money on local news and other programming so that the network programs appear on respected stations that can guarantee high ratings. A number of stations and station groups do as much local programming as Group W, but too many stations depend largely upon inexpensive reruns of old network comedy and game shows to fill the time between network offerings.

There are 93 independent stations not affiliated with networks. These operate under the handicap of having no regular source of big-time programming and make do with schedules that usually emphasize local sports and syndicated shows that already have appeared on the networks. (Syndicated shows are also sold abroad, where buyers more often are interested in action shows than situation comedies. Violence in the action shows, plus the largely negative aspects of this country shown on their nightly newscasts, help form foreign audiences' impressions of the United States.)

Network difficulties with the program producers fall into two categories—money and creative problems. The

Hollywood producers complain about "deficit financing," which means the programs they produce cost more than the networks pay for them.

Grant Tinker, whose company produces *The Mary Tyler Moore, Bob Newhart, Rhoda, Phyllis* and *Tony Randall Shows,* said a year or so ago that he might be forced out of business because each episode of his programs cost more than the networks paid him. "They just don't understand how impossible this business is," he said.

The networks have been increasing measurably their payments to producers. They also point to the rather large salaries some producers draw—from the program budgets—and hint that perhaps they're not quite approaching penury. "They're drawing salaries of thousands of dollars a week," said one network head, "living in mansions with swimming pools and a flock of fancy cars. It's hard to feel too sorry for them." Since the producers remain in business year after year, and fight to get new shows on the air, it would appear that "deficit financing" is not yet breaking them.

Creative arguments between producers and networks center around network insistence on supervising stories and casting, and ordering series tailored to network needs. The network has the last word in determining which performers are used. The decisions sometimes depend upon surveys purportedly proving which actors are recognized by the audience, which are popular. One such survey, TvQ (for television quotient), reportedly is used extensively by the networks, especially in approving casts of movies made for television. And it is true that the same faces are seen again and again in TV movies. Such decisions leave little room for producers to develop new talent, to employ their own experience and judgment.

Stories must be discussed with network programming executives, and scripts are approved by them, sometimes with extensive changes. Scripts must also be approved by network censors, euphemistically known as "program practices" people. The decisions of these departments, which have chiefly to do with just how far a script can go in portraying sex and violence and in use of mild obscenities, are frequently baffling to Hollywood writers.

A program shown in "Family Viewing Time"—before 9 P.M. (ET)—cannot have as much sex or violence as one shown after 9 P.M., even though just as many children may be in the audience. (A federal court recently outlawed any real enforcement of Family Viewing Time, but networks and stations are expected to continue it on an unofficial basis—at least for the time being.) The censors generally permit violence up to the point where a knife or bullet actually enters the victim. In beatings, the camera may not linger on the bloody results, a practice that frequently tends to trivialize the horror of real violence. The censors are well aware that, to network programmers, violence is an essential ingredient of some programs. The trick is to permit just enough violence to satisfy the network program people but not enough to draw direct attack from critics. The result often has censors telling producers they can have one stabbing but not two, a couple of pistol-whippings but not shootings,

one car crash during the chase but not three.

As for sex, it is obvious from the programs being shown that pretty girls in as few clothes as possible, and even suggested but not explicit nudity, are now acceptable. A recent episode of *Charlie's Angels* had the three Angels arrested. A sadistic and obviously homosexual matron insisted that they strip before being assigned a cell. As the Angels stood in profile, apparently naked behind towels they held up between themselves and the camera, the leering matron stood in front of them slowly "disinfecting" their bodies with a spray can.

Arbitrary restrictions and the incessant pressure for higher ratings often result in use of violence, sex and obscenity where they are not really required for the dramatic situation, and rather stilted use of them where they might naturally be called for.

Each network allocates tens of millions of dollars each year for "program development." One network alone last season went through 2500 show ideas, considered 150 scripts, and financed 37 pilots. From all this came nine new shows, of which perhaps one or two will last beyond this season.

It is an expensive, nerve-racking, highly competitive business. It is a business controlled by three networks whose top executives usually hold their jobs for relatively short periods, but who during those short periods exercise an effect upon their country and its people rarely equaled—even by the President of the United States.

PART III
PROGRAMMING FOR PROFIT
A look at the values that prevail
in the frantic competition
to build audiences

Television's success lies in its strength as an advertising medium. Its programs attract huge numbers of viewers who are sold to advertisers at $6 to $7 a thousand in prime time. The more viewers, the more money. It's that simple—and that complicated, because there is competition for viewers.

Drawing by Bill Charmatz

Most of the standard questions the audience has about the medium can be answered with the facts in that paragraph.

- "Why is there so much violence on television?" Because many programs that feature violence attract large audiences.
- "Why must they have so many commercials?" Because commercials mean money, and the networks and stations are in business to make money.
- "Can't they make money with fewer commercials?" Yes, but networks and stations are corporations. Stockholders want dividends to increase. The more money the corporation makes, the happier the stockholders are, and the more likely the men who run the corporations are to keep their jobs and make more money themselves.
- "Why, if one network schedules a good special, do the other networks schedule good specials at the same time?" Because competition involves keeping the other fellow from getting a big audience, and sometimes it's just as effective to ruin your competitor's blockbuster as it is to schedule a blockbuster of your own.

The networks have developed audience-building into a fine art. In the early days it was believed that creative people should have an important voice in setting a network's schedule. That was when men like Pat Weaver, who created *Today* and *Tonight* for NBC, were on that network; and Hubbell Robinson and Mike Dann—who depended upon writers and producers—were at CBS.

As competition increased, along with television's financial rewards, sales experts were brought into programming positions. They were thought to be knowledgeable about what the advertisers wanted, but before long it was not really necessary to suit advertisers.

Researchers came next because they were informed as to what viewers were watching, what performers they liked, the trends that lay ahead. One such researcher, Paul Klein, left NBC for a time, then returned late last year as chief of the network's special programming. His predictions as to which shows will succeed each year have won him a reputation as a television seer—and somewhat of a gadfly, for Klein insists that viewers don't necessarily watch programs they like, but programs that are the "least objectionable" among those on at that time.

Now the networks depend upon men who are experts in several areas, especially at gauging the audience and manipulating it. Today's most successful programmer is ABC's Freddie Silverman, whose uncanny ability to sense public tastes has raised ABC from the third network to the first, in ratings.

He did not do it with particularly innovative programming, but with program—and audience—manipulation. He built Fonzie from a supporting role to star of *Happy Days*. He featured two occasional *Happy Days* characters in a spinoff called *Laverne & Shirley*. He spun *The Bionic Woman* out of *The Six Million Dollar Man* (and has a Bionic Boy waiting in the wings). Because last year's eight-episode dramatization of Irwin Shaw's *Rich Man, Poor Man* did well, he decided to make a regular series of it.

For the opening week of the season he started a story on Sunday's *The Six Million Dollar Man* and concluded it on Wednesday's *The Bionic Woman*; placed a *Welcome Back, Kotter* star, a *Laverne & Shirley* star and Wonder Woman on the Bill Cosby show; had two *Kotter*, one *Laverne & Shirley* and several *Happy Days* performers on *The Captain & Tennille*; introduced Mr. T of *Mr. T and Tina* on *Kotter*; and the following Sunday had one of Charlie's Angels on *The Six Million Dollar Man*. He also ran two sky-terror films, "Murder on Flight 502" and "Skyjacked," on Saturday and Sunday to take some of the steam out of NBC's broadcast of "Airport 1975"; and presented an hour-long *Happy Days* that ended in a cliff-hanger to be completed on the next week's half-hour *Happy Days*. All this, in programming parlance, is known as "stunting." It uses the popularity of one show to plug another show. And, at the same time, it blocks out the opposition.

Silverman's programming philosophy (which his competitors say is to turn cartoon ideas suited for Saturday morning kiddy programs into live-action shows for prime time) and his early stunting worked well. ABC got off to a quick lead in this season's ratings. Part of his success is in knowing exactly where to schedule his programs (running *Roots* eight consecutive nights was a brilliant gamble), how to zero in on a competitor's weakness, how to bolster his own new or sagging programs by scheduling them between strong ones. Programming is a fine art and Silverman, once its most successful practitioner at CBS, is now repeating his success at ABC.

At the other networks his counterparts have the same motivation and are using the same techniques to try to catch up and pass him. They did some stunting too that first week of the current season, cross-pollinating some programs by exchanging stars, expanding some half-hour series episodes to an hour, "front-loading" the movie schedule with hit films.

Since the season opened, there have been a number of indications that ABC and, inevitably, the other networks are beginning to realize that the public may be bored with standard prime-time schedules. Viewers' enthusiastic response to the unusual scheduling of *Roots* helped prompt ABC to announce a new "living schedule" philosophy, "living" meaning more innovative programming and scheduling on a year-round basis—more excitement, more variety in the network's prime-time line-up. If ABC succeeds, NBC and CBS won't be far behind.

Still, all of them appear to be more concerned with audience manipulation than the showmanship that begins with outstanding entertainment, more involved with scheduling technique than creativity in programs. It is as if the programs themselves are only incidental to putting together the schedule that will attract most of the $6-$7-a-thousand audience, most of the time.

Complaints about violence or sex or too many commercials can hardly have an effect on men who can judge the popularity of violence and sex by the size of the audiences for *Starsky & Hutch*, *Hawaii Five-O* and *Charlie's Angels*. As for too many commercials, the people watch, don't they? And they must be buying the products or advertisers wouldn't be lining up to buy more time, would they?

Appeals to the government by groups convinced that television violence contributes to crime, or has made us a nation of paranoids, have little effect either. The Federal Communications Commission cannot, by law, concern itself with programs. The Congress is limited by the First Amendment.

One of the networks' most important profit centers is Saturday morning. Children watch television at all hours (a million of them under 11 years old watch after midnight—on week nights!), but on Saturday mornings the audience is concentrated.

A campaign by Action For Children's Television and jawboning from the FCC chairman persuaded the networks to reduce the amount of advertising during Saturday morning children's shows and prompted several attempts to try at least a few more substantial programs. But the substantial programs are up against cartoons, and there is no contest. CBS offers short segments of news for youngsters, and there are some movies and sugar-coated educational efforts, but Saturday morning still is nothing television can be proud of.

Daytime television consists of soap operas and game shows, both forms excellent for advertisers with products to sell to women, the shows and the commercials strong evidence that women's lib still has a long way to go.

Some idea of the power of the medium, and proof that others besides the networks are interested in money, is given by the fact that television has succeeded in changing the rules of football and baseball to make those sports more suited to television's commercial needs.

Football carefully measures three timeouts per half for each team. But television commercial timeouts may be called by the referees (promoted by a television technician) whenever the ball changes hands. Baseball play in a televised game does not resume after an inning is ended until the commercials are over.

Football games start at odd times Saturday and Sunday afternoons to make it possible for television to present double-headers. They're playing night games in the World Series now. Last October, because the network had football scheduled on Sunday afternoon, both players and stadium audience shivered in 20-degree cold in Cincinnati so that a World Series game could be played on a Sunday night: the only comfortable man in the stands was Bowie Kuhn, the baseball commissioner, who sat there with his coat off to show it really wasn't a bit chilly.

It is of some interest to note that last year commercial television paid about as much for the rights to televise football games as our government paid the Corporation For Public Broadcasting for the entire public-television system in this country.

Although the subject of these articles is the state of commercial television, it is fair to mention that the audience for public television is growing, although it still is only a small fraction of that enjoyed by commercial

television. The networks are rather ambivalent about public television, grateful for the fact that, by presenting serious programming, public TV takes some of the pressure off the networks, but rather displeased because a number of large corporations spend money to underwrite excellent public-television programs. The commercial networks would prefer to have that money flow their way.

It is prime-time commercial television that is most disappointing to those who are aware of the medium's power and who believe the medium could raise America's standards of entertainment. It is possible that innovative programming, perhaps even a regularly scheduled dramatic series in prime time, might attract enough viewers to warrant the expense. We have all too few truly "special" programs, although the networks frequently prove that they can present quality programming well. But innovation is risky in series television.

Obviously most new programs—about two-thirds of them—fail each season, but these are not really creative risks. They are mostly variations on past themes that have succeeded and therefore are more easily explained away than the failure of an innovative series. *Mr. T and Tina* can flop and not even an eyebrow is raised because so many *Mr. T and Tina*s under different names have worked before. But when something even as mildly different as *Beacon Hill* (actually an American version of the BBC's *Upstairs, Downstairs*) fails, there is consternation in high places.

The ratings show that Americans are watching television possibly more than ever before. This does not mean they are satisfied with what they are offered. It may even mean, as NBC's research expert Paul Klein suggests, that they are watching the "least objectionable" programs. Under the present network philosophy, the level of programs cannot change unless tens of millions of Americans simply turn off their sets.

Paddy Chayefsky, who wrote the biting motion-picture satire of television, "Network," pessimistically described television as "democracy at its ugliest." Television cannot be dismissed that easily or that cynically, for it is much too important to our society and our culture. And, besides offering an inordinate amount of mediocre entertainment, it does cover news events and sports well, it does give us entertaining hours of series shows, it does offer good as well as bad movies and occasionally presents a remarkable movie made especially for television. If, as seems to have happened, the medium has lost its excitement, it may be time for the networks to set aside a few prime-time hours a week to reach those who are becoming bored with routine television.

Red Skelton used to thank his audience each week for "permitting me to come into your home." The popular comedian, and many others in those adolescent days of the medium, considered television to be a guest in the nation's living rooms.

The guest has become—to some eyes, at least—pushy and ill-mannered, almost contemptuous of its host. It still is welcome in our living rooms, but it is like the loud-mouthed neighbor one invites and puts up with because his wife is so pretty and charming and adds so much to the party.

We put up with the clutter and the inanity of much of television because it serves our needs and the rewards are worth the discomfort they entail.

New technologies—pay-cable, two-way cable, home video tape and video-discs, and all the other promised electronic miracles—would make possible a much wider variety of programming than the commercial networks now are able to present. But whatever new services may be offered, commercial television still will be needed to provide mass entertainment and cover news and sports.

Until the new technologies come into use, those who are dissatisfied with much of commercial television have their choice of watching public television or switching off their sets. Despite commercial television's faults, most Americans will not switch off their sets. We will continue to watch the medium that informs and entertains us just about as well as we deserve.

NIGHTLY NETWORK PROGRAMS—FALL SEASON

All times shown were for the New York City Metropolitan edition.

1953

SAT

	6:30	7:00	7:30	8:00	8:30	9:00	9:30	10:00	10:30
ABC	Local	Paul Whiteman's Teen Club	Leave It to the Girls	Talent Patrol	Music From Meadowbrook	Saturday Evening Fights	Music From Cedar Grove	Local	Local
CBS	Local	Meet Millie	Beat the Clock	Jackie Gleason Show		Two For the Money	My Favorite Husband	Medallion Theater	Revlon Mirror Theater
NBC	Local	Local	Ethel and Albert	Bonino	Ted Mack's Original Amateur Hour	Your Show of Shows All-Star Review (once a month)			Your Hit Parade

SUN

	6:30	7:00	7:30	8:00	8:30	9:00	9:30	10:00	10:30
ABC	Georgie Jessel Show	You Asked For It	Frank Leahy Show	Notre Dame Football		Walter Winchell / Orchid Award	Jukebox Jury		Hour of Decision (Billy Graham)
CBS	You Are There	Quiz Kids	Jack Benny Show alt. w/Private Secretary	Toast of the Town		The General Electric Theater or Fred Waring	Man Behind the Badge	The Web	What's My Line?
NBC	Roy Rogers	Paul Winchell Show	Mr. Peepers	Colgate Comedy Hour (Martin & Lewis, Cantor, O'Connor, Abbott & Costello)		Philco-Goodyear Playhouse		A Letter to Loretta	Man Against Crime

MON

	6:30	7:00	7:30	8:00	8:30	9:00	9:30	10:00	10:30
ABC	Local	Local	John Daly—News / Jamie	Sky King Theatre	Of Many Things	Junior Press Conference	The Big Picture	Racket Squad	Local
CBS	Local	Local	Douglas Edwards—News / Perry Como Show	George Burns & Gracie Allen Show	Arthur Godfrey's Talent Scouts	I Love Lucy	Red Buttons Show	Studio One	
NBC	Local	Local	Arthur Murray Dance Party / John Cameron Swayze—News	Name That Tune	Voice of Firestone	Dennis Day	Robert Montgomery Presents		Who Said That

TUE

	6:30	7:00	7:30	8:00	8:30	9:00	9:30	10:00	10:30
ABC	Local	Local	Taylor Grant—News / Cavalcade of America	Local	Local	Make Room for Daddy (Danny Thomas)	ABC Album or U.S. Steel Hour		Name's the Same
CBS	Local	Local	Douglas Edwards—News / Jane Froman Show	Gene Autry Show	Red Skelton Show	This Is Show Business	Suspense	Danger	See It Now
NBC	Local	Local	Dinah Shore / John Cameron Swayze—News	Milton Berle Show		Fireside Theater	Armstrong Circle Theater	Judge For Yourself (Fred Allen)	Bob Considine / It Happened in Sports

WED

	6:30	7:00	7:30	8:00	8:30	9:00	9:30	10:00	10:30
ABC	Local	Local	John Daly—News / Mystery Theatre	At Issue / Through the Curtain	Answers for Americans	Take It From Me	Dr. I.Q.	Wrestling	
CBS	Local	Local	Douglas Edwards—News / Perry Como Show	Godfrey & Friends		Strike It Rich	I've Got a Secret	Pabst Blue Ribbon Fights	Sports Spot
NBC	Local	Local	Eddie Fisher / John Cameron Swayze—News	I Married Joan	My Little Margie	Kraft Theater		This Is Your Life	Rheingold Theatre (Douglas Fairbanks Jr.)

THU

	6:30	7:00	7:30	8:00	8:30	9:00	9:30	10:00	10:30
ABC	Local	Local	John Daly—News / The Lone Ranger	Quick as a Flash	Where's Raymond? (Ray Bolger)	Back That Fact	Kraft Theater		Local
CBS	Local	Local	Douglas Edwards—News / Jane Froman Show	Meet Mr. McNutley	Four Star Playhouse	Lux Video Theater	Big Town	Philip Morris Playhouse	Place the Face
NBC	Local	Local	Dinah Shore / John Cameron Swayze—News	You Bet Your Life (Groucho Marx)	Treasury Men in Action	Dragnet	Ford Theater	Martin Kane, Private Eye	Foreign Intrigue

FRI

	6:30	7:00	7:30	8:00	8:30	9:00	9:30	10:00	10:30
ABC	Local	Local	John Daly—News / Stu Erwin	The Adventures of Ozzie & Harriet	Pepsi Cola Playhouse (Arlene Dahl)	Pride of the Family	The Comeback Story	Showroom	
CBS	Local	Local	Douglas Edwards—News / Perry Como Show	Mama	Topper	Schlitz Playhouse of Stars	Our Miss Brooks	My Friend Irma	Person to Person
NBC	Local	Local	Eddie Fisher / John Cameron Swayze—News	Dave Garroway Show	The Life of Riley	Big Story	Campbell Sound Stage	Cavalcade of Sports	Greatest Fights

1954

Day	Net	6:30	7:00	7:30	8:00	8:30	9:00	9:30	10:00	10:30
SAT	ABC	Local	Local	Compass	Dotty Mack Show		Saturday Night Fights		The Stork Club	Local
	CBS	Local	Gene Autry	Beat the Clock	Jackie Gleason		Two For the Money	My Favorite Husband	That's My Boy	Willy
	NBC	Local	Mr. Wizard	Ethel and Albert	Mickey Rooney Show	Place the Face	Imogene Coca	Texaco Star Theater (Donald O'Connor/Jimmy Durante) A special every 4th week	George Gobel Show	Your Hit Parade
SUN	ABC	Local	You Asked For It	Pepsi-Cola Playhouse (Polly Bergen)	Flight Number Seven	The Big Picture	Walter Winchell | Martha Wright	What's Going On?	Break the Bank	Local
	CBS	You Are There	Lassie	Jack Benny or Private Secretary	Toast of the Town (Ed Sullivan)		The General Electric Theater	Honestly, Celeste!	Father Knows Best	What's My Line?
	NBC	Roy Rogers	People Are Funny	Mr. Peepers / Max Liebman "Spectacular" monthly	Colgate Comedy Hour		TV Playhouse		Loretta Young Show	The Hunter
MON	ABC	Local	Local	John Daly—News | Name's the Same	Come Closer	Voice of Firestone	College Press Conference	Local	Boxing	
	CBS	Local	Local	Douglas Edwards—News | Perry Como Show	George Burns & Gracie Allen Show	Arthur Godfrey's Talent Scouts	I Love Lucy	December Bride	Studio One	
	NBC	Local	Local	Tony Martin Show | John Cameron Swayze—News	Caesar's Hour		Medic	Robert Montgomery Presents		Local
TUE	ABC	Local	Local	John Daly—News | Cavalcade of America	Local	Twenty Questions	Make Room For Daddy (Danny Thomas)	U.S. Steel Hour or Elgin TV Hour		Stop the Music
	CBS	Local	Local	Douglas Edwards—News | Jo Stafford	Red Skelton Show	The Halls of Ivy	Meet Millie	Danger	Life with Father	See It Now
	NBC	Local	Local	Dinah Shore | John Cameron Swayze—News	Texaco Star Theater (Milton Berle, Martha Raye, Bob Hope & others)		Fireside Theater	Armstrong Circle Theater	Truth or Consequences	It's a Great Life
WED	ABC	Local	Local	John Daly—News | Disneyland		Stu Erwin Show	Masquerade Party	Enterprise, U.S.A.	Local	Local
	CBS	Local	Local	Douglas Edwards—News | Perry Como Show	Arthur Godfrey and His Friends		Strike It Rich	I've Got a Secret	Blue Ribbon Bouts or Best of Broadway	
	NBC	Local	Local	Eddie Fisher | John Cameron Swayze—News	I Married Joan	My Little Margie	Kraft Theater		This Is Your Life	Local
THU	ABC	Local	Local	John Daly—News | The Lone Ranger	The Mail Story	Treasury Men in Action	So You Want to Lead a Band?	Kraft Theater		Local
	CBS	Local	Local	Douglas Edwards—News | Jane Froman	Ray Milland Show	Climax! or Shower of Stars		Four Star Playhouse	Public Defender	Name That Tune
	NBC	Local	Local	Dinah Shore | John Cameron Swayze—News	You Bet Your Life (Groucho Marx)	Justice	Dragnet	Ford Theater	Lux Video Theater	
FRI	ABC	Local	Local	John Daly—News | Rin Tin Tin	The Adventures of Ozzie & Harriet	Where's Raymond? (Ray Bolger)	A Dollar a Second	The Vise	Local	Local
	CBS	Local	Local	Douglas Edwards—News | Perry Como Show	Mama	Topper	Schlitz Playhouse of Stars	Our Miss Brooks	The Lineup	Person to Person
	NBC	Local	Local	Eddie Fisher | John Cameron Swayze—News	Red Buttons Show or Jack Carson Show (every 4th week)	The Life of Riley	The Big Story	Dear Phoebe	Cavalcade of Sports	Greatest Moments in Sports

1955

		6:30	7:00	7:30	8:00	8:30	9:00	9:30	10:00	10:30
SAT	ABC	Local	On Your Way	Ozark Jubilee or Grand Ole Opry			Lawrence Welk		Tomorrow's Careers	Local
	CBS	Local	Gene Autry	Beat the Clock	Stage Show	The Honeymooners	Two For the Money	It's Always Jan (Ford Star Jubilee every 4th week)	Gunsmoke	Damon Runyon Theater
	NBC	Local	Local	The Big Surprise	Perry Como Show		People Are Funny	Texaco Star Theatre (Jimmy Durante)	George Gobel Show	Your Hit Parade
SUN	ABC	Paris Precinct	You Asked For It	Famous Film Festival			Chance of a Lifetime	Ted Mack's Amateur Hour	Life Begins at 80	Local
	CBS	You Are There	Lassie	Jack Benny or Private Secretary	Ed Sullivan Show		The General Electric Theater	Alfred Hitchcock Presents	Appointment with Adventure	What's My Line?
	NBC	Roy Rogers	It's a Great Life	Frontier	Colgate Variety Hour		Alcoa Hour or Goodyear Playhouse		Loretta Young Show	Justice
MON	ABC	Local	Local	John Daly—News	Topper	TV Readers' Digest	Voice of Firestone	Dotty Mack	Medical Horizons	Local	Local
	CBS	Local	Local	Douglas Edwards—News	Adventures of Robin Hood	George Burns & Gracie Allen Show	Arthur Godfrey's Talent Scouts	I Love Lucy	December Bride	Studio One
	NBC	Local	Local		Tony Martin	John Cameron Swayze—News	Caesar's Hour		Medic	Robert Montgomery Presents
TUE	ABC	Local	Local	John Daly—News	Warner Brothers Presents		Wyatt Earp	Make Room for Daddy (Danny Thomas)	Du Pont Cavalcade Theater	Talent Varieties	Local
	CBS	Local	Local	Douglas Edwards—News	Name That Tune	You'll Never Get Rich (Phil Silvers)	Navy Log	Meet Millie	Red Skelton Show	The $64,000 Question	My Favorite Husband
	NBC	Local	Local		Dinah Shore	John Cameron Swayze—News	Milton Berle Show or Martha Raye Show or Bob Hope Show or others	Jane Wyman's Fireside Theater	Pontiac Theater or Circle Theater	Big Town
WED	ABC	Local	Local	John Daly—News	Disneyland		MGM Parade	Masquerade Party	Break the Bank	Wednesday Night Fights
	CBS	Local	Local	Douglas Edwards—News	Brave Eagle	Arthur Godfrey & His Friends		The Millionaire	I've Got a Secret	20th Century-Fox Hour or U.S. Steel Hour
	NBC	Local	Local		Eddie Fisher	John Cameron Swayze—News	Screen Directors' Playhouse	Father Knows Best	Kraft Television Theater		This Is Your Life	Midwest Hayride
THU	ABC	Local	Local	John Daly—News	The Lone Ranger	Bishop Fulton J. Sheen	Stop the Music	Star Tonight	Down You Go	Local	Local
	CBS	Local	Local	Douglas Edwards—News	Sergeant Preston of the Yukon	Bob Cummings Show	Shower of Stars or Climax!		Four Star Playhouse	Johnny Carson (Variety)	Wanted
	NBC	Local	Local		Dinah Shore	John Cameron Swayze—News	You Bet Your Life (Groucho Marx)	The People's Choice	Dragnet	Ford Theater	Lux Video Theater
FRI	ABC	Local	Local	John Daly—News	Rin Tin Tin	The Adventures of Ozzie & Harriet	Crossroads	A Dollar a Second	The Vise	Ethel & Albert	Local
	CBS	Local	Local	Douglas Edwards—News	The Adventures of Champion	Mama	Our Miss Brooks	The Crusader	Schlitz Playhouse of Stars	The Lineup	Person to Person
	NBC	Local	Local		Eddie Fisher	John Cameron Swayze—News	Truth or Consequences	The Life of Riley	Big Story	Star Stage	Cavalcade of Sports

1956

Day	Net	6:30	7:00	7:30	8:00	8:30	9:00	9:30	10:00	10:30
SAT	ABC	Local	Local	Famous Film Festival			Lawrence Welk		Masquerade Party	Local
	CBS	Local	Beat the Clock	The Buccaneers	Jackie Gleason		Gale Storm Show (or Ford Star Jubilee monthly)	Hey Jeannie!	Gunsmoke	High Finance
	NBC	Local	Local	People Are Funny	Perry Como Show		Caesar's Hour		George Gobel Show	Your Hit Parade
SUN	ABC	Local	You Asked For It	Ted Mack and the Original Amateur Hour		Press Conference	Omnibus			Local
	CBS	Air Power (started at 6:00)	Lassie	Jack Benny or Private Secretary	Ed Sullivan Show		The General Electric Theater	Alfred Hitchcock Presents	The $64,000 Challenge	What's My Line?
	NBC	Roy Rogers	Tales of the 77th Bengal Lancers	Circus Boy	Steve Allen		Alcoa Hour or Goodyear Playhouse or The Chevy Show (monthly)		Loretta Young Show	National Bowling Champions
MON	ABC	Local	Local	John Daly—News	Bold Journey	Make Room For Daddy (Danny Thomas)	The Voice of Firestone	Life Is Worth Living (Bishop Sheen)	Top Tunes and Talent		Local
	CBS	Local	Local	Douglas Edwards—News	Adventures of Robin Hood	George Burns & Gracie Allen Show	Arthur Godfrey's Talent Scouts	I Love Lucy	December Bride	Studio One	
	NBC	Local	Local	Nat King Cole / Huntley Brinkley—News	The Adventures of Sir Lancelot		Stanley	Medic	Robert Montgomery Presents		Local
TUE	ABC	Local	Local	John Daly—News	Conflict or Cheyenne		Wyatt Earp	Broken Arrow	Cavalcade Theater	Polka-Go-Round	Local
	CBS	Local	Local	Douglas Edwards—News	Name That Tune	Phil Silvers Show	The Brothers	Herb Shriner	Red Skelton Show	The $64,000 Question	Do You Trust Your Wife?
	NBC	Local	Celebrity Playhouse	Jonathan Winters / Huntley Brinkley—News	The Big Surprise	Noah's Ark	The Jane Wyman Theatre	Circle Theater or Kaiser Aluminum Hour		Break the $250,000 Bank
WED	ABC	Local	Local	John Daly—News	Disneyland		Navy Log	The Adventures of Ozzie & Harriet	Ford Theater	Wednesday Night Fights	
	CBS	Local	Local	Douglas Edwards—News	Giant Step	Arthur Godfrey Show		The Millionaire	I've Got a Secret	U.S. Steel Hour or 20th Century-Fox Hour	
	NBC	Local	Local	Eddie Fisher / Huntley Brinkley—News	The Adventures of Hiram Holiday	Father Knows Best	Kraft Television Theater		This Is Your Life	Twenty-One
THU	ABC	Local	Local	John Daly—News	The Lone Ranger	Circus Time		Wire Service		Ozark Jubilee	Local
	CBS	Local	Local	Douglas Edwards—News	Sergeant Preston of the Yukon	Bob Cummings Show	Shower of Stars or Climax! (monthly)		Playhouse 90		
	NBC	Local	Local	Dinah Shore / Huntley Brinkley—News	You Bet Your Life (Groucho Marx)	Dragnet	The People's Choice	Tennessee Ernie Ford Show	Lux Video Theater	
FRI	ABC	Local	Local	John Daly—News	Rin Tin Tin	The Adventures of Jim Bowie	Crossroads	Treasure Hunt	The Vise	Ray Anthony Show	
	CBS	Local	Local	Douglas Edwards—News	My Friend Flicka	West Point	Dick Powell's Zane Grey Theatre	The Crusader	Schlitz Playhouse of Stars	The Lineup	Person to Person
	NBC	Local	Local	Eddie Fisher / Huntley Brinkley—News	The Life of Riley	Walter Winchell Show	On Trial / The Chevy Show (monthly)	Big Story	Cavalcade of Sports	

1957

		6:30	7:00	7:30	8:00	8:30	9:00	9:30	10:00	10:30
SAT	ABC	Local	Local	Keep It in the Family	Country Music Jubilee		Lawrence Welk		The Mike Wallace Interview	Local
	CBS	Local	Local	Perry Mason		Duke & the Duchess	Gale Storm Show	Have Gun, Will Travel	Gunsmoke	Playhouse of Mystery
	NBC	Local	Local	People Are Funny	Perry Como Show		Club Oasis or Polly Bergen Show	Gisele MacKenzie Show	What's It For?	Your Hit Parade
SUN	ABC	Local	You Asked For It	Maverick		Bowling Stars	Open Hearing	Football Film Highlights	Scotland Yard	Local
	CBS	The Twentieth Century	Lassie	Jack Benny or Bachelor Father	Ed Sullivan Show		The General Electric Theater	Alfred Hitchcock Presents	The $64,000 Challenge	What's My Line?
	NBC	My Friend Flicka	Ted Mack's Amateur Hour	Sally	Steve Allen Show		Dinah Shore Chevy Show		Loretta Young Show	Local
MON	ABC	Local	Local	American Bandstand	Guy Mitchell	Bold Journey	Voice of Firestone	Top Tunes and Talent		Local
	CBS	Local	Local / Douglas Edwards—News	Robin Hood	George Burns & Gracie Allen Show	Arthur Godfrey's Talent Scouts	Danny Thomas Show	December Bride		Studio One
	NBC	Local	Local	The Price Is Right	Restless Gun	Tales of Wells Fargo	Twenty-One	Alcoa-Goodyear Theatre		Suspicion
TUE	ABC	Local	Local	Sugarfoot or Cheyenne		The Life & Legend of Wyatt Earp	Broken Arrow	Telephone Time	West Point	Local
	CBS	Local	Local / Douglas Edwards—News	Name That Tune	Phil Silvers Show	Eve Arden Show	To Tell the Truth	Red Skelton Show	The $64,000 Question	Assignment Foreign Legion
	NBC	Local	Local	Nat King Cole	Eddie Fisher Show or George Gobel Show		Meet McGraw	Bob Cummings Show	The Californians	Local
WED	ABC	Local	Local	Disneyland		Tombstone Territory	The Adventures of Ozzie & Harriet	Walter Winchell File	Wednesday Night Fights	
	CBS	Local	Local / Douglas Edwards—News	I Love Lucy	The Big Record		The Millionaire	I've Got a Secret	Armstrong Circle Theater or U.S. Steel Hour	
	NBC	Local	Local	Wagon Train		Father Knows Best	Kraft Television Theater		This Is Your Life	Local
THU	ABC	Local	Local	Circus Boy	Zorro	The Real McCoys	Pat Boone Show	O.S.S.	Navy Log	Local
	CBS	Local	Local / Douglas Edwards—News	Sergeant Preston of the Yukon	Harbour Master	Climax! or Shower of Stars		Playhouse 90		
	NBC	Local	Local	Tic Tac Dough	You Bet Your Life (Groucho Marx)	Dragnet	The People's Choice	Tennessee Ernie Ford Show	The Lux Show (Rosemary Clooney)	Jane Wyman Show
FRI	ABC	Local	Local	Rin Tin Tin	Jim Bowie	Patrice Munsel	Frank Sinatra Show	Date With the Angels	Colt .45	Local
	CBS	Local	Local / Douglas Edwards—News	Leave It to Beaver	Trackdown	Dick Powell's Zane Grey Theatre	Mr. Adams & Eve	Schlitz Playhouse	The Lineup	Person to Person
	NBC	Local	Local	Saber of London	Court of Last Resort	The Life of Riley	M Squad	The Thin Man	Cavalcade of Sports	Red Barber's Corner

1958

Day		6:30	7:00	7:30	8:00	8:30	9:00	9:30	10:00	10:30
SAT	ABC	Local	Local	Dick Clark Show	Jubilee U.S.A.		Lawrence Welk		Sammy Kaye	Local
	CBS	Local	Local	Perry Mason		Wanted—Dead or Alive	Gale Storm Show	Have Gun, Will Travel	Gunsmoke	Local
	NBC	Local	Local	People Are Funny	Perry Como Show		Steve Canyon	Cimarron City		Brains & Brawn
SUN	ABC	Local	You Asked For It	Maverick		The Lawman	Colt .45	Interplay		Local
	CBS	The Twentieth Century	Lassie	Jack Benny or Bachelor Father	Ed Sullivan Show		The General Electric Theater	Alfred Hitchcock Presents	The $64,000 Question	What's My Line?
	NBC	Chet Huntley	Saber of London	Northwest Passage	Steve Allen Show		Dinah Shore Chevy Show		Loretta Young Show	Local
MON	ABC	Local	Local	Don Goddard—News / Polka-Go-Round		Bold Journey	Voice of Firestone	Anybody Can Play	This Is Music	John Daly—News
	CBS	Local	Local	Douglas Edwards—News / Name That Tune	The Texan	Father Knows Best	Danny Thomas Show	Ann Sothern Show	Lucille Ball—Desi Arnaz Show or Desilu Playhouse	
	NBC	Local	Local	Tic Tac Dough	Restless Gun	Tales of Wells Fargo	Peter Gunn	The Goodyear Theatre or The Alcoa Theatre	Arthur Murray Party	Local
TUE	ABC	Local	Local	Don Goddard—News / Sugarfoot or Cheyenne		The Life & Legend of Wyatt Earp	The Rifleman	Naked City		John Daly—News
	CBS	Local	Local	Douglas Edwards—News / George Burns & Gracie Allen Show	The Invisible Man	To Tell the Truth	Arthur Godfrey Show	Red Skelton Show	Gary Moore Show	
	NBC	Local	Local	Dragnet	Eddie Fisher Show or George Gobel Show		George Burns Show	Bob Cummings Show	The Californians	Local
WED	ABC	Local		Don Goddard—News / Lawrence Welk		The Adventures of Ozzie & Harriet	Donna Reed Show	The Oldsmobile Show (Patti Page)	Wednesday Night Fights	
	CBS	Local	Local	Douglas Edwards—News / Twilight Theatre	Pursuit		The Millionaire	I've Got a Secret	Armstrong Circle Theatre or U.S. Steel Hour	
	NBC	Local	Local	Wagon Train		The Price Is Right	Milton Berle or Kraft Music Hall	Bat Masterson	This Is Your Life	Local
THU	ABC	Local	Local	Don Goddard—News / Leave It to Beaver	Zorro	The Real McCoys	Pat Boone Show	Rough Riders	Traffic Court	John Daly—News
	CBS	Local	Local	Douglas Edwards—News / I Love Lucy	December Bride	Yancy Derringer	Dick Powell's Zane Grey Theater	Playhouse 90 or Du Pont Show of the Month		
	NBC	Local	Local	Jefferson Drum	Ed Wynn Show	Concentration	Behind Closed Doors	Tennessee Ernie Ford Show	You Bet Your Life (Groucho Marx)	Masquerade Party
FRI	ABC	Local	Local	Don Goddard News— / Rin Tin Tin	Walt Disney Presents		Man with a Camera	77 Sunset Strip		John Daly—News
	CBS	Local	Local	Douglas Edwards—News / Your Hit Parade	Trackdown	Jackie Gleason Show	Phil Silvers Show	Schlitz Playhouse or Lux Playhouse	The Lineup	Person to Person
	NBC	Local	Local	Buckskin	The Further Adventures of Ellery Queen		M Squad	The Thin Man	Gillette Cavalcade of Sports	

1959

SAT

	6:30	7:00	7:30	8:00	8:30	9:00	9:30	10:00	10:30
ABC	Local	Local	Dick Clark Show	John Gunther's High Road	Leave It to Beaver	Lawrence Welk		Sports	Local
CBS	Local	Local	Perry Mason		Wanted—Dead or Alive	Mr. Lucky	Have Gun, Will Travel	Gunsmoke	Markham
NBC	Local	Local	Bonanza		The Man & the Challenge	The Deputy	Five Fingers		It Could Be You

SUN

	6:30	7:00	7:30	8:00	8:30	9:00	9:30	10:00	10:30
ABC	Local	Colt .45	Maverick		The Lawman	The Rebel	The Alaskans		Dick Clark's World of Talent
CBS	The Twentieth Century	Lassie	Dennis the Menace	Ed Sullivan Show		The General Electric Theater	Alfred Hitchcock Presents	Jack Benny or George Gobel Show	What's My Line?
NBC	Saber of London	Riverboat		Sunday Showcase (Specials)		Dinah Shore or The Chevy Show		Loretta Young Show	Mike Kovac, Man With a Camera

MON

	6:30	7:00	7:30	8:00	8:30	9:00	9:30	10:00	10:30
ABC	Local	Local	John Daly—News	Cheyenne		Bourbon Street Beat		Adventures in Paradise		Local
CBS	Local	Local	Douglas Edwards—News	Masquerade Party	The Texan	Father Knows Best	Danny Thomas Show	Ann Sothern Show	Hennessey	June Allyson Show
NBC	Local	Local		Richard Diamond	Love & Marriage	Tales of Wells Fargo	Peter Gunn	Alcoa Theatre or Goodyear Theatre	Steve Allen Show

TUE

	6:30	7:00	7:30	8:00	8:30	9:00	9:30	10:00	10:30
ABC	Local	Local	John Daly—News	Sugarfoot or Bronco		Wyatt Earp	The Rifleman	Philip Marlowe	Alcoa Presents	Keep Talking
CBS	Local	Local	Douglas Edwards—News	Local	Dennis O'Keefe Show	The Many Loves of Dobie Gillis	Tightrope!	Red Skelton Show	Garry Moore Show or CBS Reports
NBC	Local	Local		Laramie		Fibber McGee & Molly	The Arthur Murray Party	Startime		Local

WED

	6:30	7:00	7:30	8:00	8:30	9:00	9:30	10:00	10:30
ABC	Local	Local	John Daly—News	Local	Hobby Lobby	The Adventures of Ozzie & Harriet	Hawaiian Eye		Wednesday Night Fights	
CBS	Local	Local	Douglas Edwards—News	Lineup		Men into Space	The Millionaire	I've Got a Secret	Armstrong Circle Theatre or U.S. Steel Hour	
NBC	Local	Local		Wagon Train		The Price Is Right	Perry Como's Kraft Music Hall		This Is Your Life	Wichita Town

THU

	6:30	7:00	7:30	8:00	8:30	9:00	9:30	10:00	10:30
ABC	Local	Local	John Daly—News	Gale Storm Show	Donna Reed Show	The Real McCoys	Pat Boone Show	The Untouchables		Take a Good Look
CBS	Local	Local	Douglas Edwards—News	To Tell the Truth	Betty Hutton Show	Johnny Ringo	Dick Powell's Zane Grey Theater	Playhouse 90		
NBC	Local	Local		Law of the Plainsman	Bat Masterson	Staccato	Bachelor Father	Tennessee Ernie Ford Show	You Bet Your Life (Groucho Marx)	The Lawless Years

FRI

	6:30	7:00	7:30	8:00	8:30	9:00	9:30	10:00	10:30
ABC	Local	Local	John Daly—News	Walt Disney Presents		Man from Blackhawk	77 Sunset Strip		The Detectives	Black Saddle
CBS	Local	Local	Douglas Edwards—News	Rawhide		Hotel De Paree	Desilu Playhouse		The Twilight Zone	Person to Person
NBC	Local	Local		People Are Funny	Troubleshooters	Specials		M Squad	Cavalcade of Sports	

1960

		6:30	7:00	7:30	8:00	8:30	9:00	9:30	10:00	10:30
SAT	ABC	Local	Local	The Roaring Twenties		Leave It to Beaver	Lawrence Welk		Fight of the Week	
	CBS	Local	Local	Perry Mason		Checkmate		Have Gun, Will Travel	Gunsmoke	Local
	NBC	Local	Local	Bonanza		Tall Man	The Deputy	The Nation's Future		Local
SUN	ABC	Walt Disney Presents		Maverick		Lawman	The Rebel	The Islanders		Walter Winchell Show
	CBS	The Twentieth Century	Lassie	Dennis the Menace	Ed Sullivan Show		The General Electric Theater	Jack Benny Program	Candid Camera	What's My Line?
	NBC	People Are Funny	Shirley Temple Show		National Velvet	Tab Hunter Show	Dinah Shore or The Chevy Show		Loretta Young Show	This Is Your Life
MON	ABC	Local	Local	John Daly—News	Cheyenne		Surfside 6		Adventures in Paradise		Peter Gunn
	CBS	Local	Local	Douglas Edwards—News	To Tell the Truth	Pete & Gladys	Bringing Up Buddy	Danny Thomas Show	Andy Griffith Show	Hennessey	Face the Nation
	NBC	Local	Local		Riverboat		Tales of Wells Fargo	Klondike	Dante	The Barbara Stanwyck Theater	Jackpot Bowling Starring Milton Berle
TUE	ABC	Local	Expedition!		Bugs Bunny	The Rifleman	Wyatt Earp	Stagecoach West		Alcoa Presents	Local
	CBS	Local	Local	Douglas Edwards—News	Local	Father Knows Best	The Many Loves of Dobie Gillis	Tom Ewell Show	Red Skelton Show	Garry Moore	
	NBC	Local	Local		Laramie		Alfred Hitchcock Presents	Thriller		Specials	
WED	ABC	Local	Local	John Daly—News	Hong Kong	The Adventures of Ozzie & Harriet		Hawaiian Eye		Naked City	
	CBS	Local	Local	Douglas Edwards—News	The Aquanauts		Wanted—Dead or Alive	My Sister Eileen	I've Got a Secret	U.S. Steel Hour or Armstrong Circle Theatre	
	NBC	Local	Local		Wagon Train		The Price Is Right	Perry Como's Kraft Music Hall		Peter Loves Mary	Local
THU	ABC	Local	Local	John Daly—News	Guestward Ho!	Donna Reed Show	The Real McCoys	My Three Sons	The Untouchables		Ernie Kovacs' Take a Good Look
	CBS	Local	Local	Douglas Edwards—News	The Witness		Dick Powell's Zane Grey Theater	Angel	Ann Sothern Show	Person to Person	June Allyson Show
	NBC	Local	Local		Outlaws		Bat Masterson		The Ford Show (Tennessee Ernie Ford)	You Bet Your Life (Groucho Marx)	The Third Man
FRI	ABC	Local	Local	John Daly—News	Matty's Funday Funnies	Harrigan & Son	The Flintstones	77 Sunset Strip		The Detectives	The Law & Mr. Jones
	CBS	Local	Local	Douglas Edwards—News	Rawhide		Route 66		The Garlund Touch	The Twilight Zone	Eyewitness to History
	NBC	Local	Local		Dan Raven		The Westerner	Bell Telephone Hour or Specials		Michael Shayne	

1961

SAT

	6:30	7:00	7:30	8:00	8:30	9:00	9:30	10:00	10:30
ABC	Local	Matty's Funday Funnies	The Roaring Twenties		Leave It to Beaver	Lawrence Welk		Fight of the Week	
CBS	Local	Local	Perry Mason		The Defenders		Have Gun, Will Travel	Gunsmoke	
NBC	Local	Local	Tales of Wells Fargo		The Tall Man	Saturday Night at the Movies			

SUN

	6:30	7:00	7:30	8:00	8:30	9:00	9:30	10:00	10:30
ABC	Maverick		Follow the Sun		Lawman	Bus Stop		Adventures in Paradise	
CBS	Mister Ed	Lassie	Dennis the Menace	Ed Sullivan Show		The General Electric Theater	Jack Benny	Candid Camera	What's My Line?
NBC	1, 2, 3, Go!	The Bullwinkle Show	Walt Disney's Wonderful World of Color		Car 54, Where Are You?	Bonanza		Du Pont Show of the Week	

MON

	6:30	7:00	7:30	8:00	8:30	9:00	9:30	10:00	10:30
ABC	Local	Expedition!	Cheyenne		The Rifleman	Surfside 6		Ben Casey	
CBS	Local	Local / Douglas Edwards—News	To Tell the Truth	Pete & Gladys	Window on Main Street	Danny Thomas Show	Andy Griffith Show	Hennessey	I've Got a Secret
NBC	Local	Local	Local	National Velvet	The Price Is Right	87th Precinct		Thriller	

TUE

	6:30	7:00	7:30	8:00	8:30	9:00	9:30	10:00	10:30
ABC	Local	Local	Bugs Bunny	Bachelor Father	Calvin and the Colonel	The New Breed		Alcoa Premier	
CBS	Local	Local / Douglas Edwards—News	Local	Dick Van Dyke Show	Dobie Gillis	Red Skelton Show	Ichabod and Me	Garry Moore Show	
NBC	Local	Local	Laramie		Alfred Hitchcock Presents	Dick Powell Show		Cain's Hundred	

WED

	6:30	7:00	7:30	8:00	8:30	9:00	9:30	10:00	10:30
ABC	Local	Local	Steve Allen Show		Top Cat	Hawaiian Eye		Naked City	
CBS	Local	Local / Douglas Edwards—News	The Alvin Show	Father Knows Best	Checkmate		Mrs. G. Goes to College	U.S. Steel Hour or Armstrong Circle Theatre	
NBC	Local	Local	Wagon Train		Joey Bishop Show	Perry Como's Kraft Music Hall		Bob Newhart Show	David Brinkley's Journal

THU

	6:30	7:00	7:30	8:00	8:30	9:00	9:30	10:00	10:30
ABC	Local	Local	The Adventures of Ozzie & Harriet	Donna Reed Show	The Real McCoys	My Three Sons	Margie	The Untouchables	
CBS	Local	Local / Douglas Edwards—News	Frontier Circus		Bob Cummings Show	The Investigators		CBS Reports	
NBC	Local	Local	Outlaws		Dr. Kildare		Hazel	Sing Along with Mitch	

FRI

	6:30	7:00	7:30	8:00	8:30	9:00	9:30	10:00	10:30
ABC	Local	Local	The Racer	The Hathaways	The Flintstones	77 Sunset Strip		Target: The Corruptors	
CBS	Local	Local / Douglas Edwards—News	Rawhide		Route 66		Father of the Bride	The Twilight Zone	Eyewitness to History
NBC	Local	Local	International Showtime		Robert Taylor's Detectives		Bell Telephone Hour or Dinah Shore	Frank McGee's Here and Now	

1962

SAT

	6:30	7:00	7:30	8:00	8:30	9:00	9:30	10:00	10:30
ABC	Local	Local	Roy Rogers—Dale Evans Variety Hour		Mr. Smith Goes to Washington	Lawrence Welk Show		Fight of the Week	
CBS	Local	Local	Jackie Gleason's American Scene Magazine		The Defenders		Have Gun, Will Travel	Gunsmoke	
NBC	Local	Local	Sam Benedict		Joey Bishop Show	Saturday Night at the Movies			

SUN

	6:30	7:00	7:30	8:00	8:30	9:00	9:30	10:00	10:30
ABC	Winston Churchill	Father Knows Best	The Jetsons	Hollywood Special				Voice of Firestone	Howard K. Smith
CBS	Password	Lassie	Dennis the Menace	Ed Sullivan Show		The Real McCoys	General Electric Theater	Candid Camera	What's My Line?
NBC	McKeever and the Colonel	Ensign O'Toole	Want Disney's Wonderful World of Color		Car 54, Where Are You?	Bonanza		Du Pont Show of the Week	

MON

	6:30	7:00	7:30	8:00	8:30	9:00	9:30	10:00	10:30
ABC	Local	Local	The Cheyenne Show		The Rifleman	Stoney Burke		Ben Casey	
CBS	Local	Local	To Tell the Truth	I've Got a Secret	The Lucy Show	Danny Thomas Show	Andy Griffith Show	New Loretta Young Show	Stump the Stars
NBC	Local	Local	It's a Man's World		The Saints and Sinners		The Price Is Right	David Brinkley's Journal	Local

TUE

	6:30	7:00	7:30	8:00	8:30	9:00	9:30	10:00	10:30
ABC	Local	Local	Combat!		Hawaiian Eye		The Untouchables		Bell & Howell Close-up!
CBS	Local	Local	Marshall Dillon	Lloyd Bridges Show	Red Skelton Show		Jack Benny Show	Garry Moore Show	
NBC	Local	Local	Laramie		Empire		Dick Powell Show		Chet Huntley Reporting

WED

	6:30	7:00	7:30	8:00	8:30	9:00	9:30	10:00	10:30
ABC	Local	Local	Wagon Train		Going My Way		Our Man Higgins	Naked City	
CBS	Local	Local	CBS Reports		Dobie Gillis	The Beverly Hillbillies	Dick Van Dyke Show	U.S. Steel Hour alternating with Armstrong Circle Theatre	
NBC	Local	Local	The Virginian			Perry Como's Kraft Music Hall		The Eleventh Hour	

THU

	6:30	7:00	7:30	8:00	8:30	9:00	9:30	10:00	10:30
ABC	Local	Local	Ozzie and Harriet	Donna Reed Show	Leave It to Beaver	My Three Sons	McHale's Navy	Alcoa—Astaire Premiere	
CBS	Local	Local	Mister Ed	Perry Mason		The Nurses		Alfred Hitchcock Hour	
NBC	Local	Local	The Wide Country		Dr. Kildare		Hazel	Andy Williams Show	

FRI

	6:30	7:00	7:30	8:00	8:30	9:00	9:30	10:00	10:30
ABC	Local	Local	The Gallant Men		The Flintstones	I'm Dickens He's Fenster	77 Sunset Strip		Local
CBS	Local	Local	Rawhide		Route 66		Fair Exchange		Eyewitness
NBC	Local	Local	International Showtime		Sing Along with Mitch		Don't Call Me Charlie!	Jack Paar Show	

1963

SAT

	6:30	7:00	7:30	8:00	8:30	9:00	9:30	10:00	10:30
ABC	Local	Local	Hootenanny		Lawrence Welk Show		Jerry Lewis Show		
CBS	Local	Local	Jackie Gleason's American Scene Magazine		New Phil Silvers Show	The Defenders	Gunsmoke		
NBC	Local	Local	The Lieutenant		Joey Bishop Show	Saturday Night at the Movies			

SUN

	6:30	7:00	7:30	8:00	8:30	9:00	9:30	10:00	10:30
ABC	Local	Local	The Travels of Jaimie McPheeters		Arrest and Trial			100 Grand	ABC News Reports
CBS	Mister Ed	Lassie	My Favorite Martian	Ed Sullivan Show		Judy Garland Show		Candid Camera	What's My Line?
NBC	Local	Bill Dana Show	Walt Disney's Wonderful World of Color		Grindl	Bonanza		Du Pont Show of the Week	

MON

	6:30	7:00	7:30	8:00	8:30	9:00	9:30	10:00	10:30
ABC	Local	Local	The Outer Limits		Wagon Train			Breaking Point	
CBS	Local	Local	To Tell the Truth	I've Got a Secret	The Lucy Show	Danny Thomas Show	Andy Griffith Show	East Side, West Side	
NBC	Local	Local	Monday Night at the Movies				Hollywood and the Stars	Sing Along with Mitch	

TUE

	6:30	7:00	7:30	8:00	8:30	9:00	9:30	10:00	10:30
ABC	Local	Local	Combat!		McHale's Navy	The Greatest Show On Earth		The Fugitive	
CBS	Local	Local	Marshal Dillon	Red Skelton Hour		Petticoat Junction	Jack Benny Program	Garry Moore Show	
NBC	Local	Local	Mr. Novak		Redigo	Richard Boone Show		Bell Telephone Hour/Andy Williams Show/NBC News Specials	

WED

	6:30	7:00	7:30	8:00	8:30	9:00	9:30	10:00	10:30
ABC	Local	Local	Ozzie and Harriet	Patty Duke Show	The Price Is Right	Ben Casey		Channing	
CBS	Local	Local	CBS Reports alternating with Chronicle		Glynis	The Beverly Hillbillies	Dick Van Dyke Show	Danny Kaye Show	
NBC	Local	Local	The Virginian			Espionage		The Eleventh Hour	

THU

	6:30	7:00	7:30	8:00	8:30	9:00	9:30	10:00	10:30
ABC	Local	Local	The Flintstones	Donna Reed Show	My Three Sons	Jimmy Dean Show		Edie Adams alternating with Sid Caesar	Local
CBS	Local	Local	Password	Rawhide		Perry Mason		The Nurses	
NBC	Local	Local	Temple Houston		Dr. Kildare		Hazel	Kraft Suspense Theatre/Perry Como Show	

FRI

	6:30	7:00	7:30	8:00	8:30	9:00	9:30	10:00	10:30
ABC	Local	Local	77 Sunset Strip		Burke's Law		The Farmer's Daughter	The Fight of the Week	
CBS	Local	Local	The Great Adventure		Route 66		The Twilight Zone	Alfred Hitchcock Hour	
NBC	Local	Local	International Showtime		Bob Hope Show and Dramas		Harry's Girls	Jack Paar Program	

1964

		6:30	7:00	7:30	8:00	8:30	9:00	9:30	10:00	10:30
SAT	ABC	Local	Local	The Outer Limits		Lawrence Welk Show		The Hollywood Palace		Local
	CBS	Local	Local	Jackie Gleason's American Scene Magazine		Gilligan's Island	Mr. Broadway		Gunsmoke	
	NBC	Local	Local	Flipper	Adventures of Mr. Magoo	Kentucky Jones	Saturday Night at the Movies			
SUN	ABC	Local	Local	Wagon Train		Broadside	The Sunday Night Movie			
	CBS	Mister Ed	Lassie	My Favorite Martian	Ed Sullivan Show		My Living Doll	Joey Bishop Show	Candid Camera	What's My Line?
	NBC	Profiles in Courage		Walt Disney's Wonderful World of Color		Bill Dana Show	Bonanza		The Rogues	
MON	ABC	Local	Local	Voyage to the Bottom of the Sea		No Time For Sergeants	Wendy and Me	Bing Crosby Show	Ben Casey	
	CBS	Local	Local	To Tell the Truth	I've Got a Secret	Andy Griffith Show	The Lucy Show	Many Happy Returns	Slattery's People	
	NBC	Local	Local	90 Bristol Court Karen, Tom, Dick and Mary Harris Against the World			Andy Williams Show/ Jonathan Winters Specials		Alfred Hitchcock Hour	
TUE	ABC	Local	Local	Combat!		McHale's Navy	The Tycoon	Peyton Place	The Fugitive	
	CBS	Local	Local	Local	World War I	Red Skelton Hour		Petticoat Junction	The Nurses	
	NBC	Local	Local	Mr. Novak		The Man From U.N.C.L.E.		That Was the Week That Was	Bell Telephone Hour/NBC News Specials	
WED	ABC	Local	Local	Ozzie and Harriet	Patty Duke Show	Shindig	Mickey	Burke's Law		ABC Scope
	CBS	Local	Local	CBS Reports/CBS News Specials		The Beverly Hillbillies	Dick Van Dyke Show	Cara Williams Show	Danny Kaye Show	
	NBC	Local	Local	The Virginian			Wednesday Night at the Movies			
THU	ABC	Local	Local	The Flintstones	Donna Reed Show	My Three Sons	Bewitched	Peyton Place	Jimmy Dean Show	
	CBS	Local	Local	The Munsters	Perry Mason		Password	The Baileys of Balboa	The Defenders	
	NBC	Local	Local	Daniel Boone		Dr. Kildare		Hazel	Kraft Suspense Theatre/ Perry Como Specials	
FRI	ABC	Local	Local	Jonny Quest	The Farmer's Daughter	The Addams Family	Valentine's Day	12 O'Clock High		Local
	CBS	Local	Local	Rawhide		The Entertainers		Gomer Pyle, USMC	The Reporter	
	NBC	Local	Local	International Showtime		Bob Hope Show and Dramas		Jack Benny Show	Jack Paar Program	

1965

SAT

	6:30	7:00	7:30	8:00	8:30	9:00	9:30	10:00	10:30
ABC	Local	Local	Shindig	King Family	Lawrence Welk Show		The Hollywood Palace		ABC Scope
CBS	Local	Local	Jackie Gleason Show		Trials of O'Brien		The Loner	Gunsmoke	
NBC	Local	Local	Flipper	I Dream of Jeannie	Get Smart	Saturday Night at the Movies			

SUN

	6:30	7:00	7:30	8:00	8:30	9:00	9:30	10:00	10:30
ABC	Local	Voyage to the Bottom of the Sea		The FBI		The Sunday Night Movie			
CBS	Local	Lassie	My Favorite Martian	Ed Sullivan Show		Perry Mason		Candid Camera	What's My Line?
NBC	Bell Telephone Hour/NBC News Specials		Walt Disney's Wonderful World of Color		Branded	Bonanza		The Wackiest Ship in the Army	

MON

	6:30	7:00	7:30	8:00	8:30	9:00	9:30	10:00	10:30
ABC	Local	Local	12 O'Clock High		The Legend of Jesse James	A Man Called Shenandoah	The Farmer's Daughter	Ben Casey	
CBS	Local	Local	To Tell the Truth	I've Got a Secret	The Lucy Show	Andy Griffith Show	Hazel	Steve Lawrence Show	
NBC	Local	Local	Hullabaloo	John Forsythe Show	Dr. Kildare	Andy Williams Show/Perry Como Specials		Run For Your Life	

TUE

	6:30	7:00	7:30	8:00	8:30	9:00	9:30	10:00	10:30
ABC	Local	Local	Combat!		McHale's Navy	F Troop	Peyton Place	The Fugitive	
CBS	Local	Local	Rawhide		Red Skelton Hour		Petticoat Junction	CBS Reports/CBS News Specials	
NBC	Local	Local	My Mother, the Car	Please Don't Eat the Daisies	Dr. Kildare	Tuesday Night at the Movies			

WED

	6:30	7:00	7:30	8:00	8:30	9:00	9:30	10:00	10:30
ABC	Local	Local	Ozzie and Harriet	Patty Duke Show	Gidget	The Big Valley		Amos Burke, Secret Agent	
CBS	Local	Local	Lost in Space		The Beverly Hillbillies	Green Acres	Dick Van Dyke Show	Danny Kaye Show	
NBC	Local	Local	The Virginian			Bob Hope Show and Specials		I Spy	

THU

	6:30	7:00	7:30	8:00	8:30	9:00	9:30	10:00	10:30
ABC	Local	Local	Shindig	Donna Reed Show	O.K. Crackerby	Bewitched	Peyton Place	The Long, Hot Summer	
CBS	Local	Local	The Munsters	Gilligan's Island	My Three Sons	The CBS Thursday Night Movies			
NBC	Local	Local	Daniel Boone		Laredo		Mona McCluskey	Dean Martin Show	

FRI

	6:30	7:00	7:30	8:00	8:30	9:00	9:30	10:00	10:30
ABC	Local	Local	The Flintstones	Tammy	The Addams Family	Honey West	Peyton Place	Jimmy Dean Show	
CBS	Local	Local	The Wild, Wild West		Hogan's Heroes	Gomer Pyle, USMC	Smothers Brothers Show	Slattery's People	
NBC	Local	Local	Camp Runamuck	Hank	Convoy		Mr. Roberts	The Man From U.N.C.L.E.	

1966

		6:30	7:00	7:30	8:00	8:30	9:00	9:30	10:00	10:30
SAT	ABC	Local	Local	Shane		Lawrence Welk Show		The Hollywood Palace		ABC Scope
	CBS	Local	Local	Jackie Gleason Show		Pistols 'N' Petticoats	Mission: Impossible		Gunsmoke	
	NBC	Local	Local	Flipper	Please Don't Eat the Daisies	Get Smart	Saturday Night at the Movies			
SUN	ABC	Local	Voyage to the Bottom of the Sea		The FBI		The Sunday Night Movie			
	CBS	Local	Lassie	It's About Time	Ed Sullivan Show		Garry Moore Show		Candid Camera	What's My Line?
	NBC	Bell Telephone Hour/NBC News Specials		Walt Disney's Wonderful World of Color		Hey Landlord!	Bonanza		Andy Williams Show	
MON	ABC	Local	Local	Iron Horse		The Rat Patrol	The Felony Squad	Peyton Place	The Big Valley	
	CBS	Local	Local	Gilligan's Island	Run, Buddy, Run	The Lucy Show	Andy Griffith Show	Family Affair	Jean Arthur Show	I've Got a Secret
	NBC	Local	Local	The Monkees	I Dream of Jeannie	Roger Miller Show	The Road West		Run For Your Life	
TUE	ABC	Local	Local	Combat!		The Rounders	The Pruitts of Southampton	Love on a Rooftop	The Fugitive	
	CBS	Local	Local	Daktari		Red Skelton Hour		Petticoat Junction	CBS News Specials	
	NBC	Local	Local	The Girl From U.N.C.L.E.		Occasional Wife	Tuesday Night at the Movies			
WED	ABC	Local	Local	Batman	The Monroes		The Man Who Never Was	Peyton Place	ABC Stage 67	
	CBS	Local	Local	Lost in Space		The Beverly Hillbillies	Green Acres	Gomer Pyle, USMC	Danny Kaye Show	
	NBC	Local	Local	The Virginian			Bob Hope Show and Specials		I Spy	
THU	ABC	Local	Local	Batman	F Troop	Tammy Grimes Show	Bewitched	That Girl	Hawk	
	CBS	Local	Local	Jericho		My Three Sons	The CBS Thursday Night Movies			
	NBC	Local	Local	Daniel Boone		Star Trek		The Hero	Dean Martin Show	
FRI	ABC	Local	Local	The Green Hornet	The Time Tunnel		Milton Berle Show		12 O'Clock High	
	CBS	Local	Local	The Wild, Wild West		Hogan's Heroes	The CBS Friday Night Movies			
	NBC	Local	Local	Tarzan		The Man From U.N.C.L.E.		T.H.E. Cat	Laredo	

1967

Day	Net	7:30	8:00	8:30	9:00	9:30	10:00	10:30
SAT	ABC	The Dating Game	The Newlywed Game	Lawrence Welk Show		Iron Horse		ABC Scope
	CBS	Jackie Gleason Show		My Three Sons	Hogan's Heroes	Petticoat Junction	Mannix	
	NBC	Maya		Get Smart	Saturday Night at the Movies			
SUN	ABC	Voyage (starts at 7)	The FBI		The ABC Sunday Night Movie and Specials			
	CBS	Gentle Ben	Ed Sullivan Show		Smothers Brothers Comedy Hour		Mission: Impossible	
	NBC	Walt Disney's Wonderful World of Color		Mothers-in-Law	Bonanza		The High Chaparral	
MON	ABC	Cowboy in Africa		The Rat Patrol	The Felony Squad	Peyton Place	The Big Valley	
	CBS	Gunsmoke		The Lucy Show	Andy Griffith	Family Affair	Carol Burnett Show	
	NBC	The Monkees	The Man from U.N.C.L.E.		Danny Thomas Hour		I Spy	
TUE	ABC	Garrison's Gorillas		The Invaders		N.Y.P.D.	The Hollywood Palace	
	CBS	Daktari		Red Skelton Hour		Good Morning World	CBS News Hour	
	NBC	I Dream of Jeannie	Jerry Lewis Show		Tuesday Night at the Movies			
WED	ABC	Custer		Second 100 Years	The ABC Wednesday Night Movie and Specials			
	CBS	Lost in Space		The Beverly Hillbillies	Green Acres	He & She	Dundee and The Culhane	
	NBC	The Virginian			The Kraft Music Hall		Run For Your Life	
THU	ABC	Batman	The Flying Nun	Bewitched	That Girl	Peyton Place	Good Company	Local
	CBS	Cimarron Strip			The CBS Thursday Night Movies			
	NBC	Daniel Boone		Ironside		Dragnet 1968	Dean Martin Show	
FRI	ABC	Off to See the Wizard		Hondo		The Guns of Will Sonnett	Judd, For the Defense	
	CBS	The Wild, Wild West		Gomer Pyle, USMC	The CBS Friday Night Movies			
	NBC	Tarzan		Star Trek		Accidental Family	NBC News Specials/Bell Telephone Hour	

1968

		7:30	8:00	8:30	9:00	9:30	10:00	10:30
SAT	ABC	The Dating Game	The Newlywed Game	Lawrence Welk Show		The Hollywood Palace		Local
	CBS	Jackie Gleason Show		My Three Sons	Hogan's Heroes	Petticoat Junction	Mannix	
	NBC	Adam-12	Get Smart	The Ghost and Mrs. Muir	NBC Saturday Night at the Movies			
SUN	ABC	Land of the Giants (starts at 7)	The FBI		The ABC Sunday Night Movie			
	CBS	Gentle Ben	Ed Sullivan Show		Smothers Brothers Comedy Hour		Mission: Impossible	
	NBC	Walt Disney's Wonderful World of Color		The Mothers-in-Law	Bonanza		Beautiful Phyllis Diller Show	
MON	ABC	The Avengers		Peyton Place	The Outcasts		The Big Valley	
	CBS	Gunsmoke		Here's Lucy	Mayberry R.F.D.	Family Affair	Carol Burnett Show	
	NBC	I Dream of Jeannie	Rowan and Martin's Laugh-In		NBC Monday Night at the Movies			
TUE	ABC	The Mod Squad		It Takes a Thief		N.Y.P.D.	That's Life	
	CBS	Lancer		Red Skelton Hour		Doris Day Show	News Hour alt. with 60 Minutes (news show)	
	NBC	Jerry Lewis Show		Julia	NBC Tuesday Night at the Movies/News Special (once a month)			
WED	ABC	Here Come the Brides		Peyton Place	The ABC Wednesday Night Movie			
	CBS	Daktari		The Good Guys	The Beverly Hillbillies	Green Acres	Jonathan Winters Show	
	NBC	The Virginian			The Kraft Music Hall		The Outsider	
THU	ABC	The Ugliest Girl in Town	The Flying Nun	Bewitched	That Girl	Journey to the Unknown		Local
	CBS	Blondie	Hawaii Five-O		The CBS Thursday Night Movies			
	NBC	Daniel Boone		Ironside		Dragnet 1969	Dean Martin Show	
FRI	ABC	Operation: Entertainment		The Felony Squad	Don Rickles Show	The Guns of Will Sonnett	Judd, For the Defense	
	CBS	The Wild, Wild West		Gomer Pyle, USMC	The CBS Friday Night Movies			
	NBC	The High Chaparral		The Name of the Game			Star Trek	

1969

		7:30	8:00	8:30	9:00	9:30	10:00	10:30
SAT	ABC	The Dating Game	The Newlywed Game	Lawrence Welk Show		The Hollywood Palace		Local
	CBS	Jackie Gleason Show		My Three Sons	Green Acres	Petticoat Junction	Mannix	
	NBC	Andy Williams Show		Adam-12	NBC Saturday Night at the Movies			
SUN	ABC	Land of the Giants (starts at 7)	The FBI		The ABC Sunday Night Movie			
	CBS	To Rome With Love	Ed Sullivan Show		Leslie Uggams Show		Mission: Impossible	
	NBC	The Wonderful World of Disney		Bill Cosby Show	Bonanza		The Bold Ones	
MON	ABC	The Music Scene		The New People	The Survivors		Love, American Style	
	CBS	Gunsmoke		Here's Lucy	Mayberry R.F.D.	Doris Day Show	Carol Burnett Show	
	NBC	My World and Welcome to It	Rowan and Martin's Laugh-In		NBC Monday Night at the Movies			
TUE	ABC	The Mod Squad		Movie of the Week			Marcus Welby, M.D.	
	CBS	Lancer		Red Skelton Show		The Governor and J.J.	News Hour alt. with 60 Minutes (news show)	
	NBC	I Dream of Jeannie	Debbie Reynolds Show	Julia	NBC Tuesday Night at the Movies/First Tuesday (once a month)			
WED	ABC	The Flying Nun	The Courtship of Eddie's Father	Room 222	The ABC Wednesday Night Movies			
	CBS	Glen Campbell Goodtime Hour		The Beverly Hillbillies	Medical Center		Hawaii Five-O	
	NBC	The Virginian			The Kraft Music Hall		Then Came Bronson	
THU	ABC	The Ghost & Mrs. Muir	That Girl	Bewitched	This Is Tom Jones		It Takes A Thief	
	CBS	Family Affair	Jim Nabors Hour		The CBS Thursday Night Movies			
	NBC	Daniel Boone		Ironside		Dragnet	Dean Martin Show	
FRI	ABC	Let's Make A Deal	The Brady Bunch	Mr. Deeds Goes to Town	Here Come the Brides		Jimmy Durante Presents the Lennon Sisters Hour	
	CBS	Get Smart	The Good Guys	Hogan's Heroes	The CBS Friday Night Movies			
	NBC	The High Chaparral		The Name of the Game			Bracken's World	

1970

SAT

	7:30	8:00	8:30	9:00	9:30	10:00	10:30
ABC	Let's Make a Deal	The Newlywed Game	Lawrence Welk Show		The Most Deadly Game		Local
CBS	Mission: Impossible		My Three Sons	Arnie	Mary Tyler Moore Show	Mannix	
NBC	Andy Williams Show		Adam-12	NBC Saturday Night at the Movies			

SUN

	7:30	8:00	8:30	9:00	9:30	10:00	10:30
ABC	The Young Rebels	The FBI		The ABC Sunday Night Movie			
CBS	Hogan's Heroes	Ed Sullivan Show		Glen Campbell Goodtime Hour		Tim Conway Comedy Hour	
NBC	The Wonderful World of Disney		Bill Cosby Show	Bonanza		The Bold Ones	

MON

	7:30	8:00	8:30	9:00	9:30	10:00	10:30
ABC	The Young Lawyers		The Silent Force	NFL Monday Night Football (to be replaced after Dec. 14 by movies)			
CBS	Gunsmoke		Here's Lucy	Mayberry R.F.D.	Doris Day Show	Carol Burnett Show	
NBC	Red Skelton Show	Rowan and Martin's Laugh-In		NBC Monday Night at the Movies			

TUE

	7:30	8:00	8:30	9:00	9:30	10:00	10:30
ABC	The Mod Squad		Movie of the Week			Marcus Welby, M.D.	
CBS	The Beverly Hillbillies	Green Acres	Hee Haw		To Rome With Love	News Hour alt. with 60 Minutes (news show)	
NBC	Don Knotts Show		Julia	NBC Tuesday Night at the Movies/First Tuesday (once a month)			

WED

	7:30	8:00	8:30	9:00	9:30	10:00	10:30
ABC	Eddie's Father	Danny Thomas	Room 222	Johnny Cash Show		Dan August	
CBS	The Storefront Lawyers		Governor and J.J.	Medical Center		Hawaii Five-O	
NBC	The Men from Shiloh			The Kraft Music Hall		Four-in-One	

THU

	7:30	8:00	8:30	9:00	9:30	10:00	10:30
ABC	Matt Lincoln		Bewitched	Barefoot in the Park	The Odd Couple	The Immortal	
CBS	Family Affair	Jim Nabors Hour		The CBS Thursday Night Movies			
NBC	Flip Wilson Show		Ironside		Nancy	Dean Martin Show	

FRI

	7:30	8:00	8:30	9:00	9:30	10:00	10:30
ABC	The Brady Bunch	Nanny and the Professor	The Partridge Family	That Girl	Love, American Style	This Is Tom Jones	
CBS	The Interns		Headmaster	The CBS Friday Night Movies			
NBC	The High Chaparral		The Name of the Game			Bracken's World	

1971

		7:30	8:00	8:30	9:00	9:30	10:00	10:30
SAT	ABC	Local	Getting Together	Movie of the Weekend			The Persuaders	
	CBS	Local	All in the Family	Funny Face	New Dick Van Dyke Show	Mary Tyler Moore Show	Mission: Impossible	
	NBC	Local	The Partners	The Good Life	NBC Saturday Night at the Movies			
SUN	ABC	Local	The FBI		The ABC Sunday Night Movie			
	CBS	The CBS Sunday Night Movies				Cade's County		Local
	NBC	The Wonderful World of Disney		Jimmy Stewart	Bonanza		The Bold Ones	
MON	ABC	Local	Nanny and the Professor	Local	NFL Monday Night Football (to be replaced by movies after Jan. 24)			
	CBS	Local	Gunsmoke		Here's Lucy	Doris Day Show	My Three Sons	Arnie
	NBC	Local	Rowan and Martin's Laugh-In		NBC Monday Night at the Movies			
TUE	ABC	The Mod Squad		Movie of the Week			Marcus Welby, M.D.	
	CBS	Glen Campbell Goodtime Hour		Hawaii Five-O		Cannon		Local
	NBC	Ironside		Sarge		The Funny Side		Local
WED	ABC	Local	Bewitched	Eddie's Father	The Smith Family	Shirley's World	The Man and the City	
	CBS	Local	Carol Burnett Show		Medical Center		Mannix	
	NBC	Local	Adam-12	NBC Mystery Movie			Night Gallery	
THU	ABC	Local	Alias Smith and Jones		Longstreet		Owen Marshall: Counselor at Law	
	CBS	Local	Bearcats!		The CBS Thursday Night Movies/CBS Reports (once a month)			
	NBC	Local	Flip Wilson Show		Nichols		Dean Martin Show	
FRI	ABC	Local	The Brady Bunch	The Partridge Family	Room 222	The Odd Couple	Love, American Style	
	CBS	Local	The Chicago Teddy Bears	O'Hara, United States Treasury		The New CBS Friday Night Movies		
	NBC	Local	The D.A.	NBC World Premiere Movie/Chronolog (once a month)				Local

1972

		7:30	8:00	8:30	9:00	9:30	10:00	10:30
SAT	ABC	Local	Alias Smith and Jones / Kung Fu (once a month)		The Streets of San Francisco		The Sixth Sense	
	CBS	Local	All in the Family	Bridget Loves Bernie	Mary Tyler Moore Show	Bob Newhart Show	Mission: Impossible	
	NBC	Local	Emergency!		NBC Saturday Night at the Movies			
	PBS	Zoom	The Electric Company	Playhouse New York			Special of the Week	
SUN	ABC	Local	The FBI		The ABC Sunday Night Movie			
	CBS	Anna and the King	M*A*S*H	Sandy Duncan Show	New Dick Van Dyke Show	Mannix		Local
	NBC	The Wonderful World of Disney		NBC Sunday Mystery Movie / Hec Ramsey (once a month)			Night Gallery	Local
	PBS	The Just Generation	The Family Game	The French Chef	Masterpiece Theatre		Firing Line	
MON	ABC	Local	The Rookies		NFL Monday Night Football (to be replaced by movies in January)			
	CBS	Local	Gunsmoke		Here's Lucy	Doris Day Show	New Bill Cosby Show	
	NBC	Local	Rowan and Martin's Laugh-In		NBC Monday Night at the Movies			
	PBS	Local	Special of the Week			Book Beat	Local	
TUE	ABC	Local	Temperatures Rising	Tuesday Movie of the Week			Marcus Welby, M.D.	
	CBS	Local	Maude	Hawaii Five-O		The New CBS Tuesday Night Movies		
	NBC	Local	Bonanza		The Bold Ones		NBC Reports / America / First Tuesday	
	PBS	Local		One Nation	Behind the Lines	Black Journal	Local	
WED	ABC	Local	Paul Lynde Show	Wednesday Movie of the Week			Julie Andrews Hour	
	CBS	Local	Carol Burnett Show		Medical Center		Cannon	
	NBC	Local	Adam-12	NBC Wednesday Mystery Movie			Search	
	PBS	Local	A Public Affair	Playhouse New York			Soul!	
THU	ABC	Local	The Mod Squad		The Men		Owen Marshall, Counselor at Law	
	CBS	Local	The Waltons		The CBS Thursday Night Movies			
	NBC	Local	Flip Wilson Show		Ironside		Dean Martin Show	
	PBS	Local	The Advocates		International Performance		World Press	Thirty Minutes with . . .
FRI	ABC	Local	The Brady Bunch	The Partridge Family	Room 222	The Odd Couple	Love, American Style	
	CBS	Local	Sonny & Cher Comedy Hour		The CBS Friday Night Movies			
	NBC	Local	Sanford and Son	The Little People	Ghost Story		Banyon	
	PBS	Wall Street Week	Washington Week in Review	The Just Generation	Masterpiece Theatre		Local	

1973

SAT

	7:30	8:00	8:30	9:00	9:30	10:00	10:30
ABC	Local	The Partridge Family	ABC Suspense Movie/The Six Million Dollar Man (once a month)			Griff	
CBS	Local	All in the Family	M*A*S*H	Mary Tyler Moore Show	Bob Newhart Show	Carol Burnett Show	
NBC	Local	Emergency!		NBC Saturday Night at the Movies			

SUN

	7:30	8:00	8:30	9:00	9:30	10:00	10:30
ABC	The FBI		The ABC Sunday Night Movie				Local
CBS	The New Perry Mason		Mannix		Barnaby Jones		Local
NBC	The Wonderful World of Disney		NBC Sunday Mystery Movie (Columbo/Hec Ramsey/McMillan & Wife/McCloud)				Local

MON

	7:30	8:00	8:30	9:00	9:30	10:00	10:30
ABC	Local	The Rookies		NFL Monday Night Football (to be replaced by movies in January)			
CBS	Local	Gunsmoke		Here's Lucy	New Dick Van Dyke Show	Medical Center	
NBC	Local	Lotsa Luck	Diana	NBC Monday Night at the Movies			

TUE

	7:30	8:00	8:30	9:00	9:30	10:00	10:30
ABC	Local	New Temperatures Rising	Tuesday Movie of the Week			Marcus Welby, M.D.	
CBS	Local	Maude	Hawaii Five-O		The New CBS Tuesday Night Movies/Hawkins/Shaft		
NBC	Local	Chase		The Magician		Police Story	

WED

	7:30	8:00	8:30	9:00	9:30	10:00	10:30
ABC	Local	Bob & Carol & Ted & Alice	Wednesday Movie of the Week			Owen Marshall/Doc Elliot (monthly)	
CBS	Local	Sonny & Cher Comedy Hour		Cannon		Kojak	
NBC	Local	Adam-12	NBC Wednesday Mystery Movie (Banacek/Tenafly/Snoop Sisters/Faraday and Co.)			Love Story	

THU

	7:30	8:00	8:30	9:00	9:30	10:00	10:30
ABC	Local	Toma		Kung Fu		The Streets of San Francisco	
CBS	Local	The Waltons		The CBS Thursday Night Movies			
NBC	Local	Flip Wilson Show		Ironside		NBC Follies	

WED

	7:30	8:00	8:30	9:00	9:30	10:00	10:30
ABC	Local	The Brady Bunch	The Odd Couple	Room 222	Adam's Rib	Love, American Style	
CBS	Local	Calucci's Dept.	Roll Out!	The CBS Friday Night Movies			
NBC	Local	Sanford and Son	Girl with Something Extra	Needles and Pins	Brian Keith Show	Dean Martin Comedy Hour	

1974

		7:30	8:00	8:30	9:00	9:30	10:00	10:30
SAT	ABC	Local	The New Land		King Fu		Nakia	
	CBS	Local	All in the Family	Friends and Lovers	Mary Tyler Moore Show	Bob Newhart Show	Carol Burnett Show	
	NBC	Local	Emergency!		NBC Saturday Night at the Movies			
SUN	ABC	Local	Sonny Comedy Revue		The ABC Sunday Night Movie			
	CBS	Apple's Way		Kojak		Mannix		Local
	NBC	The Wonderful World of Disney		NBC Sunday Mystery Movie (Columbo/McMillan & Wife/McCloud/Amy Prentiss)				Local
MON	ABC	Local	The Rookies		NFL Monday Night Football (to be replaced by movies in January)			
	CBS	Local	Gunsmoke		Maude	Rhoda	Medical Center	
	NBC	Local	Born Free		NBC Monday Night at the Movies			
TUE	ABC	Local	Happy Days	Tuesday Movie of the Week			Marcus Welby, M.D.	
	CBS	Local	Good Times	M*A*S*H	Hawaii Five-O		Barnaby Jones	
	NBC	Local	Adam-12	NBC World Premiere Movie			Police Story	
WED	ABC	Local	That's My Mama	Wednesday Movie of the Week			Get Christie Love!	
	CBS	Local	Sons and Daughters		Cannon		The Manhunter	
	NBC	Local	Little House on the Prairie		Lucas Tanner		Petrocelli	
THU	ABC	Local	The Odd Couple	Paper Moon	The Streets of San Francisco		Harry O	
	CBS	Local	The Waltons		The CBS Thursday Night Movies			
	NBC	Local	Sierra		Ironside		Movin' On	
FRI	ABC	Local	Kodiak	The Six Million Dollar Man		The Texas Wheelers	The Night Stalker	
	CBS	Local	Planet of the Apes		The CBS Friday Night Movies			
	NBC	Local	Sanford and Son	Chico and the Man	The Rockford Files		Police Woman	

1975

		7:00	7:30	8:00	8:30	9:00	9:30	10:00	10:30
SAT	ABC	Local		Saturday Night Live with Howard Cosell		S.W.A.T.		Matt Helm	
	CBS	Local		The Jeffersons	Doc	Mary Tyler Moore Show	Bob Newhart Show	Carol Burnett Show	
	NBC	Local		Emergency!		NBC Saturday Night at the Movies			
SUN	ABC	Swiss Family Robinson		The Six Million Dollar Man		The ABC Sunday Night Movie			
	CBS	Three for the Road		Cher		Kojak		Bronk	
	NBC	The Wonderful World of Disney		The Family Holvak		NBC Sunday Mystery Movie (Columbo, McCloud, McMillan & Wife, McCoy)			
MON	ABC	Local		Barbary Coast		NFL Monday Night Football			
	CBS	Local		Rhoda	Phyllis	All in the Family	Maude	Medical Center	
	NBC	Local		The Invisible Man		NBC Monday Night at the Movies			
TUE	ABC	Local		Happy Days	Welcome Back, Kotter	The Rookies		Marcus Welby, M.D.	
	CBS	Local		Good Times	Joe and Sons	Switch		Beacon Hill	
	NBC	Local		Movin' On		Police Story		Joe Forrester	
WED	ABC	Local		When Things Were Rotten	That's My Mama	Baretta		Starsky and Hutch	
	CBS	Local		Tony Orlando and Dawn		Cannon		Kate McShane	
	NBC	Local		Little House on the Prairie		Doctors Hospital		Petrocelli	
THU	ABC	Local		Barney Miller	On the Rocks	The Streets of San Francisco		Harry O	
	CBS	Local		The Waltons		The CBS Thursday Night Movies			
	NBC	Local		The Montefuscos	Fay	Ellery Queen		Medical Story	
FRI	ABC	Local		Mobile One		The ABC Friday Night Movie			
	CBS	Local		Big Eddie	M*A*S*H	Hawaii Five-O		Barnaby Jones	
	NBC	Local		Sanford and Son	Chico and the Man	The Rockford Files		Police Woman	

1976

		7:00	7:30	8:00	8:30	9:00	9:30	10:00	10:30
SAT	ABC	Local		Holmes and Yoyo	Mr. T and Tina	Starsky & Hutch		Most Wanted	
	CBS	Local		The Jeffersons	Doc	Mary Tyler Moore Show	Bob Newhart Show	Carol Burnett Show	
	NBC	Local		Emergency!		NBC Saturday Night at the Movies			
SUN	ABC	Cos		The Six Million Dollar Man		The ABC Sunday Night Movie			
	CBS	60 Minutes		Sonny & Cher Show		Kojak		Delvecchio	
	NBC	The Wonderful World of Disney		NBC Sunday Mystery Movie (Columbo, McCloud, McMillan, Quincy)			The Big Event		
MON	ABC	Local		The Captain & Tennille		NFL Monday Night Football			
	CBS	Local		Rhoda	Phyllis	Maude	All's Fair	Executive Suite	
	NBC	Local		Little House on the Prairie		NBC Monday Night at the Movies			
TUE	ABC	Local		Happy Days	Laverne & Shirley	Rich Man, Poor Man—Book II		Family	
	CBS	Local		Tony Orlando & Dawn Rainbow Hour		M*A*S*H	One Day at a Time	Switch	
	NBC	Local		Baa Baa Black Sheep		Police Woman		Police Story	
WED	ABC	Local		The Bionic Woman		Baretta		Charlie's Angels	
	CBS	Local		Good Times	Ball Four	All in the Family	Alice	The Blue Knight	
	NBC	Local		The Practice	NBC Movie of the Week			The Quest	
THU	ABC	Local		Welcome Back Kotter	Barney Miller	Tony Randall	Nancy Walker	The Streets of San Francisco	
	CBS	Local		The Waltons		Hawaii Five-O		Barnaby Jones	
	NBC	Local		Gemini Man		Best Sellers		Van Dyke and Company	
FRI	ABC	Local		Donny & Marie		The ABC Friday Night Movie			
	CBS	Local		Spencer's Pilots		The CBS Friday Night Movies			
	NBC	Local		Sanford and Son	Chico and the Man	The Rockford Files		Serpico	

1977

		7:00	7:30	8:00	8:30	9:00	9:30	10:00	10:30
SAT	ABC	Local		Fish	Operation Petticoat	Starsky & Hutch		The Love Boat	
	CBS	Local		Bob Newhart	We've Got Each Other	The Jeffersons	Tony Randall	Carol Burnett Show	
	NBC	Local		The Bionic Woman		NBC Saturday Night at the Movies			
SUN	ABC	Hardy Boys/Nancy Drew Mysteries		The Six Million Dollar Man		The ABC Sunday Night Movie			
	CBS	60 Minutes		Rhoda	On Our Own	All in the Family	Alice	Kojak	
	NBC	The Wonderful World of Disney				The Big Event			
MON	ABC	Local		The San Pedro Beach Bums		ABC Monday Night Football			
	CBS	Local		Young Dan'l Boone		Betty White Show	Maude	Rafferty	
	NBC	Local		Little House on the Prairie		NBC Monday Night at the Movies			
TUE	ABC	Local		Happy Days	Laverne & Shirley	Three's Company	Soap	Family	
	CBS	Local		The Fitzpatricks		M*A*S*H	One Day at a Time	Lou Grant	
	NBC	Local		Richard Pryor Show		Mulligan's Stew		Police Woman	
WED	ABC	Local		Eight Is Enough		Charlie's Angels		Baretta	
	CBS	Local		Good Times	Busting Loose	The CBS Wednesday Night Movie			
	NBC	Local		The Life and Times of Grizzly Adams		The Oregon Trail		Big Hawaii	
THU	ABC	Local		Welcome Back, Kotter	What's Happening!!	Barney Miller	Carter Country	Redd Foxx	
	CBS	Local		The Waltons		Hawaii Five-O		Barnaby Jones	
	NBC	Local		CHiPs		The Man from Atlantis		Rosetti and Ryan	
FRI	ABC	Local		Donny & Marie		The ABC Friday Night Movie			
	CBS	Local		The New Adventures of Wonder Woman		Logan's Run		Switch	
	NBC	Local		Sanford Arms	Chico and the Man	The Rockford Files		Quincy	

INDEX